This is your book for finding and exploring your place in this vast universe.

**YOU ARE THE CENTER OF YOUR UNIVERSE.**

You contribute your essence to the entire universe.

This book will help you understand how wonder-full the universe is and how you can participate more fully in making this the best universe you and all other consciousness on this planet can experience.

You might find it a helpful reminder of your special place in this universe to write in your name or place a photo of yourself in the center of the cover of this book.

*This is the most comprehensive publication about the HSP trait from the perspective of wholistic psychotherapy. I highly recommend this book.*

— Ted Zeff, PhD

# Wholistic Healing for the Highly Sensitive Person (HSP)

✦

## *Finding Your Place in the Universe*

✦

## A Mini-Encyclopedia of Ways to Develop and Deepen Wonder-full Relationships

## Daniel J. Benor, MD, ABIHM

All statements made in this book, including suggestions, recommendations and advice, are for informational purposes only. No professional relationship has been established between the author and the reader/user of these materials, and there is no intent to provide a professional service through the contents of this book.

The author and publisher do not assume and hereby disclaim any liability to any party for any loss, damage, or disruption caused by acting on information contained in this book. The skills described in this book may be practiced differently by each individual, and the author and publisher take no responsibility in how they are practiced by the reader. The author and publisher advise readers to take full responsibility for their choices and actions, and any and all results of their choices and actions.

Copyright © 2019 Daniel J. Benor, MD

All rights reserved

No part of this book may be reproduced, stored in a retrieval system, or transmitted by any means, electronic, mechanical, photocopying, recording, or otherwise, without written permission from the author.

Wholistic Healing for the Highly Sensitive Person (HSP)
Book 201805
978-1-7753506-0-6 (Hardcover)
978-1-7753506-1-3 (Paperback)
978-1-7753506-2-0 (Electronic Book)


Wholistic Healing Publications
P.O. Box 1021
Guelph, ON N1H 6N1
(519) 265-0698 (Canada)
(609) 714-1885 (US)

# ENDORSEMENTS

This book is the most comprehensive publication about the trait of high sensitivity from the perspective of wholistic psychotherapy. I highly recommend this book.

> **- Ted Zeff, PhD**
> Author of *The Highly Sensitive Person's Survival Guide*, *The Strong Sensitive Boy* and *The Power of Sensitivity*

Dan Benor, MD, psychotherapist, has been an iconic pioneer in the wholistic healthcare movement for five decades. His wide clinical experience and deep wisdom have led him to an understanding of the highly sensitive person — HSP. As Benor shows, HSPs, who constitute around 20 percent of the population, are gifted yet vulnerable individuals who have unique talents and needs. Benor's insights into this domain are a major contribution. This book is the go-to volume for HSPs, their spouses and partners, psychotherapists and counselors, and anyone seeking greater awareness of what it means to be human.

> **- Larry Dossey, MD**
> Author of *One Mind: How Our Individual Mind Is Part of a Greater Consciousness and Why It Matters*

Daniel Benor's book is an incredible source of wisdom and supplies us with what we all need, a life coach. His wisdom is presented in a way that we can all understand and utilize. When we are presented with the truth it is easy to accept and utilize. All you have to do is show up for practice. You have the potential and Benor's book can bring it forth for you. This is about fulfilling your potential, understanding and healing through the mechanisms which Benor makes clear are a part of our being.

> **- Bernie Siegel, MD**
> Author of *The Art of Healing* and *365 Prescriptions For The Soul*

In today's chaotic world, highly sensitive individuals are subject to increasing stress. Do not allow yourself to be made worse by the standard psychiatric nonsense of mood killing drugs. Read and heed the advice in this excellent book!

- **C. Norman Shealy, MD, PhD**
CEO, International Institute of Holistic Medicine
Author of *Conversations with G: A Physician's Encounter with Heaven*

Dr. Benor is a highly gifted psychotherapist and healer. His wholistic approach to understanding, diagnosing, and treating the highly sensitive person is masterful. Dr. Benor offers insight into the dynamics affecting not only the highly sensitive person but those in relationship with HSPs.

Dr. Benor has expanded our understanding of the HSP. He not only examines the mental, emotional, physical and relational manifestations, but also explores the energetic, spiritual, and psychic expressions of the HSP. This is required reading for anyone seeking a comprehensive and insightful understanding of the HSP. Moreover, the interventions and therapies Dr. Benor recommends are practical, effective, and easy to implement. This is a wonderful guide for helping the HSP move through life with grace and ease. Dr. Benor's wisdom, insight, and deep compassion shines brightly!

- **Lucia Thornton ThD, RN, MSN, AHN-BC**
Past-President American Holistic Nurses Association
Developer of the Model of Whole-Person Caring

This book should be the go-to guide for surviving and thriving, in our increasingly stressful world, especially for those of us who are gifted with sensitive natures. Emotional sensitivity needs no longer be a handicap, but can be cultivated as a strength, using the simple exercises he describes. A deeply fascinating journey into the world of intuition and mind/body/spirit medicine, covering everything from neuroplasticity to near-death experiences, from brains to biofields. Highly recommended!

- **Eric Leskowitz MD**
Department of Psychiatry, Harvard Medical School (1995-2017)

# CONTENTS

ENDORSEMENTS ................................................................................................................. 5
ACKNOWLEDGMENTS ........................................................................................................ 12
Abbreviations and notations ............................................................................................ 13
    *Frequent abbreviations* ................................................................................................ 13
    *Other abbreviations* ..................................................................................................... 13
Awakenings ........................................................................................................................ 15
SECTION I. FOUNDATIONAL INTRODUCTION ................................................................. 21
1. Highly Sensitive People (HSPs) and their Companions (HSPCs) ............................... 22
    *Technical points* ........................................................................................................... 23
2. The author .................................................................................................................... 24
3. Wholistic healing, an introduction ............................................................................. 26
4. Sections of this book ................................................................................................... 33
SECTION II. UNDERSTANDING THE HSP AND HSPC: EXPLANATORY FRAMEWORKS .... 45
5. Background .................................................................................................................. 46
6. Wholistic healing frameworks to understand HSPs and HSPCs ............................... 49
    *Body* ............................................................................................................................... 50
    *Emotions (HSP wholistic issues)* .................................................................................. 53
    *Mind* .............................................................................................................................. 55
        *Meta-anxieties* ...................................................................................................... 59
        *Dealing with meta-anxieties* ................................................................................ 60
        *Distractions, misperceptions, errors and delusions of Mind* ............................. 62
    *Relationships with other people (HSP wholistic issues)* ........................................... 65
    *Relationships with the environment (HSP wholistic issues)* ..................................... 67
    *Spirit (HSP wholistic issues)* ......................................................................................... 68
    *Engaging in wholistic healing* ..................................................................................... 69
        *Mainstream attitudes to wholistic healing* ......................................................... 71
7. Jungian Perspectives ................................................................................................... 73
    *Shadow aspects of personality* .................................................................................... 76
    *Synchronicities* ............................................................................................................. 79
8. Left and right brain hemisphere preferences ............................................................ 81
    *Ultradian brain hemisphere rhythms* ......................................................................... 87
    *The mind and the brain* ............................................................................................... 88
9. The High Sensation Seeker (HSS) ................................................................................ 89
10. Neuroplasticity ........................................................................................................... 91
    *Neuroplasticity for thoughts and feelings* ................................................................. 92
    *Meta-awarenesses and forgetting vs. neuroplastic forgetting* ................................ 98
11. Freudian dissections of our awarenesses - Eric Berne's Transactional Analysis (TA) .... 101
    *Levels of intimacy* ...................................................................................................... 106
        *HSPs and levels of intimacy* ............................................................................... 106
12. Inner child awarenesses .......................................................................................... 108
    *Lessons for HSPs and HSPCs about inner child awarenesses* ................................. 111
13. Observing Ego .......................................................................................................... 113
    *Partial observing ego awareness* .............................................................................. 114
    *Full observing ego awarenesses* ............................................................................... 115
    *Finding your center and being centered* ................................................................. 117
    *Developing observing ego* ........................................................................................ 118
14. Building and keeping or changing habits of consciousness ................................. 120
    *Body (Habits of Consciousness)* ................................................................................ 121
    *Emotions (Habits of Consciousness)* ........................................................................ 121
    *Mind (Habits of Consciousness)* ............................................................................... 122
    *Relationships with other people (Habits of Consciousness)* .................................. 122
    *Relationships with the environment (Habits of Consciousness)* ........................... 123

  *Spirit (Habits of Consciousness)* ................................................................................................ 123
  *Reinforcements – positive and negative* ................................................................................ 124
  *Cognitive dissonance in building and changing views and behaviors* ............................. 125
   *Relevant to HSPs and HSPCs* ............................................................................................ 130
**15. Psychological trauma** .................................................................................................................. 133
  *Dealing with traumas* ............................................................................................................... 138
   *Bullying, belittling, pathologizing and traumas of rejection experienced by HSPs* ....... 138
   *Resentments, oppositional behaviors and vengefulness* ............................................ 144
   *Trauma residues – mild to moderate* .............................................................................. 146
   *Trauma residues – severe trauma reactions and long-term residues* ....................... 149
   *Research on long-term physical and psychological residues of PTSD* ...................... 152
   *Treating long-term effects of traumas* ............................................................................ 158
   *Suicide with severe traumas* ............................................................................................ 161
   *Alcohol and substance use and addictions following trauma* ..................................... 164
   *Helping HSPs and HSPCs deal with traumas* ................................................................ 165
**16. Grief** .................................................................................................................................................. 171
  *Unresolved grief* ......................................................................................................................... 174
   *Unresolved initial stages of grief* ..................................................................................... 175
   *Unresolved middle stages of grief* .................................................................................. 176
   *Unresolved resolution stage of grief* .............................................................................. 177
  *Good grief* .................................................................................................................................... 180

**SECTION III. UNDERSTANDING THE HSP: ALTERNATIVE OR ADDITIONAL DIAGNOSES** .............. 183
**17. Attention Deficit Hyperactivity Disorder (ADHD) / ADD** ........................................................ 184
**18. Oppositional Defiant Disorder (ODD)** ........................................................................................ 186
  *Helpful approaches for getting along with oppositional children* ................................... 186
**19. Obsessive Compulsive Disorder (OCD)** ..................................................................................... 188
**20. Attachment styles** ......................................................................................................................... 190
**21. Borderline Personality Disorder** ................................................................................................. 192
**22. Narcissistic personality disorder (NPD)** ................................................................................... 194
  *Post Traumatic Stress Disorder (PTSD)* .................................................................................. 194

**SECTION IV. HSPS, THEIR HSPCS AND OTHER FAMILY MEMBERS** ............................................... 197
**23. Companioning the HSP: Relationship gifts, challenges and benefits** ................................ 198
**24. What is life all about?** ................................................................................................................... 201
  *How did we get where we are?* ................................................................................................ 201
**25. Companioned HSP – HSPC relationships: Detailed wholistic considerations** .................. 203
  ***Body*** *(HSPs and their HSPCS)* ................................................................................................... 203
   *Building positive physical aspects of your relationship* ................................................ 203
  ***Emotions*** *(HSPs and their HSPCs)* .......................................................................................... 204
   *Love and caring* ................................................................................................................... 208
   *Overwhelm* ........................................................................................................................... 209
   *Anger* ...................................................................................................................................... 213
  ***Mind*** *(HSPs and their HSPCS)* ................................................................................................... 218
  ***Relationships with other people*** *(HSPs and their HSPCS)* ................................................ 218
   *Building and maintaining positivity* ................................................................................ 219
   *HSPs' challenges in close, personal relationships* ....................................................... 220
   *How close is close enough?* .............................................................................................. 226
   *Deepening sensitivity to the 'how' of relating* ............................................................... 228
   *Parent Effectiveness Training (P.E.T.) – Problematic and better ways to express ourselves* ................... 232
   *Legal precautions and remedies* ..................................................................................... 233
  ***Relationships with the environment*** *(HSPs and their HSPCs)* ....................................... 235
  ***Spirit*** *(HSPs and their HSPCs)* ................................................................................................. 236
**26. HSP children – detailed wholistic considerations** ................................................................. 237
  ***Body*** *(HSP children)* ................................................................................................................... 237
  ***Emotions*** *(HSP children)* .......................................................................................................... 238
  ***Mind*** *(HSP children)* ................................................................................................................... 239
  ***Relationships in general with other people*** *(HSP children)* ............................................ 241
   *Relationships with extended family (HSP children)* ..................................................... 246
   *HSP Children in separation and divorce (HSP children)* .............................................. 247
   *HSP Children in school (HSP children)* ........................................................................... 249

  *Relationships with the environment (HSP children)* .................................................. 250
  *Spirit (HSP children)* ...................................................................................................... 250
**SECTION V. SUPPORTS FOR THE HSP AND HSPC: RESOURCES AND THERAPIES** .......... 253
  *Background* ..................................................................................................................... 254
**27. First aid for HSP distress, anxieties and triggered states** ............................................. 254
**28. Your place of peace and safety and healing (PPSH)** ..................................................... 260
  *For children* ..................................................................................................................... 260
  *For adults* ......................................................................................................................... 261
**29. TWR/ WHEE and other wholistic Energy Psychology methods** ................................... 263
  *TWR1/ WHEE: Dealing with symptoms and building positive resources* ..................... 263
  *TWR2/WHEE: Listening to body messages* ................................................................... 266
  *TWR2/WHEE: Deeper Clearings* .................................................................................... 270
  *Bundling issues to facilitate releases of current and earlier memories and to address*
   *the wholistic spectrum of issues* ................................................................................ 272
  *WHEE for children* .......................................................................................................... 273
**30. Marital/ couple therapy and family therapy** ................................................................ 275
**31. Two-chair explorations and clearing** ............................................................................ 282
  *Body symptoms and their messages in two-chair work* ............................................... 285
  *Reparenting ourselves through two-chair work* ........................................................... 287
**32. Neurolinguistic Programming (NLP): anchoring issues and discharging anchors** .... 292
**33. Vibrational medicine** ..................................................................................................... 293
  *Homeopathy* .................................................................................................................... 293
   *Homeopathic practice* ................................................................................................ 294
   *Homeopathic research* ............................................................................................... 297
   *Self-help with homeopathy* ........................................................................................ 298
  *Flower Essences* ............................................................................................................. 299
   *Help for HSPs with flower essences* .......................................................................... 300
**34. Acupuncture** .................................................................................................................. 301
  *Western scientific acupuncture research* ..................................................................... 302
   *Help for HSPs with acupuncture* ............................................................................... 303
**35. 12-step programs** .......................................................................................................... 304
  *Benefits of 12-step programs for HSPs and HSPCs* ....................................................... 306
**36. Family constellations awarenesses and therapy** ......................................................... 307
  *Family constellation therapy for HSPs and HSPCs* ........................................................ 311
**37. Active listening** ............................................................................................................. 316
  *Active listening in HSP and HSPC relationships* ............................................................ 318

**SECTION VI. GENERAL WHOLISTIC APPROACHES** ........................................................... 321
**38. Touching base with each other** .................................................................................... 322
  *Focusing on positives* ..................................................................................................... 322
  *Extending your positives into the collective consciousness* ........................................ 323
**39. Giving each other some space** ..................................................................................... 324
**40. Body health and healing** ............................................................................................... 326
  *Healthy, regular eating* ................................................................................................... 326
  *Vitamin deficiencies and contaminants in foods and the need for supplements* ....... 327
  *Exercise* ............................................................................................................................ 327
  *Relaxations* ...................................................................................................................... 328
   *Muscle relaxation* ...................................................................................................... 328
   *Systematic desensitization* ........................................................................................ 328
   *The energy body* ........................................................................................................ 329
**41. Emotions** ....................................................................................................................... 331
  *Food cravings, overeating, comfort eating and obesity* ............................................... 331
  *The five love languages* .................................................................................................. 334
**42. Mind** ............................................................................................................................... 336
  *Preventive clearing of negativity, AKA wholistic housecleaning* ................................. 336
  *Preventive installing of positivity and meta-positivity, AKA investing in my*
   *wholistic internal bank account* ................................................................................ 338
  *Clearing meta-negative expectations in repeating situations* ..................................... 340
  *Broader applications of preventive positivity and wholistic housecleaning* ............... 343
  *Broader applications of proactive positivity and wholistic housecleaning* ................. 349

  *Meditation* .................................................................................................................. 350
  *Clearing trauma* ......................................................................................................... 352
  *Journaling* ................................................................................................................... 353
**43. Relationships** ................................................................................................................ 354
 *Relationships with other people* .................................................................................... 354
  The what and the how of communicating ..................................................................... 354
  Forgiveness ................................................................................................................ 355
  Collective human relationships ................................................................................... 359
 *Relationships with the environment* ............................................................................. 362
**44. Spirit** ............................................................................................................................. 364
 *Personal spiritual awarenesses* .................................................................................... 364
 *Collective consciousness* .............................................................................................. 364

**SECTION VII. SUBTLER SENSITIVITIES, BIOLOGICAL ENERGY MEDICINE**
**AND COLLECTIVE CONSCIOUSNESS** ................................................................................. 365
**45. Background** ................................................................................................................. 366
**46. Intuition: A brief overview** .......................................................................................... 369
**47. Inspiration and creativity: pattern recognition, intuition and more** ......................... 371
**48. Intuition as retrieved memory** ................................................................................... 375
**49. Intuition as psychological pattern recognition** ......................................................... 377
**50. Intuition as wholistic bioenergy pattern recognition** ............................................... 379
**51. Psychic intuition that is well researched** .................................................................... 380
 *Intuitive perceptions of believers and of 'skeptics'* ...................................................... 382
 *Intuitive perceptions from a distance* .......................................................................... 384
  Dowsing ..................................................................................................................... 386
 *Understanding ESP and intuition* ................................................................................. 389
  HSPs and intuition ..................................................................................................... 390
**52. Psychokinesis (PK): Intentionality interacting with matter** ....................................... 391
**53. Psychic factors in health and healing** ......................................................................... 392
 *Ethics in intuition* ......................................................................................................... 393
**54. Biological energies (biofields)** ................................................................................... 394
 *Bioenergy field assessments* ........................................................................................ 396
  Research on biofield assessments ............................................................................. 397
 *Unusual properties of biological energies* .................................................................... 400
  Biological energies can be imprinted in various materials ......................................... 400
  Bioenergies interact with solar and planetary energy fields ....................................... 401
  Personal exploration of your own bioenergy sensitivities .......................................... 401
 *Healing powers of objects* ........................................................................................... 402
  Crystals ..................................................................................................................... 402
  Consciousness appears to interact with matter ......................................................... 402
 *Healing powers of places* ............................................................................................. 404
**55. Psychic healing – as psychic intuition and psychokinesis** ......................................... 408
 *Locus of control in healing* .......................................................................................... 410
 *Research on healing* .................................................................................................... 410
 *Negative effects of healing* .......................................................................................... 411
 *Using bioenergies with negative intentions* ................................................................. 412
 *Explaining healing* ....................................................................................................... 412
**56. Spirits and channeled information** ............................................................................ 414
**57. Activating and using our personal intuitive perceptions** ........................................... 416
 *Learning and practicing intuitive awarenesses* ............................................................ 417
 *Body indicators for intuitive awareness: Muscle testing* .............................................. 418
  Pendulums offer another form of muscle testing ....................................................... 420
  Dowsing rods may be used instead of pendulums ..................................................... 420
**58. Integrity: wholistic perspectives** ............................................................................... 424
 *Body (Wholistic Integrity)* ............................................................................................ 427
 *Emotions (Wholistic Integrity)* ..................................................................................... 429
 *Mind (Wholistic Integrity)* ........................................................................................... 431
 *Relationships with other people (Wholistic Integrity)* ................................................. 434
 *Relationships with the environment (Wholistic Integrity)* .......................................... 439
 *Spirit (Wholistic Integrity)* ........................................................................................... 440
 *Wholistic, broad-spectrum healings (Wholistic integrity)* ........................................... 443

*Placebo reactions are wholistic, broad-spectrum healings* ....................................................... 445
**59. Collective consciousness of humanity** ............................................................................ 447
**60. Family constellations therapy - accessing collective consciousness** ........................... 450
**61. Manifestation: Activation of our individual and collective consciousness** ................ 452

**SECTION VIII. SPIRITUAL AWARENESSES** ................................................................................ 457
**62. Spiritual awarenesses within Western scientific perspectives** ..................................... 458
**63. Spiritual awarenesses – accepting the Spiritual as real** ................................................. 463
    *Spirit guides* ............................................................................................................................ 464
    *Awakening and deepening our Spiritual awarenesses* ........................................................ 465
    *Spiritual emergence and Spiritual emergencies* .................................................................. 466
    *Angels* ...................................................................................................................................... 468
    *Demons* .................................................................................................................................... 470
**64. Reincarnation and past life therapy** ................................................................................. 472
    *Spontaneous reincarnation memories* .................................................................................. 472
    *Past life therapy* ...................................................................................................................... 474
        *Research on past life hypnotic regressions* ........................................................................ 476
        *HSP benefits from past life recall and past life therapy* ..................................................... 477
**65. Life in Spirit dimensions** ................................................................................................... 480
    *Bridging between physical and Spirit life* ............................................................................ 480
    *The near death experience (NDE)* ......................................................................................... 480
        *Reports from NDEs on a spirit life between physical lives* ............................................... 482
        *Pre-death experiences* ........................................................................................................ 483
        *Deathbed experiences* ......................................................................................................... 484
        *Lessons from NDE's, pre-death and deathbed experiences* .............................................. 486
    *Life after physical death, between physical lives, and before birth* .................................. 488
        *Relationships of spirits with people who are physically alive* ........................................... 489
    *Gaia, our planet* ...................................................................................................................... 490
    *The Infinite Source / All that Is / God* ................................................................................... 491
        *Theodicy: The study of good and evil* ................................................................................ 494
**66. Spirit inspires every aspect of our existence** ................................................................ 497
**67. Grief and trauma in the collective consciousness of humanity** ................................... 499
    *Grief and trauma in the collective consciousness of our planet* ........................................ 501
**68. Offering healing for the collective trauma and suicidality of humanity** ..................... 503
    *Suggestions for offering healing for the collective planetary consciousness* .................... 505

**SECTION IX. SUMMARY** ............................................................................................................ 507
    *So, again, what's it all about?* ................................................................................................ 508

**SECTION X. MY JOURNEY IN WRITING THIS BOOK** ................................................................ 511
    *Appreciations* .......................................................................................................................... 512

**ENDNOTES** ................................................................................................................................. 516

**REFERENCES** ............................................................................................................................. 530

**INDEX** ......................................................................................................................................... 541

**ABOUT THE AUTHOR** ................................................................................................................ 550

# Acknowledgments

I give thanks to the countless caregivers and care seekers who have been my teachers through a major part of my lifetime of studying the human condition. I give thanks to the many authors of books in the rainbow spectrum of wholistic healing, of poems, pithy sayings, heartwarming and humorous quotes who have given me information, insights, inspiration, pleasure, solace and spice to add to this book.

I give thanks to Elaine Aron for her pioneering exploring, researching and writing about the Highly Sensitive Person (HSP), and to Ted Zeff for writing about boys and men as HSPs. Their books have been invaluable to countless care seekers I've helped to deal with their HSP issues. They have also been invaluable to me, personally, in connecting with my HSP awarenesses and in dealing with them.

I give thanks to Roger Callahan for developing Thought Field Therapy (TFT) and to Gary Craig for developing Emotional Freedom Techniques (EFT), both of which approaches are included in the Association for Comprehensive Energy Psychology (ACEP), along with other Energy Psychology methods such as TWR/WHEE. These self-healing methods have the ring enormous healing to people who are suffering pain and trauma in this world, and to transform their lives.

Energy Psychology and EMDR have transformed my life and my wholistic healing practice enabling me to help more people, more quickly and deeply.

I give thanks to other therapists of various backgrounds and training who have helped me enormously over the years. See appreciations at the end of Section X for more people to whom I am enormously grateful for their wholistic healing assistance. I feel you will understand and appreciate what I am sharing with far greater depth and breadth of understanding after having read my discussions of wholistic healing, along with sharing details of my personal journey in this book.

I give thanks to Francine Shapiro who developed Eye Movement Desensitization and Reprocessing (EMDR), another method for releasing trauma and pain.

I give thanks to Heather Poole Dragoman and Paul Reeve for their help with editing this mini-encyclopedia.

I give thanks to those who have treated me harshly, giving me the challenges that led me to seek out those who have offered me love, caring, support, wise teachings, therapy and healings, all of them helping me find places of love, acceptance, forgiveness and healing within myself that I probably would not have found alone.

I give thanks to the Infinite Source and the spiritual beings who have often wakened me in the wee hours of the morning with insights that furthered the writing of this and my other books.

## ABBREVIATIONS AND NOTATIONS

I've taken the liberty of expanding upon Elaine Aron's HSP abbreviations for the sake of brevity in what has turned out to be another of my long books.

*Frequent abbreviations*

    HSP – Highly Sensitive Person

    NHSP – Non-Highly Sensitive Person

    HSS – High Sensation Seeker

    NHSS – Non-High Sensation Seeker

    HSPC – Highly Sensitive Person's Companion

    NHSPC – Non-Highly Sensitive Person who is an HSP's Companion

*Other abbreviations*

    CBT – Cognitive Behavior Therapy

    EFT – Emotional Freedom Techniques

    EMDR – Eye Movement Desensitization and Reprocessing

    EP – Energy Psychology

    ESP – Extrasensory Perception

    HuTiST – Hunger, Tiredness, Stress, Trauma

    NLP – Neurolinguistic Programming

    PK – Psychokinesis (mind influencing matter)

    PPSH – Place of Peace, Safety and Healing

    SUSS – Subjective Units of Distress Scale

    TFT – Thought Field Therapy

    TWR – Transformative Wholistic Reintegration

    TWR1 – symptom focus

    TWR2 – underlying causes addressed

    WHEE – Wholistic Hybrid of EMDR and EFT

**ALERT FOR HIGHLY SENSITIVE READERS ABOUT POSSIBLY DISTURBING REPORTS OF TRAUMAS IN THIS BOOK**

A CAUTION FOR ANYONE WHO HAS A HISTORY OF TRAUMA, OR IF YOU ARE SENSITIVE AND FIND YOURSELF EASILY TRIGGERED INTO SERIOUS DISTRESS BY LISTENING TO OR READING ABOUT OTHER PEOPLE'S TRAUMAS AND EMOTIONAL UPSETS: I SUGGEST THAT YOU READ THE SECTION ON THE PLACE OF PEACE AND SAFETY AND HEALING (PPSH) FIRST.[*1] THIS WILL GUIDE YOU IN DEVELOPING CALMING AND HEALING POSITIVES TO USE FOR SELF-HEALING, AND WILL PROVIDE RESOURCES TO CALM AND SOOTHE YOURSELF IN CASE YOU GET TRIGGERED BY READING ANYTHING IN THIS BOOK.

# FOREWORD

## *Awakenings*

I jerk awake to the roar of Israeli jets flying low over our rooftop,
heading out over the Mediterranean.
It's Yom Kippur, 1973, the holiest day in the Jewish calendar,
and always the quietest day of the year,
with only emergency traffic on the road.
So this can't be a good thing that's happening.**[1]
I'm still tense and shaking with the sounds of these jets at rooftop level,
but the house isn't shaking in the wash of the jet engines.
And I'm in bed, just an hour outside Toronto, on a cold, snowy
Canadian day in 2018.
Oh, my goodness! It's just the sound of snow plows I'm hearing,
scraping a bunch of snow to clear the parking lot outside our windows.
What a relief!
But wait! I'm much too rattled by these sounds, waaaaaay more than I need to be.
Oh, my goodness again! I'm in the midst of being triggered into a post traumatic
stress memory I never knew was lurking inside me.

Every book ever written contains the story of its author
in one way or in many ways
that reveal some aspects of this person's beingness.

It's humbling, to realize yet again that the same applies to me
in such a glaring way.
As a psychiatric psychotherapist,
specializing in pain and trauma
of children, adults, couples and families,
I often see such trauma responses
and teach people to understand and clear them,
so they can again live more normal, happy and fulfilling lives.

So the good news is that I have the tools that I need
to clarify further and to clear my own traumas.
And this brings me more intimately into all that I share in this book
about understanding ourselves
on every wholistic level of our being:
Body, Emotions, Mind, Relationships (with other people and the rest of the world)
and Spirit.
And about healing ourselves,
and each other,
and every other aspect of this beleaguered and threatened planet.
And this includes healing of the collective consciousness
of our families, communities, nations and the entire planet.
Because there are traumas at each of these collective levels
that have been crying out for healing for many years.

You, dear reader, can play a far more significant role
than you might have imagined in these healings.
Through your own healings you contribute to the collective healing
of every aspect of this beautiful but beleaguered world.
And you can extend these healings across space and time.
Read on and learn how to do this for yourself
as well as for others.

I've been waiting for inspiration to guide me in writing this introduction.
I'm daunted by the challenges of condensing into just a few lines,
or even in the many lines of this mini-encyclopedia,
what is the essence of my 76 years of life lessons
on this planet that is itself deeply scarred
by its many traumas during four and a half billion years.

And still counting
the decades or centuries remaining,
if not just the months and years,
till we learn whether we are actually witnessing
the definitive evidence of its sixth major extinction,
which will be called the human extinction,
that will at some point become apparent to all.

There is a slim thread of a chance we might avert the extinction.
But if not, we can at least learn
to identify and clear the residues of past traumas
and to prepare ways forward for better futures
in lives we have not begun to imagine.

## *My personal background*

I was born in 1941 and raised by my mother in New York City till age four. As she told it, I was the reason she had been seasick on the boat trip from British Mandate Palestine to New York to get her degrees in Occupational Therapy and Rehabilitation. At the end of WW II, I met my father when we returned to Palestine.

We lived in Jerusalem during the war leading to the establishment of the State of Israel. My brother, David, was born just before the end of the war. So I had a strong taste of some of what it is like to live in a war zone, with limited food, and water distributed by trucks between air raids and shellings.

I returned with my mother and brother to New York in 1949. My parents were divorced a year later and I had minimal contact with my father till much later in life.

I was a bookworm and strongly drawn from an early age to learn about animals. Our New York apartment allowed a series of parakeets but no other pets. I read everything I could find in the library about animals, thinking I would be a veterinarian. My mother eventually convinced me to shift my goals to being a medical doctor, pointing out that people were animals too, and could make my work much easier by letting me know what they felt was wrong with them. I capitulated, not unwillingly, as I became fascinated with psychosomatic medicine – reading about some of the ways the mind could influence the body.

When I was 15 we moved to Los Angeles, where I completed high school half a year early by taking summer courses, and a BA in Psychology in two and a half years by taking 22 units a term plus summer courses again. Money was limited and my contribution towards family finances was to shorten the time I was a dependent.

Medical school at UCLA was exciting because they had an excellent department of psychiatry and inspiring psychiatrists teaching in the medical school. This largely compensated for my enormous disappointments in much of the rest of my medical training, which focused on bodies rather than on the people who inhabited the bodies.

I married Vivian, who was completing her studies to be a high school chemistry teacher, at the end of my second med school year and took a year off to settle into our relationship, while exploring my interest in psychiatric research on a National Institute of Mental Health fellowship in psychiatry. This helped me to confirm I was on the right career track.

I then completed medical training, Internship, and my first year of psychiatry residency before volunteering as a psychiatrist and being assigned to a US Air Force base in a rather desolate part of Texas. I was not pleased to do this, but it was a better alternative by far than waiting to be drafted and quite likely being sent to Viet Nam as a medical doctor. (Almost all the new graduates of medical schools were Medical Corps fodder.) And I learned a lot about war trauma, and very clearly confirmed my views and opinions on the foolishness and futility of military options as ways of solving problems.

I enjoyed being father to my two daughters, Debbie and Becky, born during these years. In hindsight, though, I regret that I let my career interests and studies overshadow their earlier years, including the rest of my training in psychiatry.

In part to correct this, and in part to pursue Vivian's wishes to have a year's sabbatical in Israel, when I finished my psychiatric training we relocated to Ashkelon, a small city on the Mediterranean coast, just north of Gaza. I recall in particular enjoying being part of a synagogue community, walking along the Mediterranean beach and swimming on weekends, and hiking the hills and deserts around the country. We found this experience so positive that we stayed there for six years. For me, a greatly healing part of this experience was getting to know my father for the first time.

But again, the foolishness of military solutions to problems was strongly highlighted by the Yom Kippur War of 1973 and the continued, smoldering hostilities between Israel and its neighbors. This was all the more sharply focused for us in an unanticipated benefit of learning to appreciate the Arab points of view, as my father was an administrator for Israeli Arab education.

I fast forward my life story, as it is not the primary focus of this book, but rather to provide a context and some frames for understanding how I came to my broader understandings of health and healing than most of my medical, psychiatric and psychotherapy colleagues. Highlights include:

– I learned through donating a replacement pint of blood after my father's surgery that our blood types were incompatible with his being my biological father.

– My mother, reluctantly, admitted that my biological father had been a lover she had had for many years during her marriage and after her divorce. He had passed on when I was a teenager.

– I dealt with these emotional and relational challenges with the help of several psychotherapists.

– We returned to the US for a fellowship in family therapy, and ended up staying there.

– My interest in healers and healing was sparked by observing a physical change (that was medically impossible!) in response to 30 minutes of healing. A young man presented with a lump under his nipple that was 1 x 1.5 cm, firm and rubbery to touch, not as mobile as I'd like to see in a lesion of this sort (suggesting the possibility of an invasive growth) and exquisitely tender. After 30 minutes of touch healing on his chakras and in his energy field, accompanied by strong emotional releases, the lump shrank by a centimeter, was soft, mobile and non-tender. Another physician was there with me and we both agreed on our palpated observations before and after the treatment. This was a cure for my strong skepticism about healing as well as for his lump!

– My interests in healing that challenged my wife's scathing skepticism, added to other issues in the marriage that had not responded to five years of individual and marital therapies, led to my divorce from Vivian. I remained in the area till Debbie and Becky were in university.

– I went to England in 1987 on a sabbatical and ended up staying for 10 years, with two marriages and divorces along the way. I founded and chaired the Doctor-Healer Network, where healers and physicians met periodically to explore how best to work together. I started writing my Healing Research series of books.[2]

– I returned to the US in 1997, wanting to do more teaching of complementary/alternative therapies than was possible in the UK. I thought I had found a perfect place to practice, teach and research CAM therapies and healing, but the clinic closed shortly after my arrival due to financial challenges.

– I was forced, very reluctantly, to return to practicing psychiatry in order to put bread on my table. By this time, psychiatry had shifted from being primarily psychotherapy to being exclusively medication prescription and management. The worst of this was that I had only 20 minutes a month for office visits. This made it impossible to practice psychotherapy, which is what I had signed on for in becoming a psychiatrist.

– These apparently negative circumstances turned out to be the best thing that could have happened to me! I was forced to seek and develop simple, rapidly effective methods for helping people within the limited timeframes available. This led me to develop WHEE (Wholistic Hybrid of EMDR (Transformative Wholistic Reintegration) and EFT (Emotional Freedom Techniques), which has been enormously helpful to my clients as well as to myself in releasing stress, pains, traumas and distress, beyond all expectations.*[3] Much more on this throughout this book.

– In 2006 I moved to Canada, near Toronto, as I felt the US was heading into difficult times. Here, I happily work as a wholistic psychotherapist, with a worldwide practice via phone and Skype.

This narrative offers a factual outline of my life.

The qualitative, wholistic aspects of my life are shared, as relevant, throughout the book. Here are a few general notes as orientation to my opening to wholistic understandings of life, the universe and everything.

– Though I feel I was born as an HSP, in order to deal with my life challenges I relied on my thinking and intuitive gifts and skills far more than on my emotional awarenesses in the first 40 years of my life.

– Gradually, I watched healers at work and observed the broad, wholistic improvements in people they helped. I dabbled at first in healing as an objective observer, but eventually began to swim myself in the deeper waters of human existence and consciousness. I learned a bit of Therapeutic Touch and Reiki healing, and then explored how blending healing with psychotherapy enhanced my therapeutic practice.

– The more I explored healing, the more I came to see the entire world as much more interconnected than I had ever been taught it could be.

– As I observed the deepening of my wholistic awarenesses, I came to sense that the people I was helping were also teaching and helping me to understand myself more fully and deeply.

– As I wrote this book, I realized it could actually be seen as Volume IV of the Healing Research series published ten and more years ago.[4]

You will find much more on these and related wholistic observations in this book, and more on my personal development as relevant to the discussions of wholistic healing and HSP issues.

This book is truly an encyclopedia of HSP issues and how to deal with them. If you've read anything in encyclopedias, you'll know there are likely to be entries that are very helpful to you, and others that you will find irrelevant or even impossible to understand. This may be the case for you in this mini-encyclopedia as well.

So don't feel bad if you come upon items that either don't interest you or even feel odd or strange and worth skipping. HSPs are not, by any means, all the same. Some are introverted, others are outgoing and social. Some are active and like stimulation, and others are quiet and sedentary. And there are many, many other variations in the universe of HSPs.

So you might make use of the Table of Contents and the Index to hone in on what really resonates with you, the unique being that you are. And feel free to skip about in this mini-encyclopedia to sections that are particularly interesting to you and relevant to your unique life.

Or you might just make your way slowly and gently through the entire book, perhaps learning about aspects of yourself and other HSPs you were never aware of before.

And if you're a non-HSP but curious or needing to learn what HSPs are all about, you might just push yourself to read straight through this mini-encyclopedia. You may then be prepared to help the HSP in your life to understand and deal with their life challenges with greater understanding and healing.

I wish you good reading, good insights, and good self-healings.

And please feel free to contact me to let me know what resonates particularly with your unique, special HSP life, or what you would like to know even more about.

# SECTION I. Foundational Introduction

*In this book I offer you a broad spectrum of observations and suggestions for understanding and living your life to your fullest capacity – whether you're a Highly Sensitive Person (HSP) yourself or someone living with an HSP.*

*Writing this book has felt to me many degrees more challenging than explaining a complicated board game. In the game of life, as I understand it, we are given a broad invitation to choose and develop the roles we will play and the rules by which we will interact with others. We can discover hidden doorways into magical realms; find allies who will help us deal with our challenges; and have many opportunities to choose between good and evil. We have far more abilities to direct the courses and outcome of our lives than we generally realize or are taught in conventional educational and healthcare systems.*

*The complexity of life is such that we need to consider and understand many different pieces of the puzzle. Each piece has its own complexities. So in Section I you are invited to consider some of the important pieces of the puzzle and some of the ways that help to explain it. Following sections will take you deeper into the mysteries of life, enabling you to consider where you fit in this wonder-full world we inhabit, how to maximize your enjoyments and successes in life, and how to deal successfully with challenges that may confront you.*

*I wish you good journeys and healing explorations!*

## 1. Highly Sensitive People (HSPs) and their Companions (HSPCs)

*Highly Sensitive People offer great gifts of healing for this ailing world.*
*Let's explore how we can all understand and benefit from their gifts.*

Have you ever felt that this world is more than just a little mad? That it's getting worse instead of better? That it's hard for you to find a place of calm and sanity and safety? The more you can relate to these questions, the more likely it is that you're the sort of sensitive person this book is about, and that this book is going to help you discover ways to understand what is happening in this world, and to figure out better ways to deal with your life and with this world gone mad.

HSPs often have above average sensitivity of vision, hearing, smell, taste and touch. We also process our sensory perceptions in great detail. This can leave us prone to overstimulation, which many control by avoiding highly stimulating situations and arranging for regular quiet time in their lives.

I find the HSP trait to be extremely helpful to me, personally, and also in my practice of wholistic psychotherapy. It is an enormous blessing to HSPs to identify and understand our HSP characteristics. This enables us to clarify and comprehend the ways we feel about ourselves, and the ways we respond to others and to the world in general. It enables us to make adjustments so that we feel more comfortable within ourselves and in our interactions with others.

HSPs are also strongly connected to their emotions – both within themselves and in their interactions with others. They enjoy processing their emotions and emotional nuances of situations in conversations with others who have similar awarenesses. In general, they may be impulsive in small matters, following their emotions, but tend not to be unduly adventurous and prefer to explore all their options before moving into new situations or making serious life changes.

While 15-20 percent of the population are HSPs, a much higher percent of HSPs are found among those engaging in psychotherapy. This is because they are generally more prone to introspection, to self-analysis and to working hard at developing, maintaining and improving relationships than non-HSPs (NHSPs) are.

Much more will be shared about HSPs in this section and throughout this book, considering various experiences and situations that may be challenging, as well as pointing out a broad spectrum of blessings that come with being an HSP.

This book will help readers who are well aware of being HSPs themselves or of being in close relationships with HSPs. It will also expand your awareness if you are new to exploring HSP issues – for yourself or as a friend, partner, spouse, therapist or school teacher working with HSPs.

We'll start with a detailed consideration of what it's like to be an HSP and what it's like to be a companion (HSPC) to an HSP. We'll then explore varieties of ways to address issues that may arise in your lives – both individually and between an HSP and HSPC, as well as between an HSP and other people in general. I'll also share many approaches that I've found helpful in decreasing anxieties and tensions in our lives, improving the ways we feel about ourselves and each other, sorting out and dealing with residues of painful issues from the past. Even better, I'll suggest ways for acquiring and strengthening habits and feelings of positivity.

Explaining all of this is somewhat similar to explaining a very complex cooperative board game. You have to understand a lot of different bits and pieces in order to come out happy. To understand how to address your life issues within a wholistic framework, you need first to understand the issues. However, descriptions of the issues do not prepare you to understand the underlying wholistic issues involved in how these experiences in your life developed, nor the different ways they can be addressed – with self-healing or with the help of various caregivers. Furthermore, much of our understanding of how specific issues developed comes from dealing with them through various therapies. So I will guide you through explorations of life challenges and therapies, weaving a tapestry of deepening understanding as we consider both.

### Technical points

I often make observations and suggestions on how HSPs and their companions, partners or spouses get along with each other. For the sake of brevity, I mention only 'companions' or 'partners' in many of the discussions. I trust that spouses will understand and will not take offense to be included under these terms.

Endnotes have often frustrated me, because they may indicate several different types of information, and I have no way to know, other than checking each one, what awaits me at the end of my search. To help readers of this book, I use the following notations. Plain endnotes indicate outside references.

✦ A single asterisk indicates further information on the subject in other parts of this book

✦✦ A double asterisk indicates additional comments on the subject

✦✦✦ A triple asterisk indicates the author's experiences

You may want to read this book slowly, a section at a time. I strongly recommend that you take notes as you read, particularly where there are suggestions that may enable you to say and do things in the most healing ways possible for your situation. You will be encouraged to personalize the issues and approaches explained in this book and it is very easy to forget a terrific idea you may have, one that might transform your relationships and your life, if you push quickly on to read further, new and different observations and suggestions.

*YOU MIGHT START THINKING ABOUT WHAT THE SPECIFIC ISSUES ARE THAT LEAD YOU TO READ THIS BOOK.*

*JOT DOWN YOUR FEELINGS, THOUGHTS AND EXPERIENCES THAT YOU WOULD LIKE TO UNDERSTAND BETTER AND TO IMPROVE.*

*LEAVE SOME SPACE AT THE END OF YOUR LIST, AS WE COMMONLY REMEMBER MORE ISSUES WHEN WE'VE GIVEN THIS QUESTION A BIT OF TIME TO PERCOLATE.*

*If you are new to the awareness of the HSP trait, you are probably wondering whether you're an HSP yourself. Elaine Aron developed a questionnaire for this.*

*CHECK TO SEE HOW YOU FIT WITHIN THE COMMON CHARACTERISTICS OF THE HSP TRAIT.*
*http://hsperson.com/test/highly-sensitive-test/*

## 2. The author

> *I learned that medicine does not merely consist in taking care of body parts. Treating a disease and treating a person are very different concerns, because recovery depends in large part on the mind and spirit of the patient. Suffering, a state of mind, involves the entire person.*
> — Philip Yancy & Paul Brand

It is an enormous challenge to present the materials in this book because you and I and everyone else are such complex beings. I'll share with you a very broad range of perspectives on understanding ourselves and dealing with our problems in life – from minor irritations to major issues. These sharings are based on my wide-ranging explorations in Wholistic health and healing – addressing issues of body, emotions, mind, relationships and spirit:

- Formal education and training
  - I have BA in Psychology and MD at the University of California, Los Angeles, with a 1-year National Institute of Mental Health Psychiatry Research Fellowship, also at UCLA;
  - Medical internship at the University of Kansas Medical School
  - Conventional psychiatric training at the University of Cincinnati, University of Colorado, and Colorado General Hospital (back in the days when Psychiatry was primarily psychoanalytically oriented psychotherapy)
- Five decades of practicing clinical psychotherapy (including two years in the US Air Force Medical Corps at an Air Force psychiatric hospital
- Very broad explorations in wholistic healing therapies over 45 years – reading, attending workshops, extensive discussions with complementary/alternative therapists (many of them having diverse gifts of healing), exploring these approaches for helping clients and for dealing with my own issues, teaching wholistic healing workshops, and wholistic healing research
- Practicing as a psychotherapist for six years in Israel, ten years in England, and the remainder of my career in the US and Canada
- Researching and writing over 200 articles and a series of five books on wholistic healing and spiritual awareness, plus other books on methods of self-healing that I developed.[1]
- Serving as Editor-in-Chief of the International Journal of Healing and Caring, an open access, peer reviewed journal since 2001
- Participating in the American Holistic Medicine Association (AHMA) and the British Holistic Medical Association (BHMA) over a period of 20 years
- Joining with like-minded colleagues as a Founding Diplomate of the American Board of Integrative Holistic Medicine (ABIHM)
- Founding and for a dozen years serving as Coordinator of the Council for Healing, a non-profit organization that promotes awareness of a broad spectrum of healing
- Extensive experience in presenting lectures and teaching workshops at professional meetings
- I have served for many years on the advisory boards of professional journals

All of these formal studies and clinical practice experiences have given me very broad perspectives on health, illness and healing. I'm impressed that there is no single way to understand health or illness. My best teachers, my clients, have taught me that each person is unique and therefore the processes involved in navigating through life are as varied as are the personalities and lives of each and every person. Every aspect of our lives contributes to who we are today and to who we become. Positive experiences enrich us, help us trust the world and invite us to engage more openly and intimately with the world. Negative experiences, such as personal rejections, traumas, injuries and illnesses can discourage us from engaging with the world and from getting the most out of life.

Each experience in life will play out in unique ways within the life of each person. Each of us will also adopt and carry our personal rules for how we respond to our life experiences. These personal laws for relating to our inner and outer lives may be trusting or distrusting; encouraging openness and engagement with others, or defensive and keeping us on the alert against being hurt or harmed and distancing ourselves from others. When we are unaware of our self-limiting inner rules, we may miss seeing and developing options and possibilities for bringing more joy, love and successes into our lives. Worse yet, we may adopt varieties of negative self-images that make us feel bad about ourselves and interfere with our enjoyment in life. We may even end up harming ourselves.

I write as an HSP myself, sharing my personal experiences as relevant. I find life an exciting journey of discovering ever-new awarenesses about who I am, on every level of my being. I hope what I share will stimulate your curiosity to explore yourself and your relationships with your worlds, too.

WRITE DOWN SOME OF THE RULES YOU'VE DEVELOPED TO GUIDE YOU THROUGH LIFE FOR:

- *YOUR MAXIMUM ENJOYMENT*

- *YOUR GREATEST BENEFITS TO YOURSELF*

- *THE GREATEST HELP YOU CAN OFFER OTHERS*

- *YOUR SAFETY FROM BEING HURT, ON EVERY LEVEL OF YOUR BEING*

- *YOUR WAYS OF DEALING WITH HURT – IN YOUR BODY, EMOTIONS, MIND, RELATIONSHIPS AND SPIRIT*


A glance at the table of contents will give you a sense of the maps and tools I use in my personal and professional understandings of what it is to be an HSP. I present the various topics in this particular order because the first ones are my basic building blocks for explaining the personal and collective evolution of our consciousness, relationships and interactions with the world at large. Later topics cover broader relationships we have with the world, both in learning our personal place in the universe as well as in sorting out our highest contributions for the greatest good of all. Each of these building blocks contributes to our understandings of consciousness in general, and specifically relating to HSPs and their companions in life (HSPCs) – whether they are part of the HSP's biological family, their family of choice, a friend, colleague or even a stranger in a brief encounter.

## 3. Wholistic healing, an introduction

> *If a living system is suffering from ill health, the remedy is to connect it with more of itself.*
>
> - Francisco Varela

I offer in this book many windows of perception into ways HSPs come to experience life, feel, behave, relate and comprehend who we are. Several basic psychological factors guide my understanding of HSPs and how we live and experience our lives and relationships.

Wholistic healing is core to how I conceptualize the human condition. Body, emotions, mind, relationships and spirit are inseparable aspects of everyone's essence. Although Western society has subdivided these aspects of our being into separate categories of health, illness and healing, they are in fact parts of a unitary wholeness in every human being. Through this wholistic perspective I will show you how to better understand yourself and your life companion, family and friends, and how to get along with them better in every possible way.

I use the word 'healing' frequently. This word has many varieties and shades of meanings in popular, therapeutic and scientific usage. Dictionary.com defines healing, the adjective, as curing or curative; prescribed or helping to heal; growing sound; getting well; mending. As a noun, it is "the act or process of regaining health." These definitions focus on a return to a more normal state, presumably starting from a dysfunctional or diseased state.

While I accept and follow these uses of the word 'healing,' and consider many ways in which we can return to more normal and functional states, I also use it in the sense of healing being a search for and pursuit of a state of greater 'wholeness' within the wholistic spectrum of our beingness. So I am inviting you here to consider how to understand and harmonize body, emotions, mind, relationships with other people and with the environment, and spirit.

'Healing' is also used as a verb by people who apply various forms of interventions such as Therapeutic Touch, Healing Touch, Reiki, and related ways of identifying and adjusting the biological energy fields in and around the body.**[2]

I frequently refer to spirit in my discussions, and want to define my use of this word in this book and in my practice of wholistic healing. Spirit is the aspect of ourselves that extends beyond our physical selves. It transcends our ordinary sensory, emotional and cognitive awarenesses of the physical world. It may connect us with wholistic aspects of other living beings, with what we call the inanimate world (which actually is also conscious), with the consciousness of other people who have passed on from the physical world and are now in spirit dimensions, and with God/ The Infinite Source/ The All. Spirit also gives us access to memories of past lives – of our own and of other people. Spirit is not merely a belief about connecting with these dimensions. Spirit is an actual experience of knowing them experientially.**[3]

While it is instructive to examine the wholistic elements of each and every issue we consider, if I did so then this would make the book much longer than it is already. I therefore expand only selected, important sections into the full spectrum of wholistic consideration, to demonstrate the expanded awarenesses and options this broader perspective offers for dealing with varieties of situations. That's the good news.

Further good news is that both the issues of HSPs, along with those interacting with them, and the ways I suggest for understanding and dealing with these issues, are for the most part relatively easy to understand.

The challenging news is that there are many pieces to the puzzles of health and healing. To come to a solid understanding of the issues involved, to see the whole picture, we sometimes need to consider pieces of the puzzle that we haven't yet considered in detail in this book. So you will find cross-references within the book to other relevant pieces of the puzzle in the endnotes, along with references for further reading to help you fill in the picture.

Another bit of good news is that many of the approaches I write about are available as self-healing. You may be able to see immediately how you can use the relaxations, meditations or the techniques of energy psychology (EP),*4 along with other methodologies, to understand and relieve the stress or distress in your life. In some cases, you may find it helpful to take a workshop or a course, or to consult a therapist for a jump-start with counseling or therapy as you learn to apply these methods in your life. This will provide you with tools and help you sharpen them to use for your self-healing.

Each level of our being offers an explanation for who we are and why we feel and function as we do. Each level also opens doors to how we can get along better with ourselves and others. While we all know that something has to change when we find ourselves stuck in our lives, it's not always easy to identify where the sticking points are or how to alter our perceptions, understandings, behaviors or relationships in order to improve our condition.

I will repeatedly discuss various HSP, NHSP and HSPC issues within wholistic perspectives. While this might seem repetitive at times, my intention is three-fold:

1. Though we discuss various components of wholistic healing individually, each is intricately connected with all of the others. Each is like the face of a clear, six-sided crystal. When you examine any single face of the crystal, you also see all of the others.

2. It takes some effort to come to a fuller and deeper understanding of the unity of wholistic healing. The repetitions will help you develop the habit of expanding your wholistic considerations of issues in various aspects of your life. This will be enormously helpful to you in understanding what is out of harmony – on any and every level of your being or of another person in your life. So, if you start with an issue of body disharmony, your will know how to expand your considerations to include the other five facets of the crystal as well, and the same applies if you start with an issue that draws your attention first to any of the other facets of the crystal.

3. Wholistic perspectives will also offer you vastly expanded resources to heal what bothers or hurts you.

Understanding and changing ourselves is usually the best place to start when we want to comprehend and change our ways of being and relating in the world. While this may sound simple, it is usually rather challenging. Transformative Wholistic Reintegration (TWR) is the best approach I know for feeling better, for clearing problems and for building more positivity into our lives. TWR is a self-healing method that is easy to learn and use, yet rapidly and deeply effective. It is truly transformative.

This involves:
- alternately tapping on the left and right sides of your body
- focusing on the feelings and thoughts that bother you
- followed by focusing on a strongly positive statement.

I explain TWR in detail later, and illustrate how it can help you to build a happier life for yourself and those who are near and dear to you.[5]

TWR is also known as Wholistic Hybrid derived from EMDR and EFT (WHEE). Various therapists complained that 'WHEE' seemed too trivial a name for such a profoundly transformative approach. They were often asked, for instance, whether it had anything to do with the home video game called Wii. For that reason, WHEE is being rebranded as TWR.*[6] TWR/ WHEE is one of a family of Energy Psychology (EP) methods.*[7]

Characteristics of HSPs are explored in Section II. One of the more prominent aspects of HSPs is that their sensory organs are often very highly responsive to stimulation. Sounds or visual stimuli that NHSPs experience as normal may feel too jarring to HSPs.

Many HSPs live, breathe and interact within their emotions. They are not lacking in abilities to think, but their sensitive emotions, sensory awarenesses of everything in their surroundings, and intuitions usually come first and foremost in their awarenesses of every aspect of their lives. They are truly human BE-ings. Emotions are sometimes sufficiently strong and their intensity is so powerful that HSPs may feel stressed or even overwhelmed by them. It is in the unfolding processes of beingness within their feelings that they learn what is real, relevant and important to them... in each moment.

This spectrum of sensitivities may put some HSPs out of synch with the majority of people, who live as NHSPs through their thoughts, communicate through statements about thoughts, and often minimize or avoid awareness of their own and others' emotions. When they connect with their awarenesses of their emotions, they may often stand outside their emotions, observing them as feelings (mental constructs applied to emotions). NHSPs also tend to live by rules, while HSPs live through what feels right at that moment.

These differences may lead to mutual misunderstandings between NHSPs and HSPs. NHSPs who are out of touch with their emotions may perceive HSPs' sensitivities as over-reactions or unnecessary, overly dramatic reactions to situations that the NHSPs find innocuous. Conversely, NHSPs tend not to notice or to ignore emotional aspects of situations and relationships. Often, they are uncomfortable with expressing their emotions. Emotional reactions of HSPs therefore make the NHSPs uncomfortable.

Throughout the book, I offer many typical, illustrative examples of how various people have dealt with such challenges. The following examples from people I've worked with will help you understand how problems develop and how you can best deal with them. To protect the anonymity of those I have worked with, I altered identifying details and created composite examples in their reports. I indicate case reports with an asterisk (✦). Reports that continue after some discussion about the points that they illustrate are indicated with a double asterisk (✦✦). A triple asterisk indicates a report of my own experiences (✦✦✦).

Here is an example of some of the many ways that HSPs come to awareness that they are more sensitive than other people, and some of the challenges that their sensitivities may present.

✦ 'Avis' was a petite, charming stenographer in a secretary pool of a large corporation. She was usually bright and cheerful, a pleasure to have around. She was exquisitely sensitive to the moods and needs of her co-workers, often seeming to anticipate their wishes even before they articulated them. But she had difficulties with some of the management who were tense, loud, irritable or at times easily angered. Despite her best efforts to remain calm and centered in their presence, she would quickly become rattled and anxious herself, making silly errors that worsened the situation.

She managed to miss as many of the official office functions as she could get away with, making every excuse under the sun. The truth was that she felt over-stimulated to the point of overwhelm in group meetings or parties. She even found it difficult to tolerate her tensions when she was in the same room with the manager who understood and valued her for her strengths, and ran interference for her, assigning her as much as possible to the more pleasant and considerate managers. She was constantly worried he would give up on her and decide she was too much of a burden for him to bother with.

Avis had had similar experiences during her school years, but had managed fairly well to avoid getting stressed by loud or aggressive classmates and teachers. She simply withdrew into a self-absorbed silence, often keeping her nose buried in a book. She was not socially withdrawn, but was known as a pleasant but generally quiet person.

If HSPs like Avis are fortunate, they grow up in families that accept their sensitivities and accommodate to them. They are allowed to have their quiet times and safe places for retreat from stress and overwhelm, and for de-stressing as needed – in order to avoid over-stimulation and to calm down.

If they are unfortunate and grow up in surroundings that are lacking in understanding of their highly acute senses and emotional sensitivities, they may become irritable, oppositional and angry. These HSPs' habits of perception and responses to their life situations and interactions become shaped by what they perceive and experience as countless minor and major stresses, criticisms and rejections from NHSPs. Even when the negativity of NHSPs is not intense, HSPs may suffer because they experience frequent or even constant small criticisms and rejections, which may be traumatic for them due to their sensitivities. More about Avis shortly.

I digress here briefly to introduce a little bit about traumas. Understanding trauma is absolutely essential when we're sorting ourselves out. Trauma is a negative experience that seriously impacts us. It can be a major problem like a serious physical injury, loss of someone close to us, being in a car crash or other traumatizing situation, experiencing a very difficult failure or disappointment, or witnessing the trauma of someone else. It may appear to be a relatively minor issue, like being criticized or shamed in school, family members or friends not accepting us, or failing in a task or a relationship. The problem is that we respond intensely to the experience, feeling frightened, sad, unaccepted, rejected or badly hurt in any other way.

Most people are able to shrug off or sort through varieties of minor or even moderately disturbing experiences of these sorts and move on in their lives. But for some people, in some situations, a particular trauma has more impact. In many cases, even with an intense response, most people can find ways to sort through it, resolve the issues, release their hurt feelings, and move on. But sensitive people may respond much more intensely. And if the trauma leads us to feel overwhelmed, and we don't find inner resources or outside supports to deal with the overwhelm, we may end up with emotional scars.

HSPs' sensitivities leave them particularly prone to psychological traumas. In part, this is due to their sensitivities making them feel vulnerable and easily overwhelmed. Another cause is that they are easy targets for bullies, who prey particularly on people whom they see as weak and whom they can easily upset – thereby venting their frustrations and hurts on others in order to feel stronger themselves.

Without supports, HSPs' challenges in interacting with the community at large often border on or extend into traumatic experiences. They may have difficulties concentrating, forgetfulness, difficulties dealing with school expectations and requirements, avoidance of social interactions, fears, phobias and even post traumatic stress residues that are commonly labeled as psychiatric disorders. I discuss various psychiatric labels that may be mistakenly applied to HSPs in Section III.

If you are a family member, friend, teacher, or partner of an HSP, this book will offer you a wide array of resources for yourself and for your HSP. If you are an HSP companion to an HSP, you will naturally share similar spectrums of sensitivities, and will find this book similarly helpful for yourself. If you are an HSP companion (HSPC) and are an NHSP, you will also find much of this book tremendously helpful. This book will aid you both in understanding and in getting along with your HSP friends, family and/or partner.

> ✦✦✦ I (Dan) was not aware of the HSP as a specific typology until about ten years ago, and I am now 76 years old! I was well aware that there were people who were open to feeling and expressing their emotions, and those who avoided consciousness of and expressions of their emotions, but I had not crystallized this into anything like an awareness the HSP trait Aron describes and has defined so well. Looking back on my many years of helping people through psychotherapy, I can identify numerous clients who were certainly HSPs. Since reading Aron's books, and then finding Ted Zeff's books, I've recommended that many of my clients read them. They have come to thank Elaine Aron and Ted Zeff for these contributions to their healing as well! Zeff's books are particularly appreciated because he writes as an HSP himself.
>
> I have also found HSP awareness enormously helpful in my personal life and relationships. I survived a very difficult, traumatizing childhood by living in my thinking self, while minimizing and suppressing my feelings. My sensitivities expressed themselves rather subtly. For instance, I've always had a very strong sense of rightness and wrongness This is like an inner radar and compass that has guided me in my life from early childhood, helping me recognize signs of lovingness and healing, as well as dissonance and negativity in people's attitudes, behaviors and ways of relating to others. I gave a wide berth to anyone who exhibited danger signals of being aggressive or bullying. More on this later in this Chapter and in further Chapters of this book.

Knowing we are extra-sensitive in many areas also enables HSPs to explain ourselves to those with whom we interact, so that they can understand us and can accept and accommodate to our sensitivities, comfort levels and needs.

The good news is that many HSPs are gifted with emotional sensitivity to other people. This enables us to appreciate what others are feeling and why they respond as they do. HSPs often gravitate, appropriately, to work in the caregiving professions. As HSP caregivers, we resonate and empathize deeply with the stresses, traumas and pains of others. That's the good news. This enables us to understand people more quickly and deeply, so that we can help them more quickly and deeply.

The bad news is that HSPs are also sensitive to the fact that we are more sensitive than others. We often respond more quickly and deeply to stressful and painful experiences. This can be unsettling to others, who may not yet be consciously aware of their own stresses while we HSPs are stressing out from sensory overloads, from intensities of emotionality in these people and in ourselves, and from insensitive emotionality, behaviors and reactions of NHSPs in difficult and challenging situations.

*WHAT ARE SOME OF YOUR PARTICULAR SENSITIVITIES?*

*WHAT ARE HELPFUL WAYS THAT YOU CAN EXPLAIN YOUR SENSITIVITIES TO NHSPs?*

This brings me to the issue of meta-awarenesses, to which I will refer frequently in this book. For instance, primary anxieties will often produce meta-anxieties. A meta-anxiety is a worry about a worry.

✦ 'Tessa,' an HSP, got extremely anxious because another person in her office was frustrated and muttering out loud, angrily, about how no one is listening to him when he is warning that a crisis is building in their department.

Tessa's anxieties shoot waaay up whenever anyone around her gets anxious. This is worse when they are loud, and worse yet when there is any hint that they might be getting out of control.

Tessa's father was an angry man with volatile emotions. Until Tessa left home, as soon as she could after her 18th birthday, he had shouted and screamed at her mother and the children if they made noise of any sort, even if they were arguing in a distant part of the house. Often, he would storm out of the house after he'd had such an outburst, coming home drunk after drowning his feelings at a bar.

Throughout her life, Tessa's internal alarm bells went off whenever someone around her became emotional. I call these sorts of inner alarm bells 'meta-anxieties.'

Meta-anxieties are the "OMG!" feelings we have when problems are threatening to get worse than they are, or when we think and feel we may be getting into a situation where we'll be out of control, in danger of being hurt physically or emotionally, and perhaps even beyond help.

✦✦ Tessa had learned that she was an HSP, without naming this as such. She always felt on guard to do her best to hold her feelings in – so that her father didn't get upset with her, and her family didn't give her a hard time for upsetting him.

The ways Tessa's father behaved are examples of the sort of bullying that people do in order to avoid their own anxieties and meta-anxieties about having uncomfortable feelings. On top of their challenges in dealing with whatever upsets them, people who displace their feelings like Tessa's father did are behaving in these ways due to their unfamiliarity with emotions and incompetence in dealing with them. Being unaware of the sources of their over-reactions leaves bullies vulnerable to being triggered very quickly into bullying behaviors, or into other ways of avoiding or controlling other people so that those who are expressing their feelings don't continue to trigger and upset these bullies.

Meta-anxieties are often very strong in people who have had traumas. A woman who has been attacked in a dark alley may hold onto anxieties about going out at night because her meta-anxieties are triggered: "If I let go of these anxieties I might let my guard down and stray into harm's way again in some dark place." A man who was blindsided in an auto accident might become anxious about getting into his car, fearing that he could again be hit by another car.

HSPs are prone to meta-anxieties about getting emotional. They fear they will upset other people, which can then spiral into a vicious circle of making the HSPs more anxious, making others more upset, making the HSPs more upset. I'll share more observations on meta-anxieties as they are relevant to other HSP and HSPC issues.*[8]  Many HSPs are also gifted with intuitive awarenesses, providing us with a radar that helps us navigate a world which is often quite challenging. These HSP qualities are discussed separately, in detail, in Section 2, on explanatory frameworks for understanding the HSP, and in Section VII on intuition. I give a lot of attention to HSP sensitivities because this is a complex issue and deserves acknowledgment, exploration and support.**[9]

*CAN YOU IDENTIFY ANY META-ANXIETIES THAT BOTHER YOU?*

*IN SIMPLER LANGUAGE, ARE THERE ANY ANXIETIES YOU HAVE ABOUT CHANGING HOW YOU DEAL WITH ANXIETIES OR WORRIES?*

# 4. Sections of this book

*It is more important to know what sort of person has a disease than to know what sort of disease a person has.*
- Hippocrates

Section II, understanding the HSP and HSPC, explores a variety of ways to understand HSP sensitivities, emotionality, mentality, relationships, behaviors and responses in various situations.

✦ 'Cara' came to me for help in dealing with 'Stan,' her fiancé, who was charming and considerate but very much a thinking type rather than a feeling type. As they moved beyond occasional dating to spending more time together, his patience was increasingly wearing thin because of what he called her moodiness – which she explained were not moods but rather her emotional sensitivities.

It is for these sorts of situations that I've written this book. Cara was clearly an HSP. HSPs often run into relationship problems because the majority of other people are so much less emotionally aware that it becomes a painful bone of contention to decide which person in a challenged relationship is the one who should adapt his or her behaviors – around a particular issue or situation, or in more general ways.

✦✦ Cara and Stan just needed to understand that Cara was an HSP to enable them to sort out their discord and conflicts. One couples session and reading Elaine Aron's HSP book provided the necessary explanations for them to understand themselves and each other.

✦✦✦ I have found the HSP awareness helpful in my personal life in many unanticipated ways. I started out in life without a father and with a mother who was probably an HSP. She was moody, easily irritated, and intense in venting her angers at me. She had marvelous sensitivity and insight in understanding others, but was very poor at appreciating her own emotional volatility and at understanding herself and her very fraught family relationships. How I wish I had found someone to help me understand her, as well as myself, in my childhood, teen or early adult years!

I've been blessed with a good mind and I buried myself in studies for the first 30 years of my life. I remember, as a child, coming to believe that adults know everything, and that someday I'd know everything too. Well, even today there's a part of me that hasn't given up on that notion!

Gradually... ever so slowly, tediously and painfully... I've come to realize that I too am an HSP. And memories of being sensitive have come back, as in crying easily as a child; not tolerating being in large groups, particularly if they are noisy; and being very sensitive to what others are feeling.

My thinking functions have also stood me in good stead. My awareness and understanding of psychological models for analyzing and explaining emotional experiences and behaviors has been an enormous help – to me and to those who come to me for explorations of their psychological and relationship issues.

My ongoing, omnivorous curiosity has led me to explore many ways of analyzing inner and outer experiences, and to enable me to better help clients understand themselves through my broadly eclectic psychotherapy perspectives and approaches.

Section II also describes and discusses a variety of psychological models that I find are helpful to myself and my clients in explaining problems that are common to HSPs, or that may be similar to HSP behaviors. For instance, there are models like:
- The worldviews of Carl Jung, particularly on personality types
- Right and Left Brain Hemisphere functions, which may differ considerably between HSPs and NHSPs
- Attention Deficit Hyperactivity Disorder (ADHD), with high sensitivity to distractions from what is going on in one's environment
- Anxieties and traumas and varieties of problems that can be created in our lives by recurrent, prolonged and/or severe stresses, and single or recurrent traumas, including post traumatic stress disorder (PTSD)
- The short and long-term processes involved in grief
- Inner child awarenesses
- Transactional Analysis, which identifies Adult (logical), Parent (self-aware), and child (spontaneous, emotional) ways of relating to the world
- and more...

You may find that some of these ways of analyzing and explaining behaviors help you to identify common issues relevant to HSPs, who are more sensitive and delicate, and therefore more vulnerable to suffering from such issues. Each of the above models (and conventional psychiatric diagnoses that are also discussed in Section III) can help understand aspects of the challenges that you and other HSPs and HSPCs face. Not all of these models are relevant to any one person. They do, however, offer a broad spectrum of possibilities for exploring, understanding, and addressing various problems, if and when they are present. And many people find that different methods are helpful for dealing with different problems. So a method that helped with one issue may not help with the next one, and conversely, methods that you did not find useful in one situation may be helpful in addressing other challenges.

Such models are also of enormous help in broadening and deepening the understandings of HSPs and their partners – about what they are experiencing in their relationships, and in improving how they get along with each other. The understandings alone that these behaviors are due to identifiable issues may alleviate tensions stirred by HSPs in irritating behaviors that appear willfully negligent, perverse, uncaring or even insensitive. Very often, such behaviors are just reflections of the HSPs' very different modes of perceiving, being, behaving and relating to others.

For instance, in some situations HSPs may be insensitive to the feelings, wishes or needs of others – at times when the HSPs are deeply immersed and narrowly focused on their own intense feelings. When such apparent insensitivities are identified, discussed and understood, HSPs can often address and clear them. HSPCs can also benefit from awareness of such factors – accommodating to them or negotiating mutually acceptable compromises around their bones of contention with the HSP.

Section III, Understanding the HSP: Alternative or additional diagnoses, explores alternative diagnoses to the HSP trait. More often than not, conventional therapists and doctor who are unfamiliar with the HSP trait will misdiagnose HSPs who come to them with psychological challenges. They might label them with Attention Deficit Hyperactivity Disorder (ADHD), Oppositional Defiant Disorder (ODD), Obsessive Compulsive Disorder (OCD), Attachment styles, Borderline personality or Narcissistic Personality Disorder (NPD). The issues involved in these diagnoses, and many other difficulties experienced by HSPs, are often seen as symptoms to be treated with medications.

> *If all you have is a hammer, then everything looks like a nail.*
> *- Bernard Baruch*

On the other hand, I have seen HSPs who had some of the above diagnoses in addition to being HSPs, and it is not uncommon for psychotherapists who recognize the HSP trait to miss such problems. Conversely, it is very common for conventional therapists who are unfamiliar with the HSP trait to label HSPs with some of the above diagnoses.

✦✦ Avis, the sensitive secretary, had learned early in life that she did better in quiet environments. Loud school lunchrooms and playgrounds jarred her so much that she avoided them whenever possible. She chose her friends carefully, preferring quiet, calm, gentle girlfriends. In high school, even with an understanding and accommodating date, she refused to go out to a loud disco or to stay out much later than her usual bedtime. She had very low tolerances for noise and tiredness. She had learned from many experiences that pushing beyond her limits made her irritable and argumentative. Some of these lessons she learned from her mother, who had a measure of HSP qualities herself. Other lessons were learned from personal, difficult experiences over time.

Avis was surprised and pleased to learn that she had many symptoms and characteristics of ADHD. She was easily distractible at some times, but over-focused in others. She had even greater difficulty concentrating on tasks at hand if her environment was even mildly bustling or noisy. While many HSPs have some of these characteristics, which tend to be closely related to the intensity of ambient emotional stimulation, both internal and external, Avis was constantly bothered by them. Noise or visual distractions were always intrusive, regardless of how emotionally stimulated Avis was at the time.

While Avis wasn't delighted she had these concentration issues, she was very pleased to be able to identify them so that she could then explore ways to deal with them. I was able to guide her to identify foods that worsened her ADHD, and by eliminating sugar and red dye (the most common triggers for worsening ADHD) she found herself much more calm and focused, and did not need medications to deal with her ADHD.

Few doctors take the time to explore dietary factors in people presenting distractibility as Avis did. This is not a willful avoidance of addressing dietary contributions of health and illness, so much as gross ignorance on this subject. The sum total of time devoted to diet in my medical school education was a one-hour lecture by a dietician – mostly focused on how she could help patients address a few of the countless medical issues that we medical students were learning to understand and treat.

Similarly, the medical approach to high sensitivity is too often to drug people in order to make them less sensitive and/or less emotionally reactive. While drugs may reduce symptoms and distress of overwhelms, they also severely diminish the quality of life of an HSP. Not only are excessive stimuli and overwhelm decreased, but also their general sensory awarenesses and responsiveness. Most HSPs feel that when taking drugs, they are not themselves. The self-healing methods detailed in this book are blessings to HSPs needing relief and calming from overstimulation and help to reduce their emotional reactivity and enhance their abilities to focus, think clearly and make good decisions, both small and large.

A few further words about pathologizing HSPs are appropriate here.

Being strongly connected to emotions and sensitive to emotions in others is one of the highlights of being an HSP. This is in many ways a blessing. HSPs and their HSPCs are more readily able to identify emotional factors contributing to problems and then to deal with them. This is the primary focus of this book.

HSPs are strongly empathetic and quickly see the emotions others are experiencing, and are then able to identify what is upsetting them and making them feel that way. These sensitivities serve HSPs well when in their personal relationships. If you are an HSPC, you may be fortunate in having this human mirror into your feelings and relationships. However, being constantly in a hall of mirrors may sometimes be stressful. Sections IV – VI offer resources for HSPs and HSPCs for finding the best ways to deal with these sensitivities.

HSPs choose frequently to work in the helping professions. They often make excellent caregivers because of their great sensitivity in understanding and addressing the problems people bring for "fixing." This book will be enormously helpful to those in the therapeutic community who are open to expanding their horizons beyond their primary treatment focus.

The down side of this emotional sensitivity is that some HSPs may resonate with everyone's emotions most of the time, leaving them drained and tired. Nearly every human situation and interaction is colored by associated emotions, and the HSP will very frequently respond to the emotions much more strongly than to the factual issues being addressed. This is where the HSPC can be particularly helpful – by pointing out that yes, these challenges are upsetting, but that it may be possible to address the issues in various ways to make them less upsetting. Section IV details ways to understand issues experienced by HSPs in themselves and in their relationships, and section IV offers many suggestions for ways to reduce the intensity of these issues and in many cases to clear them completely and permanently.

Work situations are another area where HSPs may often find themselves seriously bothered by their sensitivities. HSPs find it difficult having to be constantly in thinking mode, with no time for absorbing, digesting and responding to emotional aspects of the work environment. HSPs also find it wearing to deal with stresses of deadlines, brusque interactions that feel abrasive, and angry ones that may also be abusive. They may find it intolerable just being in a work environment that does not offer them any place to find peace and quiet from the normal hustle and bustle of a workplace. NHSPs in the work setting often have no awareness of HSP's sensitivities, and take any explanations of these to be signs of weakness or emotional instability. Sections IV – VI also offer many suggestions for dealing with these sorts of concerns.

Section IV, HSPs, their HSPCs and other family members, is about helping through understanding. This section introduces a variety of ways of comprehending HSP sensitivities. When we know what is going on in ourselves and in each other, this is enormously helpful to HSPs, HSPCs and others with whom we interact. When you are resourced with a spectrum of viewpoints and ways of understanding each other on every wholistic level of your being – as well as understanding the differences between HSPs and HSPCs – you will find it easier to get along.

Section IV provides suggestions that are particularly helpful for an NHSP in getting along with an HSP when you experience challenges in your relationship. To an NHSP, an HSP may seem delightful, spontaneous, expansive, creative or spiritual – on a good day. On a bad day, this same person you care for may seem too subjective, overly emotional, illogical, immature, unaware of your issues and needs, unfocused, and over-reactive. Or you may find that the switches between positive and negative relationships with your HSP occur much more quickly, as in waking to a smiling, warm, fuzzy morning that can switch to a bad hour with only minimal misunderstanding or provocation on your part, or without your having any clear understanding of what brought about the sudden shifts in mood and irritability.

Similarly, as an HSP you may find that while your intentions are wholly positive, the responses you get from others, particularly from NHSPs, are at times surprisingly negative. Exploring the approaches in this Chapter will help you understand and deal with such issues.

> ✦✦ In her early dating days, Avis very soon realized that she would quickly shift to being somewhere on the spectrum of unhappy to miserable if she was in the company of any boy who was loud, insensitive, belittling or irritated by her expressions of emotions and her rapid mood changes. She got along much better with guys who were themselves sensitive and therefore understood her better.
>
> Avis came to me for help when she found she had dated a series of three men at her office, each of whom had appeared warm and supportive initially, but all of whom became irritable and rejecting after a few dates. She had become depressed, feeling there must be something seriously wrong with her.
>
> Self-calming techniques of TWR and meditation were immediately helpful with her distress and depression about her situation. But it took a while for Avis to come to understand her HSP sensitivities, in particular her being easily irritated, agitated and fearful in what she experienced as stressful or threatening situations with people who did not accept her sensitivities. This included the more loud and aggressive managers in her workplace.
>
> Avis was able to see very quickly how practicing meditation and being in her inner place of peace and safety and healing (PPSH)*[10] enabled her to feel a more solid foundation of quietness, peace and safety within herself during much of the day, so she was less easily triggered into distress. She was highly motivated to do better in her personal relationships and at work, and practiced these methods regularly.

Practicing the methods you choose in this book is key to making improvements in most people, but even more so with HSPs. HSPs are wired for immediately responding emotionally to most situations. Re-setting your emotional thresholds and intensities for responses to triggers you experience may take numbers of repetitions of these exercises. It's rather like building up your body's tone and strength and endurance with dancing, yoga or jogging. But once you find yourself in a better psychological space, those skills are available for your use forever.

I've focused in this introduction mostly on HSP issues in adults. Children are often able much more easily to change their responses and behaviors and to absorb and use these skills. They don't have the years of repeated challenges and emotional burdens to clear that adults do.

In Section IV we also consider in detail how to help HSP children deal with their normal life and with stresses in various situations. It may often be challenging for parents to figure out how best to support their HSP children, even when one or both parents are HSPs.

> ✦ 'Garve' was a lovely, sweet baby, smiling readily and loving to be cuddled. At the age of 9 months, he became more and more irritable and less and less cuddly. This coincided with his aunt (his mother's younger sister) moving in to live with his family, along with her 6 and 8 year-old children. Garve's mother reported that her niece and nephew had been traumatized by the difficult separation of their parents. They were often loud and agitated. They were born and raised in India, and the process of moving to the US had also been stressful. On top of that, they experienced a lot of further challenges in adapting to their new school.
>
> Keeping Garve in a quiet space as much as possible, separated from his cousins, brought about immediate improvements. He was restored to a great degree to his former, cheerful self. This was, quite literally, the creation of a place of peace and safety and healing.*[11]
>
> Teaching everyone else in the family to de-stress with WHEE (children generally prefer this name over TWR) was also enormously helpful to everyone. Within a few weeks, the whole family was back to being more calm and less agitated and loud.

This example may seem to some readers so straightforward and obvious as to hardly warrant comment. But people who have never previously experienced a major stress, or a child or infant who is upset because she is sensitive to noise and stress, will all benefit very quickly with such self-calming methods.

Garve appeared to be an HSP. He was easily startled and rattled by loud noises, was intolerant of rough clothing (even bothered by labels at the back of his neck), and loved to be held and rocked gently. Garve was fortunate to be identified early in life as a sensitive baby, and likely an HSP, with parents who accepted his sensitivities and readily accommodated to them.

Boys who are emotionally sensitive and easily upset may often find it particularly difficult to gain social acceptance among their peers, even at an early age, and frequently are teased or bullied at school because they are sensitive.

> ✦✦✦ I would cry with what appeared to be very little stress or provocation when I was in kindergarten. My mother was very accepting of my behaviors, saying "His eyes were just born in a wet place." So even though I was called a sissy by my peers and was initially bullied, as well as being berated by my teacher for crying so readily and so often, at least at home my expression of emotional sensitivity was accepted.
>
> Having my own room at home to which I could retreat as needed – an actual place of peace and safety and healing (PPSH) – also enabled me to recover and adapt to being in a school environment that I found more stressful than other children did.

As we saw with Avis, HSPs are also commonly gifted with awarenesses of and sensitivities to subtle energies and intuitions. They walk into a room and immediately sense whether the general atmosphere is positive or negative, calm or agitated, happy or sad. They may sense others' energies and be aware of disturbing emotions before people themselves are aware of them. The up side is that HSPs use their sensitivities as a radar for choosing where they want to engage and participate in the positive vibes, and where they want to distance themselves and avoid the negative ones.

The down side of these HSP intuitive qualities may manifest as challenges in tolerating various environments and relationships. An HSP may feel the need to walk around an entire restaurant to find the spot that has the most positive vibrations, or the least negative ones. Choosing an HSP-congenial place to live or work may similarly prove challenging – for reasons that many NHSPs would have difficulty understanding and accepting. Pollutants and toxic chemicals in the environment or in foods may feel intolerable, when NHSPs have no sense whatsoever that these even exist. And lingering vibrations of angers, conflicts, sadness or grief may taint a place from experiences of people who suffered there in the recent or even in the distant past.

Section IV also offers you resources and therapies that are particularly helpful in sorting out many of the personal and interpersonal issues that often make it a challenge to be an HSP and an HSPC. In particular, the understanding and resolution of our cognitive and emotional challenges are enormously facilitated by having the Energy Psychology (EP) tapping techniques. These help to clear the immediate, intense emotions. And even more importantly, they enable us to identify and clear their roots. Most commonly the origins of present day issues reside in traumas from earlier in our lives. Once we learn to use these tools, then current day issues gradually come to be opportunities for identifying and clearing trauma patterns that lead us to repeat the unresolved issues of the past in our current behaviors – rather than just being stresses. These approaches offer you both understandings and remedies for many issues that challenge HSPs.

While I am trained as a medical doctor and have practiced for years as a psychiatrist, and am fully aware of the many benefits that medications can offer, I strongly advise HSPs to search for non-medical approaches if at all possible – prior to taking pills for the problems they wish to address. Medications most often help by dulling us to the intensity of our issues. HSPs are very often also extra-sensitive to medications and liable to suffer from side effects. The good news is that if you come to need medications, you may need lower doses than are usually prescribed. The bad news is that you are more likely to experience negative side effects of medications that are prescribed in doses that are appropriate for NHSPs, compared to the doses needed by people who are not as sensitive as you.

I also recommend avoiding medications wherever and whenever possible because they can actually be dangerous. Few doctors will warn you that medications which are properly prescribed and properly used may cause fatalities, or that conventional medicine is the third leading cause of death in the US and in other countries where this has been investigated.[12] So this book can help you avoid participating in the game of medicinal Russian roulette.**[13]

Section V, Supports for the HSP and HSPC: resources and therapies, details varieties of approaches to help HSPs and HSPCs deal with their challenges. Clinical examples illustrate ways these approaches work. Many are self-healing methods you can practice and use on your own.

One of the best parts of acquiring these resources is that you will have these skills available as and when you need them. The other good news is that you are unlikely to need drugs to deaden your anxieties, angers, pains, depression or grief. In addition, you will avoid the risks of medication side effects – which often deaden your ordinary consciousness, lead you to put on weight, or may even be fatal.

NHSPs are much less responsive to many of these therapies, particularly the ones that invite or require insights into the roots of their feelings, thoughts, relationships and traumas. NHSPs may be more responsive to therapies like acupuncture, homeopathy, massage or other approaches where the caregiver actively facilitates the intervention and the careseeker is passive.

> *Alternative or complementary therapies which require*
> *higher sense perceptions in the client are not likely to work with people who*
> *are not so sensitive, but this is not an absolute.*
> *They just work far better with wizards than with muggles.*
> — Robert Alcorn

The important thing is that you know they are available and how they can be of help to you, your families of birth and of choice, and others who may be challenged with difficulties that they will be able to handle better with these methods.

The approach I find most helpful is the EP one I've mentioned, TWR/ WHEE. This is incredibly easy to learn and use, yet deeply and rapidly effective in relieving stress, distress, trauma, pains and more. In addition, TWR/WHEE enables you to install positive feelings and thoughts to replace the negative ones you have released. Prominent among these is the inner Place of Peace, Safety and Healing (PPSH), where you can retreat to relax, de-stress and release tensions, anxieties and trauma memories.

Other methods I discuss include two-chair work, Neurolinguistic Programming (NLP), homeopathy, flower essences, 12-step programs, family constellation therapy, and active listening.

Section VI, General wholistic approaches to facilitate health and healing, adds a spectrum of wholistic approaches that HSPs and HSPCs can use to enhance their lives – both personally and in their relationships.

- These include, for example:
- Building and maintaining a healthy body
- Preventive emotional hygiene, with routine clearing of negativity and transforming chronic, low grade rubs and challenges in close relationships
- Mental exercises of meditation, trauma clearing and journaling
- Fine tuning your relationships for greater harmony and closeness
- Connecting with your spirit and deepening your awarenesses of your participation in the collective consciousness
- And much more…

Section VII, Subtler sensitivities, biological energy medicine and collective consciousness, examines more refined sensitivities and biological energy medicine. Our bodies are material objects. But quantum physics teaches us that matter and energy are inter-convertible. Like all other physical matter, we are also energy beings.

As energy beings, we can connect with other dimensions of consciousness. These realms are difficult to describe in everyday language. Quantum physics is just beginning to nibble at the edges of these dimensions with more technical understandings of the energies that are associated with matter. Research summarized in Section VI confirms that our consciousness can connect with and through these dimensions.

A substantial body of information confirms that not only are we able to sense information through these dimensions, but we are also able to activate healings through our wishes and intentions – in ourselves and in other people and other species of living beings.

By building our bioenergy awareness we broaden and deepen our consciousness and connect with subtle, higher sources of healing. As well as drawing healing from the collective human consciousness, we also contribute our personal healing to this collective.

On the positive side, many HSPs spontaneously connect personally with intuitive dimensions. They may be in touch with their higher self, with past lives, and with spirits of others who have passed on, all of which offer them broader perspectives on what is going on in their personal lives and relationships. On the challenging side, HSPs may find themselves vulnerable to the influence of negative energies.

Through our personal intuitive awarenesses, we connect as well with the collective consciousness of the world upon which we dwell. This gives us access to information and avenues for offering healing to others through the collective consciousness.

The more sensitive among us can also connect with other worlds and with the universe as a whole. Conversely, each of us is a tiny pixel on the big screen of total cosmic consciousness. Just by improving our personal lives, we contribute to the well-being of the All.

Section VIII, Spiritual awarenesses, explores consciousness that transcends our current lives. While non-believers consider such reports to be no more than fantasies or wishful thinking, there are many who report personal experiences of transcendent realities. Several varieties of these reports have been studied, demonstrating consistencies among them, with research evidence confirming aspects of these perceptions.

For many, particularly NHSPs, spirituality is a set of beliefs and practices related to one of many established religious traditions. In most cases the choice of a particular religion is determined by one's family of birth or marriage. Others believe that spirituality is just a wishful creation from the imaginations of people who invent explanations, without any substance to them, in order to help themselves deal with the uncertainties of life and death.

The personal spiritual awarenesses discussed in this book are more than beliefs. They are personal experiences of perceiving, communicating with, or being an intimate part of a transcendent reality.

It may come as a surprise to some readers that there is scientific research confirming spiritual awarenesses. Research is reviewed on intuition, knowing the future, mind interacting with and deliberately influencing matter, biological energy fields, psychic healing (also called spiritual healing), collective consciousness, and more.

For instance, past life memories have been reported in Eastern countries, where their religions accept and teach about reincarnation as a reality. In Western as well as well as in Eastern countries, research has confirmed details of past life memories of children as well as of adults in locations where there were no ordinary sources for the information reported by the children. Traumas recalled in past lives have been similarly validated. Treating people for traumas from their past lives has been shown to relieve post traumatic stress residues (such as fears and phobias of being burned) left over from their a previous life or several lives in which they were burned at the stake as witches, which had no basis in their current life experiences.

They may sense the presence of spirit beings, commonly called ghosts – of humans, animals and other parts of the natural world. They may feel a strong connection with God/ The Creator/ The All or other variations of the Transcendent. And they may have a deeply felt personal awareness of their purpose in their incarnations in this lifetime – and in the interactions with other lives they have experienced in the past or will live in the future.

In discussions of spiritual awarenesses the concept of a supreme consciousness, most commonly designated in English as God, is found in all of the major Western religions. Because each religion has its own description of God and ways of relating to this God, I use a variety of designations for that which we most commonly use the word God. The word 'God' has enormous varieties of different connotations for different people. In some cases, where people were raised in restrictive, punishing religions, the term God may even be associated with negative connotations. Personally, I prefer "The Infinite Source" as a more neutral designation for this transcendent consciousness.

People around the world report they had near death experiences (NDEs) in which they were declared medically dead but returned to life. During this sojourn in afterlife dimensions, they report encountering the spirits of deceased relative and friends, angels and a 'Being of Light' that is totally and unconditionally accepting of them. Again, research shows consistencies in these reports from all over the world. The most dramatic aspect of the NDEs is that those who return from their NDEs are utterly transformed. They no longer fear death and are clear that consciousness survives physical death.

Research also shows it is very common for people to report seeing, hearing or sensing the presence of relatives and friends after they have passed on. Similarly, when people are approaching the end of their lives, they often see the spirits of relatives and friends coming to greet them.

These spiritual awarenesses can be enormously helpful in guiding us through the challenges and lessons in our lives. They provide a deeply healing perspective within our wholistic awarenesses of who we are, both individually and collectively.

While I know of no research on the spiritual consciousness of HSPs compared to those of NHSPs, my personal and professional encounters with those who report personal spiritual awarenesses strongly suggest that again, HSPs are far more likely to experience and report personal spiritual awarenesses, compared with NHSPs.

So, I invite you to join me on this journey of exploring the personal worlds and relationships of Highly Sensitive People. Even if you were not born an HSP, or have had to suppress your HSP qualities in order to get along with the NHSPs in your life, you can find many windows of perception and understanding in this book that will enable you to appreciate the wonderful spectrum of universes of HSPs. And if you wish and work hard enough, you will discover doorways through which you, too, can venture into these wonderful realms.

*O wonderful, wonderful, and most wonderful wonderful!*
*And yet again wonderful, and after that, out of all whooping.*
- William Shakespeare
As You Like It

Section IX summarizes wholistic healing and invites you to consider what life is all about and briefly summarizes the journey through this book.

Section X rounds out my experiences in writing this book.

# SECTION II. Understanding the HSP and HSPC: Explanatory Frameworks

*And why is it, thought Lara, that my fate is to see everything and take it all so much to heart?*
— Boris Pasternak

## 5. Background

Highly Sensitive People are usually sensitive on many, if not every level of their being. This often makes it a challenge to them to understand themselves, and presents multiple challenges to those around them. This is not a choice that they are expressing about how they want to be or behave. It is how they are 'wired' to be; how their body, emotions, mind, relationships and spirit sense and respond to the world.

HSPs have heightened sensitivities to most of their life experiences. Any or all of their senses may be exquisitely acute. This enables them to perceive their environment with much greater intensity of sight, hearing, smell, touch and/or taste. The good news is that they have a much broader and deeper appreciation of whatever they are attending to in their lives. The bad news is that this often makes it a challenge to them to deal with all of this sensory stimulation and not to feel overwhelmed.

HSPs may find it difficult to understand themselves because they often respond with great intensity to situations that NHSPs would hardly notice. This also presents multiple challenges to those around them. NHSPs feel that HSPs are being dramatic, over-reacting, excessively sensitive, or intolerant of people who are different from themselves.

They also have exquisitely keen sensitivities to emotional awarenesses, of their own and of others' feelings. When they are sad or sensing the sadness of others, they feel it totally. There may be little or no other awareness of feelings during that period of sadness consciousness. With happiness, they are intensely joyful, absolutely brimming over with pleasure. NHSPs rarely, if ever, experience these levels of intense emotions.

Elaine Aron (2010) also points out that this is not a trait unique to human beings. Twenty percent of animals are markedly more sensitive than the other eighty percent. The figures about animals come from studies of more than 100 species. Aron speculates that this trait enables animals "to process information thoroughly before responding." This broader species sensitivity is designated as sensory processing sensitivity (SPS).

On the positive side, HSPs are often very open in sharing their feelings and responses in interactions with other people. They care deeply about other people and are enthusiastic and passionate about whatever they, themselves, and others are experiencing, doing and planning. HSPs are sensitive to others' emotions of sadness, hurt, anger or disappointment, and often share how much they resonate and offer their support to people they care about. HSPs even reach out to strangers who are struggling or in need of assistance. Sometimes they are so attuned and more rapidly responsive to non-HSPs that they may pick up on other people's emotions before the others are aware of their own feelings.

Non-HSPs are much more often engaged with and absorbed in their thinking processes. They are minimally aware, if at all, of their emotional feelings or of the feelings of others around them. NHSPs often find it unsettling to be aware of emotions in themselves and others. NHSPs who have grown up in families and communities where emotional expressions are muted or even avoided may find it unsettling to be around HSPs who are being expressive and demonstrative with their feelings. HSPs very frequently are accused by NHSPs of over-reacting or being over the top, and chided for being a drama queen.

As children, HSPs are much more interested in exploring their worlds of inner awarenesses, in stories, creative arts, fantasies and dreams, or socializing with other, carefully selected, sensitive, kind and considerate people. Sitting still for lessons to memorize facts and manipulate numbers may be boring to them – even when they are good at these mundane tasks.

If HSP children are fortunate to have family and friends who accept and like them, they flourish. They are often very original and creative thinkers. They see patterns in the bits and pieces of information available for dealing with work tasks, working relationships, and challenges in any given situation. They understand complex situations to a level of depth that is way beyond the ordinary. They are very caring people and are dedicated to helping others.

Parents who are NHSPs may often be distressed and worry about their HSP children. Not understanding their children's emotionality, they may scold them for daydreaming, being 'babies' or sissies, or for "making a fuss over nothing." They may worry that their otherwise bright children seem likely to fail in school if they don't 'shape up' – or in other words, conform to the norms of the NHSP majority. They may pressure their children to get higher grades in subjects that HSPs find uninteresting and boring, and to participate in competitive sports and other activities that are boring or even distasteful to them.

Sadly, many HSPs frequently report their school experiences were not positive because the majority of teachers and school administrators are focused on the content of their lessons. HSP children are often much more interested in the 'how' of the world than in the 'what.' They will resonate with the personalities of characters and their relationships in a story, and ponder the 'whys' of their choices of actions and reactions as much as (or more than) they will relate to the facts of what they did and in what year this was. They may therefore appear distracted, daydreaming, uninterested in the average school lessons, or even be labelled rebellious and oppositional when they refuse to focus on the bare facts that the teacher (most frequently a non-HSP) wants the class to memorize, recite back to her, and – most importantly – to imprint in their minds so that they can achieve high scores on tests. Similarly, this makes it difficult for many HSPs to work in ordinary, routine jobs that demand constant attention to details and repetitive behaviors that HSPs find boring and uninteresting.

In relationships, HSPs often find themselves strongly challenged on many levels. Their emotional sensitivities open them to keen awarenesses of their partners' feelings and thoughts. They strongly resonate with their partner's ongoing emotional states and will spend a lot of time reviewing their interactions with them.

If the HSPC is also an HSP, there is often a mutual understanding and appreciation for each other's sensitivities, and a mutual engagement in processing them – individually and in their relationships. When the HSPC is an NHSP, it is not uncommon to see misunderstandings and conflicts arising between the couple. The NHSP may complain about the HSP being too emotional, not wanting to do things together in various situations, wanting a lot of quiet time, and talking way too much about the spectrum of alternative choices before making decisions. The HSP complains about not being heard or understood, being pressured and rushed into making decisions, and not being given enough space and quiet time for contemplation and meditation.

Elaine Aron[1] and Ted Zeff[2] each do masterful jobs of exploring and explaining many of these HSP issues, so I won't belabor them here. They provide diverse perspectives to help understand, appreciate and deal with various sorts of situations between HSPs and NHSPs, as well as between one HSP and another.

There is no one model or theory that alone explains all aspects of HSPs' psychological makeup or functioning, either personally or in their relationships. In different people and under different circumstances there may be various models that are particularly useful. In this section I describe and discuss some of the many models I have found helpful:

– for myself personally and as a therapist;
– for helping my HSP clients understand themselves;
– for helping HSPs' families and HSPCs to understand them better and get along better with them.

There are many perspectives we can take for examining the unfoldings of the HSP ways of being and relating in the world. Each is a window of perception that offers its own views and understandings of what being an HSP is like. And in peering through each window of awareness about what it's like to be an HSP we also can see new doors leading to different ways of sorting out issues that are specific to HSP sensitivities and ways of being in the world. For HSPCs there are also new doorways for understanding and sorting out their own issues, as well as for relating and interacting with the HSP.

## 6. Wholistic healing frameworks to understand HSPs and HSPCs

> *The good physician treats the disease;*
> *the great physician treats the patient who has the disease.*
> — Sir William Osler

I find it helpful to organize my understandings and approaches to working with HSPs through using a wholistic framework that addresses body, emotions, mind, relationships (with other people and with the world at large) and spirit.

Each of these wholistic levels of experiencing and interacting with the world offers its own set of perspectives, approaches and rules for analyzing what is going on within ourselves and in our interactions with others.

At the same time, all of these aspects of ourselves are intimately interlinked and interactive – to the point that to discuss them separately is actually a distortion of the reality of who we are within ourselves and in our interactions with the world around us.

For the convenience of narrowly specialized caregivers, approaches for dealing with each wholistic level have commonly been split off from most or all of the other levels.

- The body is addressed as a physical object, to be brought in for tune-ups and repairs by specialists such as medical doctors (general practitioners, specialists in various parts of the body, and surgeons), osteopaths, chiropractors, physiotherapists, massage therapists and others who minister to skin, flesh and bones.
- Emotions and mind are addressed by coaches, counsellors, social workers, and psychotherapists who identify dysfunctional feelings and thoughts; and by psychiatrists who prescribe chemicals to alter the functions of mind, moods and emotions.
- Mind is also addressed separately by family, educators, politicians, clergy, and individuals and groups promoting vested interests.
- Relationships between people are addressed by family therapists (who may also be any of those trained in addressing emotions and mind), and may include epidemiologists for attending to health issues of large numbers of people. On the collective social levels, relationships between individuals, groups of consumers, groups of corporate exploiters and the government may have enormous influence over our personal lives.
- Relationships with the environment are the territory where environmental specialists advise us – doctors and scientists (again including epidemiologists).
- Connections and participation with Spirit may be sought and sensed within religious contexts. Various religions instruct their members in the teachings of their founders, clergy/ priests/ religious leaders and followers, thereby introducing the members to varieties of concepts and examples of spirituality. Many people report personal spiritual awarenesses within religious contexts that may arise spontaneously or may be the rewards of deliberate religious practices.

Many others report direct, personal spiritual awarenesses with no connections to organized religion[3]. In any setting, people may report that their spiritual awarenesses have a feeling of real perceptions, although usually they are of a distinctly different quality from outer-world perceptions that we have through our ordinary senses (Benor, 2006).

In Western society, many others consider spirit to be a wishful, fantasy creation of people seeking to make some meaning out of a world of random causalities, and serving to counter their anxieties about the finality of physical death.

When we explore and deal with the entire wholistic spectrum that people are experiencing, they can identify and address the issues that are challenging or troublesome on any and all levels of their being.

*In summary*

Wholistic healing expands and deepens the range of issues addressed in dealing with challenges of HSPs and HSPCs. TWR/WHEE and other approaches detailed in this book enable people to address these issues on every level of their being. You will be introduced to approaches enabling you to decrease and eliminate negativities and to install and strengthen positivities in your lives. Resourced with these tools, you will be able to transform every aspect of the wholistic spectrum of your life.

Let's see how these wholistic categories relate specifically to HSPs and HSPCs.

**Body** *(HSP wholistic issues)*

> *My belief is in the blood and flesh as being wiser than the intellect. The body-unconscious is where life bubbles up in us. It is how we know that we are alive, alive to the depths of our souls and in touch somewhere with the vivid reaches of the cosmos.*
> — D.H. Lawrence

Many HSPs have heightened, advanced sensitivities in their ordinary senses.
- These senses include sight, sound, smell, taste and touch, plus sensitivities to pressure, pain, temperature, thirst, hunger, and time.
- There is also the spectrum of inner awarenesses that include intuitions about oneself; telepathy; direct intuitive perceptions about states of health and illness in ourselves and other; of inanimate objects; of things that happen in the future or past; of spirits and angels in other dimensions; and of a loving, accepting consciousness that we call God.*[4]

Many of our outer sensory senses are very well researched. The intuitive and spiritual ones are also well research but are not well accepted by the NHSP majority.*[5]

HSPs may often be aware of sensations that others don't notice. Their bodies may respond to specific foods with nausea, abdominal pains, gassiness or allergic reactions. Common culinary culprits include milk and milk products, wheat products, gluten, and the hosts of additives and chemicals commonly found in junk foods.

They are easily startled, jarred and distracted by strong or sudden sensory stimuli (which may even be experienced as painful), or they may feel rattled in busy surroundings such as shopping malls and markets, and on streets and roads during rush hours. Stimulation they find irritating or even intolerable may include loud noises (voices, music or TV, movie theaters, restaurants, and other loud public places, emergency services sirens), bright lights (especially fluorescent lights – even if they are not flickering), strong smells (as in perfumes, strong disinfectants, gasoline or automobile fumes, or being seated in a restaurant next to the toilets), coarse fabrics, wrinkles or labels in clothing or tiny particles of anything in their shoes.

They may want or even need to avoid or withdraw from intense situations, in order not to get jarred, upset or to feel overwhelmed. They need down-time to allow rattled nerves to unwind and muscles to relax. Falling asleep may be difficult after being over-stimulated or jarred.

Due to HSP sensitivities, pains may feel overwhelming, even from minor causes. This may be an extra-troublesome issue, as there can be major bruising and swelling with minor injuries.

HSPs respond strongly to caffeine and may easily become habituated. Strong headaches are common when missing a regular fix or with withdrawal from caffeine. To decrease anxieties and stress reactions, they may engage in comfort eating (also comfort purchasing and other such behaviors), alcohol, marijuana or more dangerous prescription or street drugs.

Chemical hypersensitivities can be severe, even to the point that some HSPs are unable to live in most modern urban environments. Sensitivities to mercury, fluorescent and the new LED light bulbs may also be severe.

They are easily aroused and triggered by issues that stir their emotions; moody, irritable and short-tempered when hungry, tired, stressed or triggered. And their thresholds for feeling stressed may be quite low, particularly with intense stimulation of their senses. These are situations in which HSPCs can most frequently be of enormous help to their HSPs – simply by reminding the HSP to check whether these easily-addressed issues are bothering them.

You may question whether dealing with stress, worries and allergies should be included on a list of easily-addressed issues, and rightly so when people are unfamiliar with the varieties of recently developed, self-healing approaches. But there are now many methods for de-stressing that will be identified, illustrated and explained in Sections IV – VII of this book. We can alter our sensitivities and responsivities to over-stimulation, hunger, tiredness, and other stressors. The more we practice these methods, the more quickly we become able to decrease our irritabilities.

HSPs often are aware of their biological energy bodies as well. Your body can also be addressed through its energetic aspects – by healers and other practitioners of what is broadly identified as Energy Medicine.*6

Many HSPs cannot ignore their biological energy awarenesses. They sense the energy fields of other people, of a room or of a place in nature. When other people are in a positive state, the HSP may feel their contentment, happiness and loving presence. When out in nature, HSPs may feel calming and healing vibrations in certain geographic locations, next to particular rocks, trees, or bodies of water.

Someone who is upset, hurt, sad or angry will send out vibrations that are palpably unpleasant to those who are sensitive to these energies. This may be a part of why HSPs are intolerant for being in crowds, for eating foods and water that are contaminated with harmful chemicals, and for chemicals in makeup, clothing, and various chemicals and sprays used in cleaning products – among countless other sources of disturbing vibrational energies.

HSPs often want or even need to avoid and withdraw from intense situations, in order not to get upset or to feel overwhelmed. They need down-time to allow rattled nerves to unwind and tensed muscles to relax.

✦ 'Lottie,' a non-HSP second grader, was an 'easy' child. Sitting in class on a Monday morning, she was focused on her teacher, Miss Brown, eager to hear her little welcoming story for the day, and to see what her schedule for that day would be. Johnny was arguing with his neighbor, and Katy, at the back of the room, was having difficulties settling down, having dropped her pencil box and creating a lot of noise and disturbance in gathering up its contents. Lottie sighed, patiently, while Miss Brown put off talking to the class as she helped these children settle down.

✦ 'Bonnie,' a strongly HSP student sitting next to Lottie, had made her usual early entry to class so she could settle herself as quietly as possible at her desk and bury herself in a book. She usually managed with this strategy to avoid or ignore a lot of the noise and hustle and bustle and banging about of the other children, particularly the three loud boys who sat in the front row so Miss Brown could keep a close eye on them. The noise of Kay's pencil case jarred her out of her book, and she was then aware of the boys in the front of the room starting to poke each other; the label at the back of her new shirt irritating her neck; the body odor of Bruce, the boy in front of her, being worse than usual; and the sounds of several late students running down the hallway as the bell rang for the start of classes.

✦ 'George' was a high school English teacher who was much admired and liked by students and by his fellow teachers as well. He was outgoing, sensitive, and caring in relating to everyone. His greatest strength was in his listening skills. With just a few, penetrating questions he let people know he deeply understood and resonated with what they were discussing. You could guess by this description that George is an HSP.

Few knew that George suffered from serious stomach pains. He only spoke of these with those who needed to know, such as his wife, his doctor and his school principal. He had had extensive workups for ulcers, colitis and other abdominal disorders, with never a definitive diagnosis. George came to me in desperation. He had been recommended by a mutual friend who knew of my successes in helping people with pains of all sorts, but who didn't know precisely how my methods worked. George was anxious because he expected a psychiatrist would diagnose him as a severe hypochondriac or some other sort of nut case, and that I would recommend stronger drugs than the many over the counter pills he had taken – all to no avail.

My approach with pain is to invite the person in pain to ask the pain what it wants him to know about his life. Opening this door almost always leads to rapid reductions in the pain. In medical school, I was taught to prescribe pain killers to reduce or eradicate pains of all sorts. I've come to understand that this is almost always terribly wrong. Pain is (at least in part) a messenger from our inner selves about disharmony in our lives. Rather than killing the messenger, it is much more productive to dialogue with it.

✦✦ The pain as messenger concept was immediately effective with George, reducing his pain intensity by more than half in just a few minutes. Over a series of three sessions, He was able to learn to use this, plus related methods that I describe in Section IV, such as TWR/WHEE, relaxation and imagery exercises to eliminate his pains completely. In this process, he came to understand that he had been 'swallowing down his feelings' for much of his life. Though he was willing and able to help everyone else, he didn't feel he deserved to be helped himself, and rarely asked anyone for assistance.

This pattern had started in childhood, when his mother suffered from such severe depression that she was incapacitated. As the oldest child, He was called upon to help at home in ways that were way beyond what would normally be expected, and certainly more than was appropriate for a young child. This habit had then persisted into his current life situations.

George accessed the wisdom of his body, which had worked very hard to get his attention. The intimate links between the body, emotions and mind are again and again demonstrated by people who come to me for help because they are suffering physical and/or emotional pains. The pains are like phone bells, clamoring to get the person's attention – to attend to buried issues and feelings from unfinished business from the past.*[7]

The residues of traumas from earlier in life are pernicious in how they can burden us and cripple us. Whenever possible, I strongly recommend that a caregiving person should take a detailed life history, starting with people's earliest available memories. Similarly, HSPCs may find increasing understanding about the problems their HSPs have experienced in life – which will enable them to understand particular areas of sensitivity and reactivity in their HSP. That is why I offer many examples of children's issues in this book. The basis for many of our strengths of character, as well as the seeds for later issues, are often planted in childhood, and an inner child awareness of these residues persists throughout life.

The person who is suffering with pains and other debilitating problems and issues is often quite surprised when the therapist puts two and two together, identifying earlier life roots of current day issues. It is often difficult to unravel the tangled threads of our own lives. As a companion to an HSP, you can be enormously helpful in such ways as your abilities grow and deepen your understanding of your wholistic awarenesses, which can help you to increasingly understand and help your HSP. And you, the HSP, can also be helped as the HSPC grows in awareness and understanding – as you get more familiar with yourselves and with each other.

Later Chapters in Section IV offer many more windows for understanding HSP issues manifesting through the body (and other aspects of yourselves), and Section V suggests varieties of ways to deal with your personal and interpersonal challenges. And when we are open to even deeper levels of self-awareness, the body can be a vehicle for connecting with spiritual dimensions as well.

### *Emotions* (HSP wholistic issues)

HSPs experience life and communicate largely through their emotions. This is not a choice. This is how they are wired and how they function. This is in no way to suggest that they are limited in their thinking or communicating capacities. It is just that their emotions come first, both in their awarenesses and in communications.

Deep absorption in emotions is such a pervasive aspect of HSP existence that this deserves a detailed discussion. HSPs experience their inner and outer worlds first and foremost through their emotions. This is far more than saying that they are just sensitive to their own emotions and to their emotional interactions with others. Their sensory awarenesses and thoughts are processed through their emotions to an enormously greater degree than NHSPs can generally appreciate or even imagine.

In different words, HSPs not only experience but to a great degree also conceptualize their personal worlds through their emotions and feelings. This is not to say that they don't hold the awarenesses of their senses as experiences that they can conceptualize and express in thoughts and words. But their thoughts come a far second to their sensory and emotional engagements with whatever they are experiencing.

HSPs live in and through their feelings and emotions. They organize their perceptions, wishes, plans, and actions around how they feel. Their subjective experiences of feelings is often heart-centered. They are not just experiencing emotions. They are their emotions at the time they experience them.

This may make it challenging for HSPs to make decisions. They may connect emotionally with an issue, sort through their feelings about it, and come to a plan of action. But the next time they revisit the issue, they are in a different emotional and feeling place. So the issues have different colors and shapes and smells and appear different from how they seemed the first time the HSP visited the issues under consideration.

This can be very confusing to an HSPC who is an NHSP. NHSPs generally process issues through thoughts and logic. When analyzed through such lines of reasoning, without much consideration for one's feelings about them, once a decision is made it is pretty firm and remains consistent the next time it is mentally revisited. The HSP's repeated revisiting of an issue, often coming out with different decisions with each sorting through of feelings about the issue, can be utterly confusing, bewildering and frustrating to an NHSP.*[8]

HSPs are easily influenced by other people's moods, both positive and negative. They may be easily startled, jarred or upset by tensions and discord of any sort. They often find themselves somewhere between uncomfortable and rattled when in a bustling room, crowded bus, theater or other public place where many people are sensing and expressing varieties of emotions. Violence in the news, films and TV shows is often upsetting or even intolerable. It is very common for HSPs to avoid watching news shows for these reasons.

When they are strongly stimulated, HSPs may experience what they are going through as intense waves, or even floods of emotions that require a while to process, absorb and digest. While in such overwhelms, they may find it hard to put what they are experiencing into thoughts and concepts that can explain in feeling words what they are going through. This is all the more true when the stress is related in any way to past traumas the HSP experienced, because residual memories and feelings associated with the trauma may linger long after the traumatic incident(s) and may get triggered by stresses, even many years later.

When stimulated to the point that they are overwhelmed, HSPs may find it difficult to focus their thoughts. This is something that can happen to NHSPs as well, though usually NHSPs will reach a point of overwhelm mostly when their stresses are very severe.

HSPs' emotionality can be confusing to others, particularly when the HSPs demonstrate when not stressed or overwhelmed that they are able to process their feelings and thoughts similarly to ways that an NHSP does – by saying what they are feeling.

NHSPs generally hold the center of their awareness of themselves in their thoughts. They may be thinking about what they are experiencing as they experience their perceptions, which are mostly focused on the outer world. They may be unaware of their emotions, even when they are experiencing and expressing them in ways that are obvious to outside observers. When they connect with their awarenesses of their emotions, they may often stand outside their emotions, observing them as feelings (mental constructs applied to emotions). Often, they expect HSPs to do the same, and have a hard time understanding and accepting that HSPs are simply wired and function differently.

HSPs develop strategies to avoid feeling flustered, such as sitting in a quiet spot at school with a single friend during recess or on a play date, rather than joining a crowd on the playground; avoiding action films and TV shows; and wishing their NHSP partner a good time at the basketball game, while they stay home to read a good book or to write in their personal journal.

✦✦ Lottie, the NHSP second grader, was somewhat amused by the unexpected hubbub in the classroom. She looked over at 'Mandy,' rolled her eyes, and both of them smiled.

✦✦ Bonnie, the HSP, was jarred by the fuss over the dropped pencil box, finding that the commotion reminded her a lot like the loud argument between her two younger brothers at home that morning about whose hat was whose, and where the second one had disappeared to. She thought she had done well to avoid getting upset by that one, but the classroom hubbub stirred it up again. Her mom, also an HSP, didn't handle last minute stresses well and had shouted at her brothers. Bonnie had bolted out the door to avoid this hubbub, to sit on the tree stump in the front yard till the schoolbus arrived.

HSPs may need quiet time to themselves after even modest stimulation, such as a walk through crowded streets, a trip to the supermarket, or a ride on crowded public transportation. Greater intensity or duration of stress often require longer down time for recuperation.

This discussion isn't complete without mentioning (prior to a much fuller discussion in Section VII) that spiritual awarenesses markedly deepen our connections with emotions. In fuller spiritual dimensions, emotions are much stronger, shared, and vital aspects of all communications.[9]

There are many ways an HSPCs can be of help and support to HSPs when their emotions are strongly triggered. These are discussed in Section IV.

**Mind** *(HSP wholistic issues)*

> *Your mind develops into a perceptual organ of the soul.*
> – Robert D. Waterman

HSPs often sense subtleties in people's conversations, emotions, moods and relationships. They often enjoy pondering and discussing awarenesses about the nuances of their own thoughts and feelings. They may prefer an immersion in a topic rather than a skim across its surface; a feast of factual and emotional details and analyses rather than a light dab and a taste of the issues.

HSPs often have excellent pattern recognition, quickly seeing links between people, experiences and issues that may offer explanations and theories about unclear situations. This makes them appreciated conversationalists and valuable resource in their workplace. They also make excellent therapists, and maintain their caring attitudes to much greater degrees than NHSPs.

Even though HSPs live in a world where the majority of people are NHSPs, it may still often be jarring to them to have to deal with and relate to people who are focused on Mind, to the exclusion of Emotions. In retrospect, one of my strongest personal Mind lessons as an unknowing HSP (at that time) occurred in medical school.

✦✦✦ My experience of medical school was enormously disappointing. The strong, caring attitude that most of my fellow students expressed on entering school was eroded very quickly and very thoroughly in the majority of these budding doctors within the first year of studies. In part, this was due to the overwhelming focus in the first year on anatomy, pathology, biochemistry and all the other building blocks essential in the making of a doctor. But at the same time there was very little focus on the people – as individuals – we were to treat.

The exception to this was our first-year course in psychiatry, which focused on the development of the person from gestation in the womb to end of life issues and death. From the first week of studies, the instruction focused on one aspect at a time of personality development and stages of life experiences, with a live person discussing the issues under consideration. In the first week, we had an expectant mother talk about her feelings of bringing life into the world; in the second week, it was a mother with a newborn; and so on. This series ended with an octogenarian who spoke about resigning himself to the end of his life, having lost all of his contemporary family members and most of his friends. I absolutely loved this class, where we discussed people and weren't just analyzing bits and pieces of people. It's not surprising that about 25% of the classes in those years declared they wanted to go on to specialize in psychiatry!

And this became the general medical student attitude – to focus on 'what is wrong in this case' rather than 'how are we going to understand the problems this person has and how can we best help her?

One of my most striking memories demonstrating this depersonalizing of the patient was that my clinical instructors, from the initial course in physical examination, would regularly refer us to "the interesting liver in bed #3" or the more generic "come see this fascinoma" (which could be any interesting manifestation of disease or abnormality). No mention was made of the person who had the liver or the fascinating problem, and no time was allotted for discussing that person's experience of having the problem nor how they were dealing with it.**[10]

And this is very typical of how people in all walks of life wrap their minds around physical and psychological issues – to the exclusion of much, if any, of their awarenesses of relevant emotions, relationships or spirit.

My HSP empathy was often deeply stirred by the patients' conditions but regularly frustrated and disappointed by theclinical instructors' attitudes and clinical approaches to patients, without my fully understanding at that time why I was feeling as I did.

HSPs frequently have strong intuitive gifts that extend beyond pattern recognition into psychic and personal spiritual awarenesses.*[11]

HSPs often have a poor sense of clock time, with difficulties planning to have enough activities but not too much to fit into the time available. They are easily rattled when on a tight schedule and frequently unsettled in the face of demands for completing multiple tasks within a given time frame.

✦✦✦ I can again attest to this issue personally. As I opened more and more into my intuitive and feeling awarenesses in the later part of my life, I found that my time management faltered. I now have more difficulty estimating correctly how many activities I can fit into a given timeframe. It appears to me that I have been moving along the spectrum from thinking to feeling.

Delays often occur when HSPs address unpleasant or unwanted tasks. That which is felt to be distasteful or annoying, likely to involve stress, conflict or rejection, to be tedious or boring, may be scheduled last in a series of jobs on the 'to do' list. Immersion in the more enjoyable tasks puts off the tougher ones. Distractions can also lead to delays in getting the tougher jobs done, much less started. So, the jobs with lower priority may get bumped to another day's list, consciously or unconsciously. This can snowball into irritability over difficulties hanging over the HSPs head – with little or no appreciation of how they keep getting there through this sort of process. Such delays are often as frustrating to the HSP as to those around them.

HSPs sincerely want to fit in and be accepted. But they have serious difficulties with the generally held expectations that they must live within the normal bounds of the NHSP majority expectations and behaviors in order to be accepted. On the one hand, they may be disappointed in themselves for failing to be like others and to do what is usually expected of others – but which can be extremely challenging or impossible for themselves because of their HSP characteristics. On the other hand, they are very, very, very frustrated because they are not understood as being different in many ways from the average person. Most of all, they are frustrated for not being accepted as okay in their differences, or worse, for being pathologized because they are different.

HSPs can be quite self-critical about perceived shortcomings. They may even be more severely critical of themselves than others are critical of them. They often worry about making mistakes and berate themselves severely when doing less than they expect of themselves or less than they believe others expect them to do or be.

HSPs often become anxious in situations of uncertainty, feeling they are now or are soon going to be out of control or will fail. They may obsess for long periods of time over alternate possible options, plans and outcomes, seeking to feel more certain and in control. What is most difficult, for them and for those around them, is that they sort through their issues primarily through their feelings *about* their situations – whether objectively realistic, fantasied or feared. And it may take them a long time to resolve their ambivalences and to come to a decision on a course of action. Even after finally reaching a decision, they may have lingering doubts, second-guesses, regrets and recriminations about their choices.

✦ 'Sidney' was a successful business consultant who was always meticulously attentive to details in his work and home life. His HSP qualities served him well. He was popular, liked by all, and was appreciated for the caring and support he brought to all he encountered. He generally got along well with his wife, Leslie. They were a devoted couple, married for six years. The only major issue they reported was that his wife, Leslie, a NHSP, had had to learn to be patient with him when he obsessed over decisions. She found it particularly difficult when he took a very long time to choose between alternative options.

I saw Sidney and Leslie for a brief series of consultations over a three-month period, precipitated by his inability to make a decision about buying a new home. The couple came when she was nearly four months pregnant with their second child. They were feeling the urgency to move prior to the birth as they wanted to have more rooms for their growing family. They had reached agreement about their desired specifications. They were clear about their price range and had no serious differences in their preferences for what to include in the new home.

The problem was that Sidney simply could not commit to buying a specific home. Even when it met all their essential requirements, he kept chewing and obsessing on the possibility that this specific home wasn't really going to be the best one for them. Leslie, a practical NHSP, was at a loss for how to proceed. She was growing impatient to the point that she had uncharacteristically lost her temper with him several times.

Two issues from earlier in his life appeared highly relevant. The first was that Sidney had great difficulties in making decisions when he felt these would affect other people. The second was a series of memories from childhood. When Sidney was nine years old, his father had lost his job and had great difficulty finding employment. His family had to vacate their home when they defaulted on their mortgage payments. Sidney, his parents, and four younger brothers and sisters all lived for over a year with his father's elderly parents. It was two years before they could relocate to a very small, rented home of their own and another two years before they managed to find adequate lodgings.

Sidney had found it extremely difficult to live in the crowded accommodations for those four years. He had difficulties falling asleep, became nervous and edgy, and had difficulties concentrating on his homework. After a few weeks, he also developed difficulties concentrating at school. It was also a stress having to change schools twice when they moved.

Sidney was able to clear his childhood trauma memories about moving homes with the help of TWR/WHEE within two sessions. The difficulties dealing with the decision about choosing a home took another two months. This was because the core issue had many related roots and branches, each of which required identification and then using tapping and related methods.*[12] We found that he had had to take on serious babysitting responsibilities during the family relocations in childhood, when his mother had to work part time to help make ends meet. He always worried about making the right decisions in sorting out his brothers and sisters' issues when he was babysitting. The habit of worrying about decisions generalized to other decision-making situations and persisted in gradually decreasing degrees over the ensuing years. They had remained a mild to modest issue until the home purchase decisions triggered him back into more serious worrying about making decisions.

I've found that many of the decision-making challenges experienced by some HSPs and witnessed by those close to them are often of two principal origins.

1. The nature of HSPs is to process perceptions, issues and decisions through their feelings. They immerse themselves in the feelings they anticipate they will experience with each option under consideration, and may keep alternating back and forth between the options until they reach a

point where they feel reasonably comfortable with one option more than with the others. With serious decisions, this process may take weeks and months of wavering back and forth between options.

Needless to say, this can be enormously stressful both to their HSPCs and others who are close to them. NHSPs may find it excruciating to witness the deliberations and agonizings of the HSP around feeling issues. NHSPs usually approach these sorts of decisions with what they call a cost-benefit analysis (CBA) in the business world. They draw a line down the middle of a sheet of paper, list the costs in one column and the benefits in the other column, weigh the positives compared with the negatives, and make a decision on their best assessment of the situation. Finished! Well, maybe they sleep on the decision. Perhaps they consult others who are involved. But the long and the short of it is that this is often a much shorter, more direct process than deciding according to how you feel about each of your options.

2. Residues of trauma memories and feelings from the past may get triggered, along with meta-anxieties attached to the trauma residues, because they resonate with issues associated with the current decision options.

*Meta-anxieties*

Let me expand a bit further about meta-anxieties. These are our worries *about* our worries. Meta-anxieties will often add intensity and stress to the feelings experienced by HSPs as they wade through their feelings. Very often, the specifics of the triggered trauma memory feelings are not within the conscious awareness of the HSPs, even though the feelings are quite strong. When these are cleared, the decision-making becomes much easier. However, arriving at a decision will still by no means be as simple as the ways NHSPs make decisions.

And after a decision is finally made, that may not be the end of the story of the decision-making agonies. HSPs may have waves of doubts, and recriminations, and worries, and second and third thoughts about the paths chosen and not chosen.

With afterthought worries, too, we can also lessen the intensity of our distress and agitation. Here are a few suggestions for HSPC immediate, first aid responses when your HSP is in agonies of indecision or distress, worrying about making the right decisions or avoiding wrong decisions:

- Invite your HSP to check regarding hunger, tiredness, stress or being triggered (HuTiST)
- Listen patiently
- Ask for further details
- Ask what she is feeling
- Acknowledge the emotions being experienced.
- Reassure your HSP that these feelings are very understandable under the present circumstances.
- Remind your HSP, if relevant, that these may be (in part or whole) also resonating with or triggering similar feelings and/or related traumas from the past.
- Suggest that your HSP might lessen his intensity with de-stressing techniques.*[13]

## Dealing with meta-anxieties

As an HSP, you may become anxious and distressed about being anxious and distressed. You may worry or obsess over possible outcomes, and may replay again and again your memories of events, emotions, thoughts and interactive experiences, analyzing alternative ways you could have responded in particular situations.

*Once burned, lessons learned.*
– Anonymous

✦✦ Part of Sidney's distress in childhood was cause by meta-anxieties. As a child, he worried that his anxieties showed he wasn't up to meeting the duties his parents expected him to perform. At times when his anxieties and meta-anxieties felt overwhelming, he also worried that he would become incapacitated by his worries and thereby add to his parents' burdens instead of relieving them of some of theirs. Some of these could even be described as meta-meta-anxieties.

In agonizing over his adult decisions about their buying a new home, Sidney worried that his worries were going to overwhelm him; that they were going to become intolerable burdens to Leslie; and that he was going to be unable to make a decision in time to buy a really good home they had seen – before it was sold to someone else.

Once we identified his meta-anxieties and trauma residues, tapping enabled Sidney to clear his past and current issues systematically. He was then able resolve his ambivalence over his current home purchase – much to this couple's mutual relief.

Anxieties and meta-anxieties include emotions along with thoughts. Anxieties may feel overwhelming to HSPs, even under seemingly minor stresses. They may have difficulties focusing on tasks at hand due to their anxieties. I address the meta-anxieties here in the section on Mind (within the Wholistic spectrum) because most people find it much easier to develop and utilize cognitive plans for dealing with their emotions rather than to resolve the emotional issues through addressing the emotions primarily by experiencing them. The aroused emotions tend to disrupt linear thinking, reasoning and planning. So, it is usually better to focus initially on the reasons for the stresses, tensions, anxieties and other feelings, and to sort out how to deal with them through reasoning.

This is not to say that we ignore the distressed emotions. On the contrary, it is essential to identify what they are and why we're experiencing them – and better yet when we do this without interferences from meta-anxieties.

For instance, we may have *anxieties or fears of letting go of fears* because we feel that our fears keep us safe. A typical meta-anxiety of this sort may be: "If I let go of my fears, I might not be careful enough and put myself in danger again."

✦ 'Ken' was an HSP third grader who was bullied because he was easily upset to the point of crying. He felt anxious to the point of withdrawing into silence most of the time he was in his classroom, despite his school counsellor's support with Cognitive Behavioral Therapy (CBT). Under pressure from his therapist to practice being more assertive in the class, as they had discussed and role-played successfully in counselling sessions, he became so anxious that he refused to go to school. His mom had to drag him physically to the car, lock the car doors, and drag him physically to the door of the school, where the assistant principal met her and physically restrained him from running back to the car, so his mother could drive away.

His mom brought him to me for deeper help in dealing with his school avoidance issues. Using TWR/WHEE, Ken was rapidly able to lower the intensity of his school phobia from '60' on the Subjective Units of Distress Scale (the 'SUDS' has a normal maximum of 10), bringing it down to 25. And there it stuck. It would not go any lower, though Ken had been successful in reducing several other issues to zero.

When I asked Ken what might be one or more reasons for holding onto his fears of going to school, he readily answered, "If I don't keep my radar on high alert, I'm likely to get hurt by the bullies." This 'meta-anxiety' had a SUDS of 20. He also acknowledged that he felt so much safer at home that he didn't want to leave home and face his anxiety state in school. (Not wanting to leave home had a SUDS of 8.)

Despite knowing cognitively that his teacher was on the alert to stop any bullying, and that she had spoken with the bullies and with their parents, Ken had been traumatized to the point that it was hard from him to get out of his 'high alert' state when he was in school.

The same meta-anxieties were aroused in his fear of leaving the safety of home. Focusing on the fear of letting go of these meta-anxieties, he was able to use his tapping to reduce their SUDS to zero. Re-focusing on his school phobia, he found its SUDS to have gone down from 25 to a 6, and was able to reduce it all the way to zero in only two further rounds of tapping.

The positive tapping exercises then enabled Ken to install a series of positive images of going to school with his mother and of functioning comfortably and competently in the school setting. With the help of his school counsellor, he had built detailed behavioral plans he could follow in class, and we strengthened his confidence that these would work with his tapping therapy.

Then he came up with another meta-anxiety about feeling overwhelmed if some of his old anxieties returned when he went back to class. We set up a signal to use with his teacher: raising his hand and waving it slightly from side to side, rather than holding it steady. This was to ask permission to go to the toilet, where he could sit in a stall and use his tapping without anyone seeing him doing it. (This was before another young client had stimulated the TWR/WHEE variation in which you gently alternate tapping with your left and right feet on the floor, or alternate tighten the toes on one foot and then on the other – so no one can tell you are using self-healing tapping in public.)

This series of interventions worked marvelously well. Ken was able to return to school the next day, and after two weeks he no longer needed to ask to be excused to the toilet.

School phobias are among the few true psychological emergencies.**[14] Once a child develops a fear of going to school, it's like falling off a horse. If you don't get back on immediately, or return to school promptly, the fears tend to snowball into bundles of meta-anxieties along with the primary traumas. Tapping therapies are excellent in resolving these issues.

Other examples of meta-anxieties include:
- Anxieties about how people would relate to you if you revealed you have particular issues
- Doubts about being able to cope with your issues, or anxieties about being overwhelmed by them
- Doubts about being able to find help for dealing successfully with your challenges
- Anxieties about who you would be and how you would relate to the world if you didn't have your problems

The good news in all of this is that meta-anxieties usually release much more quickly and easily than primary anxieties, other feelings, and trauma memories. And another good aspect of this is that you can develop and practice installing meta-positives.

*Distractions, misperceptions, errors and delusions of Mind*

Mind offers us the tools to perceive, analyze and choose options, and then to select which to act upon in our outer and inner worlds. We like to believe that our mind can stand, clear and firm, in the midst of various internal and external pressures that can influence it, lead it astray, and even betray it, without our conscious awareness that this is happening. But this is far from the truth. Mind may get distracted, deceived or deluded into making poor choices on one or another wholistic level of awareness.

- Body may distract or mislead our mind when hormones drive us to seek short-term sexual gratifications with poor choices in partners; with premenstrual and menstrual tensions; and with other hormonal challenges
- The brain matures very gradually throughout the early part of our lives. The prefrontal cortex, which analyzes memories and current perceptions and situation, does not mature till our early or mid-twenties. This is why young people are liable to make impulsive, rash and poorly conceived decisions, such as:
  - Buying into the dream of becoming a model, performer or media star: Teenage pop culture promises glamorous careers that are statistically very unlikely to be unattainable, yet modern day teens dream of this and pursue it – with little thought of more substantial alternatives for making a living and having a decent life.
  - Deciding to train for a career in professional sports: The chances of making a living in professional sports or the performing arts are infinitesimally small. Waaaay less than 1 percent of people who aspire to do so are able to get anywhere near succeeding. For example, 15 people will make it onto a professional hockey team, while 30,000 work very hard but get nowhere near their career goal (Caulfield, 2015).

And this is a dangerous career choice. American football, soccer (the rest of the world's football), hockey, lacrosse, and several other contact sports carry very severe long-term risks from repeated brain concussions and injuries[15] that may be as severe as the more acute risks of serving in the military in wartime (Omalu, et al., 2005). Yet the optimistic bias that leads people to pursue glamor, fame and fortunes blinds them to these limited prospects and serious dangers.

- It is primarily the young, with their immature faculties for reasoning, who go to war.

*CAN YOU REMEMBER DREAMS YOU HAD OF A GLAMOROUS CAREER WHEN YOU WERE GROWING UP?*

*HOW DID YOUR DREAMS UNFOLD AND CHANGE?*

- HuTiST may distract and distort our thoughts.
- In the course of our lives, mind is formatted throughout our formative childhood and maturing years by circumstances of chance. Our interpretations of the world and beliefs about it are strongly shaped by our family, religion, education, community and the media.
- Other people have different experiences from ours, and are just as likely to be certain as we are that their views and understandings of the world are the correct ones, and that our views are misguided and wrong.
- We acquire and shape our belief systems largely without conscious awareness that we are doing this.
- We tend to have meta-beliefs and rules about the rightness and worthiness of our own beliefs, along with questions and doubts about the validity and worthiness of the beliefs of others.*[16]
- Our minds resist questioning or changing our beliefs and meta-beliefs, even when we find that they are misleading us and even getting us in trouble.[17]

*WHAT FAMILY AND CULTURAL BELIEFS OR BIASES HAVE INFLUENCED YOUR LIFE?*

*WHAT OR WHO WOKE YOU UP TO SEE THAT YOUR INHERITED BELIEFS WERE NOT NECESSARILY OR EXCLUSIVELY RIGHT?*

– Emotions may similarly be driven by hormones, for instance, misleading our mind into making poor choices in love, anger and aggressive behaviors. Emotions may also be stimulated by the wholistic spectrum of life experiences, coloring and biasing our thinking.
  - Anger is a particular mischief-maker in derailing our thinking.
  - Love or jealousy may blind us to warning signals that others see as obvious, and that we, ourselves, may see similarly – though perhaps in retrospect.
  - Traumas may leave us with emotional triggers that bypass our thought processes.

*ARE YOU AWARE OF PARTICULAR EMOTIONS THAT ARE PRONE TO DERAIL YOUR RATIONAL THINKING?*

*WHAT HELPS YOU SENSE YOUR EMOTIONS ARE TRIGGERED?*

*WHAT HELPS YOU DEAL WITH YOUR EMOTIONS ONCE THEY ARE TRIGGERED?*

– Relationships with other people often sway our emotions and mind, as group mentality may default to low denominators, with negative or even disastrous consequences.

- As noted under 'Body,' above, parents encourage their children to join teams and persevere in playing dangerous contact sports that produce high rates of concussions.
- Participation in any social group often includes expectations of allegiance to beliefs and thinking biases of group members.
- Bullying is often a group activity, frequently with traumas in bullies' experiences that they are venting on people weaker than themselves in order to boost their damaged personal sense of power.*[18]
- Politicians inflame passions, blaming 'others' for difficulties in their home country, and sending them to wars that benefit arms dealers and other businessmen, while distracting people from domestic issues.
- Allegiance to religious leaders, both the founders of the religions and their current priesthood, encourages 'us vs. them' beliefs and attitudes that can be triggered and fanned into flames of inter-culture and inter-faith conflicts and wars.
- The rich grow ever richer and more powerful, to the point that they control the economy, the government and the media (McQuaig & Brooks, 2010). Relatively few people in the general public appear to be aware of these issues and dangers.
- Banks are among the leading beneficiaries of these trends, passing laws and insinuating themselves into power that gives them incredible boosts in earnings and in financial and political powers.
- Until serious breakdowns occur in the economy and the workplace, people continue to believe and hope all will be for their best, despite indications of impending serious environmental collapses.

*HAVE YOU FOUND YOURSELF PRESSURED OR SWAYED BY PEOPLE IN YOUR SOCIAL GROUPS?*

– Relationships of humans with the environment are horrendously destructive, largely due to the prevalent attitude that humans have been given dominion, for their own benefits, over all the other living beings on the planet, as well as over the natural resources of the planet. The alarms are ringing to warn us that tipping points in environmental collapse are approaching, or may have even been passed, beyond which there will be no return.*[19]

*WHAT ARE YOU DOING TO PROMOTE AWARENESS OF THE NEED FOR ENVIRONMENTAL HEALING?*

- Spirit, as filtered through diverse interpretations by various religions, often is explained and promoted as a set of beliefs in the exclusive views of each religion that puts itself forward as the only true and correct way of understanding and relating to the world.

> *God created Man in his own image, and Man,*
> *being a gentleman, returned the compliment.*
> – Jerome Lawrence, Robert Lee

In my explorations of these issues of spirit, personally and in my work as a psychotherapist and teacher, I find that NHSPs generally tend to be either:

- Locked into religious beliefs about spirit, which often exclude possibilities of personal spiritual awarenesses, or

- Wedded to logical proofs that can be measured in some scientific manner that is regularly and reliably repeatable. It is difficult for them to accept that their disbelief in spiritual awarenesses is a belief that is as incapable of the absolute proof they demand of believers in spirit.

HSPs tend to connect personally with spirit, with varying degrees of trusting in their own awarenesses. When their perceptions are honored by family and friends, and better yet when they are consensually validated by others, then HSPs usually find spiritual awarenesses to be of enormous importance and benefit.

Sadly, many HSP children suffer from the disbeliefs of parents, other family members, teachers and peers regarding their HSP intuitive and spiritual awarenesses. This trauma is particularly damaging in childhood because it occurs in their formative years, when beliefs and disbeliefs are being learned for personal maps for navigating the continents and oceans of life. Some HSPs simply learn to remain silent about their awarenesses. Others may come to doubt or even to dismiss their own experiences.

*WHERE ARE YOU ON THE SPECTRUM FROM DISBELIEVING TO BELIEVING PERSONAL SPIRITUAL AWARENESS?*[*20]

*IF YOU'RE TUNED INTO PERSONAL SPIRITUAL AWARENESSES, HOW HAVE YOU DEALT WITH DISBELIEVERS?*

### Relationships with other people *(HSP wholistic issues)*

Many HSPs are very keenly aware of subtleties in their own and in other people's emotions, moods, behaviors and relationships. These HSPs show great interest and pleasure in pondering and discussing the specifics and nuances of all of these in great detail.

The good news is that these HSPs are usually very caring and conscientious about people's feelings, needs and preferences, and eager to please others when they engage in interactions with them. They enjoy immersions in the creative arts, such as literature, drama, visual arts, music and singing, and take great pleasure in exploring these with others.

The bad news is that HSPs are often highly sensitive to abrasive interactions, criticisms or rigid demands in family, school or work situations, taking them to heart and often obsessing over their difficulties in living with them. They may be easily hurt or even traumatized by such experiences.*[21]

Sensitivities to relationships may pose burdens to HSPs. Many HSP qualities are intensified with stresses such as loud or strong emotionality in people around them; changes in routines; having to move to a new living or work situation; or needing to adapt to new people and circumstances in their lives.

✛✛ Bonnie had bolted out the front door, to sit on the tree stump in the front yard of her home till the schoolbus arrived. She resented her parents' expectations that she should take more of a role as the 'big sister' in sorting out her brothers' bickering and arguing, which she was relieved to have left on the other side of the door of their home. Bonnie felt lucky that this year she was one of the first children picked up on her schoolbus, which allowed her to sit at the back and avoid a lot of the rowdiness of the other children. She wished that her friend, Selma, lived closer to her, so that they could ride the bus together, or that Selma could be in her class. Selma was her constant companion at breaks and in the lunchroom. She was gentle and sensitive, like Bonnie.

Bonnie worried on the way home from school on the bus about whether her mom would scold her for running out when her brothers had their argument that morning. She was enormously relieved when her mother smiled and gave her a hug as she came in the door, telling her she had been wise to stay out of the silly argument that morning. She then started to worry that she worried too much about some things. Her mother was actually a very understanding mom.

Relationships are experienced through our whole selves with the whole selves of those with whom we are interacting. It is through relationships that we come to know ourselves – through differences and contrasts in our words, thoughts, feelings and spiritual awarenesses. We learn about ourselves through our interactions with each other on all levels of our being.

We'll consider much more about HSP and HSPC relationships in many sections of this book.

> *Our feelings are not ours, any more than… our thoughts are ours. We locate them in our heads, in our selves, but they cross interpersonal boundaries as though such limits had no meaning for them: passing back and forth from one mind to another, across space and time, growing and breeding, but where we do not know. What we feel arises out of what I feel for what you feel for what I feel about your feelings about me – and about many other things besides: it arises from the betweenness, and in this way feeling binds us together, and, more than that, actually unites us, since the feelings are shared. Yet the paradox is that those feelings only arise because of our distinctness, our ability to be separate, distinct individuals, that come, that go, in separation and death.*
>
> – Iain McGilchrist

**Relationships with the environment** *(HSP wholistic issues)*

> *We are a part of, not apart from nature.*
> – Anonymous

HSPs often take great pleasure in being out in the beauty and quiet of natural surroundings, enjoying their surroundings through all of their keen senses. They may like gardening, walks and drives in nature, and may spend hours just sitting and enjoying a field of flowers, a lake or a mountain. They like homes with a view of nature.

They can be keenly aware of negative aspects of the environment, and may respond strongly to coming across a dying or dead tree; to other people's disregard for the environment in minor and major ways – as in seeing trash discarded on a trail; passing an animal killed on the road; or seeing evidence and effects of pollution. Conversely, they can be spiritually centered and at peace with a dying tree, animal, or person, with direct awarenesses of their spiritual paths.

I've seen numbers of HSPs who developed environmental allergies. These may be no worse than mild hay fever (which I suffered myself when living in northern Kansas City and Texas), or may be more severe – including skin, digestive or respiratory track sensitivities, or even pervasive multiple allergy syndromes. Any of these allergies may be partly or largely caused or worsened by physical and/or emotional stresses and traumas. They may be markedly decreased with listening to what the allergies want us to know about our lives and then clearing the associated stresses. In other words, allergies are no different from any other body symptom (as discussed earlier in this section).

While I know of no way to prove this, my personal sense from speaking with varieties of environmentally concerned people, is that a high percent of HSPs have strong feelings and awarenesses about environmental issues.

Under this category, I also include relationships with other living beings. Many HSPs take great pleasure in having pets, growing plants, and gardening. Some have innate gifts or develop their abilities to sense the energies of animals and plants, and some have stronger gifts yet and can communicate with them. These communications may be with individuals or with the collective species.

HSPs often have a deep awareness of the ongoing, escalating destruction of our planet's environment, which is seriously threatened by an impressive array of human projects:

- Increasing carbon emissions that are causing global warming
- Exhausting our natural resources
- Polluting our waters, land and air so that they are increasingly poisonous to ourselves and to most other life on our planet;
- Overpopulation
- Genociding other species, with numerous extinctions that are escalating at unconscionable rates – to our own detriment and at our own peril in many cases, as with the approaching likely extinction of bees needed for pollination
- Building and continuing to run nuclear plants with no way to totally assure their safety or to safely dispose of spent nuclear fuel
- Engineering the weather with highly toxic sprays
- There are also issues that have obvious secondary effects on the environment,

through failures of governments to take the necessary measures to protect it from destruction.
- Waging useless wars on contrived pretenses that benefit the rich arms dealers and other suppliers of the military on the one hand, and that distract the public from the real issues in government at home on the other hand
- Allowing the concentration of resources into the hands of corporations and individuals who are obscenely rich – at the expense of the 99% of the rest of the population, which leaves no funds for protecting, much less restoring the environment

HSPs are often drawn to support movements to protect and improve the environment

Some HSPs also have awarenesses of consciousness in gemstones, rocks, aspects of nature such as lakes, rivers, oceans, positive and negative energies in given locations (energetic earth power points), and energy lines (ley lines) in the earth.
- On the more sensitive end of the HSP spectrum (overlapping with the realms of spiritual sensitivities, discussed next) they may sense the pain of those species that are going extinct – both in the suffering of individual members of those species and in the species as a collective consciousness.
- They may similarly feel the hurt of Mother Earth when they connect with mining operations and oil spills that disrespect, disrupt and poison the environment.
- The very highly HSP may also connect with Gaia, the living being that is our planet, who may well be approaching the sixth major extinction of most life as we know it today on planet Earth (Benor, 2014).

IN WHAT WAYS ARE YOU AWARE OF YOUR BEING INTIMATELY CONNECTED WITH NATURE?

HAVE YOU SENSED A CONSCIOUSNESS IN NATURE?

**Spirit** *(HSP wholistic issues)*

*When the soul is at peace, so will the body be.*
– Arama

As mentioned above, in Western society, spirit is considered by many to be a wishful, fantasy creation, serving to counter anxieties about the finality of physical death. This view is furthered by Western education that emphasizes evidence-based research to validate beliefs and understandings about the world. If you can't measure it or record it in some objective way, it is assumed to be no more than a theory or a belief.*[22]

Various religions instruct their members in the teachings of their founders and followers. Spirit may be sensed by some, within these contexts, through prayer or other devotional practices, and within the fellowship of a spiritual community. For other religious followers, spirit is a concept, perhaps a goal to be reached upon death or in an afterlife, but not something they currently know as a personal experience.

Numerous people report spontaneous, direct, personal spiritual awarenesses that have a feeling of real perceptions, although usually they are of a distinctly different quality from outer-world awarenesses through sight, sound, smell, taste or touch. They are also different from daydreams or dreams experienced during sleep.*[23]

Research reports validate many of these intuitive awarenesses.*[24] The numerous studies confirming the existence of extra-sensory perceptions and spiritual awarenesses are ignored or rejected by those firmly wedded to their conventional ways of thinking and of understanding the world.

Heightened intuitive awarenesses may leave HSPs vulnerable to sensory overloads that create challenges by drawing the HSPs' attention away from their outer world awarenesses:

- Intuitions in general may strongly draw their attention, interfering with, overriding or preventing other sensory awarenesses from coming into their present-moment consciousness.
- Intuitions about the feelings, intentions, motivations and levels of honesty and integrity of the person speaking may distract HSPs from attending to the content of the conversation.

I believe the spiritual dimension is a tremendously important aspect of HSP awarenesses. I discuss this in greater depth in Section VII, exploring personal spiritual awarenesses and collective spiritual participation; and in Section VIII, which considers the more subtle sensitivities of HSPs and of others who open to direct consciousness of spiritual dimensions.

## Engaging in wholistic healing

Even when we may be familiar with wholistic healing, it is easy to overlook portions of our wholistic potentials, even when we most need them. When we are stressed and distressed, we may easily over-focus on limited aspects of ourselves, while ignoring other parts that may be crucial to understanding our situations and to resolving them.

- If you injure your foot, your pain may draw most of your attention. You may forget to ask your pain and your foot what each one wants you to know about your life.
- When you're seriously upset with someone, your emotions may overwhelm any other aspect of your being.
- Challenged by a problem, you may wind yourself up in logic and reason, ignoring your frustrations, worries and emotions that get in the way of your thinking clearly, but which might alert you to important elements in the issues you're dealing with.
- In a heated argument with your friend, you may lose sight of the importance of the friendship while over-focusing on the facts in your disagreement.
- In the business of your engagement in the nitty-gritty details of getting on with life, you may stray from the perspectives of the spiritual aspects of your existence, which would give you a totally different perspective on the issues you're struggling with.

There are various ways to bring ourselves back into wholistic awareness when we notice we've strayed from being 'centered.' Sometimes it is enough just to catch ourselves straying and we can bring ourselves back into this centeredness.*[25]

When I'm really rattled, I find the following invocation can help bring me back into wholistic harmony and focus:

Wholistic harmony invocation: I invite the Infinite Source, archangels and angels, spirit guides, spirits, my soul, my spirit, the collective consciousness, all my relations (in the sense that Indigenous people use this term, to include all, interrelated, conscious beings), my mind, my emotions, my energy body and my physical body to participate in dealing with [INSERT YOUR DETAILS]. Collectively, we have the wisdom and knowledge to address this competently, to bring about the best healing that is for my greatest good and the greatest good of all, starting right *now!*

The complexity of this statement helps me to refocus, away from the unwanted and distrubing distractions and back into a more healing space.

*YOU MAY CHOOSE TO EDIT THIS TO MATCH YOUR PERSONAL PREFERENCES, OR, BETTER YET, WRITE YOUR OWN REMINDER FOR CENTERING YOURSELF.*

There is also a caution here when you're seeking help for your physical challenges from conventional, Western caregivers who address any of the individual levels of our being. Conventional therapists tend to focus exclusively on the body, which is a very limited portion of the wholistic spectrum.

The clearest and most important examples that come to mind are from the practice of conventional medicine. Medical doctors will prescribe medications and surgical procedures for symptoms and for identified, diagnosable physical abnormalities. They usually ignore the entire remainder of the wholistic spectrum. There may be psychological stresses which cause imbalances of muscle tensions, nervous system overloads, immune system dysfunctions and so on, but most doctors are not trained to identify or treat these. For these medical practitioners, the body is the only thing needing fixing.

✦✦✦ I still squirm with embarrassment and shame when I think back on how, despite my intentions to help the whole person rather than just address the physical issues, I nevertheless sometimes have found myself overly immersed in the conventional medical mode of relating to people's problems.

I was in the neurology clinic during my internship when 'Selma,' a 10 year-old girl was brought in by her parents for help with recurrent grand mal seizures. She was terribly embarrassed when they occurred in public and she lost control of her bladder and wet herself. The seizures were less frequent with her anticonvulsant medication but still occurred every few weeks. She was developing a reluctance to socialize with friends after she'd embarrassed herself at a friend's house in front of the whole family at dinner time. I had just read about a new medication that was found effective for children's seizures and prescribed this for her.

On her follow-up visit two weeks later, her parents reported Selma was tolerating the medication well and had had no seizures or side effects. They missed their next appointment, a month later, and I never gave her another thought. Several months further on, she appeared at the clinic with her parents without an appointment. They had to move to another city due to her father's work and were unable to get an appointment with me on short notice, but wanted to be sure to thank me for the miracle I had facilitated. She had been seizure free since starting the new medication and was beginning to blossom socially. She was actually looking forward to starting a new school and building new friendships where no one would know she had epilepsy and no one would have seen her wetting herself during a seizure.

I shudder as I recall my response. Coming totally from the thinking side of my brain, I said that I really couldn't take credit for a lucky guess in prescribing this new medication. I hardly responded at all to her enormous relief in being seizure free at last, nor to her parents' enormous gratitude as well.

In my defense, I can only mention that this was after having been on emergency room duty the previous night, which meant I was about 30 hours into my work period, having had only 2-3 hours of sleep. And I have a very low tolerance for tiredness, which I now realize is another of my HSP characteristics.

Were I able to turn the clock backwards, I would share in Selma's celebration, perhaps giving her a high five or a hug to acknowledge her delight and relief in which I had played such an important role.

## WHAT ARE YOUR WAYS OF ENGAGING IN WHOLISITC HEALING?

### *Mainstream attitudes to wholistic healing*

Conventional psychotherapists may focus just on the cognitive and behavioral aspects of people's stress and distress – ignoring or minimizing the contributions of the body, emotions, relationships and spirit to the presenting problems that brought the person for help.

In these regards, conventional doctors and psychotherapists may actually cause harm, representing themselves as offering the best and only legitimate approaches for physical and psychological issues. They even lobby (often successfully) local, state and national authorities to legislate restrictions against anyone practicing healthcare or psychotherapy approaches that differ from their own.

HSPs are particularly prone to suffer from stresses that are related to their sensitivities. Their responses to these stresses may manifest in any and all areas of the wholistic spectrum. These stresses often contribute to physical and psychological problems. So I recommend that HSPs seek medical and psychological consultations with practitioners who are open to the broadest possible spectrum of wholistic care that you can find.

It is also important to know that so-called 'skeptics' about complementary and alternative medicine, wholistic healing, intuition and personal spirituality are highly vigilant to disseminate their disbeliefs. They are not actually skeptics but are rather ardent disbelievers.**[26] They are very active in the media and on line, discounting and disparaging reports of successes with wholistic healing approaches. They are also active in promoting legislation that limits or excludes the availability of wholistic healing practices.

✦✦✦ Here is a glaring example of ardent disbeliefs. Along with other wholistic healing practitioners, teachers and researchers, I have found that Wikipedia is strongly biased against complementary/ alternative therapies, commonly also labeled as holistic healing. Within hours of anyone making an entry in Wikipedia that supports these approaches, they are diligently edited out of Wikipedia.

I repeatedly made a Wikipedia entry noting the safety of complementary/alternative therapies. There are only extremely rare instances of fatalities with these approaches. In marked contrast, modern Western medicine is acknowledged as the third leading cause of death (with cancer and heart disease being first and second). The entries I made about this, which I confirmed with references from respected medical journals, were deleted each time in less than 24 hours.[27]

While I won't belabor this point further here, interested readers can find more information on line, with diligent sleuthing, about systematic biases and disinformation to be found on Wikipedia.

*In summary*

Wholistic considerations empower us to engage in self-healing and to clear our own problems. By connecting with our issues at each of these levels, we often identify many details that we can address for ourselves. We can then decrease stresses that are creating and worsening these issues, and increase our comfort and competence in dealing with them.

We've considered various components of wholistic understandings of ourselves and of the world. These help us to analyze how challenges develop in our lives, and also suggests various doorways into approaches for sorting out rough edges in ourselves and in our relationships.

We can begin to appreciate that our consciousness is an incredibly complex essence of our states of being. It is no wonder that we sometimes find ourselves challenged to understand what is going on in our inner lives and in our relationships.

Having made these distinctions within the wholistic framework for understanding our places in the world, I hasten to reiterate that each of these levels of our being is intimately interlinked and interactive with all of the other levels. The dissection above of the various wholistic levels is merely for convenience of discussion – within frameworks that are familiar from our conventional ways of thinking about ourselves and the world we live in.

# 7. Jungian Perspectives

*The sad truth is that man's real life consists of a complex of inexorable opposites – day and night, birth and death, happiness and misery, good and evil. We are not even sure that one will prevail against the other, that good will overcome evil, or joy defeat pain. Life is a battleground. It always has been and always will be; and if it were not so, existence would come to an end.*
— Carl Jung

Carl Jung, in the early 1900's, developed a broad awareness of psychological functions that are helpful in understanding and accommodating to HSP sensitivities. Jung focused on the polarities of psychological functions he identified as Thinking vs. Feeling and Intuitive (inner awareness) vs. Sensate (outer awareness). Jung pointed out that everyone has a personality type that is dominant in one or two of these four parameters. Though these are labeled as polarities, each pair is actually a continuum. At any moment, we may find ourselves engaging with our inner and outer worlds from different points on each of these spectrums. (See Figure II-1.) Jung also noted that there are Introverted and Extraverted styles of relating to the world.

In many ways, these polarities parallel the qualities that distinguish HSPs and HSPs. HSPs tend to be strong and comfortable on the Intuition and Feeling sides of these polarities, while NHSPs are generally stronger and distinctly more comfortable on Thinking and Sensation polarities.

**Figure II-1. Jungian polarities**

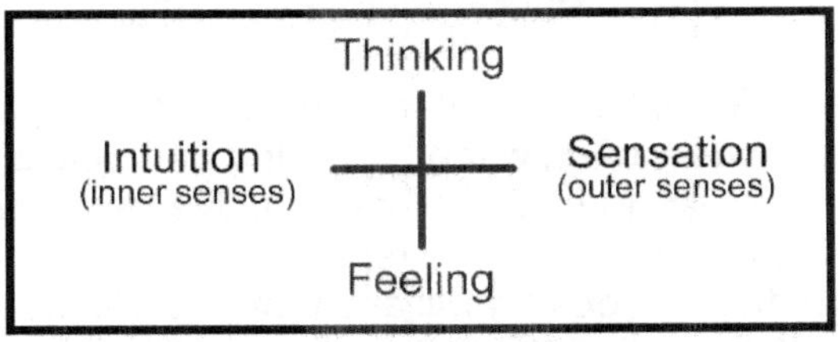

```
                    Thinking
                       |
    Intuition    ——————+——————    Sensation
  (inner senses)       |         (outer senses)
                       |
                    Feeling
```

I'm puzzled that Elaine Aron's research shows as many men as women HSPs. My personal experience is that women tend to be more often on the intuitive and feeling ends of the spectrum, and men more often in thinking and sensation awarenesses.

What I particularly like about the Jungian polarities is that they don't suggest that HSPs are incapable of activating Thinking and Sensation functions, nor that NHSPs are incapable of perceiving, expressing and responding to their Feeling and Intuition functions, as well as recognizing and relating to those functions in HSPs. By pointing out that these functions are experienced on a spectrum – rather than either being present or being absent – there is more of an invitation for HSPs and NHSPs to meet somewhere along a commonly-experienced/ understood/ negotiated/ accepted middle zone of each continuum.

Many languages (including English) are limiting in the concepts that they encompass and the realities that people can conceptualize within their linguistic boundaries. In Russian, *da* means 'yes' and *nyet* means 'no.' But in slang there is the delicious word, *danyet*, that acknowledges there are some things and situations and relationships where both yes and no are equally applicable. This is the ultimate in accepting polarities.**[28]

*Thinking type* people organize their perceptions of the world and their responses to it through logical analysis and planning. They usually do not pay much attention to their feelings, and may even dismiss feelings as *illogical, unreasonable*, and *unreliable*. A scheduled, predictable world is most comfortable for the thinking types.

Western society overvalues and over-emphasizes the thinking mode of relating to the world. Our educational systems is almost totally focused on left brain studies. Emotions are dismissed as being 'melodramatic,' 'over the top,' 'histrionic,' 'excessively sentimental,' 'saccharine,' 'soppy,' 'syrupy,' 'sickly', and more…

> *The great enemy of the truth is very often not the lie, deliberate, contrived and dishonest, but the myth, persistent, persuasive and unrealistic.*
> – John F. Kennedy

*Feeling types* experience life as a montage of emotions and values. Experiences that are emotionally charged feel real and alive, interesting and exciting, and are highly valued. Thoughts alone are colorless and dull. Plans are acted upon, wherever possible, if one is in the right mood, and communications are engaged as much or more through the tones and nuances of interactions than through their content. The Feeling types respond with attraction to most events, activities and experiences that stimulate and excite them positively, or with withdrawal to those that turn them off or repel them. In language of feeling people, this is often identified as relating through the heart rather than the head.

> *The heart has reasons that reason knows little of.*
> – Blaise Pascal

*Intuitive types* grasp information in patterns and mental maps. They sense and intuit their way through situations, often without thinking or verbalizing to themselves the processes by which they make their decisions. Intuitive perceptions come in wholes – and any individual part they might analyze represents less than the full truth. They instinctively know the right thing to do in familiar situations. Faced with new challenges, the intuitive may simply know rather than deduce solutions, relying on specific details and leaps of inspiration rather than step-by-step reasoning. I've been amazed and amused to see intuitive people who come up with the accurate answers to challenging problems in mathematics or the sciences but can't even begin to explain how they arrived at their answers. Intuitives may suffer in school when they come up with correct answers on their exams but are unable to explain how they arrived at them, and may be unfairly accused of cheating.

> *The intuitive mind is a sacred gift and the rational mind is a faithful servant. We have created a society that honors the servant and has forgotten the gift.*
> – Albert Einstein

*Sensation types* notice every detail in the world around them: form, color, sound and their patterns. These factors are the threads with which they weave the fabric of their reality. Everything has its place. Shaping, organizing and moving bodies and objects around is important and satisfying. Everything has its cause and effect, and if these are not apparent in the present, it is merely because insufficient efforts have-been applied to understanding and fitting things into their proper order. Fixing anything that is not working is a welcomed challenge, addressed with an immediate analysis of what's broken or jammed and seeing the obvious ways it can be fixed.

*A wise man's goal shouldn't be to say something
profound, but to say something useful.*

— Criss Jami

It is worthy of mention that relatively few HSPs I know appear to be strong on this polarity. I have found that many who are strong HSPs have clear (and sometimes awkward) difficulties connecting with their sensate functions. This is particularly noticeable in issues related to time management and to dealing with mechanical malfunctions or space management.

Just as the term NHSP is useful, so I find that the term 'non-sensate' can be helpful to HSPs and HSPCs to identify areas where patience, on both sides and support on both sides be needed and much appreciated.

In addition, Jung also identified another polarity: Introversion vs. Extroversion. This, too, can be very helpful for understanding the HSP.

*Introverted* people prefer to be guided by their personal awareness, heeding their feelings, thoughts, wishes and intentions for guidance in their actions and responses to the world around them. The expectations and demands of the outer world will not influence them as strongly as their own inner worlds. Such people will appear thoughtful, introspective and quiet, if they are moderately introverted. They are often their own worst critics, setting their inner barometers for behavior and response per their own opinion of themselves, and not so readily influenced by external pressures. Extremes of introversion are seen as deviant from psychological and social norms, and may include excessive shyness, social isolation, depressed withdrawal, disregard for expectations of friends and family, and the like.

*Extroverts,* In contrast, are outgoing and highly responsive to social situations. They seek interactions with others, care about others' opinions and expectations, and want to conform in order to be accepted.

Within each of these polarities there are varying degrees of insightfulness and wide ranges of behavior, so the basic polarities explain some but not all aspects of people's various ways of being in the world.

It is important to emphasize that although people may express varying degrees of preferences for some polarities over others, they are not restricted to any polarity in all situations or at all times. People who are generally introverted may be more extroverted when in the presence of people from whom they feel greater acceptance. People who are extroverted may feel more introverted when lacking confidence in their knowledge or skills to deal with a given situation. A person who is primarily a sensate may still have excellent intuitive abilities.

These Jungian descriptive polarities have been formalized into the Myers-Briggs psychological scale (Web ref), which can be helpful to HSPs and their companions in identifying, comprehending and sorting out their differences – particularly when people are unsure of where they fit on the spectrum of Jungian polarities. This is a fast, easy way to get a sense of where you are on the spectrums of these qualities.**[29]

YOU MIGHT FIND IT HELPFUL TO EXPLORE WHERE YOU ARE ON THE MYERS-BRIGGS SCALE IF YOU'RE IN A RELATIONSHIP WITH SOMEONE DIFFERENT FROM YOURSELF IN THESE WAYS.

### Shadow aspects of personality

Jung pointed out that while we tend to experience and express ourselves predominantly on one or another polarity of a spectrum, we all experience the entire spectrum on some levels of our awareness. Those parts of ourselves that are not being expressed are still present within us, but they are in the 'shadow' parts of our consciousness – outside of our conscious observation.

Until recently, we have been encouraged to maintain cultural stereotypes of men as thinking/ sensation primaries, and women as feeling/ intuitive primaries. Women's Liberation has been a transforming force in helping to acknowledge our neglected polar opposites, giving women permission and encouragement to express and develop their thinking and sensation aspects, while HSP awarenesses and men's groups encourage boys and men to acknowledge and express their feeling and intuitive sides.

Unconsciously, people may choose a friend or mate with opposite polar preferences not only because they find this stimulating and balancing, but also because they can let the other express the aspects of themselves that they would rather not acknowledge or deal with. For example, a husband with primary introverted, thinking/ sensation functions may be happy to see his wife – with primary extroverted, intuitive/ feeling functions – handle the decorating and entertainment at home. His wife may likewise leave the finances and mechanical repairs to her husband. Thus, each avoids engagement with their own shadow or inferior polarities.

This kind of partnership of polarities can work in the opposite direction as well. For instance, the feeling partner can help the thinking partner to be more aware of his own feelings.

*If my heart could do my thinking, would my brain begin to feel?*
— Van Morrison

While some may readily acknowledge their own primary traits, they may not be aware that their polar opposites are also alive and active in the shadow aspects of their being – those parts of themselves that exist outside of their conscious awareness.

The shadow aspect of our unconscious mind shuts away those parts of our awarenesses that make us uncomfortable, and that we would rather not experience or acknowledge to ourselves and to others. This shadow carries all of our forgotten, unacknowledged, deeply buried old hurts, along with accompanying angers, resentments and grief; all the little and great envies and desires that parents, teachers and religious institutions tell us we ought not to have, though we very often do, and more negativities besides.

In addition to managing *shadow* aspects of our emotions and personalities, our unconscious mind serves as a vast storehouse for factual memories. While the unconscious is very much a part of us, it is extremely challenging to perceive and comprehend its functions within ourselves.

The shadow aspects of our personalities seek expression just as our conscious polarities do. For instance, a thinking primary person will also have feelings that want and need to be expressed. If the feelings are held in, they tend to build up until they find some outlet, often under conditions of pressure or stress, when the dominant polarity loses some of its control. When these repressed feelings finally do come to expression, it is often through interactions with other people that stir the shadow to strong responses, and many times the eruption into consciousness and expression in words or actions occurs in ways that are counter-productive. Such explosions of emotion or other aspects of shadow, in turn, often generate negative reactions in others. These sorts of experiences may then discourage people from giving expression to their shadow sides.

> *The Unconscious is not unconscious. It is only the Conscious that is unconscious of what the Unconscious is conscious of.*
> – Francis Jeffrey

Our shadow also is a storehouse for memories and feelings we would rather not be aware of. Disappointments, failures, rejections, betrayals and other negative experiences are buried outside of our conscious awareness. Even major traumatic experiences may be hidden from our conscious mind. And despite the fact that we don't recognize that they are there, the buried, unpleasant memories and emotions often influence our thoughts and feelings.

There are many ways that shadow feelings can affect a person's life. They may lead to depression, anger, negative beliefs about one's ability to succeed, or poor interpersonal relationships.

✦ 'Todd' was a highly successful businessman who had been married for 14 years to 'Julie,' a music teacher. Over the years, Todd found himself developing an increasing irritation with Julie's emotionality. She was completely up-front in saying what she felt, when she felt it, and had no hesitation in expressing joy and laughter, tears or anger. Whenever they argued, which was becoming more and more frequent, Todd was upset as much by how she expressed her feelings as by whatever it was they were arguing about. Julie, for her part, felt that he was increasingly cold and distant, as well as less and less interested in spending time with her. She was increasingly enraged when they disagreed, which was highly out of character for her.

A marriage counsellor suggested that each might do well to sort out some of their feelings in individual psychotherapy. Todd reluctantly accepted this suggestion, overcoming his unhappiness with the referral because the counsellor came very highly recommended and he truly wanted to save their marriage, as much for their children's sake as for his own.

Over several months, Todd was surprised to discover that a lot of the anger he was venting on his wife was actually buried anger that came from a deep well of negative feelings he was carrying inside himself from his childhood. Julie's emotionality frequently stirred these buried feelings about his parents. But before he became conscious of them, he simply vented them at the source of their arousal, Julie, rather than at their original sources – his own parents, who had argued and fought each other bitterly for many years, sometimes getting into physical fights. These had terrified him and he had buried the memories of these experiences in order not to suffer the fears, sadness and general distress he often experienced – in those early years of his life when he had no better recourse for dealing with them.

Both of Todd's parents had had to work long hours to support their four children. While they said that they loved Todd, he never felt sure they really meant it because they were rarely there to help him when he was upset or feeling needy. Being a bright student, Todd sought approval and gratification by earning good grades. This also served him well later in his work.

Todd buried his feelings of hurt and anger in what I call 'the emotional trash basket' of his unconscious mind. As a child, this was the best he could do. He couldn't change his parents, couldn't fire or replace them, and couldn't leave. Had he not stuffed these feelings away, he would have suffered much more emotional distress and pain of feeling unloved and unwanted by his parents. This didn't stop him from being much more sensitive than other children, nor from getting teary-eyed or easily triggered into frustration and anger in class and with his peers. With the passage of time, he managed to gain more and more control over showing his feelings as he matured into adulthood.

As he grew up, he became increasingly able to control his emotional responses to other people and to hide his stress reactions. This became such a habit that he was able to function most of the time without others being aware of how sensitive he was. In fact, he himself became less aware of his HSP qualities.

Early in their relationship, Julie's emotionality had appealed to Todd because he could vicariously enjoy seeing her expressing and releasing feelings that he himself had learned to suppress. Over the years of living together, however, his unconscious mind gradually absorbed (through the freedom exhibited by Julie in expressing her feelings) that it did not have to keep the lid shut so tightly on Todd's emotional trash bucket. So when Julie stirred his feelings, they started to leak out and sometimes to overflow.

As Todd was able to recall and release in therapy the feelings from his emotional trash basket that had been stored away since his childhood, the load of painful buried feelings was lightened in his unconscious mind. Then, when Julie became emotional, his current frustrations no longer overflowed in emotionality that was as intense as before.

In her individual psychotherapy, Julie learned as well about feelings she had been carrying from her childhood. She had always felt frustrated that her father was cold and distant most of the time, but highly volatile and explosive when he was drunk, at which point she became frightened of him. While Todd had not been withdrawn when they married and never had a drinking problem, his increasing discomfort with Julie's feelings had led him to withdraw emotionally in their relationship, as their arguments became increasingly heated. This stirred her buried childhood fears and angers about her father's behaviors, which were vented initially on Todd. She, too, was able to sort through and release her childhood feelings in psychotherapy so that they no longer intruded inappropriately in her marriage.

Todd's and Julie's individual trauma residues from earlier in their lives came out in the course of their marriage. This happens quite frequently, to varying degrees, in many relationships. When people are ready to explore the unconscious issues that are creating the tensions and frictions between them, as Julie and Todd did, there is a good likelihood that they can be resolved. Too often, however, people lock into their surface issues and are unable to get to the roots of the issues in order to reconnect their conscious awareness with the buried memories and feelings and to resolve them. It is difficult for most people to do this sort of healing work individually and in relationships without the help of a trained therapist.

*CAN YOU IDENTIFY ANY FEELINGS, MEMORIES, HABITS AND/OR BEHAVIORS IN YOUR RELATIONSHIPS THAT YOU EXPERIENCE IN YOUR CURRENT LIFE, WHICH MAY BE INFLUENCED BY PAINFUL REMANANTS OF ISSUES FROM EARLIER IN YOUR LIFE?*

*WHAT ARE YOUR WAYS OF REACTING WHEN THESE COME UP?*

*In summary*

What I see as most helpful in Jungian teachings is that psychological polarities are identified within each of us. Each pair is expressed along a spectrum. This is so within a single person and also evident in interactions with others. Generally, introverts will be quiet in public, but there are times when they will be more open and extroverted. People who are primarily thinking types may still be moved by their emotions. And so on.

Similarly, the HSP and NHSP characteristics may be considered as a spectrum of ways of being, both within ourselves and in relationships with each other, rather than a cast-in-stone description of characteristics that are fixed and immutable. Yes, people may be primarily either HSP or NHSP, but each individual person presents a spectrum of intensity and rigidity of these characteristics. In various situations and relationships there also may be differences in how strongly the HSP or NHSP characteristics are evident.**[30]

### *Synchronicities*

Synchronicity is the label applied by Carl Jung (1955) to the "simultaneous occurrence of two meaningfully but not causally connected events." The classic example is from Jung's experience as a therapist with a difficult patient who was making no progress in therapy because she was having difficulties in allowing her unconscious mind to speak to her. In one of her therapy sessions she reported dreaming about a golden scarab beetle. At that very moment there was a tapping on the window of the therapy room. When Jung investigated this, he found the tapping was caused by a golden scarab beetle, which was extremely rare for that climate. This highly unusual event, so perfectly timed to coincide with the patient's dream, stimulated her to make important connections that markedly facilitated her progress in the therapy.

The meanings of synchronistic occurrences may be obscure in terms of everyday logic and reasoning but often resonate within the involved individual(s) on deeper levels. A lovely example of synchronicity can be seen in the following anecdote, which includes many interwoven coincidences.

Allan Vaughan (1979) reports:

In 1974 I gave a lecture on synchronicity and dreams in Monterey, California.

The next morning, I was standing at a bus stop in a suburb, becoming very impatient at the poor service. Deciding to hitchhike, I stuck out my thumb. The very first car that came by stopped.

"Oh, Mr. Vaughan," the voice of the driver called, "I so enjoyed your lecture last night on synchronicity. To add to it, I'm Mrs. Allen and I live on Vaughan road."

We both laughed about that, and I got into the car. She asked me where I was going. "The San Carlos Hotel," I replied. "Oh," she remarked, "I'm going to the San Carlos today for a wedding reception."

She invited me to the reception, and later she told me about some very moving synchronistic experiences of her own. It was a very synchronistic day.

The similarity in names of the woman in the first car driving past the person hitchhiking is striking, yet has no particular meaning in and of itself. But to the participants who were interested in synchronicity it was meaningful. The fact that the woman was also going to be on that day in the very hotel required by the hitchhiker is particularly striking.

Synchronicities may be complex and yet entirely without apparent meaning or practical significance to the participants. People have struggled to understand and explain these magical occurrences.

In experiencing such incidents of synchronistic nature, participants often feel an intuitive sense of meaningfulness, which is hard to describe, surrounding or attached to them, or guiding them into manifestation. From our everyday perspective, they may make us wonder whether there isn't at work some level of order and/or causality which is beyond the reach or grasp of our ordinary, everyday consciousness. Synchronicities often stimulate people to ponder about deeper levels of awarenesses and meaningfulness in their lives and relationships.*[31]

✢✢✢ In my personal experiences, the quality of feelings associated with synchronicities has considerable similarities with the quality of feelings of spiritual experiences. Though somewhat hard to put into words, with both I experience:

- Heart feelings, difficult to put into words, of something shifting; of large, internal energetic wheels and cogs turning to new settings, working in new ways
- Touching into deep awarenesses and wisdom that I can just begin to identify in principle, but the details of which elude me as yet
- Inviting me to explore the related issues more deeply

These similarities suggest to me that synchronicities may be aspects of spiritual experiences, perhaps even hints and invitations for us to look more closely through these windows of perceptions or to walk through the doorways between our everyday realities and spiritual realities.*[32]

## 8. Left and right brain hemisphere preferences

*If you want to be truly understood,*
*you need to say everything three times, in three different ways.*
*Once for each ear... and once for the heart.*
*The left ear represents the ability*
*to apprehend the nature of the Whole,*
*the wholeness of the circumstance, the forest.*
*The right ear represents the ability to select a sequential path.*
*And the heart represents a balance between the two.*\*\*[33]
— Paula Underwood Spencer

We focus here on studies in neuroscience and psychology that explore broad functions of the brain. These observations suggest vastly expanded and deeper appreciations for differences found in HSPs compared to NHSPs. While the studies of brain functions are often presented in either/or, black/white polarities, my own observations are that these, similarly to Jungian polarities, tend more to express themselves on a spectrum between the polarities – both within individuals and in their interactions with each other.

The large, outer portion of the brain, called the cortex, is divided into two sides (hemispheres) communicating with each other via neural pathways called the corpus callosum. Each hemisphere connects to the outer-world senses and controls the muscles of the opposite side of the body.

Relevant to HSPs, the left hemisphere focuses on thinking, analyzing, step-by-step order and logic, dissecting events and decisions of the past and planning for the future. The right hemisphere is more focuses on the present moment, with emotions and whole patterns of awarenesses, and with creativity.

HSPs generally appear to experience their lives more strongly through their right hemisphere awarenesses and expressive functions than those of their left hemisphere. They have very keen awarenesses of emotions (their own and those of others), strongly intuitive thought processes, are overall extremely sensitive, and have low stimulus thresholds and intense arousal levels. They are most comfortable accepting that there are many ways to experience the world, and that each may be right for them at different times. They are very engaged with what they are feeling and thinking in the present moment.

This is in no way to suggest that HSPs are weak in intelligence or in abilities to use their thinking functions. It is just that they prefer to engage the world through their feelings as their primary mode of interaction and with thinking as their secondary mode.

NHSPs very often are much more connected with their left hemisphere consciousness than that of their right hemisphere. They experience the world through rational thoughts and logical deductions and live in an either-or world where something is right or wrong, with little or no middle ground. They are very absorbed with the past and their plans for the future, often overlooking or ignoring the present moment. In Western culture, NHSPs are strongly allied with the prevalent majority culture that values, nurtures, and promotes thinking as the primary and preferred channel for engaging with the world.

These basic differences in the hard-wiring of the brains of left and right hemisphere dominant people may create great misunderstandings and conflicts between them.

Being aware of these differences enables us to see and accept those who are different from ourselves as being okay and acceptable in their differences, rather than weaker or lesser in whatever respects we see ourselves as being stronger or better.

There are many differences between right brain and left brain dominant people. These differences are complex and may be expressed in very obvious or in subtle ways. Some are very apparent and easy to describe. Others are complex and may be very difficult for both HSPs and NHSPs to identify and to sort out.

For a start, let's consider Table 8-1 for details of the differences between the expressions of the two hemispheres.[34] As detailed above, HSPs fit the profile of right brain dominance, and NHSPs fit that of left brain specialization.

**Table 8-1. Brain Hemispheric Functions**

| Left | Right |
|---|---|
| Rational/ logical/ thinking | Intuitive/ instinctive / feeling |
| Differentiating | Existential |
| Detail-oriented/ exclusive | Gestalt-oriented/ inclusive |
| Time sense focus (past, present, future) | Present-oriented |
| Directed/ controlled by rules (acts with long-term awareness) | Spontaneous, impulsive (acts on present-time awareness) |
| Aims and goals-oriented, plans progress before acting | Focuses on the present moment, acts on present awarenesses |
| Works to rules/ bound/ static | Expansive, changeable, 'in the flow' |
| Proceeds to goals per plans, often ignoring experienced processes | Acts per sensory and experienced processes and patterns |
| May steamroll towards set objectives, ignoring emotions | May get bogged down in emotions or overwhelmed |
| Cautious/ inhibited | Enthusiastic/ impulsive/ over-reacting |
| Product | Process |
| Temporal/ partializing - step by step | Spatial/ wholistic - gestaltic |
| Sequential (slow) | Parallel (fast) |
| Discrete – piece by piece | Continuous/ sense of being in a flow |
| Sequential, successive (either/ or) | Simultaneous (both/ and) |
| Focal | Diffuse |
| Explicit, defining steps and objectives | Tacit, combining many details |
| Objective/ sensory world orientation | Subjective/ intuitive, spiritual orientation |
| Divergent approach | Convergent approach |
| Self-centered/ selfish, hoarding | One with others and the All, sharing |
| Conscious of sensory world/ Uncomfortable with unconscious | Conscious of many levels of awareness, including the Unconscious |
| Language comprehension abstract | Language comprehension concrete |
| Attends to speech content, grammatical | Attends to voice intonation, non-verbal expression, kinaesthetic, musical |
| Abstract models | Perceptual-synthetic |
| Synthesis of goal-related concepts | Creativity, openness to new options |
| Relatively narrow arousal level range over which hemisphere can function | Relatively wide arousal level range over which hemisphere can function |
| Evolutionarily newer | Evolutionarily older |

This discussion of the brain functions is based on a logical analysis, so the left hemisphere is considered first, placed in the left column. This constitutes a left brain baseline for comparison with right hemisphere functions. This is how the brain hemispheres are almost always described, because the vast majority of neuroscientists are primarily living their lives and pursuing their studies and research through left brain modes of functioning in the world.

HSPs, by the nature of their being, prefer to engage their awareness through their right hemisphere functions. After looking through Table 8-1, see how it feels to read through Table 8-2.

See whether this shift in order of the presentation gives you a different feeling for how we can perceive, experience and engage with the world around us. (For brevity's sake, I list only some of the items in this replication of the table.)

Left brain orientations to the world are deeply entrenched in Western society. Those in the left-brain dominant group tend to disparage people who have ways of thinking that differ from their own. Those who prefer left brain world views often perceive HSPs as illogical, unreasonable, over-emotional, impulsive, and 'woo-woo' (vague term that may mean anything from 'ungrounded in defined steps and processes'; or 'too emotional'; to 'alleging to be inspired by some vague, indefinable, unproven, higher source or powers'). And these labels are generally applied judgmentally, as criticisms and as dismissive put-downs.

### Table 8-2 (abbreviated). Brain Hemispheric Functions

| Right | Left |
|---|---|
| Intuitive/ Instinctive / Feeling | Rational/ Logic/ Cognition |
| Existential | Differential |
| Gestalt-oriented/ inclusive | Detail-oriented/ exclusive |
| Present-oriented | Time sense focus (past, present, future) |
| Spontaneous, Impulsive (acts on present-time awareness) | Directed/ Controlled by rules (acts with long-term awareness) |
| Focuses on the present moment, acts on present awarenesses | Aims and goals-oriented, plans progress before acting |
| Acts per sensory and experienced processes and patterns | Proceeds to goals per plans, often ignoring experienced processes |
| May get bogged down in emotions or overwhelmed | May steamroll towards set objectives, ignoring emotions |
| Impulsive, may over-react | Cautious, inhibited |
| Process | Product |
| Spatial/ Wholistic | Temporal/ Partializing |
| Simultaneous (both/ and) | Comparative (either/ or) |
| Tacit, combining many details | Explicit, defining steps and objectives |
| Subjective/ intuitive, spiritual orientation | Objective/ sensory world orientation |
| One with others and the All, sharing | Self-centered/ selfish, hoarding |
| Conscious of many levels of awareness, including the Unconscious | Conscious of sensory world, Uncomfortable with unconscious |

HSPs, being a minority, may feel they are somehow wrong to feel, engage, experience and act primarily through their right brain functions. Conversely, many HSPs criticize non-HSPs as being rigid, insensitive to emotions, dense when it comes to feelings and intuitions, and controlling.

Having noted these issues, we should also acknowledge they are unlikely to go away any time soon. HSPs generally have to learn to speak the language of left brainers in order to communicate with NHSPS, who constitute the majority of the population. Barrie Jaeger's excellent book (2004) on HSPs offers suggestions for dealing with these issues in the workplace. She addresses some of the ways that logic and reason can be very helpful to HSPs in explaining themselves and in adapting to the commonly left-brain atmosphere and organization in their work environment.

As I was looking at the two variations of the right and left brain functions table, I realized yet again how I was mired in left hemisphere thinking in considering HSP functions. When we examine research showing which are left and right hemispheric functions, the tables provide helpful contrasts. But when we consider HSPs, Table 8-2 is still misleading, as it again presents a polarized, left brain list of either-or alternatives. Everyone has both right and left brain hemispheres – barring those with damaged brains. And while most people have either a right or left brain hemisphere preference for relating to the world, they still express themselves at times through their non-dominant brain hemisphere functions.

Table 8-3 presents a more accurate picture of the spectrum of preferences for these functions. This version emphasizes that each person will have tendencies for engaging with the world through a combination of both hemispheric modes. Different situations may elicit responses that differ in the degree to which right or left brain preferences are expressed.

**Table 8-3 (abbreviated). Spectrum of Brain Hemispheric Functions**

| Right | Left |
|---|---|
| Intuitive/ Instinctive / Feeling | Rational/ Logic/ Cognition |
| Existential | Differential |
| Gestalt-oriented/ inclusive | Detail-oriented/ exclusive |
| Present-oriented | Time sense focus (past, present, future) |
| Spontaneous, Impulsive, acts on present-time awareness | Directed/ Controlled by rules, acts with long-term awareness |
| Focuses on the present moment, acts on present awarenesses | Aims and goals-oriented, plans progress before acting |
| Acts per sensory and experienced processes and patterns | Proceeds to goals per plans, often ignoring experienced processes |
| May get bogged down in emotions and Interaction processes or overwhelmed | May steamroll towards set objectives, ignoring emotions |
| Impulsive, may over-react | Cautious, inhibited |
| Process | Product |
| Spatial/ Wholistic | Temporal/ Partializing |
| Continuous | Discrete |
| Simultaneous (both/ and) | Comparative (either/ or) |
| Tacit, combining many details | Explicit, defining steps and objectives |
| Subjective/ intuitive, spiritual orientation | Objective/ sensory world orientation |
| One with others and the All, sharing | Self-centered/ selfish, hoarding |
| Conscious of many levels of awareness, including the Unconscious | Conscious of sensory world, uncomfortable with unconscious |

Jung acknowledged this, saying that it is helpful to be able to come to a place where we can hold two opposing views at the same time. As noted earlier, the English language is misleading because it only includes the polarities of yes and no in its lexicon. The Russian slang word, 'danyet,' which is both *yes* and *no* is much more accepting of the space between polarities. How wonderful the world would be if more cultures allowed for this duality of realities!

It is often enlightening and very helpful to HSPs, as well as to the non-HSPs with whom they closely interact, to consider and discuss the differences between them that are indicated in these tables and how these may lead to misunderstandings or conflicts in their relationships.

✦ 'Rose' and 'Jerry' came to me because they were often at odds with each other, to the point that they were starting to argue and fight. They had been living together for six months, and what had seemed like a promising relationship was beginning to feel more like a disaster. Rose had just been promoted to assistant manager at a MacDonald's restaurant and was a very organized, purposeful, logical person who planned each week carefully on her calendar. Jerry played violin in a band at weddings and other festive occasions. He was a warm, funny, easy-going guy who lived one day at a time. He was very changeable in his emotions, lived in the moment, and resented Rose's insistence that they stick by the calendar that she had set up each week. Sometimes he just didn't feel like doing what they had scheduled, even though he had previously agreed to it. Each was sure they were right and the other was very obviously wrong, but was refusing to admit it.

Jerry was clearly a very gentle soul, a warm and fuzzy, laid back, right-brain-dominant HSP. Rose was a very organized person, living to schedules and within set and structured routines, clearly a left-brain-dominant NHSP. Going over the Right and Left Brain characteristics was an enormous help to each of them in understanding themselves, as well as each other. They were able to see that it wasn't a matter of being right or wrong, but of each of them being very different from the other. They agreed they needed to learn to better understand each other's characteristics and preferred ways of relating to each other and of how they each lived life in general, and needed to learn to accept and make accommodations for their differences.

What seemed to help the most here was my validating each of them as being OK and 'right' within their different ways of perceiving, experiencing and living in the world. At a followup visit three months later they were getting along much more amicably, though still needing to explain themselves at times to each other and to work out compromises over their differing preferences.*[35]

I sigh when I think how much better it would be if we had education in our schools for recognizing, understanding and dealing with our emotions. I believe that many more young children than are generally appreciated have capacities to connect with their emotions. The majority of children are not fortunate enough to have modeling, mentoring or even simple validation of the existence of their emotional awarenesses; to have instructions from family or school to listen to their inner selves; to be aware of and respond to the emotions of others; or to attend in other ways to their emotions. So while most of these abilities are innately present in many people in childhood, they are rarely nurtured or developed in deliberate ways. In the home, children learn through modeling themselves on their parents' instructions, emotional expressions, behaviors and relationships. Relatively few parents have themselves been raised or educated to be sensitive to and aware of their own thinking and feeling processes, much less in how to instruct their children in connecting with these awarenesses. So most people grow up in home environments where our emotional intelligence (EQ) is not even acknowledged, named or discussed.

And then we go out into a world in which the prevalent culture is one in which NHSP habits of awarenesses, behaviors and preferences prevail. The generally accepted norms in schools, in public and in the workplace are that we don't display or discuss our feelings. We focus on the left-brain business at hand, whether it be:

- Schooling for knowledge, as in who ruled, led and won or lost the battle, and how we put strings of numbers together to get the correct answers tests. We memorize facts, manipulate figures, and regurgitate these in exams for which we cram factual information... and very soon forget much, if not all of it. Even the minimal right brain classes, such as music and art, as well as extracurricular activities, have fallen by the wayside in budget cuts in most North American public schools.
- Conversation focus upon factual information, such as who scored higher on tests or in sports, who in our social circles is doing what with whom, who said or did what in the social media, entertainment media and political arenas, or what the next business agenda will be.

So modern society generally fails to nurture or educate its citizens in psychological or emotional intelligence. NHSPs have very little, if any, exposure to discussions or analyses of the feeling, intuitive and spiritual experiences that are so prominent in the worlds of HSPs. Lacking such experiences, many NHSPs have no frames of reference for understanding and accepting these aspects of human experiences, much less having grounds for accepting HSPs who experience much of their lives through greatly heightened sensitivities. So it is no wonder that NHSPs find HSPs different from themselves, odd, strange, or abnormal – to their ways of understanding and engaging with the world.

*IF YOU HAVE CHILDREN AT HOME OR YOUNGER SIBLINGS OF SCHOOL AGE, YOU MIGHT FIND IT INSTRUCTIVE AND THEY MAY FIND IT INVALUABLE, IF YOU CONSIDER WAYS IN WHICH YOU CAN PROMOTE INCREASING AWARENESSES OF THEIR RIGHT BRAIN FUNCTIONS.*

To bring much of this discussion alive, I highly recommend a book and a Ted Talk by Jill Bolte Taylor, a neuroanatomist. She had an amazing, wonderful demonstration of left and right brain awarenesses through an uninvited but enormously impacting series of lessons in brain functions – with a massive stroke that developed slowly. Thanks to her professional training, she was able to observe her movement, speech and consciousness fading, leaving her with half of her body paralyzed. These and further lessons were profoundly transformative over the eight years of her recovery. Prior to her stroke, she had strongly favored her left brain functions. In the process of recuperation, she came to appreciate her right brain functions.

Sadly, for most people who are wedded to their left brain functions, there are few motivations or opportunities they are likely to encounter that would broaden their worldviews and life experiences in these ways. The most common exception is when an NHSP has an intense relationship with an HSP.*[36]

On a collective level, there is also the factor of long-standing, historical, male dominance in most of the cultures around the world. Men tend more to left-brain, thinking modes of relating to the world. This creates a cultural bias against feeling modes of awareness and interactions. Overall, modern Western culture appears to be showing a trend towards including more women in positions of prominence and power.

But don't think for a minute that the die-hard, left-brain preferring, masculine, dominant people are not actively promoting their preferences. A Ted Talk by Christopher Bell (2015) reveals that six companies in the US own 90 percent of the media: NBCUniversal Comcast, AOL Time Warner, the Walt Disney Company, News Corp, Viacom and the CBS Corporation. These corporate moguls are systematically eliminating images of feminine superheroes in their publicity. They go so far as to edit out female superheroes like Princess Leia of Star Wars from film scenes on T-shirts, substituting Luke Skywalker instead. And you can rarely find a female superhero toy in stores!

These masculine preferences that are being promoted in our modern world are not just cultural and media trivia. Women and HSPs (remember that there as a many male as female HSPs) are far more likely to talk through their issues and confrontations, rather than to square off and go at each other with their fists, or to claw at each other verbally. They are far less likely to vote for military appropriations. So the HSP trait itself can be healing on a cultural level.**[37]

## Ultradian brain hemisphere rhythms

Another fascinating characteristic of the brain is the alternating predominance of right and left hemisphere activities. Either your right or left brain will be more active roughly every 90-120 minutes. This is one of the ultradian rhythms, involving cyclical shifts in body functions within the 24 hour day.**[38] You can tell which side of your brain is active by checking which nostril is more open to the flow of air. If your right nostril is more open, then your left brain hemisphere is more active at that time, and conversely with your left nostril connecting with your right hemisphere.

> ✦✦✦ When I first learned about the ultradian rhythm, I checked periodically to see whether my left or right nostril was more open. I was at first surprised, and then dismayed to find that every single time I checked, it was always my right nostril that was more clear, which indicated that my left hemisphere was active. I had known for many years that I generally tended to be more in thinking than in feeling mode, but didn't think (or feel) that I was so exclusively locked into my left brain as my apparently complete persistence in left hemisphere activity seemed to indicate.
>
> It was only several days later that I came to wonder whether perhaps I was more likely to remember to check which nostril was active when I was in the active left brain swing of my internal thinking-feeling brain rhythm pendulum, and less likely to check when my right hemisphere was engaged. So I set a timer to ring every hour to remind me to check my nostril/ hemispheric activity. I was tremendously relieved to find that indeed, my hemispheric activity shifted regularly, about every 90 minutes, and that my right and left hemispheres were alternating equally, as expected.

You may find that you do better at certain tasks when the appropriate hemisphere is engaged. To check this out, you can simply wait till the shift occurs naturally – but if you want to catch yourself with the left nostril open, you might do better to set an alarm clock. If you don't, you are more likely than not to neglect this intention when your non-linear, right hemisphere is active.

As a more controlled alternative, it is possible to force the nostril of your choice to open more, by lying on your side on a pillow, so that the nostril you want to be open is not next to the pillow. Within a few minutes, you will find the nostril you choose is opening up, while the opposite one is closing down.

Research shows that by choosing which hemisphere is active, or by timing your tasks to coincide with the rhythmic activation of your hemispheres, you might find yourself more in harmony with your chosen work and play.*[39]

More importantly, the late renowned hypnotherapist, Milton Erickson, found that the 3-5 minutes during which the hemispheres were both active at the same time, between shifts from dominance of one side to the other, was a special time when people were extra-receptive to hypnotic suggestions. If a person has problems with tapping away particularly challenging memories and/or feelings, tapping during this window of dual hemispheric activity may work more quickly and deeply. Using the head-on-pillow technique, it is also possible to induce and prolong the windows of increased suggestibility.

### *The mind and the brain*

It is broadly assumed in Western cosmology in general, and in Western science in particular, that consciousness is the product of brain cell activity. This is a logical deduction, based on countless observations that if parts of the brain don't function, then various awarenesses of consciousness and initiation of actions won't occur.

However, evidence from research reviewed in Sections VII and VIII on intuitive and spiritual awarenesses strongly suggests that our personal consciousness originates in spiritual dimensions. Our brains appear to be physical world receivers, processors and memory banks for this spiritual consciousness. Whereas we had assumed consciousness was produced in the brain, it appears that our brains are actually like very advanced and sophisticated audio and video receivers, recorders and information processors. Malfunctions of sections of the brain block various awarenesses that originate outside the brain, and interfere with processing and memory functions within the brain.

This concept will be a stretch for many readers of this book. If this is a challenge for you to consider, you may want to skim or read Sections VII and VIII, particularly for the research evidence that confirms consciousness that precedes birth and survives after physical death.

## 9. The High Sensation Seeker (HSS)

> *I think I'm greedy, but I'm not greedy for money... I'm greedy for an exciting life. I want it to be exciting all the time.... On the other hand, I can find excitement... in raindrops falling on a puddle... and a lot of people wouldn't. I intend to have it exciting until the day I fall over.*
> – David Hockney

Elaine Aron (2000) and Marvin Zukerman (1994) highlight the High Sensation Seeker (HSS) as a distinct trait, genetically independent of the HSP trait. The HSS trait may influence the lives of HSPs and HSPCs, either of whom may be HSS or non-HSS (NHSS). This is a helpful trait to be aware of in considering who we are and how we get along with each other.

HSSs like and crave strong or even intense stimulation. They will seek new, exciting, changing situations, such as spectator and participatory sports, loud discos and high-powered cars, and the challenges of new relationships. They often get bored and restless when they are in calm and familiar (unstimulating, unchallenging) environments, and will repeatedly seek challenges and thrills of all sorts. Taking risks is thrilling for an HSS. These preferences may predispose the HSS to frequently seek new relationships, which may make long-term commitments less likely.

The HSP who is a non-HSS (NHSS) prefers quiet environments, periods of contemplation, meditation and solitude, and likes walks in the quiet of nature. It is very likely that HSS and HSP traits are likely to conflict with each other.

If you are both an HSP and an HSS, you may find yourself in conflict within yourself. Some parts of you crave intensity, while other, equally essential aspects of your being may be rattled, uncomfortable or disturbed with some kinds of sensory intensity and you may then prefer calm and quiet surroundings and experiences. So your HSP in-depth engagement with whatever you focus on, with a preference for not jarring some of your senses, may conflict with your HSS tendency to seek highly stimulating thrills and participation in new situations, and you may find you are unhappy with yourself at times.

HSPs who are HSSs may habitually create situations of tension and conflict. On some levels, these interactions are unpleasant, but on other levels they satisfy their cravings for strong exchanges with other people. Internally, there may be an inclination to dwell repeatedly on situations of tension and conflict.

I've seen numbers of HSPs with this sort of craving for intensity, who discovered in long-term therapy that this was trauma-related. When the traumas were identified, addressed and cleared, the intensity-seeking behaviors diminished significantly. It appeared to me that in some of these people their cravings for intensity were more a defense to distract away from and avoid conscious awareness of their trauma residues. The tensions of the trauma residues were not only re-enacted through the emotionally intense interactions, there was also a partial discharge of these tensions, along with a modest feeling of having released and resolved some of the old, underlying trauma issues – though these were not directly addressed. I have not seen this succeed in actually clearing the trauma residues significantly. This high sensation generating behavior keeps cycling through repeated intense interactions that are generated by the HSS HSP, though the HSP often blames others for triggering the HSP emotions, particularly anger.

If either you or your partner (or another family member) are an HSS and the other is not, you are likely to experience interpersonal irritations in your relationships. Patience and tolerance are required in order to resolve such dissonant personal preferences. If you can each take space for pursuing your interests that offer your preferred levels of intensity, you may find your relationship manageable. Counselling or psychotherapy can be helpful as well in sorting our areas of stress and conflict. EP and other stress management approaches can contribute by decreasing your irritability or annoyance with each other over your divergent intensity likes and dislikes.

The HSS preferences for intensity are aspects of your being that are to a great extent wired into your sense of who you are and these are your preferences for how you function in the world. Understanding these aspects of yourself enables you to figure out where the rubs and challenges are in your life, and helps you zero in on what you may want to address in order to feel better.

*THINK OF PEOPLE YOU KNOW WHO HAVE THE HSS TRAIT. ASK YOURSELF IF YOU CAN SEE ANY SIMILARITIES BETWEEN THEM AND YOU. IT IS OFTEN EASIER TO NOTICE HSS QUALITIES IN OTHERS, BEFORE WE SEE THEM IN OURSELVES.*

In contrast with the more fixed HSS characteristics, the following issues relate to aspects of yourself that are more subject to changing – though this is not to say that changes are easy to make. First, let's consider the neurobiology of learning and changing.

## 10. Neuroplasticity

*The measure of a person's strength is not his muscular power or strength, but his flexibility and adaptability.*
— Debasish Mridha

When we learn anything new, it is stored in our brains in ways very similar to computer records. Different areas of the brain store specific types of data. When we don't for a long time use something we learned, such as how to roller skate or to juggle, we tend to lose some or all of these skills. Recent research in neurology is explaining how this happens in our brains. In the spectrum of human capacities, whatever skills are not used and practiced tend to fade from consciousness and are soon lost. Our memories of having had the skills remain, but the ability to demonstrate these skills with the proficiency we had achieved is lost. The rates of decay of these memories vary with different skills in different people.

Modern neuroscience is showing that the loss of such memories is due to how the brain allocates the use of its nerve cells. If the nerves dealing with a skill are not being used, the brain gradually reallocates these nerves to other tasks.

The concept of neuroplasticity explains how we remember our experiences and develop competence in various tasks. It may also help us understand what happens when we haven't developed major skill sets, such as expressing our emotions or recognizing and responding to the emotions of others. For instance, NHSPs, who tend to have more muted experiences of emotions, have difficulties in relating to HSPs, whose primary ways of experiencing and relating to the world are through their emotions. The NHSPs may totally lack the skill sets for emotional awarenesses and expression because they have never allocated brain cells to these skill sets.

Neuroplasticity for learning to speak is well researched. We acquire our language from those around us, coming to comprehend the sounds we hear and mimicking them ourselves. Each language has its unique spectrum of included and excluded sounds.

Infants in every culture are born with a capacity to produce the full spectrum of vocal sounds appropriate for any language. Children learn to mimic the sounds they hear and will readily learn the spoken language of this family.

Infants who move with their parents to a new country and grow up in a culture different from that of their parents' country of origin will also learn to mimic the sounds of the local language they hear – although these may include a different sound spectrum from those of the parents' language that is spoken at home. Japanese children growing up in an English-speaking community will learn to pronounce the sound of 'R' accurately, even though their parents, born and raised in Japan, may have difficulty pronouncing this sound.

But after the age of five, our brain plasticity for mimicking new sounds gradually diminishes, narrowing the range of possible comfortable verbalizations. By the middle to late teen years it becomes difficult to acquire and use sounds that are not common in the language(s) we are used to using.

The language parts of our brains gradually lose their abilities to make sounds that that we've never used, and also lose the capacities to adapt familiar sounds in the new combinations of a foreign language.

Similarly, we may experience disuse atrophy with larger muscle functions. For instance, we may lose our skills for playing physical games when we don't play the games or practice the game moves over a period of time.

It is logical and reasonable that the brain should function in these ways. This enables the brain to divert less-used and unused nerve cells to take on our currently-active tasks, while reducing the numbers of nerve cells assigned to functions that are not being used, and presumably are no longer needed. If we are good at baseball or tennis (or any other sport) but don't go on playing and practicing our skills, we find that our sports abilities suffer from disuse atrophy. even though we might have been quite good players.

I call such losses of abilities to acquire new information "neuroplastic disuse atrophy."

✦✦✦ Although I am well aware of such disuse atrophies, I was still startled by how awkward I was, and how clumsy I felt, when I experienced it myself. I had played racquetball, squash and tennis from my teen years into my early thirties and was a passably good player. But when I went out on a court with my grandson, Sammy, after several decades of not playing tennis, it was like I was starting from square one. I was embarrassed at how unable I was to hit the ball. I could remember myself having swung the racquet in forehand and backhand strokes, but was incredibly awkward with both of these. My eye-hand-arm coordination was that of a crass beginner on the tennis court.

Another fascinating example of neuroplastic disuse atrophy comes from the late Oliver Sacks (1998), a neurologist and author of many delightful and fascinating books on aspects of neurology. In A Leg to Stand On, he shares how he severely fractured his left leg at the hip and was in an immobilizing cast for two weeks following surgery. He found it increasingly difficult during these two weeks to sense his connection with this leg. When they removed the cast, he reported that the 'white thing' hanging from his hip seemed to have no connection to him, nor he to it. In that short period of time, he had completely lost all sensory and conceptual relationship with his own leg. His surgeon was pleased with his physical repair and utterly uninterested in Sacks' sense of disconnections from his leg.

A physiotherapist helped him reconnect his conscious awareness with his leg, and he was able fairly quickly to relearn how to move it so that he could walk again.**[40] Being the curious person he was, he researched this in the medical literature. To his surprise, he found that there had been numbers of earlier reports about this, but very few neurologists or orthopedists seemed aware of it. The earliest reference he found was from the Greek physician, Hippocrates, in the third century BCE.**[41]

### *Neuroplasticity for thoughts and feelings*

If we can lose our conscious connection with our own limbs in less than two months of disuse, I see no reason not to expect that we would lose our connections with thoughts, concepts and feelings that go unused for much longer periods of time.

We develop practical understandings and various beliefs from childhood, building our concepts about how the world around us functions, and about what our places and roles are in our world. These are recorded in our brain cortex and become the accepted rules for perceiving and responding to repeating situations. These rules are the equivalent of a personal, internal navigation system for our journeys through life.

Similarly, we experience emotions in the limbic system in our brain and our autonomic nervous system that is distributed over various parts of our body. The same processes of neuroplastic atrophy would be found in these parts of our nervous system as well.

Emotional blindness is very common in Western society. We can reasonably speculate that several steps may contribute to this personal emotional blindness, as well as to limited perceptions and awarenesses of emotions.

Neuroplastic blindness to emotions may seem rather speculative but there is evidence to support its existence. First, though, let's examine psychological phenomena that are similar to neuroplastic blindness but distinctly not caused by neuroplasticity – although with time, they may lead to neuroplastic changes.

People very often block out traumatic memories from their conscious awarenesses in order to not suffer from deep emotional wounds. This is a survival mechanism, which enables them to avoid overwhelm at the time of the trauma, which could leave them vulnerable to various dangers. They completely focus on whatever is needed for survival in those moments of great danger. Soldiers who are seriously wounded or who see others who are wounded or killed may find themselves numb to any emotions during and immediately after the traumas. They do whatever is needed to deal with the threats to their lives, and do not allow the horrors they are going through to impact their conscious awareness. This survival mechanism is a form of dissociation of consciousness from awareness of painful physical and psychological experiences. The unconscious mind blocks out the intense perceptions, emotions and thoughts about the horrors being experienced, protecting the conscious mind from the overwhelm, so it can gather more resources to cope with whatever is needed for survival when we are in dangerous situations.

Similar dissociations may occur in non-military citizens who are traumatized by real or perceived dangers or painful physical and/or emotional experiences. These could occur in an auto accident, in being attacked physically or psychologically, or in any other highly upsetting situation.

Such dissociations may last minutes, hours or days, sequestering the perceptions – of both external events and internal reactions to them – so that they don't come into conscious awareness even after the danger is past. In other cases, the memories may be kept from conscious awareness over months and years, or even for a lifetime. Any of these healing entombings of memories may occur as part of severe post traumatic stress (PTS) experiences.

In these cases, the memories are not lost. They are filed away in vivid detail, but thoroughly walled out of reach of the conscious mind. Under hypnosis, or when a person suffers trauma or sees someone else suffering another trauma years later, the buried memories may surface – in vivid, graphic details and with considerable emotional intensity. So in these cases, the interim forgetting is not because the memories were lost but because they were thoroughly locked away, outside of conscious awareness.

We can learn further from hypnosis how we may become blinded to aspects of our experiences:
- People may develop complete amnesia for their experiences under hypnosis, either spontaneously or under deliberate hypnotic suggestions.
- The memories to which they have been blinded may be retrieved by new hypnotic suggestions.

– During the hypnosis sessions people can be hypnotized to be blind to something within their range of vision, or deaf to sounds that are present and available to their ears, and evident to anyone else in the room. These are called "negative hallucinations" (Dabney & Bruce, 2006).

So it is evident that one or more parts of our unconscious minds can decide that we will ignore and deny with our conscious minds the presence of some of our sensory, emotional and cognitive experiences and memories These are further ways that we may come to ignore aspects of the world we live in.

The programs to maintain unawareness and blindness to feelings and thoughts are often surprisingly effective. People turn down their inner 'dimmer switches' for emotions, thereby protecting themselves from triggering painful memories of traumas. Often, their unconscious does a very thorough job of this by shutting down their emotional sensitivities. At the same time, they develop habits of approaching their perceptions and interactions with people and various life situations through logic and reasoning.

Generalizing their defenses further, they may then avoid information and situations that are new and different from their accepted norms, out of unconscious anxieties that these can or will be uncomfortable, painful or traumatizing. This feels safer than peering through the windows or opening the doors in the protective inner walls they have erected for their protection.

With time and repeated practice of ignoring uncomfortable issues, it becomes less and less likely that their defensive inner rules will be modified in the light of new information that appears dissonant within their established, accepted maps of normality. So even though they may be in friendly new company, traumatized people remain on guard lest they prove to be dangerous.

So we may be carrying outdated navigational maps for guiding ourselves. To a great extent, we don't update our general rules for recognizing and responding to new situations. We are satisfied to live within the limits of the familiar territories of our brain maps of the world. Such negligence in not updating our inner screening systems often leads to inabilities to perceive and absorb aspects of our world that don't fit our personal perceptual and conceptual maps. Even when we are capable of understanding new ideas and methods for dealing with the world, we often prefer to continue along the paths well-travelled, rather than risking anticipated dangers along these paths.

This appears to be a variation of neuroplastic blindness. Having not utilized their awarenesses to perceive or experience these aspects of their world, these people are blind to various portions of the spectrum of reality.

I believe this explains some of the challenges experienced in communications and relationships between NHSPs and HSPs. We can see how emotional awareness could atrophy if it is not developed and practiced – much like verbal language does. Over many years of their lives, NHSPs have been much less sensitive to emotions than HSPs and have ignored their inner feelings. Likewise, they are insensitive to the feelings and emotions of others. I believe that on top of their natural aversions for emotional awarenesses, NHSPs have neuroplastic conceptual atrophy from disuse in those portions of their brains that engage consciously with emotions, express emotions and recognize emotions – in themselves and others.

✦✦✦ I've explored numerous approaches for bringing people rapid relief from stress, pains, distress and traumas. Most people with whom I speak about these methods are somewhere on the spectrum of uninterested to incapable of discussing them. I believe this is due to neuroplastic blindness and deafness to ideas and approaches they have not been exposed to, have not chosen to explore, or have chosen to exclude from their lives.

This neuroplastic blindness may help to explain further why many NHSPs are clueless about how to relate to HSPs, who are very emotionally sensitive, aware of and expressive of their emotions. The NHSPs don't understand the language of emotions. On top of their inherently low sensitivity to emotions, they have a disuse atrophy for awarenesses and expressions of emotions. And that which is unfamiliar and not understood tends to be ignored, belittled, dismissed and rejected.

*The only thing worse than being blind is having sight but no vision.*
— Helen Keller

I've seen countless HSPs who suffered from being in the company of NHSPs who were so unaware of and insensitive to their feelings and the feelings of the HSP as to make communications for the HSP extremely difficult with them. This can be so serious a challenge as to lead HSPs to find it impossible to relate to members of their families, who are strong NHSPs, with little awareness of their own emotions, much less the emotions of others.

✦ 'Nicky' was a bright, outgoing, cheerful young teenager in her eighth grade class at the start of the school year. Her homeroom teacher, 'Cheryl,' was a friend of mine. She phoned me about two months into the first semester to ask for an informal consultation. As the year was progressing, Nicky was becoming more and more depressed. Cheryl had invited her for a chat during a lunch break and she was distressed to hear Nicky's story of difficulties she was facing at home.

Cheryl reported that Nicky had blushed as she shared the feelings she was experiencing in her first strong attraction to a boy in her classroom – who was not showing any interest in her. This wasn't her main issue, though. What was frustrating and depressing her were the responses of her family members after she had mentioned her attraction to her classmate. Her father, her two older sisters, and her younger brother were teasing her mercilessly at home over this infatuation. And while her mother was largely silent on the subject, she had completely sided with the others when Nicky complained to her about the teasing. All of this would have probably passed as water under the family bridge, but the added event of their aging German shepherd, Sheba, losing control of her bladder and having to be put down, was the precipitating event in the start of Nicky's depression.

Nicky had come to realize she was an alien in her family. She was very open in showing her emotions, while none of the others would ever utter a word about their feelings. She had learned early in life to shrug this off, but when she cried openly as they buried Sheba, and her whole family disparaged her for being such a crybaby, she suddenly realized that in ways very important to her she truly was an alien in this family. She started to feel she was living with a bunch of emotionless zombies. As she withdrew from participating in much of the family chit chat, which suddenly seemed to her to be very shallow and superficial, they started teasing her about being moody, speculating that she was mooning over her unrequited love. Nicky withdrew more and more into herself.

I had not yet read the books by Elaine Aron and others on the HSP, but this trait of sensitivity was certainly an obvious aspect of Nicky's life. I had helped others to deal with such disparities in emotional sensitivities and expressions of their feelings during my several decades of doing family therapy, so I was able to suggest a course of action for Cheryl, which helped Nicky with her depression.

✦✦Cheryl helped Nicky to understand how she connected strongly with her feelings and was open in expressing them, while Nicky's family's ways of recognizing and dealing with emotions were to disconnect from them and to bury them outside their conscious awareness. One of their ways of doing this was to discourage Nicky from speaking about such things. While this was frustrating and upsetting to Nicky, Cheryl pointed out that in all fairness, Nicky couldn't demand that her family members engage in discussions of feelings with her when this was largely outside her family's conscious awarenesses, and certainly outside their comfort zones – which was a mirror image to Nicky's own unhappiness with their discomforts and behaviors towards her for expressing her emotions openly.

Cheryl also made times available for Nicky to chat with her about her feelings, and encouraged her to find friends with whom she could do the same. Just having Cheryl's understanding and support was enormously helpful and validating to Nicky, enabling her feel more comfortable in her sensitivities. Gradually, she came to perceive and understand these as normal and acceptable parts of who she is. Cheryl was also able to help Nicky to express and release much of her grief over the death of Sheba. Her depression cleared in just a few weeks.

While I've focused on challenges in HSP-NHSP relationships, by no means do I wish to imply that NHSPs are incapable of being kind, considerate and accepting with HSPs. Let me offer a common example that I've seen quite a number of times, in many variations.

✦ NHSP 'Albert,' an accountant, had been married for many years to HSP 'Jenny,' a music teacher. Al grew up in a home with NHSP parents, but had a very warm and supportive, HSP older sister with whom he has always remained close. Jenny is a devoted wife, housewife and mother to their four children. While Al will occasionally help wash dishes and pick up some groceries on the way home, he has little interest in or sensitivity to further details of homemaking and child rearing. He leaves almost all of that to Jenny. But he takes great pride in providing a solid, regular income; in handling the family finances and investments; and in planning, booking and managing all the details of vacations, when he leaves his business affairs behind and is fully there for his wife and children.

It also helps that he and Jenny share the same love languages of touch and words of affirmation.[42] Al also compartmentalizes his attentions to the children, giving a lot more time to their two sons and leaving much of the parenting of their daughters to Jenny, though being fully and enthusiastically supportive to his daughters whenever he is asked to pitch in.

Over time, neuroplastic atrophy leads to neuroplastic emotional blindness. Having lived without awareness of emotions, intuitions and personal spiritual awarenesses of their own, many NHSPs find these subjects completely alien to their cognitive maps and experiences of the world. Yet the portions of the brain that normally deal with emotions are still present in NHSPs, and subconsciously they still experience emotions. I have seen NHSPs displaying sad and angry feelings, commonly at funerals, but they are generally unable to identify these emotions consciously, or perhaps they are very uncomfortable admitting that these feelings were present.

People with such neuroplastic blindness for their feelings may be extremely uncomfortable with HSPs who often express strong emotions – as in Nicky's family. I've seen many NHSPs belittle, disparage, and pathologize HSPs for being overly emotional, drama queens, and mentally unstable – when the HSPs are just being their normal, emotionally sensitive, deeply reflective selves.

> *Just like some NHSPs have a hard time accepting feelings,*
> *it can be difficult for HSPs to accept people who are afeelistic.*
> — Daniel Benor

I've also counseled many HSPs gifted with various aspects of intuition who had to learn similar lessons of dealing with the disconnects of family and friends from their intuitive awarenesses.[43] Fortunately, while it is distressing to experience these rejections from members of our family and friends whom we expect and hope will be supportive to us, it is generally easier to learn not to mention information that comes in on one's emotional and intuitive channels than it is to shut down one's sensitivities to and expressions of emotions and intuitive awarenesses.

Some HSPs, on their sides of these interactions, may come to wonder or worry whether they are actually crazy. They may have been so beaten down, over so much of their lives, by family and/or friends who say that they care for them, that they may come to question their own emotional sensitivities, their intuitive perceptions and even their sanity.

HSPs may be faced with difficult choices between going to battle with the NHSPs over the right to have, experience and express their feelings; shutting up and pretending they are similar to the bullying NHSPs on the one side, and on the other side denying their true awareness of being the sensitive people they are; or cutting off these abrasive, bullying relationships.*[44]

The important takeaway lessons here are that HSPs may have to build families of choice that consist of people who are happy to befriend right-hemisphere dominant, feeling and intuitive people just the way they are. And here is where a loving, caring HSPC can be of inestimable help to the HSP who has struggled with these sorts of issues. I've known many HSPs, personally and professionally, who are blessed with deeply accepting and appreciating NHSP HSPCs. And their relationships are all the more meaningful for the negative experiences that taught the HSPs to be thankful beyond words for having those who accept, appreciate and love them, just the way they are.

> *The most valuable gift of all is the sentence, "You are perfect for me,*
> *exactly the way you are." A confirmation that I'm the best version of*
> *me that could possibly exist brings a gratification deep in the soul.*
> — Bert Hellinger

*AS AN HSP, CAN YOU IDENTIFY PEOPLE AMONG YOUR CURRENT OR PAST RELATIONSHIPS WHO APPEAR TO HAVE PSYCHOLOGICAL BLINDNESSES?*

*WHAT ARE YOUR WAYS OF COPING WITH PEOPLE WHO ARE BLIND AND DEAF TO EMOTIONAL ISSUES?*

*AS AN NHSP, CAN YOU IDENTIFY AREAS OF DISCOMFORTS YOU EXPERIENCE WHEN COMMUNICATING WITH AN HSP?*

*CAN YOU IDENTIFY EARLIER LIFE EXPERIENCES THAT MIGHT HAVE SENSITIZED YOU TO AVOID CONNECTING WITH PSYCHOLOGICAL AND/OR EMOTIONAL ISSUES?*

### Meta-awarenesses and forgetting vs. neuroplastic forgetting

How we think and feel about how we think and feel is another level where forgetting occurs. This is different from neuroplastic unawareness and forgetting.

One place where we see this relatively clearly is in our stress and trauma responses. When we have strong negative experiences, we often come away with painful, frightening memories. In many cases, our unconscious mind works hard to protect us from remembering the unpleasant details of these very painful experiences – by creating amnesia for some of the gruesome details, or even for all them. It appears that we have forgotten what happened, but the truth is that we have blocked our conscious mind from accessing the memories – which are still present and may be actively influencing our unconscious awareness.

At the same time, our unconscious mind wants to protect us from getting traumatized again. So, for instance, it might leave us with only vague memories related to the trauma incident.

*A CAUTION HERE: IF YOU HAVE ANY HISTORY OF TRAUMA, OR IF YOU FIND YOURSELF EASILY TRIGGERED INTO SERIOUS DISTRESS BY LISTENING TO OR READING ABOUT OTHER PEOPLE'S TRAUMAS AND EMOTIONAL UPSETS, I SUGGEST THAT YOU READ THE SECTION ON THE PLACE OF PEACE AND SAFETY AND HEALING (PPSH) FIRST.*[*45] *THIS WILL GUIDE YOU IN DEVELOPING CALMING AND HEALING POSITIVES TO USE FOR SELF-HEALING, AND WILL PROVIDE RESOURCES TO CALM AND SOOTHE YOURSELF IN CASE YOU GET TRIGGERED BY READING ANYTHING IN THIS BOOK.*

✦ 'Jason' was mugged and robbed by two teenagers when taking an ill-advised shortcut through a dark alley on his way home from an evening class. He was unable to recall many of the details of being beaten up. In the emergency room they attributed his memory loss to a brain concussion, as he had several bruises on his face from the beating he had received.

'Gary,' Jason's gay partner, noticed a variety of changes in Jason following this unfortunate incident. Darkness made Jason uncomfortable. He insisted on keeping lights on at night. He refused to go out to their favorite arts film theater, as he couldn't imagine himself staying in the theater when the lights would be dimmed for the showing of a film. And he made every possible excuse to avoid going out after dark.

It didn't take a lot for Jason, an HSP and Gary, an NHSP, to put the pieces together and for Jason to find his way to my office. EP tapping enabled him to develop an inner place of peace and safety and healing,*[46] to which he could retreat if he began to feel overwhelmed by residual fears from his mugging. Knowing he had the self-healing capacity to calm his fears of overwhelm was a meta-positive awareness that encouraged Jason to trust he could also deal with the residues of fears from his trauma experiences. He then needed only two sessions of tapping, plus practicing on his own at home, to release the trauma fear residues from his beating in the dark alley.

With the retrieval of his buried memories of the mugging, Jason had no trouble holding onto the lesson learned about not going through dark places where he might stray into harm's way. His unconscious mind no longer needed to cue him indirectly to avoid all dark places that might be dangerous – once he got the specific warning message. But still his SUDS did not go lower than a 3.**[47]

In taking his life history, I noted that Jason's father was an alcoholic who had been physically abusive to his mother. Jason recalled lying in bed at night, putting his pillow and covers over his head to dim the sound of his mother's screams from down the dark hallway of their apartment. These memories were also cleared with the tapping. At that point, his SUDS went all the way to zero and he was able to install replacement positive thoughts and feelings.

This is a complex chain of processes of fear about feeling the full memories of several different layers of separate fearful experiences. Jason's unconscious mind maintained awareness of important cues to keep Jason safe, while protecting him from the full, painful and frightening impact of his beating in the dark alley.

I would also speculate that on a deeper level, Jason's unconscious mind may have held off alerting him, or may even have led him into the danger zone of the dark hallway – as a way of helping him release painful, long-buried memories of his secondary trauma from his childhood.

Jason's story is shared here to illustrate some of the complexities of our minds. We have varieties of ways of keeping unpleasant or uncomfortable information from disturbing our conscious awareness. Considering personal intuitive and spiritual awarenesses more closely, I would speculate that the unconscious mind is incredibly adept and clever in getting us in touch with buried traumas and feelings in these sorts of ways.*[48]

*In summary*

The important takeaways about neuroplasticity are that both HSPs and HSPCs can:
- Change how we understand ourselves and each other
- Change how we react to our innate responses, particularly to our heightened sensitivities and to when we respond to our emotions and those of others
- Change how we relate to ourselves and each other
- Accept that some people are stuck in neuroplastic blindness

More on meta-awarenesses in the neuroplasticity of our thoughts and feelings after we consider further ways of analyzing and understanding our thinking and feeling processes.*[49]

# 11. Freudian dissections of our awarenesses - Eric Berne's Transactional Analysis (TA)

*Only I can change my life. No one can do it for me.*
— Carol Burnett

Sigmund Freud, an Austrian neurologist, is credited with being the father of psychoanalysis and of clinical psychological awareness. The three principal elements of our consciousness identified by Freud are of great help in understanding psychological states in general, and HSPs in particular:

- The *ego* is the rational, thinking part of our awareness.
- The *id* expresses our basic desires and feelings.
- The *superego* is our critical self that contains our beliefs and understandings of what we should and shouldn't do.

These aspects of our selves were translated into everyday language by Eric Berne as Parent (superego), Adult (ego) and Child (id) in his framework of Transactional Analysis. Berne further simplified explanations of these terms with diagrams of the parts of ourselves, as in Figures 11-1 and 11-2.

When we analyze our personal issues and our relationships through TA, we can quickly identify and address some of the personal and interpersonal issues and feelings that get us in trouble. For instance, as in Figure 11-1, we may be in conflict within ourselves over how to behave. By clarifying what each ego state is saying, we can more easily decide which option, which part of ourselves, we want to express. And if we have difficulties in adhering to our reasoned decisions, we have already made a start at identifying what issues within ourselves are causing our challenges.

**Figure 11-1. Transactional Analysis ego states**

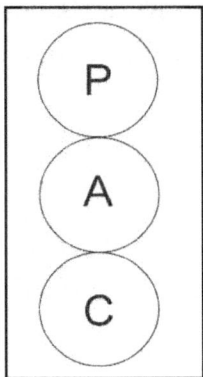

For instance, you might experience inner dialogues like this:

- Child: I'd really like to munch on some of those doughnuts!
- Parent: How could you even think of abandoning your diet like that?
- Adult: Let's put just one away for dessert this evening.

**Figure 11-2. Detailed Transactional Analysis ego states**

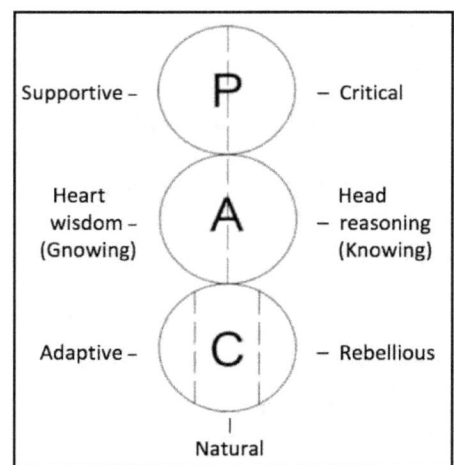

As with most psychological observations, the basic explanations for how our mind and emotions behave can be expanded to include nuances and factors along a spectrum. Figure 11-2 illustrates some of the subtleties and nuances of the Parent/ Adult/ Child ego states.

These diagrams point out ways you perceive yourself, how you analyze your awarenesses, and suggest alternatives you can choose when you're dissatisfied with your ways of addressing your issues and/or with how you get along with others. For instance, your inner parent may speak to you with supportive messages and a supportive tone of voice about what you should or shouldn't do. Alternatively, it can be harsh and critical.

Supportive: "You might remember next time to say 'thank you'."

.... vs. ....

Critical: "OMG! How ungrateful can you be, neglecting to send a 'thank you' note for Sally's gift?"

Your Adult ego state may speak from the heart, with awarenesses of your emotional wisdom, or may comment from your thinking side.

"I'll just give her a big hug and explain how much I appreciate her presence in my life."

.... vs. ....

"How can I say this in the best possible way, so that Sally will understand that I truly care for her and am grateful for her thoughtful gift?"

An inner message that is conveyed from your Supportive Parent is likely to elicit a response from your Adaptive Child (wanting to please) or Natural Child (responding emotionally) ego states.

"She's an HSP with a big heart. I'm sure a hug and a brief explanation will correct my oversight."

.... vs. ....

A message that is spoken from your inner Critical Parent is likely to elicit a response from your Rebellious Child.

"I screwed that one up so royally, there's no way I'm going to set this right! I'm just going to clam up and hope she forgets this in good time."

In these kinds of inner dialogues, often it's the tone of the message, even more than its content that dominates our responses, particularly in an HSP. Often, it takes a while for HSPCs to learn to pay careful attention to the feeling aspects of messages.

By reviewing the ways you speak with yourself about your behaviors, you can identify how supportive or critical you are towards yourself. If you're unhappy with your attitudes, you can immediately identify alternatives that are gentler and more supportive.

Here's another illustrative series of options you might find yourself considering.

Your inner Parent could express itself in various ways along the spectrum of Supportive to Critical, in your inner dialogues. For example, you could say to yourself or to your HSPC anything along a spectrum, from:

"You've done so well on your journaling this past month, you really should keep it up. Even a brief entry before you go to bed – after watching this TV show – would make you feel better."

To: "Come on, now, can't you be serious and resist this frivolous temptation?"

To: "You know that if you start to break your habit even a little bit, you're going to slide backwards and fall into depression (or anxiety states, self-defeating thinking, etc.) again!"

To: "You're really stupid to even glance at that TV guide!"

Your inner Adult might respond from right hemisphere or left hemisphere wisdom, starting from:

"You're feeling a little depressed and lonely right now because you're away from home at this business meeting, but surely you could choose a better option than a pacifier like this silly sitcom and this bag of potato chips – such as tapping away your loneliness and cravings."

To: "You just know this 1-hour dose of escapism is going to be followed by hours of self-recriminations. Why don't you save yourself from that torture and just stick with your resolution to limit your TV time during the work week?"

To: "Why don't ever think of better choices? You're so self-destructive! You might juggle a modest entry in your journal, which would allow you some fun/ relaxing/ rejuvenating down-time during this conference that's been all work and no play."

To: "You always make the most piss-poor excuses to break your healthy resolutions!"

Your inner Child might respond to some of the above supportive and feelings-acknowledging advice with:

Adaptive Child: "Yeah, that's right. I really can do better than to vegetate mindlessly in front of the TV, and then have to face my endless recriminations yet again!"

Natural Child: "One hour of Downtown Abbey won't ruin my successful journaling streak. I've really earned it! And if feel tempted to watch anything more, I can tap those craving habits away."

Rebellious Child: "Screw, it! I'm tired and fed up with our committee chairman being so bossy and unreceptive to any of my suggestions! I deserve to have a little treat!"

TA diagrams can be of enormous help in mapping what is unfolding in your interactions with others. Increasing awareness of your inner ego states and how they speak in your inner dialogues with yourself can help an HSP or HSPC clarify what is going on inside himself when he gets upset. Often, his emotions are triggered intensely, leading to strong statements, colored by strong feelings. These elicit strong reactions from others.

Awareness of the options to choose TA ego states from which to state your opinions and feelings can help you identify how your messages to and from others may be better understood on the one hand, or misperceived and misunderstood on the other.

Often, your tone of voice and/or body language may convey a very different message from the surface content of what you are saying – completely outside your conscious awareness. Similarly, the person you're speaking with may interpret what you say as coming from a different ego state than the one you intended. You may be surprised when your partner responds to your tone of voice rather than to the content of what you said.

Teenager: "May I have the car keys?"

Father: "Are the dishes done? And where are you off to?"

Teenager: "Yup! I want to go over to Sammy's to compare our answers on the chemistry homework. Then we're competing on a new video game he got for his birthday.

Clarification: This is a congruent communication, Supportive Parent to Child and responses from Adaptive Child to Parent. This could also be seen as Adult– Adult ego states communication, clarifying factual information.

In contrast, here is a crossed communication:

Partner: "I think it's getting late, dear. Shouldn't we be going home?"

HSP: "Stop treating me like a child! I know when it's time to go and it's not now!"

Clarification: This HSP heard his partner as speaking from Critical Parent rather than Adult, as was intended. He responding from Rebellious Child.

Similarly, these PAC diagrams can be used to identify what was said in words and in tone of voice or body language in order to clarify the ego states that were activated in people's interactions. Figures 11-3 and 11-4 illustrate how different aspects of our PAC could express themselves in an interaction between two people. Father tells daughter to do the dishes. He is unaware his tone is critical. Daughter responds to his tone of voice, from a place of hurt in Natural Child. She is assuming he is speaking from Critical Parent, and responding to this rather than to the information he wanted to convey from Adult.

**Figure 11-3. Father gives orders with an angry tone**

Father speaks to Daughter

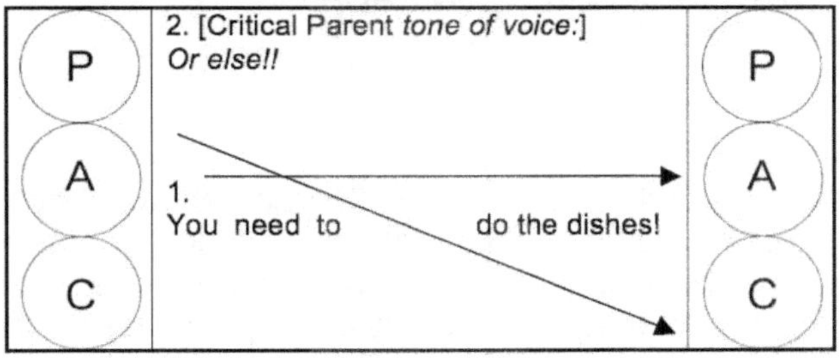

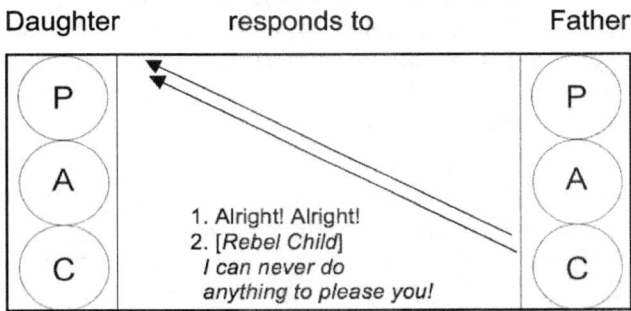

**Figure 11-4. Daughter responds to tone of voice more than to content of message**

Daughter responds to Father

Many miscommunications occur between people who are not HSPs because they respond to the perceived ego state from which the message is assumed to originate. In the diagrams above, father was unaware of his angry tone of voice. He thought he was simply telling his daughter it was time to do the dishes.

Very often, statements from HSPs are not intended to be as intensely impacting as they turn out to be, due to the characteristic sensitivity of the HSP. But when HSPs are upset, their sensitivities may lead them to know unconsciously exactly how to annoy or hurt the person who triggered them. Interactions may unfold more gently when the HSPC can respond by addressing the content of the communication rather than getting triggered by the intense emotions that accompany the communication.

Diagramming the communications between our PAC ego states and the PAC ego states of others can be enormously helpful in suggesting alternative ways of interacting that may lead to happier, more productive, and harmonious responses and outcomes. [50]

1. Identify the feelings that are being expressed, including their intensity, and then
2. Address the message content separately.

> *WHEN YOU FIND YOUSELF IN CONFLICT WITH YOUR PARTNER, CHECK WHICH EGO STATE IS SPEAKING IN EACH OF YOU.*

### Levels of intimacy

To tell you the truth, I was at first put off when I learned about TA because it seemed to me a bunch of very superficial and facile restatements of psychoanalytic theories and practices. Very quickly, however, I saw that this simpler language made it possible for anyone and everyone to understand and apply these principles in ways that are rapidly and deeply corrective and healing.

Another series of observations, taking us beyond the basics of TA, are steps in the hierarchy of relationships through which we seek and address intimacy, and how we select and take these steps. In TA terminology, 'strokes' are the coins we use for interactions between people. Strokes are the ways we acknowledge and respond to each other. Strokes may be positive or negative. In TA these are identified as "warm fuzzies" or "cold pricklies." Strokes serve people's needs for receiving and offering acknowledgments, praises, acceptance, caring attention, love, nurturing, encouragements, feedback on behaviors, alerts to over-stepping boundaries, and expressions of dissatisfactions, disapprovals, hurts, rejections and angers.

People need strokes to satisfy every level of their wholistic beingness. Strokes may be offered and received through varieties of wholistic expressions.

- Touch: ranging from caresses, to playful tickling or poking, hugs and kisses, and sexual intimacy on the positive side of the spectrum; to pushing away, slapping, spanking or hitting on the negative side
- Expressions of emotions: smiles, nods of the head, 'high fives' and other gestures of caring and appreciation, or frowns, angry gestures and words, walking away from or ignoring others
- Words: from requests for attention, approval and praises, gratitude, expressions of emotions, endearment, caring admiration, and love, and direct requests for help, to expressions of dissatisfaction, disapproval, criticisms, rejections, gossip and disparagements
- Acts of support and service: letting others go first, holding a door open, offering to carry some or all of a person's burdens (literally and figuratively), volunteering time, offering gifts and grants
- Spiritual offerings: prayers for the wellbeing of other people, of all of the beings on our planet, and of our planet herself

People crave for and thrive on such strokes, and express their presence in the world through offering and receiving them. The craving for attention in the form of strokes is so strong, that many will provoke negative strokes rather than be ignored, as being ignored is often experienced as rejection and abandonment.

### HSPs and levels of intimacy

HSPs generally crave intimacy. We purr when we feel accepted and understood, when we can offer others strokes and when we receive them from others. And here you can see that intimacy can be expressed through a whole spectrum of the levels:

- Withdrawing into a quiet, inner space with a book or holding hands in silence with a close friend or partner, by the fireplace or a brook; or petting your cat
- Enjoying sharing the rituals of reviewing in the evening three nice things that happened to you today and in the morning anticipating three nice things in the new day
- Passing a few quiet moments checking in on selected social media with a group of close friends
- Engaging in heart-centered activities, such as volunteering to visit people in a hospital who have no relatives or friends available at the time of their illness or surgery; Taking pleasure in watching Heartland, Grey's Anatomy, or any other heart-centered soap opera with your partner or spouse or family
- Playing the game of "Ain't It Wonderful" (a positive game I see played in warm, caring relationships), where the wife shares responsibilities for household and childhood duties with her husband, and both enjoy contributing to their smoothly running household.
- And of course, enjoying personal intimacy with partners, close family and friends.

## 12. Inner child awarenesses

> *So, like a forgotten fire,*
> *a childhood can always flare up again within us.*
> – Gaston Bachelard

As we grow into our lives in our physical universe, each of us builds our personal pictures and maps of the world. The unique collection of perceptions of each person form the basis for a highly individualized existence as a physical being.

From the time of conception, each of us has unique experiences and makes individual decisions and choices. Each of these contributes bricks and mortar to the structure we create that is our life, defining what and who we are. The experiences we have and decisions we make throughout childhood create memories of information and programs for behaviors that are the basic frameworks upon which our personality and life course are built.

In a normal family, children learn how to relate to parents, brothers and sisters, to extended family and friends in nurturing, supportive ways. Most importantly, from their personal experiences of being loved and cared for, they learn how to love and care for others. These ways of relating become templates for their own behaviors.

Often, there is a special person or several people in their lives with whom children have particularly close relationships. The memories of these special relationships persist throughout life. They can be wonderful resources in building an inner place of peace and safety and healing (PPSH) in times of stress, distress, or trauma.*[51]

Conversely, when a person's childhood is fraught with negative experiences, tensions or traumas, these experiences may similarly leave strong imprints that persist throughout life. Childhood programs are usually childish. When we're young and inexperienced in life, we have very basic and only partial understandings about what we experience and what it means. But our later memories are built upon our initial impressions and childhood comprehension of our experiences. And here brews mischief!

These inner childhood programs for perceiving and interpreting negative experiences may lead us to believe that life is a burden we have to bear – with no recourse for improving it, or that the world is a dangerous and unsafe place. We may behave accordingly, avoiding experiences that feel unsafe in the light of our inner programs. Because of such memories, we may seriously short-change ourselves in the course of the rest of our lives.

As children, we may mistakenly interpret what is happening to us as being more dangerous than it actually was. This may influence our feelings and self-image in ways that persist through the rest of our lives. In some cases, the lessons are mild, but still troublesome.

> ✦ 'Josh' was a young executive who appeared to have everything going for him. He was smart, hard-working, innovative, good with people, had a warm sense of humor, and above all was noted for being very caring and supportive when anyone needed help. In his family, social circles and company, he had always been told he was a good catch. But when he reached his 35th birthday and still hadn't found a serious partner, he sought a psychotherapist to help him figure out why he could never find anyone to share his life.

Long story short, Josh came to understand that his issues had started in early childhood. His sister, Kari, born when he was a year and a half old, had serious allergies and many bouts of pneumonia. She also suffered from colic (crying at night) till she was close to a year old. His father, a policeman, working long hours and changing shifts, was minimally available at home. His mother was utterly exhausted from the attention she had to give Kari. Without any reason related to Josh, she simply could not give him the attention he deserved. In fact, she often asked him to help at home. He started with small fetching and carrying chores. By four he was helping with cleaning, by six buying occasional groceries from the corner store. His father, whom he adored, praised him highly for being a good young man for helping his mother. Though his father was not present much of the time at home, he had good, 'quality' times with Josh, playing games with him and always asking about his school work and performance, and after-school activities.

Josh grew up with the inner understanding of a child that he was there to help others. His father was a further model for self-sacrifice in public service, and his mother a model for devotion to her responsibilities as wife and mother. Josh continued with his own service to family and to all and sundry as an adult. However, women who welcomed these sorts of attentions did not appeal to him. Some unconscious part of him seemed to know he could do better for himself. But on the other hand, the women he was attracted to found his attentions somewhere on the spectrum of over-flattering to over-attentive to smothering.

I referred Josh to a therapy group for singles who were exploring varieties of questions similar to the ones he was addressing about getting along better in personal relationships. His therapist shared that he did well in the group, and after about a year of weekly group sessions he had a good handle on his issues and was much more appropriate in his dating relationships. I heard from his therapist again, several years later that he had gone on on to find a partner with whom he could get along in ways that were less influenced by his childhood experiences.

Josh was fortunate in having caring parents who demonstrated their love and devotion for him in appropriate ways from childhood and throughout their lives. He grew up feeling loved and safe. So he had the inner psychological and relationship programs which resourced him for developing caring relationships as an adult.

In other cases, childhood experiences may leave us with more serious psychological scars. Worse yet, they may leave us crippled within ourselves and in our relationships.

✦ 'Mary' had a normal childhood development until she was 13 years old and in seventh grade, when her life went off the rails. She had been a very sensitive, caring child in her home, getting along well with her two sisters, 4 and 6 years younger than her, but often needing private time and space to herself. She was an excellent student and popular among her classmates. By this history I would guess she was most probably an HSP.

Mary was raped by 'Clarence,' a teenage neighbor who stood in as a replacement baby sitter when his sister had the flu. He told her if she made any noise and woke her sisters upstairs in their bedroom, he'd tell them they were just doing "big kid things" and to go back to sleep, and if she ever told anyone about him he would hurt her little sister very badly, in ways that would probably cripple her for life. Terrified, Mary's mind seemed to freeze, and after that she only remembered seeing the chandelier in the living room, feeling pain in her vagina, and waking up in her bed the next morning.

Next morning, Mary told her mother she had a bad headache, was feeling achy all over and weak. Her mother assumed she was coming down with the flu and kept her home, in bed that day. She assumed Mary's red eyes were further evidence of the flu, having no suspicion of anything else going on. Mary stayed home a second day, still crying quietly when no one was around, feeling enormous shame and guilt. On the third day she decided she had to return to school.

Mary never told anyone about what happened, but her life just wasn't the same after that. The family pediatrician ordered some blood tests, after finding nothing on his brief physical exam of her ears, nose and throat, chest and abdomen to explain her lingering tiredness and brain fog. When her symptoms persisted, he suggested a consultation at the local university pediatrics department. Again, nothing was found, and Mary remained silent about the rape. After many months of lingering lassitude and mild depression, along with withdrawal from non-required social activities, she was diagnosed with chronic fatigue syndrome. A series of antidepressants were prescribed, which produced many side effects but no relief from depression.

Mary struggled through her middle school and high school years, just doing passing work. She gained a lot of weight, which led her doctors to order further tests of various hormones and antibodies. Nothing showed up that would in any way explain her tiredness and depression.

It was only when Mary went for a consultation with a very thorough careers counselor that the truth finally came out. Dr. 'Gordon' was dismayed to see that no one had ever asked Mary about sexual trauma. Mary's story is absolutely classic for this sort of post traumatic syndrome. Everyone had focused on possible physical causes for her depression, tiredness and then her obesity, but no one had considered psychological issues.

It is extremely common for people who have suffered sexual assaults to have depression, serious changes in their personalities, social withdrawal and obesity. The weight acts as 'armor,' making the survivor of trauma less attractive and therefore less likely to suffer another sexual assault.

Mary was very lucky to have had her sexual assault diagnosed by Dr. Gordon. It is not uncommon for women and men to carry such traumas through several decades of their lives, if not through most of their lives, before they are identified. And the longer they are present, the more damage they can do and the more challenging it can be to release them. Dr. Gordon recommended that Mary take a year off from studies after high school to focus on treatment for her trauma, which she did.

With appropriate psychological counselling over a period of eight months, Mary recovered not only from her depression, but also from her social withdrawal and armoring. Her parents describe her as being like a butterfly emerging from her cocoon. A major focus of her therapy was on inner child work, in which she reconnected with that part of herself which had frozen into a state of withdrawal, self-blame, depression and armoring through putting on a lot of weight.

Mary's therapy did not focus to any great extent on her eating as related to her weight gain. Dealing with her underlying issues was sufficient to eliminate her need for armoring, which cleared her overeating. By addressing her inner motivation for putting on weight, her weight decreased without direct efforts on her part.

Her recovery was further facilitated by her parents following up on her rape, confronting Clarence in front of his parents when he returned home from university on summer holiday. While he at first denied it, his parents took the allegations seriously, and after several discussions with him he confessed what he had done. Mary and her parents decided that legal action would probably be more traumatic than helpful for Mary, so they did not pursue that route to redress the trauma and suffering she had experienced. Clarence's family were so ashamed of what he had done that they moved away shortly after.

I saw Mary several years later for a brief period of further counselling. She had found herself getting emotionally attracted to 'Connor,' another university student, but was unable to proceed past casual dating because of anxieties that were triggered any time she thought about getting close with him. Using inner child healing, facilitated by a combination of TWR/WHEE and two-chair work, Mary was able to clear the trauma residues she had frozen inside herself at age 12, including releasing her terror at the sexual assault, the betrayal of trust in a person her parents had chosen as a caregiver, and the fears engendered by Connor's threats to hurt her and her sister. She also released a large load of grief and regrets over the years she had lost following the rape.*52

Mary was then able to move on to fully explore her attraction to Connor. Though they ended up not pursuing a long-term relationship, Mary reported in her final session with me that she felt she was now over her trauma and could get on with her life.

It is very often possible to help survivors of sexual abuse, rape and other childhood traumas to clear their trauma residues as Mary did. Inner child work is tremendously powerful for such challenges, particularly when combined with two-chair work, Energy Psychology (EP) and other trauma release methods.*53

*It's never too late to have a happy childhood.*
– Tom Robbins

Sadly, it is relatively rare to find happy, spontaneous resolutions to severe traumas such as physical, emotional and sexual abuses, particularly when they occur in childhood and have festered, without being addressed, for several decades.

## Lessons for HSPs and HSPCs about inner child awarenesses

The inner child each of us carries within our deeper consciousness can be a wonderful resource. Its memories of positive experiences offer many levels of inner healings. These qualities are invaluable in our relationships. Our inner child has a freshness, an openness, and a wonderment about the world that we can access and activate in our learning and interacting – offering joyfulness, playfulness and unconditional love to each other.

Our inner child has habits that were learned in childhood in our family, peer and school relationships. Our adult relationships with another person who comes from different childhood experiences will offer us many mirrors of personal awarenesses – some of them harmonious with ours and others that may be disturbingly dissonant. Our approaches to life and attitudes that we took for granted, as "the way things are in the world" will be brought into question as we explore how to get along with and understand our significant other. And it is quite common for the inner child to want to assert its accepted and preferred ways of doing things – rather than accommodate to someone else's inner child attitudes and accustomed approaches to life.

✦ 'Ella' and 'Isaac' moved in to live together after dating for two years. They had always found each other easy-going and comfortably compatible. They were totally surprised to find themselves arguing over silly little things, like whether the knives should be put in the dish drainer with their points up or down, or whether a bar of soap or liquid soap was more appropriate for the guest washroom.

✦ 'Dylan' and 'Lilly' got along wonderfully well until they were expecting their first child. For reasons they could not understand, they argued often over details about decorating the nursery and about countless other issues on how they wanted to raise their son. This was in total contrast to the ease of discussions and decision making they had had with countless details involved in their moving in to live together.

Points of transition in life often raise awarenesses of territoriality, along with re-allocations of responsibilities, authority and decision-making. Establishing a home and deciding on how to raise a child are common issues that require serious consideration and discussion, and may bring out differences between couples that had been there all the time but were never relevant or important enough to discuss or argue about. At times like these, HSP-NHSP differences in perceptions, responsivity and relationship styles that were established in childhood and tend to be taken for granted as "the way it's supposed to be" may emerge into unexpectedly sharper focus. Discord and conflicts may ensue.

It is ever so much easier to manage these differences in views and understandings that crop up in periods of change and stress if you have taken some time to consider your differences and have developed ways to bridge these during the process of developing your relationships with each other. I hope this book is raising your awareness in these regards and offering you helpful resources for dealing with such issues.

As we have seen, on the challenging side of our inner child memories, most of us will carry bruises and scars from the wear and tear of our life experiences and relationships in childhood. These often remain outside our conscious awareness until events in our relationships waken us to their presence. While these may be anywhere on the spectrum from surprising to annoying to frustrating to painful or even destructive in our relationships, they are always invitations and opportunities to clear the wounds and scars we carry from earlier in life. It is enormously helpful in dealing with such issues to consider them from a wholistic perspective.

## 13. Observing Ego

> *Until you make the unconscious conscious,*
> *it will direct your life and you will call it fate.*
> – Carl Jung

'Observing ego' is a psychoanalytic concept that deserves more attention than it has received in the recent evolution of psychological awareness and psychotherapy. Strictly speaking, this term has been used to indicate our camera-like memories, and the focus has been on memories from our outer-world experiences. But our observing ego also takes 'selfies' and gives us memories of what goes on in our inner lives, including issues from every level of our wholistic selves.

Observing ego may provide a spectrum of awarenesses, depending on people's self-awareness capacities, such as:

- The meta-awareness that we are experiencing various thoughts and feelings
- A wise, inner observer who understands that we have choices in how we respond to our outer and inner worlds
- Memories about ourselves and of other people's parallel awarenesses of themselves, providing a spectrum and norm for grading the appropriateness, dissonance or dangers in our current experiences
- The observer with x-ray vision, who watches our interactions with others and interprets what we or they really meant to convey with certain words and actions; that is, what intentions, motivations and meta-messages may accompany what we say and do
- The deliberator that can pause, even for an instant, and consider which actions and responses to others' words and actions are in our best interests and theirs, and where we may be overstepping a line
- The inner librarian who archives our awarenesses, who may (or may not) compare in deliberate details our current views of what is going on in our lives with various previous snapshots we have taken, and can weigh in with cautions or encouragements about acting on our current thoughts, feelings and emotions

For example, when we're strongly challenged, offended or hurt and want to tear into someone, some of us have the capacities to take a few deep breaths that can give us time to recall other occasions when we felt positively or negatively towards this person. We may then consider the best alternatives and options we can choose for the most positive, long-term scenarios and relationships we would like to compose in our lives. This more reflective mode is the way HSPs use their observing egos.

There is a spectrum of awarenesses in observing ego capacity:

- Complete blindness about your having options and choices in how your thoughts and emotions are stimulated, how you can modulate your responses to your thoughts and emotions, and to what degrees you can be aware of other people's emotions
- Occasional insights that in particular circumstances and situations you have choices in how you respond to the situation and your feelings about them
- Frequent awarenesses that your beliefs and past experiences color your current observations and your responses to them

- Insights that in particular circumstances you have choices in how you respond to that situation and your feelings about it
- Layers of insights about underlying causes for the ways your thoughts are being stimulated and your feelings are coloring or causing what you are thinking
- Keen and constant awareness of where you are in parts or in the entirety of the wholistic flow of beingness and relatedness
- Here are a few examples of observing ego blindness – which could be found either in an HSP or HSPC blaming their partner:
- "You give me such a headache when you keep complaining about being upset over anything and everything."
- "You make me sooo angry (or upset, sad, frustrated, etc.)!"
- "My back (or neck, stomach, or other part of my body) is hurting sooo much ever since the auto accident (or funeral, rape or other difficult experience), and none of the doctors or therapists or medications or remedies anyone has offered or suggested have been able to fix it."
- There is little or no consciousness in the ego awareness blinded people who make these sorts of statements about their personal participation in:
- Creating and holding onto their pains
- Having these feelings triggered in response to whatever is going on between them and the person they are relating to (rather than assuming it is something wrong with their physical body, for which they can take responsibility)
- Expecting that someone else will 'fix' them

### Partial observing ego awareness

✦ 'Barry' complains, "My shoulder pain went down by half when I tapped on it at work, but it wouldn't go down any further. TWR works so much better in your therapy office than at home."

Barry learned TWR1, tapping on the symptom directly, but hasn't yet understood TWR2 principles of inviting the pain to reveal what his inner self is complaining about through the symptom. In other words, he saw the symptom reflecting the state of his body, but did not understand yet that his body is a reflection of who he is and how he thinks, feels and relates to other people and to the rest of the wholistic spectrum.

✦ 'Jerry' reports, "That last therapy session we had was wonderful! My knee was so much better after you guided me in tapping on the pain, which we discovered is a leftover from the traumas of my auto accident and hospitalization and litigation. But the next day it came back almost as bad as before."

What Jerry missed was the lesson that there were multiple underlying feelings, memories, or traumas which were not yet cleared and were still making him up tight and triggering the pain.

✦ 'Dora' complained, "I know that when I'm tired, hungry or pre-menstrual, my patience is shorter and my temper is more likely to flare up. But when my temper comes out, I can't control it. Tapping has been helping me clear some of my sensitive points so they don't get triggered as easily or as often any more. I've been that way all my life. But most of the time I'm not yet at the point where I can catch and restrain myself from lashing out when I feel provoked.

Dora's inner filing cabinets are seeking releases for many buried irritations and several significant traumas that she experienced when she was a child, growing up in a difficult home, in a difficult neighborhood. Her childhood trauma memories and feelings are happy for the opportunities that various provocations in her current life provide – allowing her to release some of her buried childhood stresses and traumas that she had been unable to deal with so far. Dora is aware of these connections in theory, but not yet connecting with these awarenesses at the times when her angry outbursts are provoked and her general irritation loads are high. She is starting to connect with these in some instances a little while after her anger outbursts.

Another variant of partial ego awareness is being conscious of one's own issues but being blind to other people's psychological problems, or to their responses to your words or actions.

### *Full observing ego awarenesses*

✦ 'Paula,' an HSP, shared, "I'm amazed at how the bullies in my high school have stopped picking on me, ever since I learned to release all my feelings of being hurt, ashamed and different over being born an HSP. I now know how to tap in good feelings about myself and stand up to them without being ashamed that I'm more sensitive than they are, and I can show my feelings more openly and intensely than they do."

✦ 'Derrick' apologized to his wife. "I'm sorry I got angry and started to dump on you just now when I was triggered into hurt, anger and trauma memories by what you said. I could see myself doing this but the feelings were so strong that I couldn't control my overwhelm. I was feeling hurt, angry and abandoned and just went into my porcupine protective response. I'm glad we agreed to the 'time out' signal you gave me and that I was able to take a few moments of quiet space to calm myself."

Derek is well on his way to doing much better, as he increases his observing ego awarenesses.

It may take a fair amount of practice to reach a place where people who are hurt and triggered can control themselves more fully through enhanced observing ego consciousness. Practice and persistence are essential to changing our defensive habits.

*HOW WOULD YOU RATE YOUR LEVELS OF OBSERVING EGO AWARENESS?*

*ARE THERE SITUATIONS IN WHICH YOU HAVE GREATER OR LESSER OBSERVING EGO AWARENESSES?*

Many children can develop observing ego quickly in counseling and are able to make rapid, deep changes – even in difficult situations. This is because they are open to learning new ways of understanding the world and then relating better to whatever comes their way. They also don't have barnacles on their problems from decades of behaving in various unhelpful ways, avoiding thinking about these awarenesses, and burying the emotions attached to them.

✦✦✦ I grew up with an abusive mother and absent father. No other family members were present. Looking back on those early years, I understand that my observing ego worked overtime to help me navigate the many challenges I faced. Somewhere in my early years I realized I had to parent myself because no one else was going to do this with or for me. I developed a strong, intuitive and observing ego for rightness and wrongness about my decision points in behavior. I can recall this from the age of 3 or 4. I have always been a strict parent with myself (mostly, speaking inwardly with a critical parent voice), choosing not to hurt others because I suffered from my mother's abuse and didn't want to inflict pain or suffering on others.

Most helpfully, I learned which behaviors of mine would trigger my mother's criticisms, anger or calmer responses, and that I could, at least sometimes, influence how our interactions unfolded – so that I avoided triggering some of her abusiveness. My most intense memory was from age 8, where I became aware of my sensing her anger building towards abusiveness. I came to realize I could provoke her into discharging it, rather than continuing to suffer by sitting on a smoking, rumbling volcano and not know when the eruption would occur.

My keenly developed observing ego has served me well in my interactions with my parents, my several wives, my children, and with friends and family of choice. My training and practice in psychotherapy has further sharpened and deepened these abilities to understand and interact in more healing ways under stress. And my clients have often stirred me to waken to ever deeper layers of lessons, mirroring in the issues they struggle with the very same issues I need to work on further.

And this is by no means any pretense of having 'arrived' at some psychological pinnacle of enlightenment or full control of my emotions and reactions. I am constantly peeling the layers of the onion of my life. And I strongly suspect that my onion grows at night when I'm sleeping, because there always seem to be more layers to peel and understand when I wake up in the morning and am wakened to greater awarenesses by some blessing or discord in my life – that alerts me to further layers of issues inviting/wanting/needing identification, clarifications and clearing.

My observing ego has of course also been enormously helpful as well in my psychotherapy work, enabling me to watch my interactions with clients. I can use my observations of my emotional responses in clinical interactions as tools for understanding what my clients are experiencing. For instance, if they are provocative, needy for approval or playing the role of 'poor me' I can zoom in on this quickly because my observing ego notes my emotional responses to their behaviors and stirs memories of how I've learned to deal with these issues.

And of course, in HSP-HSPC relationships our self-awareness is an invaluable tool in sorting out better ways to get along.

✦ HSPC 'Dorothy' notes: "I'm learning to catch myself when my partner, Cindy, gets triggered and goes into high anxieties, fear mode, anger or overwhelm. I used to get anxious myself when she flared up like that, and could also get triggered into anxiety, annoyance or even into anger. Now I take a deep breath, zip up my protective bioenergy shield,*[54] and use tapping with my toes*[55] in order to lower my stress levels. Then I'm in a calmer place to consider the best ways to help her calm down and find her center again."

✦ HSP 'Cynthia' observes: "I used to think I was really aware of myself and my relationships because I can so keenly sense what I'm feeling and what everyone else is feeling. It wasn't till I got together with Dottie that I began to appreciate that sensory and emotional awareness is not where our full spectrum of awareness ends.

I found that I often couldn't understand why Dottie was upset with me when I was honestly sharing what I felt. It wasn't till we learned WHEE in a webinar workshop that we both began to be sensitive to the 'hows' of what we were saying to each other and not just the 'whats.' Some of the other bits that really helped our relationship were saying "Ouch!" or signaling a time out when things are heating up between us, and tapping to take the steam out of our reactions before resuming our discussions.

Clearly, both Dorothy and Cynthia are developing their observing ego capacities. This is enormously helpful in relationships!

### Finding your center and being centered

We all have options in how we respond to stresses and provocations on the one hand, and to feeling empathy for someone who is upset on the other. We can be much more supportive and helpful when we develop our observing ego awareness for when we ourselves are feeling stressed, when we understand and empathize with others about their being stressed, and when we express our thoughts and feelings in the most healing ways we can muster.

Doing all of this may be challenging when we are dealing with someone else's negative feelings, since our own negative feelings may be intense as well. Usually it is easiest to learn to recognize and deal with our own feelings first, so that they are not overwhelming and so that we don't get into vicious circles of someone else's negativity triggering our own negativity, which then escalates the other person to even more negativity.

Clearly, observing ego can be developed and strengthened. At times when you aren't stressed or triggered, you can practice deliberately reconnecting with your own traumas, triggering issues, and hurt feelings in order to learn to recognize and deal with them, using whatever de-stressing methods work for you. Then, when you encounter situations in your daily life that could stir you towards overwhelm, you have both the habits of observing ego you've exercised to recognize them and tools to deal with them. A personal therapist and/or marital therapist can be enormously helpful in approaching and learning to deal with them.

This is called 'being centered.' This term is taken from the potter's craft, where a glob of clay is placed in the center of the spinning wheel and the artist shapes it with fingers and tools into various cups, vases and other artistic creations. As long as the clay remains in the center of the wheel, it can be easily manipulated into utilitarian and beautiful creations. But if it slips even a bit off-center, the centrifugal force of the rapidly turning wheel splatters the clay in all directions.

So, when you are centered, the world may be spinning around you, yet you remain calm and can sort out what you need to within yourself. But if you are off-center, you may be thrown in any and all directions.

Being centered enables you to enjoy your own life and your relationships much more. When you are centered you are in a space where you feel safe and secure, connected with all aspects of your being. You can sense if and when your partner is off-center, empathize with her, support her, and still remain centered and not triggered by whatever is stressing her. You can ask yourself whether anything that she is experiencing resonates with residues within yourself that are still waiting to be identified and cleared. If you find old file-drawers that still need emptying, you can use whatever methods work best for you to clear them.

Whether you're an HSP or NHSP companion to an HSP, the more you can hold your connection with your observing ego, the more energies you have available for healing yourselves and your relationships. Doing this challenging work on yourselves and with each other enables you to improve how you get along with each other.

When you clear your own triggering issues, traumas, fears or other issues, and come to a place of centeredness, your inner self less often gets pushed or triggered into alarm mode – either because of your own sensitivities or because you are resonating with your partner. You then have more energies and time to enjoy the positive aspects of your relationship.*[56] **[57]

### Developing observing ego

We've noted that sensitive children often march to different tunes from those of the majority of their peers. NHSPs are solidly rooted in the prevalent left hemisphere culture. The average NHSPs will just shrug and roll their eyes over HSP sensitivities and behaviors. But some NHSPs will belittle, ridicule or bully those who display HSP qualities in order to silence them. In many cases the NHSPs do this to protect themselves from connecting with their own feelings that are deeply buried, outside their conscious awareness.

Many HSP children assume there is something wrong with them when they are ridiculed or bullied for doing something that is perfectly normal for them, such as being intensely emotional or totally absorbed in their reading, thinking, creative activities, and daydreaming – disconnected from the outer world. This can set up a vicious circle in which the HSP child becomes anxious with dismissive or bullying NHSPs, making the HSPs more intensely emotional, which stirs the bullies to further bullying.

The same challenges may be experienced by adult HSPs, with NHSP classmates or instructors in higher education, co-workers and supervisors in places of employment, and other acquaintances who fail to understand our HSP qualities and behaviors.

Developing and strengthening tools for calming and de-stressing can be an enormous help to HSPs. The exercise I most often recommend for children is visiting "your safe place." For adults I call this your place of peace and safety and healing" (PPSH). This is a very highly recommended calming and safety essential for HSPs.*[58]

*In summary*

Observing ego is an enormous benefit in clarifying what is happening in our lives and in formulating and implementing plans for changing how we respond to what is distressing us. Most people can develop and strengthen their observing ego, and can apply it to making their lives less stressful and more harmonious. If you are among the more sensitive HSPs, and often are completely immersed in your emotional awarenesses, this may be a challenge. However, even if you find it difficult to connect to your observing ego when you are triggered into high alert or distress modes of relating to the world, awareness of issues identified by your observing ego can be of substantial help in your understanding what is happening in your life and a help in your relationships with your HSPC and with others.

*ARE YOU AWARE OF WHEN YOU ARE CENTERED?*

*WHAT ARE SOME OF THE WAYS YOU CAN IDENTIFY THIS?*

*HOW CAN YOU BRING MORE OF THIS INTO YOUR LIFE?*

*WHAT ARE INTRUSIONS AND DISTRACTIONS THAT PUSH YOU OFF CENTER?*

*WHAT ARE HELPFUL WAYS TO DEAL WITH THESE?*[*59]

*WHO ARE PEOPLE YOU KNOW WHO ARE CENTERED?*

*WHAT CAN YOU LEARN FROM THEM?*

## 14. Building and keeping or changing habits of consciousness

> *I had the good fortune (Karma) to want to be free*
> *more than I wanted to be right.*
> *Then I could admit*
> *that I had gotten caught in old habits…again.*
>
> – Ram Dass

We've explored some of the basic ways we absorb information and how we organize our awarenesses of the world. In this section I invite you to consider some of the ways we evaluate new information and change what we hold to be true or choose to persist in our beliefs.

HSPs and HSPCs take an awful lot for granted when they consider how they assess what is relevant, important and good for them. For the most part, we go through our lives on our inner, automatic pilots. We navigate our ways with cognitive maps and response patterns that we've developed through trial and error, plus enormous, conscious and unconscious memory banks of experiences we would like to repeat or to avoid, augmented by the opinions that we've taken on board from other people. So each of us has arrays of well-established habits that make us who we are.

Let's briefly consider how we get to be who we are in terms of learned behaviors. This is a process with many layers:

- Our world is a very complicated place.
- Our sensory organs are very complex translators of diverse aspects of the world that come to our attention.
- Our brains have to interpret the sensory data taken in by our eyes and ears and other senses.
- We have two tracks for separating out the few items that are important to us from the countless ones that are not worth repeating or particularly relevant.
  - The track of rewards and punishments that teaches us what is worth repeating or avoiding, which is largely automated and unconscious.
  - The cognitive track in which we seek the advice of various experts on the subjects under consideration and then we decide on responses to our interpretations of the information we have selected
- Then we have to sort out the best ways to put our decisions into effect.

And this is not where it ends…

- We have to monitor our responses to the world.
- We have to monitor the world's responses to our responses.
- We want to remember what our responses were, and what the outcomes were to our responses – so that we can repeat the successful ones and avoid those that led to negative consequences or failure.
- And we continuously repeat these loops of perception, interpretation, analysis, decisions, actions, monitoring and remembering.
- So, we've worked pretty hard to reach the place where we are today, and even the thought of re-writing our internal operating manuals is rather daunting, to say the least. This has been called confirmation bias, the process whereby we become prisoners of our own assumptions.

Now add the intricacies of interacting with other people who are going through similar sorts of experiences – to all of the above processes we are experiencing – and you can begin to appreciate the mind-boggling complexities and challenges in sorting out how to get along in our relationships with other people.

This is a long way around to saying that it can be a serious challenge to understand HSPs and HSPCs individually, and to figure out how to relate with our partners, our families, and with other people in general in the most productive and healing ways. Sometimes we deal with these challenges competently and well. At other times we serve ourselves poorly because, although the world around us has changed significantly, we are reluctant to change our selections of sensory perceptions, our habits of interpreting what we perceive, and ways we relate to the world.

Navigating our ways through our lives is a very complex business. You can readily guess that the habits of perceptions and of responses that we develop provide very welcome shortcuts for dealing with the numerous complex situations we are constantly facing. The good news is that we are very adept at developing these sorts of habits, on every level of our being.

Habits enable us to pull from the shelves of our past experiences a previously-explored set of perceptions, plus memories of our responses and how they worked out. Here are examples of habits we all learn:

**Body** *(Habits of Consciousness)*
- Learning, in the earliest years of our lives, the basics of how to interpret our sensory inputs and to use our muscles for moving our bodies around
- Attending to bodily needs of nutrition, cleanliness and other protections of our body
- Shaping sounds with our mouths, tongue, throat and lungs to communicate
- Manipulating objects in our environment, from clothes to utensils to electronic equipment and more
- Pleasuring ourselves and each other through our various senses

**Emotions** *(Habits of Consciousness)*
- Learning to recognize and express our various emotions
- Expressing ourselves so that our emotional wants and needs can be attended to and satisfied – by ourselves and others
- Reading the emotions of others, so that we can respond in appropriate ways, for their benefit and ours
- Sensing the bioenergies of emotions, a radar system that picks up subtle clues*[60]

**Mind** *(Habits of Consciousness)*
- We develop mental maps and navigating manuals for our personal world to help us navigate
  - With appropriate communications
    - To express and explain our wants and needs
    - To understand the wants and needs of others
    - To know and to obey rules and regulations
  - Going from place to place for specific needs
  - To understand causes and effects
  - To maximize our formal learning experiences in schools and other learning situations
  - To pass on information to others
    - For our benefit
    - For their benefits
- We develop our memories
  - To acquire and retain information
  - To decide when and how to allow for editing of our memories
  - To decide when to reject new information

**Relationships with other people** *(Habits of Consciousness)*
- Identifying nurturing, supportive people
  - Among our family, friends and acquaintances
  - In our community and society
- Identifying unfriendly, threatening or dangerous people
- Learning the rules of our
  - Family of birth or adoption
  - Families of choice
  - Community and society
  - Meta-rules about how strictly we're expected to obey the rules we've acquired
  - Learning how to amend or delete outmoded rules, in the light of new situations

**Relationships with the environment** *(Habits of Consciousness)*
- Recognizing pleasant, helpful and safe vs. unpleasant and unsafe places to visit and live
- Identifying nurturing, healthy, safe foods to eat
- Identifying harmful or dangerous animals, plants and other substances to avoid

**Spirit** *(Habits of Consciousness)*
- Learning the beliefs and disbeliefs of your family, community and nation about
    - Religion and religious practices
    - The Infinite Source
- Experiencing personal spiritual awarenesses and learning to discern the differences between real and fantasy experiences
- Finding our personal spiritual path and navigating our ways through life's challenges and lessons

This is a lot to learn! This is even more of a challenge to remember and apply in our daily lives. It would be impossible to manage our daily routines if we had to review all of the maps and rules and taboos every time we interact with any of these aspects of the world and all it contains.

Enter the world of rewards and punishments. We tend to repeat behaviors that are rewarded and to avoid behaviors that are punished. These sorts of lessons begin in our family relationships and continue throughout our lives.

Much of what children are taught is for the practical purposes of surviving, thriving and enjoying their lives. We need to learn about
- Skills, ranging from crawling and walking, feeding ourselves, understanding spoken words and talking
- Dangers, such as handling sharp objects and electrical devices, what is safe to eat or not to be put in the mouth, and navigating stairs and street corners
- Sources of nurturing and guidance
- Social cues and culturally congruent and 'proper' vs. unacceptable behaviors
- Personally enjoyed/ preferred activities and distasteful or unpleasant ones
- As we mature, our range of learning broadens to include
- School lessons
- Life skills
- Career choices
- Partnering and raising a family of our own

Unspoken lessons are also learned from our families and social milieu. I'm reminded of the poignant verses from *South Pacific*, by Rodgers and Hammerstein:

> You've got to be taught to hate and fear
> You've got to be taught from year to year
> It's got to be drummed in your dear little ear
> You've got to be carefully taught
>
> You've got to be taught to be afraid
> Of people whose eyes are oddly made
> And people whose skin is a diff'erent shade
> You've got to be carefully taught
>
> You've got to be taught before it's too late
> Before you are six or seven or eight
> To hate all the people your relatives hate
> You've got to be carefully taught

We are constantly being programmed in very complex ways by our families, peers, schools and religious institutions, and end up with beliefs and disbeliefs that we tend to take for granted. The good news is that these lessons prepare us to get along comfortably with our social milieu. The bad news is that it is rare to be taught critical thinking skills, so that we can better assess what is for our highest good and for the highest good of all.

When we find ourselves uncomfortable with the discrepancies between our inherited social lessons, many of us lack the skills to identify and address the challenging issues in our lives. So let's consider some of the basics of psychological approaches to learning and changing our behaviors.

### *Reinforcements – positive and negative*

When a behavior is rewarded, we tend to repeat it. When it is punished, we tend to avoid it. This is the basis for much of conventional psychology.

It all started in the 1890s, when a Russian physiologist, Ivan Pavlov, noticed that his dogs would start salivating when he entered the room, even when he wasn't coming to feed them. He realized they had been conditioned to respond to his presence with salivating because he was the one who brought them their food. He then found that they could be conditioned to salivate with the ring of a bell, and so the psychological science of rewards and punishments was born.

Anything that feels positive can be such a reward, like a smile and saying kind words, a gentle voice, praise, success in a video game, and getting good grades. Food is one of the best rewards. Behaviors that are followed by positive reinforcements tend to be repeated.

Anything that feels negative can be a discouragement from repeating whatever behaviors were associated with the negative experience. Negative reinforcements may include a frown, criticism, a harsh voice, failure or rejection in what you say or do, electric shocks (in the laboratory), a spanking or trauma.

And these rewards and punishments may be effective even when people are not consciously aware they are perceiving them.

✦ Students in a Psychology 101 class learned about positive and negative reinforcements. One day, before the professor arrived in class, they agreed that students on the right side of the room would smile and nod as the professor lectured, and those on the left side of the room would frown and look bored. They were amused to see that by the end of the lesson, the professor was facing almost all of the time towards the side where students were smiling.

And chance occurrences that are positive or negative may have similar effects.

✦ A researcher set a timer to dispense a kernel of bird food for a series of caged pigeons at random times, videotaping what happened. Pretty soon each pigeon was doing something odd, such as turning round and around in one direction, or scratching its head constantly. Reviewing the videos, it was clear that the pigeon had been scratching its head or turning around just as a food kernel arrived. The researcher surmised that the pigeon responded as though his turning in circles or head scratching had caused the food kernel to arrive. Having repeated the behaviors often enough, he was again rewarded, which further strengthened his initial, randomly reinforced behavior.

So we can see that positive and negative reinforcements can occur outside our conscious awareness. And we develop habits for going through the routines in our lives. Habits make life sooooo much easier! That is the good news.

## Cognitive dissonance in building and changing views and behaviors

The bad news is that our habits may keep us locked into set patterns and ways of perceiving and understanding the world and for interacting with it. Then, even when something attractive comes our way, if it is novel and different from what we are accustomed to, we may reject it out of hand because we rely on our well-established habits and rules to guide us in our responses. This is called 'cognitive dissonance.'

And when the new people or circumstances that appear might invite or require new and different responses from us in order to engage with them and enjoy them, we may reject them out of hand because of our cognitive dissonance. They don't feel right, or don't fit the patterns we are used to thinking about or to responding to automatically. And then we miss out on new, helpful, profitable, enjoyable and healing opportunities because we rely on our established. routine libraries of habitual reactions to guide us.

✦ 'Pat' was a vivacious, outgoing, sensitive, fun-loving, first year university student who was the life of the party and of most other gatherings in which she participated. 'Jeff' met Pat at a Halloween event in the children's wing of their university medical school. Pat had come out of an interest to serve her school community. Jeff had come because his introductory Social Science course required five community volunteer hours.

Though he was strongly attracted to her, and thought she was also attracted to him, he held back from responding to her several attempts at starting conversations with him. The rules he carried from his family culture were very restrictive when it came to showing emotions. He couldn't see any way that he would be comfortable with someone who was so effusively outgoing.

A year later, they happened to meet again in the university cafeteria. Living at the university, away from home for these several months, had offered Jeff new perspectives on what he felt personally were acceptable and comfortable social behaviors. Though still rather introverted, he was able to enjoy Pat's company this time without discomfort or anxieties. They started dating and were married two years later.

They got along well with Pat's family. Sadly, however, Jeff's family was rattled by Pat's emotional exuberance and let him know in subtle and direct ways that they did not enjoy her company. By then, Jeff had shifted his inner rules about expressing feelings to the point that he was uncomfortable being back in his own family. So, the last I heard from them, Jeff and Pat were having very little to do with his family.

Habits on the spectrum of emotional openness and closedness are developed largely from one's personality plus one's family rules for what levels of emotional expressiveness are expected, tolerable, proper or prohibited. There will also be meta-rules about how much flexibility in bending or ignoring rules is acceptable within the family. This is especially so in strongly NHSP families, where rigid rules often evolve about not mentioning, much less exhibiting emotions or intuitions. Such rules may be comfortable for the NHSP family as a group, but uncomfortable for family members who may be more emotionally sensitive and extroverted, or more intuitive, and particularly for HSPs.

Jeff had initially experienced cognitive dissonance in meeting Pat. He was both attracted to her but also uncomfortable being in her presence because of his personality and his family rules. He resolved this dissonance initially by not engaging with her, thereby remaining loyal to his internalized rules about unacceptable levels of feeling and expressing emotions, both within his personal (unexpressed) awarenesses and outwardly, in private as well as in public social settings. Over time, living in social settings among others who had more permissive rules for experiencing and expressing emotions, Jeff shifted his personal rules to be more flexible and open in these regards.

I've seen numbers of NHSP families where major distancing occurred after one of the flock strayed from the family fold, where there were rigid rules that emotions had to be muted, avoided and/or silenced. In a few cases, compromises were found after the grandchildren arrived and the grandparents wanted to be involved. But for the most part, the divides between strongly left and right brain preferences proved to be more than these NHSP families could or would tolerate.

These sorts of social rules also apply within academic and work settings. An example of highly unusual right brain functions is the story of Srinivasa Ramanujan, a peasant from Madras, India, who had an astounding natural gift for mathematical calculations, which he developed largely on his own. Though he studied mathematics in a Madras college, his work exceeded the knowledge of his instructors, and he had to leave the college because he focused only on mathematics and did not complete his other required courses.

He eventually made his way to Cambridge University, where he worked with the ambivalent support of G. H. Hardy, one of England's leading mathematicians. The movie titled *The Man Who Knew Infinity* portrays his struggles to gain the acceptance of the mathematics faculty for the validity of his advanced theories. They roundly rejected him and would not even consider his brilliant contributions because he had not come the route of academic studies that all the other mathematicians in this bastion of higher learning had taken.

This is a good example of cognitive dissonance. The Cambridge mathematics professors initially dismissed his work categorically and refused to even look at it, despite the fact that Hardy reported Ramanujan's theories were well ahead of the leading edge of the mathematics of their day. Hardy, himself, had difficulty accepting Ramnujan's explanation that his mathematical abilities derived from Divine inspiration. His theories were studied for many decades after his death, contributing to the development of numbers theory, mathematical analysis, continued fractions and infinite series.

The rejections of Ramanujan's brilliant work by the Cambridge University mathematicians is a very clear demonstration of cognitive dissonance, and far from uncommon in society in general and in academic circles in particular. Despite his acknowledged brilliance and successful proofs of mathematical theories that no one else had been able to figure out before, his work was rejected by some of the best mathematicians of his day. And these were the only people qualified to sit in judgment on his work.

How and why such rejections occur can be partially explained by cognitive dissonance. Another notable historical example is Ignaz Semmelweis, a Viennese physician in the mid-19th century, noticed that women delivered by midwives were far less likely to die of puerperal fever ("childbed fever") than mothers delivered by medical doctors, who had a 10-35% mortality rate. The only difference he could identify in the obstetric procedures of midwives was that they washed their hands prior to attending to the births. When he did likewise then he, too had far fewer deaths among his patients. Semmelweis wrote a book and numbers of articles about this, and spoke with many of his colleagues, but all of them rejected his simple suggestion to wash their hands. Part of the issue was that he had no explanation for how washing one's hands could make a difference because germs and antisepsis had not been discovered yet. He ended up being hospitalized in an asylum at age 47, where he was beaten to death by the guards.**[61]

These sorts of rigidities are in the same categories of rejections that HSPs experience from NHSPs. The NHSPs are absolutely certain that their perceptions and understandings of the world are accurate and that any alternative views are flawed and unworthy of their consideration, much less acceptance.

Similarly, the reluctance today of medical doctors to consider new approaches that could be of enormous help to their patients might seem odd. One might think that in the century and a half since the time of Semmelweis we would have seen more openness to innovative healthcare methods. But this is far from the case.

Doctors and other conventional healthcare practitioners today, along with most other people in all walks of life, are reluctant to change their established beliefs – in matters large and small. They will find some rationalizations and reject new information rather than re-examine what they currently hold to be true and valid.

Worse yet, they will even refuse to look at, much less to consider, any evidence that contradicts their beliefs. Patients will sometimes report they have recovered from incurable diseases, and the most common medical response is that they must have had the wrong diagnosis. And doctors give all sorts of rationalizations and excuses for ignoring evidence from well designed and well run studies as well.

Tim Hartford, in a Ted Talk, calls this "the God complex." He shares a fascinating experiment showing how people tend to persist in their opinions, and to resist all efforts that might contradict their cherished beliefs. This research study was conducted in a hospital by Archie Cochrane, MD.

> ...it's so hard to admit our own fallibility. It's so uncomfortable. And Archie Cochrane understood this as well as anybody. There's this one trial he ran... He wanted to test out the question of, where is it that patients should recover from

heart attacks? Should they recover in a specialized cardiac unit in hospital, or should they recover at home? All the cardiac doctors tried to shut him down. They had the God complex in spades. They knew that their hospitals were the right place for patients, and they knew it was very unethical to run any kind of trial or experiment.

Nevertheless, Archie managed to get permission to do this. He ran his trial. And after the trial had been running for a little while, he gathered together all his colleagues around his table, and he said, "Well, gentlemen, we have some preliminary results. They're not statistically significant. But we have something. And it turns out that you're right and I'm wrong. It is dangerous for patients to recover from heart attacks at home. They should be in hospital." And there's this uproar, and all the doctors start pounding the table and saying, "We always said you were unethical, Archie. You're killing people with your clinical trials. You need to shut it down now. Shut it down at once." And there's this huge hubbub. Archie lets it die down. And then he says, "Well that's very interesting, gentlemen, because when I gave you the table of results, I swapped the two columns around. It turns out your hospitals are killing people, and they should be at home. Would you like to close down the trial now, or should we wait until we have robust results? ..."

Rigidities in opinions and behavioral patterns are very common aspects of the human repertoire of ways of thinking and behaving. My best guess for why this is so are that

- People usually prefer to take the easiest way forward, involving the least amount of effort, which means simply coasting on automatic pilot rather than putting their minds into gear and thinking about various choices and options
- Habits are hard to change
- People are embarrassed to admit they are doing something poorly, as they feel criticized when someone suggests a better way to do it
- People don't want to put in efforts to learn new approaches
- Many people would rather avoid changing how they do things, as this can be at the very least tedious, and may also require retraining and learning new approaches from scratch

This is true as well for courses of action people have chosen out of their own free will, and not just those that were learned through formal training. Rather than re-examine their reasons for deciding to go in a certain direction, people will justify and argue to preserve and pursue their initial choices in what they are continuing to do – even if this may appear far-fetched to outside observers.

✦✦✦ I've had experiences similar to those of Semmelweis in exploring fresh ways to understand and deal with psychological and physical problems. I've been studying complementary/ alternative therapies, especially bioenergy healing and self-healing, for four decades. I have considerable expertise on how healers can

Identify people's difficulties on every level of their being: body, emotions, mind, relationships and spirit

Offer healing for these issues by holding their hands on or near the body of the healee;

- Offer healing through mental intention, meditation or prayer.

I've done many things to confirm and document the powers of healers and healing:
- Over the past 35 years I've observed hundreds of healers helping transform people from illness to health without known medical interventions
- I clarified with countless healees how the healings helped them or not
- I wrote two books reviewing 189 research studies of healing, and of the 50 most rigorous studies, 74 percent demonstrated significant effects (Benor, 2001; 2002)
- I've written over 150 articles on various aspects of healing
- I've lectured and given experiential workshops on many aspects of healing

I've personally studied
- Conventional medical diagnosis and treatments
- Conventional psychological interventions, including behavior modification, psychodynamic psychotherapy, hypnotherapy, group therapy, Transactional Analysis, two-chair work (gestalt therapy), and more.
- A broad spectrum of complementary/ alternative therapies, including muscle relaxation, meditation, imagery, intense emotional release therapy, Neurolinguistic Programming, Reiki, LeShan healing, Therapeutic Touch, past life therapy, Energy Psychology, and more.

Through my lectures and workshops I've found numerous complementary/ alternative therapists, nurses, and non-therapists who have been ready, willing and eager to learn about healing so that they can refer people to healers for help. Many have also have gone on to develop their own healing gifts.

And I've found only a very few hands-on conventional therapists, medical doctors, and fewer psychologists who have been anywhere near open to even listen to anything about healing. When the subject is mentioned, their eyes glaze over and they immediately come up with reasons why none of these newer (in Western healthcare) approaches could be anything more than suggestion, placebos or quackery.

In each of these examples, new ideas and evidence for understanding and interacting with the world were rejected by the majority of people who heard about them. The new ideas contradicted their conventional logic and everyday practices, and the consensus was that they simply could not be valid or true. For conventional clinicians and the average person in Western society, cognitive dissonance rules out the possibility that healing could be anything more than a placebo. To them, this means that healing is just a suggestion something is being done, which activates 'spontaneous changes'. And there is little or no interest in exploring how people are able to do this, nor in how to enhance the effects of the suggestions inherent in the placebos.

I've pondered for several decades on how and why people become so rigidly entrenched in their habits of perceiving the world and of interacting with it. More importantly, I've been troubled by how repressive people are in discouraging others from exploring new therapeutic perspectives and practices that are developed by others.

*It ain't so much the things we don't know that get us into trouble.*
*It's the things we know that just ain't so.*
— Artemus Ward

Cognitive dissonance is probably neuroplastic blindness under another name. Cognitive dissonance is the tension we experience when something in our outer or inner worlds contradicts our habitual perceptions and how we are used to interpreting them.

> *A new scientific truth does not triumph by convincing its opponents and making them see the light, but rather because its opponents eventually die, and a new generation grows up that is familiar with it. A variation of which is: Science advances one funeral at a time.*
> — Max Planck

*Relevant to HSPs and HSPCs*
- Rigidities in people prone to dismissive beliefs as ways of dealing with their cognitive dissonance about emotions and emotionality may include that women are second class citizens. This is very disempowering, to say the least, and can be traumatic to women in general and HSP women in particular.**[62]
- Similarly, there are those who believe that boys and men who show their emotions are weak, effeminate, crybabies, wimps (and other derogatory descriptions). HSP boys are frequently targets of teasing and bullying. Surprisingly, a study of newborn children shows that boys are actually more emotionally reactive than girls (Kindland & Thompson, 1999). This strongly suggests that beliefs about boys being less emotional are culturally specific myths. Ted Zeff (2010) makes this point repeatedly in his excellent discussion on *The Strong Sensitive Boy*.
- NHSPs in many cases have often grown up in families and/or cultures in which the expression of emotions is discouraged, dismissed, belittled, and pathologized. Many HSPs have suffered from these sorts of attitudes in their own families. Some HSPs have been seriously traumatized and their lives scarred and limited because they cannot fully actualize their potentials within these cultures of emotional and intuitive repressions. Even when they distance themselves from these negative relationships, these HSPs almost always come away scarred and hesitant, or even scared to explore, express and assert their full potentials because they expect to be discouraged, dismissed, belittled, and pathologized by others.

CAN YOU SENSE WAYS IN WHICH THE RIGIDITIES OF OTHER PEOPLE IN YOUR LIFE MAY HAVE IMPACTED YOU?

HAVE YOU EXPERIENCED REJECTIONS BECAUSE YOU ARE DIFFERENT FROM OTHERS IN YOUR FAMILY?

AMONG YOUR FRIENDS, CLASSMATES, CO-WORKERS OR PEERS?

WHAT HAVE YOU FOUND HELPFUL IN DEALING WITH THESE CHALLENGES?

Many such criticisms are commonly leveled by specialists in diverse professions against anyone believing and/or practicing differently from themselves. These critics have boxed themselves into restrictive beliefs through their education, training, life experiences and/or wanting to protect their earnings and job security. They assert that:

- They have reached a pinnacle of understanding and absolute truth about some aspect(s) of human experience and existence.
- Their explanatory systems and therapeutic approaches are more valid than any other explanations for the same phenomena, and other explanations are erroneous and even dangerous for people to espouse or apply to their life issues.

In these categories are found conventional doctors, psychiatrists, psychotherapists and other practitioners who warn patients against alternative methods – about which the practitioners actually know little or nothing, but which their equally ill-informed instructors during their training told them are just rubbish.

I have many times shaken my head in disbelief over such self-restricting cognitive dissonance, with totally unfounded dismissals of innovative and new approaches. Such claims about therapeutic approaches are refuted by strong evidence that is very plainly available to anyone who is not part of the 'in' group that dismisses any evidence that is not consonant with their own rigid beliefs.

I have come to see these people as very much like cats-in-the-box that were described in a Toronto tweet by Danielle Matheson that went viral, with over 11 million forwards in less than a week (Kwong, 2017). Pinterest reported that if you put a square of tape on the floor, a cat will come and sit inside this box. (See Figure 14-1.) I can't think of a more appropriate image to illustrate this sort of cognitive dissonance! People park themselves on a box that they've drawn in the sands of time and defend it against all existing rectangles, circles and even more against newcomers who might have multi-dimensional figures – that of course they, too, will champion – in similarly rigid manners.

**Figure 14-1. Cat in a box**

In medical school I was taught that my job was to arrive at an accurate diagnosis, following which I could then prescribe the recommended treatments. The diagnosis was based on my best clinical assessment of the patient's presenting problems, derived mostly from the history, augmented by a physical examination, laboratory tests, x-rays and other measurements. Today, computers augment each of these steps, reducing the likelihood of overlooking important questions or lab studies. But the medical focus is almost exclusively on the body the patient brought in for examination. The rest of the wholistic spectrum is ignored. This oversight is convenient for promoting medical treatments, which are highly lucrative for doctors, hospitals and clinics, not to mention the pharmaceutical companies.

However, having invested so heavily in focusing on the physical body, the ignoring of the rest of the wholistic spectrum becomes an ignorance that creates a distinct cognitive dissonance in doctors for anything related to the rest of their patients' beingness. Many doctors who disparage the various rainbows of other treatments, of which they know little or nothing, are completely sincere. They really believe what they are saying and that this is the best course their patients can follow.

This is a serious caution to you when you are seeking help for your issues. If you are considering complementary/ alternative therapies, take any disparaging opinions that your doctor presents with a serious grain of salt. Helpful questions to ask are:

"Are you speaking from opinion or from knowledge?"

"Have you experienced or studied these methods personally?"

"Are you familiar with the research on these methods?"

*In summary*

When people are deeply invested in their beliefs and disbeliefs, they will deal with contradictory beliefs that generate cognitive dissonance by seeking or even inventing confirmations, however far-fetched, to justify these beliefs. And they will do this even in the face of very strong evidence contradicting their views.

Much of the above is to put in perspective and explain some of the difficulties that many NHSPs experience in considering that it might be acceptable to have heightened sensitivities and emotions and to express them openly.

*WHAT ARE SOME OF YOUR POSITIVE AND NEGATIVE BELIEFS: IN YOUR FAMILY?*

*IN YOUR CHOICES OF FRIENDS?*

*ABOUT RAISING CHILDREN?*

*IN YOUR PROFESSION?*

*IN THE WHOLISTIC SPECTRUM?*

*HAVE YOU EVER FOUND SOMETHING OF VALUE OUTSIDE YOUR COMFORT ZONES?*

*WHAT ARE SOME OF THE APPROACHES AND ISSUES MENTIONED SO FAR IN THIS BOOK THAT FEEL LIKE THEY ARE OUTSIDE YOUR COMFORT ZONES?*

*IF YOU IDENTIFY COMFORT OR DISCOMFORT ZONE ISSUES YOU FEEL ARE OUTMODED, YOU CAN SHIFT THESE BY USING EP METHODS, DECREASING NEGATIVITIES AND STRENGTHENING POSITIVITIES.*

## 15. Psychological trauma

*Unlike other...psychological disorders, the core issue in trauma is reality.*
— Bessel A. van der Kolk

Many of their HSP sensitivities and behaviors may bring HSPs to ask, when considering the frequent and varied challenges they experience in getting along with the NHSP majority, "How did I get into this challenging situation?" and "How in the world am I going to deal with this?" Very often, the answers to these questions are related to traumas HSPs have experienced, both recent and in earlier periods in their lives.*[63] HSPs are very, very sensitive to being hurt and traumatized, and in my clinical experience are more prone to suffer from residues of their traumas that significantly impact their lives, for longer periods of time than NHSPs generally will experience. If we want to understand HSPs, we absolutely must have a solid grasp on what happens when people experience traumas, both major and minor.

People respond to stresses and negative experiences in varieties of ways. Conventional medicine, psychiatry and psychotherapy have developed detailed diagnoses to categorize the residues of traumas.

Let's examine a spectrum of problems that result from traumas. An impending trauma initially sets off alarms in a person's mind, emotions and body. Anxieties and fears trigger the body into releasing stress hormones, such as adrenaline and cortisol. These make the heart beat faster, raise the pulse rate and blood pressure, and tense up the muscles – preparing us to fight or flee. At the same time, anxieties heighten our sensory awarenesses so that we can better see and hear any dangers that might threaten us.

Because HSPs are very sensitive, they may respond with considerable intensely to these inner alarms. They may feel overwhelmed – far more quickly and strongly than NHSPs who are responding to similar situations. HSPs tend to experience the traumas more intensely. It also takes HSPs longer to calm down and unwind, unless they have learned to use de-stressing techniques, in which case they may calm down much more quickly than the average NHSP.

Most importantly, HSPs retain intense and vivid memories of the impacts of stresses and traumas. If they find themselves in situations that are in any ways similar to those of the original trauma scenario, their inner alarms go off very quickly and loudly. It can also take them a long time to calm down when they are triggered.

*AGAIN, A CAUTION TO ANY SENSITIVE READERS: GRAPHIC DETAILS ARE DESCRIBED IN THE NEXT CASE.***[64]

When you have scary, upsetting experiences or witness others undergoing such challenges, it may be difficult for you to recover from these. You may respond with serious distress even when something dangerous didn't really happen, because this scared you as though it had actually happened. Precipitating events might include:

- Violence of any sort
- Experiencing trauma, such as being in an auto accident or war zone
- Being threatened by someone or by circumstances, such as being the victim of a holdup or nearly having a traffic accident

- Experiencing or witnessing someone's anger getting out of control, even if it isn't directed at you
- Experiencing emotional, physical or sexual abuse
- Feeling or being out of control
- Nearly falling down a flight of stairs, going into a hospital for surgery, or being in a crowd that gets rowdy
- Having someone out of control in your family, due to their poor controls over their emotions or behaviors – including alcoholism or drug abuse
- Having someone in your family seriously ill
- Losing someone close to you
- Death of a family member or friend
- Moving to a new home and losing touch with family or close friends

You may find it difficult to recover from such experiences, which are formally labeled as a post traumatic stress disorder (PTSD). They may replay in your memory and feelings and you may get triggered back into these scared reactions by similar occurrences in the future. Seeing a film or being exposed to a news report about violence could be such a trigger.**[65]

You might even forget the original issue that started you along this path of being traumatized, as part of your inner defenses in dealing with your trauma. At a subsequent time, even years later, these feelings might surface without apparent reason, or might be triggered by anything similar that you experience.

You may experience a variety of trauma symptoms, including:
- Vague distress, anxieties and fears that are out of proportion to what is going on in your life
- Flashbacks to the trauma
- Difficulties concentrating
- Phobias around things that remind you of the original situation.
- Irritability, restlessness, agitation, impatience, anger, insomnia – without apparent cause, or with minimal irritations
- Feeling 'out of it,' disconnected or unable to experience pleasant and/or unpleasant emotions
- Feeling distanced from people, unwanted, unlikable, unacceptable, unsafe, or being unable to trust anyone
- Isolating yourself and pushing away people who reach out to you
- Dulling your senses with alcohol, drugs, mindless computer games or TV shows
- Depression – from a mild but apparently unprovoked 'downer' to full-blown blues, with difficulties mustering energies to do anything, loss of appetite, insomnia
- Engaging in self-injury, such as cutting yourself, overeating
- Struggling with suicidal thoughts and plans

✦✦ Bonnie, the sensitive child described earlier, had experienced relatively mild traumas at home with her brothers. She was upset and agitated when they were loud or angry, and moreso when they got into physical fights. She was both relieved and again frightened when her father stepped in and yelled at them to settle down. Her most intense stress reactions were when her father physically pulled them apart when they were fighting. It could take Bonnie several hours to calm down after witnessing an altercation like that.

Any time the boys got loud or angry, Bonnie felt flooded with anxieties. She couldn't think straight, and found modest relief in occupying herself with a physical activity like walking the dog, doing her bathroom cleaning chores, or volunteering to help her mom by picking up something at the convenience store. Her mother understood and supported her in distancing herself from these situations that upset her, and in releasing some of her anxieties through physical exertions. Her father was much less understanding, and would berate her for not participating in keeping the peace at home, since she was the older sister.

These sensitivities carried over to Bonnie's experiences in school, as well as in social activities. She was jarred into silence when her peers were loud, rowdy or aggressive. Her anxiety levels rose so high, so quickly, that she couldn't think clearly.

✦ 'Ken' was a gentle, quiet, sensitive child. He suffered all through his lower school years from being bullied by other children, who called him a crybaby and would tease him mercilessly to make him cry. His father and several teachers urged him to stand up to the bullies, but he would never resort to aggression himself, no matter what the provocations. At home, his older brother and two sisters kept telling him he just had to get over it and move on, and not dwell so much on his feelings.

In middle school he was finally referred to a counsellor by a teacher who realized Ken was much brighter than his grades showed him to be, and who realized how traumatized Ken was by the bullying she witnessed herself. When Miss 'Baker,' his counselor, spoke with Ken's other teachers, they were dismissive and disparaging of Ken's problems, blaming him for not controlling his emotions and saying it was about time he learned to grow up. So Miss Baker got the vice principal to intervene with the bullies' parents, which significantly lessened the bullies' harassing of Ken.

Though the bullying was decreased, as far as his counselor could see, Ken remained very quiet in his classes. He was fortunate to have Miss Baker available to help with tapping methods for releasing his trauma memories and ongoing fears of being bullied again. Ken was particularly grateful to be able to tap quietly and discretely in class, when he felt he was under the spotlight and when he experienced further incidents of bullying. Both his participation and grades improved significantly before the end of the school term.

Children often release any of their issues very quickly. It would be wonderful if EP methods could be taught in schools as preventives for suffering and overwhelm with anxieties, stress, distress and trauma.

✦ 'Jerri' was an extroverted, popular, HSP young woman who was very sensitive to emotions in herself and in others. She had enjoyed a happy childhood and had warm memories of her school years, where she excelled academically and had a busy and satisfying social life. Jerri's first job was with a theater promotions agency. Her outgoing, pleasant personality made her a natural in this work. She ran into a serious snag, however, when a producer was very brusque and angry with her when she misunderstood what he was saying. Jerri managed to sort out the issues he raised in a satisfactory way. However, she couldn't let go of worrying about this incident, replaying the scenario again and again in her mind, asking herself what she had done wrong and how she might have done better. She found the whole experience so stressful that she decided to quit her job.

Fortunately, Jerri's NHSP partner, Bob, had a sister who was a policewoman and had experienced serious traumas in the line of duty. Though Jerri's trauma was much milder, Bob recognized the similarities in Jerri's stress responses to those his sister had experienced. He was able to help Jerri calm herself, recommending that she see a therapist to learn to deal better with stressful situations.

As with many HSP people I've helped, Jerri very quickly learned to release her anxieties with TWR/WHEE. It was not a surprise to find that she had also had a negative interaction at age 8 with an after-school dance instructor. This teacher was a strict disciplinarian and an angry person. The issue was resolved in that case by Jerri's mother immediately removing her from the class. However, Jerri was still carrying a level 9 (out of 10) intensity of painful memories from this childhood experience, which is why she probably had such a strong reaction to her theater agency incident. A single tapping session sufficed to clear Jerri's troublesome issues from her current and earlier experiences and to resource her with tools for dealing better with any future encounters of these sorts.

Self-criticism is a common issue for HSPs, as they replay their experiences in their minds repeatedly. Their emotional sensitivities leave them vulnerable to being stressed and traumatized more easily on the one hand. Their strong connections with their feelings may also lead to worsening of the effects of the traumas with time, as they keep replaying them in their memories or as they get triggered by further experiences that are similar to the original trauma. On the other hand, their keen awarenesses of their emotions can enable them to connect with, identify and clarify their issues and clear them relatively quickly when they have the self-healing tools and/or therapy enabling them to do so.

HSP and NHSP companions can be enormously helpful to traumatized HSPs in these sorts of situations, offering feedback, suggestions, and support to enable HSPs to identify, address and clear their issues more quickly.

AGAIN, A CAUTION TO ANY SENSITIVE READERS**[66] The next example is of a severe post traumatic stress reaction.

✦ 'Ted' returned from his tour of duty in the infantry in Iraq a broken man. He had witnessed seven of his buddies killed, and more serious injuries than he could count. He shook his head slowly when asked how he managed to survive, saying, "I don't know why God didn't take me out of my misery along with the others who didn't make it."

At 22, he was devastated to find himself such a wreck of a man. He was irritable, easily triggered into violent rages by minimal provocations or, when drinking heavily, by his moodiness and depression. Most nights, he had to drink himself into a stupor to fall asleep, but he still often woke, screaming, with nightmares that replayed bloody scenes he had witnessed.

Ted was unable to tolerate being around his family, who were terribly distressed and saddened to find him in this condition. Prior to his tour of duty, he had been very close with his parents and his older and younger sisters, but now he stayed away from them because he felt too guilty for lashing out at them in anger over little or nothing. They did everything they could to facilitate his going to a Veteran's hospital for treatment, but after his first experience with heavy duty psychiatric drugs he refused, saying "If I'm going to be halfway dead, I might as well go the whole way. I don't want to have the easy means to overdose myself."

Ted was very lucky. His family persisted in searching for ways to help, and were able to connect him with an EP therapist who specialized in helping people with post traumatic stress disorders (PTSDs). In under two months, he was sometimes beginning to be recognizable as his old self – friendly, warm and caring. He couldn't praise his tapping treatments too highly. They not only enabled him to release his trauma memories and feelings during his sessions, but he was also able to do the tapping on his own, whenever he needed it. He felt that tapping away his horrors after waking from nightmares was absolutely the best part of it, though his family were quick to point out the many other benefits, including his being able to visit with them for brief periods before he 'lost it' by being triggered with what they felt were inconsequential issues, but which he obviously found intolerable.

Ted was truly lucky in another way. His therapist warned him ahead of time that his recovery might come in waves and stages, with occasional setbacks. And indeed, this is what he experienced. The worst of these were the waves of grief he had to work through over the deaths of his closest buddies.

Long story short, Ted was able, four months into his therapy, to return to the factory job he had held prior to enlisting, and his improvements continued steadily to a point of pretty full recovery by his sixth month. He reported wryly to his family that he seemed to be a slow learner, because other veterans in his therapy group had managed fuller recoveries in 2-3 months. It was only later, when Ted met another very sensitive veteran in his group, that he could come to accept that he, himself, was an HSP. At that point he stopped being so critical of himself.

Ted was indeed lucky. Not only did he survive his tour of duty, but he also found the help he needed for a full recovery from his PTSD. A lot of credit goes to his family, who had always supported him and continued to be so throughout his return from the horrors of war traumas. More on this below.

*HAVE YOU HAD TRAUMAS THAT LEFT YOU EXTRA-SENSITIVE TO PARTICULAR SITUATIONS OR ISSUES?*

*WHAT ARE WAYS YOU CAN CLARIFY AND CLEAR THESE?*

A word of caution here to therapists, family members and friends of veterans. Veterans have a very high rate of suicide. More soldiers in the US and Canada are dying of suicide than died on the battlefields. To a great extent, this appears to be a largely unnecessary outcome of military PTSDs. Recent research in EP shows that these soldiers can be helped to rapidly and thoroughly release their severe trauma residues with tapping techniques (Church, et al., 2017). Sadly, the military and veterans' associations have been resistant to the inclusion of EP in the treatment of soldiers' and veterans' PTSDs. Other approaches that they use demonstrate very limited benefits for PTSD. So here is yet another case of cognitive dissonance or neuroplastic blindness. Similarly, EMDR can help with deep releases of PTSDs.[67] *[68]

### *Dealing with traumas*

It is very sad that the most common approach to dealing with trauma in conventional healthcare is to medicate the trauma symptoms. It is reprehensible that conventional medicine and many psychotherapists very commonly overlook the person's experienced traumas behind their current symptoms.

Yes, it is helpful to control strong reactions to trauma. But this is like tightening the lid on a pot that is boiling over rather than turning the fire down under it. Clearing trauma memories and symptoms is far better than putting a lid on them.

This is more here than just a question of clinical preferences for different approaches to dealing with traumas. Medications are actually not indicated as the best option for treatment of traumas in many cases where pediatricians, family doctors, and psychiatrists prescribe them. Yes, drugs can make it somewhat more possible for people to function in their schools, jobs and homes. In war zones these may be lifesaving, preventing self-injury and suicide. Often, however, in civilian settings, these medications not only dull the stress and trauma responses, they dull the whole of a person's consciousness. And the side effect of increased weight is hugely problematic, particularly to younger people. These criticisms are valid regarding the majority of people receiving medication prescriptions for trauma symptoms, but this is an even more severe challenge with HSPs.

HSPs are often very sensitive to medications. Even when medications might be appropriate for easing the psychological symptoms of traumas, HSPs very often get serious side effects with normal doses of drugs – whose normality is determined by their effects on the majority of the populations tested. These norms are based for the most part on the 80-85% of the population who are NHSPs.

And even if the medications do function appropriately when they are prescribed, they are still seriously contraindicated because they do not eliminate, and may actually mask the awareness of the severity of the psychological traumas that are experienced. This leaves people vulnerable to enormous risks of extremely serious long-term effects of the traumas, including suicide. And the drugs give people the most commonly used method for suiciding. More on this below.

### *Bullying, belittling, pathologizing and traumas of rejection experienced by HSPs*

Bullying is an enormously important but too commonly neglected and ignored form of trauma. Sadly, many NHSPs are very uncomfortable with emotions in general, and with their own emotionality in particular. And if they weren't born with this NHSP tendency to avoid emotions, this is a common attitude acquired by children who are discouraged from expressing their feelings. This is done with good intent (on the conscious level) by the NHSPs, who want to help their children not suffer from uncomfortable feelings. But then the children come to see any expression of emotions as a weakness.

NHSPs will often tease, belittle and bully HSPs who express their feelings openly. In silencing HSPs, the NHSP bullies experience a degree of control over other people's feelings. This offers a small measure of compensation for their own unconscious feelings of inadequacy and helplessness to deal with their own emotionality or traumas. HSP boys in particular suffer from this form of bullying. They are often teased and taunted for being crybabies, wimps and wusses. By putting others down, the bullies feel themselves to be stronger.[69]

Another stimulus for bullying comes from traumas that the bullies experienced. It is very typical for traumatized people to traumatize others.

Bullying often occurs in school or in other places outside the home. If you have no one to protect you or at least to comfort you, you are at risk of carrying varieties of buried trauma memories and feelings from such painful experiences – particularly if you are an HSP.

Such bullying may occur as well among family members. HSPs may be bullied by their NHSP siblings, or criticized and belittled by parents and other adults in the family for being emotional. These HSPs may come to feel there is something wrong with them because they can't control their emotions like others in their family are doing.

Of course, there are expectations that we won't be pouring out our feelings on every occasion when we experience them. But it is frustrating and painful to sensitive individuals to be coerced into limiting their expressions of feelings to suit the comfort levels of other people. And when HSPs are pressured to not be themselves this may be traumatic – leaving them with fears of expressing their emotions and with meta-anxieties that they are somehow abnormal for having feelings. And for strong HSPs, this is an exquisite torture, because feeling their emotions and expressing them is core to the essence of their being.

And you may continue to carry such leftover hurts and traumas, festering inside you like pus in a boil. When people hurt you, this can also stimulate the memories of other hurts from the past. As a part of your trauma response, you may then strike out at others without even being aware of the buried feelings that are being triggered, adding fuel and intensity to your fired-up emotions. Such misdirected feelings, which have their origins in angers at people and situations that are not directly related to your current situation, are typical of PTSD. They can erode and damage your relationships.

*A CAUTION TO ANY SENSITIVE READERS: GRAPHIC DETAILS ARE DESCRIBED IN THE NEXT CASE.*\*\*[70] *BUT IT HAS A LOT ABOUT CLEARING NEGATIVITY AND CREATING POSITIVITY IN ONE'S LIFE.*

✦ When 'Gail,' an HSP, was 18, in the middle of her senior year in high school, her parents died in an auto accident. She had no other family or close adult friends and had to fend for herself.

In a way, it was a relief to have her father gone, because he had been a verbally abusive alcoholic all of her life, on frequent occasions punctuating his abuse of Gail and her mother with slaps, and of Gail with spankings. Her mother had been abused similarly in childhood and was unable to offer more than a shrug in support, with the advice that Gail just had to suck it up because it was never going to change.

And you probably won't be surprised to hear that when Gail entered puberty, her father came home drunk one Saturday night and raped her. She never knew where she got the crazy idea or the courage to do this, but the rape was a last straw that somehow, somewhere in her consciousness just snapped her into the determination that this was an insult she simply wasn't ready to tolerate happening again. She knew her mother would do nothing, which was going to add further insult to injury. So she literally took matters into her own hands. When her father passed out after the rape, lying on his back, snoring on her bed, she got a kitchen knife and scraped a shallow arrow, pointing from his upper belly down to his pubis. He hardly moved as she did this. When he woke up next day she told him, "If you ever do anything to me like that again, I will cut off your dick when you pass out, before I call the police. And if they put me away for doing that, well at least I won't have to lose sleep over its ever happening again."

And it didn't. His verbal abuse continued, but he never laid a hand on her again. And after that, she found she was also less scared by his verbal abuses, though she still found it impossible to concentrate and hard to fall asleep when he came home drunk.

She buried herself in studies and as many organized after-school activities away from home and study nights with classmates at the nearby university library as possible. She had only a few friends who, like her, suffered from severely dysfunctional families, and would come to the library till closing hours, like Gail did, just to avoid being at home. She commiserated with them about her awful home life, but was never very close with any of these girls.

Gail had to leave school to work as a waitress in a hotel restaurant to support herself. Her ex-schoolmates were initially supportive to a very modest degree, but she had little time or inclination for socializing, and very quickly lost touch with them. She was very bright and had good survival skills. Situations that were challenging in the restaurant were a piece of cake to her, compared to the difficulties she had faced and survived at home. Over a period of six years she was given support and training by the hotel manager, who had taken a liking to her. She was promoted to be the youngest restaurant assistant manager in the hotel chain. She was very proud of herself for working, getting her high school diploma, and successfully completing courses in business management and accounting, in addition to the hotel's training.

While work and studies were islands of stability in Gail's life, her personal life was very disappointing. She contacted me for help at age 22, after a careful internet search. She liked the idea of having self-healing tools for her problems. Her presenting issue was that she couldn't seem to find a man to date who didn't turn out to be abusive in some ways. "Even when a guy looks perfectly good and kind, every single one I pick turns out to have a temper, or a mean streak, or is basically selfish and self-centered – once he gets past first base and into my pants. I always end up uncovering the disappointing loser buried behind what seemed to be a promising winner."

Gail's lifelong experience of abuse took two years of individual sessions to address to a point of resolution. Gail, for all of being a smart and successful survivor of abuse, and perfectly competent in handling confrontations in her professional life, was unconsciously drawn to men who turned out to be abusive in one or more ways. Gail used to explode in anger when she came to feel she was just being used as a sexual partner or an emotional punching bag, and quickly terminated these relationships. She would then spend weeks analyzing and re-playing her mental tapes of what had happened. She so wanted to get it right and have a decent relationship! Gradually, Gail learned to recognize the warning signs in her potential boyfriends' attitudes and interactions and was able to end the relationships before they reached a flashpoint of explosive anger.

Here are some of the approaches Gail particularly appreciated:

- Building a place of peace and safety and healing where she could feel nurtured and safe*71
- Using two-chair work,*72 combined with TWR/WHEE*73 to re-parent 'Little Gail' to:
  - Release her memories of constant, low-grade fear, with episodes of terror and pain when her father got violent and slapped or spanked her and raped her
  - Vent her buried feelings of helplessness and being unloved and unwanted – other than as a beating post
  - Release her deep disappointment and despair over her mother's passivity, realizing her mother had probably suffered as much as she had, or more.
  - Feel safe, accepted, loved and protected by "Gail of Today"
  - Forgive her mother for when Gail sensed her feeling relieved that Gail was the target of her father's anger at times, rather than her mother being the beating post of that day
  - Forgive herself for sometimes in childhood thinking that by 'letting' her father abuse her she was helping him feel better
  - Install positive thoughts and feelings about herself as Little Gail and as Gail of Today.
- Releasing meta-anxieties and negative beliefs that blocked Gail from making better choices in dates and potential partners, using her tapping*74
- Going back in her memories to times she had felt particularly vulnerable and abused as a child and using Two-chair explorations and TWR/WHEE for clearing her trauma memories and feelings
- Her relationship with me as her therapist was enormously helpful and healing to Gail in:
  - Finding acknowledgments of and validations for her suffering throughout her childhood
  - Experiencing acceptance of her HSP traits, particularly her emotional sensitivity, empathy (even for her father and mother – in retrospect), and her disappointments in many of her childhood friends for their insensitivities to her suffering

- The experience of being in a therapeutic relationship with a male therapist was particularly healing, though not without a lot of testing and checking on whether I was being humanly honest – and not just playing the supportive role that a therapist was supposed to play with clients.

– Helpful wordings and imagings in Gail's clearing and healing process:
  - PPSH – An isolated, absolutely impregnable mountain retreat built of steel. Doors opened only on Gail's voice command. A self-contained inner environment, included endless supplies of anything and everything needed to support a comfortable and safe life. "I'm perfectly safe here. Always!"
  - Releasing – "I always have to be careful and on guard, looking for early warning signs of anger in people around me, just like I always did any time daddy was at home."

  "There is no one I can ask for help when I'm being treated unfairly or being abused."

  "There is no one I can trust to protect me."

  "If I trust someone I'll only get hurt."
  - Installing – "It was my father's own trauma that led him to abuse me and my mother, rather than something about me and my mother that was bad or wrong and deserved his abusive punishments."

  "I can know a man cares about me without the intense negativity I experienced from my father, and which I witnessed from my father towards my mother."

  "Gail of Today is smart enough and strong enough to protect me."

  "I can (later, replaced by "I will") allow myself to be with someone who will love, honor and protect me."

But Gail continued to make poor choices in dating men and could not see how to further refine her interpersonal radar to pick a winner from the endless pool of losers she seemed to attract. It was not until she realized she had given up hoping she would ever deserve or have a positive, loving relationship and also installed and strengthened a variety of positive thoughts and feelings about herself that she was able to find and establish dating relationships with the kind, considerate, caring men she was seeking.

– She then worked on identifying and releasing meta-anxieties and beliefs, such as:
  - "No matter what I say or do, I could never change my father from being the angry, abusive person he was, and I'll never be able to have anyone else in my life who shows he cares for me in positive ways."
  - "I have to resign myself to the fact that I'll never be free of being abused."
  - "There's something basically wrong with me, because my father was totally rejecting of me and abusive, and my mother never loved me enough to protect me from his abuse."

– Helpful, positive affirmations she installed:
  - "I deserve to have a deeply caring, kind, considerate man as my friend and partner."

- "I am a kind, considerate, sensitive person, lovable just the way I am."
- "My boyfriend can and will like me for who I am."

− Particular attention was given to stating the positives as positives, rather than as negatives of negatives. For example, "I don't have to be on guard with a boyfriend all the time to watch for the earliest signs of anger." was reframed as "I can let go of looking constantly for signs of anger and impending abusiveness."

To her deep delight, Gail started to be attracted to and to attract to herself more positive, caring, considerate men, who demonstrated their caring through gentle, kind words and actions. Within a year she was in a committed relationship with 'Bill,' who was six years older than her. However, she still was very cautious in continuing to test the as-yet unfamiliar waters of a deepening relationship with this gentle, supportive, caring man. While she consciously hesitated to commit to a marriage, after two years in this relationship she "forgot" to take her birth control pills and found herself pregnant. She had continued to check in with me about every 3-6 months and was able to see that her unconscious mind was giving her a green light to finally tie the knot and commit to marrying. The last I heard from Gail, about four years into her marriage, she was deeply satisfied with her relationship and smilingly able to accept my compliments on the good work she had done on herself.

Gail was unusual in being able sort out her life as well and as relatively quickly as she did. Many HSPs end up more seriously and deeply scarred emotionally and have greater difficulties in recovering from such traumas. The earlier we can intervene, the more we can offer help to HSP children and young adults who have experienced such traumas, as well as disparagements and discouragements about their being sensitive. It is extremely helpful to deeply wounded children and adults when you:

− Acknowledge they're feeling hurt, angry, rejected or upset in any other ways
− Invite them to share what is upsetting them
− Help them identify the feelings that were triggered that led to their anger
− Guide them in using releasing methods such as Energy Psychology to decrease the intensity of the issues they were upset about their traumas
− Role-play with them what happened, inviting them to alternate taking each side of the situation.
− Install positive feelings and thoughts to replace the negative ones they have released.
− Invite them to consider what they might say or do differently if they 'rewind the video of what happened'.
− Review what happened, putting it in a framework such as "I know you are sensitive and reacting to what is happening around you."
− Review any memories they may have of similar upsets in the past. Clear these as well with similar approaches.
− With practice, it becomes easy to 'bundle' issues from the present with issues from the past, clearing both at the same time. For many, particularly HSPs, clearing with bundling of past and present issues works more quickly and deeply than clearing each on its own.

Imagine what our world might be like if such self-healing methods were taught in schools. EP self-healing approaches are particularly helpful for dealing with emotional upsets, bullying, exam anxieties, social anxieties, fears of shootings, and other issues.

Imagine if schools devoted time for developing emotional awareness and emotional intelligence. You might think at first that the average school curriculum wouldn't have time for teaching emotional intelligence on top of all the required subjects. You may be interested to know that in Finland, whose schools are rated as the best in the Western world, classes are held only 3-4 hours per day (Moore, 2015). There can be plenty of time for learning life lessons in a school curriculum, in addition to learning the essentials of basic reading, writing and number manipulations!

Once you have ways to calm yourself, you can look for your best options in dealing with bullies. Responding with anger may be helpful if you are coming from a place of strength and centeredness – letting the bullies know you're not a meek or helpless scapegoat. If you are not physically strong enough, centered and confident, anger may work to your disadvantage, as bullies love to wear a person down in order to build themselves up.

There are simple methods you can learn to counteract bullying. Brooks Gibbs, a bullying expert points out that responding to the bullying with humor, compliments and acceptance can completely disarm the bully. He has videos that are well worth watching to start you on your path of being able to stand up to a bully.[75]

Bullying or sexual harassment in schools and in the workplace should not be tolerated. People in charge should be held accountable for dealing with bullies.

*Resentments, oppositional behaviors and vengefulness*

Much as we would like to have everything go well between us in our close relationships, our human nature and psychological makeup are such that there can be times when we have issues with those who are close to us. This can happen in HSPC-HSP relationships.

Some of the issues develop out of differences between HSPs and HSPCs in personalities, lifestyle habits and ways of communicating. Often, we didn't pay attention to these little issues initially, as they hardly seemed worth mentioning. In the glow of early times of togetherness, these differences paled in comparison with the good experiences we were enjoying together. You may have agreed tacitly to modify your behaviors or to tolerate behaviors of your partner out of sincere consideration for his sensitivities and preferences. And you may have been on your best behaviors with each other, watching out for each other's needs and preferences, and slowly, with the passing of time, you've come to accept your togetherness as solid, and relax your attention to these relatively minor details.

With time, however, such issues grate upon us and we can build up resentments. Or there may be particular interactions that trigger us into trauma feelings and memories. In either case, we may become irritable, angry and vindictive over issues that we accepted without issues in the early blooming of our relationships.

Another path may open into resentments in HSPC-HSP relationships at times when pressures build up and caring feelings are not shared, or perhaps inconsiderate or disrespectful things are said or done, and any of these may generate resentments. Or bunches of little hurts may accumulate, which then feel like big ones.

It's not unusual to want to hurt someone else back when you have been hurt. This is a common experience but not one that is commonly considered in discussions of healing. I feel it is well worth addressing here because the methods we've been considering are so rapidly, deeply and thoroughly effective in clearing and transforming such issues.

We may be surprised to find that what we accept as normal for ourselves, and was normal in our families of origin, is not acceptable to the special person we're living with. And resentments and disagreements can be stirred over serious issues or about the most trivial choices that trigger us into unexpectedly, and sometimes unexplainably sharp resentments. I've seen this happen with:

- Leaving breakfast and lunch dishes in the sink, to be washed with dinner dishes
- Hanging towels out over the shower curtain rod to dry rather than on the towel rack
- Driving within the posted speed limits – to save gas, as a matter of environmental responsibility
- Paying bills when they are received – to avoid forgetting them, rather than on their due dates
- Visiting with family of origin relatives vs. celebrating on your own as a couple, with friends and family of choice, and common points of friction over frequency, duration and/or timing of visits, e.g. on state or religious holidays

Resentments that arise but are not expressed, clarified and sorted out can often be like gritty dirt that somehow got into an otherwise smoothly working machine. There may be many reasons for holding back your expressions of resentment. Some are wise and considerate, such as:

- You, the HSP, could feel jarred by the loudness of music that your NHSP husband revels in, but you might hesitate to complain about this in the early stages of your togetherness.
- You, the NHSP HSPC might hold back from playing the loud music you enjoy, knowing your HSP is bothered by loud sounds.
- You may hold back from arguing over visiting your partner's family when there is illness or other stress in his family.
- You might accept that your partner, who left home for the first time when you and she moved into your own place, is homesick and needs to learn to adapt to new relationships with family. Her pace may be slower than you, yourself can easily manage, as you went away to university and sorted out those issues much earlier.

With time, and as the first glorious bloom of togetherness starts to fade, these and similar concessions may start to grate on you. You may feel you are making a lot of concessions but are not having your special sensitivities and wishes honored sufficiently. Resentments start to fester and build up, like pus in a boil. You may feel tense (emotionally and physically), irritable or out of sorts. You may occasionally forget to honor your commitment to do or not do this or to show her consideration in particular ways.

Avoiding speaking about these or not sitting down to deal with them is like ignoring a boil on your elbow. After a while you may find painful red lines of infection spreading ominously up your arm. You will realize that something has to be done, or this may grow into a serious challenge between you.

And these negativities can be infectious. Your behaviors then generate resentments on her part. She starts to ignore promises and commitments, or lets you know – either verbally or through other behaviors – that she is upset. You may get upset and vent your angers with each other over anything or everything. Moving into vengefulness can become quite nasty and painful.

*WHAT ARE RESENTMENTS YOU'VE FELT IN YOUR RELATIONSHIPS?*

*WHAT ARE YOUR USUAL WAYS OF DEALING WITH THESE?*

*WHAT MIGHT BE BETTER WAYS YOU COULD HANDLE YOUR RESENTMENTS?*

The first time something like this happens is often the worst you'll experience. Once you sit down together and discuss the issues you're experiencing and your feelings about them, you can often come to understandings about how your problems came about, why you each felt upset in the ways you did, and how you can move forward with renewed or revised agreements for dealing with what has festered and come to a boil.

Again, I recommend using self-calming methods to release stresses, angers, resentments and other negativity. This can enormously facilitate your sorting out your issues with each other in more gentle, caring and harmonious ways. Particularly helpful self-healing approaches are EP, NLP, P.E.T., relaxation and meditation.*[76]

*Trauma residues – mild to moderate*

Psychological traumas, for instance, from physical injuries, may leave emotional scars. In many cases the residual painful memories and feelings are minor and, again like physical injuries, these heal without leaving much of a memory or emotional trace. This can be true even when the experienced issues and your emotional responses felt like major, life-changing experiences when they occurred. Think of some of the transitions in your life that may have been challenging and difficult to deal with:

- Giving up your role of favorite, favored or youngest child when a younger brother or sister is born
- Graduating from one school year or level to the next
- Moving from one neighborhood/school/city to another
- Good friends moving away and disappearing from your life
- Parents separating and/or divorcing
- Losing a job you like and/or find satisfying and profitable

Changes such as these can trigger various intensities of stress reactions. Mild traumas tend to dissipate on their own. We often heal from these mild emotional wounds without great efforts or attention to them.

What feel like hugely important and impacting events at the time can mellow and lessen substantially, as you adapt to your new circumstances. You are then able to release the hurt and move on to feel better about your losses, whatever caused or contributed to them, and about yourself.

- Learning to appreciate and enjoy being an older brother or sister

- Discovering and enjoying the benefits or your new neighborhood, school and geographic location
- Finding ways to keep touch with your good friends who moved away
- Coming to understand and accept the reasons your parents separated or divorced
- Finding new, unexpected benefits and enjoyment in a new job

Moderately intense trauma may leave us feeling wounded and in need of support and healing. We may not have the energies or inclination to engage in our new surroundings and situations. Strong trauma reactions may leave us incapacitated. In such cases self-healing methods and therapy may be enormously helpful.

Grief may also play a part in such trauma situations. In many cases, the process of grief may simply be a natural part of recovering from trauma. However, if the current grief stirs other experiences of grief that were not processed to a point of resolution, this may markedly worsen the trauma and require additional attention and energies for healing.*[77]

HSPs often find the changes involved in life's transitions more challenging than NHSPs do. HSP trauma reactions are stronger, and there may be more trauma residues, even with what NHSPs would consider milder losses. Traumatized HSPs may have difficulties concentrating and remembering, may be slow and reluctant to speak up, and may be hesitant to engage in new relationships, all of which may make poor impressions on new acquaintances and in new situations. These are some of the reasons HSPs may find transitions and other life changes difficult to deal with.

Worse yet, when HSPs find themselves in group transitions, as in family moves, changes of schools or disruptive reorganizations in their workplace, they may suffer in comparison with NHSPs who just take these challenges in stride. These are times when HSPs are particularly vulnerable to being belittled, criticized for making mountains out of molehills, and put down as immature or attention seekers. These setbacks add insults and further injuries to the stresses of HSPs' transitions, which may become seriously traumatizing.

NHSPs as well as HSPs who are traumatized in these ways develop various strategies for dealing with their unhappy and painful feelings. Rather than fester in our trauma and hurt, we may bury the pain in our unconscious mind. With time, we put warning signs at some distance from the psychological memory file cabinet, to protect ourselves even more from going anywhere near this place of inner pain. So we may forget how painful it was to be hurt. But our unconscious mind remembers the whole story, and keeping it buried may prevent us from living our life to our fullest potential.

Paradoxically, by not feeling and releasing our traumas, rather than protecting ourselves from further pain:
- We never get to clear out and release the hurts we buried.
- We never feel our full spectrum of grief reactions.
- We never process the grief through to a point of resolution.
- The grief festers like a pus pocket of emotional infection.
- We wall off the buried feelings more and more.
- Our anti-feeling protective walls grow thicker and thicker.
- Our emotional life overall may be dimmed and muted behind these walls.

- We then avoid others who are expressing emotions.
- When those expressing emotions are family members who can't be avoided, we may discourage them from expressing their feelings altogether – to protect us from stirring the buried feelings we've been avoiding.
- In time, when there are several NHSPs in a family doing the same thing, it can become a family rule that "We don't express emotions in this family."
- This rule then makes it easier to bully the emotionally sensitive and emotionally open members of the family into not expressing their feelings, which would be outside the family rules and would make us uncomfortable.
- This rule then also serves to decrease cognitive dissonance that may be present around bullying a family member, as the bullies feel they are contributing to the family by standing by its unspoken rules.
- Sadly, when bullying occurs at home it may leave scars that cripple HSPs for much or all of their lives.

Bullying of HSPs is so common that it deserves further discussion. Outside the home, bullying is often better dealt with by persons in charge of the setting in which it occurs. Teachers and school administrators are often called upon to respond to bullying. Remedies include setting firm limits, encouraging other students to report the bullies, and involving the parents in setting limits on the bullying. Bullying in the workplace is also common. Sadly, some people in managerial positions are themselves bullies.

Bullies are unlikely to seek help themselves to deal with the underlying issues that lead them to be nasty to others. Remedies generally involve counseling and therapies for traumas that they have themselves experienced.

Bullying is traumatic to those who are the targets of the bullying. Therapies such as EP methods and EMDR are very effective in dealing with the emotional scars and damage to self-image that are commonly seen.

An HSPC can be enormously supportive in these life adjustments.
- First and foremost, acknowledging the HSPs expressions of feelings as legitimate, whatever they are, negative or positive.
- Just listening and letting your HSP verbalize the concerns and fears that are troublesome is helpful.
- If the feelings are intense, acknowledge they are strong ones.
- If they are upsetting, acknowledge that, too, and offer some reasons why you sense these feelings are understandable in the context in which they are being stimulated.
- If your traumatized partner has shared any details about his traumas, bullying or grief earlier in life, you might ask whether the feelings of today that are upsetting are resonating with those earlier experiences.
- For transition anxieties, you can invite descriptions, speculations and expectations of what might occur in the new situation.
- Ask about any feelings of loss over having left the old, known and comfortable situation.
- Ask whether your HSP ever went through a similar situation in the past. If this source of disappointment, anger, fear, sadness or other feelings is a repeating issue, you might point that out, as a clue that might clarify further whatever is going on.

- In cases of repeating traumas, you might invite exploration of what is the first memory of a repeating issue your HSP can recall. Working on the 'bookends' of similar traumas, that is, bundling the most current and earliest remembered instance of such issues and tapping on both together will often ease the intensity of memories of the intervening experiences as well. Bundled issues and feelings often clear more rapidly and deeply than individual ones do.
- If your HSP has acquired and successfully used particular de-stressing methods, you can ask if this might be a good time to practice them.
- You might offer or remind your HSP of the potential for self-calming by visiting their place of peace and safety and healing (PPSH).
- You can suggest using releasing techniques, such as alternating left and right tapping on the body for further releases of the emotions.
- When your HSP has released her anxieties and other feelings, invite her to picture positive situations and outcomes developing. Have her tap on these so that they are strengthened.

*Trauma residues – severe trauma reactions and long-term residues*

Various factors can contribute to more severe reactions to current traumas, such as: greater intensities of stress, greater sensitivities of the person experiencing the trauma, fewer inner and outer coping resources, and a past history with unresolved trauma issues.

A CAUTION TO ANY SENSITIVE READERS: DISTURBING DETAILS ARE DESCRIBED IN THE NEXT CASE.**[78] BUT AGAIN, THERE ARE HAPPY OUTCOMES.

✦ 'Manuel' and 'Maria' were in in their mid-fifties, having recently celebrated their thirty-fifth wedding anniversary. Manny was an HSP who had suffered many traumas in his life. His parents had immigrated from South America before he was born, and he was their oldest son. His mother had died of a rapidly growing brain tumor when he was eight years old. His eleven year-old sister had taken on the role of mother in his family, and his father had to work extra shifts to make ends meet. No other relatives were available to help. Manny had had to grow up quickly, taking on a paper route, then a grocery delivery job, and then construction work – as soon as he became able to manage these jobs.

Manny was both lucky and unlucky that his body matured early – lucky because he was better able to stand up for himself in a rough neighborhood, and unlucky because people expected more of him than he was ready or able to offer emotionally.

Manny was bright, and with the encouragement of his construction boss got his high school diploma in night school, seeking to gain just enough of an education to be able to be a construction foreman. His HSP sensitivities served him well in getting along with people, and his accelerated maturity into adulthood had offered him good opportunities for honing his social skills.

It was in night school that he met Maria, who had been raised in foster care because her father was violently abusive and had killed her mother in a drunken rage when she was six years old. Maria had been placed in a good foster home, with parents who were loving but of very limited means. She started working at age 14, helping her mother with housecleaning jobs after school, and then quit school at 16 to work full time. Like Manny, Maria was bright and had been encouraged by her family and friends to return to get her high school diploma, but had not managed to pull this together. With Manny's support and further encouragement, she was able to set up a modestly profitable cleaning business.

They were a very happily married couple. Each worked hard but they always kept their weekends free to have time with each other. And without putting words to their relationship, they were warmly supportive of each other. Though Maria was an NHSP, she was patient with Manny's moods and sensitivities. But they were disappointed in not having children despite many years of doing their best to conceive, with no apparent reasons for the infertility, despite extensive medical evaluations. And then, when Maria was 41 and they had given up all hope of being parents, Maria was almost afraid to believe that her missed period was not an early menopause.

They were wonderfully happy, devoted parents to their daughter. But their joy was cut short when 6 year-old Ariana, the light of their life, was struck and killed by a drunk driver on a Sunday morning, while playing on the sidewalk in front of their home.

Their grief was beyond description, beyond uttering or imagining. Maria, who had returned to work when Ariana entered first grade, was unable to manage even to get out of bed for many weeks. Manny did the housework in the evenings and on weekends. But he quietly turned to drinking wine and then whiskey to dull his emotional pain. Their family doctor's antidepressants and tranquilizers and sleeping pills just made each of them dopey and dull, but did nothing for their inconsolable grief. Manny's insurance paid for a brief series of psychotherapy sessions for each of them, but these had no effect on his moodiness, sadness and grief, nor on Maria's crying every time she looked out the window to the front of their home, where Ariana had crumpled in a bloody heap, never regaining consciousness.

A friend of Maria's recommended Kelly, an EFT practitioner, who saw them immediately, in consideration of their intense grief. As it turned out, this practitioner came for a WHEE workshop a few weekends later, and asked for suggestions on how to help these deeply bereft people – who were barely responding to EFT. I suggested, on principle, to explore whether there might be additional, unresolved grief in their lives, which Kelly confirmed in principle, based on their family histories.

By bundling and tapping on the earlier grief residues together with the current grief over the loss of their daughter, there was a distinct deepening of the releases. I also suggested they might work together for one or more of their EFT sessions, and this, too, facilitated their releases. Following their second joint session, they continued using the tapping therapy at home together, finding that this helped both of them much better than working on their own.

They were each very surprised to discover the depth and intensity of the residues lingering inside them from their own childhood traumas. Maria, in particular, had completely forgotten most of what she had witnessed and experienced with her father's violence. She had been terrified of being injured by her father for as long as she could remember, suffering repeated strappings and witnessing repeated beatings of her mother – culminating with his murder of her mother – the sounds of which she heard from another room, but the full import of which she did not understand until the next day. She stayed silently in her room that night, hoping to avoid her father noticing her and venting his anger upon her as well. The next morning, her father had gone out, and Maria found her mother crumpled on the sofa and unresponsive to Maria speaking to her or shaking her. Maria was the one who made the 911 call that started the process of her being placed in foster care. She never saw her father again – much to her relief. She later learned that he had been hospitalized in an institution for the criminally insane, where he died shortly after of unknown causes.

The loss of a child is ranked as the most intense grief a person can suffer. Few couples remain married after such a loss. Any previous, unresolved grief or traumas are almost always triggered as well by the loss of a child, thereby intensifying the grief reactions – as happened with Maria and Manny. What appears likely in retrospect is that the support which each had received following their childhood losses had also resourced them with skills for dealing with their later, tragic loss of their only child. And the solid bonds they had developed through the years of their devoted marriage were further strengths that sustained them and enabled them to be there emotionally for each other.

In my many years of clinical experience, the tapping therapies are the best interventions that I've ever found for most traumas. This couple were extremely fortunate to have had the benefits of EFT, taught by Kelly, a skilled therapist, to deal with their catastrophic loss of their daughter. Installing and strengthening positive thoughts and feelings was one of the benefits of EP to which they responded to best.

In addition, Manny's having grown up with loving, supportive parents; Maria's having had the good fortune to be in a good foster home; and having had each other's support for so many years, were all enormously helpful life experiences that enabled them to offer their continued support to each other and in their being able to accept each other's help. And making regular times to do their tapping together was very supportive as well.

> ✦✦ It took close to three years for Maria and Manny to work through their devastating grief to the point that they were able to sleep through most nights and no longer get triggered into crying by random reminders of their loss. They found it helpful to move to another home in the same neighborhood, maintaining relationships with supportive friends, while leaving many of the reminders of Ariana's tragic absence behind. Maria had had to sell her cleaning business, and in coming out of her depression decided she wanted to do something different. After much hesitation, deliberation, and soul-searching, she decided with Manny that they would become foster parents. When I last heard about them several years later, they were pleased with their decision – to the point of berating themselves for having resisted this option prior to Ariana's coming into their lives.

I have never ceased to marvel at the unexpected resilience of some people in dealing with horrendously devastating experiences. Had I been their therapist, I would have almost certainly cautioned this couple very strongly to carefully consider and ponder and reconsider their decision to become foster parents. In fostering children, there are very frequent unexpected events that create enormous pressures on the foster parents and children.

While foster parents may do everything they could reasonably be expected to do to create a nurturing environment and provide support for the children placed in their home, I've seen countless circumstances arise that led social services to remove children from foster placements. I would have anticipated that even the possibility of such an occurrence would be a serious deterrence to this couple taking on foster children. But Kelly, their EFT therapist, made a good call in supporting them in their decision. At the point when I last heard about them, around 10 years after Ariana's death, Kelly reported that they actually did extremely well in helping foster children with difficult trauma issues, teaching them EFT as a resource for dealing with current issues and ones triggered from the past.

*Research on long-term physical and psychological residues of PTSD*

While psychological residues of trauma were recognized as residual damage following experiences with disastrous impacts on people, there was little or no awareness in the conventional medical and psychological communities that PTSDs could have long-term negative effects on physical health as well. In 1998, research was published that identified serious, long-term, residual effects of childhood traumas. The Adverse Childhood Experiences (ACE) study was organized by doctors at Kaiser Permanente's San Diego care program and the US Center for Disease Control (CDC). The following summary is taken from a reader-friendly article in the Huffington Post (Stevens, web ref).

It all started when Vincent Felitti, MD, at Kaiser's obesity clinic in California, discovered that about half of his seriously obese patients had been sexually abused in childhood. He stumbled on this when he was seeking to clarify why people who were 300 to 500 pounds overweight would lose weight while actively engaged in the Kaiser weight loss program, but would then immediately regain the weight upon leaving the program – either upon completing it or by dropping out.

By coincidence, one of his obese patients disclosed that she had been sexually abused as a child, and that by being obese she was making herself unattractive so that she felt safe – because she was then unlikely to be sexually abused again.

Once he started to ask other obese patients about this, it became rapidly clear that a very high percent of them had been sexually abused early in life. For these women and men, the weight was a protection against repeated abuse because looking unattractive made them feel safer. Being overweight was also helpful to people who had been bullied, because they literally couldn't be pushed around as easily.

> Felitti didn't know this at the time, but this was the more important result – the mind-shift, the new meme [viral idea] that would begin spreading far beyond a weight clinic in San Diego. It would provide more understanding about the lives of hundreds of millions of people around the world who use biochemical coping methods – such as alcohol, marijuana, tobacco, drugs, food, sex, violence, work, thrill sports, or drugs like methamphetamines – to escape intense fear, anxiety, depression or anger.

Robert Anda, MD, an epidemiologist from the US Center for Disease Control (CDC), joined Felitti in setting up formal research at the Kaiser Center Care Program, where 50,000 people were seen annually for health assessments. They surveyed 17,421 people between 1995 and 1997 to explore the severity of their childhood traumas.

Their findings totally surprised them. The greater the numbers of childhood traumas, the greater the likelihood of developing adult diseases of just about every possible type.

Here is how they assessed the severity of childhood traumas. (You might be curious to see how you score on this test. Score 1 point for each of the following 10 factors you have experienced in your life. You are only scored one point per *type* of abuse you experienced, not per the number of multiple times you experienced abuses of any one kind or another.)

ABUSE
  Verbal/ psychological/ emotional
  Physical
  Sexual

NEGLECT
  Emotional
  Physical

DYSFUNCTIONAL HOUSEHOLD
  Mental illness
  A mother who experienced domestic violence
  Loss of a parent through separation, divorce or abandonment
  A family member who was incarcerated
  Substance abuse

The researchers were amazed to discover that the majority of people with a score of 4, "... were twice as likely to be smokers, 12 times more likely to have attempted suicide, seven times more likely to be alcoholic, and 10 times more likely to have injected street drugs..." Similarly, high scores were found for people with obesity and with drug use.

In addition, they were truly astounded to discover that people with serious *physical* problems also had ACE scores that were significantly higher than the scores of people without these physical problems. "Compared with people with zero ACEs, those with four categories of ACEs had a 240 percent greater risk of hepatitis, were 390 percent more likely to have chronic obstructive pulmonary disease (emphysema or chronic bronchitis), and a 240 percent higher risk of a sexually-transmitted disease." See Table 15-1 for further problems in later life that correlate with ACEs.

So it is now very clear that trauma in childhood contributes to a broad variety of very serious psychological and physical challenges later in life.

**Table 15 – 1. Adverse Childhood Experiences predispose to:**

| | |
|---|---|
| Fetal death | Risk for intimate partner violence |
| Depression | Suicide attempts |
| Poor academic achievement | Smoking |
| Poor work performance | Early initiation of smoking |
| Financial stress | Alcoholism and alcohol abuse |
| Early initiation of sexual activity | Illicit drug use |
| Adolescent pregnancy | Health-limited quality of life |
| Multiple sexual partners | Chronic obstructive pulmonary disease |
| Sexually transmitted diseases | Ischemic heart disease |
| Unintended pregnancies | Liver disease |
| Risk for sexual violence | |

This summary to my discussion of trauma is intended to alert you to the great importance of this topic.

It would also be interesting to know what percent of people in ACE studies are HSPs, and whether their experiences with trauma are any different in their long-term effects from those of NHSPs. I have found no research addressing these questions.

From the wholistic perspective of trauma, it is a natural assumption that the body reflects effects of psychological traumas. As noted earlier, emotional tensions are often locked into the body following physical trauma.

One mechanism for demonstrating links of trauma with physical symptoms is fairly simple and straight-forward. This is illustrated in a therapy called Neurolinguistic Programming (NLP).*[79] In NLP, you think of an emotionally painful or traumatic experience. At the same time, you touch a convenient part of the body with a finger. You might choose a spot on your thigh to do this. Hold the pressure with one finger on your thigh for a few seconds and then release the pressure but don't move your finger from just above that spot. Now release your attention from the emotionally painful or traumatic experience. Focus on thoughts and feelings of something that is neutral (such as what you ate at your last meal) and contemplate this for a few moments. Then press on the same spot you pressed before. See what you experience before reading further.

Usually, the negative issues and their associated feelings will return to your awareness as you press again on the original spot. In psychology, this is called classical conditioning. This was identified in the 1890's by Ivan Pavlov, a Russian researcher. He showed that when he rang a bell while feeding dogs, the dogs became conditioned to salivate at the sound of the bell, even when no food was presented to them.

So it appears very likely that in experiences of emotional trauma, a tension present somewhere in the body at the time of the trauma would become conditioned to memories and emotions associated with that trauma. If memories of the trauma persist, which they often do, then that part of the body is likely to become tense repeatedly. Eventually this may cause chronic pain. This could conceivably also create more serious problems through classical conditioning of the body to release stress hormones in association with the trauma memories and feelings. Stress hormones are known to contribute to the development of such problems as cardiovascular disorders and diabetes, among others.

The methods detailed in this book can offer enormous benefits to people with ACE traumas, and can thereby contribute as well to their physical recoveries and wellbeing.

While these associations between traumatic memories and feelings have been generally acknowledged in the complementary/ alternative therapies community, they have not been widely taught to conventional doctors, nurses and other conventional therapists. Physical symptoms are therefore almost always treated as physical problems of the body, ignoring the rest of the wholistic spectrum of associated issues.

You might wonder why I'm presenting such detailed discussions on wholistic aspects of trauma. I do so because trauma responses are so common and widespread that most people will experience them to some degree at some time in their lives. And HSPs are, because of their sensitivities, more prone to experience trauma when they are in tense, abusive or traumatic situations.

Trauma can often have horrendously destructive consequences in the lives of those who experience it. The psychological scars from traumas may become grossly obvious. The serious levels of trauma I am discussing are formally diagnosed as Post

Traumatic Stress Disorder (PTSD) in the Diagnostic and Statistical Manual (DSM-V) of the American Psychiatric Association (Staggs, web ref). The following description of PTSD is for people aged 7 and older.

*Criterion A: Traumatic event*
- Trauma survivors must have been exposed to actual or threatened death, serious injury or sexual violence
- The exposure can be direct, witnessed, indirect (by hearing of another person who has experienced the accidental or violent event), repeated or extreme indirect exposure to qualifying events (the latter usually reported by professionals).**[80]
- Many professionals who work in trauma differentiate between "big T-traumas," the ones listed above, and "little-t traumas." Little-t traumas can include complicated grief, divorce, media exposure to trauma, or childhood emotional abuse, and clinicians recognize that these can result in post-traumatic stress, even if they don't qualify for the PTSD diagnosis.

*Criterion B: Intrusion or re-experiencing the event as*
- Intrusive thoughts or memories and nightmares related to the traumatic event
- Flashbacks, feeling like the event is happening again
- Psychological and physical reactivity to reminders of the traumatic event, such as an anniversary

*Criterion C: Avoidant symptoms, as in efforts to avoid any memory of the event, which must include one of the following:*
- Avoiding thoughts or feelings connected to the traumatic event
- Avoiding people or situations connected to the traumatic event

*Criterion D: Negative alterations in mood or cognitions, such as a decline in someone's mood or though patterns, which can include:*
- Memory problems that are exclusive to the event
- Negative thoughts or beliefs about oneself or the world
- Distorted sense of blame for oneself or others, related to the event
- Being stuck in severe emotions related to the trauma (e.g. horror, shame, sadness)
- Severely reduced interest in pre-trauma activities
- Feeling detached, isolated or disconnected from other people

*Criterion E: Increased arousal symptoms, with the brain remaining "on edge," wary and watchful of further threats, as in:*
- Difficulty concentrating
- Irritability, increased temper or anger
- Difficulty falling or staying asleep
- Hypervigilance, with anticipations of further negative experiences
- Being easily startled

### Criteria F, G and H

The symptoms listed above have to have lasted at least a month, seriously affect one's ability to function and can't be due to substance use, medical illness or anything except the event itself.

#### Trauma subtype: Dissociation

In dissociated states, people split off some part or parts of themselves from their ordinary consciousness of who they are. This is an imagined distancing of oneself from the traumatizing experiences and memories of the trauma. While there are several types of dissociation, only two are included in the DSM:

– Depersonalization, or feeling disconnected from oneself

– Derealization, a sense that one's surroundings aren't real

Post traumatic stress disorder (PTSD) is the lingering result of unresolved trauma experiences. Single events that are experienced as intensely stressful may cause PTSDs. Repeated traumas (severe bullying, being repeatedly verbally abused, physically beaten, sexually abused, or neglected) or multiple traumas of different sorts may produce a more profound, 'complex' PTSD.

Judith Herman (1997), a psychiatrist who has been active in feminist movements, discusses Complex PTSDs, which may occur in repeated and ongoing child or spouse abuse, repeated sexual abuse, wartime horrors and incarceration. Rupert Ross (2006; 2014), a Canadian Crown attorney also has painfully excellent descriptions of individual, family and cultural Complex PTSDs resulting from severe abuses in the Canadian residential schools for Indigenous children.

In Complex PTSD the symptoms are much more severe, pervasive, persistent, more challenging to live and deal with, and more difficult to treat and clear. Notably, they may include a dense lack of conscious memories of many or all details of the traumas, extreme difficulties in developing or maintaining normal relationships with family members and friends, alcoholism and drug abuse, and severe, brutally violent temper outbursts without awareness or empathy for the suffering that is caused.

Bessel van der Kolk (2005) identifies Developmental Trauma Disorder as a subset of Complex PTSD. These are severe traumas, experienced in childhood as repeated, often ongoing neglect and abuse, usually perpetrated by parents. They may also be caused by repeated medical and surgical procedures. In the case of the Canadian residential school abuses, the parental neglect was caused by the government and by the church and secular school authorities and staff. The effects of the Complex PTSD trauma may be far reaching, on many levels.

> Chronic trauma interferes with neurobiological development... and the capacity to integrate sensory, emotional and cognitive information into a cohesive whole. Developmental trauma sets the stage for unfocused responses to subsequent stress..." (van der Kolk, 2005).**[81]

In the normal course of development, children learn to handle stress by observing how their parents and other family members cope with life challenges. When their family members deal competently with various stresses and traumas, the children learn to deal with them effectively. But when the parents cope poorly with stress and traumas, and even moreso when they are the perpetrators of traumas, children grow up without models or personal positive experiences in these areas of their lives. So when they are faced with severe stresses and traumas in the future, not only are they unable to cope with practical issues, but "...the relevant sensations, affects and cognitions cannot be associated – they are dissociated into sensory fragments – and, as a result, these children cannot comprehend what is happening or devise and execute appropriate plans of action" (van der Kolk, 2005). In other words, the victims have not acquired the patterns of recognition or comprehension required for assimilating the meanings of their severe, later life challenges. And the patterns they have from their Developmental Trauma are not adequate for coping with new, serious challenges.

Such people also don't know how to ask for or accept help from others. This is also outside their range of experience and expectations. They have enormous difficulties developing positive later life interpersonal relationships because their trauma responses are so quickly aroused when they experience stress and distress. The responses of panic and emotional overwhelm they learned in childhood are then repeated when they are seriously stressed in their remaining childhood years and in adulthood.**[82]

My experience in helping HSPs in therapy is that they may be vulnerable to Developmental Trauma Disorder. Because of their very high emotional sensitivities, the intensities of stresses that generate these disorders in HSPs may not appear on the surface to have been sufficient to warrant consideration of a PTSD spectrum diagnosis. NHSPs who experience such traumas are often not as seriously impacted.

HSPs may be vulnerable to these challenges for additional reasons as well. HSPs have strong right brain functions.

- HSPs are strongly connected with their emotions, focused on what they are experiencing in each moment, with high arousal levels that distract them away from their left brain thinking functions – while NHSPs hold to left brain goals and plans and can navigate better through stressful situations without being overwhelmed and derailed by their emotions.
- HSPs are strongly focused on present time processes of their interactions, whereas NHSPs are more focused on goals and steps towards achieving them.*[83]

These characteristics make it very difficult for HSPs to develop strategies to deal with serious trauma. Their levels of distress are overwhelming, and their thinking abilities to develop plans for dealing with the traumas are therefore hard for them to access. Being so rooted in the present also makes it hard to look beyond their current suffering to a future time when things may be better – even if this is only until the next episodes of abuse.

Periods between abuses are not much of a respite for HSPs because they hold onto their emotional memories of emotional and physical traumas. Where NHSP victims of traumas may be able to calm and distract themselves to some degree between abusive episodes, or even shut them out of their consciousness completely, HSPs are much less able to do so.

PTSD symptoms of any sorts may persist for the victim's entire life, perniciously interfering with their inner and outer world life. Worse yet, when PTSDs are experienced by many people together – as in wars or natural disasters, they may lead to collective suffering, aggression as a group or as a country, and to self-destructive behaviors.*[84]

Due to the same sensitivities, the residual psychological effects of such Developmental Trauma Disorders may also be expressed more overtly in HSPs throughout their lives than in those of NHSPs. HSPs, due to their general sensitivities, can be more easily triggered into distress and trauma reactions by later stresses in their lives.

*Treating long-term effects of traumas*

Judith Herman notes that recovery from Complex Trauma in therapy occurs in three stages.

1. Establishing safety
   - The therapist provides a safe therapeutic environment and helps trauma victims to come into a place of feeling they have a measure of control over their lives.
   - The traumas are acknowledged and victims are helped to recall them in detail, in the safety of the therapy room. For some people, there may be partial or total amnesia for traumas, even when they were repeated over periods of years. This is one of the ways the unconscious mind avoids pain and suffering.
   - An important part of control and safety is to learn methods for dealing with trauma responses of fear, panic and violent reactions that are part of the PTSD.
   - A safe living environment is sorted out.
   - All of this is done with respect for the victim's degrees of understanding of the trauma and for their wishes and autonomy in deciding on each step in the process.

2. Remembrance and mourning
   - The entire details of the trauma are methodically retrieved from the memories that were often obscured when the victims shut them out of their consciousness in order to avoid suffering the shame, shock, fears, terrors, pain and other trauma experiences.**[85]
   - Memories in which victims feel their competence to deal with life shredded and torn away; self-blame, and guilt for allowing the trauma to happen and to incapacitate them; helplessness in the trauma situation and during their subsequent struggles to recover.
   - They mourn the loss of their previous whole and competent selves; their having suffered social shame and blame in sexual traumas; losses of physical functions due to injuries; losses of relationships; and losses of other people who were killed in war or group assaults.
   - They go through all the stages of grief over losses of their former selves, of opportunities to grow and flourish, of relationships and other options they missed, and of years of their lives spent in trauma reactions.*[86]
   - Slowly but surely, they regain their sense of personal power, competence and control in their lives.
   - Not mentioned by Herman, but very commonly in my experience of helping people through their traumas, is a period where old trauma-related habits have been released but new, healthier ones have not yet been developed to replace them.
   - David Gersten (1997), a psychiatrist, identified this as 'going through the void.' This can be experienced as a serious confusion and is often anxiety-provoking. It is most helpfully addressed by relabeling it as a good sign of progress, with successful relinquishing of old patterns of fears and trauma residues, and opening up spaces for more healthy habits to be developed. This is an example of a meta-anxiety and of installing meta-positives.**[87]

3. Reconnection
   - Having processed much of the trauma feelings and memories, survivors recreate a new self and leave the ashes of the past behind them for the most part.
   - In some programs, assertiveness training is offered. This helps to overcome their self-image of being helpless victims and the terrible sense of powerlessness that PTSD victims suffer. They are then taught experientially how to deal with abuses such as belittling and bullying, so that they can handle future confrontations with abusive people without allowing themselves to be retraumatized.
   - Feeling strong enough to be assertive, they take control over their lives and learn to fight, if necessary, to redress wrongs in their current and earlier lives.
   - They create new selves, building on pre-trauma memories of themselves and/or on current-life choices of who and how they want to be.
   - Resolving their traumas to the best of their abilities, they build new lives. They are now ready for healthy friendships and for resuming relationships with supportive family members and with their own children.
   - Social action may offer channels for exploring one's new self.
   - Herman notes that with severe trauma there is no final and definitive resolution of PTSDs. Memories of previously unrecalled experiences may surface, old trauma patterns may get triggered, and fears of moving forward may re-surface. But at these later points in their lives they have many more resources to deal with such issues, and confidence from positive, healing experiences that they can clear these new challenges as they cleared the previous ones from which they healed. This can then be turned around to say to oneself, "Look how well I'm doing! I'm able to think clearly and to choose healing responses to my issues now!" In effect, this is the installation and strengthening of meta-positives.

Herman observes that group therapy can add enormously to the healing of traumas and to post traumatic growth. However, she offers detailed suggestions and strong cautions about structuring the content and process of each group very carefully, according to the particular issues of the participants and according to each of the three stages she identifies in the processing of traumas. Anyone considering running or participating in a group for dealing with trauma issues would be wise to review her excellent observations, suggestions and warnings.

Rupert Ross (2006, 2014) notes that Indigenous people respond to trauma treatments better through discussions in groups with other trauma victims from their own culture, rather than with Western approaches to trauma treatments. This is congruent with their cultural ways of offering help to each other in respectful ways, without telling anyone what they should or shouldn't be doing. There is no pressure for anyone to disclose their issues until they feel ready to do so. Often, the therapists in these groups have also experienced severe traumas and will share these, as appropriate, in the group sessions.

The various types of 12-step programs for dealing with addictions are similarly helpful in dealing with the challenges of habituation as well as with the stresses and traumas that most often accompany alcohol and drug problems. The various groups have a considerable range individuality in offering assistance within the broad spectrum of support, understanding, acceptance, community and instruction in their 12 steps for addressing addictions. They tend to discourage use of medications for psychological and physical issues commonly seen with alcoholism, as they generally advise not relying on any chemical crutches.*[88]

For many decades, doctors blithely have prescribed medications for various symptoms of people suffering after experiencing traumas. Many doctors have little or no training in identifying or dealing with the traumas behind the symptoms. The medications sometimes dull trauma symptoms such as severe anxieties, panic attacks, insomnia, physical pains, cravings and other problems, but very rarely eliminate them. Side effects of the medications are often so serious that many cannot tolerate the drugs, even when further medications are prescribed for the side effects. Worse yet, these side effect medications often have their own side effects. Overall, medications provide symptomatic relief but often do not serve trauma survivors well in the long run. Addictions to the prescribed drugs and street drugs and alcohol have also been serious issues in many trauma victims.

Various forms of trauma relief therapies have been developed:

*Exposure therapy* was designed to get people used to the memories of the original traumas so that they no longer were triggered into their symptoms that replicated how they felt and reacted in the original trauma situation. Generally, this was not very successful, and many were and still continue to be seriously retraumatized by the therapy itself.

*Eye Movement Desensitization and Reprocessing (EMDR)* was developed in the 1990's. EMDR involves:

1. Focusing one's mind on whatever memories and emotions one wants to release (such as trauma memories),

2. While alternating stimulating the left and right sides of the brain by:

   – Moving one's eyes back and forth, right and left, or

   – Alternating auditory stimulation of the right and left ears, or

   – Alternating tapping anywhere on the right and left sides of the body.

For reasons that remain to be explained, this process evokes intense emotional releases of the trauma memories and feelings, which eventually diminish and clear. Positive thoughts and feelings can then be installed to replace the negative ones that have been released. The downside to EMDR is that the releases are so intense that people are strongly recommended to use this therapy only in the therapist's office, so that the therapist can provide support for the heavy emotional releases.[89]

Energy Psychology (EP) includes a group of therapies that can similarly release trauma memories and feelings, without the risk of heavy emotional releases.[90]

– Emotional Freedom Techniques (EFT) is the most popular EP. It involves

1. Focusing the mind on the feelings and memories to be releases,

2. Followed by a strong positive statement, such as "I totally and completely love and accept myself."

3. Tapping on a long, standard series of acupressure points on the head, chest and hand.

These steps release trauma memories and feelings without heavy emotional releases, so EFT is safe to use on one's own. The downsides of EFT are that in seriously triggered states of anxiety or trauma release, when people most need to use EFT, it may be difficult for them to recall the complex tapping procedures. Also, many are embarrassed to use EFT in public because it looks strange. Children, in particular, complain about this because they get teased or bullied for doing something odd that their peers don't understand.

- Thought Field Therapy (TFT) also involves tapping on a series of acupressure points, with a different series of points being prescribed by the therapist according to the issues being addressed. TFT is also safe to use on one's own. The downside is that with different issues one has to have the guidance of the therapist as to which points to tap on. Despite the last issue, TFT has been enormously helpful to people with serious traumas in Africa and elsewhere (J. Edwards, 2016; Hamne & Sandström, 2017).
- TWR/WHEE is enormously helpful in releasing the memory and emotional residues traumas. It is safe to use on your own. It is easy to learn and use, yet rapidly and deeply effective. It is so simple a procedure that people remember how to use it when they are stressed, and it can be used discretely so that no one knows you are de-stressing when you use it in public.[*91]

HSPCs can be tremendously helpful to their HSPs who are dealing with trauma residues.

- First and foremost, just acknowledging your HSP's feelings of distress is enormously comforting.
- Helping her to verbalize what distressed her can focus her on the present issues and is then a first step towards dealing with them.
- If he uses self-treatments for de-stressing, you can ask whether this might be a good time to use them
- If you are both aware of earlier life traumas, again this might be a time to ask whether he could clear some of these, along with his current issues.
- Rounding out the self-treatment, you could invite her to consider what positive thoughts and feelings she could install to replace the negative ones she released.
- Remembering to compliment her for dealing well with her issues can add to the positivity.
- And last, but not least, you can take the opportunities offered in coaching her for using whatever self-treatment methods you use yourself to deal with your own issues that resonate with hers.

*Suicide with severe traumas*

There is a serious risk of suicide in people with severe post traumatic stress. The emotional pain and distress involved in PTSD may be more than people are ready or able to bear.

If you have any inkling of suspicion that a person you know is or may be contemplating suicide, the first and most helpful thing you can do is to invite them to speak about it. Many people who have not had experience in conversing about or helping with people's suicidal thoughts may hesitate to even raise the subject – out of anxieties that mentioning it might be planting seeds of thought or intentions where none had existed before. This would very rarely be the case.

In fact, the opposite is true. In decades of helping people with serious depression and traumas, I have confirmed the general experience of the majority of caregivers that if the thought crosses my mind that the person I'm speaking with might be considering suicide, then more often than not that person has already been thinking about it. And the response is almost always one of great relief and gratitude that I asked about it. In most cases, people contemplating suicide hesitate to mention it to others unless they are asked about it – because either they don't want to upset anyone or they are serious about their intents and do not want to be stopped from carrying through their plans.

While it may be distressing to you to learn of this, be aware that you are in a position to be of enormous help to this person. If you are not feeling overwhelmed by their sharing these details, then once this door is opened you have the opportunity to enable the person thinking of suicide to unburden themselves of whatever experiences and feelings are leading them to these thoughts of ending their life.

Many people who are seriously depressed have occasional thoughts of suicide. If you are not a professional caregiver, and if what you hear leaves you unclear whether the depressed person is firmly committed to not following through on their suicidal thoughts, please, please consider yourself obligated to connect the person contemplating suicide with someone who can help them deal with their distress. This can be lifesaving!

If they have a therapist or doctor treating them for their depression, you can stand by while they phone and speak with that person. If they do not connect with that person, and you feel any question about the seriousness of their suicidal intent, your next step is to connect them with an emergency service where they can be properly evaluated.

A phone call to an emergency service, in your presence, may be the easiest next option. If they repeat their report to the emergency service with the full details they shared with you, this is a positive sign that they are on board with the plan to get help. If you hear that they are not sharing all of the details they disclosed to you, this is a matter for concern. Before they put down the phone, ask to speak with the emergency service person and explain your concerns. These suggestions may feel a bit impolite, but in matters of possible suicide, better safe than sorry.

If they report not only thoughts of suicide but have been thinking of ways and means to carry through on their intention to end their life, it is imperative that they go personally to an emergency psychiatric service for help. Their doctor or therapist may recommend a particular emergency service. If they don't have this sort of recommendation, then they or you need to clarify what their best options are for getting this help.

If they are willing to go along with you, your best next step is to accompany them to an emergency service immediately, where they can get a professional assessment and whatever supports are needed to prevent their carrying through with their suicidal thoughts or intentions. Do not leave this to a later time.

If you are a professional caregiver, then you at this point bear the responsibility for making an assessment of the seriousness of the potential for this person's carrying through on the thoughts, feelings and intentions they shared with you. I strongly recommend leaning towards erring on the side of caution rather than being polite or too readily accepting reassurances that all is well. Some of the more serious danger signals include:

– There is a plan in place to proceed with the act of suicide.
– The means to carry through on this plan are available.

- There were serious attempts at suicide in the past.
- The person has been having a hard time resisting following through on the plan.
- The person had been using alcohol and/or street drugs.
- There are few or no ongoing psychological and social supports available.
- There are various other warning signals as well.[92]

Should you, a caregiving professional, decide that the risk does not warrant immediate emergency care, it is important that you still:

- Remove any means for following through on the suicide that can reasonably be eliminated.
- Arrange with the suicidal person to have at least three phone numbers they can call, listed on their refrigerator with a copy by the bedside, to be used if they are feeling seriously suicidal, and at least one of these numbers must be an emergency psychiatric service.

For HSPs and HSPCs, much of the discussion above is similarly applicable. If you have been in a relationship for a while, the surfacing or worsening of suicidal thoughts and feelings are important to discuss. While this may be distressing for either or both of you, it can be enormously helpful to the one who is depressed to have someone with whom to share some of his feelings.

While you, the listening partner in the relationship, cannot take responsibility for the feelings or actions of your partner, you can offer enormous support.

- First and foremost, being available to listen is a tremendous help. People who suicide usually feel they are alone and without sufficient supports or people who care about them. Your listening presence can make a big difference.*[93]
- You, the listening partner, can agree to be on the list of people the depressed person will contact if suicidal thoughts become strong or worrisome.
- Very often, depression and suicidal thinking have evolved out of earlier life traumas. This is an opportunity for you, the listener, to learn more about your partner's life history.
- People who have chronic depression sometimes have found ways of dealing with it in the past that were helpful. Asking about these and reminding her about these can be surprisingly helpful, as part of a depression often involves over-focusing on the negative and ignoring or forgetting about the positive in one's life.
- One of the simplest and most effective preventives and aids in dealing with depression is physical exercise. While feeling depressed, this may be a difficult option to implement. Accompanying the one who is depressed when they exercise is an excellent way to be supportive.

Tapping therapies are enormously helpful in clearing depression, trauma memories and feelings, and treating insomnia. The old saying that "Misery loves company" takes on a different meaning here. Tapping along with someone who is depressed is supportive in many ways.

- This serves as a reminder to tap.
- The partner who is not depressed can tap on his own issues, which makes the joint tapping a joint benefit.

- The partner who is not depressed may be able to activate more positive energies than the depressed person can muster, which can serve as a reminder or a model for the depressed person to move into more positive healing mindsets and energies.
- The partner who is not depressed can add the momentum of healing intentions and energies of her tapping to those of the depressed person, as a proxy healing.*[94] In this method of healing, our own healings are offered as energetic, intentional templates to give a boost to another person in their healing.
- The partner who is not depressed may be able to suggest and support ways to use tapping that the depressed person finds difficult to muster or does not think of while in a depressed state. These could, for instance, include doing inner child work to bring healing to the roots of the traumas that many depressed people have experienced earlier in life;*[95] considering experiences with other family members of the depressed person who are also depressed;*[96] and to past life traumas and depressions that may be resonating with current life traumas and depressions.*[97]

*Alcohol and substance use and addictions following trauma*

People who are traumatized often find that alcohol and sedative drugs provide relief from some of their distresses. They feel more relaxed and at ease, their anxieties and hurt feelings are numbed, and they sleep better. Some find it easier to socialize and others to withdraw from contact with people, These are early responses to these sorts of self-medication with alcohol and drugs. Others find that stimulant drugs offer them temporary relief from depression or a temporary 'high' feeling. There is also a camaraderie among drug and alcohol users.

The price for using alcohol and drugs can be high, and the consequences severe. Habituation and addiction often lead heavier users into downward spirals that can include difficulties in thinking, lack of motivation to work or even to attend to their health needs, depression and suicide.

HSPs are far from immune to these challenges. Being emotionally sensitive can be a major burden, particularly when people have been traumatized by disparagement or bullying. Low self-esteem predisposes to alcohol and drug use and abuse.

It is a serious challenge to help people acknowledge and halt their addictions and to come into a place of recovery. The alcohol and drugs provide immediate relief and distraction from psychological traumas and pains, so those who are addicted often turn to their substances of choice when they are stressed or distressed. Often, they are unaware of the connections between their addictions and the traumas and related feelings that underlie their addictions.

For HSPs who have addictions, their emotional sensitivities are two-edged swords. On the one hand, they are more easily triggered into feeling hurt, angry or depressed – and therefore likely to turn to their addictions. On the other, they have the advantage of being more in touch with their emotions, so they may be more responsive to accepting therapeutic alternatives to drugs to relieve their anxieties and distresses.

An HSPC can be enormously helpful to an HSP with alcohol or drug issues. With mild or modest habits, emotional support is enormously beneficial and may be curative. It is best to focus on the emotions in supportive ways rather than harping or scolding about the alcohol or drug use.

Alcoholics Anonymous and Narcotics Anonymous can add social supports, with people who are working in a community that understands addictions and drug dependencies. Alanon provides supports for families of addicts, and can be tremendously beneficial to HSPCs dealing with these issues.*[98] One word of caution regarding HSPs attending these groups: They vary enormously in how aware and sensitive their members are to emotional aspects of addictions and recovery.

With more severe addictions, professional counselling and therapy groups can be helpful, though relapses are very frequent and success rates are limited. In my experience, successes are much more frequent when Energy Psychology is used by addicts, in addition to participation in therapy groups and groups such as Alcoholics Anonymous and Narcotics Anonymous.**[99] Wholistic EP not only can reduce cravings, but may also transform the addiction from being a burden to being a teacher. Instead of being enemies, the cravings can be transformed into alerts or alarm bells about emotions and trauma issues being triggered – which can then be reduced and cleared by the EP. In addition, wholistic EP invites people to install positives to replace the negatives that have been released.

An HSPC can be a great help in supporting their HSP in using EP.
- Asking whether a particularly stressful issue might be reduced in intensity with EP
- Non-verbally tapping for the HSPC's own anxieties as a hint to the HSP to tap on their addiction-related issues.
- Tapping along with the HSP to reduce the HSPC's anxieties
- Suggesting tapping prior to entering a situation that is likely to be stressful
- Asking and clarifying with their HSP how the HSPC can best be of further help

Dealing with addictions is usually a long-term project. Keeping in mind that the addict's behaviors are often based on trauma can be enormously helpful to addicts and those supporting them.

Those supporting the addict are usually seriously stressed themselves. Counseling, stress reduction methods and ALANON groups can be enormously helpful here.

We should also acknowledge that electronic games and sex can also become addictive, distracting people from their stresses and traumas.

*Helping HSPs and HSPCs deal with traumas*

In my experience, the entire range of traumas – from modest upsets to major horrendous events – are best treated with Energy Psychology (EP) or Eye Movement Desensitization and Reprocessing (EMDR). TWR/WHEE combines elements of EMDR and EFT.

Let me share a few reports of clients' experiences in dealing with their HSP trauma issues.

While bullying to suppress people's feelings is very common, it often goes unrecognized or unlabeled as such by HSPs because they feel they are not like other people and are therefore actually weak or wimpish because they are so sensitive and open in expressing their emotions, just like the bullies say they are. This is especially true when HSPs grow up in NHSP families, and even moreso when they suffered from bullying or from physical, emotional or sexual abuses.

✦ 'Cathy' was a recently divorced, 42 year-old, successful clothing designer who worked with me by phone on her long-standing depression and her struggles with increasingly frequent suicidal thoughts. She is an intense HSP who grew up in New York City. Both of her parents, two of her three older sisters and her younger brother and sister were NHSPs. Cathy's oldest sister was an HSP who had been taught by her parents to minimize, hide and deny her feelings and who had learned to live by their rules.

Cathy's father, 'Ben,' was a badly traumatized war veteran who had overcome serious addiction problems with the help of Narcotics Anonymous. What had helped him the most was "letting the past be the past and moving on." Cathy's mother, Fran, was a warm, caring woman who had grown up in a large family. Her parents had both immigrated with their traumatized families from post-World War II Europe. Fran was utterly devoted to Ben, and although she might have been an HSP, had hidden and suppressed her feelings for so long that they were no longer evident in expressions of emotions, but strongly suggested by her kindness to everyone and sensitivities to their needs.

Cathy was struggling to hide her depression from her young children, her parents and her siblings. She felt no one could or would understand her or accept her feelings of deep sadness and despair over her failed marriage.

'Allan,' her ex-husband, was a strong NHSP. Like her family, he was uncomfortable with emotions and disparaging when Cathy expressed or talked about her emotions. Cathy's feelings were markedly worsened by the fact that her family liked Allan because he was very much like them in suppressing emotions. Cathy had worked hard to convince Allan to go with her for marital or family therapy. She had desperately wanted to find ways to resolve their differences but he had steadfastly and adamantly refused. In this, too, Cathy felt herself a failure, ruminating on what she might yet have done to make things better.

The last straw that led to her filing for divorce started as a seemingly small thing, but it had a huge impact on Cathy. Cathy's sexual relationship with Allan was a fraught one. She was sensitive to the atmosphere surrounding lovemaking, and Allan was not. He expected his 'marital rights' to be granted whenever he demanded sex, regardless of Cathy's feelings at the time. Cathy had grown up in her emotionally repressive home, with no discussions on sex, nor any sex education in her school, and no sense that she could find much enjoyment in an intimate relationship. It was an article on women satisfying their sexual needs, which Cathy read with nervous, blushing interest while waiting for her annual dental checkup, that set her on a path of one woman's liberation. And this was the beginning of the end of her marriage, because in this, too, Allan was totally unresponsive to Cathy's feelings, desires and needs.

Cathy was surprised at how depressed she was after her divorce. She had expected to feel much more relief and even pleasure at being free from the emotional indifference and abuse she had suffered with Allan. But she was plagued by self-blame, guilt and depression, even to the point of sometimes having fleeting suicidal thoughts.

It took Cathy several years of therapy to overcome her habits of cowering when interacting with her family. She found it impossible to stop abiding by the family injunctions to remain unemotional. Her way of dealing with this was primarily to develop a 'family of choice' that included people who were warmly emotional HSPs or accepting NHSPs, who were supportive of her openness in HSP ways.

TWR/WHEE enabled Cathy to release a lot of her accumulated traumas, both in addressing various specific memories and in clearing 'bundled' experiences of many rejections from childhood and from her marriage. She was particularly grateful to have an immediately available way of using this de-stressing discretely, when struggling with her family's repressive attitudes. She did this by alternating contracting the toes of her left and right feet inside her shoes.

During Cathy's journey out of her abusive family of origin and into a family of choice, it was enormously helpful for to her have the support of a variety of complementary/ alternative therapists to help her deal with some of the many aspects of her HSP traits. She often suffered from stomach aches after contacts with her family. She realized that her chronic abdominal pains, which her family physician had diagnosed as irritable bowel syndrome, and which had been unresponsive to all of his medications and to several restrictive diets, were related to her 'swallowing down her feelings.' TWR/WHEE was modestly helpful in dealing with these somatic symptoms when they arose unexpectedly. But it was the little drops of vibrational essences that provided Cathy with the most striking and permanent relief. A good naturopathic doctor (ND) prescribed a series of homeopathic remedies*[100] and flower essences*[101] that were everything Cathy had hoped to find in her many years of searching for help with her gut issues.

Cathy's backaches responded similarly in modest ways to the tapping and affirmations of TWR/WHEE when they flared up unexpectedly, but it was frequent massages that relieved her back pains the most. Cathy realized she had internalized her father's repeated criticisms about her being too sensitive and emotional, which he complained was 'a pain in the back,' and she had then locked away many of her feelings of frustrations and hurt in that part of her anatomy. Having massages lessened her back pains over the next few days but did not provide permanent relief. It was when Cathy did two-chair work, dialoguing with her back pains to listen to their complaints, and then released them with tapping, that she found her deepest and more permanent relief from her backaches.*[102]

As Cathy's depression diminished, she became more assertive and avoided family gatherings, where she not only couldn't be herself, but was often derided, belittled and pathologized for expressing her emotions openly. She also avoided these gatherings because Allan, her ex-husband, continued to attend her family's holiday and birthday celebrations.

Cathy's children were both HSPs but were uncomfortable expressing their feelings, having been raised in this family where anyone open with their emotions was labeled a 'woos', a 'drama queen' or in other ways ridiculed and ullied into silence. With Cathy's support, her daughter, Donna, very gradually came to accept a little more that she was emotionally sensitive, like her mom. However, her son, John, remained entrenched in the family pattern and increasingly chose to spend more time with his father and less with Cathy. Cathy was deeply distressed by this parental alienation, but found no ways to counteract the rigidity of her ex-husband's and her own family's avoidances of emotionality.

Cathy is typical of many HSP people I have helped through the years. They had been so traumatized by their family, friends, fellow students or co-workers that they had come to feel there was something seriously wrong with them. Some even became depressed to the point that they were at times suicidal. Most were greatly disappointed in the treatments provided by their family doctor and several specialists they had seen. Many doctors have little training or understanding about emotional issues and their manifestations as physical symptoms. Today's medical doctors are specialized in treating various parts of the body, with little or no appreciation of the psychological issues influencing the person who inhabits that body. They are also focused primarily upon the medications they can prescribe for each symptom. The limitations of 10-15 minutes per visit further narrow and restrict the benefits they can offer. Worse yet, when medications produce side effects, they prescribe further medications for the original side effects, but patients then run into side effects of the new medications and interactive effects between the original meds and the secondary ones.

And it is no better with psychiatrists. Today, many psychiatry training programs offer psychotherapy as an elective, because psychiatry has come to focus so heavily on medications. A high percent of psychiatric trainees see little or no relevance of psychotherapy to their jobs. And again, it is worth cautioning that because of these ongoing issues of habituation to using medications for anything and everything, modern medicine is the third leading cause of death in the modern world. Few doctors will warn you about this!

All of this is horrendously disempowering to people seeking healing for their physical symptoms. HSPs are very responsive to guidance in connecting with what their bodies are wanting them to know about their lives and in listening to what their bodies are suggesting they might do differently in order to eliminate their symptoms.

An HSPC can be enormously helpful in these situations. HSPs tend to focus on what they are feeling at the moment. Even when they know how to listen to their body symptoms, they may forget to do this when they are experiencing pains or other issues with their bodies. A reminder from their HSPC to consider what might be stressing them at that moment; to dialogue with their symptoms; and to tap on the stressors and other issues they identify can enable them to engage in the self-healing methods they are learning to use.

✦ ✦ A year and a half after Cathy's divorce, she literally bumped into a sensitive, considerate man – in of all places, another waiting room. Her naturopath worked in a group practice, and Fred was waiting to see his massage therapist for persistent, severe spasms in his neck following a whiplash injury. She apologized for being clumsy when she tripped over her own feet and nearly fell into his lap as she was turning to sit down, and he graciously forgave her. They started chatting, hit it off nicely, made a date for coffee following their appointments. And this was the start of the caring, accepting relationship Cathy had only begun to dream of.

While Fred was an HSP, he was more left-brain centered and able to stay more focused on processes and outcomes under stress than Cathy was. This enabled him to remind her to look for the issues behind what was upsetting her, whenever she became immersed in a back spasm or was triggered into emotional intensity that blurred her own abilities to access the approaches and tools she was learning to use.

Cathy, in turn, was pleased to be an HSPC to Fred, introducing him to some of the approaches that were proving helpful to her. This was a relationship she had not even ventured to fantasy during most of her life!

✦ 'Josie,' an HSP, had a Skype session with me because she had left a seriously abusive relationship with 'Gino,' an NHSP, six months earlier. He had been verbally, emotionally and physically abusive, but she could not stop berating herself for failing to work harder at fixing the relationship. She realized when she left Gino that she had actually endangered her life by getting into the relationship in the first place, ignoring his sharp, snide remarks bordering on verbal abuse, not long after they had first dated. Josie had known these warning signs from her stepfather's verbal abuse towards her, and had observed his verbal and physical abuse as well towards her mother.

Following Josie's breakup, she had experienced difficulties concentrating, insomnia, nightmares, and had no tolerance for even modestly loud noises. She also had a horrendous time maintaining a semblance of normality at work in the university research lab. She frequently was reduced (under even moderate stresses that had not bothered her before) to having difficulties in keeping her thoughts straight, and sometimes even had to withdraw to the ladies' room to sob quietly while sitting in a toilet stall. It was the danger of losing her job that finally led her to seek therapy.

Josie later reported that her first TWR/WHEE session was the turning point in her life. After providing a thorough history, she spent the remainder of the session building and connecting with her place of peace and safety and healing (PPSH) and learning how to relieve tension and to decrease anxieties with TWR/WHEE1 – addressing her frequent anxiety reactions under stress. The tapping was highly effective because Josie had a good observing ego*[103] in addition to being a psychologically aware HSP. She also felt supported and reassured with my email support to clarify how to best use these methods to deal with her PTSD issues of getting triggered unexpectedly on many occasions.

At her second session, she reported that she was now able to stop most of her anxiety attacks very soon after they were triggered. This was a tremendous relief to her, because she had been spiraling into vicious circles of work stresses → high anxieties → anxieties about becoming anxious → inability to concentrate and focus on her work → worse anxieties → etc.

I helped Josie start a list of her major anxieties and fears on her notepad, to be re-ordered from worst to least intense at home. She then picked the first one she wanted to work on, which was her anxiety about becoming incapacitated by her anxieties and losing her job. Her initial anxiety intensity was 35 on a scale of '0' = not at all, and '10' = the worst it could be. Within 15 minutes, she brought this down to a '0'.

In these ways, Josie worked through her list of anxieties in her present life. She then elected to clear the trauma memories and feelings from her childhood experiences of direct and secondary abuses. She could see that these trauma residues from earlier in her life had unconsciously predisposed her to choose her recent abusive relationship with Gino. On the one hand, her choice had been to connect with a person who felt familiar because he was abusive like her father. On the other hand, she also senses that her unconscious mind had guided her to be with a person like that in order to invite her to clear her trauma residues.

A high percent of people with trauma also suffer from physical symptoms, often related to the types of trauma they experienced. Being hit or beaten can leave emotional scars locked into the body, manifesting as chronic pains. Sexual trauma can leave symptoms related to the sexual organs or to other parts of the body that were tensed or physically traumatized during the abuses or assaults.

Our relationships often appear to be chosen by the deeper awarenesses of our unconscious mind in order to help us sort out residues of difficult, challenging and traumatic experiences earlier in our lives.*[104] Sometimes the same types of dynamics draw us to connect with past life awarenesses as well.*[105]

*HAVE YOU EXPERIENCED TRAUMA(S)?*

*HAVE YOU EXPLORED TWR/WHEE OR ANY OTHER ENERGY PSYCHOLOGY (EP) APPROACHES FOR DEALING WITH TRAUMA RESIDUES?*

*IF DRINKING OR DRUGS ARE A PART OF YOUR TRAUMA RESIDUES, HAVE YOU EXPLORED WHOLISTIC EP FOR DEALING WITH THESE?*

# 16. Grief

*To weep is to make less the depth of grief.*
— William Shakespeare

Grief is a serious challenge that faces most of us at some points in our lives. How we experience and process our grief makes an enormous difference in how we live the rest of our lives. HSPs will usually feel grief deeply and will often express their grief with intensity. NHSPs tend to avoid feeling and expressing their grief. A time of grief can become a time of stress for everyone in families where the HSPs are showing their feelings and the NHSPs are doing their best to avoid their feelings.

We usually think of grief as relating to the death of a person, but there are other issues that we grieve in life that will sit in the same inner 'graves' where we bury experiences and memories we would rather not deal with. These can include losses of friends when we or they move away, loss of a job, loss of body functions due to injuries or as we age, loss of a pet, and so on.

Grief in its many variations is such a common and frequently difficult experience that I discuss it in some detail. This is also because modern Western society is often very poor at processing grief. When it is not processed, it can be as traumatic as any other stress that causes a PTSD.*[106]

Every time we experience another dose of grief, or anything that reminds us of our grief, we build thicker, denser inner walls around our buried griefs to keep us from stirring the painful feelings buried there. The grief grave is rather like a filing cabinet in a vault that is securely locked away from our conscious awareness. An individual grief may be located in one of our inner 'psychological memory filing cabinets.' The walls we build around the cabinet or around the entire vault may also isolate and hide portions of our general memory files that are in some ways related to the buried griefs. In these ways, we can shut ourselves off from many, if not most or even all of our emotional awarenesses. Often this will include the factual memories of the trauma incidents and experiences that led to the grief as well – in order to be as careful as possible not to stir these painful memories to come back and haunt us.

This process may spiral into our bullying family members who do not bury their feelings like we are doing, because when witnessing others grieving it makes those who do bury these awarenesses very uncomfortable. Rather than deal with such discomforts, people often disparage, bully and reject these family members.

With time, we put the equivalent of police-style warning signs around our psychological memory file cabinet, to protect ourselves even more from going anywhere near our place of inner pain. Paradoxically, by not going there, we create further challenges, some of which may be difficult to deal with. Buried grief is like a psychological cancer that slowly grows and saps the energies of the person and family that is carrying it. Major grief reactions produce effects similar to those of other traumas.*[107]

Elisabeth Kubler-Ross (1975) identified five steps in the process of grieving: denial, anger, bargaining, depression and acceptance. I have worked with many individuals who experienced varieties of losses, large and small, in their lives. I find that these stages can be expanded helpfully to include seven distinct steps, divided into three major stages of grief:

1. Initial stages of grief responses – Generally in the first 24-48 hours, but in some circumstances, may extend longer. Residues of these initial stages may sometimes linger or recur episodically, usually with ever diminishing intensity, through the middle stages of grief.

   A. Shock: "Oh, my God!" or "What terrible news!"
   B. Denial: "It can't be true! It must be someone else who died." or "I just saw ___ a week ago!" or "The Infinite Source wouldn't have taken someone so [young/ good/ needed/ important] in this world!"
   C. Bargaining: "Please let this not be true!" or "I pray that this is a mistake!" or "I won't believe this till….!"

2. Middle stages of grief – Generally 3-12 months for a friend; 2-5 years for a close family member, with loss of a child generally acknowledged as the most severe trauma

A. Depression:
– Sadness, crying, missing and longing for the person
– Loss of appetite, difficulties sleeping, troubled dreams and nightmares
– Apathy, lack of energy to carry on with life
– Feeling empty and that life is incomplete without the deceased
– Wishing to die oneself, in order to be reunited with the one who is now missing or in order to stop suffering the painful grief of having lost the deceased
– Sometimes the pain of the loss or the longing to be reunited with the deceased is so great that suicide is contemplated, attempted or completed.

B. Anger:
– At the deceased for 'abandoning' us, for not having taken steps to live a healthier or safer and longer life
– At ourselves for acts of omission or commission that might have contributed to the death; for not having helped the deceased enough; or for not having visited enough
– For feeling guilty even when there was really nothing substantial we could have done to prevent the death
– At other people who might have treated the deceased poorly or who failed to offer support
– Anger may be so great in cases of murders that the bereaved want to kill someone in revenge. In tribal societies people often act upon these feelings of anger and it is not uncommon to see revenge killings or even battles developing out of such situations.
– At The Infinite Source for allowing the deceased to be ill or to suffer in illness, or through trauma, and to die

C. Guilt:
– Over our acts of omission or commission that might have

- contributed to the death, such as not having helped the deceased enough
- Over being alive ourselves when the deceased is no longer alive
- Over feeling angry, especially at The Infinite Source
- Over having vengeful feelings and even wishes to hurt or kill others in retaliation when the grief is about a death caused by someone else

And here it is worthwhile to mention the differences between guilt and shame. Guilt tells me "I did bad." Shame tells me "I am bad." (B. Brown, Web. ref). Shame associated with grief is often based more on residues from experiences in life that are not related to the grief itself, but to more serious and chronic traumas, frequently from childhood, in which the grieving person was bullied or in other ways abused. Being chronically abused, the person came to feel they must have been bad to have deserved such treatment. In these instances, the resolution of the grief offers opportunities for the grieving person to clear their shame along with the grief.

Little-acknowledged among conventional therapists, though extremely common experiences during this stage, are profoundly moving encounters with the spirit (ghost) of the deceased. Bereavement apparitions, as these are called, usually visit in the first few weeks after the loss, and are more common when the deceased person was psychologically close to the grieving person. This may include seeing and/or hearing the deceased or just sensing they are present.*[108]

3. Resolution/ Acceptance stage of grief – 3 months to several years, overlapping with (2)

A. Recalling more of the positive memories about the deceased

- Adjusting to a world where the deceased is no longer physically present
- Finding other relationships and ways to deal with life – without the presence, participation, or strong intruding memories of the deceased

B. The bereavement apparitions lead many to understand that physical death is not the end of existence. This is one of the blessings of a good grief.*[109]

The above are very general outlines of grief reactions. In each experience of grief, the process will vary uniquely in many details.

Specific aspects of each stage may occur in any order. Each of the aspects of grief may surface repetitively at any time in the grief process, often with considerable intensity.

It is most common to find waves of feelings alternating and repeating along our paths to resolution and healing. It is helpful for people in grief to hear that they may experience their feelings in waves; that emotions may be triggered by issues related to the death, but also by apparently unrelated issues that resonate somehow with the death. Common triggers for recurring feelings of grief include birthdays, anniversaries and holiday times when we used to get together with the deceased.

Gradually, the waves of grief get less intense and are of shorter duration, though it is fairly common to find occasional, more intense waves of feelings wash over and through us.

When we have someone close who is suffering from a severe injury or illness, and death appears likely or inevitable, we may suffer from anticipatory grief.

We may then find ourselves experiencing any or all of the grief stages prior to the physical demise of the person we're grieving.

All of these are natural psychological processes for letting go of parts of our lives. And we may mourn many types of losses, not just the deaths of people we have known. We may grieve:

- Relationships we have had with other people that change –such as when we or they move away
- Routines we have had for a period of time – such as our employment (including parenthood, the waning of which many of us grieve, as our children grow up and leave home)
- Terminations of a school or activity group, or moving on through the stages of our lives (as in grieving the loss of our childhood)
- Physical aspects of our world that we lose, including body functions or body parts that are lost to injury, illness or surgery, or that simply no longer work they way they used to as we age

I usually don't recommend using EP on current, fresh experiences of grief. Grief is a natural, normal process. In most cases it does not require treatment, unhappy and painful as it may be. Over a period of several weeks or months, grief usually lessens and finally diminishes to more tolerable sadness. Eventually is becomes a memory that is simply there but no longer troublesome or burdensome.

In many cases, once the pain of a loss wanes, our attention shifts and we connect with positive memories of the person or other object of our loss. We remember the happy and nurturing times we had together.

TWR/WHEE or other therapies may be appropriate, however, when grief becomes so intense that it intrudes and interferes with our lives, perhaps even to the point that we are hindered in our normal functions or drained by our mourning to a point of being incapacitated or suicidal.

### *Unresolved grief*

Sometimes our journeys through these stages of grief are interrupted by life circumstances or by our reluctance or fear of delving into the pain, anger, sadness, loss, and other feelings and issues associated with our loss. We may have to force ourselves to sideline or even bury our grief in order to deal with our family issues, show up for work, and attend to general necessities of life. In other cases, we may find our grief issues so painful that we avoid or block them. Then, if our emotions are not processed up to and through the phase of resolution, our residual feelings may fester, grow increasingly intense and worsen. We may end up feeling angry, empty, drained, depleted, helpless, depressed and even suicidal.

Buried and unresolved griefs may also compound other unresolved life issues. For instance, when we are carrying buried traumas, we tend to avoid anything related to our grief. Our unconscious mind protects us from experiencing the pain and distress of stirring our buried feelings into awareness.

To deal with such issues:

- We may avoid discussing issues related to our grief or resonating in our unconscious minds with any grief that touches our life
- We might look for whatever excuses we can find or devise that might support our avoidances

- We could end up avoiding other people who are sad or grieving
- We may avoid interactions and relationships in which we feel there are potentials for meaningful attachments – because we fear to build bonds that could be sundered by another separation or death. In this way we do our best to avoid further grief, which might lead us to resonate so strongly with our repressed memories and feelings from our unresolved grief that we could no longer avoid feeling them.

It is not surprising that HSPs quite often suffer intensely in their grief reactions. When death is approaching in someone close to an HSP, as in terminal illnesses, anticipatory grief can be quite strong. Any residues of unresolved grief reactions from the past may be stirred as well, with similar intensity.

It is often surprising to both the grieving HSP and HSPC, that the HSP may be carrying considerable unresolved, buried residues of grief over losses that occurred in the recent and distant past. While one might expect that the emotional sensitivities and awareness of an HSP would lead them to feel and process their grief intensely and thoroughly, several factors mitigate against this.

HSPs are often distractible, so they may allow themselves to shift their attention away from their losses. In addition, if their ordinary lives include strong stimulations of their emotions, they may unconsciously allow themselves to focus more on the less painful triggers of their emotions than on their grief. This may leave them with buried, unresolved grief.

Many HSPs learn to avoid speaking with NHSPs about issues associated with intense feelings. If their HSPC or other family members are NHSPs, then when the HSPs are grieving they may be pressured or bullied into "not being such a crybaby," "standing strong" (particularly boys and men), "don't upset everyone with your moaning and wailing," or may voluntarily tone down their emotional expressions of grief. Even when others who are uncomfortable with their emotionality say nothing to the HSPs, the HSPs quickly pick up that speaking about their grief is painful to the NHSPs, and will mute their responses out of consideration for others' discomforts. With constant toning down, the HSP's unconscious mind will conform and bury portions of their painful feelings.

Old, buried grief usually responds very readily to tapping therapies. So when there is a very intense mourning over a current loss, it is helpful to inquire about past losses that have left residues of unresolved grief. By lightening the load of such old, buried burdens, we often are able also to lighten the intensity of responses to current losses.

Here are some examples of working through grief reactions:

*A CAUTION TO ANY SENSITIVE READERS: GRAPHIC DETAILS ARE DESCRIBED IN THE NEXT CASES.*\*\*[110]

*Unresolved initial stages of grief*
✢ 'Ellen,' the 58 year-old divorced mother of 'Gabriel', a 20 year-old soldier missing in action in Iraq, was unwilling or unable to accept that he was almost certainly dead, even though it had been five years since he disappeared during an intense battle. She felt she would be disloyal to Gabriel if she grieved for him. She kept hoping beyond waning hope that word would arrive that he had been held captive rather than killed. She was unable to move beyond the denial stage of grieving. Yet after four years, ten months and three days, by her careful count, there was no shred of evidence her son was alive.

Ellen came to me for help because in a single day she had found herself angry at the bus driver, the postal clerk and the market checkout girl. She realized she was carrying a load of excess anger over her lost son and was getting triggered to vent it inappropriately in many situations. She had also withdrawn from social interactions because she was embarrassed over crying with minimal provocations and sometimes for no apparent reason.

I was able to help Ellen connect with and start to release her devastating grief and anger over the loss of her only child, while still holding a little ray of hope in her heart that Gabriel might someday be found alive. Within two weeks she was no longer venting anger inappropriately; after three months, she was starting to socialize again; and after a year she found herself most of the time only occasionally sad – to a manageable degree. It was several more years, though, before she felt she had returned to a life in which she didn't feel a frequent heartache over the loss of her son.

Ellen was a Holocaust survivor, and had suffered the losses of many members of her family and community earlier in her life. In working with older people who carry grief and/or trauma residues, I have learned to proceed very gently. Many older people lack the resilience to change their habits of repressing old hurts – even though they may clearly see the benefits of doing so and may wish to do so. Here, dreams and synchronicities – the projections of their intuitive and higher selves into their awareness and experiences – would have to strongly suggest that they are truly ready to proceed with such psycho-archeology before I would be tempted to encourage them to peer behind the walls they have built around their past traumas and griefs.

✦✦ Ellen had excellent gifts of observing ego. She very quickly learned de-stressing and emotional clearing techniques and used them very appropriately, with excellent results. She had even taught several of her friends to use them as well. I had great confidence that Ellen would have the tools to deal with issues that might trigger her into reconnecting with buried griefs, should these surface. I was also confident that she would seek appropriate professional help and support if she ever needed it again.

### Unresolved middle stages of grief

✦ 'George' lost his second wife to breast cancer after eight years of a very close relationship. 'Rose' had been a wonderfully loving and supportive wife. She had been a warm, accepting stepmother as well to George's two young children, whose mother (Betty) had died in a car accident, three years before George married Rose.

Everyone had praised George for how strong he was to carry on working in a challenging job and caring for his children (8 and 11 years old) after the death of their mother. He was fortunate to have had the help of his older, married sister who lived nearby. George was an accountant in a big business, a person of modest means. He had to work extra hours at home to make ends meet. He had little time to grieve the loss of his first wife. His children followed his lead and pretty much buried their feelings soon after their mother was buried.

George came to me with his two children for help, seven months after Rose's funeral. 'Bob,' age 20, had taken a break from university because he couldn't concentrate enough to manage his studies. He was also irritable and easily angered, which was very uncharacteristic for him. 'Sue,' a junior in high school, had withdrawn socially and was irritable, depressed and angry – with herself and often with others. The consultation was precipitated by Sue's revealing to her aunt that she was feeling suicidal at times. It was clear to all that the double losses of mothers were more than the children could manage on their own.

In further explorations for symptoms of grief reactions, George reported that he often felt considerably more drained of energy and tired at the end of a day's work – more than he had ever experienced prior to Rose's death. He, too, admitted he sometimes had mild, transient suicidal thoughts – wanting to die in order to be with Rose again. This had occurred on the anniversary dates of their wedding, Rose's birthday, and the one-year anniversary of her death.

I chose to see all of them in weekly family sessions because they all acknowledged they were struggling with issues of a grief they experienced in common and because George and Bob also wanted to be of support to Sue. As with most people in grief, the initial work was to open themselves to their neglected and buried feelings. Sue was the most open in sharing her emotions, and this was a help to the others to connect with and to express theirs. She clarified that her suicidal thoughts and wishes were expressions of missing her stepmother and mother and longing to be with them.

Because they had not grieved the earlier loss of Betty, their feelings about her death were also explored and released. After six weekly sessions, followed by four monthly sessions, they were all in much better emotional spaces. Sue was no longer having suicidal thoughts and Bob was fully able to return to his studies. All reported they felt more energy in general in their daily lives.

Sue elected to continue monthly sessions, having become aware in the course of our family sessions that she is an HSP, and that she had consciously felt her suffering more intensely than her brother or father, who were NHSPs.

What was most helpful to Sue was to identify and clear her meta-anxieties about expressing her feelings, to release buried traumas of feeling rejected and abnormal because she was so openly emotional, which also upset other people, and to install positive thoughts, feelings and self-image awarenesses to replace the negatives she had released. There were also very deep elements of grief from her childhood, from having come to feel she would never be accepted by people with whom she was close because she was so easily triggered into feeling and expressing her emotions so intensely.

When people have not grieved through to the point of resolution over several years from the time of their losses, it is often helpful to them to use a releasing technique. It is very common for people to realize they have been functioning at considerably less than their full capacities after clearing such buried emotions. George was enormously grateful for having learned TWR, which he was able to use if any of his residual feelings of grief were again stirred over losing both of his wives.

*Unresolved resolution stage of grief*
✦ 'Wilma's' husband of 22 years, 'Joe,' was killed in a street robbery. This childless couple had been extremely close with each other and Wilma was utterly devastated. She came for help because she felt she was "just not herself" since she had lost Joe, four years earlier. Wilma appeared to have processed her grief, with recurrent periods of deep sadness; anger at the robber; anger at

God for having allowed Joe to be killed; guilt over blaming God; and many other such feelings in the spectrum of grief. It is quite common to experience these sorts of responses in any grief process – both normal and prolonged. But Wilma never returned to being the fully warm and caring person she had been prior to this tragedy. She avoided socializing, isolating herself from colleagues at work and also from extended family – in ways she had never done prior to Joe's death.

As frequently seen in unresolved grief, Wilma had also experienced prior, unresolved grief. She had lost a twin sister at birth and later on lost her father when she was in college. Both had been ungrieved losses. Her father had been estranged from the family after running off with his secretary when Wilma was in her early teens. Wilma recalled having sided completely with her mother when her father left, and having felt no grief at that time. She also felt no grief for her twin.

While the loss of a twin at an early age is generally dismissed as irrelevant to the surviving twin, we are learning that this is far from true. Even the death of a twin in utero may be experienced by the surviving twin as a serious loss, consciously or unconsciously (McCarty, 2012).

✦✦ Wilma found herself experiencing the whole gamut of grief emotions, in sessions focused on both of her earlier losses. She also released many more layers of her most recent grief, including hurt, abandonment, anger, betrayal, and most importantly, distrust and avoidance of relationships – due to unresolved elements of grief over the loss of her husband, Joe. TWR/WHEE was a great help to her in connecting with, processing and releasing these feelings. After clearing the issues that had been blocking her resolution of her grief over losing her husband, and then working through her mourning over losing her sister, she soon felt herself back to being her full self – though still missing Joe at times. (Periodic residual grieving is normal after losing someone very close.)

The above are examples of people who were fortunate enough to live in modern times and in places where understanding of grief and help to deal with its resolution were available. On the whole, these are a minority of people – even in settings in which such grief counseling is available.

Extended family supports often help in dealing with grief, particularly in traditional societies where family members still reside nearby and/or remain in close contact with each other. Grandparents and other extended family, friends, elders, and others provide social, emotional and material supports. These can bring healings in many ways to those who experience trauma and grief. Where people grieve together, they often bond more deeply and continue to be supportive of each other.

Sadly, there are many who do not have such supports for dealing with their grief processes. Their life circumstances, past and present, do not provide them with outer or inner resources or supports for releasing their grief. Unresolved grief often remains and festers as an enormous burden of drained energies. It also tends to distort people's feelings, behaviors and lives. The above examples provide just small windows into the challenges that can develop through lingering residues of grief.

Dealing with grief is an enormously complex subject. A few further references deserve high mentions.

Catherine Sanders (1992) details a summary of stages of grief slightly different than those of Kubler-Ross, who is generally seen as the definitive reference on this subject. Sanders offers excellent observations and advice for dealing with parental bereavement, death of a spouse, dealing as an adult with one's own parents' death, family grieving, and transcending death and grief.

Tranquilizing medications (such as valium), antidepressants and sleeping pills are often prescribed shortly after people suffer the loss of someone close to them. While they have the good intention of alleviating the distress of grief, many doctors have had very little, if any, education or training in the management of grief, and are far too quick to prescribe drugs for symptoms of sadness, hurt and anger that are perfectly natural and not valid indications for these prescripts. Such drugs may end up preventing people from feeling, expressing, working through, and releasing their distresses over their losses. Medications can thus set them up to be more vulnerable when they encounter future losses because they will be carrying buried, unresolved feelings from their current grief that leave them vulnerable to being triggered into more intense grief by their later losses. We saw that with Ellen, whose soldier son was missing in action, which undoubtedly triggered some of her deeply buried feelings of losses from the holocaust.

Grief may, however, spiral into a serious, suicidal depression, particularly in someone who has a personal and/or familial history of serious depression. In these cases, antidepressants have a definite place in people who are struggling to deal with their grief. It is highly recommended to seek the help of a psychiatrist in these cases.

Unrecognized grief is worth mentioning again here, now that we've considered in detail what grief is about and how we feel, process and gradually clear it. Grief doesn't always burden us in clear and obvious ways. Particularly with losses that many people consider and would experience as relatively minor. This is the sad news for HSPs. Having increased sensitivities, we respond more strongly to challenging issues in our lives. Consider the grief you may feel in leaving a place of work; moving to a new home; breaking up when you've been in a steady dating relationship;[111] watching elderly parents and other relatives and friends fade into old age; watching your children grow up, and, in essence, pushing you into parental unemployment when they leave home.

Fear of dying is another aspect of grief that often weighs on people and may create difficulties. This is particularly true in modern societies where we distance ourselves from death. In the West, for instance, people commonly die in the hospital. Their bodies are transferred by family with a phone call to a mortuary, and the funeral is held with the body neatly arranged in the coffin or even with a closed coffin. People may never see or touch a dead body, and come to fear death because it is unfamiliar.

Thus, there is in many of us a strong motivation to distance ourselves from the anticipation of our own death. The greatest part of these anxieties appear to be due to fear of an experience that is largely unknown to us. Grief over the death of others will thus resonate with fears of our own death. Burying one's feelings of grief may help to distance people from considering their own mortality and the uncertainties that lie beyond physical life. Thus, many will distance themselves from the whole topic of death. This is particularly true in societies where physical death is believed to be the end of existence for a person.

On a personal basis, one of the greatest losses in our avoidance of dealing with awarenesses of death is that we then lose opportunities to experience evidence that physical death is not the end of life. The pre-death and deathbed apparitions reported by many people suggest that physical death is not the end of existence.[112]

Our individual and collective reluctance to even acknowledge that global warming may be well on its way might be explained in part by anxieties and fears of deaths of massive numbers of people in this impending disaster, along with the increasingly possibilities of our own death and/or that of our descendants. These fears we experience would be markedly enhanced by any unresolved griefs we are carrying. This may be one of the reasons that humanity is not taking active steps to deal with the multiple causes of the mass extinction that looms ever more possible as time passes and little or nothing is done to avert it.*[113]

HSPs often have very strong experiences when they grieve. In many ways HSPs are actually fortunate to feel their emotions of grief so intensely. This makes it more difficult to ignore and bury these sad emotions, which might otherwise fester until they are triggered into awareness at some later date.

HSPs often become totally immersed in their feelings, particularly if these are intense. As an HSPC you can be most helpful by just being present and acknowledging the feelings of grief. If you and your HSP have explored the uses and found benefits from the de-stressing methods described in this book, then you, the HSPC, may also be supportive in suggesting to your HSP that she use those approaches that proved helpful previously on her current issues.

### *Good grief*

Grief can be a celebration of fond farewells and appreciation of life rather than primarily being a sad occasion.

A good start in this direction can be instructions from the person being celebrated, detailing his or her preferences in funeral and burial ceremonies. This is a preventive against arguments between the family members about such details. It is best to include wishes for advance directives regarding terminal care and organ donations, the preparation of the body after death, type of service and/or celebration (including specific prayers, music and songs), disposition of the remains, and last will and testament. The more detailed these instructions are, the less likely it is that there will be discord and grief over sorting out these issues. Naming a person among several people, in order of preference, to be in charge is also helpful.

Without such guidance, conflicts may arise due to different opinions and preferences of various survivors regarding the customary family, cultural and religious funeral arrangements and preferences of family and friends. At times, these can become serious points of contention, arguments and bitterness.

When death is approaching through serious illness, injury and/ or waning of strength and life energies, a celebration of the person's life prior to their impending death, with their participation, can be a blessing to all. Sharing of love, fond memories, gratitude and sadness, along with apologies and forgiveness over conflicts or transgressions, will all contribute to making this a healing experience. Even when the dying person is unconscious, this can be a powerful experience for all.

Electronic communications, including phones, cellphones and Skype can broaden the participation in these celebrations, particularly when an impending death was unexpected.

Celebrations of these sorts can bring a lot of healing into the grieving process.[114]

Robert Romanyshyn (1999) shares a poetic description of his path through mourning the death of his wife. I found this an inspirational book.

*... there were stories to accompany me along the path, tales told by those who had returned from the land of grief and who had brought with them an account of their travels. Such stories were not prescriptions for action. They were testimonies which told me that, while I had to find my own way through grief, I was not alone...*

*So often in these moments of rest, I felt that my personal grief intersected with a collective one. On these occasions, I was lost in a kind of reverie. Time would slip away, and for a while the boundaries between myself and the world were erased, easing somewhat the cold feeling of isolation which grief brings. In reverie before these warming fires, I could hear those other. Voices whispering that grief arises because we have dared to love, that grief is the mark of the power of love, to love even when we know that life is loss, to love even though we know that those whom we love will one day pass away.*
– Robert Romanyshyn

# SECTION III. Understanding the HSP: Alternative or additional diagnoses

*Symptoms are perceived through the categories of psychiatric medicine at a given moment in history, categories which are continually shifting and being named or renamed.*
- Siri Hustvedt

Doctors and therapists who are unfamiliar with the HSP trait may mistakenly diagnose HSPs with any or several of the diagnoses below. In other cases, HSPs may actually have these problems but the doctors miss the characteristics of the HSP trait that may also be present, making it appear that the disorders are more severe than they actually are.

## 17. Attention Deficit Hyperactivity Disorder (ADHD) / ADD

Many HSPs present some of the symptoms commonly found in ADHD, including any of the following: mild to modest hyperactivity, distractibility, impulsivity in expressing emotions and/or in their actions, and at other times being over-focused. When the hyperactivity is absent, the syndrome is called Attention Deficit Disorder (ADD). These problems are often worsened by the high levels of sensitivity, emotionality and arousal of HSPs and may generate varieties of challenges for HSPs and HSPCs.

If these symptoms are prominent and troublesome, it is well worthwhile exploring how to reduce or eliminate them – assuming they may be due to ADHD/ADD, separately from HSP qualities. There are standardized psychological tests for ADHD. If resources permit, it is well worth while having a formal assessment if there is a suspicion that this may be the cause of a child's or an adult's difficulties in functioning.[1,2]

The majority of children who have ADHD or ADD outgrow it in their middle or late teen years. But a significant percent continue to suffer from these symptoms into adulthood. This is a diagnosis often missed by family doctors, who are frequently not trained to deal with psychological issues or to make psychiatric diagnoses.

As noted above, many of the symptoms of ADHD and ADD overlap with HSP issues that can be problematic. Examples come readily to mind, such as being distractible, impulsive, and having difficulties in activating left brain thinking functions. So it may take some detective work to clarify whether ADHD is truly an issue. As mentioned above, various screening scales have been developed for children and adults and may be helpful to you.*[3]

NHSPs may experience ADHD-like symptoms under serious stress and traumas, but with them these are uncharacteristic relative to their normal ranges of emotional sensitivities and behaviors. HSPs often experience these sorts of symptoms with much milder stresses – ones that most NHSPs would ignore or just take in stride. So the lack of awareness of the HSP trait is clearly the cause of these confusions.

I am puzzled by Elaine Aron's (1996) report that she has almost never seen an HSP with ADHD. My best guess is that my experience of years of diagnosing and treating ADHD and ADD in children and adults makes me more ready to apply these labels, while Aron's vast experience with HSPs leads her to see typical HSP qualities when she observes these.

Regardless of the diagnosis, for HSPs it is helpful to be aware of such symptoms that may be troublesome. Distractibility and over-focusing are the most common of these.

It is enormously helpful to have an HSPC who is aware of such issues and able to point out to your HSP that she is stuck in a groove of over-focusing, or that she has gotten distracted and strayed from the subject under discussion or from a task he has begun.

Preventive measures for dealing with ADHD are worth pursuing. First and foremost is to check whether sugar or food coloring (especially red or yellow dye) in one's diet are causing the ADHD/ADD or making it worse. Other food sensitivities may also do this, but it takes careful detective work to identify them. Sometimes it is not a single food but a combination of foods that produce ADHD symptoms. Two weeks of a very bland diet in order to identify troublesome food items, as these are added one at a time, may be a challenge to live with but can be of sufficient benefits as to make it worth the efforts.

Stress and anxieties can also worsen ADHD/ADD, so lowering stress levels and learning anxiety reduction methods may be very helpful.

The next approach is to explore homeopathic remedies. My experience is that these are only sometimes helpful, and are more likely to succeed with prescriptions from a homeopath who has a lot of experience in treating ADHD.

After the above steps, medication is another possibility. But a caution here. Many doctors are not well trained in managing ADHD. Pediatricians and Psychiatrists often (but not always) are more familiar with the medications that can help. In choosing a doctor to help with ADHD, you are best off seeking a recommendation from satisfied and grateful patients.

As mentioned above, stimulant medications such as Ritalin (effects lasting 4 hours) and Adderall (lasting 8 hours) are frequently prescribed by pediatricians and family physicians for these symptoms, although they may have had little training in using these medications.

I have seen numerous sensitive people who did not do well on these medications because they were under- or over-medicated. HSPs may be extra-sensitive to such stimulants, so smaller doses may be advisable for initial trials of stimulants. The generic version, Methylphenidate, is often the gentlest form available.

Side effects may include loss of appetite, stomach pains, headaches, nervousness, insomnia and more.[4]

## 18. Oppositional Defiant Disorder (ODD)

There are numerous children and some adults who are highly oppositional, will frequently balk as a reflex when asked to do something, and resist cooperating when someone appears to be telling them what, how or when to do anything. They insist on doing things their own way. They are highly irritable, easily angered, and will argue about anything and everything. They are often defiant and may take pleasure in provoking others into joining them in arguments, mischief and misbehaviors. They may also hold grudges and be vindictive. They set themselves up to perpetuate and worsen their challenges because they provoke others to be angry with them. These are symptoms of ODD. Research has shown that boys outnumber girls in this diagnostic category by 3 or 4 to 1.[5]

HSPs sometimes may be given this diagnosis because they often hold back from jumping into activities, strongly preferring to feel and contemplate their ways into participating – or into deciding not to join in. They may be labeled as being ODD due to their insistence on doing things their own way or due to taking a long time to make decisions, as they feel their way through analyzing whether they want to accept or do things.

Those HSPs who are also HSS may be oppositional when asked to participate in repetitive routines, which they find boring. They may also creatively stir mischief in their searches for intense experiences.

Recommended treatment of ODD, per the DSM-V, involves psychotherapy, training of the children with ODD and those who interact with them to build positive family, peer and teacher interactions and skills to manage their behaviors. Medications may be helpful to treat the irritability, anxieties, and related mental health conditions.

### *Helpful approaches for getting along with oppositional children*

We often create and worsen issues by how we identify and label them. Calling a person oppositional and defiant is often an invitations to set up a power contest with them. Think how Johnny will respond if he's in an oppositional frame of mind (for whatever reason) and you say to him, "You WILL obey me! NOW!" The two of you are heading for a power struggle that is likely to be frustrating and unpleasant for both of you.

Consider, instead, how you might approach Johnny if you perceive and identify him as a 'fiercely independent person.' You absolutely know that whatever you tell him, he's very likely to oppose you.

How about using what I call 'mental judo'? In judo, we use a person's own movements and strengths to get him to move in the direction that WE want him to move. So, knowing that Johnny is going to move in a direction he perceives as opposite to what we want, ask or tell him to do, we can use reverse psychology and say something like:

- "I don't expect you're in a mood to [do whatever you're wanting Johnny to do] right now…"
- "The other children are going [to do 'x'] but you look like you're probably not ready to join them."
- "I don't know if you'd want/ are ready to do 'x', because I see you're working on 'y' and might want to continue doing that, rather than [doing whatever 'x' you're wanting Johnny to do].

When I first learned about paradoxical interventions in my family therapy training, I was horrified. This seemed like a deliberate manipulation of people and I expected they would feel I was 'messing them about' or 'playing with their heads.'

I was very pleasantly surprised to experience just the opposite with them. They felt acknowledged and accepted in being fiercely independent. They would generally bite the bait and move in the opposite direction to what I was suggesting or asking them to consider doing – which was actually the direction I was hoping they would choose, on their own, without an argument.

This mental judo is also helpful with HSP or NHSP children who are oppositional. Often, this is not because they are habitually negativistic, but rather that they are bothered by HuTiST, absorbed in thought or totally absorbed in an activity, and likely to resist shifting into whatever activity you want or need them to do. It is a challenge to you to develop whatever creative modifications of paradoxical suggestions you find that work with them. A variation I've often seen working successfully, to the benefit of everyone, is to offer several choices, all of which are acceptable to you.

- "Would you like a sandwich or a bowl of chili for lunch today?"
- "Do you want to have your shower before or after [your sister/ me/ other]?"
- "Are you ready to go to bed now or in [x number of minutes/ at a specified time]?"

Once they have agreed to their choice among the options on offer, they feel more in control. If they choose to act immediately, the problem is solved. If they chose a later time, then a reminder about the agreed time may be all that is needed. But again, ask ahead of time, "Will you keep an eye on the clock or do you want me to remind you?"

If they are still oppositional, you can offer them choices such as:

- "You chose to [fill in appropriately] and you and I agreed on this. You and I can have a pleasant time doing this now or we could have a good argument about it."
- If they choose the argument, you might bet them that they can't guess what you're going to say next. If you keep the tone playful, you can often have a relatively pleasant, pretend argument. Stay firm in your insistence that they abide by their agreement.

I have seen numbers of HSPs who are strongly independent in the above ways. They come for help but resist therapeutic suggestions and present creative excuses for not following their therapy plans. Accepting their behaviors and giving them choices in how to proceed with their treatment plans is often very helpful. Holding a reluctantly skeptical attitude regarding the likelihood of change for the better is both realistic and supportive, as discussed above.

Such oppositional behaviors can be quite challenging for HSPCs to accept and to respond to in constructive ways. Much patience is required. TWR/WHEE is highly recommended for the HSPCs for dealing with these sorts of challenges to their patience.

## 19. Obsessive Compulsive Disorder (OCD)

People with OCD often seem to have a mental needle that tends at times to get stuck in a groove. They obsess and ruminate repeatedly (if not endlessly) over issues, develop avoidances for certain situations, and/or engage in habitual or ritualized behaviors – particularly when they become anxious. Some may exhibit these behaviors in specific situations; others will do so at apparently irregular intervals. Common OCD behaviors include frequent handwashing, re-checking that doors are properly locked, avoiding certain things, and precisely placing certain objects in particular locations.

HSPs may appear to have OCD because they will return repeatedly to the same feelings that are distressing them, mulling over what they did wrong or what they haven't yet done right. They can be hypersensitive to irritations to their sensory system and will go to great lengths to avoid these irritations – which most NHSPs will not even be aware of. Generally, these are not manifestations of OCD type ritual avoidance, but in rare instances these ruminations may be incorporated into OCD thinking and behaviors. I have seen a few HSPs who develop OCD habits as coping mechanisms for dealing with their anxieties.

Similarly, when faced with decisions they find challenging, they may vacillate back and forth between several options, getting wound up emotionally on each side of their emotional ambivalences.

For the most part, however, while HSPs may ruminate and obsess over their emotions and concerns (personal and interpersonal), may develop avoidances for situations they find stressful, and engage in habitual or ritualized behaviors when anxious, they generally do not continue to focus on the same issues and behaviors endlessly. Within minutes, hours or days they resolve the issues about which they are ruminating. They may be prone, however, to pick up other issues over which they will fester for periods of time.

Such habits of ruminating repeatedly over the same issues, again and again, often in ritualized ways, are very persistent and difficult for people with OCD to control or alter. Therapies that are sometimes effective, in order of their success rates (in my personal experience and reading) include:

- Cognitive Behavioral Therapy (CBT) has been the most recommended psychological for the control of the OCD behaviors. In particular, Exposure and Response Prevention (ERP) can help to overcome the OCD habits and the anxieties that arise when people even think of resisting their compulsions. With the firm support of a therapist, a person with OCD will be guided to start thinking about their OCD thoughts and rituals. They will then be guided in resisting them through relaxations, distractions and sheer willpower (or in this case won't-power). With time and persistence this can markedly lessen the frequency and intensity of these behaviors. Serious persistence is needed! [6]

- Energy Psychology (EP) can be very helpful for dealing with anxieties that trigger OCD behaviors. TWR/WHEE also helps by focusing on meta-anxieties, such as the anxieties that arise when people are struggling between their OCD habits and their wishes and efforts to resist them. They worry that if they resist doing the behaviors they will become more anxious – which becomes a self-fulfilling prophecy, generating a vicious circle of worries. By tapping on this worry about what will happen when they resist, some can significantly reduce their OCD habits.

– Another contribution of TWR/WHEE is through building and strengthening a Place of Peace and Safety and Healing (PPSH). This provides an inner space where people who are wound up and very anxious can relax and calm themselves – enabling them to persist in addressing their OCD thoughts and behaviors.[7]

✦ Gina was a bright, second year university psychology student who was getting above average grades and generally well adjusted. She had always been meticulous in her personal hygiene, strongly influenced by her mother's strict rules at home about cleanliness being important in order to stay healthy.

Gina came to me for help because she was finding herself worrying about getting sick because her roommate, Lisa, was very untidy and insensitive to matters of cleanliness. This bothered Gina, particularly in Lisa's messiness in their shared dormitory bathroom. What started out as a difference in preferences rapidly escalated to Gina's obsessing about dirtiness and worrying about getting infections or illnesses. She developed compulsive cleaning rituals, scrubbing the sink and bathtub three times prior to using them. This had continued for the better part of her school year, and started to generalize to having to wash public sinks before washing her hands. What precipitated her seeking help was her discovering that she felt compelled to do the same cleaning rituals when she visited her home for Spring break – since she clearly did not need to be cleaning up when her mother was keeping her home spotless.

Gina was aware of her behaviors as fitting the OCD diagnosis, and came for help very shortly after starting to feel she could not stop herself from washing the sink or shower prior to using them, even when she knew her roommate had not used them in the interval since she herself had washed there. With TWR/WHEE she was able to calm the anxieties that were stimulated when she imagined herself at the sink or in the bathtub, and to build her confidence that she could wash herself without having to scrub the bathtub or sink three times.

The fact that Gina came for help very soon after developing her OCD anxieties and behaviors made it much easier for her to stop these behaviors than it generally is for others with OCD who had come after finding themselves stuck in OCD ruminations and compulsive actions over much longer periods of time. Gina's psychological awareness was also much higher than those in my years of experience in helping most other people with OCD have been. It is uncommon for people with OCD to recall a precipitating trauma or predisposing factors that contributed to the development of their OCD. My personal impression is that people who develop OCD often are low on the spectrum of observing ego abilities.

Antidepressant medications can significantly decrease OCD thoughts and behaviors, but about half the people with OCD who use these have to stop due to side effects.[8]

## 20. Attachment styles

There are four attachment styles that are helpful to consider in looking at potential compatibility harmonies or challenges in relationships (Diehl, et al, 1998). These are based on the Freudian observations, well-documented in many decades of research, that early life experiences imprint patterns in people beliefs and behavior about how safe or unsafe the world is for them, and how they should respond to other people.

- The secure style, present in close to 50 percent of Western populations, is developed when children have adequate, regular, and reliable attention to their needs from infancy and throughout childhood. This consistency in early relationships creates a solid sense of selfhood in the person, including feeling good in the company of others, as well as knowing they are able to trust others and be trusted by them.

- The preoccupied style, present in around 10 percent, wish they had good relationships but their childhood experiences were uncomfortable enough to make them uncertain from early in life about trusting others. This style is usually due to one parent alternating between being uninvolved and over-involved and over-controlling in the care of the child. This leads children to grow up with great insecurities and anxieties about whether they are worthy of being loved and accepted. They hold the wishes and hopes of finding relationships that will be satisfying, safe and reliable but are very anxious and doubtful of succeeding in doing so. These anxieties lead to holding back from full commitments to a relationship.

- The dismissive-avoidant style, present in around 30 percent, includes people who develop with similar parental relationships to those with the preoccupied style, but with more severe trauma. In these cases, the lack of acceptance of the child and the lack of attention to their childhood needs for acceptance and encouragement led to more severe doubts about the possibility that anyone could like them or accept them. These people grow up seeking satisfaction in life through a focus on work and career, avoiding close involvements with other people. They tend to deny the need for emotional attachments and to dismiss or even disparage the feelings of others. These distancing ways of relating increase with age.

- The fearful-avoidant style, present in about 10 percent, have responded to the poor parenting they received with strong yearnings to have friendships but being very fearful of rejections. In this style, when opportunities for closeness arise, the fearful avoidant people may become anxious even to the point of being disorganized. Sometimes the label of 'disorganized' is applied to this sub-group. Parents or other caregivers of members of this group often behaved in ways that generated in the child feelings of being in danger, physically or emotionally. The children in these situations wanted to help their caregivers but were frightened by them and confused about how to behave. The same uncertainties and ambivalence carry over into their adult relationships.

Understanding these styles of relating may explain some of the challenges you are experiencing when you are encountering major conflicts in your relationships. However, it may be difficult for you and your partner to confirm whether these are relevant to your situation when you are in the midst of sorting out your challenges in getting along. If you sense that there may be an attachment style issue, consulting a psychotherapist who specializes in helping people with these sorts of issues may be advisable and very helpful.

Conventional psychotherapists commonly view attachment style problems as extremely unlikely to respond to anything but very long-term, intensive therapy – if at all. The recently developed EP approaches can be of enormous help here. Wholistic EP may greatly facilitate the releasing of residues of traumas, even from early in life, which can be causal factors in attachment disorders. This is not to say that attachment disorders can be easily cleared, but that these EP approaches offer tools that can be helpful when diligently applied to such issues.

HSPs may be labeled with this diagnosis when they have experienced difficult and traumatic relationships in their families, due to their high sensitivities and to having to protect themselves from the pathologizing and bullying from their family members, as discussed earlier.

## 21. Borderline Personality Disorder

People given the diagnosis of borderline personality have seriously difficult personalities and are challenged in developing and maintaining interpersonal relationships. They are stubborn and easily triggered into anger. They will distance themselves from others, though many of them crave closeness with others. This cluster of traits makes it difficult for them to get along with just about everyone in their lives and are prescriptions for depression.

HSPs frequently ruminate and obsess over their emotions and concerns (personal and interpersonal), develop avoidances for situations and relationships they find stressful, and may engage in impulsive avoidant behaviors when anxious. Most troublesome, and overlapping with some of the characteristics of borderline personality, HSPs may have difficulties in developing and maintaining many close relationships. They often tend to have one or just a few close friends.

Some of those HSPs I've seen had emotional lability, irritability and anger outbursts, along with troubled relationships that raised the possibility of borderline diagnosis in my mind. These HSPs had very high emotional sensitivity and low tolerance for other people's insensitivities. Many also had suffered traumas that left them with post traumatic stress disorders. These challenges in their lives left them with high levels of distrust in other people and the defensive habits of pushing people away.

Criteria for a diagnosis of Borderline Personality have been made more complex than previously, per the latest version of the Diagnostic and Statistical Manual of the American Psychiatric Association (Oldham, 2015). They include:

1. Fear of abandonment
2. Difficult interpersonal relationships
3. Uncertainty about self-image or identity
4. Impulsive behavior
5. Self-injurious behavior
6. Emotional changeability or hyperactivity
7. Feelings of emptiness
8. Difficulty controlling intense anger
9. Transient suspiciousness or 'disconnectedness'

Each of these items has detailed aspects that must be considered. Not every person with this disorder manifests all of these characteristics. Many parents of people labeled as borderline personality describe them as having had difficulties getting along with other people from very early on in life. Many also report there were stresses that impacted these children.

My personal impression is that serious trauma may be present far more frequently than is generally appreciated where this diagnosis is applied. These people often have great difficulties functioning with any sort of stability. Their emotional instability makes it difficult for them to work or to stay in long-term relationships, including therapeutic relationships.

Conventional treatments for borderline personality are primarily through behavioral therapy that teaches how to identify, understand and control disturbing and disruptive emotions, thoughts and behaviors. The severity of the challenges experienced by people with borderline personalities makes it difficult for them to work their ways through psychotherapy to learn better ways of relating with others. Medications such as antidepressants and antipsychotics, often in small doses, may help (Mayo Clinic, Web ref.).

Wholistic EP can be of significant help to these people. Working on meta-anxieties and expectations of rejections is particularly important because the prickliness of their ways of relating leads them into situations and interactions where they feel repeatedly rejected.*[9]

HSPs may be labeled with this diagnosis when they have experienced difficult and traumatic relationships in their families, due to their high sensitivities and/or due to pathologizing and bullying from their family members, as discussed earlier, with other diagnoses.

## 22. Narcissistic personality disorder (NPD)

Narcissistic personality disorder (NPD) includes grandiosity, a lack of empathy, and seeking excessive admiration. The prevalence rate in the general population is under 1 percent, yet within groups of people in psychotherapy, this number has been estimated between to be as high as 2 to 16 percent, with 3 times as many men as women having this diagnosis. Many teenagers are prone to exhibit narcissism at some points along their paths to maturity, but this is generally a passing developmental phase and in many cases may be responsive to psychotherapy. NPD in adults is very difficult to treat and often present with other psychological challenges, such as substance abuse (Ronningstam & Weinberg, 2013). Without long-term therapy, which few people with NPD are willing to pursue, change in their NPD is highly unlikely.

Narcissistic personality disorder (NPD) may be identified in people who have anxiety, depression, relationship challenges, or other challenges. NPD is often resistant to conventional psychotherapy approaches. It is found more often in men than in women. Typically, these people are self-righteous, insist on having their way or no way, are controlling and dismissive of others. Despite these outer appearances of enormous self-confidence, these people suffer strong feelings of low self-esteem and inadequacy. They have very low tolerance for criticisms or disapproval and generally lack empathy and respect for others. Their personal and professional relationships are generally poor, because their condescending and dismissive attitudes are difficult to tolerate.**[10]

While it may seem contradictory that an HSP might be insensitive to other people's feelings, I have seen this fairly often as a part of responses to trauma. Some HSPs who grow up in a family where they were not accepted for who they are or were rejected by others because of their sensitivities, may compensate by over-valuing themselves. They may also absorb some of their family's attitudes and behaviors of dismissing and de-valuing others, starting with family members who the HSPs devalue because these family members devalue them. Whether to identify this as NPD or as part of a trauma reaction may be a difficult call.

In clarifying whether a diagnosis of NPD is warranted and helpful, a therapist may find it useful to clarify whether the HSP has more of an observing ego*[11] than an NHSP with NPD diagnosis typically has. Typically, HSPs are much more self-aware and capable of introspection and insight, despite their traumas that led them to focus more on their self-interests.

An HSPC can be enormously helpful to HSPs with NPD characteristics, particularly when these are due to trauma. Acceptance of your HSP's emotional sensitivities and expressivity will be deeply healing. This will require a lot of patience on your part, though, because countless repetitions of your inputs over many months and perhaps even years will probably be required.

### *Post Traumatic Stress Disorder* (PTSD)

This is a diagnosis that is often missed in HSPs, who may be traumatized by experiences that NHSPs could tolerate but the HSPs find intolerable. This has been discussed above, in ch. 15 on Trauma.

*In summary: Alternative or additional diagnoses*

Some HSPs may exhibit symptoms and behaviors that warrant some of these diagnoses. In many of these cases, however, what appear to be symptoms of ADHD, ODD, OCD, etc. are aspects of their being HSPs and their responses to how people have related to them. In other cases, they may be HSPs and also have symptoms that do warrant these diagnoses. Much of this confusion arises because many HSP characteristics can overlap with symptoms of such more widely recognized psychological challenges as anxiety disorder, OCD, and others detailed above. This is particularly true when HSPs have experienced serious traumas, especially earlier in life. Resourcing with stress management tools can be very helpful.

It is not surprising that the conventional medical and psychological communities, who are largely unfamiliar with the HSP trait, would give HSPs such diagnoses – sometimes, but not always justified by the symptoms – but would still completely miss the heightened sensitivities that contributed in these cases to the development of the trauma issues.

It is quite common for HSPs to receive prescriptions for stimulants (for ADHD symptoms), or tranquilizers or antidepressants that are intended to help them deal with symptoms of ODD, OCD and so on. Sadly, the medications may diminish or dull the symptoms, but they don't get to the roots of HSP difficulties to alleviate or eliminate these.**[12]

# SECTION IV. HSPs, Their HSPCs and other family members

*It is because I think so much of warm and sensitive hearts, that I would spare them from being wounded.*
- Charles Dickens

## 23. Companioning the HSP: Relationship gifts, challenges and benefits

In Section II we explored a rainbow of general factors at play in the lives of HSPs and of their HSPCs. In close relationships, HSPs will often be sensitive in many, if not all, of the wholistic aspects of body, emotions, mind, relationships and spirit, which is the focus in this section of this book.

The quality of relationships is a tremendously important issue to HSPs in general, and in close relationships in particular. Sensitivity has many layers and nuances that we do well to pay attention to, both in ourselves and in each other. Even though we are aware of this issue, it may often be a challenge to deal with some or all of the levels of sensitivities of another person, particularly when these differ from our own. This is particularly true when an HSP is partnered with an NHSP.

We've considered how being in a relationship with an HSP can feel like an immeasurable treasure of deep awarenesses, with intense feelings of caring and loving, It can also be enormously challenging or stressful, for the very same reason that it is often complex and intense.

If you are an NHSP, you are signing up for all sorts of lessons, many of them totally unanticipated. You will be invited through living with a highly sensitive person to experience and understand feelings, closeness and intuition as you would probably never be able to achieve on your own. And these will also be lessons about yourself and how you perceive and interact with the world in general.

If you are an HSP, you will be challenged to explain yourself. You will come to awarenesses of your own sensitivities through the contrasts between the two of you, and to better understand your NHSP's lower levels of sensitivity, despite caring for you. Thus, you can both be doubly enriched through your HSP qualities in your relationships.

An NHSP may find the relationship with an HSP stressful, awkward, unpleasant and even at times hard to bear. Being pushed in the process of being in the relationship to engage in feelings and emotions that are outside your comfort zones may be anywhere from difficult to unpleasant or in some instances intolerable.

These observations also apply to your relationships with parents, siblings, partners, children, friends, co-workers and acquaintances. They apply as well to various settings, such as your place of work, where your relationships with other employees in general can be a major factor in your job satisfaction, or lack therof. The learning curves at the start of any of these relationships may be quite steep. Be patient and persistent. The rewards are incalculable, but the challenges and frustrations may be equally beyond your expectations.

In this section we consider a broad spectrum of approaches and tools for exploring and clarifying the challenges that may arise in your relationships, and explore methods for sorting them out. Remember always that challenges in life need not be solely experienced as burdens. Even the most difficult life experiences almost always offer opportunities to better understand yourself, your HSP or HSPC and your relationships, and to deepen and strengthen your enjoyments and satisfactions with each other and with life in general.

*The heart has a mind that the brain struggles to understand.*
— Blaise Pascal

This section begins to address deeper questions about which ways are best for exploring and developing our lives, and what are the true meanings and purposes of our lives. These questions often arise in significant relationships, where we interact closely with other people who are sufficiently similar to ourselves so we have the ease and comfort of common interests and activities, and with whom we are deepening our trust, but where we are at the same time sufficiently different so that we challenge each other to re-examine our own understandings about the meanings and purposes of our lives.

Relationships are so important that I give this topic its own section, despite the fact that we consider broad ranges of HSPC – HSP wholistic issues throughout our explorations in this book. Here, I invite you to consider some core matters that are likely to come up and ways you may choose to deal with them to achieve the most helpful and healing outcomes.

If you are an HSP yourself, you will each be exploring and discovering ways in which your sensitivities and responsivities overlap and harmonize with each other. Even though you are both highly sensitive, your ranges of sensitivities and life experiences will probably differ sufficiently that each of you can share awarenesses that your partner has not yet explored, or to which your partner has not been particularly sensitive. Where your experiences as HSPs differ, you will each become aware of your partner's particularly keen awarenesses, as well as understanding and appreciating your own spectrum of HSP gifts. You will certainly be enriched by expansions and deepenings of your enjoyments in music, visual arts, films, theater, literature and other creative arts.

Being an HSPC with an HSP is an enormous gift. Your relationship is going to raise your awareness in varieties of ways. The differences in your sensitivities are going to invite discussions and clarifications between you. Through learning more about your NHSP partner, you, the HSP, will have windows of perceptions into how the majority of people experience their world – with less sensitivity and reactivity to their physical senses, emotions, thoughts, relationships and spirit. This can also be enormously instructive to you regarding your own sensitivities, in varieties of ways. Having a partner who wants to understand you will invite you to understand and explain yourself more clearly – first and foremost to yourself, and then to your partner.

You, the HSP, may often come up with much clearer awarenesses and understandings of possible new ways to deal with your own, more keen and reactive sensitivities. I have championed and explained the often-overlooked and neglected characteristics and needs of HSPs that make them different from the NHSP majority. I have clarified how these differences often lead others to criticize HSPs and how these criticisms are often unjustified.

However, there are also situations in which HSPs may come to feel they are over-reacting, particularly in feeling it is difficult or impossible to tolerate and deal with sensory and emotional stimulation. Having a loving and caring NHSP as your partner may motivate you to work on toning down or modifying some of your reactivities to your sensitivities. You may choose to use varieties of de-stressing approaches to take the edges off stresses and strains you experience that make it difficult to tolerate the lower levels of sensitivities in your special NHSP. You will then be invited to explore in these contexts how to explain your sensitivities and needs, in an atmosphere of caring and with both of your wishes to be clear in your explanations and understood by your partner. And compromising is an invaluable skill that you will both develop.

You, the NHSP in this relationship, will learn about sensitivities of your partner in physical sensations, emotional and mental awarenesses, subtleties in relationships that promote closeness or invite distancing, and spiritual awarenesses that you may never have dreamed existed. You may choose to be in this relationship primarily as an NHSPC, supporting your HSP. You may also come to question your basic beliefs and habits of perceptions, your limits of sensitivities in those areas where you and your HSP clearly differ, and your choices in the ranges and depths of engagement you are willing to explore through your relationship.

And each of you is likely to come to points of stress and challenges that push you to ask why you ever chose this partner of yours who differs in so many ways from yourself. And here you are being invited – in your personal life experiences – to seek answers to questions that have challenged the best and brightest and most intuitive of people to explore and to share their observations, explanations and recommendations.

*WHO IN YOUR RELATIONSHIPS IS AN HSP?*

*WHO IS AN NHSP?*

*AS AN HSP, WHAT ARE SOME HELPFUL WAYS YOU CAN EXPLAIN YOUR SENSITIVITIES?*

*AS AN NHSP, WHAT ARE HELPFUL WAYS YOU CAN CLARIFY HSP ISSUES THAT ARE CHALLENGING FOR YOU TO DEAL WITH?*

*WHAT ISSUES BETWEEN YOU MAY BE DUE TO HSP-NHSP DIFFERENCES?*

*ARE THERE ISSUES THAT MAY BE STICKING POINTS BETWEEN YOU, DUE TO YOUR TRAIT DIFFERENCES?*

*WHAT ARE HELPFUL WAYS YOU CAN ADDRESS THESE DIFFERENCES?*

## 24. What is life all about?

> *God explained that, in order to experience anything at all,*
> *the exact opposite of it will appear. "It is a great gift," God said,*
> *"because without it, you could not know what anything is like."*
> *"You could not know Warm without Cold, Up without Down,*
> *Fast without Slow. You could not know Left without Right,*
> *Here without There, Now without Then."*
> *"And so," God concluded, "when you are surrounded with*
> *darkness, do not shake your fist and raise your voice and curse*
> *the darkness. "Rather be a Light unto the darkness,*
> *and don't be mad about it. Then you will know*
> *Who You Really Are, and all others will know, too.*
> *Let your Light shine so that everyone will know*
> *how special you are!"*
> — Neale Donald Walsch (2004-2006)

Let's pause here for a brief, broader consideration of relationship issues that we are addressing, in order to put our immediate, day-to-day issues into broader, wholistic perspectives.

There is nothing like a close, meaningful relationship to bring out deep, important questions about what life is all about and what you want or don't want in your life. Hitching a team of horses to a wagon forces each horse to accommodate to the strengths, weaknesses, pace and personality of the other horse. So, in being a couple, we hitch ourselves to the relationship wagon of experiences, rubbing elbows and moving forward together, engaging in discussions, emotional exchanges, and sorting out the baggage, experiences and habits that each of us brings from the previous wagons to which we've been hitched. And this confronts us with the challenges of dealing with life's inevitable questions and lessons as a couple, which will differ from how we each responded in our previous routines and habits of doing these things from the perspective of being individuals, as well as from being hitched to previous wagons.**[1]

### *How did we get where we are?*

> *I take Michael in contradiction and in mayhem. In grief and delight. To cherish, dismay, and split burritos with. For good company and daily comfort. For the tornado of rage and for love. I take him. I do.*
> — Catherine Newman

I want to reverse my usual order of discussion here in order to put our personal relationships into the context and perspectives of our participation in a larger reality than just our individual selves.

Connecting with the spiritual and spirit awarenesses of our lives and strengthening them can often be an enormous help to us, stimulating us to pause and take the deep breaths we need to sort out the difficulties that life inevitably invites us to face and deal with. There really are few life experiences that are better than our personal and relationship stresses and conflicts that invite us, or actually push us, to seek the deeper meanings of our lives. Taking a deep breath, we can step back from our relationship challenges with our distressed feelings and thoughts, and connect with our spiritual awarenesses. We can then ask for whatever inner help, outer guidance and spiritual inspiration we need to support and aid us to clarify what our current issues are, to discover the lingering traumas from the past might be waiting for us to clear them as well, and to find the emotional strength, insights and compassion to move forward in the best healing ways possible.

Looking beyond our personal existence, each of us contributes individually to the unfolding of the collective reality. By bringing more healing into our personal lives, making our contributions as healing as they can be, we help to counteract and clear our personal portion of the pain, suffering and other negativity in the collective consciousness. In these ways, our personal clearing of negativity and our enhancements of positivity contribute not only to the healing of ourselves and our personal relationships but also to the collective wellbeing of our family, community, nation and planet.*[2]

- Our opening to awareness that we are more than just a body with a physical brain can be a lesson and an inspiration to others to do the same.
- Demonstrating and teaching others how to understand and address their troublesome emotions, thoughts, relationships and personal spiritual awarenesses, as we do so ourselves, offers them benefits in learning to heal their current difficulties and to prevent the development of further, personal wholistic dysfunctions.
- We generate collective healing by informing others of broader ways to conceptualize where we are as individuals, and by helping them see that they are each contributing to broader realities in which we all participate, whether we are consciously aware of this or not.
- Coming from the opposite direction, we may develop awarenesses of some of the ways that many of our thoughts and feelings are derived from the collective consciousness of our family, community, country and world. Western views and attitudes in many countries encourage and promote selfish self-centeredness. The measures of success for many people are the personal wealth and power they have accumulated. As we explore and develop our personal and interpersonal healing awarenesses and gifts, many are moved to focus more on how they, as individuals, can bring greater healing to others.
- With wholistic awarenesses, our focus on helping others can extend further, to include healing other nations, other species, our environment, and our entire planet as well.

You will see much more on this as you continue reading.

*If you want to go fast, go alone. If you want to go far, go together.*
                                                                    - African Proverb

*DO YOU NOW OR HAVE YOU EVER HAD DIFFERENCES IN YOUR RELATIONSHIP(S) WITH OTHER PEOPLE, FROM WHICH YOU HAVE LEARNED OR ARE STILL LEARNING HELPFUL LESSONS?*

*DO YOU HAVE ANY SENSE OF A HIGHER PURPOSE IN YOUR LIFE AS A RESULT OF YOUR RELATIONSHIP WITH AN HSP?*

# 25. Companioned HSP – HSPC relationships: Detailed wholistic considerations

*What counts in making a happy relationship is not so much how
compatible you are, but how you deal with incompatibility.*
— Daniel Goleman

In your intimate relationships you'll find great satisfactions in life, as well as great challenges. Here are suggestions to guide you on these journeys.

**Body** *(HSPs and their HSPCS)*

*And your body is the harp of your soul,
It is yours to bring forth sweet music from it or confused sounds.
And forget not that the earth delights to feel your bare feet
And the winds long to play with your hair.*
— Kahlil Gibran

*Building positive physical aspects of your relationship*
− A healthy diet is tremendously important to HSPs. Organic food, though expensive, enables you to avoid toxic or allergic reactions, or serious poisonings by chemical fertilizers, pesticides, herbicides, preservatives, food coloring, flavor enhancers, appetite stimulants, GMO foods, and enormous varieties of cheap food bulk expanders. Any and all of these could exceed your HSP sensitivity thresholds or even NHSP thresholds for serious reactions. Foods from China and some other countries in the Far East may be particularly challenging because they are not regulated for the above dangers.

Sadly, we can't rely on US grown foods either unless they are organic. For instance, monosodium glutamate (MSG) is an appetite enhancer that can lead "to a host of health issues, including obesity, fatty liver, high insulin and blood sugar, high cholesterol, metabolic syndrome, high blood pressure, disturbances in the gut-brain connection, fibromyalgia, neurological and brain health issues, and much more" (Douillard, web ref.). MSG is so infamous as an unhealthy appetite stimulant that its presence in lists of ingredients on food container is often disguised by food manufacturers under pseudonyms such as Glutamic Acid (E 620), Glutamate (E 620), Monopotassium Glutamate (E 622), Calcium Glutamate (E 623), Monoammonium Glutamate (E 624), and more.**[3]

If the price of organic foods is too high for your budget, you will do well to do some serious scouting in your community among eaters of healthy foods to get recommendations for the cleanest food sources available.

− Exercise is essential for maximizing the functioning of your body and for increasing longevity. Barring disabilities, which require exercises personally designed for your needs and limitations, you will do best with a serious workout at least 3 times weekly, to keep your cardiac system in good shape.
− Proper rest is important. Some people need 9 or even more hours a night, while others can feel fine with only 6-7 hours or less.
− For injuries and serious illness, conventional surgery and medical diagnosis have a lot to offer. Beware of medications, however, as conventional medicine is the 3rd leading cause of death – largely due to medication side effects and interactions.*[4]

Respecting your nervous system's sensitivities and getting to know those of your family members is important. If you are an NHSP coming into a relationship with an HSP, it is very helpful to explore your individual preferences for sensory stimulation and intensities in ambient sound and music; in physical activities and exertions; in food tastes; in intimate relations; sleep rhythms; and any other areas of sensitivities you feel are important to you.

There will be an initial period of adjustments when you are in the getting acquainted phases of your relationship. It may be advisable as an HSP to share your highest HSP priorities first, rather than stating all of your sensitivities at once, especially if you are with an NHSP who is new to being with someone as sensitive as you. On the other hand, holding back and suffering from insensitivities to your preferred ways of experiencing the pleasures of lovemaking and to your other personal needs can build up frustrations and resentments. The most important part of your communicating is to develop the greatest openness between you that is within your comfort zones. That will enable you to find ways to understand and accommodate to each other's needs.

Your sexual relationship deserves special attention. Here, where you are both enjoying the pleasures of sexual stimulation and learning the desires, needs and responsiveness of your partner, great sensitivity may be required. HSPs may want particular types of stimulation and may be strongly uncomfortable with others. Many HSPs tend to prefer a set routine for lovemaking and to be uncomfortable with surprises.

When engaging in sex, the usual precautions to be alert for irritability or triggering of sensitivities in any encounter when HuTiST are present might apply here as well. HSPs' sensory sensitivities may also interfere where smells or the textures of bedclothes or of a partner's rough hair against her skin could be off-putting. Room temperature, noise, or a phone intrusion could likewise be issues that derail what could have been much more than just a moment of platonic physical closeness.

Emotional readiness is clearly important, again being alert to an HSP's sensitivities and preferences for particular intensities of approach, touch, loudness or other stimuli that could be facilitating or jarring. Developing a language for cuddling, sex, lovemaking or other ways of talking about your intimate relationships can also contribute to your pleasures and satisfactions.

It is enormously helpful if you can make all of this a matter for open discussion. Be honest in sharing your preferences, likes, tolerances and dislikes. As you are warming up and as you get passionate, ask for what feels good to you and offer similarly to pleasure your partner. The more you can make this a topic of mutually supportive conversation, the easier you will develop your sex life.**[5]

### *Emotions* (HSPs and their HSPCs)

> *The best and most beautiful things in the world cannot be*
> *seen or even touched. They must be felt with the heart.*
> — Helen Keller

The word 'feelings' is often used interchangeably with 'emotions' but I see them as being different. Feelings are our interpretations of our emotions. For instance, we may experience emotions of happiness, sadness, hurt or anger. We contextualize these emotions, associating them with inner and outer world experiences in order to convey to others what we are experiencing subjectively. So we say we are feeling:

- Happy upon getting good news; seeing our children or partner smile; or succeeding in choreographing our cooking of a good meal
- Sad when we reach the end of a happy experience; someone fails to keep a promise they made to us; or we unintentionally hurt someone
- Hurt by, and angry with others who don't understand our sensitivities and needs; or who criticize and belittle us for being unable (or in their views, unwilling) to do what they do without particular thoughts or unusual efforts
- Angry when someone lies to us; cuts close in front of us on the road; or when we make a mistake

Feelings can be our mental, outer expressions of what we are sensing emotionally:
- We may cheer out loud upon getting good news; mirror our children or partner smiling; or share our pleasure in words upon succeeding in cooking a good meal
- We may express our love for each other through words, amorous eye contact and touch
- We may heave a big sigh and make a comment when we reach the end of a happy experience; or may groan and complain when someone fails to keep a promise they made to us; or we may say how sorry we feel for unintentionally hurting someone and demonstrate our sorrow on our face and in our words and gestures
- We may blow our horn and yell out the window when someone cuts close in front of us on the road; say how upset or angry we are if someone disappoints us; or say we feel sorry when we make a mistake

Thoughts are often mingled with feelings. We may be:
- Frustrated with ourselves when we find we cannot do what NHSPs do without particular thoughts or unusual efforts, as in being unrattled by situations that we find stressful, hurtful and deeply unsettling; or in being able to deal better with practical and boring tasks.
- Weary of our struggles to explain ourselves, and hesitant to ask for the considerations and accommodations we need in a relationship, classroom or workplace so that we can function at our HSP best
- Longing for environments such as quiet, un-busy, peaceful work spaces or regeneration time in nature, with quiet music, or other nurturing elements that help us remain centered and restore our frazzled energies and patience

Fortunately, wholistic EP offers you excellent, highly effective tools to deal with all of these issues of emotions, feelings and thoughts. Even more helpful may be your installing and strengthening positive feelings and thoughts to help you deal with your immediate responses or to cope more effectively with ongoing, repeating situations that are challenging.

It's enormously helpful to talk with each other about our feelings. And it's helpful to explain factors that color our feelings, such as sensitivities we have that are based on natural, inborn traits, as well as those that have been acquired through life experiences.

It's important to affirm and reaffirm our positive feelings for each other, as in finding words to express our love and caring; love notes; little touches and caresses; flowers, or a specially prepared meal or a meal out together. These gestures and sharings are enormously helpful in building and maintaining our loving relationship.

*One can give without loving, but one cannot love without giving.*
                                                        - Amy Carmichael

You may learn that when either or both of you are upset, it is more difficult to address your issues in constructive ways. When feelings are running high because one or both of you are feeling unheard, hurt, angry or in any other ways distraught, it is often difficult to formulate or say what you're feeling in constructive ways. At such times, when feelings are running high in the midst of a discussion, it can be helpful to call a pause in the discussion or argument. A 'time out' gesture may be helpful (as is commonly used in sports): one palm-open hand pointing up to the center of the other, palm-open hand that is held horizontally, miming a 'T' for 'time out'.

Emotions, particularly anger, may often blur the issues and how you present them and how your companion hears them. If either of you senses this happening, you might do well to bookmark the issues and wait for a calmer time to consider and discuss them. It's very much like exercising discretion and not responding immediately when you receive an upsetting email. When you take a little space from your upsets, when you calm down and reconsider the situation, you will very often perceive and respond to issues in more helpful and healing ways.

Preventive uses of tapping can markedly enhance your relationships. It is very easy, especially early in your togetherness, to spiral into feeling unheard or misunderstood, particularly when you are likely to be taxed with adjustments to demands of new jobs or studies, relocation and new living accommodations, and having also to adjust to each other's schedules, needs and preferences. And prevention is far easier and more pleasant than sliding into disharmony and frustration from feeling your needs are not being met.

✦ 'Gemma,' an HSP, was married to 'Larry,' an NHSP, for a bit over a year when they came to me for help in sorting out their relationship. Larry had seemed to Gemma to be an ideal partner. He appreciated her sensitivities and complimented her on being the emotional 'radar' for the two of them. He was familiar with this arrangement because his parents had the same partnership in reverse – with his father being the HSP. But Larry was now complaining that he felt the relationship was too unbalanced, and that he was always having to accommodate to Gemma's moods, feelings and preferences, with insufficient consideration for his own needs and likes and dislikes.

I was relieved to see that Gemma was not as closed to listening to Larry's issues as he felt she was. It appeared to be more about his hesitations to present and assert his needs than her unwillingness to listen to or consider them. With just a little bit of encouragement and support from me he was able to clarify some of his wishes and needs, including wanting some time apart from Gemma for sports activities that he had missed since their marriage, after he had agreed to abandon these intrusions into their weekend time together. Gemma acknowledged readily that he had been very considerate and generous in supporting her HSP needs for a quieter and slower pace than he had been used to. She had little difficulty accommodating to his requests.

In the course of discussing Larry's parents' relationship, it had also been clarified that his father was quiet, meek and unassertive. His mother, despite not being an HSP, was a very kind, thoughtful and considerate person, who had learned to ask about her husband's sensitivities to be sure she could accommodate and support him. Larry had modeled himself to a great degree on his father's meek ways of asserting himself.

It continues to surprise me how many conflicts and impasses in couples and family relationships, like those of Larry and Gemma, could be resolved with explorations of communication styles and negotiable agreements. It is generally easy, as it was here, to identify the issues of conflict, in the context of thorough, detailed family histories as were explored with each of these participants in the two couples' sessions we had.

✦✦✦ Though I (Dan) was sensitive and easily cried when I was upset as a child, for much of my teen years and early adult life I repressed my feelings. I did such a good job with this that I wasn't even aware I was holding in my feelings, avoiding conscious awareness of them.

Gradually, through learning and practicing psychotherapy, I came to see that much of the time I was holding my feelings in, just like the people who came to me for help with expressing their feelings. What was most helpful to me in this regard were my personal, close relationships with several HSPs.

At first, when I was more in my head, I was often puzzled and confused in my HSPC role because my HSPs would frequently change their minds and preferences, often quite radically. A strong preference for going somewhere, getting together with someone, or making a significant purchase on one day would often change completely. It would become a rejected and strongly disparaged non-option. This was very most confusing, in particular, when it came to preferences and dislikes for ways I expressed myself and behaved within our relationship

I've been a very caring HSPC. Though I didn't have HSP concepts or terminology in my earlier relationships, I saw myself as a dedicated companion/ partner, especially as our relationships deepened to the point of serious commitments and in a few instances to marriages. I wanted to do my best to support my HSP. But often as not, as I started out making plans in the directions very clearly indicated by my HSP as absolutely essential, I very soon might feel jerked around by totally contradictory feelings and preferences, stated by my HSP with similar intensity and enthusiasm, explaining how the initial preferences had been so clearly and firmly laid out.

Early in these relationships, I responded with confusion, irritation, and sometimes with outright anger. "How can you change your mind so completely?" I would ask. "Yesterday you wanted nothing more, whatsoever to do with 'X' but today you say you think we should be making X part of our life." And X could be as trivial as a choice in home decorations, a menu for dinner or a weekend destination, or as important as pursuing or calling an end to our relationship.

With time and countless experiences of these sorts, I vary gradually came to understand that my HSP's definitive statements were not based on reasoned choices but rather on the feelings these options aroused at one time, contrasted with the feelings aroused at a later time.

With my gradually growing understandings about HSPs and HSPCs, I've learned to look for factors like HuTiST that could influence emotions at one time or another; and above all, to be patient and wait for the pendulum to swing as it will between various options until it comes to rest in a place of contentment with an option.

And I realize repeatedly that I, myself, am now more prone to vacillating opinions and feelings, as my own connections with my emotions and feelings gets stronger. Which I take to be a compliment to my releasing my avoidances of awarenesses and expressions of my emotions due to my personal trauma history.

WHICH EMOTIONS DO YOU FIND IT EASIEST TO EXPRESS?

HOW DO YOU AND YOUR PARTNER EACH EXPRESS YOUR FEELINGS?

HAVE YOU NOTICED DIFFERENT WAYS EACH OF YOU HAVE FOR DEALING WITH EMOTIONS – THAT ARE RELATED TO THE WAYS YOUR FAMILIES OF ORIGIN EXPRESSED EMOTIONS WHEN YOU WERE GROWING UP?

DO YOU SAY 'OUCH' WHEN YOUR FEELINGS ARE HURT?

DO YOU APOLOGIZE WHEN YOU REALIZE YOU'VE HURT EACH OTHER?

DO YOU ENCOURAGE EACH OTHER TO PUT WORDS TO YOUR FEELINGS WHEN YOU SENSE YOUR PARTNER IS GETTING UPSET?

*Love and caring*

Many people hold to the romantic notion that love and caring are just naturally part of a close relationship, and in some measure they are right. It's the words 'just naturally' in the last sentence that may be misleading.

Our attractions to each other are based on compatibilities that we may or may not feel on every level of our wholistic beingness. Physical attraction is usually a strong and essential part of being together. This is usually more intense in the early part of our togetherness. In these 'honeymoon times,' the novelty and wonderment of finding more than just a physical attraction is strong as it unfolds in new and deeper ways that enhance the physical attraction. And when this is a solid part of the relationship, there is not only the physical buildups and releases of our own sexual tension, but also the loving learning of how to stimulate and satisfy the sexual needs and preferences of our partner.

Our physical relationship may bring and hold us together, but it is the emotional that more deeply binds and bonds us to each other. And when our relationship is solid, this is an ongoing process of ever-deepening bonding.

For the HSP it is important to have repeated expressions and affirmations of love and caring. As an HSPC you will experience the reaffirmations of love and caring from your HSP. It is equally important for you, especially if you are an NHSP, to make it a point to reaffirm your connections with your HSP. Here it may be helpful to you both to learn which of the five love languages[6] speaks loudest to each of you. If you purr most readily with words of affirmation, you may need to remind your HSP that you just love to hear him whisper in your ears sweet appreciations and excitement at your togetherness – if his preferred love languages differ from yours. Likewise, he may need to remind you that physical touch is what cues him most strongly to know that you care for him.

It is important to schedule time for chats and discussions about how things are going and developing and deepening, or how your relationship is feeling strained, distanced, or soured by interactions and events in your lives. A loving relationship, like a garden, needs watering, weeding and nurturing in order to remain strong and healthy and to grow ever stronger and deeper yet.

And deliberate attention to the nurturing of your spiritual lives deserves attention, both individually and mutually, for a rounding out of your wholistic relationship.

*Love is the threshold of another universe.*
*- Pierre Teilhard de Chardin*

WHAT ARE YOUR WAYS OF DEMONSTRATING THAT YOU CARE FOR EACH OTHER?

ARE YOU COMFORTABLE ASKING EACH OTHER FOR QUALITY TIME?

HAVE YOU CONSIDERED, DISCUSSED AND EXPLORED NEW WAYS OF BEING TOGETHER?

*Overwhelm*

Overwhelm is a common experience for HSPs. At a basic level, it is simply an overload of stimulation to sensory organs are acutely sensitive, along with their feelings and emotions that are stirred by the overload. It can occur in the most common of circumstances.

- With loud music, as in concerts and movie theaters, on busy streets and in restaurants, at family celebrations and other social events
- During travels, where the temptation is to pack as much sightseeing into the time available, forgetting to allow for quiet time, rest and recuperation
- In emotional situations, both personal, witnessed in others, and in films and theaters
- On days of celebration, anniversaries, major life changes or losses of relatives and friends

Overwhelm is the meta-feeling that you are in a situation which is approaching or has reached a place where you or others around you will be or already are out of control and in danger of being unable to cope. The earlier you realize you are heading into overwhelm, the easier it is to deal with it. Any of the approaches in Sections V and VI may be helpful to you in dealing with overwhelm. Practicing these methods to the point that they become acquired skills is a good plan for when you are in stressful situations. Relaxation, meditation, imagery (such as the Place of Peace, Safety and Healing) and tapping techniques are particularly recommended here. Meta-issues, such as overwhelm, often respond very quickly and deeply to these de-stressing techniques.

You may be traumatized in experiencing overwhelm. You may then develop meta-anxieties when you become upset, out of fears that you could again be upset to the point of overwhelm in similar situations.

Again, wholistic EP, plus the various other de-stressing approaches detailed in Sections V and VI of this book are excellent for controlling and eliminating worries about overwhelm.

HSPs may have difficulty connecting through their mind to identify what external and internal factors are stimulating their overwhelm when they feel upset. In states of HSPs' overwhelm, an HSPC can be enormously helpful just by pointing out what he perceives might be upsetting his HSP.

✦ 'Mason,' an NHSP, and 'Ava,' a strong HSP had gotten along pretty well in the first three years of their marriage. But the stress of having a baby brought them to me because they found themselves arguing much more frequently. Their 3-month old daughter, 'Sally,' was both fussy when sucking at the breast and irregular in her sleeping schedules, and they were truly frazzled by sleep deprivation and frustration over the deterioration in their relationship.

I invited them to share one of the issues they had argued about. Ava immediately responded with her distress over Mason's repeated urging that they should put Sally on regular feeding times, every four hours, so that Ava and her parents could have a less stressful schedule. They very quickly started to argue about this in my office.

I held up my hand in a "stop" gesture, and they turned to look at me again. I asked Sally what she was feeling about these issues. She replied, "I feel stressed, and tired, and frustrated, and angry and unheard.

I turned to face Ava and acknowledged each of her feelings individually, asking her to say more about them. She heaved a great big sigh and shared what it was like for her to have to be constantly on call for breast feeding and for calming Sally, who seemed to be so uncomfortable at times that nothing would quiet her. All Ava could do was to hold her and gently stroke her head and body till she fell asleep. And all the while she was soothing Sally, Ava was asking herself what she had done or not done, since Sally's birth and before her birth, that might have stressed her so much that she had these terrible difficulties in settling down after her meals.

Soon after Ava started to speak she had tears in her eyes, and she was sobbing softly when she finished. She rounded out her descriptions of her frustrations by adding that she was glad she had taken a year's leave from her teaching job for parenting, as she couldn't possibly have handled leaving Sally with a baby sitter when Sally was so irritable and crying so much.

Several times during this interchange between Ava and me I had to raise my hand in a 'stop' gesture to keep Mason from interrupting. When Ava was through explaining, I asked her how she felt. She responded, "It feels so good to be able to share what it's like for me and just have someone listen without criticizing me!"

I sighed, and responded by briefly sharing how it had taken me several years when I was first married to learn to start out by listening carefully to what was going on, before moving into exploring what we could do to make things better.

I then turned to Mason and asked him how it felt to be a new father, with a baby who was so irregular in her schedule and who cried a lot and had a hard time settling down. He, too, was close to tears as he shared his frustrations and tiredness and feeling unable to help. "I have to be at my 9:00 – 5:00 job, with nearly an hour's commute, and just don't know any more what to suggest or do to be helpful."

I asked whether Mason had heard Ava's feelings, and he responded with interpretations of her feelings as complaints. I then asked Ava to repeat her feelings about their stresses. After she did so, I repeated her feelings of being stressed, tired, frustrated, angry and unheard. I invited Mason to briefly fill in specific examples for each of these from his own experiences. Ava, to his surprise, started to relax and even smiled at one point when he shared some of his frustrations that resonated with hers.

I pointed out that each of them was feeling many of the same things, and that Mason had the advantage of being away from the stresses at home during his workday and commutes, but that Ava was pretty much stuck with them all of the time. I commended Mason for wanting to fix the situation, but shared my opinion that it was probably more helpful to Ava if he just listened to her feelings, clarified that he understood them, and acknowledged how difficult it must be for Ava to be the constant caregiver to Sally, with no relief during the day.

Ava was nodding in agreement during much of the time I was explaining this, and Mason started to relax as well.

I then asked for more particulars on how Sally was doing. I learned that she was actually sleeping noticeably more, during both her shorter and longer sleeping periods. Her crying, however, seemed unchanged in intensity or duration. Their pediatrician had explained that this is called colic, and is a problem affecting about one in five babies. It usually diminishes at the age of 3–4 months, and rarely lasts past 6 months.

My assessment, which I shared with Ava and Mason, was that they were actually doing relatively well, considering the grueling stresses they were all experiencing. I reassured both of them that we would find ways to make things better. I explained that they had one of those children who just wasn't regular in her sleeping or eating rhythms. Quite understandably, this made it challenging for her parents, who are regular in these rhythms. I recommended a book that described people's personality traits, which were often clearly identifiable in childhood – as early as the age of 2 months (Chess & Thomas, 1968).

We extended the session by half an hour so they could learn tapping for de-stressing. They were both surprised at how quickly and deeply they were able to release many of their tensions and feelings of helplessness, hurt, and annoyances – with Sally, each other, and themselves.

At the end of the session and over the next month, with weekly Skype meetings and a few emails for support I made a series of suggestions, which they diligently implemented:

- They would consult a local Naturopathic Doctor regarding dietary items that Ava might eliminate in the hopes of not irritating Sally's digestive system because of the small but allergenic residues that could enter her breast milk. Cow's milk is one of the most common offenders, and I advised Ava to stop drinking regular milk immediately in case this could help, and as it was relatively easy to do.
- They would practice TWR/WHEE daily, whenever stressed, and would bundle current stresses with memories of earlier ones.
- After clearing stresses, they would install positive thoughts and feelings to replace the negative ones they had released.

- They would take turns tapping alternately on the left and right sides of Sally's body, while saying, "Even though I, Sally, have these times when I cry and seem to be in pain, I still love and accept myself, and know my mommy and daddy love and accept me, wholly and completely."
- Mason was to listen to Ava's feelings, confirming what he had heard and understood, and without making immediate suggestions to change anything.
- After discussing her feelings, Ava would then listen to his suggestions and discuss them with him.
- If they found themselves in conflict, they would reserve further discussion for the next day, and if they still felt shaky about pursuing their discussion, then for the next therapy session.

To their great relief, they found that tapping seemed very soothing for Sally, and her crying was greatly diminished in intensity and duration over the next two weeks. I suggested that Ava might return to drinking cow's milk to see whether this could be a contributing factor to watch out for, but when she did so it didn't appear to make a difference. Nor did the Naturopath identify any other allergen that might be contributing to the crying. We also could not know whether the colic was clearing on its own, regardless of our interventions.

What Mason and Ava felt to be their most important takeaway lesson, however, was that Mason could be most helpful by simply listening patiently to Ava when she was upset. When an HSP is upset, this is frequently the help they appreciate more than any other.**[7]

They also found TWR/WHEE extremely helpful in varieties of ways. In the process of Ava's doing her tapping with my guidance, she came into memories of feeling unheard and not understood or accepted by her parents, her younger brother and sister, and most of the rest of her extended family. Clearing these painful memories was also helpful in releasing some of the steam behind her annoyances with Mason, when he was promoting his views and not acknowledging Ava's perceptions, feelings and thoughts.

Ava was also able to point out to Mason that some of his eagerness to help her find solutions to her frustrations might come from his childhood parentification – being the oldest of four children in a family where both parents worked long hours in their hardware store, and it had fallen on him to help watch after his younger brother and sisters. Mason agreed with her observation, and was able to make good use of tapping to clear some of his memories of being frustrated when he felt he wasn't adequate in his standing in as a parent, way before he should have had to take on such responsibilities.

Installing positives to replace negative experiences and memories was also tremendously helpful. Once they had done this, their trauma residues were no longer triggered by current-day stresses. In fact, the installation of meta-positives of being successful in transforming their lives brought about a tremendous improvement in their relationship. A current-life issue that would otherwise have been a trigger for the earlier trauma memories became a stimulus for feeling good about having overcome their earlier challenges.

*DO YOU OR YOUR PARTNER EVER FEEL YOU ARE OVERWHELMED?*

*WHAT ARE SOME GOOD WAYS YOU CAN DEAL WITH YOUR OVERWHELMS?*
    *INDIVIDUALLY?*
    *TOGETHER?*

*ARE THERE PARTICULAR ISSUES YOU'RE SENSITIVE TO FOR WHICH MIGHT YOU SEEK HEALING?*

*Anger*

Anger can have varieties of roots and causes.

- Anger is often an expression of your frustrations, dissatisfactions, disappointments or hurts over perceived unfairness, painful experiences or unfulfilled expectations. Most commonly, anger is a complaint that things are not going as you want or hope they will unfold.
  - You feel you are not being treated fairly or considerately.
  - You reach a point of frustration where your feelings boil over.
  - You may feel you haven't been heard, so you speak more emphatically and with more intense emotional expression.
  - You may feel you're being deliberately ignored, so you raise your intensity to make your points heard because they are important to you.
  - You may escalate higher in expressing your anger if you are still not getting the results you want or feel you deserve. You might throw or break things or vent your feelings in some other physical manners.
- Anger as a tool for controlling others
  - You feel you need to assure that you are heard and that your wishes, requests and orders will be obeyed.
  - You feel that if you are not forceful enough in your requests and demands, you will not be heard or obeyed or will lose control over your situation, relationship or life.
  - A significant other in your life is angry and you feel you have to stand up for yourself or you will be steamrolled.
- Anger is a displacement of feelings and beliefs from other sources and times that resonate with your current situation.
  - When you encounter situations in your current life that remind you of your earlier traumas, anger boils up inside you.
  - You may be unaware in your conscious mind of any of the above, but find yourself exploding with anger for reasons that are unclear to you.

These last kinds of buried angers deserve further comment. Anger, especially when it is a recurring, chronic issue, can also be an alert pointing to stresses and traumas from earlier in our lives. Many angers are generated from intense but unexpressed or inadequately expressed feelings from the past. When you were on the receiving end of someone else's anger, inconsiderate behaviors, bullying or abuse, you may have been unable to express your own fears or anger and hurt to those who upset you. Perhaps it would have been socially inappropriate, or maybe you couldn't think clearly because of your upset, much less defend yourself in a proper and adequate way. Or the person who angered or traumatized you may have been stronger than you and it was dangerous for you to speak out or express your angers. These buried angers can predispose you to be overly sensitive to particular issues in your current life that in some ways resonate with the earlier traumas and trigger you into anger. You then respond with greater intensity to your current issues than might otherwise be warranted.

Worse yet, you may have experienced emotional, physical or sexual abuse. This can leave memories and feelings locked into your body, often outside your conscious awareness. However, your unconscious mind still feels these trauma memories and feelings stored in your body.[8] This leaves you vulnerable to getting triggered into fear and anger by similar experiences at some later time.

Often, the patterns of being abused and angered begin in childhood. Parents, siblings, or other family members may be aggressive towards you. This can be extremely traumatic, especially if you had no one to turn to for protection, comforting or understanding. When you have been abused, you may even come to perceive that this is the way people show you they care for you.

> ✦ ✦ ✦ I found myself quite irritated and angered during my early years of medical training by people in authority who were rigid, demanding and dictatorial. It took me months of being in psychotherapy to wake up to the awareness that I was carrying a lot of resentments and angers over my mother's having behaved in these ways towards me throughout my childhood and young adulthood.
>
> This was a most helpful learning experience. I had been able to see such patterns in my psychotherapy clients and to help them address these sorts of anger issues, even during this period when I was myself blind to the fact that I had a very similar history and patterns of getting triggered as they did. My avoidance of the awareness of the roots of my reactivity to such authority figures was a testimony to the success of my defensive habits.
>
> By ignoring my buried angers from my childhood, I avoided feeling more helpless and beaten down. But my unexpressed feelings were also stirred at times, creating an excess of irritation to my current experiences.
>
> Back in my early years of learning psychotherapy, dealing with such trauma residues was a much slower and more tedious business than it can be today, when we have much more highly effective approaches, such as EP and EMDR. In the bigger picture, however, I can see that these personal challenges to deal with my own angers helped me understand my clients better and motivated me to seek and develop better ways to help people deal with such issues – for them and for myself.

The bad news about anger is that it is often unpleasant, distressing, hurtful, and can be corrosive and damaging in relationships. The good news is that anger can be a doorway to releasing unexpressed, pent-up, festering feelings that are otherwise undermining, destructive to our quality of life, to our relationships and to our health. Anger can uncover issues in our current lives that we are avoiding and failing to express.

The very high sensitivities of HSPs leave them open to frequently expanding or even exploding into intense, negative emotions, sometimes without clear or obvious hints about what triggered them. Someone may say something to an HSP that appears innocuous but that triggers strong objections, anger, personal attacks, crying, or other feelings. Sometimes, the HSP himself may have no clear understanding of why he reacted that way.

Almost always there will be one or more triggers to such emotional outbursts. Often, issues that were being processed shortly prior to the outburst can readily be identified.

As an HSPC you can be enormously helpful (as appropriate and relevant to your situation) if you:

- Acknowledge your HSP is upset
- Check whether HuTiST might be irritating her.
- Check whether he is open to discussing his upset now
- Check whether she wants some time and space to deal with this herself
- Check whether obviously stressful, unresolved issues from the present or recent past were lingering and upsetting her
- Ask what he feels or thinks might be helpful in dealing with the upset
- If this appears to be triggered by a recurrent issue
  - Check whether he senses this might be true
  - If yes, remind him what you perceive may have helped to resolve similar issues on previous occasions
- Ask whether approaches that have worked in the past might be helpful again here
- If yes, ask whether she wants your help in sorting out the issues, and if yes, ask how you can be of greatest support
- Suggest approaches you know
- Consider, for instance, that you might each picture yourselves spending a few minutes in your place of peace and safety and healing (PPSH)[9]

It is not uncommon for an HSP to get triggered into letting out some of her upset feelings on anyone nearby, regardless of whether that person was responsible or even involved in generating the upset. As an HSPC you may have had occasional or even ample examples of this displacement onto you.

For yourself, when you're upset, it may be helpful to:

- Check whether HuTiST might be present
- Ask yourself whether you're in a reasonable inner place to deal with your HSP's upset at the moment
- If not, then explain why and suggest that you'd feel better taking some space for a little while, to sort out how you're feeling
- If yes, take a deep breath and start using a self-treatment method to de-stress and assure that you're as calm as possible
- If you can identify issues from the past that have been triggered in you, and if you feel comfortable doing this, you may share your awarenesses with your HSP

Often, you will find that there were multiple triggers to your HSP's upset. It is helpful if one of your writes down what issues you identify. In the heat of being upset it is easy to overlook important issues or to forget issues you've identified – which is like leaving dirt in a wound that may then fester and heal slowly. Similarly, you may have a brilliant suggestion that might be forgotten in the intensity of your situation.

✦ 'Len,' an HSP, was obviously agitated and upset when he came home from work. He slammed the front door and immediately shut himself in the bathroom. His wife, 'Reggie,' could hear him banging about as he took a shower and dried himself off, stomping into the bedroom to put on some casual clothes.

Reggie, an NHSP, took a deep breath, turned off the stove, took the dinner stew off the burner, and sat down on the sofa (their most commonly shared place for chatting and watching TV). The sofa was also conveniently situated between the bedroom and the kitchen. She took several deep breaths and did several rounds of EP tapping to release her tensions from her day of teaching high school History, and her anxieties over seeing Len's upset.

Len soon emerged, and without needing an invitation, plopped himself down next to her. Reggie put a hand on his knee and said she was sorry to see him looking upset. Len took a deep breath, and pictured himself blowing out some of his tensions (as he had learned to do over several years of exploring de-stressing methods for dealing with his high sensitivities to stresses at work and in interactions with insensitive people).

Reggie could see his body visibly releasing some of its tensions. She asked him if he'd like to talk about it now, or have some dinner first. Len paused for a thoughtful moment, and asked if he might start dinner with a bit of the dessert – a leftover piece of Reggie's birthday cake from the previous weekend party that he'd been looking forward to finishing off. Reggie smiled as he patted her on the knee and got up to get his cake, acknowledging he was looking forward to her special stew that he was smelling.

A few minutes into his hunger-staving snack, which he ate slowly, with obvious pleasure and increasing relaxation evident in his posture, he shared some of his frustrations. He had spent the afternoon meeting with parents and their children to discuss applications for moving on to institutions of higher education – in the high school where he taught junior and senior level English.

"I'm sooooo frustrated!" he said. "So many of these parents want their kids to make choices based mostly on earning potentials. They don't listen to what calls to their kids' hearts or souls."

Reggie: "I really feel your disappointment! You've spoken about this several times before."

Len: "I have some very good students, who enjoy my classes and are getting into literature and poetry really nicely. Some of them could be really good as teachers, counsellors or other human resource types, and some of them can sense this. But when I hear many of their parents planning their lives for them without any appreciation of their kids' sensitivities, and when I find their parents totally closed to any discussions in these directions, I begin to ask myself, what am I doing as a teacher?!"

Reggie listened, patiently, with only occasional acknowledgments that she understood his frustrations, as Len let off a bit more steam. She silently gave thanks to the counselor who had helped them develop their communication skills – shortly after they were married.

Len's angers and Reggie's angry responses to them had gradually escalated to the point that they weren't sure they had made good choices in getting married. It had been extremely helpful to both of them to clarify Len's being an HSP and her being an NHSP, to read more about this, and to explore the best ways for them to deal with their differing personality traits. What they had learned was clearly standing them in good stead!

✦✦ And they soon moved on to dinner in a much better psychological and energetic space.

*Anger is just anger.*
- Anonymous

It may take a fair bit of work on yourself and your relationship with your partner to reach points of understanding about your differing styles of relating to each other and to the world at large. Friction points can be de-fused and your relationship markedly improved when you learn and practice communication skills; identify and clear emotional baggage that you bring with you into your relationship; build understanding and trust between you; and come into the blessings and mutual growth that good relationships support.

It can be enormously helpful to call upon some of the resources in this book to aid you when you're feeling angry and getting emotional about it. Ask yourself:

- What has triggered my anger?
- What am I upset about in this situation?
- Am I resonating here with angers from other situations in my life?
- Might I be responding with emotions that are more strong than is really warranted just by this trigger?
- What outcome do I want in this situation?
- How can I bring healing to this situation?
- If it's a person that I'm angry at, how can I verbalize my upset in a respectful way that won't antagonize and trigger the other person?

E.g., you might state your angers as "I-messages," (e.g. I'm upset with you for coming home late again.") rather than 'You-messages" (e.g. You're really making me mad by coming home late again).*[10]

- What would be the best time to approach him?*[11]

WHAT ARE SOME ISSUES THAT MAY TRIGGER YOUR ANGER? YOUR PARTNER'S ANGER?

CAN YOU REMEMBER GOOD ARGUMENTS, IN WHICH YOU EACH SHARED YOUR UPSET FEELINGS AND CAME OUT FEELING BETTER?

WHAT HAVE BEEN SOME LESSONS YOU'VE EACH LEARNED ABOUT EXPRESSING YOUR ANGERS IN BETTER WAYS?

**Mind** *(HSPs and their HSPCS)*

> *Just imagine becoming the way you used to be as a very young child, before you understood the meaning of any word, before opinions took over your mind.*
>
> *The real you is loving, joyful, and free. The real you is just like a flower, just like the wind, just like the ocean, just like the sun.*
>
> — Don Miguel Ruiz

It is fairly common for people who are developing their relationships with each other to ponder how they are getting along and what more they might do to please their partner. You will find it helpful if you get a more solid sense of your partner's opinions and preferences in all matters concerning your relationship. A set time each week to check in with each other on how things are going in your relationship can be enormously helpful. It is so easy to put off conversations on issues that you're uncertain about, or that you sense might be touchy for you and your partner to discuss. Far better to catch anything early, before it becomes a serious irritation or conflict, rather than put off a conversation that you worry might cause friction.

If you are an NHSP in a relationship with an HSP, you may notice varieties of situations in which your preference for thinking your way through problems leads to quicker and often very helpful solutions to practical issues, while your HSP is only gradually feeling her way through them.

Conversely, if you are the HSP in the relationship, you will probably find that you're far better at sizing up how the two of you are likely to get along with another person, couple or group, or how your children are going to respond to changes in plans.

Note that 'mind' is often taken to be a description of thinking processes related to outer-world observations. This is an NHSP bias. (You may have noticed this in the quote introducing this segment of my discussion.) Mind also observes our inner-world experiences. And in both inner and outer observations, mind analyzes, categorizes, compartmentalizes, and files away memories of all of our life experiences. And our inner-world data which mind observes include emotions, feelings, and inner-world experiences of relationships with other people, the environment and spirit.

Be patient with each other as you explore your own and each other's strengths and weaknesses of these sorts. And don't expect to solve your differences mainly by changing your partner's ways of dealing with challenges so that they are more similar to your own preferred modes of relating to inner and outer worlds. You will probably do better to observe and accept that in practical measures and estimates, an NHSP has innate advantages, just as an HSP has advantages in sizing up people situations and in dealing with feelings.*[12]

And again, choose wisely when you set your times for discussions and negotiations. Remember that when HuTiST are present it's usually not the best option for doing this.

*KEEP A BIT OF YOUR FOCUS ON LESSONS YOU'RE LEARNING AS YOU NEGOTIATE. JOURNALING THESE CAN BE HELPFUL*

**Relationships with other people** *(HSPs and their HSPCS)*

> *If we treat people as they are, we make them worse.*
> *If we treat people as they might better be,*
> *we help them become what they are capable of becoming.*
> — Johann Wolfgang von Goethe

*Building and maintaining positivity*

We start out in our relationships with the beliefs and hopes that how we get along will be satisfying and successful in mutually meeting our wishes, needs and dreams. Much of this book focuses on problems and challenging issues and how to deal with them. But the very best ways for dealing with life issues are to maximize their positivities, and to proactively identify and sort out our issues, doing our best to see that they don't become serious.

Building and maintaining positivity is the best way forward. I am puzzled that this is not more obvious and certainly not the primary focus or practice of most psychotherapies.

A good place to start is for each of you to write a list of what you like about your friend, companion or partner in life.

START WITH YOUR OWN LIST, BEFORE READING FURTHER.

I don't want to stifle your creativity or to or to distract you from important issues through my selected items in this discussion. I don't want you to overlook aspects of your relationship that I am unable to guess about but which are important to you.

Helpful positivities to consider include (and I hope you explore each of these items wholistically, considering every level of your being!):

- What feels good in your relationship in general?
- What speaks to each level of your beingness: body, emotions, mind, relationships and spirit?
- What first attracted you to your companion?
- What do you like to do together?
- What are your love languages?*[13]
- Is there anything that could improve your love life?
- What do you look forward to doing together?
- How do you ask for help and support when you feel frustrated, disappointed, hurt, angry, sad, or in any other way that leads you to want your special someone to be there for you?
- Are there times you hold back from asking for help? Why? What can the two of you do to make this better?
- Are you comfortable asking for your own time and space to pursue interests that you don't share with each other?
- Who in your past does your companion remind you of and does this enhance or deter your getting along with each other in any ways?
- What could make your relationship better yet?

- Is there anything that might make you more comfortable in your communications and relationship?
- Do you check with each other periodically about how high your 'positivity bank account' is, in your partner's views and feelings?

If you find your feel-good accounts are running low in any ways with each other, and if issues that are bothersome are not immediately urgent to address, it's often helpful to schedule a time one or more days later for discussion of ways to make things better. Carefully considering and sleeping on problems often sharpens our focus on what aspects of the issues are more or less important; mellows the irritations attached to our issues; and invites new perspectives and ideas for dealing with them to percolate up from our inner selves to add insights and to soften irritabilities.

And don't overlook opportunities to celebrate your successes in dealing with your challenging issues. For your encouragement, I very highly recommend Ted Zeff's (2015) wonderful collection of reports in his inspiring "*The Power of Sensitivity: Success stories by Highly Sensitive People Thriving in a Non-sensitive World*." Here you will find many more suggestions for developing and enhancing your positive investments in your relationships and your enjoyments in being together.

### *HSPs' challenges in close, personal relationships*

Deciding whether you want to enter into, continue and deepen a serious relationship is an issue that deserves careful consideration. Varieties of factors are helpful in making these choices.

The first I suggest relates to how you or a potential partner feel, in general, about being in any relationships. You are embarking on a co-creative project that will offer you many insights, experiences, and lessons. Coming into these discussions, it is helpful to hold an open mind in sharing your views, opinions and expectations and in listening to those of your partner. Even if you uncover differing points of view or different opinions, just be patient in sorting through them. Don't feel that you have to come up with immediate agreements or compromises if there is something important to either of you that seems to be a sticking point in your reaching agreement.

HSPs are very sensitive to the finest of nuances in their relationships. A close relationship with another HSP can be a very positive mutual experience, as each of you will understand the other so much better because you share the same sorts of nervous system and energetic sensitivities. You will immediately appreciate and understand the issues that your friend or partner mentions. You will have a common language and will resonate with each other's experiences of dealing with different people and situations. So each of you can be an excellent HSPC to the other. That's the good news.

The challenging news is that each of you will find degrees of responsiveness in the other's spectrum of sensitivities that differ from your own. So each of you will need to be doubly alert to those aspects of your environment that are challenging, jarring or overwhelming to yourself and your HSP-HSPC. It is helpful to anticipate some of your challenges and to know that they are normal and not necessarily signs that your relationship is a non-starter or doomed to ultimate failure due to your differences.

- Time management can be an issue, as many HSPs tend to work on schedules that reflect their feelings in the present moment.
- Sensitivities to foods can usually be negotiated, but the two of you may need separate dishes for some meals.

- Home and car temperatures may need to be negotiated, due to differing sensitivities. If you can afford a newer car model, you might look for one that includes separate temperature options in heating and air conditioning for front seat passengers.
- As much as you are a match for each other, you are likely to also want and need time to yourselves to follow your own interests and callings.
- And each of you needs to keep in mind, for yourself and your HSPC, that irritability or anger can be signs that HuTiST may be contributing to your levels of distress or overwhelm. When you encounter these situations, take a deep breath, count to 10, and check if any of these 'internal weather' factors are causing or contributing to the intense reactions you're experiencing.

There are, as well, distinct advantages to an HSP in having an NHSP as your HSPC. NHSPs tend to live much of their life experiences through the thinking side of their brains. They can be enormously helpful to HSPs in varieties of ways because their awareness is generally anchored and focused in the outer world.

- NHSPs' awareness of clock time can be a most helpful complement to HSPs focus on the present moment.
- A downside and challenge with clock time is that the NHSP may be standing with a hand on the doorknob, fretfully waiting for her HSP husband to step out on their errands – after he said, "Honey, I'm ready to leave now" – and that was 5 or more minutes earlier… and you are having a hard time feeling supportive rather than disregarded, disrespected or abused by your non-sensate (a Jungian term)*[14] HSP. Again, here are lessons in patience and opportunities to practice clearing your distress.
- An NHSP is more likely to be a 'fix-it-myself' person, as well as a map and instruction manual reader than an HSP, and again these are often helpful contributions to your relationship. Here, the HSP may need to practice patience, as the NHSP may be used to barging ahead and completing the fix without consulting or discussing the 'how it's going to look when it's done' part of the fixing it.
- While all of the above may be positive contributions in your relationships with each other, the differences between you may prove grating or annoying to either or both of you. Looking at this positively, these are great opportunities for learning and practicing patience, for using whatever de-stressing methods work best for you, and for developing your skills at negotiations.

Such discussions may be eye-openers when it comes to issues that you and your partner feel differently about. Until you actually compare your views and opinions, it may not be at all apparent that you perceive things as similarly or differently as you do. When we've grown up in our families and live according to the family traditions and rules, we may not realize that other families have rules for certain issues that differ in subtle or major ways from our own.

✦ 'Lila' was considering moving into Ben's apartment, after they had been dating regularly for a year and a half and his flat-mate was moving out. They had gotten along pretty smoothly in their time together. Both were from middle-class families.

Ben's family was unusual in that his mother was a part time luthier (repairing string instruments), working in-home, and his father was an office manager in a small moving company. So, Ben had grown up with a stay-at-home mom, with whom he and his two younger NHSP sisters were very close. Both he and his mother were HSPs, while his father was a kind but distinctly NHSP person who was good at numbers, ledgers, scheduling and home repairs.

Lila's parents were both factory workers and she taught high school math. She, her parents and two brothers were all NHSPs.

Ben and Lila thought they had generally agreed pretty well on their lifestyle preferences, but in the week after she moved in, both began wondering whether they hadn't made a serious mistake. For example, Ben knew Lila liked Pop music, and had attended a pop concert with her, and she had slept overnight at his place on many occasions. But he hadn't known she liked to wake up to a loud Pop station with the volume on her bedside radio (part of her belongings that she brought with her) turned way up. They had relied on his radio for occasional weekend wake-ups, tuned to a classical station, prior to her moving in. And she had always slept over on Friday or Saturday nights, when she didn't have to get up for work. She could see he was rattled, and explained that on workdays she didn't want to take a chance of sleeping through the radio alarm if it was tuned softly to his station.

Lila was seriously rattled by Ben's expectations, previously unspoken, that she would take over the domestic duties of shopping, cleaning and laundry, which his mother had done because she worked from home and his father worked long hours.

Lila assumed her explanation was accepted by Ben. Ben assumed his complaint to Lila was going to be honored. He was badly jarred the next morning when the loud music woke him again. He knew from long experience that responding immediately when he was really angry was generally a poor choice. He also held back from responding before breakfast, being aware that hunger inclined him towards poor choices and responses that he later regretted. And opening a serious discussion when they were both heading for work very soon was also a poor choice. That evening, after dinner, Ben asked Lila if she would be willing to discuss the radio issue.

Lila paused a moment and made a counter-offer. She'd discuss the radio if he'd discuss the issue of household chores. I'm sure you'd like to know how this all unfolded, but from the tone and content of their opening negotiations, you can pretty well guess that they were able to come to mutually acceptable solutions to their issues.

*HAVE YOU BEEN HOLDING ONTO GRATING OR IRRITATING ISSUES IN YOUR RELATIONSHIP?*

*IF YES, CAN YOU THINK OF PRODUCTIVE, HEALING WAYS YOU MIGHT DISCUSS THEM?*

*RELEASE THEM (YOURSELF OR TOGETHER)?*

*NEGOTIATIONS OR TRADEOFFS YOU MIGHT EXPLORE?*

The successes and failures in relationships just as often are dependent on the 'how' of discussions and negotiations as they are on the 'what.'

Helpful general principles include:
- With serious issues to clarify, let the other party know well ahead of time set for the discussion what the issues are that you want to consider and negotiate.
- Set a time for the discussion that will be as un-stressed as possible by other time sensitive obligations, HuTiST, and the like.
- Mutual respect and consideration are incredibly important during the discussions.
- A clear opening statement of the issue that one of you is raising saves a lot of misunderstandings and hassles.
- Having each person state what they heard and understood about the issue at hand is essential to knowing you're both on the same track.
- Stating how each of you feels about the issues is very helpful, especially if feelings are running high.
- Again, acknowledging that you heard and understood the feelings expressed by your HSP partner is enormously helpful in setting the stage for discussions and negotiations.
- Having a paper and pencil or electronic writing device to list and describe the issues, record the options you each raise, and your feelings about these can help you avoid secondary arguments about who said what about the issues you're considering.
- While taking notes may seem tedious, it is a much better investment of time, emotions and energies than spiraling off into secondary arguments over disagreements regarding various details that were or weren't raised.
- When you come to a mutually acceptable agreement, again check how each of you feels about it.
- If there is still tension or disagreement, you might want to sleep on it one night or at least give it a few hours to percolate. It's surprising how often new ideas will surface when you give the dust a chance to settle and consider the issues and options from your new positions of greater understanding of each other.
- If there is agreement, set a time a few days later to check on how it is working out.
- Be sure to express your appreciations and to thank your partner for working on these issues with you, and reassure him that you are open to further clarifications and negotiations if needed.
- If you've succeeded in settling a major issue, a little celebration is in order.
- If the disagreements are not resolved, give it a bit of time and then explore the issues again.
- If they are still unresolved, it is often helpful if each of you takes a while (could be minutes or a day or two) to ponder whether what is upsetting you or blocking your coming to an agreement might involve related issues from your past experience with other people. These might be over the particulars of your argument, or about how arguments are dealt with in general, or how you've felt in the past about the issues under consideration.

Even though I've been working on my own issues for decades, I'm repeatedly surprised at how issues buried in my inner, emotional filing cabinets can get stirred by issues in my present life.
- The good news in all this is that while it may prove somewhat challenging to sort out issues from the past that get stirred by current life situations, the benefits of doing these clearings are enormous. It's like releasing old, emotional pus from a boil that's been festering for years.

> *Stress is the trash of modern life –*
> *we all generate it but if you don't dispose of it properly,*
> *it will pile up and overtake your life.*
> — Terri Guillemets

Moving past the initial adjustments of a relationship can take several months of frequent clarifications and negotiations. You will then settle into enjoying your togetherness with only occasional discussions of the what and how of getting along with each other.

If you're an NHSP, being in a long-term, partnered or marital relationship with an HSP can be enormously broadening and rewarding – inviting you to explore parts of the world you've never known.
- HSPs are often very keenly conscious of the present moment, sensing a broad spectrum of awarenesses, sensations and feelings that add immeasurable depth and wonderment to your life experiences. For instance, you may be amazed at the ranges of nuances your partner discusses with you after getting together with some friends or seeing a movie.
- HSPs can be in tune with their feelings and yours, making life a passionate tango rather than just a routine waltz.
- Intimate and sexual relations will often have heightened qualities that reflect the sensitivities of your HSP.
- HSPs can be enormously caring about other people and all living beings. They can be wonderfully creative, seeing nuances, possibilities and options that others easily pass over and miss in the most common of situations. A ride on a bus can easily become an adventure of engaging in conversations with interesting strangers, or a stroll through a park may bring out surprising new awarenesses of sights, sounds and textures.
- HSPs can be deeply appreciative of the arts.
- HSPs can connect deeply with direct awarenesses of intuition and spirit.

If you are also an HSP, you will find mutual, synergistic pleasure in the ways that you dance through life together. Each of you can markedly enrich the life of your partner through sharing your sensitivities.

However, being in a relationship with an HSP may be challenging, as well. Because HSPs have heightened sensory and emotional sensitivities. they are highly reactive to whatever you are each experiencing. If you are enjoying yourselves and feeling safe, you can expect to be warmly responsive and stimulating with each other. But if HSPs are feeling stressed, criticized, belittled, attacked, or in any other ways unsafe, their hackles are likely to go up very quickly, their porcupine quills may bristle and their claws may come out – with very painful words and reactions to anything that stresses them.

Though repeating myself, I again emphasize my primary recommendation for HSPCs: Whatever the challenging situation may be in the moment, it is important to consider, first and foremost, what your HSP is feeling. And you will do well to clarify whether you are reading her correctly. You don't want to add insult to injury by guessing wrong when you assume you know what she is experiencing when she is upset – but you get it wrong.

> *When we honestly ask ourselves which person in our lives means the most to us, we often find that it is those who, instead of giving much advice, solutions, or cures, have chosen rather to share our pain and touch our wounds with a gentle and tender hand. The friend who can be silent with us in a moment of despair or confusion, who can stay with us in an hour of grief and bereavement, who can tolerate not knowing, not curing, not healing and face with us the reality of our powerlessness, that is a friend who cares.*
>                         - Henri Nouwen

So, your first step, whenever you are interacting with your HSP, is to check the current emotional weather report. A general statement about what you are observing, without interpretations, is helpful. This is an invitation to your HSP to clarify what he is feeling at this moment. Your acknowledgment that you hear and understand his feelings will open a door to a space in which he can feel safe and is invited to continue communications.

*Examples:*
- Your HSP has just come home from work and is abrupt, sharp and mildly to moderately critical in talking with you...
- Your HSP turns crabby and irritable when you're at a party together...

Suggestions:
- Acknowledge you sense he is irritated or upset about something.
- Don't respond immediately with suggestions for how he can fix whatever it is. Empathize and sympathize with his feelings so he knows he has been heard and understood.
- Ask whether he's ready for a snack or a meal. Remember that what appears to be an upset over external issues may often be more of a statement of general irritability due to HuTiST.
- If any of these additional items might commonly be a relaxation and pleasure for him, ask whether he might like to take a shower, a little stroll or a nap to dissipate the energies from his day, or step out together for a breath of fresh air and a chat, or have a cup of tea or a glass of wine.

Your next steps depend on your relationship. They will be influenced by many factors, which will vary with the roles you play out with each other in this grand, infinitely complex game of life that we have all signed up for.

Creating regular times to share what is going on in your lives and how you are feeling gives you opportunities for building and maintaining harmony between you.

This is particularly true if an NHSP is partnered with an HSP. Early in the building of your relationship, it may be very helpful to check in with each other frequently to clarify how each of you is experiencing being together and how you feel about the developing relationship. Having a regular time for such chats is a preventive against build-ups of tensions and worries over differences in your personalities and preferences that are becoming evident as you live together. It is really easy to misperceive, misinterpret or misunderstand the differences between you as expressions of dissatisfaction or disapproval. Practicing asking each other, "What's up?" is highly recommended when you sense tensions in your partner or between the two of you.

Planning your days and weeks so that they include balances between your differing preferences can also add to your prevention repertoire. Many HSPs often need quiet time and may prefer to have this by themselves. I've seen this frequently formalized as time for meditation or contemplation, being in nature, reading, listening to music of their preference, playing an instrument, and other solitary, soothing activities. Other HSPs enjoy more frequent joint activities with their partners.

If you're an NHSP, you may be more gregarious and may find quiet time something that is outside your usual experiences or pushing you beyond your normal comfort zone. You may find it helpful to have regularly scheduled group activities, such as participating in team sports, having a night out with your buddies or girlfriends, or whatever other stimulating activities you enjoy.

*How close is close enough?*

This is a factor often overlooked in the early stages of enjoying a closeness in your HSPC-HSP relationship. At the start of your being together you will to some extent be enjoying the glow of finding someone compatible, and exploring the many nuances of being together. You, the HSPC, will do well to keep in mind that it's very common for HSPs to want quiet time for themselves. Don't take this as a rejection. HSPs need this, both for processing and digesting their detailed sensory awarenesses and for resting and recovering when they find themselves over-stimulated.

You, the HSP, may find that you enjoy complex nuances of sensory explorations with your NHSP HSPC. Your openness to and capacities for these explorations are likely to be far greater than those of your NHSP partner. In these regards, you may both find an exploration of the five love languages enormously helpful.*[15]

These sorts of differences between you on the above issues may also impact your sexual relationship. Again, it is very important to talk with each other about your preferences, both positive and negative.

A major issue in our times may also be the question of monogamy vs. polyamory. If this is an issue on the table, it absolutely requires careful consideration between you. Elaine Aron (2000) has excellent discussions on sexual relationships. Aron is very accepting of polyamory as a lifestyle choice, and if you and your partner are in agreement that this is your preference, you may be able to live comfortably with this choice.

My own observations, over many years of doing marital and family therapy, as well as living for years on each of three continents, is that polyamory may often be a statement of a less than full commitment to your relationship, a way of withholding your full commitment from your togetherness and keeping a distinct distance from your partner or spouse. If this is an issue that divides you, you may do well to seek marital therapy. Be sure you check out the views of prospective therapists on polyamory before starting in therapy.

Ambivalence and differences of opinions about numerous aspects of close relationships are extremely common, not only in the area of sexual preferences. It's easy to find yourselves in disagreements over issues large and small in the process of exploring and developing your close relationship, one of the most precious and important adventures of your lives.

The first big argument the two of you have will probably surprise you and will very likely dismay you. It is likely to be about something minor or even silly, such as:
- Do we have our trash bin out in the open or in a closet?
- Does the sofa look better on the back or side wall of your living room?
- Do we display pictures of our families in the upstairs hall, where we'll enjoy these reminders of our relatives in privacy or do we share them with everyone who comes into our home, on the walls outside our living room?
- What color should the towels be in the bathroom?

Your first arguments are as much about meta-issues of how do we sort out our differences of opinion, and who is in charge of what areas of our combined household, as it is about the issues themselves of trash, sofas and towels. These arguments are a jockeying for who is in charge of what, and statements about how important particular issues are to each of you. These are usually not a sign of incompatibility, although one or both of you may feel some questions about such a possibility.*[16]

If you find you've set off a hidden landmine like that, call a time out to calm down and cool off. Be patient with yourself and your partner. You are experiencing a very normal part of the process of learning how to get along with each other. Again, the stress releasing and calming exercises detailed earlier can be helpful to you here.

When you are both calm, set a time to revisit what happened between you. How you conduct these discussions is every bit as important as the specific details you will clarify between you.
- A good place to start is for each of you to review briefly what you felt, thought and experienced as you engaged in your disagreement and in your friction.
- It is truly helpful if each of you takes a turn critiquing your own behaviors first.
- Then take turns asking each other, "What could I have done differently about ____?" (naming one specific issue at a time).
- Discuss each suggestion.
- Write them all down, with asterisks beside the ones you like.
- Re-run the original argument as a calm discussion, scripting it in the light of what you have heard from each other.
- Discuss how your re-runs feel to each of you.
- Ask yourselves if you still have any negative residues from your argument.
- If you do, then use a de-stressing method to decrease your SUDS to zero.**[17]
- Install positive thoughts and feelings to replace the ones you've released.
- Congratulate yourselves and each other on having done a good job in sorting out your argument.
- Congratulate yourselves and each other on having developed ways for dealing with future arguments.

- Ask yourselves how good and positive you each feel about your success, using the SUSS scale, and share this with each other.
- Use a positivity enhancing method to strengthen the positivity of how you feel about your success.*[18]

You may be surprised to find you can have good arguments in which you both come out feeling much better about being heard, understood and having sorted out whatever points of disagreement and conflict you had.

You may also have difficult arguments that leave you feeling frustrated, disappointed, angry, and even despairing. If your relationship has been positive until that point, and if further discussions between you don't clear the air and improve your feelings about the issues and about each other, you may want to consider having couples counseling to see whether a therapist can help you sort out your challenges.

Some couples find that taking time apart provides fresh perspectives and opens doorways to moving forward in better ways. And sometimes, realizing that you are not compatible may be the outcome. For the most part, this is better recognized earlier than later in a relationship. And again, you may find that individual counseling is helpful after a breakup, to clarify issues contributing to the breakup and lessons learned.

*Deepening sensitivity to the 'how' of relating*

This may sometimes be an ongoing challenge to both the HSP and HSPC in your relationship. I address this in greater detail here because it is important on many wholistic levels.

Awareness of wholistic sensitivities is especially important for an NHSP, whose operating system works primarily through the 'mind' level, focusing on reason and with the first approach to issues being processed generally through logic. The issues that arise in relationships may often seem rather simple and clear to him. For an NHSP, steps to resolving issues usually focus on left brain approaches, such as:

- Identifying the problem
- Clarifying the components of the problem
- Prioritizing issues to address
- Deciding at what level to begin to work on the issues
- Tracking progress, as in regular verbal acknowledgments or charting completed steps
- Scheduling regular, periodic times to review progress, decide on next steps and modify the program (Weekly reviews are common, but you and your partner may decide on more or less frequent assessments)
- Acknowledging progress and completion of important steps
- Celebrating resolution of the issue(s)

For an HSP, the issues are often identified as feelings that are somewhere on the spectrum of:

- General uneasiness about how something is feeling in the relationship
- Discomfort with a specific issue or event that bothered the HSP
- Irritation over the issue, and also over the lack of a whole-hearted response from the HSPC to the HSP's feelings about it

- Frustration that it is not being resolved quickly despite your efforts to address it
- Anger over the issue, and having to repeatedly mention the issue
- Feeling that your HSP discomforts are unheard, not valued, belittled or dismissed
- Resonating with previous experiences of being ignored, belittled, pathologized or dismissed, in the current relationship or in previous ones that left a residue of annoyance or disappointment
- Being triggered into residues of past traumas, with unresolved angry or hurt feelings over similar experiences

It is very important for you, as an HSPC, to understand that the first items in your discussions to address are the feelings of your HSP about the issue – rather than going directly to exploring or working on factual details of the issue. It is essential that your HSP gets ongoing acknowledgments about her feelings. Here is a sample progression for constructive discussion. Be certain that you leave ample time for your HSP to consider her feelings before moving from one level of acknowledgment and clarification to another.

Here are various ways you, the HSPC, might proceed:
- "I sense/ hear/ see you're bothered/ annoyed/ frustrated/ very upset/ angry about _____..."
- "Am I right that you feel _____ about this issue?..."
- "Am I right that you feel that we haven't been _____ this challenge?..."
- At each step which is relevant to you, clarify and confirm that you have heard and understood her feelings accurately.
- Ask what he feels would be helpful.
- Ask whether she feels ok about your adding some suggestions.
- As much as possible, tailor your HSPC statements about your suggestions to relate to his responses and suggestions.
- If either of you is feeling or thinking you are unheard, call a time out and clarify whether you have or haven't been heard and understood accurately.
- If you want to suggest ways to deal with the issues, then as much as possible, make it clear (if this is true) that you agree with aspects of her suggestions, and specify which ones, but feel (better choice than 'think') that they might perhaps work better if _____... ending your explanation with, "and what do you feel about this?"
- Avoid pointing a finger at him or saying harshly critical things about what he is observing and/or proposing.
- If you feel she is wrong, still acknowledge (as above) that you have heard her views and suggestions. Then state that you see some additional possibilities.
- Ask whether now is a good time to bring these up, or whether first taking a bit of time to digest what you've discussed so far would be better.
- If you become frustrated and/or upset, say what your feelings are and specify what issues are winding you up.
- If your conversation is getting heated, either of you might ask for a time out to cool off.

This might look and feel rather convoluted and complicated. I've probably overstated the degrees of caution you may find feasible or necessary. But I would rather you err on the side of caution when you're looking at a disagreement between an HSP and HSPC (particularly if the HSPC is an NHSP). And even where the HSPC is an HSP, the same issues are relevant. When an HSP is experiencing an emotional upset, particularly if it is intense or involves triggered feelings from previous, similar situations (in your relationship or from a previous one), it may be difficult for her to access her thinking functions in ways that are constructive. It is far better to err on the side of caution than to get into tangles of arguments where the HSP is strongly into his feelings, despite the fact that there are concrete issues to discuss, clarify and resolve.

When the HSPC is an HSP, it's advisable for him to pick a time when he is calm and less likely to get rattled, upset or triggered himself in a discussion with his HSP, if at all possible. Helpful processes for discussion recommended under Parent Effectiveness Training (P.E.T.) are particularly useful in situations of these sorts – detailed in the following Chapter.**[19] Doing your best to use 'I' statements will facilitate smoother discussions, rather than pointing a finger with 'you' statements of the challenges. For instance, see which of the following you sense will be more likely to facilitate the resolution of a touchy situation:

– "You're not considering _____. That's what we need to address first."

Compared with: "I hear and understand your concerns about _____. What do you feel about this part of the issue?"

Or

– "I think this might be a better way to approach the issue."

Compared with: "I hear you're upset about this challenge and understand these are your concerns and suggestions _____.

Or

Have I heard you correctly?" After any necessary clarifications, and then proceed with "In addition to your suggestions, do you think that it might also be helpful for us to think about _____?"

Again, I mention that it is helpful to both HSP and HSPC to keep a written list of issues discussed and agreed, including the feelings that came up, along with the considerations of points of friction or disagreement and action plans.

In moving forward, following such discussions and agreements, it's very helpful to continue to keep in mind that an HSP's internal processing systems and internal filing systems are organized under the category of emotions. His HSP memory of previous discussions will contain feelings first, and second (possibly even a distant second), he will have files under headers of relationship issues/ factual considerations/ decisions and action options. If you are an NHSP, you most likely will recall your joint decisions first as action steps, with secondary emotional issues surrounding your clarifying discussions and the plans for resolving the difficulties. You are likely to be expecting to proceed from action step 'x' to follow-up steps 'y' and 'z'.

Again, in follow-up discussions, I suggest you (the HSPC with NHSP trait) might do well to invite discussions of the threads of feelings about the issues first. This doesn't have to be all one-sided. After you process your issues through feelings for a while, you may find it possible to ask (on a review day that is calm and pleasant) whether the two of you can touch base first on the decision points and action plans, and then move on to consider the remaining related emotion issues. If this goes well, your differing HSP-NHSP preferences for prioritizing discussions can each be honored in a balanced fashion.

And last, but by no means least, be patient with each other. We have all spent many years growing into our habits of experiencing and relating to the world. Sorting out a relationship also takes learning, time and patience.

You may be asking, "Are all of these discussions about HSPs' emotional sensitivity really necessary?" And the answer is that if they are not relevant to your relationships, then they are not needed. But if your experiences as an HSP have included rejection of your wholistic sensitivities, particularly in the emotional parts of the spectrum, then these are issues that may be enormously meaningful and helpful to you and your HSPC.

And once the difficult issues in your relationships and the friction points are identified and clarified, they can be eased and cleared and replaced with positivity, using various approaches presented in this book.

With time, HSPs who have had difficulties finding acceptance for themselves and their ways of being and relating in the world are often able to overcome what have been in the past the troublesome aspects of their sensitivities. More trust is built up, and less reassurances of acceptance of the HSP's sensitivities are needed in order to maintain a harmonious discourse and satisfying relationship.

What has been helpful to many couples working on their relationships is to remember that progress is rarely seen in a straight line from their starting point to where they are at a later time. There are high points and low spots along the way, much as in a graph of growth in financial markets or variations in temperatures over time, as the seasons shift from winter to summer. Don't give up quickly when you find yourself in what feels like a downturn in your relationship. Take a deep breath, remember the good times you've enjoyed together, and be patient. It's very likely they will return shortly.

Deliberately building positivity in yourself with your partner is another path to improving how you get along as an HSP in a relationship with an NHSP. With experience, over time, you'll have easier times sharing your feelings and thoughts with each other, and knowing they are being heard and accepted. You won't have to explain yourself as often as you would with an NHSP. In other words, you can work your ways through your issues together more readily because you are both familiar with the HSP tunes and steps.

If you are an HSP and are companioned with an NHSP, you will probably find that positivity grows and deepens as you learn to understand and speak each other's languages. But don't just sit back, waiting and hoping for your relationship to improve. Look for wholistic ways to pleasure each other, as below.

While books like the one you're reading may help you get varieties of handles on what the challenges are, it is may be difficult to sort out your relationship issues on your own. If, despite all your efforts, you don't find ways to settle your disagreements, and particularly if this is a repeated experience over a long time (what is long for you will depend on many factors), you may do well to consult a therapist trained in couples, marital and family therapy. A skilled therapist can often suggest many ways for approaching, analyzing and resolving issues that most people would rarely think of on their own.

A therapist can help you and your partner more quickly identify the issues, suggest approaches for you and your partner to use in addressing them, and can guide you through the processes of self-exploration, clearing old patterns of trauma and problematic relationships, and can guide you to solutions you might never have considered yourselves.

If you are open to exploring these difficulties but your partner is not, you might want to consider more carefully whether the partner in your relationship is someone with whom you want to develop a long-term relationship. When one person in a relationship starts these sorts of psychological explorations on their own, the process of one person changing in relation to their past ways of thinking, feeling and relating may lead to greater distancing from their partner. Though this may be stressful and painful, accepting irreconcilable differences is probably better than continuing to struggle in a relationship that is proving difficult to maintain.

*Parent Effectiveness Training (P.E.T.) – Problematic and better ways to express ourselves*

Thomas Gordon (1975) developed the approaches taught in P.E.T. These are very helpful in dealing with your relationships. Though this book by Gordon addresses parent-child issues in particular, the methods it teaches are outstanding for improving communications between HSPs and HSPCs. Here are a few of the methods recommended to facilitate harmonious relationships.

– You might picture to yourself that whenever you're speaking to someone else you are being a good neighbor, respecting an imaginary fence between you and that person.

– You restrict yourself to speaking about what is on your side of the fence. You use 'I' messages, describing what you are feeling. You may include details of what your neighbor has said or done, but do your best to use neutral, descriptive language that is not criticizing, attacking or blaming. Looking for the feelings that are generating an emotional charge and irritability or anger is also helpful.

Here are some samples of helpful phrasings:

"I can see you're tired after a long day's work, but I'm finding your edginess and blaming attitude are rubbing me the wrong way – over such small things as my leaving the refrigerator door open a crack, or leaving a bit of food on the bottom of the plate when I was washing the dishes."

"It looks like we've both had a hard day, honey. I'm finding it harder than usual to not snap back at you when you criticize me over these little things."

"I'm not used to seeing you so grumpy after you've had your dinner and get over your hunger edginess. Is there something bothering or worrying you?"

"I think we're both tired, dear one. How would a brief nap feel before we go out to the party this evening?"

Samples of several shades of unhelpful phrasing:

"Why don't you just go to bed now and sleep off some of your annoying irritability? And we can forget about going out to the party tonight!"

"Why don't you just lay off your constant criticisms! I've had a long day myself. I'm not ready to put up with your bitchiness this evening."

More helpful phrasing:

"I'm very upset/ hurt/ angry with you because I feel I am being disrespected and blamed in this conversation we're having."

"When I hear you say, 'You shouldn't take it so hard when someone in charge tells you what to do at work.' I feel you aren't appreciating how bad I'm feeling in my situation. My new boss is cracking the whip to show us who is in charge. And she simply wouldn't listen when I started to explain that if we do what she is suggesting it will end up messing up the team meetings and productions schedules."

More unhelpful phrasing:

"You never listen to me. I don't know why I'm wasting my time talking with you."

"I'm really fed up with your looking for any excuse, and finding real put-down ways to criticize me."

"Buzz off! You don't know what you're talking about!"

For further explorations on how to approach discussions of problems and issues with other people, I highly recommend Gordon's books, Parent Effectiveness Training and Teacher Effectiveness Training. TWR/WHEE blends well with P.E.T., helping you lower your levels of anxieties in dealing with other people. TWR/WHEE also adds the building of positives and meta-positives to strengthen what is going well between you and others.*[20]

YOU MAY FIND IT HELPFUL, PERHAPS EVEN FUN, TO PRACTICE VARIOUS WAYS OF SAYING THINGS TO EACH OTHER

IT CAN BE HELPFUL TO DEVELOP A SIGNAL TO CLUE YOUR PARTNER TO THINK OF A DIFFERENT WAY TO SAY SOMETHING. "OUCH!" IS PROBABLY THE SIMPLEST.

*Legal precautions and remedies*

For peace and security, and for healing relationships in a family there are numbers of legal issues that may be important to address. Some of these are universally applicable and others relate to special situations that may arise in partnered and family relationships. I only mention these here briefly, as my focus is far more on psychological aspects of relationships.

- A marital agreement identifies your preferences and intentions in the management of your estate, both within the marriage and should you come to a separation or divorce. In Canada, a marital agreement takes precedence over a will, should there be differences in the two documents. In other countries you need to check on which document has precedence over the other.

- A directive for your care is highly advisable, in case you are unable to make decisions yourself regarding you care. Do you want to be allowed to die naturally? Do you want medical treatments to prolong your life if you are no longer conscious? Again, better that you make these decisions known, in writing, to save others the agonies of deciding for you.

- A last will and testament provides clarity and security to your significant other and the rest of your family. This can also prevent what otherwise can be difficult and contentious issues from marring the relationships of the survivors

- with each other and with the deceased. Even if there are no complicated or contentious issues in the relationships of the person writing the will, the review of the drafted documents by a lawyer is usually advisable. There may be legal issues or life contingencies that are best mentioned in the documents that people who are inexperienced in writing wills wouldn't realize are best made explicit.
- A directive for your end of life care is highly advisable, in case you are unable to make decisions yourself regarding you care, do you want to be allowed to die naturally? Do you want medical treatments to prolong your life if you are no longer conscious? Again, better that you make these decisions known, in writing, to save others the agonies of deciding for you. And important to appoint someone to make any decisions you have not addressed in your directives.
- A separation agreement can be a tricky and finicky document to compose, even when the proceedings are amicable. There are many contingencies to consider, and some of them may not be obvious to anyone who is inexperienced in these matters. Consulting a lawyer is always a prudent procedure.
- If there are contested, contentious issues in a separation or divorce, and if the parties involved cannot resolve these themselves, the help of lawyers may be required for sorting out the differences.

Be aware that not all lawyers provide services in the same manner. There are lawyers who are good mediators, who will clarify what the laws are regarding the issues at hand, making suggestions for what they feel is reasonably achievable in your situation and working with the lawyer for the other party in the litigation to achieve a mutually agreeable settlement. The majority of such settlements are arranged without a court battle, though you may have to appear in court for a decision regarding contested items.

There are also lawyers who fight like barracudas to achieve what you ask them to get in your agreement. This may involve lengthy court proceedings and can be enormously costly. It may be necessary, however, if the litigating family members are not just dealing with property but also with dependent children. This is particularly true when the children have special needs, and/or when one or both of the responsible adults demonstrates attitudes and/or behaviors that may not be in the best interests of the children.

- Advance directives regarding terminal care and organ donations are strongly advised. These assure that your wishes will be known and honored. They also avoid stress and confusion among family survivors, guardians and medical personnel.

A caution regarding organ donations: It is strongly advised that you stipulate that the final decision regarding organ donations should be made by a trusted relative or friend rather than by medical personnel. If you are seriously injured and unlikely to survive, the decisions of your trusted person might be different from that of an anonymous medical person who is thinking more about the intended recipients of your organs than about you. And if you know a trusted medical intuitive or medium,**[21] you might instruct your designated guardian in these matters to consult your intuitive, if circumstances permit this, before the final decision is made.

**Relationships with the environment** *(HSPs and their HSPCs)*

To be with an HSP in the great outdoors is to re-experience with her the happiness of exploring the natural world as a child would. HSPs commonly resonate very deeply with nature. They feel more alive when they are connected to nature and can revel in the sights of sunrises and sunsets, of downpours and rainbows, of frost on leaves and branches, of plants swaying in the wind, in the sound of waves along the seashore, of smells of the salty sea and seaweed, of fresh cut grass, in the sensations of warm sun on their skin, and of wind blowing their hair while fresh air fills their lungs.

To be with an HSP may also be to sense – through his discomforts – the suffering from smoky city skies and breathing smoggy city air, of witnessing him experience physical nausea in walking through noisy, dirty streets and gutters, of having difficulties with the crowded urban human environment – as in passing by a person sitting on the sidewalk in ragged clothing and not responding to a plea for a handout because he has no small change, and of turning off the radio or TV when the latest gory, depressing news of the day is aired.

You, an NHSP, may have grown up in the same city, but you were not experiencing, and probably even unaware much of what the HSP finds impossible to ignore. For you, most of these details faded into the background and might have remained non-existent, were it not for his complaining about them. And it may still prove difficult for you to appreciate how intensely your HSP feels these sensations.

While in many cases these HSP-HSPC differences are noted, acknowledged and tolerated, there can be situations where they become troublesome bones of contention. Choosing a place to live can be one of these. The HSP may find an environment unbearable, which an NHSP could easily ignore, as in details around a home that is otherwise agreed by both to be great, in and of itself. Irritating issues might include noise, smells or electromagnetic pollution. A commute on public transportation during rush hour may be utterly draining energetically to an HSP, where an NHSP could happily read a newspaper in the same situation and not notice the negative energies.

Further along on the spectrum of greater sensitivities, some HSPs cannot tolerate ordinary US or Canadian food. They feel sick when eating it because of pesticides, preservatives and other chemicals that are intended to color, flavor or preserve the food on store shelves for longer periods of time, and they may be unable to digest genetically modified foods.

These HSP sensitivities require discussions and clarifications with your HSPC, first to clarify HSP challenges, and second to arrive at mutually agreeable decisions about how to deal with these challenges.

> IF NATURE SPEAKS TO YOU,
> - BRING SOMETHING OF NATURE INTO YOUR HOME, BE IT PLANTS, ROCKS, PAINTINGS, A BUBBLING FOUNTAIN, PHOTOS, OR OTHER ITEMS THAT CONNECT YOU WITH THE WORLD AT LARGE.
>
> - BE SURE YOU SCHEDULE TIMES FOR EXPLORING NEARBY PARKS, GARDENS, HIKING OR BIKING TRAILS, AND BOTANICAL GARDENS, AS WELL AS TAKING TIME TO LOOK FOR THESE DURING TRAVELS.

**Spirit** *(HSPs and their HSPCs)*

There is a very broad spectrum of sensitivities and awarenesses among HSPs to spiritual dimensions. I should clarify from the start that I am describing and addressing actual perceptions and experiences of HSPs, not just their beliefs about spiritual issues.

The range of these experiences may include:
- Deep, loving acceptance of people just as they are, with no wishes or expectations that they should change in order to be more acceptable
- Intuitive awarenesses, as in directly knowing what people are feeling and thinking without their disclosing through words, expressions or gestures the information perceived by the HSP
- Intuitively sensing the rightness and wrongness of a situation, in ways that go beyond logical reasoning
- Sensing biological energies around people and other living beings, as well as in the broader environment
- Communicating with spirits and/or angels*[22]

## 26. HSP children – detailed wholistic considerations

*You are the bows from which your children as living arrows are sent forth.*
*The archer sees the mark upon the path of the infinite, and*
*He bends you with His might that His arrows may go swift and far.*
*Let your bending in the archer's hand be for gladness;*
*For even as he loves the arrow that flies,*
*so He loves also the bow that is stable.*
— Khalil Gibran

If you have a child who is very sensitive, you've been given an amazing gift. It's an exquisitely sensitive gift, and one that you must be very careful and patient in nurturing. It is also a series of learnings, and these are lessons that can be profoundly deep and helpful to both of you.

How can you know if your child is an HSP? The fact that you're reading this book already puts you many steps ahead in addressing this question.

Practical steps, in brief: Look for high levels of sensory sensitivity in many aspects of their lives. High sensitivities may be present for sight, sound, smell, taste and touch, even in the first few months of their lives. Children may have difficulties in clearly identifying what is bothering them, or in expressing or explaining their irritabilities clearly, or in making themselves heard when they complain about them. Parents, brothers and sisters, teachers and others who are unfamiliar with HSP sensitivities will often think the HSPs are just tired, fussy or spoiled. As a parent to an HSP child, you can be enormously helpful – first to your child, but also with proactive explanations to teachers and parents of playmates.*[23]

Your relationships with your children will often be among the most meaningful experiences of your life. I discuss this in greater detail, considering the wholistic spectrum of children's HSP sensitivities.

### *Body* (HSP children)

High sensitivities to physical stimuli may be one of the first indications that you have an HSP child.

- HSP children's senses of sight, sound, smell, taste and touch may be very, very keen, as in:
    - She may purr with caring, loving touch.
    - She may also respond in negative ways to being touched, held, stroked or having others invade her space.
    - He may complain of discomforts with items of clothing, such as labels in collars, rough textures, wearing a belt or tight clothes.
    - He may express strong likes and dislikes in tastes and smells, complaining of feeling put off or even nauseous by some strong smells and tastes
    - She deeply enjoys gentle music or the sound of a bubbling brook, but is intolerant of loud sounds of any sort, such as boisterous groups or media.
    - Sensitivities to what is eaten
    - He may be hyperactive and/or irritable with sugared foods (very com-

mon) and other foods and/or food combinations specific to himself.

- She may feel sick, tired and/or irritable with ordinary foods that may contain any combinations of chemical fertilizers, pesticides, preservatives (including gassing chemicals used to preserve produce and fruit), and GMO food components.
- He may have allergic reactions to foods and drinks containing additives and chemicals
- She might feel and behave significantly better with a diet of organic foods.

### *Emotions* (HSP children)

Emotional awareness and sensitivity is probably the most noticed and commented on aspect of the spectrum of HSP children's sensitivities. HSPs may engage readily in friendly, calm, happy interactions with other children and adults. However, they may quickly respond to issues that upset them, displaying anxieties, frustrations, fears, crying or anger. And they may have difficulty in identifying and explaining what it is that upset them. Their very high sensitivities in all aspects of their being may leave them upset, discombobulated, and with difficulties putting words to their upsets because they are very deeply immersed in the upset and unable to connect with their observing ego*[24] in order to identify their issues and explain them.

- HSP children often become immersed and absorbed in emotions (sometimes stirred by sensations) and may be oblivious to what is going on around them. This may interfere with their attention in classrooms, social settings and time alone, such as homework time. It can be difficult to redirect their attention when they are absorbed in their feelings. This is the norm for HSP children. It's not that there is something wrong with them.
- Your HSP child's range of emotional responses may include:
    - She may connect readily and deeply with people who accept emotionality and avoid those who don't.
    - She may display keen emotional awarenesses for the feelings and moods of others and particularly those of parents, other family members and close friends.
    - He may be strongly distressed when there are tensions between parents or other family members. (Most children will react this way to high levels of family tensions, but HSP children will respond more immediately, even to low or moderate family tension levels.)
    - He may tend to cry easily when stressed, disappointed or distressed.
    - She may respond with quick and deep calming to being comforted by being held, cuddled, hugged and/or reassured that she is safe.
    - He may be deeply bothered or upset with perceived pain or distress of others, and may find it deeply disturbing to watch or hear them.
    - He is likely to be disinterested in, dislike or avoid emotionally insensitive people.
    - Competitive sports are likely to be strong turnoffs, both as a participant and as an audience.

- There are many ways you can help your HSP children with their emotions.
    - Ask about and acknowledge his emotions when he appears moody or upset.
    - Help him learn to identify, label and describe his emotions, so that he can inform others about what he is feeling.
    - Remind her that a deeply felt disappointment or other strong, upsetting feeling will soon pass, as other upsets have faded before.
    - Help him to identify stimuli and irritations that stir and intensify his emotions, so that he can understand why he is irritated or upset.
    - Clarify that he may need quiet time when he's upset and that he can mention he's a bit rattled at the moment and ask for a brief quiet time to sort out his feelings.
    - Teach her to use TWR/WHEE or other relaxation and de-stressing methods.
    - Remind her to use her de-stressing methods when she feels overwhelmed and hasn't thought to make use of them.
    - Acknowledge that everyone has strong feelings at some times, so he knows he's not odd or wrong to be having these feelings in response to whatever triggered them.
    - And last but not least, children respond very rapidly to tapping with TWR/WHEE. Even with severe traumas they may release their intense feelings down to a 0 or close to it.*[25]

WHILE THE LOVE LANGUAGES*[26] ARE USUALLY CONSIDERED IN COUPLES RELATIONSHIPS, THEY MAY BE EQUALLY HELPFUL IN PARENT-CHILD RELATIONSHIPS.

E.G. WORDS OF AFFIRMATION CAN RE-ORIENT A CHILD WHO IS OFF-CENTER.

A TOUCH OR CUDDLE CAN BE ENORMOUSLY CALMING.

**Mind** (HSP children)

Processing emotions may take much longer for HSP children than for NHSP children. They tend to become immersed and absorbed in emotions and oblivious to what is going on around them. This may interfere with their attention in classrooms, social settings and time alone (e.g. homework time). It can be difficult to redirect their attention when they are absorbed in their feelings and sorting out their understandings of what is going on and what is best for them to do about it. These are the normal responses for HSP children. They are not suffering from psychological disorders. These are their inborn traits and personalities and how they are wired.

- Adults can be enormously helpful:
    - Understand that comfortable clothing is important to children, as the irritation of rough cloth, clothing labels or tightness of fit may be distracting and irritating enough to make it hard for her to relax and concentrate on other issues and demands in her environment.
    - Acknowledge the sensitivities of his ordinary senses and discuss the

best ways to handle them.
- Help her figure out ways to deal with irritations to her senses.
- HSP children may feel anxious and worried in situations where they are not understood and accepted. To expect the more sensitive HSPs to be paying attention all of the time (especially in school), as is the norm for NHSP children, may be unreasonable for those who are on the higher sensitivities side of the spectrum.

- HSP children are usually very thoughtful about whatever they are engaged in doing. They may pause in the middle of an activity to ponder their awarenesses, understandings, feelings and whatever is going on.
- HSP children and adults often love to read about other people's lives, loves and tribulations. Stories of challenges, suffering and learning to deal with life challenges really speak to HSPs.

## MENTIONING PREVIOUS SUCCESSES IN DEALING WITH SIMILAR SITUATIONS CAN BE HELPFUL

*There are certain children who are told they are too sensitive, and there are certain adults who believe sensitivity is a problem that can be fixed in the way that crooked teeth can be fixed and made straight. And when these two come together you get a fairytale, a kind of story with hopelessness in it. I believe there is something in these old stories that does what singing does to words. They have transformational capabilities, in the way melody can transform mood. They can't transform your actual situation, but they can transform your experience of it. We don't create a fantasy world to escape reality, we create it to be able to stay. I believe we have always done this, used images to stand and understand what otherwise would be intolerable.*

- Lynda Barry

Teachers, doctors and other caregivers who are unaware of the HSP trait will often have little understanding or patience for HSP sensitivities. They often label HSP children as psychologically disturbed. To pathologize the HSP sorts of absorption in deep reflection, contemplation or fantasy as oppositional, defiant, obsessive compulsive or Attention Deficit Disorder (ADD) is to do these children a great disservice.*[27] Sadly, many conventional psychologists are not aware of the HSP trait. So, if you feel your child has been mistakenly labeled in such ways, you may want to bring this to the attention of the school counsellor or administrator. Resources to support your complaints might include books and websites explaining the HSP.[28]

A strong word of caution here. To the extent that you are able, it will truly serve your HSP child best if you adopt an activist attitude in addressing their needs. Don't leave it to wishes or hopes for the best. Whenever I think of wishful thinking, I'm reminded of the old Scottish proverb, "If wishes were horses, then beggars would ride." Your child is too important to leave to the policies, procedures and practices of people who are unavailable to offer needed attention for HSPs with special needs. Often, this is not because they are callus and uncaring, but because they are overburdened and overworked due to large numbers of students per class and because children with serious behavioral issues, including autism, are being mainstreamed without adequate supports for the classroom teachers.

Taking a step backward, this is a caution, to the extent that you are able to manage this, to choose a home in a school district that has a good reputation for attention to children with special needs, or at least to one that has smaller numbers of children per class. Beyond this, it is also an inducement for parents to scout out the teachers who offer more individual attention to their students, and to draw the attention of school authorities to your child's needs.

Becoming a known activist advocate for your child is generally a good idea. The squeaky wheel really does get the grease more often than the silent one. At the very least, checking in regularly with your child's teachers puts a spotlight on their individual personalities and needs in ways that can be of enormous help.

And if you have the time and energies, offering your assistance to teachers is often tremendously appreciated. When you are sensitive to the teachers' needs, they are more likely to be sensitive to your children's needs.

And for dealing with stress and trauma, again I recommend:

- EP for stress, worries, anxieties, traumas and other issues works wonderfully well in children.*[29]
- Children on the very highly sensitive end of sensory sensitivities may benefit from occupational therapy (Rosenshein, 2013). This involves practicing various tasks to help integrate their functioning within varieties of settings and challenges to their sensitivities.
- Absorption in emotions and thoughts is more prevalent when HSP children are anxious or upset. Wholistic EP tapping methods can be excellent for reducing emotional stress and distress rapidly, and are enormously helpful in these situations. TWR/WHEE has the extra advantage that it can be used discretely. This avoids the extra burden of children teasing or bullying the HSP for tapping on their face, body and hand when using other wholistic EP methods – which may be seen as strange in school or on the playground and could trigger bullying.*[30]

## *Relationships in general with other people* (HSP children)

This is such an important topic that I address it from several perspectives, even though this introduces a bit of repetitiveness.

At home, HSP children often need more attention than other children.

- Acknowledging and accepting your HSP child's sensitivities is enormously helpful, as HSP children commonly feel they aren't normal when they see other children are unbothered by all the stimuli the HSPs have difficulty tolerating, or when other children tease or bully them for being so sensitive.*[31]
- Make HSP awarenesses and preferences an open subject for discussion, so that she feels comfortable talking with you about it.
- Whether you're an HSP or not, share observations of your own with him about awarenesses that you have with other people, images you see, issues that stirred you to connect with your own sensitivities in music, other creative arts, and so on, so that your speaking about sensitivities is a two-way street.

*A problem shared is half a consolation.*
- Anonymous

- Pointing out benefits of being an HSP is a great support, particularly if you can share your own and/or other people's sensitivities and ways in which these have been helpful to them and to those around them.
- If at all possible, it's most helpful to give an HSP child her own space, where she can retreat and close the door to compose herself when her emotions get stirred or her senses are jarred.
- As it isn't always possible to retreat to a quiet and safe physical place, introducing and practicing being in a place of peace and safety and healing (PPSH) can be enormously helpful.*[32]
- Teach him how to tap away his anxieties and stresses, and remember to teach him to tap in positives to replace the negatives he's released.
- Brothers and sisters may need to be told that their HSP sister is highly sensitive, and that they are better able to ignore stressful stimuli and are quicker to get over upsets than she is. Putting these issues in a positive frame (for whichever child you are talking with) is important, to avoid blaming or stigmatizing.
- Let teachers know about his needs to de-stress when he is feeling challenged, and that it's her nature to think things through thoroughly before deciding what she feels is right for her to do.

In friendships and interactions where HSP children are feeling safe and positively engaged, they often develop solid, positive relationships.

- They have strong preferences for gentleness and kindness in interactions with others, and avoidance of boisterous, loud environments and engagements.
- They tend to pick friends who are similarly sensitive, or who are accepting and appreciate the HSP's sensitivity.
- They may prefer single-person interactions rather than groups, as children's group energies can at times feel too boisterous or overwhelming.
- They are sensitive to responding to redirection and correction by teachers and other authority figures, and have a strong sense of fairness and unfairness.
- They demonstrate strong empathy with others' situations, emotional states and interactions and often want to help those who are upset to feel better.

✦✦✦ I strongly preferred single-friend relationships and activities as a child. I was puzzled that one of my closer friends behaved differently with me when we were both in a group. At the time, I didn't understand that because I was not in a close-friends relationship with others in the group, the group norm for interacting with me differed from the norm I had established with the single friend, and that this friend deferred to the group norm of relating to me (which included some measure of indifference or grudging acceptance) when we were both in the group.

Being sensitive can have distinct down-sides.

- Criticisms from teachers and other adults may feel unduly harsh to HSP children when these are handed out with the intensity or harshness that an NHSP child might need in order to pay attention and comply.
- Any unfairness, to themselves or others, may seriously raise their anxiety

levels, making them feel unsafe.
- HSPs are upset by witnessing negativity, such as bullying or violence between other children, disappointments that upset peers, and any other sorts of painful experiences such as other children's failures, rejections, grief and the like.

There are many ways you can be supportive and helpful to your HSP child in getting along with other people.

- Explain that some other people aren't as sensitive as she is, or as used to discussing their feelings, and that they may be uncomfortable with discussions about some of her sensitive issues.
- Help her anticipate that there may be times when she will have to learn to accommodate to other people's ways of doing things as best she can. Acknowledge that at times this may, unfortunately, be difficult and may require patience on her part.
- Alert his playmates' parents, particularly when he is younger, that he is a very thoughtful child and that he may not have the ability in a moment of upset to explain his need for a bit of time to sort out his *thoughts* (if talking to an NHSP parent) or his *HSP sensitivities* (if talking with a parent who is comfortable with emotional issues).
- Share with them what you have found helpful to her to remain calm and to settle down when upset.
- Support her in choosing quality friends.
- If he is inclined to live a quiet, more isolated social life, support him also in not feeling he needs to bend to pressures to join groups or activities "because everyone does this." Your firm affirmation that he is not 'everyone' – and that there are other sensitive children who are like him and share his preferences – can be very reassuring to him.
- To the extent that you can, stand up for him and discuss his sensitivities with teachers and school administrators. You may need to confront attitudes such as "He has to learn he's not special and simply has to conform to the ordinary expectations for all children." Yes, this will be true in many cases. But no, this should not apply to all situations, particularly if he has something that is upsetting him. If you force him to push himself to simply accept all situations that are upsetting him, he is likely to feel rejected because he may come to feel that his sensitivities don't matter to you or to others.

HSP children's relationships in their families may at times be challenging. When their parents, sisters and brothers are understanding and accepting of their sensitivities, HSPs can feel accepted and safe. This may, however, demand a lot of efforts on the parts of parents to explain to the other children in the family why the HSP child should get special considerations and allowances for being more emotional, particularly when these dispensations are not granted to other children, who are NHSPs. Their brothers and sisters may become jealous and may treat the HSP badly. This can be terribly destructive to the self-confidence and self-image of the HSP, particularly when their siblings are older and/or stronger than they are and belittle or bully them.

> "You mean it's okay to let others see how special I am?" asked the Little Soul. "Of course!" God chuckled. "It's very okay! But remember, 'special' does not mean 'better.' Everybody is special, each in their own way! Yet many others have forgotten

> *that. They will see that it is okay for them to be special only when you see that it is okay for you to be special." "Wow," said the Little Soul, dancing and skipping and laughing and jumping with joy. "I can be as special as I want to be!"*
> *"Yes, and you can start right now," said God, who was dancing and skipping and laughing right along with the Little Soul. "What part of special do you want to be?"*
> — Neale Donald Walsch (2004-2006)

Even more challenging are families in which one parent understands and accepts the HSP child while the other parent is unaccepting of their special sensitivities and special needs. An NHSP parent may view his child as being immature, weak, spoiled by the other parent, a "fraidy cat," and needing toughening up. I've seen numbers of families where these sorts of issues led to endless arguments, sometimes even ending in divorce. Marital and family therapy can be enormously helpful in these situations.

It can be even worse for the HSP children when they are in divorced families, moving back and forth between one home where they are accepted as HSPs and another home where they are being told they have to behave differently. In these situations of repeated transitions between very different home environments, self-healing methods such as EP, relaxation and other exercises can be enormously helpful.

It can also be tremendously helpful if you take preventive measures in sorting out relationships and behavioral expectations within your family.

- Equalizing the extra attention given to your HSP child by giving your NHSP children their own private time with you is helpful in preventing build-ups of jealousies and resentments.
- Compromises of setting periods when loud activities or quiet times are agreed can be helpful. And earbuds or earphones may sometimes save the day.
- Be aware that outside your home there will be many adults and children who will not understand that your child is an HSP. Prepare your child for this, explaining that many people will not know she is sensitive and needs more time to sort out her feelings and to compose herself.

You'll also do well to keep your eyes and ears alert to your HSP child being upset or moody over a period of time, which might suggest more than normal distress.

- You might want to consider whether parental or family tensions in general, not directly related to your HSP child, are provoking him to high anxiety levels.
- Be alert to the frequent bullying that occurs, when bullies find someone who can be made to cringe and cry and won't fight back. Keep this in mind, especially if your HSP child is moody and silent over a period of time (more than you would expect from a single episode of distressing issues).
- Debriefing your child about her day in school can help her identify recurring stressors that increase her tensions. Reminding her to use her de-stressing exercises can help her to resource herself when she feels pressured or criticized.

Parents often learn incredibly valuable lessons from their children, and HSP children are particularly good teachers. They often have highly developed, intuitive senses of rightness and wrongness. They will often respond first to how they feel about the issues, not just to the logic and reasoning of the situations – which they may not even understand. They can challenge parental ways of relating – to each other as well as to the children.

From my training and decades of practice in family therapy, I'm also impressed with how quickly all children (including NHSPs) pick up on family tensions, particularly between their parents. HSPs are particularly sensitive to any parental discord. They often are not even conscious of this, but commonly will distract their parents from friction and arguments between them. Children (and family pets) may develop psychological, behavioral or physical symptoms under such circumstances.

Having regular family times together is an important way to encourage open communications and to facilitate discussions about challenging or troublesome issues, as well as to share and celebrate positive experiences. Often ignored, but equally important are the development of good listening skills, which are among the many other lessons learned in family meetings. Knowing there is a regular forum for bringing up questions and problems is a good preventive against festering issues and feelings that can cause frustrations, mischief and upsets.

How to run family meetings depends on the personality and communication styles of the participants. In many case, a simple, open format with anyone speaking their mind is fine. But where one or more of the family members is shy or hesitant to speak up, or when one or more are more dominating in conversations, a bit of structure can be helpful. Simply starting the family gathering with a report from each person on how they are feeling and doing (both are important to share!) may suffice.

In more tense or boisterous family meetings, a 'talking stick' can be helpful. The talking stick is taken from tribal cultures where formal discussions are conducted with a stick that is passed to anyone who wishes to speak. As long as this person is holding the stick, others listen respectfully and do not interrupt or comment until their turn comes to hold the stick. Any object can be used. Often, a soft toy is particularly appreciated, especially where some of the family members are younger children.

When HSPs' children are HSPs, this is a blessing to both sides. You can teach your HSP children about their sensitivities and how to deal with them. People exploring these areas are repeatedly puzzled why HSPs often do not recognize their specific sensitivities and may have difficulties figuring out how to accommodate to them. This is a common challenge in general. It is very difficult to understand and diagnose our own issues. Sharing adult wisdom, experiences and advice with HSP children can save them many years of challenging experiences and stresses.

*YOUR HSP CHILDREN MAY FIND IT VERY HELPFUL TO DISCUSS INTUITION AS A FREQUENT SUBJECT WITHIN THE FAMILY.*

*YOU MIGHT MAKE IT A RITUAL AT FAMILY MEALS TO HAVE EACH SHARE 3 GOOD THINGS THEY EXPERIENCED THE PREVIOUS DAY, AND 3 THEY ARE LOOKING FORWARD TO THE NEXT DAY.*

### Relationships with extended family *(HSP children)*

HSP children may find it challenging to get along with extended family, who may not understand or accept their high sensitivities on any and every level of their being. Emotional sensitivities are usually the most challenging, particularly with NHSP grandparents, uncles, aunts and cousins who may feel that their young HSP relatives are being coddled and spoiled because they are fussy and easily upset under stresses that most children find benign or readily manageable.

Explaining the HSP trait characteristics and challenges may be sufficient to resolve these issues. But if extended family refuse to acknowledge, accept and accommodate HSP children, it may be wise to have these children visit only when you, their parents, can accompany them. I have seen significant numbers of HSP children hurt and even traumatized by unaccepting relatives who belittled, teased, chastised, or even bullied them over being too sensitive.

Belittling and pathologizing you, as a parent of an HSP child, may also be a serious irritant – to the child as well as to you. And in some cases, carefully monitoring and/or limiting visits with such relatives may be the wisest choice.

I have seen numbers of children with separated or divorced parents who have these sorts of issues, with one parent accepting their HSP trait and the other either insensitive to or unaccepting of it. This can be enormously stressful when the children are court mandated to alternate spending time with each parent.

Resourcing HSP children with EP and/or other self-healing methods for dealing with stresses or upsets is extremely helpful to them in these sorts of situations. These methods may enable them to continue their relationship with an extended family member who is criticizing them for some aspect of their HSP trait, with the child coming to understand that this is their relative's issues of insensitivity rather than their own issue, and that you, their parent(s), will back them up and protect them from such negativity. TWR/WHEE is particularly helpful because it can be used discretely in stressful situations like these, without anyone knowing the child is de-stressing by alternating tapping their left and right feet or by alternately tightening and relaxing their toes. So even in the immediate situation of being stressed by a relative who lacks understanding, children can diminish and release their anxieties and avoid further stress or trauma from what is going on.

This sort of lesson from dealing with stresses may be a blessing in disguise for the HSPs, giving them practice in dealing with challenging situations and thereby resourcing children with skills for de-stressing in any future situations they find challenging or difficult. Once they are used to responding in this way, they can de-stress at any other time and in any other situation in which they want or need to.

*IF YOU HAVE EXTENDED FAMILY MEMBERS WHO LIKE SENSITIVE CHILDREN, MAKE IT A POINT TO GET TOGETHER WITH THEM PERIODICALLY.*

*IT'S WONDERFUL TO BUILD RELATIONSHIPS THAT BECOME FAMILIES OF CHOICE.*

*Home is the place where, when you have to go there,
they have to take you in.*
- Robert Frost

## HSP Children in separation and divorce *(HSP children)*

It is not uncommon for parents to end up in courts, fighting about custody issues over their children. Courts vary enormously from one location to another and between one judge and another, regarding their sensitivities to these sorts of issues. Sadly, many lawyers are focused more on winning cases (and, I often suspect, on generating work for themselves) than on the sensitivities and emotional needs of the parties involved.

Court proceedings can be enormously stressful on everyone, and naturally, even moreso for any of the involved children or parents who are HSPs. Again, TWR/WHEE is tremendously helpful to anyone facing these issues. Tapping quietly and discretely during family discussion, meetings with lawyers, and court appearances can be helpful.

✦ 'Naomi' had a ten year-old daughter, 'Lexi,' who was very stressed by her parents' angry separation, brought about by Naomi's discovery that 'Tom,' her husband, had been having an affair for over two years. This had involved major changes in just about every area of Lexi's life.

Tom declared he wanted nothing more to do with his wife. Naomi had to move back to a distant city to live with her elderly parents, due to financial strains. So Lexi not only lost her father, her friends, and her school, but also had to adjust to living in the same room with her 14 year-old sister, Grace. Lexi and her mother were HSPs, while Grace, Tom and Naomi's parents were NHSPs. Grace was occasionally moody and on rare occasions tearful (as when she heard her mother arguing on the phone with her father), but was otherwise adjusting reasonably well to her new home and school.

Naomi is an elementary school teacher who attended a WHEE Level 1 weekend training workshop with me. She had kept in touch occasionally over the intervening four years, and was doing a very competent job helping her fourth graders with WHEE as a part of her morning classroom start-up routine. She scheduled a brief phone session with me to get some suggestions on ways she could further help Lexi adjust to her various challenges.

Though Lexi had learned WHEE from her mother and had used it occasionally when she was upset, her degree of overwhelm was so great that she was forgetting to use it in her new surroundings. Naomi sat with Lexi and made lists of issues to help her systematically deal with what was bothering her, and reported back a week later that Lexi was much calmer. Naomi was perplexed and frustrated, though, because she expected Lexi would have done better – based on previous experiences of helping her with WHEE. I suggested that patience was in order, because the numbers and intensity of issues were so massive here, it didn't surprise me that Lexi wasn't clearing all of her issues more quickly.

Several weeks later, Naomi was even more frustrated and concerned, because Lexi was still not making much further progress from the time of the previous consult. I made an appointment for a Skype session with Lexi. I suspected that there might be issues that Lexi did not feel comfortable discussing with her mother, and indeed that proved to be true. Nancy was doing her best to cover up her deep traumas over the separation in order to not upset the children, but this was having the opposite effect on Lexi, who sensed but didn't understand her mother's distress and worried about her. I helped Lexi transform most of these anxieties into more manageable concerns with tapping, and recommended to Naomi that she share with Lexi and Grace how she was feeling and what she was doing to cope with her distress, to the extent that she felt comfortable doing so.

Naomi followed through with the girls, and Lexi responded with immediate relief from much of her distress, reducing the intensity of her collective anxieties to a '1' on a scale of '10'. This not only relieved Lexi of imagined issues of concern about her mother, but also reinforced Lexi's uses of tapping, as Naomi mentioned how the tapping was helping her, too, in adjusting to their new circumstances. Lexi was also able to tap on images of positive new friendships, along with success in her new school. In the weeks that followed, she began to make much better progress in acclimating to her new home and school.

When Naomi fretted over her daughters wanting to see their father, I recommended that Naomi make more efforts to arrange for phone contact between her daughters and their father. But Naomi was adamant that this was going to be a total and permanent termination of that relationship for all of them. My assessment (from talking with Lexi) was that a major portion of Naomi's anxieties over dangers of a continued relationships between Tom and the girls was generated more from Naomi's own conflicts with her husband than by difficulties between him and the girls. I persisted with this recommendation in the occasional communications I had with Naomi, and after a period of several years she began to allow the girls to have phone and Skype contact with him, and eventually occasional brief visits, which went relatively well for Lexi.

This family's experiences with serious stresses was quite typical of how positive inputs that are accepting of HSP sensitivities, along with appropriate accommodations to these issues can ease transitions into new surroundings and situations. Having an in-home stress management facilitator is an enormous asset! But one doesn't have to be a professional caregiver or instructor to achieve good results in these sorts of situations. I find that many HSP parents, whatever their backgrounds or training, make excellent HSPCs for their children. A major component of their help is in holding an open, accepting attitude towards the HSP family member.

This is also a typical example of how NHSPs are able to pick up the pieces after a major shift in their lives and move on. Sometimes there are distinct advantages to not having the high sensitivities of an HSP!

*IF YOU SEPARATE OR DIVORCE, MAKE TIME PERIODICALLY TO DISCUSS HOW EVERYONE IN THE FAMILY IS FEELING ABOUT IT.*

*EXPLAIN TO EACH CHILD, ACCORDING TO THEIR AGE AND UNDERSTANDING, THAT THIS WAS A DIFFICULT DECISION AND NOT ONE TAKEN LIGHTLY.*

*SHARE YOUR ANTICIPATIONS THAT THERE ARE GOING TO BE TIMES WHEN EVERYONE FEELS UPSET ABOUT IT.*

*IT IS A BIG HELP TO LET EVERYONE KNOW THEY CAN COME TO YOU TO ASK QUESTIONS AND TALK ABOUT THEIR FEELINGS.*

### HSP Children in school *(HSP children)*
Suggestions for teachers:

- HSP children may feel anxious and worried in situations where they are not understood and accepted. To expect the more sensitive HSPs to be paying attention in class all of the time, as is the norm for NHSP children, is unreasonable. An understanding teacher can be a godsend to an HSP child.
- Accept that an HSP child may be very thoughtful about anything and everything that draws her attention, knowing she may become totally absorbed and lost in thought and contemplation.
- Anticipate he may be very selective in choosing friends; may have a greater tendency to prefer single, good friends rather than groups or cliques; may be mature beyond his age in understanding people's emotions and able to intuitively and/or energetically read many details from how they express themselves (not just listening to what they are saying); tends to be meticulous in telling the truth and is unhappy with people who are not truthful.
- If your child's teacher is unfamiliar with HSPs, recommending appropriate books can be helpful.[33] You might also consider investing in a copy of one or more of these books that you can lend teachers through the years of your child's journeys through school.
- The same applies for the school counsellor, psychologist, and administrative staff.
- A teacher accepting the HSPs' behaviors in her class, just as they are, can reduce their tensions significantly. Accommodations may be needed, as in a time out space for composing himself when he's upset.
- Developing non-verbal signals between an understanding, accepting teacher and the HSP child can be boon to both. A child who is using tapping techniques or other de-stressing methods might agree a signal with the teacher to indicate she needs some time to herself outside the class. For instance, she might raise her hand and slowly but obviously (to the teacher) wave it back and forth, rather than holding it raised and steady. This would allow the teacher to nod if she feels it is appropriate to give the HSP child permission to go to the restroom, to use the privacy of a toilet stall for tapping or just for isolating from whatever in the classroom might be distressing her or triggering her anxieties. Similarly, the teacher might inobtrusively touch the HSPs left shoulder to bring her out of her absorption state and back to the classroom, or give her a different signal to suggest a time out for de-stressing in the restroom.

*IT IS A BLESSINGS IF THERE IS ANY OPPORTUNITY FOR YOUR HSP CHILD TO ATTEND A WALDORF OR MONTESSORI SCHOOL, WHERE LEARNING IS INIVIDUALIZED FOR EACH STUDENT.*

*AFTER-SCHOOL ENRICHMENT PROGRAMS IN MUSIC, DANCE, CREATIVE ARTS AND NATURE STUDIES CAN PROVIDE ENRICHMENTS THAT SUPPLEMENT AND COMPLEMENT THE ORDINARY SCHOOL CURRICULUM*

*TIME IN NATURE, SELF-STUDY PROGRAMS, AND CAREFULLY SELECTED INTERNET PROGRAMS CAN PROVIDE THE SORTS OF STIMULATION THAT HSP CHILDREN CRAVE AND THRIVE ON.*

### Relationships with the environment *(HSP children)*

> *We suffer from Nature deficit disorder.*
> - Richard Louv

HSP children are often more sensitive to the world around them than the average person.

- They may enjoy playing with your family's cat or dog, alert to respond to their needs, and forming a very strong emotional bond with them.
- Many like having their own pet or potted plant.
- They like to have windows facing green spaces and to spend time in nature.
- They often take enormous pleasure in being out in nature. They may spend hours in a garden, enjoying flowers, climbing trees, watching birds and butterflies, wading in lakeshore waters, or just daydreaming in the fresh air.
- Encourage him to identify surroundings that feel peaceful, and support him if he likes to spend time in these environments for nurturing and/or for calming when he is upset.
- Be alert to any changes in your HSP child's behaviors or health that coincide with being in a new location, as environmental allergies are not uncommon to cleaning chemicals, disinfectants, pesticides and the like.
- In these fraught times of environmental challenges, including global warming, HSPs are often sensitive to and distressed by their very keen awarenesses of the challenges faced by all living beings on this planet. Again, acknowledging her feelings about these issues can be enormously helpful to her.
- On the more sensitive end of the HSP spectrum, they may prefer a vegetarian diet, with difficulties tolerating thoughts of eating an animal.

Don't expect the same degrees or intensities of spontaneous interests in your NHSP children, but do involve them in explorations of the natural world as well, when and as you can. For many people, engagement with the environment is a learned taste, but nevertheless a much appreciated and enjoyed one. It also contributes to greater understanding and responsiveness to the climate change crises many of us are struggling to address.

### Spirit *(HSP children)*

HSP children may be sensitive in varieties of ways within the spectrum of personal spiritual awarenesses. While children aren't likely to understand general questions about spirituality, they may report direct perceptions:

- Sensing people's physical pains and other sensations, sometimes mirroring these in their own bodies
- Perceiving positive and negative bioenergies, mirrored within themselves, including people's moods and emotions, friendly or unfriendly intentions and personalities

- Being able to sense biological energies around people, either with their hands or visually – as an aura of colors around living beings and non-living objects, and sometimes being able to interpret their meanings*34
- Perceiving group energies, as in when people in a classroom, an auditorium, or a baseball stadium are in positive, supportive, healing consciousness or in negative, angry or aggressive states of mind
- Able to help others through the HSP's healing abilities – through touch or with hands held near the body, and/or through intention, meditation and/or prayer*35
- Perceiving and communicating with spirits of humans, animals, plants, and other aspects of nature
- Perceiving and communicating with angels
- Memories of their own and of other people's past lives*36
- Knowing about things that will happen, before they occur

Keep an open mind on the topic of spiritual awarenesses, so that he knows this can be freely discussed. Sharing some of your own thoughts, feelings and spiritual understandings and awarenesses can be helpful to your HSP child.*37

If you don't have these awarenesses yourself, it will still be helpful if you listen with an open mind to your child's reports of what she experiences. When the topic comes up, speak with her about her personal spiritual awarenesses, and encourage her to connect with and trust her sense of rightness about her inner, personal spiritual consciousness.

If she mentions she remembers when she lived in a different place and time, invite her to share any memories she has. Writing these down can be a help to your child and to other members of the family who are interested to know more about this. Children under four to five years old may also report such memories if you ask, "Do you remember being a grownup?"

If personal spiritual awarenesses are not part of your own world of direct perceptions, you can still be helpful by listening and letting your child know you honor his reports of his own experiences. If you are uncomfortable with such reports from your child, you can explain that not everyone has these sensitivities, including yourself, but state your level of willingness to hear about his perceptions. In this case, you can still be enormously helpful to your child if you find someone else who is willing and available to discuss these matters with him.

It is also very helpful to explain that some people are so uncomfortable with these topics that it is better not to share personal spiritual experiences with them.

Much of the above discussion assumes that if you are in a dual parenting relationship, your spouse or partner is in general agreement with the above. When you meet with objections to parenting approaches such as those suggested above, this may become a source of conflict between you and your spouse or partner. Again, discussions, clarifications, and tapping can hopefully bridge the gaps between you. A détente is also an option, where you agree to disagree but allow each other to live with your chosen beliefs. For this to work reasonably well for children of a détente couple there has to be mutual respect between the parents for their differing views, so that their child isn't caught in a crossfire of disagreements.*38

*WHAT ARE YOUR PERSONAL SPIRITUAL BELIEFS?*

*WHAT ARE YOUR PERSONAL SPIRITUAL AWARENESSES/ GIFTS?*

*WHAT ARE YOUR PERSONAL SPIRITUAL PRACTICES?*

*HOW DO YOU SHARE OR PLAN TO SHARE THESE WITH YOUR CHILDREN?*

# SECTION V. Supports for the HSP and HSPC: Resources and therapies

*The art of therapy is in sensing how rapidly the process can move without creating resistance or turning the patient away, and in allowing the patient to make his or her own discoveries.*

– John E. Upledger

## Background

HSPs, being more sensitive to emotions, are prone to feeling stress and trauma more intensely and to responding more intensely than NHSPs. As an HSPC you can be of enormous help when your HSP is stressed:
- Just listening to your HSP venting his anxieties
- Acknowledging you feel and understand her upset and distress
- Checking whether HuTiST might be present
- If overwhelm is an issue, help her clarify what she is feeling, what has upset her, what she feels her options are, and when she feels would be a good time to act on her awarenesses of the upset
- Reminding him to practice de-stressing methods that have helped in the past

HSPs in general, and anyone feeling stressed, anxious or triggered by current situations and/or trauma memories may feel stuck or helpless to deal with them. They may also be stressed by their meta-anxieties about the situations, stimulating stressful, panicky, depressed, despairing or other negative feelings. As an HSPC you can be of enormous help in varieties of ways, as detailed below.

## 27. First aid for HSP distress, anxieties and triggered states

*It is one of the most beautiful compensations in life...that no man can sincerely try to help another without helping himself.*
— Ralph Waldo Emerson

An HSPC can be enormously helpful to a distressed HSP. Let your HSP know that you hear his distress. Being heard is enormously reassuring.

If you, the HSPC, are feeling anxious, and if you know any de-stressing techniques for yourself that can be used quietly and discretely, start using them. Staying calm and just being present, listening and doing your best to understand what is upsetting your HSP, provides a calmness and safety that she can resonate with and use for psychological support, reassurance and calming. This can also be a non-verbal reminder to your HSP to start using her own de-stressing approaches.
- You might ask: "How can I best support you?"
- "Are there particular issues that are worrying or distressing you right now?"

Sometimes the issues that trigger HSPs are not the issues that are worrying them most. They may be fretting about a random event that triggered them at that moment. They may not be aware of their own deeper, more serious worries, as they may be over-focused on the challenges of their current issue that triggered and upset them.

Be generous in your support. You may want to repeat statements such as:
- "You're safe with me!"
- "I'm here for you when you need me."

These, or other statements of reassurance to your HSP that in your presence she is safe, can be very supportive and calming. As HSPs are so strongly engaged with emotions, they can easily find themselves lost in overwhelm when stressed.

If you sense or think that your HSP might be experiencing HuTiST, mention these possibilities. Again, it is reassuring to a person in distress to identify things they can do something about in order to feel better. And it's meta-reassuring that you, the HSPC, understand and support him.

HSPs may also fret and worry about choosing the right or the best option for dealing with their challenges. In sorting out HSP intense vacillations between several options, the two-chair technique can be helpful, described later in this section.*[1]

In the longer-term perspective, you, the HSPC, can be most supportive by helping your HSP to learn to identify which issues are the key ones to prioritize and address – both in a triggered situation or when discussing and planning how to handle being triggered. When possible, pick a quiet time for this, when you both can think more clearly, deliberate on the issues calmly, and speak from a place of greater centeredness.

So, your challenge as the HSPC is to be supportive – but just as helpful as necessary, and not so helpful that your HSP comes away feeling unable to sort out the issues without your help. You are a pilot advising the captain of the ship how to navigate through a storm. It is best that the HSP remains the captain of the ship.

Dealing with stressful situations will also have instructive take-away lessons for you, the HSPC. First and foremost, you'll be most helpful if you learn to remain calm yourself. Your HSP will resonate with your calmness, which will offer an immediate island of stillness where she can anchor herself to feel safe – as a helpful start to reaching a calmer, safe harbor after struggling in her sea of turbulent feelings.

Preparing yourself in advance as an HSPC for stressful situations (to each of you) can be enormously helpful to both of you.

You may develop the most productive discussions if you refrain from:

- Saying critical things, or anything that might be taken by him as critical, like:
  - "You're making a mountain out of a molehill."
  - "You're not getting your head in gear."
  - "You've said this ten, if not twenty times already."
  - "Last time we talked about and went through this, you said you could see how you were getting triggered by ____ and that you'd work on yourself so this wouldn't happen again."
- Telling him to calm down –     with any irritation or criticism in your voice or attitude.
- Getting annoyed or angry at her.

Some of the most important things you, as an HSPC, can say in order to be helpful are:
- "It looks like something is bothering you."
- "Do you want to tell me about it?"
- "You look upset. What are you feeling right now?"
- "I hope it's not something I said or did!"
- "I understand how you're feeling, because I feel ____ too."

Surprisingly to you, the HSPC, your HSP may not be conscious of the specific issues upsetting him. The overwhelm of the upset releases stress hormones and puts the nervous system into an alarm state that can be discombobulating. (This is a great word to describe how the HSP feels when he's upset!)

If you, the HSPC remain calm, despite the agitation of the HSP, this calmness will be sensed by your HSP and it will be a helpful space where he can drop anchor to help calm himself down. Then your HSP is better able to reflect on what is upsetting him and may also be able to sort it out more quickly and easily.

As an HSPC you can be of further help to your HSP as she is processing strong feelings when you:

- Acknowledge that you hear/ know/ sense she is upset. Identify how you know this:
  - "I hear by your voice that something is upsetting you."
  - "I see you're upset because you're [looking sad/ angry/ frustrated/ agitated, etc./ pacing back and forth/ drumming your fingers on the table/ etc.]"
  - "I can really resonate with how you feel [frustrated/ anxious/ sad/ angry/ etc]. about this."
- Clarify whether you've understood him correctly by reviewing the circumstances and issues in your own words. Check whether you're on the same wavelength.
- Share how you feel about what's upset her
  - Acknowledge ways in which you resonate with what she is experiencing.
  - Share ways in which you feel differently from her about the situation and explain why.
- Ask,
  - "Can I help in any way?"
  - "What can I do that would be helpful to you?"
  - "Do you just need a bit of time or space to sort this out by yourself?"

HSPs are very much immersed in whatever is going on in the moment – around them and inside them. HSPs often make definitive statements about feelings, thoughts and relationships – based on their feelings in that particular moment. Common examples might be,

- "I don't ever want to have anything to do with (whoever/ whatever jarred, disappointed or upset me)"
- "I'm calling Cindy tomorrow morning to let her know we're not going to the party on Saturday. Cindy was abrupt with me on the phone when she called to ask if we could bring a salad, and I really don't need to spend my Saturday night with her and her other inconsiderate friends."

At another time, under different circumstances, when experiencing different emotions, HSPs may express very different opinions and make very different decisions about the same issues.

- "I think I was tired and hungry when Cindy called. I probably over-reacted. I actually like her and I'm looking forward to going there on Saturday."
- At a third, fourth and fifth time, depending on his then-current feelings, he may switch his opinions yet again; and may state them just as definitively as he had done earlier, even though his current statements radically contradict his earlier ones.

Basing decisions on their HSP feelings at the moment may be misleading and/or confusing to HSPCs and to others, particularly to NHSPs – who may take HSPs' current statements as the firm opinions and decisions they are stated to be at that particular time. NHSPs often assume these to be decisions based on mental analyses and calculations, missing the fact that they are based far more on the HSPs' emotional states and feelings about the issues at the time they are presenting their current views. This is all the more confusing because HSPs may state their views with great intensity of conviction and argue against their earlier, alternative views, with equal intensity, each time they discuss the issues.

In such situations, I remind you again (as this is easy to overlook in a stressed situation) that a helpful initial strategy is to ask herself whether HuTiST might be relevant issues to her HSP or herself, or whether an upset about something else is lurking in the shadows when her HSP is making these strong, definitive statements that appear to be out of character or contradicting his previous opinions and statements.

Assuming your HSP identifies what is upsetting her, you might:
– Offer to hear more about it.
– Listen patiently, with as few interruptions as possible, until she winds down a bit.
– If she is getting more wound up by talking about it, you might:
   • Reflect to her that this is really upsetting her a lot.
   • Share any observations that come to mind that would broaden her perspectives on the upsetting issue, such as:
      "This isn't the first time this has upset you, is it?"
      "How did you feel about this when it happened before?"
      "How did you sort this out this the last time it came up?"
      "It looks like you're also upset at yourself for getting angry/ responding this way/ losing it in front of ____."
– Ask whether she feels she might set aside the issue for a few moments and
   • Take a bit of a rest/ quiet time in her place of peace and safety and healing (PPSH)
   • Tap on the issue to lower its intensity[*2]
   • If the issue sits within a complex set of circumstances, would she want to bundle the issues and tap on all of them at the same time?

If you're aware of her preferred love languages,[*3] you can connect with your HSP through the modalities that are most likely to produce positive effects.

Let me illustrate some of these approaches with the challenges experienced by a couple who had been married for six months, after having lived together in a committed relationship for four years.

✦ 'Abby' an HSP, called me for Skype sessions with her wife, 'Tara,' an NHSP, to help with their relationship, which had been deteriorating since shortly after their marriage. Abby worked for a flower shop that catered a lot of weddings. She had enjoyed her work for over 10 years but was stressed by a new partner who had joined the shop owner four months earlier and was pressing everyone to work more quickly and efficiently in order to increase their profits. This made it difficult for Abby to take the time she was used to spending with her customers in planning the floral decorations she so enjoyed creating. Abby was coming home stressed and irritable, and this was seriously impacting their marriage.

Tara, a nurse, was a very caring person. She expressed her caring particularly through acts of service. She was increasingly frustrated and becoming irritable herself as there was nothing she could do or any advice she could offer that seemed to be of any help. Abby was doubly distressed because she could see that her job stresses were carrying over into their home, yet couldn't control herself or figure out ways to behave differently.

They both felt that their relationship had been very solid prior to the changes in Abby's job. So they felt they really only needed symptom relief, rather than deeper psychological explorations.

Both were pleased with the immediate relief they experienced when they each created their special place of peace and safety and healing (PPSH) – for general centering and calming – and even moreso when they learned to decrease their frustrations, angers and other troublesome feelings using TWR1/WHEE.*[4]

Abby reported in their second session that she was both calmer at work and, for the most part, able to leave her frustrations at work and not bring them home. Tara reported she was able to reduce the intensity of her memories of recent frustrations, and anxieties about Abby coming home with a nasty mood and attitude to zero, and then also able to install replacement positives.

Abby was frustrated that she couldn't reduce her irritations over her job stress lower than a level '3' out of '10' despite her belief that she was ready to make her peace with her new work situation. We muscle tested*[5] to see whether she was ready to let go of her frustrated feelings at work, and got a 'yes.' When sore spot massage*[6] didn't release this block, and further muscle testing suggested there might be residual issues from earlier in her life contributing to her irritability, Abby agreed to explore this possibility.

In two-chair work,*[7] she discovered that the altered circumstances at work were triggering unresolved feelings of betrayal from childhood, first with her father abandoning the family to marry his secretary when Abby was four years old, and further feelings of betrayal with her mother remarrying when Abby was seven, and her stepfather turning out to be a strict disciplinarian – which utterly changed the atmosphere in her home for the rest of her childhood. When she cleared these issues with further tapping, bundling them with her current frustrations, her SUDS came down to '0.'

It felt to all of us that Abby and Tara had reached a point of resolution in their issues and were ready to move on. They were pleasantly surprised that they were able to achieve these shifts so rapidly. An email follow-up a month later confirmed that all was well on the work and home fronts.

I was also pleased to see in this email an acknowledgment on Abby's part that she thought her guardian angels were actually helping her by guiding her into her job challenges and the subsequent resolutions she achieved in clearing issues from earlier in her life. She speculated that her residual traumas from childhood might have impacted her life more seriously at some future time, in some future situations, if she had not cleared them now.

I, myself, was initially surprised when I started developing TWR/ WHEE and saw how rapidly people were able to make serious, major changes in their lives. Over the years, I've seen this happen so frequently that I've come to expect it. Delayed changes are almost always indications that there are further unresolved issues waiting to be identified and addressed.

I was also skeptical, at first, wondering whether these changes that came about so rapidly could possibly last. I'm pleased and relieved, both in my personal and professional uses of these methods, to find that the changes they help us to achieve are generally permanent. If symptoms recur, it is almost always the case that we've overlooked the equivalent of some dirt in a corner of our wound that continues to fester. Once we identify it and clear it with further tapping, we are truly through with these challenges.

If you're an HSPC, then after your HSP returns to his calmer self, you can continue to be of great help. Your support is not only helpful immediately but often includes further benefits as you move forward. You can prime that pump in various ways. For instance, you might ask what lessons you and your HSP can learn from what you went through. Some lessons will relate to the content of the upset and how it is resolved. But just as important, or even more important, may be the meta-lessons of increased confidence that you and your HSP can take away from dealing with the situations, as in:

- "I did pretty well sorting that one out!"
- "I'm gaining confidence in my abilities to deal with these issues now!"
- "I'm learning to recognize when I'm getting triggered, and can use de-stressing techniques before I reach a state of overwhelm"
- "I can trust you (my HSPC/ partner/ husband/ wife) to be here for me when I'm distressed and upset."

In many cases, HSPs' sensitivities to emotions may be difficult for NHSPs to absorb and understand. Even NHSP psychotherapists and counsellors may find HSPs challenging to comprehend and deal with, because they see HSPs as "Too overwhelmed by their emotions" or "Unreasonable in dealing with their feelings."

With HSPs, the progress through therapy is often much easier and quicker to achieve. The HSPs are able very quickly to connect with and identify the feelings that are disturbing them, making it much easier to address them therapeutically and to release them. They are able to practice the self-treatment methods on their own with equal success. They may gallop through the therapy at a very rapid pace.

Once you and/or your HSP are clearer on what the tension and upset are about, and you are past the initial, traumatizing stress and distress that can make it difficult for an HSP to focus on self-healing, you can figure out together how to deal with the stressful issues in better ways. The help of a marital or family therapist or of a trauma therapist can enormously enhance the pace and depth of healing in stressful situations, when it may be difficult for a couple alone to sort out their difficulties in the situation and/or in their relationship. This is particularly true when there is a history of trauma issues that may be getting triggered.

## 28. Your place of peace and safety and healing (PPSH)

*Fear is the foundation of safety*
— Tertullian

This is a de-stressing method in and of itself, and also the first part of TWR/WHEE, particularly for people who are dealing with trauma or other intense issues.*[8]

You can come to this inner place whenever you want or need a quiet, calming, safe space. You can come here to calm down from situations that feel uncomfortable, threatening or dangerous. Or this can be your private space where you come just for the sake of enjoying some peace, quiet and rejuvenation.

Your PPSH can be a focus for deep meditation. Coming from the other direction, your meditation can strengthen and deepen your connection with your PPSH. Even if you are in a state of anxiety, you can create and strengthen your PPSH.

If you practice preventive imagery you will be well rewarded. Think to yourself ahead of time about several different possible scenarios that you can visit. You can then explore each of them and pick the one that works best for you in a given situation, per these generic instructions that you should feel free to adapt to your preferences and needs:

– Relax your body
  - Settle yourself into your chair so you feel comfortable.
  - Take a nice, deep breath, and as you exhale, notice any tensions, anywhere in your body that you sense them, and blow them away as you breathe out.
– Scan your body, checking your jaws, mouth and neck to see whether there are any muscles that are still tight.
  - Blow away the tensions you feel there.
  - Check your shoulders and arms, your hands and fingers for tightness.
  - Breathe away tensions you feel there, so that every breath out is also an invitation to let tension out.
  - Continue down the body, a few muscles at a time until all of them are as relaxed as they can be.
– Instead of using your breath as your focus for releasing tensions, stress and negativity, you can alternatively us TWR/WHEE to tap away your bothersome issues.[9]
– Then, when your body is relaxed from head to toe, picture to yourself that you're in a place that's completely safe. It can be a memory place that you've visited or an imaginary place. Bring in whatever you need in your imagination to make this place ever more safe.
– A PPSH may take many forms.

### For children
  - A room in your home
  - Sitting on your father's or mother's lap; sitting next to one parent; or between both of them
  - Sitting in a private space that is all your own, one that you have actually visited and like

- An imaginary place, like a tree house in an enormous tree
- A castle with a secret entrance that only you know about, which you can lock so no one else can enter if you want to keep them out.
- Place yourself...in any other imaginary place that feels really, really safe to you.
- Or anywhere else you can remember where you are totally safe and have whatever you need to feel comfortable.

### For adults

- Relax in a place in nature, such as

    A secluded, private beach

    A secluded place in a forest that is guarded by angels, nature spirits, or an impenetrable barrier

    A mountain pinnacle

    A cave with a secret entrance

- Place yourself in an impenetrable fortress, protected by

    Titanium steel walls

    Electronic barriers

    An anteroom where visitors can be screened through electronic communications, and entrance is granted only on your specific voice command

- Surround yourself with protecting angels or other beings
- Surround yourself with an impenetrable force field that only you can control

– This is your Place of Peace and Safety and Healing (PPSH). You can call it whatever you wish.

– You can change any details of your PPSH at any time

– While you're enjoying being in your PPSH

- Ask yourself how safe and good you feel being there, where '0' = not at all and '10' = the safest you could feel (This is generally called the 'subjective units of success scale' or in this case could be the 'subjective units of safety scale' or SUSS.)
- Take turns tapping gently with your right and then your left hand on your opposite arms or with your right and left foot on the floor
- Say silently to yourself or out loud:

    "I feel completely and wonderfully safe in my (name and describe your PPSH)."

And [I love and accept myself/ I know (my mother and father / The Infinite Source / Jesus / other spiritual being)] loves and accepts me, wholly, completely, and unconditionally

- Take another deep breath and then stop tapping.

    Check again how safe and good you feel being there

    Repeat this process till you feel safe at a level of '10' ... or higher

    You can go to your PPSH whenever

- You want to connect with and strengthen your sense of feeling good/ positive/ safe/ protected.
- You feel HuTiST or any other negative feelings.

- You want to counteract and clear negative feelings
- You want to enhance the depth and intensity of your positive thoughts and feelings.
- You want to connect with strongly positive feelings and energies
- You want to reconnect with your higher self, Spirit the Infinite Source/ All That Is

Using your PPSH, you can release negativity, as in some of the methods described below. The strong positive feelings of the PPSH can neutralize negative thoughts and feelings and help you reconnect with the Transcendent. You may find this works most deeply to establish and strengthen your PPSH if you practice visiting there when you are as free of stress and tension as you can manage, which gives you a starting edge on the inner state you are seeking to establish and deepen.

# 29. TWR/ WHEE and other wholistic Energy Psychology methods

*Pain is a choice and suffering is optional.*
— Daniel Benor

TWR/WHEE is the best approach I've found for my clients and myself for dealing with stress, distress, anxieties, fears, trauma memories and triggers, depression, physical and psychological pains, cravings, insomnia and many other issues. This method is simple to learn and to use, rapidly and deeply effective, and easy to remember in time of stress or other needs. It is better yet if both the HSPC and HSP have each learned and practiced this method prior to needing to using it in very stressful or urgent situations. TWR/WHEE is described in detail below.

I anticipate most readers of this book will want to understand themselves, their family and friends, and/or their partners in life. Many of you will be seeking tools to deal with bothersome issues. TWR/WHEE can help you deal effectively with just about every challenge you could possibly imagine.

TWR/WHEE is easy to learn and to use, yet deeply and potently effective. By doing the simple steps detailed below, you decrease the intensity of the issues that are bothering you. When they are reduced to zero you can then install positive thoughts and feelings to replace the negative ones you have released. This is TWR1, which focuses on reducing the intensity of symptoms. TWR2 goes deeper, identifying and releasing the roots of your issues as well.**[10]

### TWR1/ WHEE: Dealing with symptoms and building positive resources

TWR/WHEE is an elegantly simple method. It enables you to choose the level at which you want to address your specific issues and to make helpful changes in how you feel about and respond in general to situations that upset you.

TWR1 is used for symptom relief. You can rapidly lower the intensity of many psychological and physical symptoms by alternately tapping on the right and left sides of your body, while focusing your mind on y our issues and reciting a positive statement to neutralize your negative issues. You can then install positive thoughts and feelings to replace whatever you have released.

Here are fuller details of the basic TWR/WHEE process for releasing negativity:

1. Alternate tapping on the left and right sides of your body, anywhere that feels comfortable to you. Convenient ways to tap might be:
   - with your index and middle finger of one hand, on the ends of your eyebrows closest to your nose
   - with each of your hands on the opposite biceps muscle (often called the 'butterfly hug')
   - with each of your hands or with one finger of each hand on your thigh, as you're sitting in a comfortable position with your hands on your lap
   - with each foot on the floor
   - tightening your toes inside your shoes of your right and left foot
   - with your tongue on your teeth on the right and left
   - the last three can be done discretely, when you don't want people around you to know you are de-stressing

2. Focus your awareness on your issue and on how you feel about it. How strong your feelings are about the issue tells you how much this bothers you. You may say this out loud or state it silently in your mind and connect with it in your heart.
   – Here is your starting point, your Setup/ Focusing statement:
      Even though I feel _____
      When I think about or remember _____
3. Assess your Subjective Units of Distress Scale (SUDS) for how strongly you feel on this issue, prior to and following each round of tapping, where '0' = it's no bother at all and '10' = the worst it could be. Write down your SUDS.
4. Shift your focus to a strongly positive affirmation or neutralizing statement that feels helpful/ supportive/ nurturing to you, such as:
   – I still love and accept myself, wholly and completely
   – and The Infinite Source/ God/ Christ/ Allah/ Buddha loves and accepts me, wholly, completely and unconditionally
   – and I remember how good I felt when:
      • I was on holiday, lying on the beach, with no cares at all, listening to the waves and birds, feeling the warm sand beneath my back, and the light breeze cooling me
      • I was sitting on my mother's lap, feeling so good and warm and protected and safe
      • Or use any other statement that feels strongly positive to you
5. After completing your counteracting statement, assess your SUDS again.
   – If the SUDS goes down, you're on your way to neutralizing the intensity of your issue
   – If the SUDS goes up, you're connecting more solidly with the intensity of your feelings
   
   In either case, continue further rounds of tapping + steps (1) – (5)
6. If there is no shift of SUDS number (up or down) after tapping:
   – Massage the acupressure releasing points (also called the 'tender spots') below your clavicles for 15-30 seconds. (See Figure V-1)

**Figure V-1. Releasing points (Tender spots)**

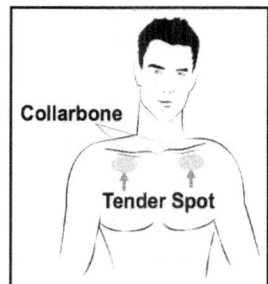

– Repeat your steps (1) – (5).
– If there is still no decrease in SUDS, look for meta-anxieties that block releases of issues and address them as in (1) – (5).

7. Meta-anxieties are worries/ fears *about* the issue you are working on. These unconscious anxieties may block the release of your issues. For instance:
   – "If I let go of these meta-anxieties/fears about my trauma memories, I may let down my guard and put myself in danger."
   – "If I drive my car again, I could get into another bad accident."
   – "If I let go of my fears of men, I might not be careful enough and might put myself in danger of being molested/ raped again."

   Continue working on your meta-anxiety as you would with TWR/WHEE in addressing any regular issue, until the SUDS for the meta-anxiety is '0' and then install a meta-positive to replace the meta-negative you have released. e.g:
   – "I'm pleased those meta-anxieties/fears about my trauma memories are a thing of the past."
   – "I can drive my car again, and will be a more cautious and careful driver."
   – "I'm now properly alert to choose carefully when I meet new men, having learned important lessons from my past experiences."

8. Return to your initial issue (with its meta-anxieties) and assess your SUDS. Often the suds for the initial issue will shift (usually going down, but occasionally rising) after the meta-anxieties are released. Continue tapping + focus + affirmations until your SUDS = '0.'

9. Replace the negatives
   – Create a Replacement Positive statement to take the place of the negative thoughts and feelings you have released about your primary issue. For instance, if you've released a fear of speaking in public, you might install something like the following:
   – "I can speak out in public and feel comfortable and confident that people will listen to me with interest and respect."

Always state your replacement positive as a totally positive phrase. The unconscious mind often ignores the word 'not.' If you used a statement like "I can speak out in public and [will not] feel uncomfortable and worried that people will listen to me with interest and respect." then your unconscious mind might perceive this as "I can speak out in public and [will] feel uncomfortable and worried etc." In this case, you would be re-programming yourself to have anxieties all over again about speaking in public.

   – Assess your Subjective Units of Success Scale (SUSS) for this positive statement, where '0' = "I don't believe or feel this at all" and '10' = "I fully believe and feel confident that this is completely true."
   – Start your tapping
   – Recite your replacement positive statement, followed by your Strongly Positive Affirmation.
   – Check your SUSS again.
   – If it has increased or decreased, then continue with further rounds of (b) – (e).
   – Continue until your SUSS is a '10'.
   – Continue with several more rounds of (b) – (e). More often than not, you will

find your SUSS going higher, beyond the point you initially thought would be the maximum positive intensity you could feel for this issue. I've known some people whose SUSS went up to '20' or '30.' This is clear evidence that they greatly under-estimated how good they could possibly feel after they released their negative thoughts and feelings!

It is often helpful to write down exactly what you are saying as you use TWR. Having your written record enables you to:

– Repeat your focus statement when it has been helpful

– Sharpen and improve your focus

– Return at later dates to use your successful TWR statements for focusing

– Reinforce your progress

Many HSPs appreciate TWR1 most because it provides tools for creating an inner place of peace, safety and healing (PPSH). This is a calming inner space to which you can retreat any time you feel stressed, triggered into negative states or overwhelmed.[11]

### TWR2/WHEE: Listening to body messages

TWR2 is often a transformative experience. TWR2 Gives you the tools to identify, lessen and often to clear the roots of your pains and other problems so they are far less likely to return to bother you.

This involves some of the deeper uses of TWR, based on principles of wholistic healing. Your body, emotions, mind, relationships and spirit are all parts of your being. Any one or all of these parts may speak to you through pains and other symptoms in order to get your attention, to help steer you through challenging experiences and to guide you through your life.

Your psychological and physical symptoms are messengers from your deeper self. They truly want to help you sort out and improve your life on every level of your being. Pain is your friend, not your enemy. Your body or your psychological distress may want to draw your attention:

– To issues you've neglected

– To point you towards actions needed for your health and wellbeing

– To alert you to other parts of your life you have overlooked or neglected, including your relationships and your spirit.

For many people, listening to your body may be a totally new concept. Conventional medicine teaches that your body is simply a vehicle like a car, with warning lights (pains and other symptoms) that alert you to take your body to the medical 'diagnostics and repair shop' for the medical experts to diagnose and fix for you. An acute pain may have a physical cause, such as a sprain or fracture or appendicitis – for which conventional medicine is a treatment of choice. It is wise to check first with your medical doctor whether there is a medical or surgical fix to treat it.

Often, when there is no clear cause for acute pains, and even moreso for chronic pains, a doctor may offer a best-estimate assessment and is likely to prescribe pain medications to help you until it's gone. With acute, short-term pains, pain medication can be a blessing.

People who have come to me for help with their pains and other physical challenges have taught me better ways to deal with many their symptoms. Thousands of clients over the years have shown me that body symptoms are most often messengers from your inner self. When you listen to your body, your inner self will no longer have to yell at you so loudly to get your attention. Your pains will offer you new understandings and directions for courses of action – to bring the needed self-healings into your life. In my discussion below I focus on pains, the most common symptom that brings people for help, but the instructions and principles apply to any other symptoms as well, from any wholistic level of your being.

In the TWR2 process you dialogue with your pains. This almost always opens doors to understanding the issues surrounding your pains. Please note that this is a discussion *with* your pains, not you complaining *about* them or telling them off for hurting you.

1. Begin by assessing your SUDS for how strong your pains are at this moment – on a scale of '0' (no pain) to '10' (the worst it could be). It helps to write down the number you get, each time you measure your pain.

2. Start your TWR2 tapping. Use whichever right-left tapping is comfortable and works best for you, as detailed above for TWR1. Using your feet, toes or tongue for left-right tapping leaves your hands free to write down the exact words you're saying, as you think them. Having a record of what you say can be an enormous help as you sharpen your TWR focus on any given issue. This is also a help in developing your skills.

   Tapping with your feet on the floor is also a private way for using TWR in public, so that no one knows you are doing it. Even if you're wearing sandals or barefoot, it's likely people won't notice you're tapping.

3. Ask yourself the following questions. These TWR questions are your keys to connecting with your inner wisdom for self-healing.

   Q1. *What does your pain want you to know about your life?*

   – Take your time to listen carefully to all the answers. Ask each question at least 3 times because there may be several answers to each one.

   – Check your SUDS level. If the number has come down after you get an answer, this is a good sign, suggesting your pain is pleased you are listening to it.

   – If your SUDS goes up, it is also a good sign. It is your inner self, saying you're connecting more fully to your pains so they can inform you better how to bring the needed healing into your life.

   Write down any answers you get.

   You may not get answers to question 1, but in this case, continue on to question 2.

   – Make sure you continue tapping.

   Q2. *What does your pain want you to do differently in your life?*

   – Consider carefully the answers you get to this one, again writing them down.

   – Check your SUDS level. If the number has come down, again this is a good sign, suggesting your pain is pleased you are wanting to listen to it and to respond to it.

   – Write down the answers you get.

   – Then, go to the next question and continue tapping.

   Q3. *What do you promise faithfully you will do in response to what your pain has just told you?*

- This is for many the most difficult question. Your promise has to cover the general issues raised by your pain, and must also be specific as to what you will do and when you will do it.
- When the SUDS goes down, it's a sign that you're on the right track. If it doesn't go down, you need to pursue these three questions further and to seek new, deeper responses in your dialogue with your body's messages. Two-chair dialogues with your pain may open insights if your pain hasn't spoken to you or hasn't been clear enough to suggest new directions you can take.*12
- Again, it's important to write down the promises you make. Broken promises may invite a return of the pains.
- After you've processed the three questions to the best of your ability, if your SUDS is not down to zero, you might choose to reduce your pain further by direct, TWR1 tapping, as detailed above.

Common sense must apply in using TWR. If your pain is due to injuries or surgery, your pain may be reminding you to be gentle with your body while it's repairing itself. In this case, you should not deliberately reduce it to zero until your injuries or surgical procedures have healed beyond your body's need to caution you to be gentle with it.

4. There are further steps you can take with TWR2 if your pain still persists. These steps are better taken with the guidance of a therapist.

Users have reported that TWR/WHEE helped them with:

- *Physical pains of all sorts*, including tension headaches, migraines, stomach aches, irritable bowel syndromes, Crohn's Disease, Ulcerative Colitis, frozen shoulders, backaches, pains after injuries and surgery, arthritis, bursitis, fibromyalgia, cancer, post-radiation pain, and more. Many have been able to decrease their pains even when they've been present for months and years.

CAUTION: As I mentioned above, Pain may also be a signal of a physical issue requiring medical or surgical attention. It is important to consider such possibilities carefully before working on removing the last remnants of pain. A medical examination is advisable to identify serious disorders causing the pain. But even when such disorders are present, TWR/WHEE can help to relieve pains. A great benefit here is that this is a self-healing method with no known side effects. In contrast, conventional medicine is the third leading cause of death, and pain medications figure prominently on the list of medical dangers.[13]

- Emotional pains: Distress after painful emotional experiences, both recent and from the distant past, such as parental conflicts, separation or divorce; worries over family stresses such as illness, injuries and financial issues; or unresolved grief and bereavement.*14
- Anxieties and fears about challenging experiences in your life, including visits to dentists and doctors; fears of flying; fears or phobias of insects, snakes, pets and larger animals, heights; test anxieties; performance anxieties, such as speaking in class or in public; writer's blocks; specific fears following frightening or traumatic experiences; anxieties and fears about recurring experiences such as oncology medical treatments, shifting between homes of parents who are not living together; calming after waking from a nightmare; dealing with underlying anxieties and post traumatic residues associated with nightmares; and the like.
- Phobias, including school avoidance – These respond rapidly, even when

they are severe.*[15] Milder fears, such as those marked by procrastination, respond well too.

- Angers, including rubs from mild annoyance, through festering and simmering resentments, and on to rages that are triggered by major or minor irritations and provocations, can be decreased and usually eliminated. Here, preventive use of TWR/WHEE is best, emptying the 'bucket of old angers' so that it doesn't overflow when new angers are stuffed inside. Preventive tapping also has further benefits. Once people have practiced using TWR/WHEE when they are not angry, then they can do their tapping more easily and successfully in the actual times of upsets, such as releasing anger and calming while sitting in a time out chair; addressing fears and hurts that may be associated with their angers; and so on.

- Post traumatic Stress Disorders (PTSDs): These are very responsive to TWR/WHEE, which can help with residual traumatic memories, panic attacks, nightmares, temper outbursts and more.

- Insomnia: Sleeplessness responds wonderfully well, even when it has been present for a long time. This, however, is a habit that may sometimes take several weeks or months to clear fully.

- Motion sickness and morning sickness of pregnancy: These can often respond immediately and can be eliminated very quickly. In some cases the meta-anxieties of repeating previous experiences of severe nausea and embarrassments experienced with vomiting in public may need to be addressed before the nausea itself will clear. Pregnant women appreciate this in addition because it is a non-medicinal treatment that is safe for the fetus.

- Allergies: Sensitivities to animals, pollens, foods and other allergens; and asthma may respond within minutes or may take several weeks of regular TWR/WHEE use to ease or dissipate.

- Cravings: Addictions to sweets, food, cigarettes, drugs, thrills, and other self-injurious behaviors may respond to TWR/WHEE. (Smoking is easier to clear than many others substance addictions, probably because it doesn't impair consciousness.)

- Comfort eating and drinking: Habits of putting something that tastes good in your mouth and gives you a feel-good in your tummy. This is often a substitute for lack of interactive and emotional sweetness on one's life.

- Weight loss: Like other body symptoms, being overweight is often a way the body speaks about anxieties, stress and/or trauma. It can also be a sort of 'armoring' against being attacked again. TWR/WHEE is helpful in reducing, eliminating and transforming the underlying issues and meta-issues behind obesity. These often include issues around psychological self-image and self-esteem.

- Reducing side effects and the need for many medications: TWR/WHEE aids in the reduction in severity of the issues for which the medications are prescribed or street drugs are used (anxiety, pain, allergies, insomnia, chemotherapy, etc.). Reductions in doses or even in the need for medications as well as in their side effects are therefore possible. These self-healing methods also help to harmonize the responses to medications, such as chemotherapy, reducing side effects for which other medications are often prescribed.

- Relationships, social issues, performance anxieties, low self-confidence:

Many of the common issues of teens respond dramatically well to TWR/WHEE. This is an extension of the uses of TWR/WHEE into beliefs and disbeliefs about our abilities to deal with our life issues. In many cases there are overlaps with reductions in post-trauma stress.

- Family members' anxieties and distress: There have been excellent responses in anxieties raised by children's, partners' and parents' issues; anxieties not caused by the children but impacting the children because children pick up on parents' worries or because parents have a short fuse; anxieties and stresses of relatives dealing with a family member's chronic illness.

In short, TWR/WHEE has been found by users to be very rapidly effective, rather like a vacuum cleaner that allows you to clear away dusty old hurts and trauma reactions that you carry around with you from traumatic experiences.

### *TWR2/WHEE: Deeper Clearings*

TWR2 allows you to explore the roots of problems, clearing the deeper issues that are contributing to or actually generating your symptoms. Behind your pains may be:

- General tensions that make you up tight emotionally, which tenses your muscles, which go into spasms or which worsen tensions and pains from injuries or other physical causes
- Metaphoric tightening of muscles, as for example if you keep saying "What a pain in the neck (or other part of your body) this is!" then that part of your body may tense up and get painful.[16]
- Your body may be "speaking" to you to get your attention about something that is out of harmony in your life, that you haven't yet identified.*[17]
- Sometimes we get so entrenched in our habits of responding from a place of being symptomatic that it is hard for us to let go of how we are responding, even though we know we are generating, perpetuating and worsening our own problems. For instance, food cravings and comfort eating may become so habitual that they are difficult to release. TWR2 gives you tools to help you sort out why you have the cravings and then to release them.

Here is an example of a deeper TWR2 clearing.

✦ 'Saul' had a neuroma on his right foot. This is a fairly common inflammation of a nerve, sometimes from poor fitting shoes, at other times from unknown causes. Saul's doctor recommended that he have it surgically removed, which he did. Saul was dismayed to find his foot hurting even more than before surgery. He was miserable with the side effects of a variety of pain medicines, which included drowsiness, muddled thinking and nausea.

One of his co-workers had had good results with tapping therapy for premenstrual pains, and suggested he might find it helpful for his foot. Though he was rather skeptical, Saul was suffering a lot because he had to walk modest distances during his workday and at home, and sometimes had to stand in the bus to and from work, so he was well motivated to try something that wasn't medicinal.

TWR1 brought his pain down from a level 8 when he was standing to a level 5, but Saul's pain persisted at that level despite tapping on his collarbone points and doing other releasing and relaxing exercises. Though this was quite a stretch for Saul, he agreed to explore two-chair work to see whether some part of his inner self might be able to clarify anything about the pain.*[18]

It took only a few minutes for Saul, sitting in the chair representing his hurting foot, to connect with the awareness that his inner self was protesting about his fear to take some important steps forward in his life. He had been offered a promotion to move up to a managerial position, but this would require further studies and retraining – some of which he would have to do on his own time, after hours. A part of Saul really wanted the promotion, but a strong part of him was hesitant and anxious about whether he would succeed if he moved forward in that direction.

He was surprised that his pain went down to a 2.5 after the two-chair discussion, without tapping. Even though he hadn't resolved the issue that his foot was complaining about, now that he was listening to what his foot wanted to tell him, it no longer had to 'yell' at him with more intense pain in order to get his attention.

Saul was sufficiently impressed with the decrease in his pain to continue his TWR2 work, exploring deeper issues behind the pain. Further two-chair work and tapping helped him clarify that some of his hesitations to accept the promotion had nothing to do with his current job situation. His father had been a factory worker with little education, who suffered severe privations of poverty that deprived him of a high school education. Though he was intelligent, his father never got very far in life, partly due as well to his drinking habit. His father (Saul's grandfather) had been an aggressive, physically and verbally abusive man. Though Saul's father was not physically abusive, he criticized and belittled Saul frequently, which Saul found devastating. These unconscious trauma residues appeared to have been the greatest underlying blocks in Saul's wholistic self that generated his foot pain. The TWR2 explorations clarified the details of these trauma residues and enabled Saul to clear them, along with his current day issues.

After only three sessions, Saul was pain free and clear that he was going to proceed with all necessary steps to achieve his promotion. Saul shared with me a year later that following his self-healing sessions, his relationship with his father had improved considerably. He was also discovering in his new managerial position that he had a gift for helping people connect with awarenesses of some of their earlier life traumas and consequent psychological blocks in their work and lives. He was, as well, volunteering to help teenagers through the Big Brothers Association, and reconnecting with his church – from which he had felt alienated in growing up because no one reached out to help him with his traumas and distress.

We can see that not only can TWR2 open into insights, but at the same time it often offers immediate suggestions for clearing both the current and the earlier issues contributing to your challenges. Single trauma experiences generally clear a lot more easily and quickly than multiple and repeated traumas. However, the period of therapy can be shortened if, along with the trauma residues themselves, we clear any meta-anxieties and meta-traumas of hopelessness about issues like:

- "I'll never be safe from these sorts of attacks."
- "I'm need to keep a basic level of tension and hypervigilance so that I won't be blindsided by another attack."
- "If my own family can't be trusted to keep me safe, I need to be sure to stay on the alert everywhere else."**[19]

It's not uncommon to find that one's relationships improve with people who were involved in the traumas that we cleared. Some people use TWR/WHEE deliberately for such purposes, through what we call 'proxy healing.' Here, healing is offered to the traumatized and/or traumatizing person through an invitation to participate in the healing of the person sending the healing. In practice, this can be done in several formats.

- A mental intent or invitation is sent to the other person to share in the tapping or other form of healing that the sender is working on, herself.
- The sender takes on the role of the person in need, tapping on himself as though he were experiencing the symptoms the target person wishes to clear.

Proxy healing is not pushed upon the recipient(s) or sent with any expectations of specific outcomes that are determined by the person(s) sending the healing. We are not doing anything to others but are rather inviting them to experience healing if they are ready to receive it and if it's for their highest good and the highest good of all.

> *...our own inner work becomes part of our offering to others.*
> Ram Dass & Marabai Bush

Not everyone is ready to do the deeper work of TWR2. Some are content to have symptomatic relief. Others have not been gifted with or haven't developed their observing ego – their inner awareness of their own psychological processes.*[20] Others come from families where psychological issues are not discussed or are even avoided, and discussions of psychological issues may be actively discouraged. Growing up in such families leaves these people without the concepts or even the language for connecting with emotional issues. In other words, some people may have the capacity to develop observing ego for psychological issues but this part of themselves has grown weak from neuroplastic atrophy, due to discouragements and disuse.*[21]

**Bundling issues to facilitate releases of current and earlier memories and to address the wholistic spectrum of issues**

Once you are familiar with methods like EP, NLP, and/or CBT, many people are able to work their ways more quickly through their lists of issues by bundling issues of greater and lesser intensity and clearing all of them together. Let's take the example of Todd, mentioned earlier in illustration of releasing buried emotions.*[22] I briefly review some of Todd's issues here.

✦ Todd is the highly successful businessman who found himself developing an increasing irritation with his wife, Julie's, emotionality. Todd was able to use tapping to release both his current life frustrations and his earlier life traumas that sensitized him to his current life issues. Todd found he was able to clear these issues quite readily. He was similarly successful in dealing with residues of problems from the past. When guided to bundle both past and present issues in order to clear them together, he found that both issues actually cleared much more quickly than when he had addressed them alone. For example, when he was feeling upset over Julie being too critical, and he bundled these feelings with residues of feelings from earlier in life about his parents being uncaring, both issues cleared much more quickly than working on either alone.

Bundling the present and past issues in the tapping process facilitated the clearing of both issues. I believe that dealing with either current or past issues alone does not work as quickly because the related issues are still being held in memory quarantine, with one's unconscious doing its best to keep them from coming into conscious awareness. The withholding of the early memories conflicts with efforts to release the similar, recent memories, when the recent ones are addressed alone. And conversely, releasing earlier hurtful memories that are similar to current conflict memories, without addressing the current ones will slow the release of the earlier ones. Bundling both sets of memories works best for releasing both.

## TWR/WHEE for children

Children usually respond much more quickly and deeply to TWR/ WHEE than adults do. Essentially, they haven't grown the sorts of habits-rust or barnacles on their issues that adults have developed over years of keeping painful feelings and memories buried outside their conscious awareness. It is common for even very high levels of SUDS in children, such as 100 (on a scale of 10), to come down to 0 with just a few rounds of tapping.

Adaptations of procedures for children, depending on their age and abilities to cooperate, may include:

- Children who don't know their numbers can indicate by holding their palms facing towards each other 'how big,' 'how bad,' 'how strong' or 'how scary' it feels, with the space between their hands showing the magnitude of what they are feeling.
- The 'butterfly hug,' in which you alternate tapping with each hand on the opposite biceps muscle, feels self-comforting, in and of itself. This has the extra advantage that it produces a simultaneous, double stimulation to left and right brain hemispheres. The tapping on your left arm sends a stimulus to the right brain from your left arm, and also from your right hand to the left brain; and conversely from the tapping of your left hand on your right arm.
- Children are vulnerable to being teased or bullied for doing anything that looks unfamiliar or odd to other children. Alternating tapping quietly with their feet on the floor, or alternating tightening and relaxing their toes inside their shoes is a more private way to use TWR/WHEE.
- Focusing statements can often be similar to those of adults, such as:
  - "Even though I'm worried about speaking up in front of the class"
  - "Even though I'm scared of the kid in the front row who talks loudly and doesn't quiet down like she should when the teacher speaks to her"
  - "Even though I'm worried about taking this exam" (Tapping feet works well while writing!)
- Calming words have to be adjusted to children's age levels
  - "I feel really good when my mommy gives me a big hug."
  - "I remember how good it feels to be tucked into bed at night by my mommy/ daddy."
  - "I remember how good I felt when I got a [insert acknowledgment or reward] from my teacher for doing well [insert occasion]"
  - "I remember how good my class/ family trip to [insert] was."
  - "I remember how good it was to go swimming/ walking in [insert location or description of nature or other setting]."

- "I know I'm safe now" (after traumatizing circumstances are dealt with and further trauma is being avoided, prevented and/or blocked).
- "I remember how great I felt at the concert last weekend." (Check to be sure you're not buying into memories of using illicit drugs or some other questionable behaviors!)

– Building an imaginary inner place "where it's always quiet and calm and safe" is enormously helpful, as detailed with the PPSH. This can be used in place of calming words.
– In a religious setting: "I know God/ Christ/ Allah/ my guardian angels/ Archangel [insert name] is always watching over me and protecting me for my highest good."
– TWR/WHEE tapping with the feet can be used during stressful situations.
– Inviting a child who knows how to use TWR/WHEE to teach one or more other children ("paying it forward") is a nice boost to their self-image and self-confidence.
– Children learn they can do this anytime, anywhere if they're feeling worried, scared or hurt.
– You will do well to explain TWR/WHEE to children's parents, so that they will not discourage or make fun of the child for doing something that is new to the parents and outside their range of experience.
– Other EP methods may be used with children as well. I have found, though, that:

Methods involving tapping on the face, chest and hands can draw unwanted attention from other children, who may tease or bully a child who is doing something they see as strange.

– Long and complicated series of tapping sequences may be difficult for children to remember when they most need to use them, because they are feeling stressed, fearful or panicky and have difficulties focusing their attention at such times.

## 30. Marital/ couple therapy and family therapy

> ...no culture has ever been able to provide a better shipyard for
> building storm-proof vessels for the journey of man from the cradle
> to the grave than the individual nourished in a loving family.
> – Laurens van der Post

Many issues presented by people coming for therapy either have their origins in difficult relationships between family members, or are worsened by these relationships. When the person coming for help is the only one in the family willing to address the troublesome issues it is entirely appropriate to proceed with individual therapy. But when the family is willing to participate in the therapy, there are many more options available for helping everyone who is involved.[23]

I trained for six months in marital and family therapy at the Philadelphia Child Guidance Clinic in 1979. I have found this approach invaluable in helping people sort out their relational challenges. Even when only one person comes for help, understanding the family dynamics enables a therapist to be far more helpful in the individual therapy because the interpersonal issues of the person being helped can be identified and addressed to some degree through that person.

This is relevant to our considerations of how best to help HSPs and their HSPCs and families. There are often misunderstandings between left and right brain dominant people that can lead to conflicts, bitterness, distancing and alienation. Family therapy can often help enormously in bridging the differences in ways of relating to the world in general and to each other in particular. The one requirement is that family members must be willing to come and look at their relationships and themselves, with a willingness to consider and explore changes that can make things better.

My training in marital and family systems therapy was the best experience of formal clinical learning I've ever had. We had lectures by gifted family therapists, videotaped live supervision through a one-way mirror, groups of students reviewing each other's work on videotape together with an instructor, and access to excellent reading and video materials.

I came away from this intensive course with a thorough appreciation that each of us is not just an individual but is also a piece of a family. This was an excellent opening into awareness of wholistic systems theory. Generally, the most healthy, basic model for families is that each generation within the family has its accepted roles.

- The two parents are partners engaged in a committed relationship. The parents form the nucleus of their family, and bear the responsibility for setting and maintaining the family rules.
- The children are individuals, growing up and learning their various roles in the nuclear family, extended family, community, world and life in general. Their normal place is to follow the directions of their parents and to provide age-appropriate supports for their parents.
- The extended family are on similar, parallel life paths. The grandparents are parents to the parents, and are also bearers of the lineages of traditions of the family that extend back in time to include legacies of experiences from previous generations. Uncles, aunts, cousins and other extended family members add varieties of awarenesses and supports.

Many family relationship challenges derive from failures in establishing and maintaining the generational roles and boundaries. Children in general, and HSP children in particular, are quick to sense when there is disharmony between their parents. It often is deeply perturbing and stressful to children that their parents are not getting along with each other. HSP children are more likely to display anxieties and tensions that are out of the ordinary for them under such circumstances. For instance, they are likely to misbehave in order to distract parents from arguing with each other. And they will sacrifice themselves in order to reduce the conflicts, as they perceive and interpret them, between the parents.

This is a burden and sacrifice that children take on intuitively. Better to have a known issue (their misbehavior) as the cause of parental discord than to live with the tensions and stresses of parents arguing and fighting over unknown issues.

The causes of family dysfunctions are often complex and challenging to identify and unravel. Parents are often unaware of the roots of their issues that are causing disharmony and conflicts between them. Often, they perceive their children's misbehaviors before their own issues are clarified.

Individual lives and family relations tend to function well when there is respect and support from the family for each person as an individual, and reciprocally, when individuals have respect and support for family traditions and expectations. There is an enrichment available for each individual from the lessons learned by members of the family, both in current life and in other generations.

Difficulties often arise when the family has developed traditions that demand conformance of every individual to rules and habits that may be unaccepting of the unique personalities and preferences of some individuals. As HSPs constitute only 15–20 percent of the population, they are often different from the 80–85 percent of the rest of their family members. Where families are flexible and accepting of such differences, HSPs can flourish and the families are enriched. The NHSP family members are exposed to broader ranges of emotional sensitivities, awarenesses and expressions. The NHSPs may learn to

- Tolerate people who say and express what they feel
- Resonate with some of the feelings being expressed and recognize that they themselves have such feelings
- Reciprocate with the HSPs who are expressing their feelings, thereby learning and experiencing a greater range of feeling awareness and expression that can enrich their lives
- Learn to initiate and share expressions of positive feelings of their own more openly and deeply, such as joy, happiness, love, compassion and more
- Learn to tolerate, express and process feelings that can be difficult to deal with, such as anxieties, fears, hurt, depression, grief and more

That is the good news. The bad news is that problems for HSPs often arise in families that are uncomfortable with people whose ways of relating to other individuals, to the family and to the world in general are different from their family norms. A very common source of discomfort, irritation and conflict is often on the spectrum of openly expressing vs not expressing feelings and intuitions.

Often, we find troubles arising where the NHSP family traditions and rules that have developed to live one's life are strongly flavored with habits and unspoken rules such as:

- We don't openly express our emotions
- We don't consciously think about or discuss feelings
- We discourage others from expressing their feelings
- People who express their feelings are weak, wimpy, looking for attention or sympathy, childish, immature, emotional basket cases, wanting to get their way by wearing us down, etc.
- If others persist in expressing their feelings we avoid, silence, isolate, disparage, or bully them into silence about their feelings.

These attitudes and behaviors protect the NHSPs from the discomforts and anxieties about being aware of their feelings. And I've found these sorts of conflicts far more commonly than I've found accepting NHSP attitudes towards HSPs.

Varieties of family therapy approaches have been developed. Some of them are wonderfully creative. The great value of all of them lies in the exploration of new patterns of perceptions, insights, understandings and behaviors in a group of people who live and interact with each other frequently. The fact that these are group shifts can markedly facilitate the rate of change in some or all of the participants because they are constantly reminding and reinforcing each other to respond in new ways to the challenges that brought them for help.

Marital and family therapy can be of enormous help to HSPs, their HSPCs and their families in coming to understand each other, in overcoming uncomfortable or negative relationships, and in getting along better together. Marital and family therapy can be enormously enhanced with varieties of uses of Energy Psychology.

Let me illustrate some of these issues with the family therapy experience of several generations that were touched by the multiple traumas of earlier generations. You will probably find it challenging to keep the details about various family members clearly in mind. It may be a help to jot down a diagram with a few noted about each member as you read this.

✛ 'Harold,' an HSP, and his wife 'Bertha,' an NHSP, came to me because the school was complaining that their teenage children were bullying other students in school. There was also a chronic, repeating pattern of Harold's periodic severe upsets with his wife that were utterly frustrating both of them.

This was a second marriage for Harold. His first wife had cut off her relationship with him following the divorce, fifteen years earlier. He had a son and daughter from his previous marriage, but they had been estranged from him since their parents were divorced, when the children were in their mid-teens. Some of Harold's family had cut off relations with him as well at the time of the divorce. His family remained friends with his former wife and included his children in their family functions.

Harold had been a devoted husband to Bertha and to her two children from her first marriage, 'Kim' and 'David,' now 15 and 13, respectively, through the six years of their marriage. Bertha had been equally steadfast and supportive as an NHSPC**[24] wife and was a caring mother.

In taking Harold's life history, it was glaringly clear that he had always found himself to be very different from all of the people in his birth family and two marriages. He was a sensitive, caring, kind HSP who had been born into a family of NHSPs, who were all strongly avoidant of acknowledging their feelings. There were also a lot of trauma residues in his family.

Harold's parents had both been orphaned in childhood. They met in a group home in their late teens, after each of them had suffered multiple rejections from foster homes. Harold's mother had been abandoned at birth and his father's parents and a younger brother had died in an auto accident that left him with a moderate limp as a residual and constant reminder of the auto accident where he was the sole survivor.

Harold's father, 'Jacob,' was a bright but angry man who was okay as long as he was sober. Jacob struggled, with fair success, to stay away from alcohol, but every few years fell off the wagon, usually following a major disappointment in his life. With the support of his wife and employers, he always regained his sobriety within a few days and returned to work with promises to all that he'd learned his lesson and would never go near the bottle again. Despite these issues, Jacob held down decent construction manager jobs for years at a time because he was bright, outgoing and a hard worker. His home life was reasonably stable, and he got along well with his wife and their five other children but not with Harold, their youngest child.

Harold's father had always seen him as a sissy, and held the attitude that he and the rest of the family needed to toughen Harold up so he would act like a man and not stay the baby of the family. Harold's family had no tolerance, much less understanding, for his being an HSP. Harold was bright and a hard worker at school and at home, like his father, but got no praises or positive acknowledgments from anyone in the family – who could only berate him and put him down frequently for being a weakling, a 'wuss' and a 'drama king.'

Bertha complained that though she was generally able to tolerate Harold's being an emotional person, she found his more intense emotions stronger than she could deal with. She was definitely not willing to put up with him when he burst into anger for no apparent reason, over issues that she didn't feel warranted such intense feelings. She had put up with this from the time of their marriage, but her patience was wearing thin as she saw her teenage children showing similar behaviors. Bertha had responded with anger to his outbursts in the early years of their marriage, and they had several times reached a point of considering separating, but she had eventually learned to just let him blow off steam and if she didn't respond with anger herself, he would get over it within a day or two.

The precipitating issue that led to their seeking help was a series of calls from the children's school vice principal, who complained they were each bullying other children, getting into fights and creating negative atmospheres in their classes.

The children were a bit sullen as we moved through the initial introductions. But the discussions between their parents created an atmosphere of working to understand their issues, so the children didn't feel put on the spot as we shifted the focus to their school issues. This wasn't to say that they were willing or able to share more than that there was a lot of bullying going on in the school, so they didn't know why the vice principal and now the principal were picking on them in particular. Bertha volunteered that she had made an appointment for the end of the following week to speak with the vice principal, so we agreed to hold off further discussion about these issues till we had more information.

Having started in a family therapy format, with both parents and the children present, and particularly as the children were having behavior problems in school, we agreed to continue with this format. They were eager to get on top of their problems as the school was pressuring them to address the bullying issues. But I let them know I expected we would meet occasionally with individuals or pairs of family members some of the time.

I returned to the parental presenting problem, asking them about what might have triggered Harold's anger in the past, but there was no clear consensus about this. I asked everyone to observe what was going on if he had any angry outbursts as we moved forward.

Session 2, two days later, included all of the family and was focused on learning the basics of TWR/WHEE for de-stressing. Everyone agreed this definitely felt like it would help, both to individual family members and to their getting along better within the family. I recommended that they each keep a record of how they were using the tapping and how it was helping.

Session 3 was with Harold and Bertha alone. I asked them to sharpen the focus for me on how the anger outbursts began, unfolded and ended. Long story short, we distilled from a detailed review of several anger outbursts that Harold was often "moodier than normal," according to Bertha, before he exploded into anger. Harold, in a tone of controlled frustration, explained that he didn't feel he was actually moody, but rather that he felt and expressed his feelings much more clearly and often than anyone whom he had ever called "family." He did, however, acknowledge that there seemed to be a build-up in his sensitivity and the intensity of his feelings in general just before his anger outbursts occurred.

I explained to both of them a little about left-brain and right-brain ways of experiencing the world and of communicating, and that some people lived more through their thoughts and others more through their feelings. I repeated this several times, in different words, with different examples. This was both to emphasize the importance of these awarenesses, and to resource them with a variety of perspectives for thinking and talking about Harold's emotional ways of expressing himself.

They both agreed that these very different thinking and feeling ways of expressing themselves could explain a lot of what was going on, and were interested to learn more. I suggested it would be helpful if both of them did some more detective work, to see whether they could figure out what might be happening when Harold started to express his feelings more strongly. They also were open to including the children as assistant detectives.

I indicated it is important in detective work to write down the details of your observations so that they will be remembered as accurately as possible. I suggested it would be helpful if they all sat down prior to the next session to share their observations, and that Harold was to write a brief summary of the observations to fill me in on them when we all met together again in the next session.

In addition to searching for details that might help to explain to all of us what was going on, I was reframing Harold's being an emotionally expressive person in several ways:

- I was helping this family to accept and normalize Harold's emotional manners of expressing himself, inviting them to just write down their observations but to minimize their responses, if possible.
- I was inviting them all to relate to his emotionality in new ways.

- I was tacitly indicating it is okay to have emotions and to express them.
- I invited everyone to accept as fact that Harold has emotions and expresses them frequently.
- I invited Bertha and the children to observe the tones and nuances of his emotionality, to start noticing when they were calmer (deliberately not using the word "normal") or might be moving into a zone of greater intensity.
- I invited Harold to observe his own process of expressing his emotions and to reflect on what might be pushing him towards expressing them more intensely.
- I was suggesting, without saying it directly to Bertha, that she might be able to help Harold clarify and deal with his emotions by taking charge of the various detectives' observations, being careful in instructing her just to observe and not yet to go to the next step of changing things before we understood what was going on.
- I gave Bertha the task of collecting everyone's observations so that she would think about and watch the expressions of emotions and feel a little more in control of issues related to emotions. This was a clear nudge to use her left brain observing abilities to sort through right brain issues.

Session 4 included everyone. Bertha summarized the two weeks of family observations, noting that Harold had had three workday evenings when he expressed his emotions more intensely, with clear irritation but not in anger. In two of these incidents he readily identified that he was anxious about work-related stresses. In the third, he noted that he was concerned because Bertha had had yet another complaint from the school that Kim was bullying younger children on the way to school, and Bertha had called him at work to be sure he would be home early that evening so they could speak with the children together about this.

Bertha and Harold wanted to focus on the school complaints but I suggested we discuss this later in the session and instead start with a review of the detective work. Everyone seemed to be on the same page with the observations as noted above. Bertha and Harold both seemed less tense, but Kim and David were squirmy and looked anxious. I asked, among several other questions, whether they had shared anything about these sessions with Bertha's family.

The parents both looked at each other and shook their heads, silently. The children became more fidgety. I asked whether they had spoken with anyone about these sessions and Kim glared at David, who stared at his shoes and started chewing one of his fingernails. It turned out the children had been to a family birthday party, and David had mentioned their detective work. He was met with intense derision and disparagement, with several of the children and an aunt chiming in that David's stepfather had always been the baby of his family and they were still hoping he would someday grow up.

Further inquiries revealed that this was not the first time Kim and David had heard these sorts of put-down comments about their stepfather. I shook my head, confirming out loud with Harold that he had indicated his parents and sisters had never understood his being emotionally sensitive, very much like everyone in the therapy room had not understood about left and right brain ways of relating to the world – before we started these discussions. I complimented David for wanting to let others in the family know some of the things he was learning in these sessions, and asked Harold if he had any suggestions for how to deal with his family.

He was thoughtfully silent for a few moments, long enough for the others to start fidgeting. Bertha spoke up and said she doubted anything anyone said would ever make a difference to Harold's family. Harold chimed in, agreeing with Bertha. He added that well before he left home for college he had given up on getting them to understand him, and that he held no hope for changing their attitudes. He added, after another thoughtful pause, that he armored himself emotionally whenever he had contact with them.

I observed that contact with his family of origin might be something that could wind him up, and he readily agreed, punctuating his response by answering rather quickly and with some tension in his voice. I asked the others, "Did you notice the tension in Dad's voice just now?" and all of them nodded. I then asked, "When he gets up tight at home, is it about like he just responded now, or more or less strong?" Here, there were differences in opinions about two out of the three times people noticed him getting up tight at home recently.

I've gone into some detail in describing these sessions, which continued weekly for three months, mostly with the parents, with about one in every four sessions including the children, and then monthly for the better part of a year. This is to give you a taste of how marital and family therapy sessions can work. What I like about seeing people together like this is that I get a more rounded picture, with everyone's perspectives contributing to better understanding for all of us about the family dynamics and individuals' dynamics. I also help them learn experientially how to explore and develop new ways to interact with each other – both in the sessions and at home.

Harold and Bertha's family all made good use of TWR/WHEE to lessen their anxieties and tensions at home, and without my having to prescribe many direct changes in their behaviors or responses to each other, they themselves came up with improved ways of getting along in general, and with Harold's emotional openness in particular.

The children's bullying issues were addressed by their parents with the school. My impression was that Kim and David were unconsciously venting some of their discomforts with their own emotions in general and with the challenges in dealing with emotions at home by letting out anger at children weaker than themselves. Children who misbehave in such ways are most often expressing indirectly something about their own feelings. This might relate to things said or done to them that were uncomfortable or painful, or might relate to issues of someone else in their family that have impacted the children. At the same time, such behaviors are commonly also very distracting tactics that children unconsciously employ – to get their parents to stop arguing with each other and to shift the heat onto themselves.

Harold's choice of Bertha, an NHSP for a wife, along with his behaviors in his current family, re-created some of the types of interactions he had experienced in his own family. This is extremely common with trauma residues. The buried psychological residues from the traumas surface in other contexts, re-created by the unconscious mind that is begging the traumatized person to wake up to the presence of these buried memories and feelings and to find ways to release them.

I hope what I've shared will give you a window into the marital and family therapy approaches that can be helpful to HSPCs and families with HSP members. Family therapy helps family members work together cooperatively towards improving their relationships. It develops and deepens the ways HSPCs can support the HSPs in the family. Similarly, it helps HSPs understand the worlds of NHSPs better. And the de-stressing methods that are used by everyone work ever so much better when all of the family members practice them.*[25]

## 31. Two-chair explorations and clearing

*Confrontation affords you opportunity to hear the other side of the story.*
— Sunday Adelaja

Fritz Perls (1969) developed Gestalt Therapy in the 1940's and 1950's. This is a wonderful way to help people clarify and resolve many of their psychological and relational issues. This method has been adopted into many other forms of therapy, including TWR/WHEE.

Whatever your issue, you can clarify and often resolve it by having a discussion with it. You place an empty chair opposite the chair where you're sitting. You may start from either your own chair, stating your question or your thoughts and feelings about the issue, or move over to the empty chair and state the thoughts and feelings that the issue itself has. You then change over to the opposite chair and respond to what was stated in the previous chair. Alternating back and forth between the chairs, you will usually come fairly quickly to new insights and understandings about the issues. Often, you will also arrive at new solutions to whatever was bothering you.

When you're vacillating between two options and having a difficult time making up your mind about which direction to take, two-chair discussions can greatly facilitate your way into making a decision.

✦ 'Mike' very much wanted to move on from his job as assistant to an assistant manager in a clothing firm in a large city. He had wanted to move on for the last five of the eight years he had held that position, but was anxious about leaving this, the first and only job he had ever held. He was bored because he knew the routines and was able to do his job competently, with little thought or effort. But he feared even mentioning his interest in going elsewhere because he felt he had very little to recommend him in the job market at that time. Mike was also reluctant to mention his wish to move on from his current position because it had been his uncle who arranged for him to get this job. Mike's wife pushed him to seek counseling because he was becoming increasingly irritable over his frustrations. This also coincided with his having started night school to finish the twelfth grade and obtain his high school diploma.

After reviewing Mike's life history in detail, Mike's inner conflict led me to suggest a two-chair discussion between the parts of himself that were conflicted. Mike was equally strong in stating his positions from either side of the argument. What he omitted, however, was his uncle's involvement in initially securing this position. When he brought that issue into the two-chair discussion, it was as though he had lanced a boil, releasing a pus-pocket of feelings related to family relationships.

Mike's uncle Sol was the oldest child in his family. He had taken over the role of father in his childhood family at age 14 when his father was murdered in a massacre of Jews in Poland, just prior to WWII. He escaped with his mother and six brothers and sisters to France and from there to the US. Uncle Sol became a successful jeweler who continued through the years to take care of his own family and to provide support to his extended family. He was the go-to person for anyone in the family needing help of any sort, from financial and career decisions to job hunting. Mike's father, Levi, had been the last child, the baby of the family. He was not very bright and had left school after the ninth grade, but was a steady and reliable worker in his janitorial job, and a devoted but very strict parent to his four children. He was very dependent on his brother, Sol, for advice on serious matters and for occasional financial assistance. For Mike to abandon the job that uncle Sol had arranged was outside the box of possible considerations in his father's family.

When Mike was sitting in the "I really want to leave this job" chair, I asked if he'd feel ok discussing with the "I mustn't disappoint Uncle Sol" chair whether his uncle might be open to Mike's asking his help in getting a job with more opportunities for advancement. It didn't take more than a few minutes for Mike to convince himself that his uncle would probably be pleased to help him with this request, especially as Mike was working towards completing his high school studies.

When I re-read some of my summaries, like this one, I often marvel at how often a simple suggestion like this one can have such a rapid and transformative impact. A lot of what I help people do is to consider new options in their lives. What I've learned, though, is that it's almost always better to let them make the decisions themselves rather than for me to push them into doing something new and different from their usual ways of being in the world. This also creates positive meta-beliefs about being competent to help themselves.

And when I recall the further unfolding of Mike's story, I also marvel at how ghosts from the past can haunt us for many years.

✦✦ I had asked Mike to check back with me to let me know how he got along in his discussion with Uncle Sol. Mike phoned to make another appointment two months later, again with the urging of his wife. He had not been able to bring himself to follow through with his plan to speak with Uncle Sol. He also mentioned that he had dropped out of his evening high school classes.

In further two-chair discussions, Mike became aware of the anxieties he carried from his father's feelings of inadequacy in this family, where everyone else had been much more successful in school and work. Mike came to realize he had felt that if he were to be more successful than his father was, he would be putting him to shame at the least, and possibly be seen by his father as demonstrating disrespect for him.

I invited Mike to go back in his memory to the first time he had felt this way about his relationship with his father. He recalled a time in the second grade when he had wanted to ask his father to help him with his homework, and his mother had told him very firmly to never upset his father by asking him anything about school work. (His mother hadn't learned to read or write English, having been raised in an Orthodox Jewish home in Belgium and immigrating to the US as an adult.) Little Mike had interpreted his mother's injunction to mean that he was not to embarrass his father by asking about school work that his father might not understand. Mike readily agreed to hold a two-chair discussion with his father about this situation. I suggested he might start by speaking as Mike of today with his father about 2 year-old Mike.

Mike (chair 1): Tatte ('father' in Yiddish), I'm sorry you didn't do well in school. Mamme told me not to ask you about my school stuff. I didn't want to hurt you back in second grade when I needed help with my homework.

Tatte (chair 2): I'm surprised to hear you held back from asking me.

Mike: Mamme said you'd be upset.

Tatte: Mamme worries about keeping things quiet and calm at home. You know how her tatte gets angry over every little nothing. I might have been a little embarrassed if I didn't know the answers, but I wouldn't be upset.

Mike (to me): Am I making this up just to feel better?

Dan: Why don't we just see how this unfolds? What comes to you to say to your tatte?

Mike (to tatte): So I held back from ever asking you about schoolwork for nothing?

Father: Oy vey! It looks like that's what happened!

Mike: Shaking his head silently, looking glumly down at the floor.

Me: What might you say to Little Mike from the second grade if he were sitting in this chair now, instead of your tatte? (And I moved chair 2 a little to one side, to indicate it is Little Mike's chair, not his father's chair at this point.)

Mike: (After another few thoughtful moments...) I'm beginning to see that we probably felt we shouldn't do well in school, so as not to make tatte feel bad.

Little Mike: He worked so hard to make things good for us! And I could see how bad he felt when the family came together and people were talking about stuff he didn't understand...

Mike: Yah! And I went on protecting him from being uncomfortable by never asking him stuff he might have actually known, and he might not have been upset about it when we were little and wanting his help with things he didn't know. (Shaking his head, and again looking down, silently.)

Mike was very thoughtful through the end of that session. I was pleased to notice that he sat up more straight in his chair as he ended the two-chair dialogues. He had uncovered a persistent childhood myth that his father would be upset if he did well in school, and had realized this was almost certainly untrue.

Setting aside the second chair, Mike then used tapping to eliminate his anxieties about upsetting or hurting his father, plus his guilt for having misunderstood the severity of these issues, and his having held back from engaging with his father in many ways since that unfortunate misunderstanding in second grade. He also installed positive awarenesses and expectations about speaking more openly with his father. He then came up with the idea to find fix-it projects around his home for which he could ask his father's help – as a way of acknowledging he valued his father's knowledge and skills, in areas where Mike himself was not adept.

With this session, Mike freed himself of the self-imposed shackles holding him back from succeeding in school. He returned to night classes and got his high school diploma. This gave him the confidence to approach his Uncle Sol, who was indeed pleased to help him find a better job.

I cannot count the number of times and the different ways that I've heard people describe such mistaken understandings from childhood that undermined or even crippled their progress in school and in other areas of their lives. Two-chair work is one of the best and fastest approaches I've found for helping these people connect with the issues and feelings that started their problems, and for helping them to release these and move on with their lives.

## Body symptoms and their messages in two-chair work

Stressing your body through physical over-exertion or injuries can leave you with tightness or pains in your muscles and joints. Muscle tightness that occurs when you're upset about something may become linked in your unconscious mind with the issues that upset you.

In addition, the words you use to describe how you're feeling and functioning can program your body into being tense. For instance, when you have anxieties and worries about issues in your life, physical tensions are generated. You get 'wound up,' 'up tight,' 'tense,' and 'hot under the collar.' An annoying problem 'is a headache,' 'a pain in the neck' or 'a pain in the ass.' Your 'blood pressure rises,' the problem 'turns your stomach', 'is a heartache' or 'gets your guts in an uproar.' Your body is prone to respond to words of these sorts by becoming tense all over or in particular areas that you repeatedly focus on – sometimes to the point of being tight and painful and functioning poorly. As you release your stress and distress, you 'unwind,' 'relax' and 'calm down.'

Coming from the other direction, when your body is tired or tense, it is hard for you to calm down psychologically. Pain 'winds you up,' 'drives you to distraction' and 'wears you down.' In short, when your body is tense, it is difficult for you to be calm, centered and at peace.

And these can become vicious circles, with physical symptoms winding you up emotionally, and psychological problems pushing your body into tensions that wind you up physically, creating symptoms that worsen your psychological states, that spiral into mind-body problems that take on lives of their own.

Another way that your body may speak is when psychological issues are not addressed. Your body will work hard to draw your attention to these buried irritants. Physical pains very often become associated with psychological issues of distress and tension in your life. It is rare for conventional medical therapists to be aware of these buried problems. Many a surgical procedure has been performed without exploring these possibilities first.

Most people don't realize their body responds to what they are thinking and saying. If you keep repeating "I have this or that pain in the neck" then your body will tense up your neck and you are likely to create muscle spasms and pains in your neck. The same process can affect many other parts of your body, creating what I call 'body-mind' or 'mind-body' problems.

Whatever the reasons for your body being stressed to the point of complaining, you can:

- Identify what is causing your physical tensions, tightness and/or pains
- Address the issues that are leading you to be up tight
  - Clear the tightness in your body
  - Install positive physical states and feeling-associations with your body

Many people can uncover the issues that are locked into their physical symptoms simply by asking their body these questions:

1. What does my body want me to know about my life?
2. What does my body want me to do differently in my life?
3. What do I promise faithfully I will do in response to the answers I have gotten from (1) and (2)?

Another excellent way to clarify what your body is suffering from and wanting you to know is to use the two-chair technique.*[26]

> ✦ 'Frieda,' a corporate secretary, suffered from pains in her back that had gotten worse and worse over a four-month period, to the point it was difficult for her to sit and do her work. The pains were relieved when she stood up and walked around but returned within minutes of her sitting back down to resume her secretarial job. She had no history of injury or strain that would explain her pains.
>
> She read my book, *Seven Minutes to Natural Pain Relief*, and used the two-chair method on her own to speak with her pain. Frieda learned that her pain was triggered by her anxieties that were stimulated by her new boss being an extremely demanding and critical man, who was rarely satisfied with her work. Her previous boss had been a kind, gentle woman with whom Frieda had gotten along well for the fourteen years she had been with the company. Sadly, her first boss had been killed in an auto accident. This was extra distressing to Frieda because she had lost an older sister in an auto accident in childhood.
>
> Using TWR/WHEE, Frieda was able to release some of her angers towards her new boss but still suffered from pain sufficiently to make it difficult to continue work. She requested a transfer to another office, but her boss refused to approve it. She contacted me to see if there was anything further I could suggest. In a single phone session, Frieda was able to release a lot of her grief over the deaths of her former boss and residuals of grief from her sister's death as well. Her pains diminished to the point that they were often barely noticeable, and she was able to tap gently with her feet on the floor when distressed by her current boss. I had a thank you note from her a few months later, sharing that her boss had been transferred to another department, which relieved her stress, but that her pains had completely stopped several weeks before her boss left.

I should add here that the dialogues above are abbreviated for this book entry. Two-chair discussions are often considerably more detailed. They may include intense exchanges and emotional releases concerning the issues in focus. The two-chair work alone may often clarify and resolve the issues that are raised.

With experience and practice, many people can do two-chair work on their own. However, the facilitation of a therapist can markedly enhance the process. A therapist will often be able to suggest issues and feelings to address, plus phrasing for stating these, that a person in the midst of the two-chair work might not think of.

Tapping works well in combination with two-chair work, as each facilitates the other. If dialogues do not suffice to resolve issues, tapping can then help to deal with the remaining feelings and conflicts. Two-chair work is also helpful when people have difficulty choosing whether to address an issue in one way or another, and when issues being addressed involve conflicts between the person tapping and others..

### *Reparenting ourselves through two-chair work*

Strong memories from our childhood often persist into adulthood. What we remember from being young creates a basic identity that in many ways defines who we are throughout the rest of our lives.

- If we had a happy childhood, we tend to be happy as adults, continuing into adulthood the joyful sense of self we experienced when we were young.

- If we experienced successes in play activities, school, and friendships as we were growing up, we usually continue to have these blessings in our lives as adults.
- If we were lonely, sad or depressed, or experienced serious losses as children, we will often carry into adulthood a collection of anxieties and expectations about being lonely, sad, and depressed that have become core aspects of our identities.
- If we experienced losses of people close to us when we were young, we may grow up with anticipations and anxieties of losing friends and/or family when we are adults.*[27]

In other words, whatever we learn to expect from life as children often persists into adulthood. These expectations are childhood memories that have come to define the character of what is commonly called our inner child. For the most part, we are unaware of our inner child. It is simply part of our life's perceptual, interpreting and operating systems that we take for granted.

These memories are usually perceived and experienced as factual, and therefore not capable of being changed – both by the person who holds the memories and by many psychotherapists. The conventional view is that memories are like video records, always reproducing whatever we experienced when we look back at these images.

Often, without our realizing it, our inner child sits at the driver's seat of our life. And it can cause us to drive through our life with serious impairments due to all the negative childhood experiences that left us with negative memories, beliefs and expectations, such as:

- No one could ever like me/ want to be close with me (because my parents never loved me).
- I can't make a good impression on people (because I was a poor student/ was too shy to speak out in public as a child/ was never part of the popular crowd in school)
- I'll never succeed in business (because I'm poor at selling my ideas/ poor with numbers/ don't make a good first impression)

These sorts of limiting beliefs keep us from doing the best we can do in life. It is generally felt that with such crippling beliefs, we'll never be able succeed. This is the bad news.

The good news is that this is not actually the case. Two-chair work combined with TWR/WHEE can enable us to identify our limiting and crippling inner child memories, beliefs and trauma residues, and then to change them in healing ways. This frees us from the shackles of disabling childhood residues.

Better yet, we can then install positive feelings, expectations and beliefs about ourselves to replace the negative ones we've released. This can be life-transforming.

✦ At 26, 'Joel' was a very frustrated librarian. He had a Master's degree in English literature but had found himself unable to pursue his chosen career of teaching in high school for several reasons. He couldn't tolerate the noisiness and boisterousness of his teenage students. Worse, yet, he was unable to control his class. His students gradually became more and more disrespectful and disruptive, to the point that teachers in adjacent classrooms were complaining of the noise and disruptive example that this was setting for their classes as well. His principal at first put this down to inexperience, but found that even with coaching, Joel was simply unable to assert the required discipline in his classes to be functional, or indeed tolerable in the school.

While being a librarian was quiet and unstressful, Joel was becoming increasingly bored and dissatisfied with his life. He came to me because his doctor had prescribed antidepressant medication, which he was very reluctant to take, and because he found himself increasingly depressed and didn't know what else could possibly help. Joel was very surprised when I suggested we might address his lack of assertiveness, but hesitantly agreed to explore how to do this.

It was no surprise that he was also frustrated in not having many friends, and in not being successful in dating. He was clearly an HSP who had grown up in a family of NHSPs, including three older brothers who were sports jocks, just like his parents were. They all lacked understanding of his sensitivities, were unaccepting of his preferences for the quiet of isolating in his room with a book or going out on solitary nature walks, and of his disinterest in anything athletic – despite their persistent efforts to encourage and engage him in countless sorts of sport activities. When he was young, they had tolerated this to some degree because he was the baby of the family. But as he grew up, they were less and less tolerant, and then became disparaging and critical. Their most frequent comment when he was upset was, "Why do you have to keep talking about having these upset feelings? Why don't you just swallow it down and move on?"

His parents at first were as critical as his brothers, but because he always got good academic grades, they were a bit less disparaging about his lack of interest in sports. But he couldn't remember their ever being solidly positive and accepting of him.

His experience in dating had been similarly a dismal failure. He was shy as a teenager to the point of blushing when around girls, and so unassertive that he found only a few girls who accepted his invitation to go out on a date. These were girls who were also quiet and unassertive, but who also turned out to be uninteresting to Jeff. When he got to university, and after he graduated and worked as a teacher and then as a librarian, he gave up any expectation of finding a satisfying date and didn't even approach women to go out with him.

He moved out of his unaccepting home as soon as he could, and lived a reclusive life, reading and watching films when he wasn't at work. He had minimal contact with his family other than occasional phone calls with his parents on holidays and birthdays. His cat was his principal companion.

Many conventional therapists would view a person like Joel as a questionable, or even as a poor candidate for individual therapy, as he pretty well knew what his difficulties were but was so strongly and habitually unassertive that there would be little expectation of achieving much of a change in him, even with assertiveness training or group therapy.

My assessment was different. I found Joel to be a pleasant, intelligent, well-read, caring HSP, despite his shyness, unassertiveness and lack of self-confidence. He was actually less depressed than I would have expected from the story he told of unremitting criticisms and rejections from his family throughout his life. I was able to tell him honestly that I actually felt he had done remarkably well to only be as modestly depressed as he was, considering the unacceptance and unremitting negativity he had suffered from his family all of his life.

I told Joel I understood how difficult it must have been for him to feel anything but bad about himself as he was growing up. I speculated from my several decades of being a therapist that I would expect that if most other HSPs had suffered what he'd been through, they would be even more depressed than he was. I speculated that he had far more inner strengths than he realized, but that they were being held back due to the traumas he had experienced from his family over so many years. I suggested we might explore a few sessions of talking therapy and he hesitantly agreed.

In his first session, I began by taking a thorough history. The major points he mentioned that I stored away for future reference included:

- Joel had a paternal grandmother whom he remembered as just loving and cuddling him when she visited for the winter holidays, as she read stories to him. This was the only unconditional love he could remember having received. He was very disappointed and sad when he was told she had gone to heaven, shortly before the winter holidays, when he was seven years old.
- He had several teachers throughout his school years whom he liked because they were good at sharing stories from literature and history, and recommended books he enjoyed reading.
- A neighbor's old cat that the family inherited when the neighbors moved away became Joel's close companion, but died just a few years after she arrived in their home.
- Joel had devastating, soul-despairing feelings when he thought of any of his immediate family members.

I then invited Joel to build an inner place of peace and safety and healing (PPSH), where he could begin to explore what it's like to feel more positive. His PPSH would also be there for him if he found himself in a depressed mood or funk. Joel's PPSH was by a pool at the base of a waterfall, where he had sat on several family holidays, watching the splashing water, with birds and an occasional raccoon coming to drink and bathe in the broad pool. We used tapping to strengthen the positivity of his PPSH. This was a surprising experience to Joel, who had had no idea it was possible to deliberately and effectively enhance mildly or modestly positive feelings and memories.

I suggested that Joel might explore what experiences and messages he was carrying in his memory from his childhood years, particularly focusing on doubts and discouragements about any prospects for success in getting along with other people and of being accepted by them. He agreed, though he was rather hesitant and skeptical that this would do anything for him other than making him more depressed. I suggested the two-chair approach, to facilitate his getting into this as deeply as possible.

Starting in his own chair (which I'll call number 1), he asked 'Little Joel' "What are some of your memories from childhood about getting along with people?"

Chair 2: "I liked when I was in a quiet place, like with mommy reading a book to me."

"I liked when Granny just held me and cuddled me and told me funny stories."

"I was soooo sad when Granny died!"

"I hated it when my brothers and father kept after me to practice throwing a baseball or a football with them."

Because the pressure to engage in sports was such a long-term, immensely irritating issue, I suggested that we focus first on this. I suggested he should shift to the chair 1, of 'Joel of today.' From this vantage point, I invited him to respond to Little Joel's distress over being pressured frequently to engage in sports activities.

Chair 1. That was a terrible bullying you suffered! They just wouldn't let up over this. They wanted you to be a jock like them. And they had no understanding or tolerance for your being different from them. And they went on, and on, and on, and on about it.

I invited Joel, non-verbally, to shift back to Chair 2.

Chair 2. I was so frustrated, I'd end up in tears. And then they'd call me a crybaby and other names. I'd just go to my room and cry into my pillow till I fell asleep.

I instructed Little Joel in using TWR/WHEE to release his feelings from the worst time he could remember this happening. He used the standard neutralizing statement, "I love and accept myself, wholly and completely" for several rounds and then added "and God loves and accepts me, wholly, completely and unconditionally." Including God noticeably enhanced his releases of negativity. He started with a SUDS of "about 200 on a scale of 10 being "the worst it could feel." With repeated rounds of tapping and affirmations over about 20 minutes, Little Joel reduced this to an 8, but it would not go any lower, even with tapping on the releasing spots and exploring meta-awarenesses.*[28]

Returning to connect with Joel of today, I invited Joel to identify his most frustrating and painful experiences of being rejected as an adult. Without hesitation, he came up with:

– Chair 1. Finding himself a failure at teaching because he wasn't strong enough to maintain discipline in his classes.
– Being turned down when he approached 'Theresa' for a date. She was a quiet, sensitive, intelligent volunteer library assistant to whom he was strongly attracted.

Tapping on his disappointment with Theresa, which started at a 9, Joel was able to reduce this to a 6 but no further. As we were at the end of his first session, and he had done so well, I suggested that he continue to tap at home on the issues he had begun to work on.

In his second session, Joel said he was pleased he was able to reduce the intensities of his Little Joel memories to 6 and of his dating frustrations to 5. I invited him to sit in Chair 1 and bundle the issues of Little Joel with the issues of Joel of Today that he had been working on and tap on both of these in the same round of TWR/WHEE. He was surprised to find each of the issues was reduced in one round of tapping to 4, and with further rounds of tapping they went all the way to 0.

Bundling current issues with similar, early-life issues, and tapping on both together markedly facilitates releases of both. This is true for NHSPs as well as for HSPs.

We then invited Little Joel to explore what positive memories from his childhood he'd like to strengthen. He chose to focus on how loved he felt when his grandmother held him and he would laugh about her stories. He said that this was the strongest he ever felt a total acceptance within his family. Little Joel rated these memories as a 10.

I suggested he could tap further on these, to see whether they might get stronger yet, because most people, and particularly traumatized ones, don't have any sense of how they could feel better than they did in their best memories. To his great surprise and pleasure, with just a few rounds of tapping, he was able to bring these up to a 28.

Surpassing a 10 in positive memories and feelings is quite common in most people who use EP, though many EFT and TFT practitioners are content to just stop after they've helped people release negativities.

We continued through three more weekly sessions and two monthly session to clear further negativities and install positivities.

The two-chair approach was particularly helpful to Joel in sorting out his anxieties about talking with women, useing the second chair for him to speak for Theresa to explore and clear his anxieties and then to explore speaking with her with positive expectations.

I was pleased to see Joel go on to date Theresa, and to continue his work with tapping and two-chair work on his issues as a teacher.

Some people are able to do two-chair work on their own, at home, when they need to clear inner child issues or to deal with other relationship challenges. Others are uncomfortable with this and find the help of a therapist essential for this sort of inner work. Joel was able to do much of this on his own, with occasional brief Skype consultations when he was hitting an impasse. He found work as a teacher in adult education, which he enjoyed enormously. Though he was fairly confident he could teach high school without his previous problems, he much preferred teaching mature students.

## 32. Neurolinguistic Programming (NLP): anchoring issues and discharging anchors

*Our bodies are apt to be our autobiographies.*
– Frank Gillette Burgess

Richard Bandler and John Grinder (1982) developed NLP in the 1970s. This is a detailed approach for assessing how people perceive their world and for bringing about deep, rapid changes in whatever bothers them.

*Anchoring* is the aspect of NLP I find most helpful and synergistic with the other approaches I recommend in this book. Anchoring demonstrates very clearly that the body participates in consciousness. You can readily experience this yourself.

1. Choose something you would like to feel better about. Focus your awareness on your thoughts and feelings about this issue.
2. Assess your SUDS level for how strongly you feel this negativity.
3. While focused on your issue, press with your index finger on the thigh of your left leg, holding the pressure for about 30 seconds while maintaining this focus.
4. Without moving your hand, release all pressure of your index finger and keep it poised above that spot you have pressed, so you can press again exactly on the same spot in a few moments.
5. Release your concentration from this negativity, taking a deep breath and releasing your breath as you do so.
6. With your right hand, press with your right index finger on your right thigh, as you focus your mind on your place of peace, safety and healing (PPSH) or on any other strongly positive memory and its associated positive feelings.
7. Keep your focus on this positivity, maintaining your pressure with your right index finger on that spot for about 30 seconds.
8. Release the pressure of your left index finger, without moving your hand, so you can press again exactly on the same spot. Release your focus on the positivity, taking a deep breath and let it go as you do so.
9. Press again on both spots simultaneously.
10. Check your SUDS again for how strong the negativity feels.

Almost always, the negativity intensity will go down. This gives you another way to decrease the intensity of bothersome thoughts and feelings.

This is another demonstration of your body participating in thoughts and feelings. It shows how negativity can link to the body and how it can be released.

## 33. Vibrational medicine

There are several varieties of treatments whose actions are based on biological energies. That is, their bioenergetic components are the effective aspects in their efficacy rather than their biochemical compositions, as in homeopathy and flower essences.**[29]

> *The idea that water has a memory can be refuted*
> *by any one of several easily understood, invalid, arguments.*
> — Brian Josephson

### Homeopathy

Homeopathy is a form of wholistic treatment that uses very dilute solutions of various substances in water to stimulate healing. For reasons yet to be explained, the more dilute the solutions are, the more potent the remedies are. Dilutions are used in which there can't even be a single molecule remaining in the remedy that is administered. It appears that the water has a memory and participates in the process of healing.

In initial sessions lasting 1–2 hours, homeopathic doctors take very detailed, broadly wholistic histories from the person being treated in order to determine the appropriate remedies. People with the same medical diagnosis are often prescribed different homeopathic remedies because the remedies are chosen according to the personality and life history of the patient, in addition to considering the particular clusters of symptoms related to the presenting problems in the individual being treated.

Despite the lack of explanation for the mechanisms of homeopathy within conventional scientific paradigms, research confirms it is an effective treatment for a variety of problems.

Homeopathy was developed by Samuel Hahnemann (1755-1843), a physician of German origin. Homeopathy appears similar to an immunization process. The body learns to deal with symptoms of an illness when it is given minute quantities of substances that produce symptoms in a healthy person that are similar to the symptoms of an illness.

A homeopathic evaluation begins with a very detailed, wholistic listing of your symptoms. These are organized according to personality types and diagnostic categories that make little sense in frameworks of conventional medicine. Homeopathic remedies are prescribed for syndromes, which are collections of symptoms, more often than for individual symptoms. These syndromes may include the presenting illness, personality factors in the patient, past traumas of a physical and/or emotional nature, relationships with others (particularly parents), patterns of likes and dislikes and much more. The syndromes are then organized into remedy symptom clusters.

The patient is not placed in a diagnostic box defined by the pathological or psychological causalities which are presumed to produce the illness according to conventional Western concepts of disease. For instance, symptoms like inertia or lack of will are viewed in allopathic medicine as defects of character or motivation. In homeopathy, these are approached as further aspects of disharmony, in addition to other, empirically derived symptom clusters for which specific remedies may be effective treatments.

Under the stimulus of these remedies, the body can learn to handle the symptoms competently instead of being overwhelmed by them as it had been previously. Oddly, this method is successful even when a person is currently suffering from the very same symptoms that are being treated. A clear example is found in the treatment of laboratory rats poisoned with lead. When given homeopathic microdoses of lead, the rats excreted greater amounts of lead in their urine than did untreated rats.

Homeopathic remedies are discovered and developed in two ways.

- In *conventional homeopathy*, various substances that might be therapeutic are given to healthy people in order to study their clinical effects. This process is termed 'proving'. The symptoms produced are then presumed to be treatable in ill people by giving them diluted solutions of these substances.
- *Intuitive homeopathy* relies on the clairsentient perceptions of highly sensitive individuals, who are able to intuitively assess the therapeutic properties of the substances.*[30]

*Homeopathic practice*

Homeopathic remedies are usually prepared by dissolving small amounts of a medication, mineral or allergen in a mixture of alcohol and water. Water may also be used alone, or it is sometimes mixed with other preservatives (especially for alcohol-intolerant patients).

Serial dilutions of 1/10 or 1/100 and greater are prepared, and then potentized by succussion (shaking). The solutions are identified by their degree of dilution. For example, the designation of 6c (or C6) means that the substance was diluted repeatedly 6 times by 1/10; 30c is diluted 30 times, etc. Dilutions of as little as one original volume per million (1M) are available. In contrast with conventional medications, the greater the homeopathic dilution, the greater the potency of the homeopathic remedy. It is generally accepted that homeopathic remedies are effective through biological energy fields rather than through chemical effects.*[31]

Clinical studies (Boyd, 1946) and laboratory tests)[32] demonstrated that a succussed remedy was effective, whereas an unsuccussed one was not. Another unusual observation is that loss of potency in aging solutions can be reversed by repeated succussion (Jones & Jenkins, 1981).

Potency can be demonstrated in remedies that are so dilute that they could not contain even a single molecule of the original substance.[33] Studies using nuclear magnetic resonance have also shown characteristics specific to the homeopathic remedies (T. Young, 1975).

Homeopathy was widely used to treat infections prior to the discovery of antibiotics,[34] and a recent report confirms that homeopathy can indeed help decrease epidemics (van der Zee, 2018).

It is of historical interest that the practice of Hahnemann's homeopathy originally spread rapidly in Europe, the US, Asia and South America. It was credited with more than halving the mortality rate from cholera in London in 1854 and from yellow fever when used during a US epidemic in 1878. It was very popular and widely used in the US till the early 1900's.

There were 22 homeopathic medical schools and over 100 homeopathic hospitals in the US prior to the publication of the Flexner Report in 1910. This report, which was promoted through lobbying by medical doctors, established guidelines for funding allopathic medical schools and led to a rapid decline in the practice of homeopathy, almost to the point of its disappearance in the US. (Naturopathic medical treatment met the same fate.) In Great Britain, the practice of homeopathy was also much reduced but not eliminated. Five homeopathic hospitals remain today and the Royal Family's support of homeopathy has helped to encourage its use.

In recent years, clinical research demonstrating the efficacy of homeopathy has helped bring about a resurgence in its popularity in the US, Europe, Asia and Latin America. Several American states have homeopathic licensing boards for physicians.

Here are some case examples to illustrate how homeopathy is prescribed for a specific issue in particular people.[35]

✦ 'Patricia' was an intense, talkative, passionate person who was very jealous and frequently angry and sarcastic with her partner. She had a history of migraines, pharyngitis, tonsillitis and colitis. She hated having anything tight around her throat. She frequently woke with a feeling of being suffocated at night, especially as she was falling asleep. She came for help because her premenstrual symptoms (irritability, jealousy, depression, headache, hot flushes) had become increasingly intrusive irritants and were threatening her relationship. She also mentioned in passing that she always had diarrhea before her periods.

Patricia's homeopath recognized that this pattern of symptoms points to the remedy Lachesis (a snake venom remedy), which has among its profile of indications the following items that appeared to fit Patricia's profile:

*Mental* – Passionate, intense people; jealousy; talkative, anger, sarcasm.

*Head* – Migraine headaches.

*Throat* – Pharyngitis; tonsillitis; Intolerance to tight collars, turtlenecks, necklaces.

*Gastrointestinal* – Colitis; diarrhea before menses.

*Urogenital* – Premenstrual syndrome, including irritable, jealous, depressed, headache, flushes of heat.

*Chest* – Wakes with a suffocating feeling at night, especially on falling asleep.

Patricia was given one dose of 200C Lachesis. When she came back for her next appointment in a month, she reported that her premenstrual symptoms just didn't happen that month and that oddly, she also did not have diarrhea before her period. Upon inquiry, she also noted that she was waking much less rarely with that old feeling of suffocation and that she just wasn't feeling as jealous anymore.

While such combinations of symptoms as a treatable entity appear strange within conventional medicine, this is not a reason to reject homeopathy. It is, rather, a criticism of the narrowness and exclusivity of conventional medical thinking and practice.

✦ A 9-year old boy named 'Johnny' was brought to the homeopath by his mother for being disruptive in school – humming and singing, getting out of his seat, standing on his chair, not paying attention to his teacher and staring out the window for long periods of time. He lacked motivation, disliked schoolwork and refused to do homework. At home he was messy and disorganized, never shared toys with others and was unfriendly with his peers. His mother reported that if he read a problem from a book he would be unable to do it, but when he heard the problem spoken by someone he could solve it correctly. Surprisingly, he was still getting good grades at school. The presumptive diagnosis was that he had an attention deficit hyperactivity disorder (ADHD).

The boy was never angry, had no strong cravings and would eat whatever his mother fixed. His mother felt that he was abnormal because nothing seemed to excite him.

In the homeopathic interview, Johnny was cooperative and pleasant but seemed distracted and only partly present. However, when describing his best friend, he became quite animated. His mother was astounded by this. She reported that the truth was, "Aside from seeing that boy in church, he has played with him only once in the whole year."

His mother had had no difficulties with the pregnancy or delivery, but she had smoked marijuana for 11 years and had stopped only when she learned that she was pregnant.

Homeopathic Cannabis indica (marijuana) in a single, very potent (1M) dose was prescribed because of the history of cannabis use by the boy's mother in very early pregnancy, combined with his present time-perception distortions and general 'spaciness.' (The basic homeopathic principle holds that the correct homeopathic prescription should be for a substance which produces symptoms similar to those exhibited by the patient.) Within a month, Johnny's ability to focus improved dramatically, he did homework without reminders, and showed enthusiasm for particular foods.

Over the course of a year his behavior remained improved, but then it began to deteriorate. Once again, he was not completing his work and he seemed less motivated. Another single 1M dose was given, resulting in a renewed remission of his symptoms.[36]

The art of homeopathy is to select key factors that are responsive to interventions of this sort. Other homeopaths might have prescribed different remedies, addressing different constellations of factors. A good homeopath will have an encyclopedic knowledge of the clusters of effects of various substances, so that the remedies can be matched to the symptom clusters of the patient. Computer programs can be a great help in suggesting remedies, as it is impossible for any one person to know the entire homeopathic pharmacopoeia.

✦ Homeopathy can be a very intricate art, as illustrated in the next case, in which the symptom complex addressed by the remedy, Calcium Carbonate. This includes physical, psychological, biological energies and metaphoric patterns. The late Edward Whitmont (1993, p., 74) beautifully illustrates the blending of symptom, substance and symbols in the clinical case of a man of about 40, whom I will call 'Henry,' who suffered from acne. After taking a detailed history, Whitmont prescribed a single dose of calcium carbonate (extracted from oyster shells) at a dilution of C1,000. This produced temporary spasms of the finger muscles, similar to tetany. This is a typical symptom of parathyroid gland dysfunction, which would produce lower blood calcium levels.

The spasms evoked memories from Henry's childhood, when his mother had taped his fingers to his bedside in a position that resembled the position people had with spasms experienced from the homeopathic remedy calcium carbonate. His mother had done this to prevent him from masturbating. During the treatment with this remedy, vivid memories arose in Henry of his anger and shame connected with this experience. As a child he had completely repressed these memories in his unconscious mind. This somehow was translated into his skin condition and a boisterous personality. With the release of these memories, the spasms in his fingers also released and this healing process furthered his progress in psychotherapy.

"...Shame, anger, finger spasm, parathyroid hormonal activity, calcium metabolism, the dynamic field of the oyster (in homeopathic practice the "personality of the *Calc. Carb.* Type can be likened to an oversensitive but heavily defended person, akin to an oyster without or with too thick a shell) and the functioning of the skin all appear here as different transduction codes of one and the same dynamic field process." (Whitmont, 1993, p. 74-75)

As Whitmont (1980; 1993) eloquently points out in his marvelous wholistic books on homeopathy, it may be impossible to clarify many of the complexities of linked energetic and imagery components that produce these effects. Every remedy has its particular spectrum of effects – its 'personality.' When a person has a cluster of symptoms and personality traits that match those of a particular remedy, then that remedy can effect a clearing of those symptoms and it may also alter the accompanying personality traits. The art and challenge of the practice of homeopathy is to ask the right questions in order to identify the relevant symptom clusters. If the homeopath did not ask the patient about specific related symptoms, many of which might not be at all obvious or likely to be reported spontaneously, the best remedy could easily be missed.

*Homeopathic research*

Clinical research on homeopathy for humans is complicated by the fact that the remedies are prescribed on an individualized basis for each person. Although two people may have the identical medical diagnosis, such as a streptococcal sore throat, each might expect to receive a different homeopathic medication, which would be determined by their symptoms, personalities and life experiences. In contrast, conventional medicine usually prescribes the same medications for all patients with a given diagnosis. Despite these difficulties, some homeopathic research has managed to conform to the requirements of randomized controlled studies.

The majority of comparative reviews of series of such controlled trials conclude that significant clinical efficacy for homeopathic remedies has been demonstrated, although three critical reviews conclude that there is only limited evidence for clinical efficacy. One of the most carefully designed is by David Taylor-Reilly, et al. (1986), which shows a 50% reduction in the need for antihistamine medication in the treatment of hay fever.

Other studies following standard, conventional medical research protocols have shown significant effects of homeopathy in treating arthritis; asthma; Attention Deficit Hyperactivity Disorder; influenza; and childhood diarrhea. This is actually remarkable, because the standard research protocol that prescribes the same dose of homeopathic medication for every patient is completely contrary to basic homeopathic practice. Other studies of series of cases in which individualized homeopathy was prescribed confirm that homeopathy can prevent infectious diseases.

The principles of homeopathy may also be relevant to other areas of medicine. A rigorous meta-analysis was made of 135 studies on the protection of various organisms from poisoning by environmental toxins, using homeopathic dilutions of 30 or greater (Linde, et al., 1997). This meta-analysis included studies of animals (70%), plants (22%), isolated organs (5%), and cell and embryo cultures (3%). Of the 26 studies that met the reviewers' stringent criteria for design and reporting, 70% showed positive effects.

So-called 'skeptics' of CAM regularly dismiss homeopathy as no more than a placebo, based on the fact that homeopathic remedies are given in very dilute solutions, and that the claim is made that the more dilute they are the more potent are their effects. I have never seen such 'skeptics' cite research of this quality!

The above-mentioned research clearly just begins to scratch the surface of the many mysteries of energy healing. As we accept, study and use it more widely, we have vast potentials to transform our understandings of the world when we.

*Self-help with homeopathy*

Self-treatment with homeopathy is very common. Arnica is probably the most popular remedy for self-help, commonly used in oral and topical forms for alleviation of pains, swelling, stiffness and other symptoms following physical trauma. I have personally experienced these benefits following injuries from falls, scrapes and random blunt and sharp traumas. And here are a few more, from lists of thousands that are available:

Aconite – for anxiety, fear and psychological shock

Apis – hives, insect bites or stings

Aurum – depression, headaches and angina

Belladonna – fever, headaches and migraines, menstrual pain

Hypericum/ St. John's Wort –depression

Lithium – depression

Lycopodium – fear of failing, fears of changes in life

Nux vomica – anxieties, bottled up emotions, chronic indigestion

Urtica – pains of burns and rheumatoid arthritis

Consultation with a homeopath will greatly broaden the spectrum of homeopathic remedies you may be able to use on your own.

Health food stores carry many common remedies in lower potencies as well as books on homeopathy for the layperson. However, while people can benefit from particular over-the-counter remedies for many of their problems, these preparations may easily miss the mark with more serious, complex or chronic problems, as would a prescription from a therapist who does not have a very thorough training in homeopathy. Computers may be a great help in identifying symptom clusters and potentially relevant remedies.

HSPs are fortunate because they are sensitive to the subtle bioenergies of homeopathy. There are the added benefits of responsiveness on all levels of the wholistic spectrum, and not only in physical symptom or illness relief.

Intuitive prescription of homeopathic remedies, in which the therapists allow their unconscious mind and intuitive powers to scan the careseeker and their life circumstances for relevant details, may offer distinct advantages in selecting the best remedies from amongst the thousands that are available. Similarly, muscle testing and other intuitive approaches may be used for self-help to identify appropriate remedies. Here, the gifts of the intuitive are crucial to the outcomes.*[37]

## Flower Essences

> *To see a world in a grain of sand*
> *And a heaven in a wild flower*
> *Hold infinity in the palm of your hand*
> *And eternity in an hour.*
> – William Blake

Early in the 20th Century, Edward Bach, a Harley Street physician in London, identified 38 flowers whose essences have curative powers. The essences from these flowers are prepared in much the same way as homeopathic remedies, except that they are not shaken and cannot be diluted more than a few times before they lose their potency.

There are two methods that are used to identify applications for flower essences. The first is through clinical testing on healthy people and on patients with physical and psychological problems. The second relies on the intuitive perceptions of gifted sensitives who are able to identify medicinal properties of plants clairsentiently.[38]

The flower remedies are intended to correct disharmonies between the personality and the higher self and soul. Flower essences are widely used and are available over the counter.

*Rescue Remedy*, a combination of several Bach flower essences, is a popular treatment for stress and trauma and is available in drops or as a topical cream. This preparation can be a good personal introduction to the efficacy of flower remedies. Taken orally, it calms anxiety and panic, counteracts emotional and physical shock, reduces pain and swelling following injuries and more. Applied topically it reduces the pain, swelling and blistering of burns and other injuries.

✦ An example of a family cat, 'Sweetie,' illustrates the effectiveness of this remedy. One day, a stray cat settled into the neighborhood. It bullied Sweetie in the back yard and even came in through the cat-flap at night, got into fights with Sweetie and had the audacity to spray all over the CD rack! Sweetie was traumatized by the intrusions and became very anxious and clinging. For two days she would not separate from her owners other than to relieve herself in very brief trips outside. She was constantly tripping up the family in the kitchen, to the point where she was getting stepped on and they were in danger of falling over her. They decided to give her some Rescue Remedy. After one dose, her behavior changed dramatically. Sweetie became calmer, stopped clinging to the family and went outside in a manner more like her usual behavior. She needed several doses daily over a period of several weeks until her responses to the stray were completely resolved.

In the past few years many new flower essences have been developed, based on plants from several continents. In addition, various gem and mineral essences have also been developed.[39]

There are helpful books that detail the indications for many of the flower essences. When the flower essence therapist recommends a remedy it is often helpful to have clients read the descriptions of the therapeutic indications and anticipated results, in order to develop their cognitive insight about their problems, which can then enhance their responses to the essences.

Flower essences may also be prescribed intuitively in cooperation with the client. The therapist will take a history and recommend essences on the basis of their known therapeutic efficacy, and will also use intuition to select additional essences that feel appropriate. In addition, clients may be encouraged to pick essences for which they sense a particular affinity. While this may seem unusual in terms of conventional practice, several factors recommend this approach. First, there are no known negative side effects of these essences so there is no risk involved. They either are beneficial or produce no apparent effects, Second, there may be subtle reasons for taking certain essences that are not apparent to logic or forethought.

'Skeptics' often criticize such practices, saying that the benefits claimed for flower essences are due to nothing more than suggestion. However, I believe that suggestion is an excellent adjunct to any therapy and can enhance people's responses to treatments of all sorts. The fact that suggestion may be present does not rule out the possibility that a treatment is also effective in and of itself.

My impression is that the essences represent far more than chemicals that interact with the physical body. Their actions, like those of homeopathic remedies, appear to be due to patterning of flower bioenergies in the solution used to make them. In the realms of energy medicine, the flower essences appear to have strongest effects at the psychological and spiritual ends of the continuum of wholistic interventions.

Steve Johnson, who developed the Alaskan flower essences, observes:

"Flower essences catalyze evolution in consciousness. They help us identify emotional and mental qualities within that need to be awakened or strengthened and stimulate our spiritual growth, which is the ongoing process of grounding our spiritual selves into our physical bodies."

Flower essences are unique in that they are a source of intelligent healing energy that is available to both empower and educate the person taking them. They are empowering because they do not do our healing work for us, but with us – they are powerful catalysts for growth and change but they respect our free will...

The gift of the plant kingdom is spiritual consciousness. Flowers are the most evolved part of this kingdom and carry positive, life-affirming patterns of conscious energy. These patterns originate in the higher dimensions and are expressed into our physical world through the specific form of each plant... (p. 5)

*Help for HSPs with flower essences*

I've been very impressed that the sensitivities of HSPs is a tremendous asset to them in being able to benefit from flower essences. Not only are the healing properties of the essences helpful for the presenting physical and psychological problems, but also for the rest of the wholistic spectrum of issues associated with the primary problems. I've seen many NHSPCs respond well to the flower remedies too. And again, the gentleness of flower essences relative to the problems of side effects and lethal effects of conventional medical treatments can be important to HSPs – who may be more sensitive to the negative effects of conventional medications than the average person.

# 34. Acupuncture

*Acupuncture is a jab well done.*
— Anonymous

Acupuncture is based on ancient Chinese observations of subtle biological energy (bioenergy) lines called meridians that run between the head and the hands and feet. This energy is called qi (pronounced kee or chee).**[40] Each meridian is related to one or more of the physical organ systems, and diseases are caused by excesses or deficits of energy, or blockage of energy flow in the meridians. Points of special sensitivity exist along the entire length of each energy line. Stimulation of these acupuncture points can influence the related organ systems by altering bioenergy flow in the meridians. The acupuncturist can stimulate the acupuncture points in several ways: by inserting needles, applying finger pressure, burning moxa herbs with the stalks held against the acupuncture points, applying mild electrical current, laser light, or through mental projection of healing to the points.

Some meridians correspond to physical organs (e.g. heart, lungs), while others are correlated with functions for which allopathic medicine has no exact parallels (e.g. the 'triple warmer'). The triple warmer is a body system that is named but poorly defined. It is that aspect of the body which controls the water-regulating organs (kidney, stomach, small and large intestine, spleen and bladder). The upper warmer governs the head and chest; the middle warmer the spleen and stomach; and the lower warmer the liver and kidneys.

Even where physical organs correspond with specific lines, the meridian reference is to energy functions of the line more than to its body functions (per Western physiology). For instance, a Chinese acupuncturist who speaks of the kidney meridian may be referring to its role in storing life energy ('jing'); to its influence on development, maturation and or reproduction; to its effects on marrow, bones and teeth; or to its interactions with respiration.

The various meridians have specific times of day when they are more and less active. Treatments may therefore be given for specific problems at particular times, even at unusual hours of the night.

Other bioenergy centers in the body that have been identified by Chinese medicine are called chakras (Sanskrit for wheels).**[41] There are many chakras around the body, but the seven major ones that are along the central axis of the body are the most important. They project as vortices of energy to the front and back of the body, as well as upwards and downwards.*[42]

For many years, allopathic medicine maintained a very skeptical or even dismissive attitude towards Eastern explanations of acupuncture because no anatomical structures were known that support Eastern theories of energy lines traversing the body. The meridians do not correspond in any way to the well-mapped peripheral or autonomic nervous system and until recently no other communication network in the body had been demonstrated that could support such theories. It seemed patently ridiculous to Westerners that needles inserted at acupuncture points on the foot or arm could influence lungs or heart or other organs at considerable distances from the sites of treatment. It was presumed that acupuncture treatments were effective purely on the basis of placebo responses or other aspects of suggestion. Yet many acupuncturists claim that they can sense acupuncture points with their fingers and others claim that they can manually detect when the meridians have a proper flow of Qi or are blocked. A few sensitives who see auras also report they can see acupuncture meridians and acupuncture points.

In addition to treatment by acupuncture, Chinese medicine also recommends self-healing through various movement and imagery exercises focused on facilitating bioenergy flow. Roger Jahnke explains that there are three states of Qi: 'jing,' related to earth energies; 'Qi,' related to life energies; and 'shen,' related to spiritual dimensions. People are seen to be an intimate part of the world around them. Energies within the body interact with and resonate with energies of the environment and of the worlds of spirit.

### *Western scientific acupuncture research*

Western science has found scientific confirmation of the existence of acupuncture points and meridians. Numerous studies have shown that acupuncture points have a much lower electrical resistance than surrounding areas of the skin. This difference is on the order of a few thousand ohms at acupuncture points, compared to millions of ohms anywhere else on the skin. Simple resistance meters are now in common use to confirm the locations of acupuncture points. These measurements are variable within short periods of time, particularly in respect to the width of individual points, but also to some extend in their locations. It seems that this variability reflects shifting energetic states in the organism rather than inaccuracies in the measurements.

Clinical studies have demonstrated correlations between predicted bioelectrical changes on various meridians and the activity of the organs traditionally associated with those meridians. For instance, conductance was found to measure nearly 20 times higher at the Liver 8 acupuncture point (located at the knee) in people with demonstrated liver disease (acute hepatitis or cirrhosis), as compared with a control group who had no liver disease. People with lung disease that had been verified with chest X-rays demonstrated 30% lower electrical conductance at acupuncture lung points.**[43]

Research on clinical benefits of acupuncture presented distinct difficulties. It was difficult at first to design acupuncture studies that conform to Western research protocols because Eastern methods of diagnosis and treatment differ substantially from those used in the West. Traditional acupuncture individualizes treatments to each person, and therefore does not lend itself to randomized controlled studies that require a standard treatment for each member of a group of subjects with the same diagnosis. Another challenge is in providing a control group. Some studies have accommodated the requirement for applying a standard treatment to subjects who share a Western medical diagnosis, and have used control subjects who receive sham acupuncture, with needles inserted at points that are not known to produce beneficial effects.**[44]

One of the best-known uses of acupuncture is in the treatment of pain. Studies have demonstrated its efficacy as a remedy for tension headaches; migraines; facial pain; dental pain; neck pain; back pain; lumbar disk protrusion; tennis elbow; osteoarthritis; renal colic; dysmenorrhea; fibromyalgia; peripheral nerve pain; knee injuries; and chronic pains of various sorts.

Another well publicized use of acupuncture is for medical and surgical procedures, with control of pain and discomforts of gastroscopy and colonoscopy, and for postoperative pain following lower abdominal surgery in women.

While individual studies may produce only modest results, a series of studies analyzed as a group provides more substantial proof. One such meta-analysis of acupuncture studies confirms that it is an effective treatment for chronic pain. Another meta-analysis was made of 14 randomized controlled studies of acupuncture for chronic pain. Pooled results according to the location of pains, the type of study, and the type of journal publishing the data showed statistically significant effects.

Studies have shown significant relief of nausea and vomiting with acupuncture after surgical anesthesia, chemotherapy, morning sickness during pregnancy, and motion sickness.

One extraordinary though little recognized contribution of acupuncture is in the treatment of strokes. Significant effects have been reported in improving muscle strength in leg and arm paralysis. Walking and balancing abilities were improved, activities of daily living (ADL) scores were higher, and days in hospital and nursing homes were halved. When treatment was started within 36 hours of the onset of the strokes, those whose condition was poorer at the start of the study showed significant improvements in neurological functions and ADL scores, while those with better initial conditions showed no significant benefits from acupuncture.

Wide varieties of other problems have also been reported to respond to acupuncture treatments.**[45]

A word of caution here to do your best to find an acupuncturist who is well recommended by people whose experience and judgment you trust, since acupuncture treatments vary with the natural skills, education and experience of the therapist.

*Help for HSPs with acupuncture*

HSPs often have the good fortune of being sensitive to acupuncture. This also makes it more likely that self-treatments with finger pressure on acupressure points can be available as needed.

In addition, the Energy Psychology systems of EFT, TFT and related therapies are available for self-treatment of psychological problems.*[46]

## 35. 12-step programs

> *The greatest mistake you can make in life is to continually be afraid you will make one.*
> – Elbert Hubbard

Where alcohol or drug habits are issues, 12-step programs can be enormously helpful to both HSPs and HSPCs. Cravings are a great challenge to deal with. Alcohol and drugs provide immediate calming of anxieties. This is such a quick relief that many people end up hooked on using these substances for stress relief. At that point, the substance itself often becomes a problem. With continued use, the physical and psychological responses to alcohol and drugs is lessened, so higher doses are needed in order to achieve the same effects. Addiction to alcohol and drugs can be very challenging to deal with!!!

Conventional therapies have had very modest success in helping people with addictions. Conventional medicine, for the most part, prescribes medications for anxiety, depression, pain, sleep and more. Most of these drugs have side effects that are troublesome, particularly weight gain, mental fuzziness and drowsiness. They also can intensify the effects of the alcohol and addicting drugs. They can also cause fatalities due to overdoses, interactive and inherently toxic effects of the medications.

Alcoholics Anonymous (AA) and Narcotics Anonymous (NA) bring together groups of people who are working on their addiction issues, focusing on being sober one day at a time. When someone joins a group, they get to ask a member they feel comfortable with to be their sponsor. Sponsors are usually members who have been participating for at least a year. Sometimes the group as a whole is the sponsor. Ideally, the sponsor is always available for support and to answer questions. Humans being who we are, it is good to have at least one backup person or phone number for support if you are feeling stressed and cannot reach your sponsor.

The 12 steps are headers for issues, attitudes, resolutions and behaviors that have been found to benefit alcoholics and drug addicts. They were created around 1940.

- Step 1: I realize that willpower has not worked to stop my dysfunctional behaviors... and continuing to do what does not work is the definition of insanity.
- Step 2: Willpower does not work because my dysfunctional behaviors come from fear and pressure. I need safety and support to overcome that.
- Step 3: I don't have to live in fear and shame. I will strive to find safety and support in connection rather than isolation.
- Step 4: I resolve to systematically face my fears in order to remove what is in the way of my finding safety, support and trust in life.
- Step 5: As I gain a compassionate understanding of my actions, I am better able to take responsibility for them.
- Step 6: I no longer identify with my knee-jerk reactions, because I know they're based in fear, not a deep sense of who I am and what I want.
- Step 7: Moment by moment, I strive to find my motivation in a deeper sense of who I really am, rather than fear and defensiveness.
- Step 8: I stop blaming and feeling blamed, with a willingness to heal the wounds.
- Step 9: I swallow my pride, and sincerely apologize to people I've hurt, except when this would be counterproductive.

- Step 10: I live mindfully, paying attention to the motives and effects of my actions.
- Step 11: I stay in touch with a broader sense of who I really am, and a deeper sense of what I really want.
- Step 12: A growing sense of wholeness and contentment motivates me to keep at it, and to share this process with others who are strugglin (Proactive 12 Steps, web ref).

Initially. it is recommended that you attend a meeting every day, so that you don't get tempted or troubled into drinking or using drugs. Gradually, most people find they need less frequent meetings.

At meetings, people speak about their issues in front of the whole group. The group listens without criticisms but with encouragements. Some meetings are open to anyone who is interested to attend, including people who are scouting for a group to join or curious to understand the 12-step programs. Other meetings are for members only and closed to any outsiders.

Al-Anon groups have meetings for people who have family members or friends with addictions. These are mutual support groups. They are enormously helpful to relatives and friends of addicts because it is often very, very challenging and stressful to be a support to someone who is struggling with addiction. Anonymity for participants is the rule. You don't even have to give your name when you speak. You can also 'pass' and remain silent, just listening to experiences of others. No one presumes to have answers to anyone else's issues. To help, people may share similar experiences of their own and how they cope with them, with the full understanding that each person's addiction is their own to sort out.

Groups may vary enormously, depending on the participants. Many individuals and some groups as a whole are strongly opposed to using medications, feeling that a drug is a drug and that people need to learn to stand on their own feet without any crutches. Acceptance of psychotherapy also varies between groups. In some you can find recommendations to particularly helpful therapists, while in others your mention of seeking or being in therapy may be met with other members' stories of therapy disappointments and failures, or with criticisms that therapy is a crutch just like drugs and alcohol are, and that most therapists don't really understand addiction because they haven't experienced it.

If you attend a meeting and don't find it helpful, check out one or more other groups. A solidly good sponsor will make a group worth attending. But the meetings are usually enormously helpful and worth attending because you will have the benefits of many people's experiences and advice, both negative and positive, and will find many gems of information, understanding and support from your group. You may also choose to attend several different groups, drawing on the particular strengths of each one.

You will find enormous support in 12-step groups. Being with people who have struggled and are still challenged with issues similar to your own helps you because you realize you are not alone. Hearing others' stories gives you perspectives on how traumas and addictions develop, varieties of ways that people respond to them, and ways to deal with them more constructively. You will find comfort in knowing that relapses are common in addicts and there are many ways to deal with these. You know you are getting into a place of substantial recovery when you begin to see newer group members who are struggling with issues you have learned to deal with in better ways.**[47]

Al-Anon groups for partners/ spouses and families of addicts are also enormously helpful.

There are other addictions that may require help to overcome, such as sexual addiction, gambling, eating, video games and data collection addictions. These are generally treated by psychotherapists. Many of these respond well to TWR/WHEE and other EP. The self-help of EP is enormously beneficial in dealing with addictions because it is immediately available and potently effective.

### Benefits of 12-step programs for HSPs and HSPCs

The 12– step programs can be tremendously supportive for HSPs and HSPCs where addictions are an issue – in themselves, in family, a partner or friend. Addictions place enormous strains on relationships.

HSPs often don't tolerate alcohol or drugs well, but with gradual use can build up to habits and addictions. As with NHSPs with drink and drug habits, there are often serious traumas earlier in life contributing to these habits. HSPs in recovery often make excellent sponsors, being sensitive to and understanding the issues of others. They may have a challenging time finding a group that doesn't have negative energies making it difficult for them to attend a whole meeting. TWR/WHEE is outstanding in dealing with such discomforts, in addition to lessening cravings and trauma responses.

The addict is likely to be a very different person when drinking or using drugs that dull the conscious mind. Feelings often come out, especially related to disappointments, poor self-esteem, traumas, moods, angers and vulnerabilities. Under the influence of alcohol or other substances, people become disinhibited and may often say and do unpleasant and hurtful things. They are often insensitive to others, even those with whom they are close and considerate when they are sober and clean. Further stresses are generated by hangovers, neglected responsibilities, missed work, financial stresses, blackouts (blanking out of memories) – including for negative behaviors and words. With repeated bouts of drinking and drug relapses, trust and positive feelings are eroded.

Energy Psychology (EP) methods can offer enormous benefits to addicts. EP tends to be well accepted because these are self-treatment methods, so that people learn better to stand on their own, to face and deal with their issues, and to trust themselves. These are cornerstones of 12-step teachings. I've seen wonderful synergies when EP methods are combined with the 12-step programs.

Here, too, the fact that TWR/WHEE can be used discretely can be a serious advantage in many situations. Also, the simplicity of left and right tapping makes TWR/WHEE very user-friendly.

With regular uses of these methods, a craving can become a friend rather than an enemy. A craving is a warning light on your inner dashboard, alerting you to feelings, memories and traumas that are being triggered. EP methods give you the tools to clear these issues. Better yet, they can also give you tools for building positivity after you have dealt with the negativity. Similarly, resourcing yourself with a place of peace and safety and healing (PPSH) can be enormously helpful.

And here I add that addictions are very often associated with psychological issues, particularly depression and traumas. These very often need to be addressed if the addict is to deal successfully with the cravings and using that bring them to the 12-step programs.

## 36. Family constellations awarenesses and therapy

> *Children are happy when their parents' love for them
> is also the parents' love for each other in the children.
> Children feel happiest when they experience their parents as a
> couple, and in that situation, they can find comfort and order.*
> — Bert Hellinger

We considered above how marital/ couple and family therapy can help when there are disharmonies between couples and within families. There are also deeper wholistic relationships at play in families that can be helpful for us to identify and address. Patterns of relationships and behaviors between ourselves and others are often influenced by residues of conflicts and traumas that shaped and scarred various individuals within our extended family, with secondary impacts on other members of the family.

Although it may seem like there was no direct connection between the currently symptomatic family member and the traumatized family member(s), on energetic and spiritual levels these connections very often exist and may perpetuate the effects of the trauma through numbers of generations.

Conventional family therapy addresses how these issues express themselves within current couples' and families' attitudes, behaviors and interactions.[48] Family constellation therapy extends ordinary family therapy into the collective consciousness of the family.[49] Family constellation therapy clearly confirms the existence of a collective consciousness. It demonstrates some of the ways that collective consciousness can function, both in carrying trauma residues through various family relatives and in healing and clearing them.

Family constellation therapy is done in workshop groups, where participants take turns in staging their family relationships with the help of the others in the workshop, under the guidance of the therapist. I use the label, 'workshop initiator' (my own term) for the focus person whose family relationships are being staged and explored. Selected workshop participants are chosen by the initiator to represent key living and deceased people in her family. These chosen family representatives have no direct knowledge of any sort about the family members they are representing.

Amazingly, each participant intuitively senses what the emotional attachments and feelings are of the family members they are representing. In most cases, the feelings they express are validated by the initiator. In many cases, they also reveal emotions, beliefs and insights about the relationships between the family members. These are surprising, instructive and healing to the person whose family is being staged.

Family constellation therapy addresses the collective consciousness of a family, as manifested in the lives of individual family members. Manifestations of symptoms whose roots were generated in individuals by stresses and traumas in other members of the family, often from previous generations, may include:

– Physical symptoms such as pains in particular parts of the body of another family member

– Emotions such as depression, fears or anger that originate from unresolved issues in previous generations

– Addictions, obesity, eating disorders and other issues where co-dependency is often a factor

- Tensions or conflicts between individuals in one generation that reflect residual, unresolved conflicts from previous generations; and more

Benefits of family constellation therapy may include:

- Family issues may manifest as a symptom or disease in a particular family member. The workshop constellation may reveal past traumas and current tensions between family members that have generated the physical problems, and this process may facilitate a clearing of the problems.
- Many of the challenges people experience in their lives derive from relationship entanglements that children experience in their families as they are growing up. These can be identified and cleared.

The clarifications of family issues that are experienced in constellation therapy are best left to bring about their effects without analyses and dissections within the group – unlike other therapies, where people discuss the issues in order to come to conscious understandings of the issues.

Michael Reddy (2012), a family constellation therapist, shares the following example (among many others) of how a symptom that defied medical diagnosis or treatment could be cleared by this method.

✦ 'Don' participated in a family constellation group, wanting help with migraines that were not responding to conventional treatments and were interfering in his work. He set up volunteers from the group to represent himself, his father, and paternal grandparents. Reddy asked whether there had been any deaths in the family. Don replied that his father's younger brother, 'Sam', had suffered a fatal concussion and died at age four after falling through a bannister railing in his parents' home. Don's grandmother blamed his grandfather for the death because he had known about the weak bannister strut but had not fixed it. Grandfather blamed grandmother for not watching their grandson properly. They had barely spoken to each other in the intervening years.

Volunteers from the group represented Don, his father, the grandparents and his deceased uncle. Invited to place themselves where it felt right, the grandparents stood off to the side, facing away from each other. Don's dead uncle lay motionless on the floor. Don knelt on the floor, looking sadly at his dead uncle. His father stood between the grandparents and Don, looking at Don.

Reddy invited each representative to share their feelings. He then invited grandfather to look at Don, asking the grandfather if he didn't want to see Don suffering less. The grandfather agreed he really would like that. Gradually, the grandparents came to face each other, and then came near to Don to comfort him. Reddy pointed out to Don that it was his uncle who had had the concussion, and that Don didn't need to suffer headaches any more in order to express the frozen, buried grief of his grandparents.

Following these interventions in the group, the real Don's migraines ceased.

This is a fairly typical example of changes that can occur in these groups. I've participated as a group member in several dozens of such sessions. There has rarely been a constellation that was not productive, and most were eye-opening in the accuracy of the impressions of the family representatives, as confirmed by the initiators. They perceived feelings, aspects of relationships, traumas and more – without having been given any details or clues that would have led them to deduce these fine details through logic or educated guesses.

The lessons from family constellation therapy groups are profound on many levels.
- The initiators open to insights about their own issues and often find deep healings through these sessions.
- Participants in each constellation enactment connect with their personal awareness of collective consciousness, as well as with that of the therapy group and of initiator's family collective consciousness.
- There are no lessons provided in how to participate in the collective consciousness. People open themselves to these awarenesses with the simple invitation of the therapist to the initiators to set up their specific family groupings, and to the rest of the group participate in whatever ways intuitively feel right to them.
- A broad spectrum of individual psychic awarenesses and elements of collective consciousness manifest in participants, as needed, to bring healing to the families of the initiators.
- There are healings in the form of opening to greater intuitive and spiritual awarenesses in the participants.

In essence, this is an exercise in exploring the family collective consciousness – through the broader collective consciousness that includes the workshop participants. This enables the unraveling of unhappy and dysfunctional patterns of relationships, and the healing of chronic, dysfunctional trauma residues and distress in the initiators who stage their family constellations in the workshop.

I quote from a book by John Payne, a gifted, intuitive constellation family therapist:

What this work reveals quite simply is that our feelings may not be our own and that we can be entangled in the fate of others, living their lives, instead of being in contact with the essence of our own unique Soul. (Payne, 2005)

What is revealed through this work is that the unresolved feelings in a person's life live on through the family collective consciousness. Often, a person in a later generation picks up unresolved feelings from family members in previous generations as though they were his or her own feelings. Thus, an unresolved grief in one generation may be expressed as a chronic depression in a child, grandchild, nephew or other relative of the person who suffered the original trauma that was unresolved in the life of the original person who experienced the trauma.

The unresolved experiences and feelings may also include relationships such as marriages or liaisons that ended poorly, miscarriages, experiences of abuse or wartime trauma, and other unhappiness that was taken to the grave by a family ancestor.

The Soul is compelled to include that which has been excluded in order to bring the family back into balance. Once these imbalances have been healed through constellation work, individuals are free to live their own lives, instead of being led by subconscious impulses. (Payne, 2005)

The person whose constellation is being staged has the opportunity, first, to witness the interactions and emotions of all family members, including those of the group member representing himself or herself; and then the opportunity to take her or his own place in the constellation and interact with the other family member representatives. The therapist guides this person to make deeply healing statements to other family representatives, such as this interchange over grief of losing a brother:

> Payne to James: Look at your brother and say, "The day you left us was terrible, it's been difficult to let you go."
>
> Payne to Brother: Look at your brother and say, "You have a family, dear brother. This is my fate, and they need you."
>
> Payne to James: Now say to your brother, "I shall leave you with the dead and go to my wife and children."

Enactments of new ways of relating to other family members and to conflict issues in the family often bring about deep, rapid changes in family relations. In conventional, individual therapy, changes come about through discussions about issues and relationships. It takes much longer for the new understandings and feelings to become parts of a person's repertoire of thoughts, feelings and habitual interactions with other people. Constellation family therapy engages people in enactments of new ways of reacting and behaving, bringing about more rapid changes.

Experiences of wartime and terrorism may be particularly challenging to deal with in family constellation therapy, because there are not only the personal hurts and traumas of the individual ancestor or ancestors, but the collective hurt, anger and traumas of the community and/or nation of that person. So, while an initiator in a family constellation workshop may reach a point of forgiveness towards the perpetrator of violence against the initiator's ancestor, the collective anger against the larger group of wartime or terrorism perpetrators may overshadow what has happened to the individual survivor.

Family Constellation work also offers healings for such societal angers and hatreds that perpetuate inter-group conflicts. For instance, people working on a constellation related to residues from a terrorist attack may experience residual feelings triggered by public responses to the attack. The public angers, hatreds and wishes for revenge may overshadow the personal feelings relating to the loss, interfering in the individual coming to closure. In such cases, the perpetrators of the attack and their survivors are also represented by volunteers in the family constellation group. So there would be one volunteer representing the collective experiences of the survivors, and another volunteer representing the collective experiences of the perpetrators. These representatives also express their feelings in the group, and the initiator in the constellation responds to them in the same manners as she responded to family members represented in the group. This frees the initiator from residues related to public feelings about the tragedy, allowing him or her to come to a place of resolution regarding the unresolved residues from the individual family member.

> …When we hold focus on a group and its descendants as perpetrators, we ourselves perpetuate our status, or the perpetrators, and there need to be victims; this is the greatest dance of fate. So when we truly honor the fate of those who were victims, the power of the perpetrators diminishes, be that real power, or the power we give perpetrators in our consciousness. (Payne, 2005)

Family constellation work closely parallels shamanic interventions, which take into account and include within the healing interventions the issues of the individual participants, their families, and the whole community. This approach to healing addresses the collective consciousness of the participating family and of the community. Payne further suggests that this process has the potential to bring healing to all of our ancestors throughout the collective consciousness.

The essence of family constellation therapy is that each person is freed of burdens of trauma residues from individual family members as well as from the collective consciousness of the family, community, and ultimately, of residues from anyone and everyone who participated in the same or similar sorts of traumas. And this really means every single participant in the collective consciousness of humanity.

My own approach to healing the collective consciousness is broader than Payne's. This includes sending healing to all beings (not only our own ancestors, but also others in need of healing who are our contemporaries) and to all living and conscious beings, through all time, to join in the healing (Benor, 2015).

*Family constellation therapy for HSPs and HSPCs*

HSPs are excellent candidates for family constellation therapy. Their sensitivities to their body, emotions, relationships and spirit enables them to connect more readily with feelings and family trauma residues that are related to family constellation issues. Their sensitivities also enable them to clear these issues more quickly and deeply. Similarly, these sensitivities enable them to identify issues in their current relationships that may be relevant to constellation patterns.

NHSP HSPCs are likely to be slower to connect with these sorts of issues. Here, the inputs of their HSPs can be a great help to them. Conversely, if HSPCs are closed to constellation and other spiritual awarenesses, this may become a point of discord and irritation in their HSPC-HSP relationships. I have seen the deepening of these awarenesses in the HSP leading to frictions severe enough to end the relationship with their partner, as well as with other family members. As HSPs come to the point of dissolving the wholistic ties that bind them to their families of origin, they may end up distancing themselves from other relationships in their current lives as well.

Conversely, I have seen such conflicts unfold in ways that lead to greater closeness, when the HSPC is open to clarifications of issues raised in family therapy constellation workshops.

Family constellation therapy can be of enormous help to HSPs and HSPCs in sorting out personal and relationship issues.

Let me offer a case example to illustrate how some of these approaches can help.

✦ 'Stan,' an NHSP was HSPC to 'Mavis.' Stan was a psychologist, specializing in grade school psychological assessments and Mavis was a social worker psychotherapist in a psychiatric clinic. Their understandings of psychological issues and clinical treatments had been enormously helpful in learning to get along with each other, despite their differing personalities and professional work. It might seem that their both being professionals in the field of psychology would give them a close connection, but psychological assessments are based on standardized testing within uniform, validated questionnaires, while clinical practice involves the art of getting people to identify and address their psychological issues and to figure out better ways to deal with themselves and the world around them. Mavis had been well aware that she was highly sensitive, but had not known of the HSP trait until Stan introduced her to this concept, from his chance reading of an article about HSPs that looked so familiar, it could have been written about Mavis.

They had been living together for about six months, with a clear deepening of their already positive relationship. They had occasional disagreements and arguments, but were getting better at sorting out their differences, recovering from their upsets with each other more rapidly and feeling increasingly comfortable being together.

Both of them were surprised and upset when Mavis got severely triggered during an argument over whether to visit with her family or his family over the winter holidays. Prior to living together, they had visited their own families separately. Don and Mavis lived in Toronto, her family lived in Vancouver (on Canada's west coast), while his family lived in Nova Scotia (in Eastern Canada). Their budget was too limited to allow them to visit both families in one year because Toronto is a very expensive place to live.

Here is an excerpt from one of their arguments.

Mavis: "I'm not going to give up this once a year time with my family! You can't ask me to do that!"

Stan: "You're not listening to me! I said we should discuss whether we're going to visit my family or yours. And the fact is, my father is getting on in years and has heart problems, so I think we need to give that serious consideration and priority. And, like with your family, my relationship with my father wasn't great when I was growing up, but it's gotten better since he's had these heart problems. And it's just June, and we've plenty of time to consider this further and come up with the best way forward."

Mavis: "You're not listening to me! You know I haven't gotten along at all well with my family. Not since I was a little girl. The past two years, with my older sister and two brothers also moving away, at least my parents were more welcoming when I spoke with them over the phone. Without my brothers and sister being there and constantly pathologizing me and belittling me for being a crybaby and a constantly seeking attention by crying, it actually felt a lot better last year, for the first time since I moved away. I was surprised to feel like my home might be a place I could visit again and not just come away feeling it was a waste of time and money. And it actually went fairly well. It means an awful lot to me to visit them, and you just don't give a damn! I don't know if this relationship is going to work out between us!"

Stan clammed up, stomped off to their bedroom, and slammed the door.

Having read my suggestions earlier in this section, I invite you to critique the discussion between Mavis and Stan. Write down different ways each of them might have responded better in their discussion with each other.

Here are some suggestions:

— Acknowledging that this is a highly charged issue and needs careful thought and consideration could be helpful, as Stan suggested. This puts the discussion in a different category from ordinary conversations. If you've been through such situations and conversations before, with positive outcomes, it can be helpful to remind each other that although this feels fraught at the moment, you've weathered several previous situations like these, so you ought to be able to deal with this one, too, in a mutually satisfactory manner.

— The Parent Effectiveness Training approaches might come to mind. Using 'I' statements, such as "I'm feeling unheard here!" or "I feel you're not listening to my concerns" are likely to be better received than a "you" statement like Mavis used.

- Self-calming methods such as TWR/WHEE, going to your PPSH, or accessing an anchored repository of positive feelings and thoughts (NLP method)[50] could be helpful in calming down before pursuing their discussion further.
- It is difficult to make plans for dealing with these sorts of issues until you've been through one or more already. But once you've come through such a challenge with a positive outcome, bookmarking what worked for you and agreeing to revisit and practice your successful conflict resolution processes is a good preventive against future meltdowns, and a helpful preparation for dealing with conflicts of these sorts.
- You might consider whether there are any other recurring, stressful issues that could be raising the emotional temperatures, contributing to your difficulties in addressing your current, hot topic. You could address these recurring ones first. This can be helpful in order to lower the general stress levels. Also, starting by resolving the less complicated or touchy issues can facilitate a calmer atmosphere. This gives you a feeling of moving together in a positive direction. Riding the momentum of this positivity can then be a help in dealing with the more challenging issues.
- Anchoring your positive feelings from dealing successfully with an issue builds further reservoirs of positivity (NLP method).
- Acknowledging that some of the tensions in your current conflict may be partly influenced by your earlier life experiences with your families is helpful. You might choose to work on yourselves individually to clear some of these residues from lingering issues, unpleasant memories that are making you tenser in discussing the current situation. Bundling the earlier issues with the current ones often works better than addressing each separately.*[51]
- If you have found other ways to reduce tension, such as calming flower essences or energetic clearing, these would be worth using prior to resuming your discussion.

Please understand that If your suggestions differ from mine, that's great! Everyone has their own way of analyzing and responding to such situations.

✦✦ Mavis contacted me a few days later for help in dealing with her relationship with Stan. I strongly encouraged her to discuss this with him and to see whether they couldn't both come for couples sessions rather than Mavis coming alone.

I explained that the outcomes in a relationship conflict are generally much more likely to be sorted out in positive ways for the continuation of the relationship if both of the involved people come and work on their issues together. When only one comes for sessions there's a much higher likelihood of the relationship ending. Undergoing any sort of therapy can bring about major transformations in people's perceptions of themselves and in how they relate to others. When one person in a relationship changes in significant ways, their relationship with their significant other may no longer feel the same as it did prior to their transformations. Mavis took this on board, and I was pleased that Stan also agreed to participate.

I took thorough family histories from each of them, noting that Stan had also had difficult relationships in his family. His mother hugely favored his sister, Vera, who was 5 years younger. His mother had died unexpectedly from heart disease when he was 12 years old. His father was devoted to the family, but his way of showing his caring was through working long hours to provide for them financially. When he was at home, he was so tired from work that he just vegetated in his own room and was unavailable to his children. After Stan's mother passed on, even though Stan's father hired an after-school childcare person, Stan ended up as a partial mother substitute, doing a lot of the shopping, some of the cooking, and helping Vera with her homework.

Mavis had not been home for six years, so the fact she felt open to considering a visit over the holidays was a big change for her. She was a bit contrite over her outburst over visiting their parents, during her argument with Stan, but added that she often felt Stan didn't want to hear about her feelings, and she had been doing her best to hold them back when she got upset in their big argument.

I invited them to share their views on what was happening between them. Mavis deferred to Stan to respond first, saying that when they were together she was usually the more outgoing one and he tended to be the listener. He countered that he tended to ponder matters a bit before he spoke up, and appreciated this invitation from Mavis to respond first.

Stan: "I like to think things through thoroughly before making any decisions. I still think we've got plenty of time to consider all the pros and cons and come up with the best solution."

Mavis: "I know I'm much more prone to feeling my way through situations than doing the logic routine you're so good at, Stan. But this is really as much about how we both feel about our families as it is about what's the most reasonable solution in this case."

Stan: "I can see your point, dear, but going through all of our feelings can lead us back down the slippery slope of getting into another argument again. And many times I've seen you have really strong feelings about things, but a while later you're feeling differently about whatever it is. I sort of expect this might happen here, too, in some measure."

I was pleased to hear their acknowledgments of their own ways of approaching issues, as well as of the differences between them.

Mavis was aware of trauma and trauma residues, and understood that she and Stan had emotional scars from their childhood and ongoing challenges with their families. She also understood about psychotherapy for trauma residues, though she did not feel competent to treat people who had these problems. Stan had only a rudimentary understanding of trauma and psychotherapy.

Again, I invite you to consider what you might have advised Stan and Mavis to do – after considering the further details I shared above, and before reading further.

I felt Mavis would be comfortable with much of the spectrum of approaches I offer, but that Stan needed some basic explanations to help him accept my suggestions. So here is how I proceeded:

I briefly explained the HSP trait, and explored with each of them whether they felt or believed that Mavis was an HSP. They readily agreed, and I recommended that they read Elaine Aron's original book (1996).

I introduced them experientially to TWR/WHEE, suggesting that they might explore it then and there for some of their current anxieties about the tensions between them. Mavis started with a SUDS of 8 and with three rounds of taping reduced this to a 2, and Stan reduced his level 6.5 SUDS to a 3.5.

Both were impressed with how quickly and easily this worked for them, and readily accepted my recommendation to practice tapping on their anxieties about their presenting problems at home. They agreed they would probably follow through better if they did this together, although both also agreed it would be best for each to do it silently. They also agreed that it would be prudent and helpful to write down what they said and to track their SUDS in writing as well.

At their next session, they reported substantial improvements in how they were listening to each other and were getting along, although they had not yet resolved the Christmas visiting conflict. With two further sessions, one after a week and the other a month later, Stan and Mavis were also able to significantly reduce the intensity of their trauma residues from their difficult earlier experiences with their families. They felt this was a very worthwhile investment of time, efforts and finances, as they were not only getting along better with each other but also finding their relationships with their families over the phone to be improving noticeably. And the last time I heard from them, Stan's father's heart condition was getting significantly better, as he improved his diet and developed a program for regular exercise. So they decided to spend the coming winter holidays with Mavis' family. And they were planning to sort out their finances so they could visit both families annually in the future.

This summary of Mavis and Stan's clearings of their personal and relationship issues is very typical of how wholistic healing can address challenges and improve relationships between HSPs and HSPCs. Best of all, once people experience these approaches, they can continue to use them in situations of further need.

## 37. Active listening

> *To listen is to hear through all the noise and discover the quiet place where both pain and promise wait to speak their healing words... Through being heard, patients can experience their own sacredness and thus enter into a process of healing.*
> – L.A. Burton

You may think active listening is out of place in the order of suggestions for how to be helpful in HSP and HSPC relationships because of its absolute simplicity. By logic it could certainly come as the first chapter in this section. However, my experience with countless therapists, clients and students of therapy is that reflective listening is actually one of the most difficult approaches for many people to absorb and use when they offer their personal support or therapeutic interventions.

In active listening, you simply reflect back the thoughts and feelings of the person with whom you are speaking, without critiques or suggestions for how to change or do anything new or different. Your intervention is to be present, listening attentively, and accepting of everything they say, acknowledging you are hearing. You do this through:

– Non-verbal responses, such as nodding, smiling, raising your eyebrows in surprise, shaking your head in sympathetic distress, frowning in parallel with sharings of negative and painful experiences, putting a hand over your heart to signal that your emotions are stirred, and so on

– Verbal acknowledgments that you understand their feelings, as in
  - "Wow, that must have been painful and difficult!"
  - "I really feel your pain and distress!"

– Rephrasing what you hear,
  - "I can really sense your sadness!" when you hear "It hit me suddenly, this feeling of being totally alone, when I returned home after the funeral." or
  - "I get a glow in my heart listening to your story!" in response to "It suddenly hit me how lucky I am to have a husband who cares about me and brings home a regular check, and grown children who visit and phone regularly, even though I'm stuck in this wheelchair, just waiting for the next symptoms of my Multiple Sclerosis to show up."

Surprisingly, many people don't need to hear interpretations for how to understand their situation differently; nor advice on something new to do that they haven't thought of; nor corrections of their beliefs, attitudes or emotions. They are deeply satisfied to have another human being affirm she understands that their situation is just what and how they perceive and experience it to be.

Equally important, there is no criticism of the person who is being helped. Taken together, these two factors create a distinct feel-good response. For many people, this brings out their innate insights and understandings of themselves and their situations. It also generates self-confidence that they are able to find their own solutions to their issues.

This 'person-centered therapy' was developed by Carl Rogers, a psychologist, in the middle of the 20th century. It is based on the understanding that by offering 'unconditional positive regard' to people, their belief in themselves is markedly strengthened.

You may find it hard to believe, but this simple atmosphere of deep acceptance has been found to be a distinctly healing experience for many people. Let me offer a few illustrations of this sort of approach.

✦ 'Gwen' was a university professor who had had a stellar career, rising to Assistant Director of her university Business department at the age of 28. She came for urgent help to figure out what had gone wrong in her marriage, after three years of what she had felt had been a good relationship.

'Brad,' her husband, was a successful accountant who had similarly risen rapidly to a managerial position in his firm. They worked long hours during the week, but did their best to keep at least one weekend day free for doing things together. Gwen was devastated when Brad told her he was very unhappy in their relationship and wanted out of the marriage. She responded with intense anger, to which he didn't respond verbally. With tight lips, he silently put a few clothes into a suitcase and walked out. He had not responded to her texts or phone messages over the three days since he walked out.

I found Gwen moderately insightful, but very controlling and highly resistant to even my most tentative inquiries about possible new ways to look at or respond to her situation. So I followed a Rogerian path of asking general questions about the marriage and accepting and reflecting back to her whatever she said.

– She reviewed possible reasons that Brad might have for wanting to separate. I acknowledged each one, and empathized with her frustration over not being able to do anything because she didn't know for sure what his reasons were. I asked which she thought were the most likely, and what she thought she might do in each case, nodding without comment on her speculations and suggestions. Her top three speculations were: Not enough fun times, compared to the two years when they were dating; not enough sex; and both of them tending to want their own way and having difficulties compromising with each other.

- She listed a variety of possible ways she could ask to him to clarify with her what had led to his decision and to talk it over with her.
- She added a list of her own dissatisfactions, which (not surprisingly) included many items similar to those she speculated would be on his list.

Up to this point, Gwen responded well to my Rogerian reflections on whatever she said. I could see she felt heard, understood, and accepted when I mirrored back to her many of the feelings she was experiencing.

– "You're feeling very, very frustrated over Brad's walking out."
– "I hear your helplessness, anger, disappointment, etc."
– "You're struggling to develop a plan but don't quite know where to begin."

I didn't hold myself rigidly to an exclusive Rogerian approach. I asked whether there were any friends or family who might mediate a discussion between them, or whether she thought they might both benefit from a joint session with me. Gwen acknowledged these were probably good ideas but she couldn't see much likelihood that Brad would agree to anyone else hearing about their problems, as he was a very private person when it came to emotions and relationships.

Gwen left this session feeling much calmer, with a clearer sense of her options and possible ways forward. She phoned me several days later to share that Brad had been freaked out by his feeling a strong turn-on when a client at work invited him to go out with her for a drink that clearly wasn't meant to be only a drink. He suddenly realized how frustrated he was by the diminished closeness in his life with Gwen, and needed some time alone to sort out his feelings. Having reviewed this in her discussion with me, she was more prepared to respond with some of her own feelings of frustration that she hadn't connected with previously, in the pressured routines of her job and his. And in another phone session with me a few months later, Gwen shared that they had come to very helpful agreements about spending more time together, and that their relationship was much improved.

✦ An unusual approach to active listening was developed by Joseph Weizenbaum in 1966. He created a computer program in an artificial intelligence lab at MIT and named it Eliza. The program would reflect back phrases that were similar to those typed by people who interacted with 'her.' Many people felt that Eliza truly and deeply understood them, although the computer had very basic programs that made this completely impossible. Eliza's programs were just responding in the most simple ways to the inputs Eliza received, according to the automated program Weizenbaum had written. It would rephrase and reflect back the feeling words and phrases the human used, or ask simple questions that invited the human to expand upon what he or she had written, thereby giving the impression that it understood and sympathized with the human.

In one situation, the Eliza program was offered as an alternative to people having to be on a waiting list to see a psychotherapist at a clinic. At the end of the waiting period, to the surprise of the researchers, some of the people said they would be happy to continue with the computer rather than to speak with a human therapist.

You can explore this yourself with an on-line versions of Eliza, a computer therapist.**[52]

### Active listening in HSP and HSPC relationships

HSPs, by the deepest essence of their very nature, tend to be caring, loving people. When they are in the company of people who accept them as they are, they express their loving and caring responses through their words, voice, eye contact, touch, biological energies, and connections of heart and spirit. For some HSPs, active listening is as natural as breathing. They are deeply present in their interactions with other people, most of the time. Other people feel heard and accepted by these HSPs.

For other HSPs and NHSPs, an accepting presence may be an acquired way of interacting – through personal experiences, modeling themselves on the examples of others who have this loving presence; through trial and error; and through connecting naturally and intuitively with people they love.

For an NHSPC, it may take a while before she truly understands that she doesn't have to keep working at doing things in order to be close and demonstrate her love and caring, Simply listening with an accepting attitude is an enormous gift that most HSPs appreciate.

## *WHAT ARE SOME WAYS YOU CAN BE MORE PRESENT WITH YOUR HSP OR HSPC?*

✦Active listening can be a helpful way to enhance your being present for those you care for. Active listening markedly enhances HSPC – HSP relationships. Active listening is particularly helpful when HSPs are sharing and discussing their emotions, which may be fairly often. But again, other factors are also relevant to how you develop closeness with each other, such as your individual preferences in love languages,*[53] whether you have stronger inclinations to be thinking vs. feeling and intuitive vs. sensation types,*[54] whether either or both of you are high sensation seekers,*[55] and so on.

# SECTION VI. General Wholistic Approaches to Facilitate Health and Healing

*The part can never be well unless the whole is well.*
                                                            - Plato

This section is about the 'what' and the 'how' of using your understandings of the wholistic unity of your being to improve your health and your relationships. Tensions in any aspect of your body, emotions, mind, relationships and spirit can disrupt the functions of all of the others. Conversely, relaxing tensions and strengthening any parts of your being will help to improve functions in all the other levels of your being.

And again, though we discuss each of the wholistic levels individually, they are all inseparably interlinked within us. This enables us to bundle issues from any aspect of our being as we are clearing them. Our focus may start with any level, and the inner threads connecting the issue being addressed will take us to any or all of the other levels. And TWR/WHEE enables us to bundle all of the threads into rounds of tapping that simultaneously reduce negativities in all of the levels, and then allow us, as well, to build positivities in all of the levels.

First, we'll look at a couple of approaches for healing through building overall positivity.

## 38. Touching base with each other

*When we seek for connection, we restore the world to wholeness.*
*Our seemingly separate lives become meaningful*
*as we discover how truly necessary we are to each other.*
- Margaret Wheatley

It is enormously helpful and healing for HSPs and their HSPCs to reaffirm our understandings and acceptance of our partner in life and our support for each other. Being an HSP minority in an NHSP world is a frequent challenge. It is enormously healing to have affirmations of our love and our caring intentions for each other, and to share with each other these confirmations of our participation in bringing more healing into our lives.

This is also a good practice for holding our awarenesses of our connections with other people and with the world at large.

### *Focusing on positives*

Share some of your intentions, anticipations and/or wishes for wholistic healings every day. This is enormously encouraging.

- Start each day telling each other over breakfast about 3 positive experiences you're looking forward to that day
- Write these on a chalk board, if one of your gets up and leaves home earlier than the other
- Phone each other once in a while just to touch base and share how your day is going for each of you
- Text each other a warm fuzzy
- Involve your children, as appropriate for their ages

*Examples*

- "I have my workout today. I've missed my exercise for several days because _____ and my body is craving it."
- "I had a wonderful dream that woke me up to realize _____."
- "I've been thinking of fixing the _____ and today's the day I'm going to do it."
- "I look over at you as I wake up and feel soooo grateful for having found you and for being together with you!"
- "I'm looking forward to meeting up with _____ today. I like her because _____."
- "Our garden is complaining about the weeds that are starting to choke some of our flowers and veggies. I'm going to start digging them out right after breakfast, before it gets hot out."
- "We made a new year's resolution to _____. Let's set a time to do that."

End each day with a sharing of 3 positives from your day is an affirmation of bringing more healing into your life and into the world

- Over dinner
- Involving your children, as appropriate for their ages
- On lying down to sleep

*Examples:*

- "The elevators were out of commission during lunchtime at work. I was surprised how my legs complained about walking down 11 stories. What a good reminder that I need to bring back some lower limb exercises into my gym routine!"

- "I finally got up the gumption to have a friendly chat with my new boss. She's a no-nonsense executive type, but far from being the dragon I thought she was."

- "I haven't told you enough how much I appreciate you for being in my life! I'm especially grateful today for _____."

- "Jimmie brought home his first quiz today. He did well. I'm so enjoying seeing him taking so nicely to first grade!"

YOUR SUGGESTIONS AND NOTES

YOUR PARTNER'S SUGGESTIONS AND NOTES

WHO KNOWS YOU WELL AND CAN SUGGEST MORE POSITIVES YOU MIGHT CONSIDER?

### Extending your positives into the collective consciousness

Each of us is a pixel in the picture of the entire world. By being the best little pixels we can be, we make the world that much better. We also inspire the pixels around us to shine more brightly.

We enormously multiply the benefits of our positive affirmations when we extend these positive interactions and healings that we experience in our relationships, to offer hope and healing for all others on our planet who need help and healing and who are open to inviting and/or accepting it for themselves.

My suggestion for sharing our positive experiences, along with our healing intentions and wishes, is to recite the following invitation when we are experiencing great positivity.

If it is for my/our highest good and the highest good of all

I / We invite anyone and everyone

Anywhere and everywhere

Anywhen and everywhen

Who is ready to [accept this healing/ clear their pain and trauma issue(s)/ etc.] with [me/ us] to do so.**[1] [2]

## 39. Giving each other some space

*Let there be spaces in your togetherness,*
*And let the winds of the heavens dance between you.*
*Love one another, but make not a bond of love;*
*Let it rather be a moving sea between the shores of your souls.*
- Kahlil Gibran

Most couples find it important to each person to have some personal time and space apart from the other. This often occurs naturally because each of us has our unique combination of interests, habits, preferences in music, art, participant and spectator sports, foods, friends, and so on. Rather than completely relinquishing activities we enjoy because our partner or spouse isn't turned on to them, we may well choose to participate alone in some of these with friends and family who have similar tastes to ours.

It's important to discuss these issues with your significant other and come to understandings and agreements about your individual and collective comfort zones in these matters. Going off to a baseball or hockey game with buddies with whom you've shared such activities, prior to being in a committed relationship, may not be an issue. This may be just the sort of time slot that she's been craving for going out to shop for clothes or cosmetics, getting together with the girls from the office or with particular members of her family – activities that you're happy to not participate in. A word of caution here, though. Going to such games every weekend may become an annoyance if your partner's comfort zone for togetherness time differs from yours.

I've seen issues arise in these areas of relationships very often because of the challenges in adjusting from life as a single person (even when having dated steadily for a period of time) and life in a committed relationship, particularly when shifting to living together. There are changes in mindsets, frames of references and expectations when making such a shift that require adjustments.

Viewing yourself as a single person, even when dating steadily, usually carries with it the expectations that you'll be free to make decisions and to run your life to some degree independently of your dating partner. Repeated, delicate negotiations may be needed as your relationship with each other grows closer. The respectful ways of expressing your feelings, needs and wishes that are detailed in Parent Effectiveness Training may be particularly helpful here.*[3]

Which of these options sounds and feels better to you?

- "You've got to give me more space to do things on my own! I'm going off to the gym on Tuesday and Thursday evening this week." or "I'm feeling a need to have a bit of personal time this week. How would it feel to you if I go on Monday and Thursday evening this week to work out at the gym?"

- "I wish you'd just let me get on with cooking our meals and not butt in where you're going to be in the way." or "I really appreciate your good intentions when you join me in the kitchen when I'm preparing our meals, but this is something I've always done on my own. I love talking with you but I get nervous and distracted when you're under foot and I'm wanting to focus on getting the food on the table."

- "OK! I get it! I'll just butt out of the kitchen and let you get on with it." or "You know, we've both been pretty busy lately, and I'm feeling a bit of my honey deficit. But I'm fine reading the paper till dinnertime."

In short, asking for more space can be really helpful in avoiding irritating each other. It's *how* we ask that makes the big difference.

When you take your space, there is then the question of what can you do for calming down. Any of the methods in this book can be of help. The most direct and effective in my experience are EP, muscle relaxation, NLP, and physical exercise. But simply taking your space and letting go of your engagement with the person and situation that was upsetting you can also work.

Next, let's explore wholistic healing approaches for every level of our being. We'll start with the body, which often is the one that first alerts us to disharmony within our wholistic selves. Body, mind and emotions are generally the easiest to address, starting with relaxations of tensions. There are wide varieties of approaches for doing this.

## 40. Body health and healing

> *If we become conscious of our wholeness,*
> *then that consciousness will manifest itself,*
> *often as a healed body, but not always.*
> *In healing it's hard to know just what is healed,*
> *and what does the individual person need...*
> *to be free of need.*
> — Rosemary Ellen Guiley

Prevention is by far the investment that offers the overall best return on our self-healing efforts. Building and maintaining a healthy body is an excellent prevention against the development of more serious dysfunctions in your body. Much of what I share here very briefly is common knowledge, but many people tend to take their bodies for granted – until their bodies start to complain or malfunction.

### *Healthy, regular eating*

Healthy, regular eating is essential for having a healthy body. In addition to a diet that is properly balanced for basic nutrition building blocks, you would be wise to take vitamin supplements. Fresh foods in the US and Canada may be stored for many months before they are put on store shelves. This diminishes the quality and potency of the vitamins they can offer you.

Foods in the US and Canada may also contain pesticides, preservatives, food additives, appetite enhancers, coloring and genetically modified products that can be harmful to your health. Foods in Europe and some of the rest of the world are far more carefully regulated, and/or less often treated with chemicals, and are therefore generally better for your health. Other countries may have much lower standards for food cleanliness, may use human waste as fertilizer, and may in other ways threaten your health.

Fast foods, in particular, are notorious for containing various substances that are on the spectrum between unhealthy to toxic. The film, *Supersize Me*, illustrates how toxic these can be.[4] The challenge here is that fast foods often offer the cheapest alternative for a stomach-filling experience.

For some people, eating becomes a habit for comforting themselves when they are distressed or when their trauma residues are triggered, leading to obesity. This is a problem I've seen in many HSPs when they have experienced traumas. Being sensitive to their feelings, they may suffer quite intense anxieties, fears, angers, grief or other emotions. When they are unfamiliar with de-stressing techniques for directly and definitively dealing with their emotional discomforts, they may end up using eating as a way of temporarily feeling better. We call this 'comfort eating.' In time, this can increase their weight, which becomes an additional challenge.

Comfort eating is a symptom that can be helpful in clarifying the underlying stresses that have triggered people into using this method for reducing stress. As with pain, the comfort eating can tell you what physical, emotional or relationship issues it is wanting to diminish. When you address these with a stress management method such as TWR/WHEE, the need for comfort eating can be diminished or eliminated. Even after eliminating the particular cause of the comfort eating, you may still need to use tapping for the general habit of eating when you are up tight or feeling other discomforts.**[5]

## *Vitamin deficiencies and contaminants in foods and the need for supplements*

A healthy body requires a broad spectrum of vitamins. People in most of the world obtain these from their everyday diet, as has been the case throughout history. The food in the US and Canada is in many cases a very poor source of vitamins. The corporatization of the food industry in these countries has led to a serious degradation of the nutritional value of food that reaches our table. Food is marketed through very large companies, whose focus is on creating good looking food for profit – for the most part without attention to its nutritional value, and often without concern for the harmful effects of preservative chemicals, food coloring, taste enhancers, sugar and/or sugar substitutes, hormones, antibiotics, and chemicals leeching out of plastic containers.

Another change that may be food-related is the markedly earlier development of puberty in girls in the US and Canada, and to a lesser extent in Europe. The average age for the start of menstruation in the US is 12-13. However, increasing numbers of girls as young as 8 years old are developing breasts and pubic hair (average for breast budding 9-10), though their menses still don't begin till 12 (Biro, et al., 2012). It is suspected that hormones used to enhance animal growth, passing through the food chain, could be causing these changes.

In the US and Canada, vitamin supplements are highly advisable unless you are careful to purchase fresh organic food or to grow your own. I don't go into details here because this is an enormously complex issue, far beyond the scope of our primary focus in this book.

## *Exercise*

Regular exercise is important in building and maintaining your body's strength, resilience and general health. Not only is exercise helpful for body functions, it can significantly lengthen your life. It can also improve the quality of your life. How much exercise is good and sufficient for you is best determined by trial and error, or by consultation with a fitness specialist. A rough general guideline is provided by the UK website, NHS Choices: "To stay healthy, adults should try to be active daily and aim to achieve at least 150 minutes of physical activity over a week through a variety of activities." Research confirms that exercise can reduce the chances of your having many serious physical and psychological challenges:

- up to a 35% lower risk of coronary heart disease and stroke
- up to a 50% lower risk of type 2 diabetes
- up to a 50% lower risk of colon cancer
- up to a 20% lower risk of breast cancer
- a 30% lower risk of early death
- up to an 83% lower risk of osteoarthritis
- up to a 68% lower risk of hip fracture
- a 30% lower risk of falls (among older adults)
- up to a 30% lower risk of depression
- up to a 30% lower risk of dementia

### Relaxations

There are countless relaxation exercises that are easy to learn and use. Here are a few examples:

### Muscle relaxation

Muscle relaxation is one of the commonest and easiest stress reduction approaches to learn and practice. Relaxation exercises can reduce and calm the vicious circles of stress → anxieties → psychological tensions → physical tensions → more stress → etc.. And just as physical tensions create and worsen psychological tensions, physical relaxation and calmness can relieve these tensions.

Here are a few wholistic suggestions for relaxations:

1. Check out your body's state of tension at this moment, using the SUDS scale.

2. Check for any thoughts or feelings of psychological tensions and check your SUDS scale for these.

3. If your SUDS is lower than '3' for physical or psychological tensions, think of a good juicy reason to worry, or of some time in the past when you were anxious or upset, and check your SUDS as you connect with this worry-reason or memory, looking for a time when your psychological SUDS was '3' or higher.

4. Check your body's SUDS again.

5. DO THIS STEP ONLY IF YOU DO NOT EXPERIENCE PAIN OR OTHER SEVERE DISCOMFORT IN THE MUSCLES YOU ARE ACTIVATING: Using your dominant hand, make a fist and tighten the muscles of your hand, wrist, forearm and upper arm, bringing your fist up towards your shoulder, and then holding the tension in all of these muscles for about 30 seconds.

6. Take a deep breath, and as you very slowly exhale, gently and slowly begin to release the tension in your right hand and arm. Continue to breathe slowly and gently. Gradually allow your fist to relax and lower your arm until it is resting without tension wherever it comes to lie – on your lap, on the arm of your chair, or hanging down at your side.

7. Check your SUDS again. Most people find their SUDS for their whole body is noticeably lower, and at the same time their psychological SUDS goes down.

8. You can repeat this as often as needed to bring your body tension SUDS down to zero.

### Systematic desensitization

Systematic desensitization is a well-established and time tested de-stressing method that is one of the backbones of Cognitive Behavioral Therapy (CBT). By repeating the muscle relaxation steps, while focusing on any issue over which you are stressing, you can systematically reduce the SUDS of your stress to zero. This can be used methodically for a thorough internal house cleaning. You can make lists of your worries, negative habits, trauma memories and the like. Then prioritize your list, giving each item a SUDS number.

In the classical approach to desensitizing the intensity of your issues, you start with an issue of your choice that has a low SUDS, reducing that to zero. Then, you systematically work your way up your list to the one with the highest SUDS. This is the gentlest way to activate your body's relaxation responses as a tool for decreasing your emotional and mental tensions.

An alternative approach is to start with the issue with highest SUDS and then work on those with lower SUDS. My own preference is to start with an issue that is somewhere in the mid-zone of SUDS intensity and see how it goes for you. Often, when you clear an issue of moderate or high intensity, the SUDS of all the issues of lower intensity will often go down without your needing to address each one individually in order to achieve these improvements. If the lower intensity issues do not go to '0' by themselves, you can address them individually, as you need or wish.

Using systematic desensitization, you can similarly install replacement positives for the negatives you have released, just as you do with TWR/ WHEE.*6

*The energy body*

Einstein's equation, $E = mc^2$, has been the modern basis for understanding our world. It tells us that matter and energy are inter-convertible. This has been fully accepted in modern science for inanimate matter. Any physical object can be described as a collection of particles or of energies.

The biological sciences in general, and medicine in particular, have been slow to absorb that a human physical body can also be described either as matter or as energy. There are healers who have been describing aspects of the human body as energy for decades, and others who have been describing the human person as a non-physical spirit for thousands of years. These concepts are explored and discussed in great detail later in this book.*7

What is relevant here is that our bodies can be understood as being made of energies. Our health and illness can be assessed according to health of its energetic states, and varieties of wholistic treatments can be offered for every aspect of our energy bodies.

The energy body can be sensed through touch. If you hold your hands close to each other but not touching, then move them 6-12 inches apart, and again move them close to each other, back and forth several times, you may be able to sense your own energy field.

DO THIS SEVERAL TIMES AND CHECK OUT WHAT YOU FEEL IN YOUR HANDS BEFORE READING FURTHER.

Many people report they feel light pressure, like a bubble, or heat or tingling in their hands when they do this. It is the biological energy field (biofield) that is being sensed.*8

Healers may be born with gifts of seeing the biofield as well as sensing it with their hands. The biofield can be accessed for diagnosis and treatment. These are skills that can be developed and enhanced with training and practice.

Varieties of therapies have been developed for assessing states of health and illness and for treating physical and psychological disorders by adjusting their energy fields:

- Acupuncture and acupressure treatments access lines of energy (meridians), running through the body. Particular acupuncture points along these lines correspond with body organs and functions.**9
- Applied Kinesiology tests the strength of various muscles to identify health and illness in various organs, related to acupuncture lines.10
- Energy Psychology (EP) accesses particular acupuncture points by tapping on them in particular sequences.11
- Chakras are energy centers along the mid-line of the body, identified originally in religious and healing traditions of India.*12
- Bioenergy healers offer healing through touch, holding healers' hands near the body, and through mental intent.13

HSPs are often sensitive to bioenergies in themselves and others. While I know of no research on this, my impression is that the vast majority of healers are HSPs.

# 41. Emotions

*The emotion that can break your heart*
*is sometimes the very one that heals it.*
- Nicholas Sparks

Stuffing our feelings down below our conscious awareness and doing our best to forget about them is a common way to deal with stresses and tensions when we're feeling overwhelmed, unsupported or helpless to deal with whatever or whoever is provoking, hurting or traumatizing us. However, doing this is like putting a bandage around an infected wound without clearing out the dirt in the wound. Our negative feelings remain in our unconscious memory and they continue to bother us.

In times of danger or intense stress, this may be the best we can do, and may be the best and most appropriate way of dealing with our situation. But these buried memories and feelings fester like pus in a wound that can come out when we're daggered the next time and we are, yet again, unable to protect or heal ourselves.

Chronic stress residues that are not cleared are major contributors to poor health. Stress interferes with the functions of our immune system, raising risks of infections. It may impair our hormonal systems, increasing incidence of asthma, diabetes, stomach ulcers, colitis and other bowel dysfunctions, hypertension and cardiac disease, and cancers. Incidence of psychiatric disorders are also increased, manifesting as anxiety, depression and schizophrenia. People who are stressed and distressed tend to put on weight.

Conversely, people who develop regular practices of exercise, relaxation, good diet and sufficient sleep time are less likely to have these challenges, and more likely to recover when they develop and enhance their health-promoting practices.

### *Food cravings, overeating, comfort eating and obesity*

Eating is a feel-good experience that is usually a pleasant part of our day and our life. But some of us have a hard time resisting reaching out for a morsel or a serious snack for a more frequent enjoyment of this pleasure than is healthy. Eating may then become a habit or even an addiction.

Eating provides what may be the only feel-good experience available for some people who have few or no other resources for decreasing their emotional stress and distress. Sweets, in particular, can be satisfying because they bring some missing sweetness into their life. Sweets may also offer associated memories of birthdays or other occasions when you felt happier, so eating in the present invokes these conditioned happy feelings from the past – thereby creating a distraction or a weak, counteracting positive experience that mitigates the negativity of unpleasant circumstances you are presently suffering.

However, each mouthful is only a little bit of temporary relief from your stress and distress. So you follow one mouthful with another, and soon you're over-eating, above the calories you need for daily sustenance and muscular activities. This is comfort eating.

One might think that putting on weight would be a deterrent to continued overeating. In Western culture, obesity is generally perceived as a detraction from desirable standards for being beautiful and handsome. However, this may be precisely why some people put on weight. Your increased body mass may be feel like armor.

- Obesity increases your size, so people who see you as bigger may be less inclined to be pick on you or take you on in a fight.
- Being obese, you may also be seen as less sexually attractive, which is another sort of armoring if you have suffered sexual abuse and traumas.*[14]
- Obesity may also be experienced as a calorie reserve if you have suffered food scarcities and starvation.

Overeating and comfort eating are among the most difficult habits to change, for varieties of reasons:
- We can't not eat.
- Cravings substances of choice are usually readily available.
- The eating habit often takes root in childhood, when we have fewer resources to deal with stresses and traumas, and when we are establishing habits for dealing with life issues.
- The preferred food, often sweet or salty, is very 'more-ish.' A small taste provides a teeny little bit of what you like, with relief through distraction from what is uncomfortable, and a boost through refocusing on something very palatable. The temptation, often irresistible, is to continue eating more to produce more of the same effects.
- The distraction usually ends when the food is swallowed, followed soon by a residual effect of disappointment because the relief was so temporary.
- This disappointment resonates with other disappointments that are parts of the trauma residues, and these awarenesses of the traumas may actually be intensified – because we have stimulated layers of trauma memories which had not been within our conscious awareness when we were triggered into reaching for that first, tasty tidbit by current stressors.
- Then, meta-memories of disappointments, failures to find relief, and inabilities to deal with the traumas play their tunes in our subconscious awareness, further increasing our food cravings. Not the least of these disappointments is often our failure to follow through on previous resolutions and plans and other valiant efforts to control our food cravings and overeating.
- And completely from outside our own dynamics, the food manufacturers (I use the term 'manufacturer' deliberately) load up much of our comfort food with non-nutritional chemical preservatives, coloring and bulk expanders. And, most relevant to this discussion, they also include appetite stimulants like monosodium glutamate.[15]

EP can relieve food cravings within minutes. This actually makes a nice demonstration at workshops. I learned this from Gary Craig, the developer of EFT. He invited a volunteer who wanted to stop his chocolate craving, to come to the front of the room. He held out a plate of Godiva chocolates (dark, light and white), acclaimed by many as one of the best-tasting sweets in the world. I could see the volunteer swallowing his saliva, anticipating the wonderful taste!

Gary then led him through the EFT protocol to decrease negative thoughts and feelings. Within minutes, I could see a shift in his eagerness to reach out and grab some of these sweets. His cravings diminished to the point that he was happy to give the chocolates a pass.

Relieving comfort eating is a much greater challenge, as this involves releasing the underlying traumas that created the craving. This may require a series of sessions plus practice on your own.

Sadly, there are surgeons who recommend bariatric surgery, in which the stomach is made smaller or the intestines are rearranged so less food can be absorbed – usually without ever exploring reasons for the overeating and obesity. This is probably why the failure rates for such surgery can be as high as 50 percent. The surgery reduces the capacity of the gut to absorb food, but the food cravings are in no way addressed. Here is an example of such a situation.

✦ 'Alma' was a pleasant, third year college student who came for help with comfort eating and obesity. She was more than 250 pounds overweight. She had explored a wide range of dieting approaches, sometimes with modest weight losses, but was never able to maintain a lower weight.

Alma, an only child, had been a normal, pretty, outgoing teenager until her father died from a sudden heart attack when she was 14 years old. She had been very close to her father, a quiet but warm and sensitive person who worked mostly from home as a TV script writer. Her mother worked in floor sales in a department store, including several evening shifts per week, and was much more outgoing. Even when her father had been alive, her mother was out socializing with women friends several evenings each week.

Alma ended up standing in for her father, helping with household chores, including cooking. This is where she started on her road to obesity. Missing her father, and often finding herself alone at home while her mother was at work or out with friends, she turned to comfort eating. She also stayed home more often and socialized a lot less. Her mother was somewhat concerned, but accepted Alma's explanation that she wanted to apply herself more seriously to her studies.

It was shortly after her mother started dating, three years later, that Alma began putting on much more weight. No form of diet seemed to work. Alma simply could not maintain her resolve to not eat for more than a week or two. Going away to college, her weight crept steadily higher. The student health doctor recommended several further weight loss diets and a dieting support group, all to no avail. He then recommended bariatric surgery, as her weight continued to creep higher and higher. In this surgical procedure, the stomach may be made smaller, and/or the small intestines may be re-routed so that less food is absorbed. Alma was appalled that she had reached this level of failure with her overweight issues, and finally sought out a psychotherapist with a good reputation for helping with weight loss.

Dr. 'Feldman' was a wise and experienced therapist. She was impressed with Alma's great sensitivity, guessing she might have suffered trauma that was contributing to her obesity. When Alma teared up as she was describing the loss of her father, Dr. Feldman saw she was on the right track. Processing the unresolved grief residues led to distinct, but modest changes in her food cravings and comfort eating.

Dialoguing with her weight in a two-chair exploration very quickly produced several helpful memories. One of the men Alma's mother had dated raped Alma when her mother was detained at work. He told Alma she was responsible for his assault because she had given him a strong 'come on,' and that if she said anything to her mother about it, he would tell her mother what a sleazy slut she was. Alma had been pleasant and polite, but in no way that she could identify did she see anything she had done or said to invite the sexual assault. But being the sensitive person she was, she assumed he, as an older person, must have seen something she missed being aware of.

Having finally spoken out in therapy about her trauma, Alma was then able to clear the residues of her rape in just a few sessions of tapping with Thought Field Therapy (TFT), another EP method, under Dr. Feldman's guidance.

It took a lot of persistence, but with her therapist's support and with participation in the dieting support group, Alma was now able to steadily diet, losing 160 pounds by the time she graduated.*[16]

I was very pleased to hear this clinical report of a successful psychotherapeutic alternative to surgery for serious obesity. Hopefully it will become the norm to offer psychotherapy first and consider surgery only as a last resort – rather than vice-versa.

### *The five love languages*

How do we show that we care about and love another person? Awareness of the five love languages identified by Gary Chapman (2007) can be enormously helpful.

Chapman found five important styles for communicating caring, affection and love. I'm surprised that most people are unaware of these – until I ask them to identify which of these five styles they favor the most: Words of Affirmation, Quality Time, Gifts, Acts of Service, and Touch. Most are able to claim their love languages immediately.

Knowing your own preferred styles and those of your significant others can enormously facilitate your getting along well with them.

These are wonderfully helpful items to pay attention to, because many people assume that other people have the same love language as their own. This can lead to great disappointment! This is an easy and fun item to address. Check out with those with whom you have close relationships what their love languages are, and share your own. That way you can connect better with each other.

- Words of Affirmation: Your heart warms when someone you're close to tells you how much they care for you and love you, why they enjoy your company, what they admire and respect you for, and how they appreciate the ways in which you show that you care for that special someone.
- Touch: You melt when your partner in life touches your hand, strokes your hair or your cheek, gives you a quick hug and a peck on the lips on the way to work, and snuggles up to you in bed to wish you good dreams. You enjoy giving your partner a foot massage, slathering on the sunscreen in spots he can't reach, or scratch his back while he purrs like a kitten.
- Quality Time: You feel so much more in tune with yourself and with the world when you are sharing quality time with the person you like or love. This might be time spent together in talking, strolling in nature, listening to music, watching a video, taking time off for a holiday, or just being in the same room

while each of you engages in your own activity. You show that you care for him by making yourself available to be with him. You listen attentively and follow up on your conversations with him, or share a laugh or an interesting item from the materials you're reading.

- Gifts: You glow with appreciation when your loved one brings you flowers, candy, a favorite quote or book, an invitation to go out to a dinner or a show, or something small and of little cost that demonstrates he's thinking of you. You enjoy keeping your eyes and ears open for indications of something your HSP wants or craves –    which you can surprise him with as a token of your affection and appreciation.

- Acts of Service: You, the NHSP may be enormously grateful when your HSP takes on the shopping, meal planning or bill-paying chores; when your HSP volunteers to be the social secretary for the two of you; or when she simply brings you a cup of coffee as you are waking up in the morning.

You, the HSP, may be relieved that your NHSPC experiences cooking as a quiet, meditative time and is happy to take on this task regularly – because you get flustered and sometimes feel embarrassed to admit you're overwhelmed with all the many details if you have to pick out the recipe, buy the food, and choreograph the timing for each dish in a meal that is more than a sandwich.

Even knowing of these love languages, HSPs who are immersed at times in very strong emotional reactions may have difficulties remembering to use the best love language with someone close to them.

An HSPC can offer words of support and appreciation, or just a touch on the arm or a hug (as appropriate to the love language of their HSP), thereby reducing the intensity of the negative experiences and helping their HSP to connect with thinking processes, and then with how to best address the troubling issues.

HSPs and their HSPCs will get along better when they check out with each other what each of their preferred love languages are. Often there is a primary one plus one or more secondary ones. Don't assume that your companion's favorites are the same as yours! Check with each other what acknowledgments, words and actions in their love language are the most pleasing and satisfying.

Be aware, if you are an NHSPC, that your quality time, words of affirmation, acts of service and/or touch may be appreciated even more by your HSP if you repeat them several times. For an HSP, the experiencing of your attention is fresh each time you give it.

## 42. Mind

> *Always think of your mind as a garden,*
> *and keep it beautiful*
> *and fragrant with divine thoughts.*
> *A mind all logic is like a knife all blade.*
> *It makes the hand bleed that uses it.*
> — Rabindranath Tagore

We've explored ways to address both acute and chronic emotional distresses. Mental distress is distinctly different, though often it is still intimately linked with emotional distress. Much of our mental distress is one or more levels removed from immediate emotional upsets. It's our thoughts, critiques, anticipations and worries *about* our distressed feelings and worries. We've explored some of these meta-issues and how to clear them when they block us from clearing the primary issues. Here, I want to invite you to use your self-healing skills proactively.

### *Preventive clearing of negativity, AKA wholistic housecleaning*

You can develop and improve your wholistic internal housecleaning with mental intent and a modest amount of practice. This involves clearing away buried clutter and tangles in your emotions and mind, as well as tidying up and putting everything in its place. Sometimes this can be in a trash bin that you quickly empty! Then you can move ahead with fuller inner resources available to you, as and when you need them, because your unconscious mind will now be free of the tasks of standing vigilantly alert to protect you from being hurt again now, as you were hurt earlier in your life.

Just as you brush your teeth in the morning and at night, I recommend that you search for any stress-grit, worry niggles, or annoyance residues you can brush away before you start and end your day. You may choose to put a quiet period into your calendar for a regularly scheduled pause some time in your daily routine. For many, a deliberate allocation of a few moments for internal housecleaning can make a great difference in your personal life and in your relationships, perhaps with an alarm clock set five minutes earlier in the morning, and again, before dozing off at night.

I'm sure you've experienced times when you're stressed or distressed over a personal challenge, and due to your inner tensions you get uncharacteristically irritable with someone who really didn't deserve to be the target of your annoyed responses. The target of your annoyance might even be yourself. You may become aware that you are fretting over issues you cannot influence or change. But your mind persists in niggling thoughts and frustrated feelings, despite your best efforts to keep yourself on task.

You can learn how to deal with such challenges competently, so that you remain calm, knowing you can sort them out. Not only is it helpful with the issues you are working on currently, but you can install and reinforce your meta-confidence that you know you will always be able to sort out anxieties, worries and distresses of any sorts. When you've done this, then when you encounter future stresses and distresses, you won't feel as upset or overwhelmed.

What I'm addressing here is how you can develop a habit of setting your emotional thermostat so that it doesn't turn on the heat when that's really not necessary, and so you don't fret or lose sleep, worrying over issues that you are unable to change, or perhaps ones that you're really able to handle comfortably but can't stop worrying about. When you develop this meta-confidence that you can manage challenges in your life, you'll find you can deal with these issues competently, without worrying about whether you can overcome them. You will simply know that you can handle them.

✦ 'Phil' was generally an easy-going, pleasant hardware store assistant manager. Sadly, his wife, 'Millie,' was diagnosed with breast cancer, and the whole family was very stressed. Phil, in particular, became unusually huffy and irritable with family members and with customers at work. His manager did her best to cover for him, but complaints started coming in and, as much as she wanted to be considerate, she had to warn Phil to shape up or he'd be demoted to doing office work.

Long story short, I saw Millie and Phil for stress management. Both were very quick to learn and use relaxation, meditation and TWR/ WHEE, and did well managing their acute stresses. Phil settled back to being his old self at work, so this crisis was sorted out.

Looking at the longer-term situation, I suggested they might find it helpful to use their tapping preventively. Millie, in particular, felt very unhappy with the prospect of months of sitting in tense waiting rooms for chemotherapy and radiotherapy. I suggested she might consider tapping preventively on her anticipatory anxieties of not enjoying these long, dreary waiting periods – so that she didn't suffer from worrying about what might or might not happen. I also suggested she could tap on her issues while sitting in the waiting rooms.

To her surprise, Millie found that by eliminating her anticipatory anxieties she was calm enough that she rarely needed to tap on worries while she was waiting for treatments or to see doctors.

She nevertheless chose to tap during those waiting periods on other stresses in her life. This changed her waiting room experience from one of not looking forward to her treatments into looking forward to times when she could sit in a place of inner calm and peace. And Phil found that by tapping while sitting in his car, before leaving the parking lot at work, first on any residual stresses from his workday, and then on anticipatory anxieties about Millie's condition, he was much calmer when he came home and more available to support Millie.

In these ways, you too can build and strengthen your positivity.

You don't have to have a serious illness, like Millie, to benefit from reducing your anticipatory anxieties. How about tapping when you're:

- Sitting in your car in heavy traffic that is moving slowly (Tapping with your tongue against your teeth on the right and left sides of your teeth or cheeks is recommended, as tapping with hands or feet could impair your ability to drive.)
- Standing in a long line at a checkout counter
- Waiting on the phone for customer service
- Waiting for the kettle to boil or for the roast to cook.
- Waiting for a family member to get ready to leave home

And once you've immunized yourself against irritability over your niggling frustrations, you can use these opportunities to focus on other irritating and annoying issues that

lower your tolerance for dealing with more important and immediate issues in your life:
- Frustrations with bureaucratic challenges
- Habits of people around you that you find irritating but can do nothing to change
- Delays in bringing your hopes and dreams and plans to rapid and satisfying fruition
- Financial limitations
- Political and economic issues that are beyond your abilities to influence

By doing these preventive clearings of irritating, annoying and frustrating issues, you leave yourself with much more energy to address the more immediate and really important issues in your life. And here, too, there may be opportunities for preventive clearing of negativities. For instance:
- If you're an NHSPC and find that your HSP gets over-focused at times on issues that stir his emotions, and he obsesses over issues he can't change or fix
- If you're an HSP and find that you have to repeatedly remind your NHSPC that in dealing with you or your HSP child she has to allow each of you time to process your feelings about situations and relationships before moving into decision-making mode

### *Preventive installing of positivity and meta-positivity, AKA investing in my wholistic internal bank account*

We've considered some of the basics of tapping to reduce emotional distress and build positivity. Here, we'll look at how you can address your meta-negative and meta-positive feelings to enhance how you deal with your emotions.

Your awareness of having negative experiences generates various feelings and thoughts – *about* feelings and thoughts that you're having. This is particularly relevant to HSPs, because our heightened sensitivities make us more reactive in general when we're feeling strongly stimulated in any areas of our lives. For instance:
- You may get anxious that your anxieties and worries about your finances are going to derail your abilities to concentrate on your studies and work.
- You may become discouraged, frustrated and angry when you find your progress in clearing an issue is slower than you hoped, or that you're finding more problems linked to your initial focus issue and needing to clear the decks of side-issues and sharpen your attention before you can address your main issue.
- You may develop a generalized 'poor me' attitude, expecting you'll never be able to overcome your challenges, feel better, or have a better relationship with your HSPC or HSP.
- You may get into a negative spiral of irritation and negativity with your HSP or HSPC, coming to a place where you put up your guard when you're together because you anticipate your interactions will be annoying, disappointing or painful.

So when we find ourselves discouraged and holding negative anticipations because our progress is slower than we had hoped, or our relationships more difficult and frustrating than we know how to address, we can ask ourselves whether we have any meta-feelings or meta-thoughts that are getting in our way of giving all we've got to helping ourselves be the best we can be and do the best we can do.

Writing down our observations about our situation can be enormously helpful. When we're stressed, it's easy to forget a brilliant insight into our challenges, or a very promising new approach to dealing with them.

The good news is that meta-feelings and thoughts usually respond much more readily to tapping and other clearing approaches than our primary issues do.

✦✦✦ I (Dan) developed a partial paralysis of my left vocal cord for no apparent reason. Medical examinations, including varieties of scans, revealed no physical cause for the hoarseness in my voice, which was worse when I was tired, dehydrated or anxious. Tapping on general and specific outer-world anxieties was only mildly effective, and minimally effective regarding my anxieties about my hoarse voice.

I developed meta-anxieties, as I became more concerned and anxious about my work on my voice being only modestly helpful. I started spiraling into despair.

Realizing I was succumbing to meta-anxieties, I started tapping on these fears. Within a day, I reduced them to close to zero. But the hoarseness remained annoyingly troublesome.

I then came into awareness that in the course of the early childhood abuse I had suffered over a period of 3-4 years, my abusers had told me that I must never speak about what I experienced, and that if I did, there would be very negative consequences. It felt as though these threats were probably reinforced with post-hypnotic suggestions never to speak about any of these experiences. I've been unable to clarify many of the precise details of this silencing aspect of the abuse I suffered, but I've had moderate improvements in my voice through clearing more general meta-statements, such as:

– "Even though I'm afraid to speak out about the traumas I've suffered because I've been told I'd lose my voice if I did…"

– "Even though I'm feeling scared that something bad will happen to me if I tell anyone about the bad things that were done to me and the terrible emotional scars I've carried from these experiences through the rest of my life…"

Gradually, my voice improved with these sorts of tapping statements, addressing the meta-anxieties and meta-injunctions to not speak out regarding the abuse I experienced, along with the memories of my suffering the abuses themselves.*[17] More on my odyssey with my vocal cord below.

WHAT ARE META-NEGATIVES YOU'VE DEVELOPED OVER THE YEARS?

HOW DO YOU HANDLE THESE?

### *Clearing meta-negative expectations in repeating situations*

You can also be proactive about dealing with meta-anxieties. Think for a few moments about meta-negative feelings and thoughts in your life.

- Do you feel unhappy or anxious when you think of particular people with whom you have to interact?
- Are there parts of your job, chores or responsibilities that you are prone to worry or fret over?
- Do issues you anticipate in the future worry you, such as finances, health or the unfolding of relationships over time?

Tapping on the meta-anxieties that are attached to your past experiences of such issues markedly facilitates the releases of thoughts and feelings you have about current issues. Tapping on meta-negative anticipations of repeating negativities can likewise reduce their intensity and ease your future repetitions of similar experiences.

EP and EMDR are outstanding for the treatment of trauma residues, including the meta-anxieties about the traumas. Prior to the development of these therapies in the late 1900's, trauma release was much more challenging and not as successful.

✦✦✦ The universe introduced me (Dan) to innovative ways for dealing with intense emotions early in my psychotherapy career. 'Greg,' a 31 year-old client who had been making nice progress addressing his feelings of social awkwardness in conventional psychotherapy for over a year, asked me one day, "Have you heard of Primal Therapy?" Arthur Janov described using this with groups in which the participants shouted and screamed at the top of their lungs, venting their feelings over abuses and traumas they had experienced. I had read Janov's book, The Primal Scream, and asked Greg why this interested him. He said he felt intuitively this was right for him, because he had suffered serious abuses from his parents as a child.

I was intrigued, as I had never considered using such an intensive therapy. I told him I couldn't imagine running a group like this, but that I'd be willing to consider doing this with him, alone. In addition, I had to explore where we might possibly hold such sessions in which his loud screams would create a disturbance, and whether the hospital where I worked would allow this.

To my surprise, neither of my concerns proved to be an issue. There was a ward that was unused, with an isolation room that had double doors, acoustically designed specifically to limit the disturbance on the locked psychiatric unit from anyone who needed to be in this room to calm down from a major emotional upset. And when I approached the Psychiatry department chairman, he was as intrigued as I was to have an opportunity to learn whether this sort of approach had any merits. He did recommend, however, that we do this after hours, to further limit any likelihood of disturbing someone.

So we held the next session with Greg lying on a padded mat on the floor of a padded room. At his suggestion, he started out yelling at his father over the abuses he had suffered from him. Following Janov's descriptions of this method in his book, I redirected Greg to focus his memory to a specific incident and express his words and emotions towards his father, as though they were back in the original situation.

To say that the results were dramatically effective would be a gross understatement. Greg went through paroxysms of anger over the hurt, fear and anger he had experienced in his relationship with his father. With minimal guidance from me, he did this with several specific incidents that opened into similar scenarios of parental abuse and Greg's deep hurt. Though we had scheduled two hours for this, he was exhausted after 45 minutes, winding down into deep sobs and tears over his disappointment and despair, as he felt he was just not good enough for his father to love and accept him.

We both agreed this had been a most encouraging start, and proceeded with weekly sessions of this sort. A notable highlight of the series occurred one night when a hospital guard knocked on the outer door, with his hand on his pistol, anxious and scared that some form of mayhem was being committed on this empty ward, behind the double doors of this isolation room!

On another occasion, Greg scared me by going into a prolonged fit of coughing, towards the end of which he spit up a little spot of blood. Though I was concerned he might have hurt himself with his intense coughing, the amount of blood was small, and appeared to me to be an unconscious message from his body – putting a physical exclamation point to follow his wailing during the session about how deeply hurt he had felt, following a particularly brutal beating at his father's hands. Greg never had any further issues with his throat or lungs while he was in therapy during the period after that single incident.

Over a period of three months, Greg cleared trauma memories and emotions from the repeated abuses he had had to endure until he left home at the age of 18. He also had several sessions where he connected with his sadness over hearing how his father had suffered horrendous abuses as an orphan from age four, through periods in an orphanage and then in a series of foster homes. He also released intense sadness over his mother's suffering similar abuses, and over her inability to stand up to his father or to provide much comfort for Greg.

We reached a point where Greg felt "I've wrung myself dry of anger and fear and hurt and despair and blaming myself for not being good enough for my father. I think I'm ready to leave all that behind me and move on with my life in a better way."

I have to say that I was glad to have several colleagues (including the psychiatry department director) with whom I could share some of what I experienced as a facilitator for Greg's clearing of these deep, intense feelings.

Over these three months, Greg had made miles more progress, and had cleared his issues far more deeply and thoroughly than he had even begun to achieve in his entire year of conventional, psychodynamic psychotherapy. By mutual agreement, we ended the therapy. A year later I had a letter from him, thanking me for being willing to go these extra miles with him. He shared that he was finding himself to be a new man, with far greater self-confidence, and now in a promising relationship with a lovely woman whom he thought might be a good marriage prospect.

I felt most fortunate to have had this lesson in helping to face trauma memories and feelings and clear them. Greg taught me that trauma residues need not continue to be obstacles in people's lives when you re-experience them in a safe and supportive setting, and have the methods and support you need for clearing them.

It appears that it is the meta-anxieties about trauma that lock people into continued suffering from these memories and feelings. And paradoxically, when people release these feelings with intensity in a safe and supportive environment, they are able to free themselves from the suffering they experience endlessly – from the battle between their meta-anxieties that warn them it would be dangerous to go near their buried memories and feelings, and even more so to exhume the horrendous pain and suffering of the buried memories themselves that are crying and begging to be released.

After helping a few more people with Primal Scream therapy, I did not pursue this further in my practice. It was terribly draining and there were few who were willing to confront their meta-anxieties and to do such intensive work of emotional releasing. But I did carry the lessons of these experiences in my awareness and was ready to explore and embrace other new approaches as they presented themselves to me.

And I'll allow myself to get a little ahead of the orderly development of my discussion of wholistic approaches here, with a modest preview of contributions of spirit in guiding our lives and in healing.

✦✦✦ I often have a sense of spiritual guidance in my life. Sometimes it surfaces to my awareness in the process of my experiences but more often it percolates into consciousness as I review in my memories what occurred.

Greg's presenting complaint when he initially came for therapy was that he had a wart on his penis, and he was seeking hypnotherapy to cure it. He had suffered a lot of pain when the wart was burned off previously, but it had returned. He was not eager for a second round of that treatment!

I had learned hypnosis during my research fellowship in medical school, at which time I also read broadly about hypnotic suggestions, placebo effects and self-healing. I was aware that warts can clear with any sort of suggestion, and Greg had found the same in his literature research over the six months following the recurrence of his wart.**[18] So the threads leading to our coming together in this healing encounter could be traced back several years.

It is a very different matter to have direct experience with a wart, rather than just book knowledge, both on the suffering end and on the treatment end of the spectrum of knowledge and understanding. I helped Greg clear his wart with light hypnotic suggestions over a period of several weeks, and he provided me with the experiential opportunity to learn more directly about physical effects of suggestions. This was one of my more impressive early introductions to the influence of the mind over the body.

And Greg continued to broaden my experiential horizons as a therapist. Having dealt with the wart, he accepted my recommendation to continue in conventional therapy to address his issues of low self-confidence and poor self-esteem, related to his childhood experiences of rejections and abuses. I would probably never have gone anywhere near suggesting to a client to explore intensive emotional releases as part of their therapy. I have to admit I had serious hesitations about doing so in this case, and saw it as rather unlikely that I would manage to get either a place suitable for doing this in my work setting, or permission within the psychiatry department to do anything like this. Yet I had no difficulties with either of these challenges.

To say that Greg became one of the more important teachers along my professional path of learning about trauma and trauma release is no exaggeration. And yet, for the most part, these lessons lay dormant and minimally influenced my practice over the next two decades.

It was 25 years later that I got interested in EMDR and then in EFT, and these threads of clinical experience and wholistic awarenesses from what I learned through Greg's therapy became stronger and clearer to me. Another thread that helped was the shift of psychiatry from the primary practice of psychotherapy to become restricted almost exclusively to drug therapies. Along with this came the decrease in patient sessions from 1-2 hours per week to 15-20 minutes per month. This led me to develop WHEE, which I could teach people to use in just a few minutes, and which they could then continue to use on their own.

And it was through my clients' successes in using TWR/ WHEE that I came to understand wholistic healing. My clients' bodies often become clear and strong indicators of the value of addressing each of the other levels of their being. In particular, pains provide a meter to measure successes in addressing issues of emotions, mind, relationships and spirit. Focusing on issues in any of these areas, while tapping on the body, would regularly reduce the pain levels – telling my clients and me we were on the right track.

And tying all of these threads of my clinical experiences together, I sense the hand of spirit guiding the flows of lessons in my life and the lives of my clients. These, too, are often validated in the tapping process. More on this to follow.

## *Broader applications of preventive positivity and wholistic housecleaning*

In the early years of my studies of how to help people understand themselves and feel better, I had difficulties comprehending why healthcare is focused so heavily on treating problems when people are sick, rather than on promoting health and preventive healing. It finally dawned on me that the answers to this question are similar from both the caregivers' and the careseekers' perspectives. Caregivers are demonstrably helpful when people are sick or in pain. Careseekers come for help when they are sick or in pain. In most cases, neither careseekers nor caregivers are particularly motivated to address how to become healthy and to stay healthy.

This is also why caregivers tend to stop their interventions when people have recuperated from injuries or illnesses. Because they are so enormously over-focused on the physical aspects of presenting problems, neither caregivers nor careseekers have the mindset to continue working on what doesn't seem to need any more fixing.

A further disincentive for caregivers is that there are enormous investments in facilities and therapies for treating people, particularly with drugs. There is far more money to be made in treating illness than in preventing it, particularly in countries with private healthcare systems. And of course there are also the factors surrounding blindness to new ways of understanding and treating problems that were discussed earlier.*[19]

In my experience, this over-focus on treatment rather than on prevention is a serious mistake. Particularly with pain, stress, trauma and other psychological problems, and especially when these impact your body and other parts of your wholistic being, you are far better off when you go the extra miles required to install positive thoughts and feelings after releasing negative ones. Whatever negativity you have released is much less likely to return when you address your issues through the broader focus of wholistic healing. Furthermore, your positivities in any areas of your life are great models for building positivity in other parts of your existence, which are suffering from positivity anemias. In addition, the habit of installing positivities develops meta-positive attitudes, expectations and skills.

And the meta-meta-positive here (that is, the meta-positive about meta-positives) is that meta-positives build your confidence in your abilities to deal with issues in general. With this awareness and confidence, you are in a much better place to install positives and meta-positives to replace the negativity you've released.

- "I'm really doing well with my _____[name issue]. I bet I can also do well with my _____ [other issues]."
- "I'm having serious challenges standing up to my [parents/ husband/ boss]. I wonder how I can apply my attitudes of positivity and positive approaches I learned to use from my successes in [school/ work/ clearing my trauma residues] to help me now in dealing with my current challenges?"

## WHAT ARE SOME OF YOUR SUCCESSES IN LIFE AND META-POSITVE TAKEAWAYS FROM YOUR SUCCESSES?

> *Many things in life are outside of our control, but the way we respond to events can shape our reality. Viewing challenges as opportunities, not misfortunes, will help you lead a productive, successful life.*
> - Jim Carrey**[20]

Similarly, you can build meta-positive thoughts and feelings as you have pleasant and enjoyable emotions and thoughts about aspects of your life, and not just when you've succeeded in dealing with negativity. These meta-positives encourage you to persist and expand your positive activities on your own and in interactions with other people, which in turn improve your chances of developing further good experiences in your life.**[21] On intuitive and spiritual levels, this also sets up vibrations that invite the universe to send more positivity your way.*[22]

We've explored building your place of peace and safety and healing (PPSH). You'll find that when you use your PPSH for enhancing your sense of being safe in the world, as well as for relaxation, meditation, and stress reduction, you'll gain confidence in how well your PPSH can help you. Just anticipating visiting and spending time there will feel positive – which is a meta-positive.

You can enhance such meta-positives by pausing as you're ending your positive experiences (like a visit in your PPSH), consciously looking forward to the next time you will be in this positive space, and tapping as you do so. This will enhance the intensity of your positive awarenesses and of your intention to remember to access this positivity whenever you wish and need to do so. You can also anchor your sense of a positive connection with your PPSH by pressing on any part of your body. This links that point which you've touched to the PPSH, so that in the future you can press on the point and it will connect you with the PPSH.*[23]

You can enhance the future effectiveness of positive experiences with the help of TWR/WHEE, two-chair work, and other approaches discussed in this book by deliberately creating meta-positives associated with these positivities.

Here's how you can do this. When you experience relief from pains, stress, trauma residues and other negativity, take a few moments to build, install and strengthen meta-positives about the benefits you are experiencing.

- "Wow! I've really had wonderful pain relief after suffering from [insert your pain experience] that I've suffered for [insert length of time]. I now know I can do this with other physical pains and for relief from other stress and distress."
- "I did so well on my last exam because I was tapping my feet quietly as I considered the questions and wrote out my answers. I'm certain I can be calm when I study for future exams, as well as when I take the exams, and I'll continue to do better and better. My exam anxiety is a thing of the past now!"

Building and strengthening your meta-positive thoughts and feelings about your HSP or HSPC can also be enormously helpful. If either of you is prone to recurrent upsets or to feeling down or hopeless, this can be very trying and wearing in your relationship. Instead of saying to yourself, "OMG! Here we go again..." You can draw upon your PPSH or anchored positivity and ask

- "What can I say that will help him feel better?"
- "What can I point out about her progress that will help her, like a life-raft would, when she's feeling she's drowning in her negative experiences?
  - "I could remind her how successful she was with_____"
  - "She's tired and frustrated with these issues right now. I could suggest setting aside the challenges for this evening, as it's getting late, and promise to help her tomorrow over breakfast. She's a morning person, anyway, so that's a better time to deal with these issues."
- "How would it be if I offered to run interference for him?"
  - "I could thank his parents for their well-meant (but inappropriate) advice, but let them know I'm here to help him, particularly in issues in our marriage, our parenting, and our life together in general, and we've been doing better and better figuring things out together."
- "What comforts can I offer when she's facing challenges from the universe?"
  - "I could remind her of Mother Theresa's complaints about the universe sending her mega-major challenges because she's done so well with the less challenging ones..."

*Acknowledging progress in the form of change over time* is another type of meta-positive. For example, if you're an NHSP, you may have to keep reminding yourself that when your HSP is upset, if you want to help her shift out of her 'down' feelings, she may feel better if she has some praises and reassurances. Helpful ego boosters might include:

"You're pretty upset, and with good reasons. [Pause for acknowledgment.] But look at the progress you've made since..."

"You're really doing well, considering how you used to get triggered by... and now you just..."

"You used to react [describe details] and now you're able to [note improvements]...

*WHAT DO YOU SUGGEST FOR BUILDING POSITIVITY?*

*WHAT ARE SOME MILESTONES AND PROGRESS YOU CAN ACKNOWLEDGE FOR DOING THIS IN YOUR OWN LIFE?*

As an NHSP, it may take you a while to truly understand how an HSP absorbs new awarenesses. An NHSP will mentally work through the details of issues, identifying and then sorting out pieces of the problems that are to be addressed. Understanding comes with new insights into details that were previously overlooked and new ways they can be comprehended and addressed. Plans are then made to address the issues as appropriate, in the light of the new cognitive understandings.

HSPs will work on their feelings about the new understandings they acquire, adjusting their emotional barometers to the newly acquired awarenesses. They are not unaware of the mental understandings that something new has been absorbed, but their inner guidance system is keyed to their emotional awarenesses much more strongly than to their mental thoughts, memories and logical understandings. In some cases, their emotional awarenesses will immediately shift significantly with new experiential and mental information. But in many instances, it takes numbers of repetitions of a new emotional experience to alter their emotional barometers and to implement new understandings. This is particularly true regarding issues around stress and trauma. That's the challenging news. HSPCs often have to remind HSPs of the new, more helpful emotional perceptions when the HSPs continue to respond out of habit with the old responses to whatever is challenging them.

The good news is that by using wholistic EP, it is possible to shift the emotional barometers much more quickly and deeply. This enables HSPs to adapt to new information and release their old, outmoded reactions and responses much more quickly and deeply.

Let me illustrate some of these observations.

✦ NHSP 'Shirley' was married to HSP 'Oliver,' who was very emotionally sensitive. They had dated in college, married shortly before graduation, and both worked as English teachers at different high schools. Though she was very outgoing and chatty, and he was much more introverted, they generally got along very comfortably and happily. They both greatly enjoyed English literature and films. Discussing books, essays, YouTubes and movies, with each other and with friends and colleagues, was one of their greatest pleasures.

When their son and daughter were born, a year and a half apart, they found themselves far more stressed and irritable with each other than they thought and felt was warranted.

Oliver had been badly bullied in childhood at home by his NHSP three brothers and two sisters and by schoolmates in grade school because he was emotionally sensitive and cried easily. He learned to cope with his sensitivity by becoming a 'turtle' and hiding in his shell of silence when he was upset. While his parents didn't condone the bullying, they didn't set any limits on it. Even as an adult, his family teased him mercilessly for the least little show of emotions. Oliver reached the point that he completely avoided family functions and would have nothing to do with his brothers or sisters or their families. He occasionally exchanged visits with his parents, but only briefly, to celebrate a birthday or anniversary.

Despite feeling a little better after he started avoiding participating in family get-togethers that were utterly depressing to him, Oliver still felt guilty that he wasn't participating as part of the family – for his parents' sake. He knew they felt hurt that he wasn't there for celebrations on family occasions.

Shirley had had more conversations about this with Oliver than she cared to count, and was feeling very frustrated that he couldn't come to peace with himself over his way of dealing with this. He would become irritable and spiky for several weeks before family occasions, and would then just make do with sending a card or a gift, or making a brief phone call to excuse himself from participating. Where she had previously been able to keep her cool most of the time over his frequent fretting, she was getting increasingly impatient and irritable, leading to unpleasant arguments between them. She found this more and more draining and irritating in their relationship. She was also frustrated and worried that it was impacting their children, who were 3 and 5 years old, and were becoming increasingly irritable and fussy. She finally convinced him they should come for a consultation with me (Dan) over their family issues.

We had a joint session, then individual sessions for each of them separately (as I frequently do with couples), and then continued with joint sessions. Towards the end of the first joint session, I introduced them to TWR/WHEE, inviting each of them to work on reducing their personal frustrations with their situation. This was immediately effective for both of them. Shirley was able to bring her SUDS down from 7 to 2, but Oliver only managed to reduce his intensity from 9 to 7.5.

In Oliver's individual session, he did well in a two-chair dialogue with himself over his ambivalence in wanting to be done with his lifelong suffering from his brothers' and sisters' bullying, vs. his guilt over cutting off his relationships with them and over disappointing his parents. His guilty side could not muster any hopes of improving the situation, nor make any suggestions for ways to deal with his brothers' and sisters' bullying that he hadn't already explored – with nothing more than further disappointments over his efforts. Nevertheless, tapping on his ambivalence reduced his SUDS to a 4.5 at that point.

In their second joint session, Shirley shared she was feeling much more positive and optimistic as she continued to tap on her current frustrations and memories of previous ones. She raised the observation that Oliver's next younger brother, Peter, seemed to be a bit less negative than the others, having grown up with Oliver as something of a father figure for him. Oliver agreed, and did several two-chair explorations around his relationship with Peter. The first was between the part of himself that lumped Peter with the rest of his siblings and the second part of himself that could muster a bit of hope for a better relationship with Peter. The second two-chair exploration was between himself and Peter. To Oliver's surprise, he found himself with much more hope than ever before that there might be some improvement in his relationship with Peter. Shirley was equally surprised, as Oliver had previously always dismissed her suggestions in this regard.

Over the course of several more sessions, Oliver clarified his feelings towards Peter. He felt more of a bond with him than with any of his other siblings. He also continued the two-chair explorations of possible ways he might address his feelings with Peter. TWR/WHEE was also helpful in reducing the various anxieties and the intensity of memories of unpleasant interactions he had had with Peter and the rest of his siblings.

Both reported they were getting along better. When they did get irritated, they would tap on their annoyances, frustrations and angers, either separately or together, with increasingly positive results.

With repeated encouragements, Oliver agreed to contact Peter. He also installed and strengthened various positive thoughts and feelings about how his discussion with Peter might unfold.

After a week of frequent tapping on this issue, Oliver connected with Peter and explained that he felt sad he hadn't discussed with him the issues that he felt were making it so difficult for him to meet up with Peter and the rest of his family, because he felt closer to Peter than to his other brothers and his sisters. Peter shared that he, too, felt sad that they had lost contact with each other. Long story short, they met and had a lengthy discussion about their relationship. To Oliver's great surprise, Peter admitted that he understood how Oliver was feeling. He also revealed he was embarrassed that he had not said anything in support of Oliver over the years, out of fear that he would end up being bullied as well by the others. As they were winding up their conversation, Peter added that in the light of his discussion with Oliver he realized he had behaved in a very cowardly manner, and apologized for this.

The other major positive that Oliver found in talking with Peter was Peter's agreement with Oliver's assessment that no changes were likely in the attitudes and behaviors of the rest of the family. Again, Oliver was tremendous relieved to have confirmation of his concerns, and to be able to stop beating up on himself for avoiding spending time with his family.

This was an enormously important turning point in Oliver's life. He came into much greater clarity of awareness of his feelings of rejection in his inner child that had built up and had been brutally and endlessly reinforced over all of his life. tapping and two-chair work were again wonderfully helpful in clearing these trauma residues. And these clearings were much deeper and more thorough than previous ones, and he was much better able to install replacement positives than ever before. And last, but not least, Oliver's relationship with Shirley was vastly improved, and their children's irritabilities disappeared as well.

Oliver's experiences of being a rejected HSP in an NHSP family is a fairly common one.*[24] Oliver's choice to avoid his family had enabled him to avoid further repetitions of their abusive dismissals and pathologizing of his being an HSP. However, this left him feeling sad and guilty for not finding a better way to cope with the situation.

As with many HSPs, Oliver had great difficulty resolving emotional ambivalence. When he felt hurt, battered, belittled and bullied, he wanted more and more to withdraw and have nothing further to do with his family. When he felt sad, frustrated, and guilty over failing to change so that his family accepted him, or over not coming to an acceptance of the situation, especially for the sake of his aging parents, he was strongly immersed in these feelings. It took two-chair work and tapping to help him move into resolving this ambivalence. Just talking about it with Shirley didn't enable him to make major, lasting shifts.

Peter's acceptance of Oliver and validation of Oliver's decision to minimize contact with their extended family was a great blessing to Oliver. With these feelings of relief, he moved into a strongly positive inner space.

HSPCs who are NHSPs may have considerable difficulties understanding both the ambivalent feelings and the HSP challenges in resolving them. Patience, persistence, and tapping are recommended!

## *Broader applications of proactive positivity and wholistic housecleaning*

If governments invested in preventive measures such as teaching and promoting healthy diets, exercise and stress reduction, trillions of dollars would be saved in long-term healthcare costs.

Similarly, when people have addressed their stresses proactively, I've seen enormous benefits with preventive uses of TWR/WHEE, both personally and professionally. My dream is to see children taught these methods from their earliest years in school. Teachers report that children are able to settle down quickly in class with tapping, and find it enormously helpful with anxieties around tests, social anxieties and bullying. They appreciate it enormously for its easy, immediate availability, ease of use, and for being able to use it discretely, without anyone else knowing they are de-stressing.

Once children (and adults too) have some of these positive experiences with de-stressing, they build up their meta-positive anticipations and expectations that they will be successful in dealing with future challenges. They also remind each other to tap on their issues when they see someone else who is getting frustrated, irritated or upset.

And let's also remember to be proactive in building, sharing and spreading general positivity. It can be a lovely warm fuzzy to share your good feelings and emotions with your partner, family and friends. And you needn't restrict yourself to these inner circles of people in your life. You can generate lots more warm fuzzies when you connect with random strangers and share little warm fuzzies with them.

- Just wearing a smile generates smiles in return.
- Smiling at babies and children and their parents costs very little, but can be a nice little boost in their day.
- Adding your positive, warm comment to something positive you see or overhear while waiting on a street corner for a red light, at a bus stop, or in a checkout lane in a store reinforces the positivity you are observing and resonating with.
- Thanking a store clerk, a telephone salesperson, or a public vehicle driver for their help is often an unexpected and much appreciated little boost in their day.

✦✦✦ I laughingly complimented a phone banking person on her precision and clarity in repeating a standard, formalized explanation of procedures to me, which was required for every customer with whom she spoke. I speculated that this was probably not the first time she had repeated these sentences. She burst out laughing, which was a total change from her tense, hurried recital of what must have become absolutely boring to her. She thanked me, with a cheerful tone in her voice, for being the first customer to have ever acknowledged this. We were both cheerful on ending what otherwise would have been a routine and boring call for each of us.

- Get to know your neighbors. Even if it's again just through smiles and little comments. This can markedly change your feeling about the physical and social place in the world where you live.

### Meditation

*If you are depressed, you are living in the past.*
*If you are anxious, you are living in the future.*
*If you are at peace, you are living in the present.*
- Lao Tzu

Meditation is probably the most widely used approach for self-healing through use of the mind. Meditation has been practiced by people around the world for thousands of years. Meditation is a discipline of the mind, which can help you to calm every aspect of your being.

There are countless ways to meditate. The core principle is to choose a focus for concentration and then practice, practice, practice – disciplining your consciousness to remain engaged only with your chosen focus, and releasing attachments to any other sensations, feelings, thoughts or other awarenesses.

When you're learning and practicing your meditation, your mind may wander anywhere and everywhere. Don't wrestle with these distractions or get engaged with the meta-awareness that you are distracted. Just return your consciousness gently to your chosen focus of breathing in and out.

While it is easy to describe the process of meditation, it is challenging for most people to get in the groove of a limited focus and remain there. Most people actually find this to be a challenge at first. The mind has been described by meditators as being like "a band of cavorting monkeys." When you start practicing, you will probably find endless distractions.

- Body sensations of every sort will draw your attention
- Emotions will arise, such as anxieties, sadness and anger.
- Thoughts will intrude, like frustration, impatience, disappointment, irritation, annoyance, self-criticism and random aware-nesses about your life and activities, including, perhaps the meta-awareness that you are successfully focusing your mind!
- You may be hoping to open into spiritual awareness, one of the ultimate goals of many forms of meditation, and frustrated that this is not happening.

There is no way around this but to practice, practice, practice!

My favorite book on meditation is by Lawrence LeShan (1974), a very wise psychologist who worked for decades to help people deal effectively with their cancers. He finds, as I do, that different people do better with different meditations. Here are a few examples you can explore.

- Observe your breath moving in and out. Say, silently, to yourself "In" as you breathe in, and "Out" as you release your breath. Nothing more to do. Just observe and acknowledge.
- Word focus: Choose a word or phrase that feels good to you, making it your mantra (meditation word(s) for focusing your mind). Anything like
  - Peace
  - Healing
  - "I am one with [Nature/ the All/ the Infinite Source/ God/ Christ/ Allah/ the Buddha]

- Or any other word or phrase that you resonate with in a positive way.

Repeat your mantra at a slow and regular pace, perhaps matching your word or phrase to your breathing.

- Focus on an object: Pick anything you find attractive and engaging, such as a flower, a picture, a meaningful symbol or whatever else appeals to you. Connect with its shape, color, texture and essence. Open your mind and heart to join and become one with it. Sense its inner essence.

- For anyone with a chatty mind which doesn't want to stop chewing on one thing after another (like my own), one of the following action meditations may be helpful:
  - Picture to yourself that you're sitting comfortably by the side of a flowing stream or river, after a brisk rain, with many little bits of branches, leaves and other flotsam floating past you. As any inner distraction draws your attention away from your image of the stream, place whatever has distracted you, gently and lovingly, on something that is floating by. Then return, waiting patiently for any further distractions that arise, and treat each in the same way.
  - Imagine yourself sitting on a bridge over railroad tracks, with an endless line of empty boxcars passing below. Drop anything that intrudes on your attention into a boxcar return to wait patiently for any further distractions that arise, and treat each of them in the same way.

- Ritualized movement can be a meditation. For instance, T'ai Chi is a Chinese series of slow motion exercises, requiring focus on your breath and on each part of the movement. Yoga can serve similarly as a physical meditation focus.

- Mindfulness meditation invites you into a meta-awareness space, to observe whatever draws your attention, without engaging with it. You simply note to yourself it is there and let it drift by your awareness, without any attachment to it.[25] Mindfulness meditation is one of the most popular and well researched in the West. It has been shown to help the brain to grow and maintain its thickness, improve interpersonal relationships, improve abilities to study, decrease anxiety, depression and chronic pains and more.[26]

- And last on this introductory meditations list, I add "the Zone," a growing awareness of sports as another form of mindfulness focus, as explained by Rick Leskowitz (2017), a Harvard psychiatrist, who has been studying measurable effects of collective consciousness in sports spectators.

"...preliminary data suggest that sport is like yoga and meditation and prayer, a powerful vehicle for entering the integral state of psychospiritual union." This is referred to "as 'the Zone' – the near-mythical state of mind-body alignment that all athletes (elite and recreational) seek... [A]chieving this state can be facilitated by a range of practices that include many modalities from the world of alternative and complementary medicine... innovators have developed training methods that enable their students to intentionally enter this so-called flow state."

There are countless other varieties of meditations. Any activity at all can become a meditation when we use it for a mental focus.

Various wholistic benefits of meditation may include

- Decreases in stress reactions, anxieties, pains and other body symptoms
- Thicker brain cortex areas serving attention and sensory processing
- Enhanced immune system functioning
- Heightened empathic awareness
- Improved relationships
- Improved school performance
- Improvement in ADHD

With any of these approaches, you will do increasingly better with a regularly scheduled meditation practice. Daily meditation is recommended. See which times of day work best for you.

You may wish to explore several of these variations on the theme of meditation. A particular one may work well for you now, but could stop being as helpful after a while. If that happens, check out another approach. It may work well at that later date, even if you didn't do well with it earlier.

Research on meditation shows an enormous range of benefits, including treatment for pain, anxiety, insomnia, ADHD, hypertension, irritable bowel syndrome, ulcerative colitis, immune system functions, smoking, substance abuse, age-related brain degeneration.[27]

As an HSP or HSPC, you may find meditation helpful in decreasing stress, in addition to enhancing your mental focus. A regular practice of meditations offers a resource similar to your PPSH. This is an invaluable tool with enormous wholistic spectrum benefits. While it may not have as great an impact in reducing the intensity of acute situations, nor is it as focused and specific in its effects as tapping, its overall effects are very deeply healing.

As an HSPC, in addition to the personal benefits you enjoy from meditation, you may also be supportive when you remind your HSP to access this resource when tensions are bothersome and your HSP is approaching or already in overwhelm.

And did you think of HuTiST here, as well?

## *Clearing trauma*

Trauma is such a common and serious contributor to difficulties on every wholistic level of our being that I mention it briefly here again, although it was discussed earlier in much greater detail.*[28] This brief discussion of trauma could clearly be placed under 'Emotions' rather than under 'Mind.' I place it here because it is generally through our conscious mind that we come to identify when we are being triggered into trauma memories and emotions, and that we can constructively address our trauma through our mental understanding, intentions and learned skills.

When you, an HSP, first become aware of your traumas, it can be very difficult to identify when you are being triggered, much less to muster resources to deal with the trauma when you are in a triggered state. Typically, something in your current life will stimulate you into an emotional reaction that other observers would call an excessively strong response. For you, however, the triggered feelings are so intense that you are very focused on your anxieties, fears, trauma memories, anger, panic or other emotions. You attribute these feelings to whatever is currently triggering them.

These observations apply as well to an HSPC. It is very common to find that people who develop close relationships have similar trauma issues in their past that are parts of the factors that draw you to each other. The similarities in your life histories give you common points of references, life experiences and understandings of each other and of the world at large. On spiritual levels, our higher selves also bring us together to help each other recognize the issues that have left us with trauma residues and to help each other learn to identify and to clear them.*[29]

### *Journaling*

> *In the journal I do not just express myself more openly than I could to any person; I create myself. The journal is a vehicle for my sense of selfhood. It represents me as emotionally and spiritually independent. Therefore... it does not simply record my actual, daily life but rather –in many cases - offers an alternative to it.*
> - Susan Sontag

Writing down the issues, emotions and thoughts you experience, and how you deal with them can be enormously helpful in many ways (Dalebout, 2016; Patel, 2015).

- Having a record of issues that trigger your trauma responses
- Calming yourself through the process of writing down your trauma responses in detail
- Exploring various self-healing approaches to see which work best for you
- Having a record of the various wordings and approaches we use in clearing traumas, so we can return to use those that were most successful, and conversely, working on improving the focus on various issues and refining the wordings that only cleared your issues partially or not at all.
- Creating a list of issues you can address through whatever therapeutic approaches work best for you
- Building habits of installing positive thoughts and feelings to replace the negative ones you've released
- Having a record of wordings you used for building positivities

In addition, HSPs often find journaling to be

- An aid in sorting out emotions that feel overwhelming
- A resource and aid in decreasing the intensity of negative triggering you experience, providing a quiet and private place to vent your feelings
- A serious help to bring in a more grounded and calmer awareness of yourself, putting more distance between your core, safe self and the intensity of your emotional reactions when you feel overwhelmed and helpless to deal with these
- A diary in which you can spot recurring patterns of issues that trigger you and ways that you deal with them
- A help in your building more positivity in your life
- An encouraging documentation of your progress

## 43. Relationships

*Since all illness is related to a negative relational experience,
it is the utmost importance for us to learn to interact
with each other in healthy, healing ways.*
— Barbara Brennan

### Relationships with other people

Most of us simply go with the flow of our relationships, enjoying the companionship, nurturing and support we find with our family, friends, acquaintances and colleagues. We also find satisfaction and joy in supporting others.

But when we find ourselves uncomfortable, stressed, disappointed or hurt in our relationships, we may do well to assess what our body, emotions, mind and spirit might want us to learn and know about our lives. Negativity isn't just negativity. It is also an invitation for us to examine what lessons the universe may be offering us. This is a very broad topic, about which many books and scripts for plays, TV serials and films are written. I offer here just a few practical suggestions that are helpful in self-healing.

### The what and the how of communicating

How you express your anger (and other feelings) is enormously important. With HSPs the feeling aspects of issues are often as important, if not more important, than the factual content. This may be a bit challenging at first, but with practice it becomes easier. While it may be difficult to control your emotions and responses in the heat of an argument, even that may be possible if you practice this till it is just part of your ways of communicating. This is particularly helpful, in fact, when working on anger within a partnered relationship. And here there is motivation and opportunity to discuss the issues that are involved.

A light-hearted way of practicing awareness in relationships is through 'conjugations' of communications. See Table VI-1 for a brief sprinkling of examples. Though this can often be funny, it is a great help in developing sensitivity to the 'how' of our communications.*[30]

**Table VI-1. 'Conjugations' in communications**

| | |
|---|---|
| "I'm slightly overweight." | "I'm sometimes distracted." |
| "You're a bit heavy." | "You can be a bit forgetful." |
| "He's getting tubby." | "She can't remember the time of day." |
| "She's simply fat." | "I'm worried he's getting early Alzheimers." |
| ---- | ---- |
| "I feel upset because you didn't phone me." | "I'm generous with my compliments." |
| "You upset me when you didn't phone me." | "You could acknowledge my help more often." |
| "You're so inconsiderate, not phoning me." | "If she says it's OK you know you've done exceptionally well." |
| "You never think of anyone but yourself." | "Don't expect him to say thank you if you block the bullet he probably deserves." |

*I INVITE YOU TO PLAY WITH THIS WHEN YOU'RE CONSIDERING SAYING SOMETHING IMPORTANT TO SOMEONE WHO MAY BE SENSITIVE TO THE 'HOW' OF YOUR COMMUNICATIONS.*

*Forgiveness*

> *Forgiveness is not about forgetting.*
> *It is about letting go of another person's throat.*
> — William Paul Young

Forgiveness offers a spectrum of healing options that are helpful for you as an HSP or HSPC, both for yourself and in your relationships. Often, this is a vitally important aspect of healing. There are countless references on this important topic, which is only lightly detailed here.**[31]

Forgiving a person with whom you currently have a relationship offers you the opportunity to discuss what upset, offended or hurt you. Forgiving a person who has wronged you in the past and is deceased or for some other reason no longer in a relationship with you, is more challenging. Here, the burden of any forgiveness is generally entirely upon you. You are not forgiving that person in order to release her from her responsibility for hurting you in whatever way she did, which could be through something she did to you or for neglecting you. You are forgiving her so that you can free yourself of resentments and hurts and move on in your life.

In situations where it is difficult for you to come to a place of forgiveness, the various releasing methods for stress and distress are again helpful. In addition, this is a type of issue where a therapist can often be enormously helpful.

✦ 'Bella' was a 48 year-old mother of two daughters, 27 and 23 years old. They had all suffered severe emotional and physical abuse from Bella's partner, 'Alex,' over the six years of her relationship with him. Bella had wanted to leave him but he had threatened to torture and kill her and the children if she even attempted to do that. She was enormously relieved when he was arrested for knifing and killing another man in a barroom brawl, and received a life sentenced in prison. This enabled her and the children at last to feel safe from his abuses and threats.

While it was a tremendous relief to Bella to be free of Alex's abuse and to know her children were now safe, she remained severely traumatized. She was able to function competently in a series of secretarial jobs, but would never trust a man more than to go out on a light date. If the relationship looked like it might be getting serious, she always found excuses to break it off, even if it meant having to change her place of work.

She did a creditable job in raising her daughters, and both had college degrees and decent jobs. She had worried that they would also have difficulties in getting along with men, but they appeared make much better choices in boyfriends than she had dared to hope. However, their relationships never lasted more than a few weeks. They always found fatal flaws in their boyfriends that led them to discontinue dating them.

Bella finally met 'Sal,' an enormously caring and supportive, second generation Mexican immigrant, who won her heart. But while she didn't run away from him as she had done with previous suitors, she still refused to live with him or even to spend an entire night with him.

She came to me asking if there was any help to get over the scars of her relationship with Alex. She made good use of tapping and two-chair work, releasing masses of horrendous trauma memories. But she was stuck with anger and resentment that Alex abused her children along with her, and she couldn't forgive him or herself for the pain that they suffered.

In working to forgive herself, she disclosed that her father had had an affair that dragged on and off for several years when she was between 6 and 11 years old. Her mother repeatedly took her father back, with promises that the affair was finished, but he never kept his word. It was only when his lover finally tired of his not staying with her and called off the relationship that he returned to stay with Bella.

This was one of those times where I had to work on forgiving myself for not having been more thorough in taking Bella's initial history. Uncovering her father's affair more quickly might have shortened the course of her therapy. Despite my concerns, her therapeutic relationship with me was not seriously damaged. And there was some good that came of this when I apologized for my negligence in this matter. The experience of my apologizing to her turned out to be enormously healing.

She was able at that point to start to forgive herself for having made such a poor choice in staying with Alex, despite having had some pretty strong hints this was not a good idea. From her current perspectives, she could see she would have been much, much better off dealing by herself with the challenges of having gotten pregnant on her first date with him.

In peeling the many layers of her trauma onion, forgiveness became a major theme. Using the two-chair approach and tapping worked extremely well for Bella.

– To decrease severe criticisms and self-blame, along with her guilt and depression over her poor choice in choosing Alex in the first place

– To reduce self-blame and guilt over not being able to help her mother more

– To reduce her guilt and self-criticisms over having been a poor model for her daughters for how to get along with men

– To reduce hurts, fears and angers at her father

With each of these, after releasing her negative feelings and installing replacement positives, Bella was able to come to a place of forgiving herself. She did this with only modest help from me, particularly by helping 'Little Bella' in one chair as 'Bella of today' from the second chair.

With many issues, forgiveness was an important part of her process of self-healing. Forgiving her father was the most difficult. Here, forgiving involved accepting that he was who he was and she was not going to carry any further burden of hurt or anger over his terrible behaviors because this was just harming herself. In her two-chair dialogue she made it clear she was not releasing him from his responsibilities for his behaviors, as these were his own issues to deal with. She also stated clearly she wasn't condoning what he had done. She was detaching from her fretting and blaming herself for the consequences of what he had done, and her participation in the unfolding of those issues. Her forgiveness was also a release of her connectedness with him.

Forgiving her mother for burdening Bella with the inappropriate responsibility of listening to her mother's repeated complaints was more of a challenge. There were layers and layers of hurt, anger, despair and abandonment to deal with. In her tapping and two-chair work, Bella was soon able to bundle clusters of issues and feelings about her parents and to clear these together, rather than addressing each one individually.

Hardest of all was her forgiveness of Alex. She realized that this load of traumas was waiting on a shelf, locked away in a remote closet of her mind and heart. But it took her a long time, with lots of practice in forgiveness of other issues with herself and her parents, to come to a place where she might be ready to address her issues with Alex.

Even as she finally moved into her Bella chair, facing the Alex chair, she found herself getting distracted away from the issues at hand. She readily admitted she still had several closets full of fears and anxieties that she might make another mistake, perhaps even with Sal, and end up again in an abusive and dangerous relationship.

Bella resonated strongly with my suggestion that these might be meta-anxieties about letting go of fears which she had heeded for many years – as protections against allowing herself to get into another dangerous relationship. And indeed, tapping away these meta-anxieties allowed her to proceed with forgiving herself for:

- Not having had the strength to confront Alex directly
- Not having found a way to leave Alex
- Not protecting her daughters more or better
- Not having sought professional help earlier to deal with these and all the other difficulties she had struggled with

And finally, Bella was ready to forgive Alex. She was clear that she was in no way condoning his nastiness or his abusive behaviors, nor absolving him of responsibilities for the pain and traumas he had inflicted. She was forgiving him as a way of fully letting go of her habits of holding onto angers, fears and memories of his abusive and traumatic behaviors. So she started her tapping with "I hereby forgive you"

- For having horribly abused me (with details)
- For having terribly abused our daughters (with details)
- For having made all of our lives frightening, miserable, distressing and painful (with details)
- For refusing therapy for your anger and drinking issues
- For refusing to go for counseling with me to sort out our marital issues
- With this piece of clearing, Bella felt free at last from the burdens of hurt, anger, guilt and other feelings she had carried from childhood.

It may take a bit of contemplation to understand this aspect of forgiveness. It is clearly not about your forgetting or just accepting what was done to you. It is about your letting go of hurt, anger, bitterness, lingering resentments, and wishes for personal revenge, justice through outside agencies or redress from outside oneself ('fixing the perpetrator') through a higher power.

It is about releasing the pains and traumas, angers and resentments, hurts suffered and wishes to hurt the perpetrator as he or she has hurt you. Forgiveness frees you to move on with your life.

*Forgiveness does not change the past, but it does enlarge the future.*
- Paul Boese

✦✦✦ As I wrote out Bella's story here, I connected with deeper resonations with her experiences in my own current life. As mentioned earlier, I suffered serious abuse as a young child from my mother. Over the years of working on my trauma issues with various therapies, I gradually came to modest acceptance of her negativity, appreciating from the ways she abused me that she must have been similarly abused herself.

However, I had not done in-depth work on forgiveness for my experiences of these abuses. After writing this section of the book, I worked with a much clearer focus on forgiving my mother, with distinctly positive results. With the intention of coming to forgiveness in mind, I again used TWR/WHEE to release terrors I experienced when she repeatedly abused me. The worst was the feeling of betrayal by my one and only adult family member, on whom I was totally dependent, with no one else I could turn to for help, comforting or healing.

As I mentioned earlier, In the process of clearing these early life memories in my mid-70's, I developed a partial paralysis of my left vocal cord. This made my voice rough, and if I have to speak loudly (as in a room with many other people talking) my voice gets rougher, to the point that my hoarseness makes my words hard to understand. I also developed a marked increase in my frequency of waking at night to urinate.

With gradual deepenings in my clearings of these trauma memory residues, I experienced modest improvements in my voice. It would stay stronger from early morning into midday, with occasional continuations into the afternoon if I did not strain it along the way.

Initially, I made no connection between these voice box symptoms with clearing specific trauma memories. Gradually, I came to a feeling awareness that my mother had told me I must never speak about how she was treating me, and reinforced these orders with threats of serious consequences if I ever mentioned any of this to anyone.

My urinary problems at night appear to suggest residues of sexual abuse as well. I had been waking every 2-3 hours to urinate over the past 5-6 years. Several strong intuitives spontaneously reported to me that they sensed this sort of abuse, without my having mentioned it to them.

Although we haven't gotten yet to a fuller discussion of spiritual aspects of wholistic healing, I still jump ahead here to include further details relevant to forgiveness.[32] My spiritual awarenesses also shifted as I worked on these trauma issues. I became aware that I had contracted with my mother prior to my birth for her to abuse me. Needless to say, this further shifted my readiness to forgive her.

However, it was only when I did a two-chair forgiveness, with more intense expressions and releases of my angers, fears, resentments, betrayal and trauma, that I understood I hadn't yet truly forgiven my mother. And when I came to this deeper place of forgiveness, following my writing about Bella's path through forgiveness, there were further changes in my symptoms. My urinary frequency decreased to 2-3 times per night and my voice became distinctly stronger and more often lasted longer through the day. My deeper forgiveness had taken my trauma releases to a distinctly deeper level.[33]

> *You only have to forgive once.*
> *To resent, you have to do it all day, every day.*
> — M.L. Stedman

There are vast resources and references on forgiveness. This is an area of human experiences that has absorbed many a good thinker, philosopher, writer and therapist.[34]

*Collective human relationships*

> *The question that continues to reverberate to this day is*
> *whether human rights trump the rights of business,*
> *or vice versa, a conflict that has been ongoing*
> *for more than three hundred years.*
> — Paul Hawken

We have serious challenges in our human relationships that extend beyond our personal family relations. There is a desperate need for wholistic healing for our global human community, to address the worldwide, collective challenges of body, emotions, mind, relationships with each other and with the environment, and spirit. As Paul Hawken notes, the growth of power in asserting corporate interests is now threatening to disempower and disenfranchise the majority of people around the world. How has this happened? The answer to this is far from simple. Let's take a look at some complexities of human relationships, and ways that we deal with them.

Even within the relationship of a couple there are often serious challenges in deciding on acceptable roles and rules for who is in charge; how decisions are made and how differences and disputes are resolved; how resources are allocated and shared; the degrees of participation of families of origin in the marital relationship; and other expectations, needs and wishes of each of the partners that may be in competition or conflict.

Our relationship issues grow exponentially as we expand our focus further, to include differences in expectations and accepted rules between different families in the same community. And as the numbers of individuals in the group increase, so do the differences in personalities, perspectives and opinions.

Humanity as a whole has not been brilliant in developing how to live in healing ways in groups larger than a single family. In family groups living as a clan, the most common way for preserving peace and order is to have a chief whose job it is to mediate disputes between individuals and families, and to enforce peace under his jurisdiction if the rule of law is disobeyed. The chief often calls upon eligible males to come together, if needed, to serve as a police force within the community, or to defend the community as a whole or to attack other communities when this appears necessary for survival or advantageous for promoting local interests.

Expanding the spectrum of relationships further, it becomes advantageous for communities to unite into kingdoms and nations, to lessen the conflicts between people within this level of organization – where the duties of mediating between communities and enforcing the law devolves upon the king or upon elected leaders and appointed officials.

Within nations today, there is a spectrum of approaches for organizing and running governments. Broadly speaking, we have dictator and election models for government, and a spectrum of socialist to capitalist governments.

In socialist governments, the laws favor the highest good of all. Those in the top earning brackets either have incomes that are limited (e.g. Japan) or taxed at a high percent (Scandinavian countries). In these ways, earnings are leveled to a great degree between workers and management. Government budgets are focused on providing health, education and welfare services for all.

In capitalist countries, a small number of individuals and corporations can accumulate increasingly high percents of the available resources, at the expense of the rest of the population. Health and happiness for the highest good of all suffer seriously. A prime example is the United States. Despite having the most expensive healthcare system in the world, the US ranks 37th in overall healthcare quality and benefits. "… in 2006, the United States was number 1 in terms of health care spending per capita but ranked 39th for infant mortality, 43rd for adult female mortality, 42nd for adult male mortality, and 36th for life expectancy" (Murray & Frenk, 2010). Canada, despite its national health service, ranks 30th in healthcare quality.

And where do HSPs fit into this picture? The sad fact for the welfare of our world is that they generally don't! It is hard core, NHSPs who are motivated by the accumulation of wealth, power over others, and political positions of power and fame, who work diligently to become heads of corporations and of local and national governments. And these people are seriously disconnected from their emotions far more often than not.

Research shows that overall health and happiness are far greater in nations where the goal is to allocate resources to provide for the highest good of all. Clearly, there is a place in government where HSPs could make great contributions – coming from a place of heart and caring in their leadership roles.

A major challenge in bringing about collective transformation on a large scale is that coordinated efforts of many people and many organizations are required. Naomi Klein (Web ref.) very clearly and succinctly summarizes many of the difficulties in doing this, and suggests ways to coordinate energies and efforts to bring about healing changes in our world.

> "…very often we think about political change in defined compartments these days. Environment in one box, inequality in another, racial and gender justice in a couple of other boxes, education over here, health over there. And within each compartment, there are thousands upon thousands of different groups and NGOs, each competing with one another for credit, name recognition and of course, resources. In other words, we act a lot like corporate brands. Now, this is often referred to as the problem of silos. Now, silos are understandable. They carve up our complex world into manageable chunks. They help us feel less overwhelmed. But in the process, they also train our brains to tune out when somebody else's issue comes up and when somebody else's issue needs our help and support. And they also keep us from seeing glaring connections between our issues."

For example, groups working on challenges of poverty and inequality are unlikely to mention climate issues – though in many cases the poor are the ones most subject to devastations under severe weather conditions. Groups who are addressing climate concerns are unlikely to mention war and occupation – despite the common link between these issues, with the constant, intense search for and development of every possible source of fossil fuels. Though the advocates for environmental issues are raising awareness that the vast majority of nations most affected by climate issues are populated by dark skinned people, these advocates rarely see a common cause with people working to address the gross biases of law enforcement authorities, with far harsher harassments of dark skinned people, and the grossly disproportionate overpopulation of North American jails with dark skinned people.

With these attitudes and disparities in priorities, the efforts of each isolated silo are not coordinated with those of other silos to implement their goals, even though each may have excellent suggestions and initiatives. Without bridging the silo walls, we come up with disconnected solutions. There is no coherence or agreement on what values or actions have priority nor how to address them. Then, "when large-scale crises hit us and we are confronted with the need to leap somewhere safer, there isn't any agreement on what that place is. And leaping without a destination looks a lot like jumping up and down."

Gradually, with ongoing discussions and explorations, there are now new, collaborative initiatives emerging. For instance, representatives of various groups in Canada gathered for several days to explore their common interests and goals.

"In that room were people who rarely get face to face, there were indigenous elders with hipsters working on transit. There was the head of Greenpeace with a union leader representing oil workers and loggers. There were faith leaders and feminist icons and many more."

Their goal was to create a brief description of how the world would look after their combined efforts came to fruition, with an economy that is clean and fair to all. So rather than frightening people with dire predictions about the consequences of doing little or nothing, they focused on inspiring people with visions of a world shaped by their coordinated actions.

Previously, the accepted norms were to focus on taking small steps toward the ultimate goal, working gradually towards the possible. They were anticipating that political changes couldn't focus on achieving perfection, but must come with one small, good step at a time.

For example, the endless striving towards the single-minded goal of more and more profits, which has been inducing many people to work over 50 hours per week, with no job security, and which is producing widespread despair, is the same striving for more and more profits and growth at the expense of our environment, with destabilization of the entire earth.

Similarly, people in Klein's forums realized what needed to be addressed and changed. The focus has to be shifted to one of caring for each and every individual, where no single person or ecological niche is ignored or overlooked. All must be considered essential and indispensable. They developed a people's platform that is detailed at theleap.org.

Here are a few details from this manifesto. The economy must be entirely renewable. Innovative trade agreements, guaranteed minimum annual wages, protection for immigrant workers, total restrictions on corporate contributions to political campaigns, day care for everyone, and electoral reforms, among other pillars for supporting a new world order

In the process of The Leap discussions, many of the participants realized that their individual vision shifted from what resembled a brand name approach to become more like a cohesive movement. Within a movement, you aren't motivated to achieve individual recognition and credit. You work to develop and disseminate productive ideas as broadly as possible.

Within The Leap movement there is no seeking to push any one agenda ahead of the others, or to tell someone else that my crisis issue has to take first priority and then you get your turn. While this was initiated in Canada, it has been well received in many other settings around the world, in both urban and rural communities where change often occurs very slowly, and where governments are failing to address the needs of the greater portions of the population.

"Here's what I've learned from studying shocks and disasters for two decades. Crises test us. We either fall apart or we grow up fast. Finding new reserves of strength and capacity that we never knew we had. The shocking events that fill us with dread today can transform us, and they can transform the world for the better. But first we need to picture the world that we're fighting for. And we have to dream it up together. Right now, every alarm in our house is going off simultaneously. It's time to listen. It's time to leap."

In listening to Naomi Klein's presentation and in reading about The Leap movement, I get the sense of droplets of water coming together to form powerful streams and then rivers of influence. This is how we can reshape our world – just as water will wear away or find ways around obstacles in its path.

### Relationships with the environment

*It is because of this split between people and nature*
*that the social justice and environmental arms*
*of the movement have arisen as separate,*
*each with its own history. Indigenous cultures*
*provide the basis for understanding the two as one.*
                                    - Paul Hawken

HSPs are generally sensitive to animals, plants, and all other living beings. They feel the land, water and air as living entities, and many have a sense of Gaia, our planet, as a collective consciousness of all living beings on our planet, including our planet herself. They feel the happiness and sadness, the health, illness and pains of other beings, just as they are sensitive to these in other human beings. Many HSPs put a lot of energies into supporting the environment – in personal and collective efforts to bring more healing into the world at large.

Sadly, the growing global focus on personal and corporate gains over all else, instigated by corporate interests, is overshadowing the efforts to deal with global heating, pollution, exhaustion of natural resources and other assaults on the environment. These are influencing most of the nations of the world to minimize or ignore the needs and healing of the environment. Without arable land, unpolluted water, reduced carbon emissions, breathable air, and global cooperation in achieving these goals with all possible haste, it is hard to see how humans and most other living beings on our planet can survive.*35

> *The exponential assault on resources and the production of waste, coupled with the extirpation of cultures and the exploitation of workers, is a disease as surely as hepatitis or cancer. It is sponsored by a political-economic system of which we are all a part, and any finger-pointing is inevitably directed back to ourselves. There may be no particular they there, but the system is still a disease, even if we created and contracted it. Because a lot of people know we are sick and want to treat the cause, not just the symptoms, the environmental movement can be seen as humanity's response to contagious policies killing the earth, while the social justice movement addresses economic and legislated pathogens that destroy families, bodies, cultures, and communities.*
> – Paul Hawken

Hopefully, increasing the healing that we can bring into this world will be effective in stopping and reversing these sad trends.*36

In these regards, western society has much it can learn from indigenous people about relating in wholistic healing ways to the environment. The absolutely best books I've ever read on this subject are by Rupert Ross (2006; 2014). Ross was a Crown attorney**37 who worked in Northern Canadian indigenous communities. He is a wonderfully keen and insightful observer of their traditional ways of conceptualizing their oneness with and ethical responsibility for the animals, plants, earth, mountains, waters, and other aspects of the world around them. In some cases, this was a connection with specific aspects of the environment. In other cases it was a more general connection.

> Indigenous knowledge is… inherently tied to land, not to land in general but to particular landscapes, landforms and biomes where ceremonies are properly held, stories properly recited, medicines properly gathered, and transfers of knowledge properly authenticated (Battiste & Henderson, 2008).

> I am now convinced by the structure of indigenous languages that people did indeed live in a spiritualized and embedding universe, speaking about the world in reverential, connecting terms, positioning everything with and within everything else and coloring daily life with a rich spirituality that almost defies western understanding (Ross, 2014, p.36).

> …Leroy [Little Bear] argued that while European languages spoke of the world with time as their central organizing theme, indigenous languages did not. Instead, they relied on place or space as their central organizing force (Ross, 2014, p. 41).

## 44. Spirit

*Discipline and letting go, the two paths as one, guide me always.*
*Work and trust, another way of saying it.*
*Knowing takes us to its limit, its edge. We go beyond.*
*We learn, come to understanding, let go of our understanding*
*and pass into the unknowable, the highest knowledge.*
*Without discipline, we increase our ignorance.*
*Without letting go we build a prison of information.*
*The two paths merge as one, breathing in, breathing out.*
— John MacEnulty

### *Personal spiritual awarenesses*

I mention just a few general items on personal spirituality here, since the next Section considers these in much greater detail, including numerous research references. While conventional Western science, medicine and psychotherapy generally relegate spiritual matters to clergy and philosophers, many people report deeply meaningful and helpful personal spiritual perceptions, experiences and understandings.

I define spiritual consciousness as perceptions about the world outside the individual, that are not based only upon our ordinary senses. Intuition includes varieties of awarenesses.

- Direct perceptions of other people's thoughts and feelings
- Intuited awarenesses of people's states of wholistic physical and mental health or disturbance
- Healing by touch, or with the hands near the body, or by mental intent, meditation or prayer
- Bereavement apparitions (ghosts/ spirits), who are seen and/or heard, or whose presence is strongly sensed intuitively by two thirds of the people who have had someone close to them pass on
- Near death experiences that include awarenesses of spirits, guides, angels, and a Being of Light that many feel is The Infinite Source

Each of these spiritual awarenesses (and others detailed in the next Sections) can contribute to healings of ourselves and of others. As an HSP, you are likely to be aware of your connections with spiritual dimensions. This can be an area of mutual growth with your HSPC, even when she is an NHSP and may have minimal or few such direct awarenesses herself. It may also be an area of discomfort, both individually and in your relationship. Much more on all of this below.*[38]

### *Collective consciousness*

Many of us are aware of our interconnectedness with other individuals, not just one at a time but also as a group. This means that we may sense the inner states of being and consciousness of collections of other people, or of humanity as a whole. Again, HSPs are more likely to be open to these levels of awareness. And again, much more on this, too, below.*[39]

# SECTION VII. Subtler Sensitivities, Biological Energy Medicine and Collective Consciousness

*Life is the only game in which the object
of the game is to learn the rules.*
— Ashleigh Brilliant

## 45. Background

Many HSPs are more sensitive than the average person in the spectrum of intuitive and spiritual awarenesses, in addition to their more commonly acknowledged sensitivities of body, emotions, mind and relationships detailed thus far. The more commonly acknowledged HSP sensitivities are described as knowing *about* our experiences. We know how a thing or a person looks, sounds, feels to the touch, and smells. These are observable details *about* the person that we know.

Spiritual awarenesses involve experiences beyond the information conveyed by our ordinary, external senses, emotional awarenesses and thoughts *about* these experiences. People describe their spiritual awarenesses as direct experiences of interacting with beings in dimensions that are beyond ordinary sense perceptions. These awarenesses are difficult to describe in ordinary, everyday language.

I call this direct perception *gnowing*. Gnowing awarenesses carry with them a sense of reality that is self-validating in ways that are very difficult to explain in words, but which are recognizable once they have been experienced. They have a feeling of genuineness and truth that feels intrinsically real. Different individuals who have had experiences of gnowing will often recognize and understand them when they are described by others who have had similar experiences. Gnowing carries with it the intuitive, 'gut feeling' of being right and true.

Those who are blind and deaf to these gnown intuitive and spiritual perceptions often label them as 'beliefs' of others. To them they are just reports of other people's odd experiences, which the disbelievers label as fantasies, wishful thinking, or perhaps even delusional or hallucinated projections of the minds of deranged people.

But to those who experience these inner gnowings, they often have the felt sense of being more real than their outer world perceptions. To those who experience gnowing, the denials of the existence of these perceptions by those who are blind and deaf to them are just their disbeliefs. Having said this, I have to add that when some people first connect with gnowing awarenesses, they may similarly question their own sanity.

Hallucinogenic drugs like LSD and psilocybin may open one's awareness to the realms of gnowing. Usually, this is a temporary window into these realms, and many have described how glorious their experiences were. Some, however, have horrendous, nightmarish experiences, and occasionally these can produce serious psychological traumas and derangements.

Research on spiritual awarenesses has identified and confirmed specific characteristics found fairly consistently in some of the personal spiritual experiences. For instance, an out of body experience (OBE) described by one person will have similar details to reports of others who have had an OBE; and similarly with Near Death Experiences, reincarnation memories, and some of the other spiritual awarenesses.*[1]

Many of the intuitive awarenesses are very well researched, though most (particularly the spiritual ones) are not well accepted by the NHSP majority. Below, I include references to many studies confirming their existence. The research is, in fact, so robust that it is extremely unlikely that it is not valid, as witnessed by the fact that the US Parapsychological Association (PA) has been accepted as a member of the American Association for the Advancement of Science (AAAS) since 1968.[2]

Section VII explores and explains the realms of personal spiritual awarenesses. For many, spirituality is experienced as a set of beliefs and practices related to one of many established religious traditions. In most cases, the choice of a particular religion is determined by one's family and culture of birth and/or marriage. This is not what I am addressing here.

Personal spiritual awarenesses involve experiences beyond the information conveyed by our ordinary, external senses, emotional awarenesses and thoughts *about* our experiences. They are not just beliefs accepted because they have been taught by religious leaders and clergy. People describe their spiritual awarenesses as direct experiences of beings and dimensions that are beyond their ordinary sense perceptions. These awarenesses have a deeply felt sense of direct connection with that which is perceived. They are difficult to describe in ordinary, everyday language.

The concept of gnostic knowledge come from Plato, around 400 BCE.

> ... Gnosis... is not ordinary knowledge, but connotes direct experience of divine reality... The gnosis is also *soteric,* that is, "saving" or healing in the sense of bestowing wholeness: it carries the power to transform and reintegrate one's life. Faith alone cannot save; one must also *know* and practice the alchemy of redemption. (Thackara, Web ref.)

The term "gnostic knowledge" has been used by various religious groups to indicate direct knowledge of the Divine as interpreted within their particular sects and branches of religions, and is not the sense in which I use it here. I use 'gnowing' as the direct, individual, personal awarenesses of intuitive and spiritual dimensions.

Some of us sense our personal spiritual perceptions within our culturally congruent ways of experiencing them. For instance, we may connect with the spiritual essence of Christ, Mother Mary, various saints, the Buddha or other religious figures. We may experience these as quintessential love and unconditional acceptance.

Others with such inner spiritual gnowings may connect with the Being of Light that is totally loving and accepting in a completely non-judgmental way. For them, this is a consciousness that is beyond words and beyond their capability to describe fully. Human language simply hasn't the words or concepts to encompass this encounter.

There are also spiritual encounters with angelic beings with similar but less intense qualities. These are often helpers in times of need. They sometimes appear spontaneously, unbidden, and at other times appear in response to wishes and prayers for assistance in times of need.

The spiritual dimensions are intermeshed with and inseparable from the physical world. They are essential aspects of our wholistic range of beingness and experiences. In Western society, only a small portion of people report such experiences. However, it appears likely that everyone participates in these dimensions, despite the fact that many do so without conscious awarenesses while they are alive in the physical world.

There is also a wide range of perceptions and experiences that overlap with spiritual awarenesses. They form bridges between our everyday consciousness in the physical world and the spiritual dimensions. Research has identified distinct aspects of gnown experiences, labeled as telepathy, clairsentience, and precognition. These are commonly grouped under the scientific label of 'extrasensory perception' (ESP) or parapsychological phenomena. In everyday language, they are commonly lumped under 'intuitive awarenesses.' Whatever we call them, these are perceptual components of gnown experiences, described in the language of our physical world of existence. And we must remember, as we discuss these in everyday language, that we have no physical world terms that adequately describe the dimensions of spirit we are discussing.

*You cannot know a strawberry from "strawberry,"*
*nor a dream from "dream."*

- Daniel Benor

We rely on interpretations of readings from various instruments in scientific laboratories to inform us about the world of molecules and subatomic particles. We have no awareness through our ordinary senses of these aspects of the physical world, and rely on the reports of others that their instruments truly do confirm that molecules and atoms exist.

Similarly, most of us have little or no awareness of the dimensions of spirit through our ordinary senses. We do not have the intuitive abilities to consciously gnow realities beyond our three-dimensional world. We must rely on the reports of others, whose personal 'instruments,' the sensitive, wholistic entities that they are, enable them to perceive and gnow these realms that exist beyond our everyday senses.

To those of us who are open-minded to the possibilities that gnown experiences are real, listening to reports of sensitive people who are spiritually aware is an invitation to explore and develop our own abilities to understand, and if possible, also to gnow the world more deeply.

I discuss this in some detail here because those who experience these usually consider their intuitive and spiritual awarenesses to be of the greatest importance in our lives. The impacts of these personal experiences are so strong that they frequently transform people's lives.

Among the majority who do not have personal experiences of transcendent gnowings, there are many seekers who wish to know about the spiritual dimensions but want to do so through the familiar paths of conventional science. They base their trust on researched evidence. Before they explore these dimensions personally, they want a map that lets them know about the territory. So let me summarize for you a spectrum of fascinating studies that are strongly supportive of the reports of the gnown experiences of the intuitively sensitive people among us. Surprisingly, these research reports show that those who deny the existence of the intuitive dimensions also have intuitive abilities themselves, and use these unconsciously in support of their denials of the existence of these abilities!

Let's start with collections of reports of spiritual awarenesses that have identified and confirmed specific characteristics which are consistently found across intuitive experiences. Their gnowing types of personal awarenesses reach into many layers of transcendent realities that are beyond our ordinary senses. In addition to telepathic communications between individuals, there are also awarenesses of the collective consciousness of groups of people; connections with the consciousness of other species; with nature in general; with Gaia, our planet; with spirits of people and other beings; with spirit guides, angels, and dark/ negative spirits; and with the Infinite Source.**[3]

# 46. Intuition: A brief overview

> *The intuitive mind is a sacred gift*
> *and the rational mind is a faithful servant.*
> *We have created a society that honors the servant*
> *and has forgotten the gift.*
>
> - Albert Einstein

At the early awareness end of the spectrum, gnowing starts with vaguely sensed perceptions, which we label as intuition. Intuition starts with a whiff of gnowing that transcends our ordinary senses and everyday experiences in the physical world. For instance, it is not uncommon to have someone show up in our lives shortly after we've thought about them – when we hadn't thought about them for months or years prior to their reappearance.

'Skeptics' will say that these are examples of pure coincidence and random reinforcements of a select few out of countless similar thoughts that we've had which were not 'verified.' In other words, we have random thoughts about many people and only occasionally do we encounter the coincidences of these particular people phoning us or showing up in person. 'Skeptics' claim that we simply don't notice having had all the other thoughts about other people because so many thoughts come and go in our minds without our ever noticing them, or we forget them.

Those who more frequently and consciously sense their intuitions report wide ranges of content that is perceived. Subjectively, intuitive gnowings are experienced with various degrees of intensity and feelings of certainty about the perceptions. They also vary in the information that is perceived, from images and awarenesses that are utterly trivial, to somewhat interesting experiences we often don't recall, to deeply meaningful and important information, sometimes even life-saving in its import.

Intuitions may surface about any and every aspect of our lives.

– Minor issues, such as

- Sensing that we're going to see someone, or hear from someone whom we haven't seen or connected with in a long time

- Needing to leave early for work, or leaving work to go home, and finding that there were important matters to attend to

- Feeling it would be good to buy extra food during a routine, weekly trip to the market, and having family or friends turn up unexpectedly the next day

- Checking on the children, who were in the yard for their regular, afternoon play time, and finding that one of them was seriously upset over a minor issue

– Serious issues, such as:

- Feeling a need to slow down when driving, and coming to the next intersection, just as a big truck comes barreling through the red light, directly in front of us

✦ My mother was standing on a hospital balcony, in conversation with a doctor who was about 8 inches shorter than her. This was in 1947, a time of serious conflict between Jews and Arabs in British Mandate Palestine. She had a sudden, inexplicable urge to ask him to change places with her. Less than a minute later, a bullet slammed into the wall just above his head. Had she not changed places with him she would probably have been killed.

- Sensing someone close has just died. This has probably been reported especially with the death of soldiers, where someone in their family knows, intuitively, that they would probably have been killed in some distant place.

- Extensive anecdotal reports document experiences of intuitive gnowing.[4]

Those who have experiences of gnowing report there is a qualitative sense about gnowing that is different from other awarenesses. Having had some of these sorts of experiences myself, I can validate that inner, meta-gnowing feeling about the validity of my gnowing awarenesses.

✦ An unusual story about gnowing was reported to me (Dan) by a physician acquaintance in England, several decades ago, before the internet had become a highway for communications:

"My mother knows when someone in the family or a close friend has died, before we hear about it by phone, telegram or postal services. She's never wrong, and over the years has become very clear and certain about these intuitions. We sort of got used to this, but were startled and concerned when she told us she had mailed a condolence letter to her distant cousin, 'Joseph,' who lived in India, over the loss of his wife, 'Mildred' – prior to our having received any notice of Mildred's passing. We were enormously relieved, though of course saddened, to have the letter announcing Mildred's passing arrive a week later."

Clearly this woman had learned to completely trust her inner gnowings about people passing on!

How can people gnow these things? There are extensive bodies of research that explore and robustly confirm the abilities of people to gnow precise information without any sensory details that would let them know this information. We'll review these studies shortly.*[5]

*WHAT INTUITIVE AWARENESSES HAVE YOU OR OTHERS CLOSE TO YOU EXPERIENCED?*

*DID YOU HAVE ANY SPECIAL FEELING OR OTHER AWARENESS THAT YOUR INTUITIVE PERCEPTIONS WERE, IN SOME INNER WAY, VALID AND REAL?*

*HOW DO YOU RESPOND TO 'SKEPTICS' WHO QUESTION YOU?*

## 47. Inspiration and creativity: pattern recognition, intuition and more

*When you are inspired by some great purpose, some
extraordinary project, all your thoughts break their bonds;
your mind transcends limitations, your consciousness expands in every direction,
and you find yourself in a new, great and
wonderful world. Dormant forces, faculties and talents
become alive, and you discover yourself to be a greater
person by far than you ever dreamed yourself to be.*
- Patanjali (c. 1st to 3rd century BC)

Let's start our explorations of intuition in areas of experiences that may or may not include gnowing that extends into spiritual awarenesses. Some of what we call intuition is based largely on our cognitive awarenesses, our memories, our emotions, and our abilities to see new and innovative connections between bits and pieces of the realities we perceive and bring together in creative ways.

Richard Feynman was a brilliant, Nobel prize winning, theoretical physicist. He was also eloquent and charming, which led to many interviews and several popular books.[6] Feynman reported that he had wonderful powers of visualization. For instance, he could picture in great detail in his mind a new device he was planning to build. He mentally put all the parts together and imagined that it was starting to work, just as he wanted and needed it to. He set his mind to fast forward in time, and returned later to observe his invention. He was able to see which parts were functioning well and which parts were wearing down, as they would have done over a period of months or years. This is an amazing example of extremely well-developed pattern recognition!

Intuition has been acknowledged for many centuries. Poets, writers, actors, painters, sculptors and others in the arts have spoken and written of inspiration that sparks and informs their creativity. Inspiration may come as an idea in words. It is as though a voice speaks to them from another dimension, planting a new idea or a new way of perceiving or explaining something they are working on. Many speak of a *muse* that has the feel of a wise entity with a distinct personality, visiting from some other dimension when they are quiet and receptive to its whispers. The muse may show them directly what is helpful or may speak through imagery – sometimes in dreams. Among those acknowledging such inspiration are poets A. E. Houseman, Longfellow, and John Masefield; authors Kipling, George Eliot, Oscar Wild; actor Sir Alec Guiness; musicians Stravinsky, Mozart, and Tchaikovsky; artists William Blake, Picasso, and Klee (Inglis & West, 1989).

Scientists have acknowledged the help of a muse, an inner voice or awareness that inspires them with new ideas. Among many others, some of the more prominent scientists have included André Ampère, Karl Gauss, Henri Poincaré, Michael Faraday, Lord Kelvin, Albert Einstein, and Nikola Tesla. Thomas Edison, one of the most prolific inventors, reported that he found inspiration particularly in the dream-like state that is between waking and sleeping. As he found it was difficult to maintain this state, he would sit in a comfortable chair in the evening, holding a heavy metal spoon in each hand, resting his arms on the arms of the chair so that the spoons were suspended over metal pots on the floor. If he fell asleep, the clang of the falling spoon would bring him back to resume his receptive state.

Where does the muse reside? Various explanations have been suggested, ranging from innate creativity in the unconscious mind of the individual; to collective wisdom accumulated over many lifetimes of an individual's reincarnations; to the collective consciousness of humanity; to spirit and angelic guidance; and to our connection with the Divine.

While we won't explore these various possibilities in great depth here, I feel they deserve acknowledgment within this discussion because HSPs are often sensitive to personal spiritual awarenesses, along with their other sensitivities. HSPs and their HSPCs also frequently state that the spiritual aspect of their lives is of enormous importance to them in many ways. For greater breadth and depth of discussion about the spiritual dimensions of life I can suggest one of my other books, *Healing Research, Volume 3* (Benor, 2006).

Let's start with a spectrum of gnowings that people report. My windows of explanation start with lighter gnowings that are related for the most part to our earthly existence, and extend into awarenesses that appear to arise in spiritual dimensions.

Gnowings and spiritual awarenesses may be reported and confirmed in

- Occasional intuitive hunches, possibly from logical reasoning, possibly from personal spiritual awarenesses that are validated in the unfolding of a situation under consideration
- Frequent intuitive hunches that are validated
- Psychic abilities that provide a broad range of awarenesses
  - Telepathy – spontaneous mind to mind communications
  - Perceiving – as a sense of gnowing – other people's thoughts and experiences
  - Intentionally sending/ projecting information to others
  - Influencing others to behave in distinctly identifiable ways
  - Clairsentience – perceiving information about the world
    
    Clairvoyance – as visual images
    
    Clairaudience – as auditory information
  - Precognition – gnowing the future
  - Retrocognition – gnowing information from the past (without identifiable inputs from one's ordinary senses or past learning and experiences)
  - Collective consciousness
    
    Group meditation
    
    Group healings
    
    Healing intent/ meditation/ prayer
    
    Family constellation therapy
  - Psychokinesis – Influencing the outer world through thoughts/ intentions, without physical intervention
  - Psychic Assessments – gnowing the issues of people or other living beings who need healing

- Psychic healing – may be performed as an innate gift of the healer or within many schools of healing traditions/ approaches, such as Therapeutic Touch, Healing Touch, Reiki, Qigong, Polarity Therapy, Ayurveda, and numerous others)

    Through lightly touching the being who is in need of healing

    Through healer's hands, held near the being in need of healing, within the bioenergy field but not touching the body

    Through reading/ interpreting the bioenergy field that is perceived visually by the healer

    Through gnowing the wholistic problems and issues of the healee psychically, which enhances healing through the healer's and the healee's awarenesses

- Treatments

    Through lightly touching the being needing healing

    Through holding the healer's hands near the being in need of healing, within the bioenergy field

    Inviting healing to occur psychically, over any distance

    Mentally projecting colors, energies, images or just the intent to heal

    Inviting participation in the healing by The Infinite Source/ Christ/ Buddha/ Allah/ angels/ saints/ or other healing presences or energies

– Past life awarenesses – may occur spontaneously or as part of specific quests for this information

- Self-awareness of one's past life

    Spontaneous memories common in children 2-5 years old, less common thereafter

    Particularly helpful in clearing trauma residues from your past lives that are influencing your current life issues

    Also helpful in clarifying issues in your relationships with other people

- Past lives of other people

    May surface in the process of your past life therapy, particularly in exploring traumas from those past lives that involved other people who also reincarnated in your current life

    Also helpful in clarifying issues in your current relationships with other people

– Karmic lessons that carry over from one life to another

- General themes, rather than memories of interactions with specific people, e.g. you may suffer abuse in this lifetime when you were abusive to others in previous lifetimes

– Spirit existence that continues after physical life and precedes the next rebirth

- Angels
  - Bringing information for healing and personal/ collective psychological/ spiritual growth
- The Infinite Source - A Being of Light who is so vastly wiser, all-knowing and unconditionally accepting than humans that we cannot begin to comprehend more than a minute portion of our awarenesses of it.

Regardless of any explanatory mechanisms for spiritual experiences, diverse collections of personal reports, plus impressive bodies of research confirm that certain aspects of intuition and spirituality exist. These will be discussed below.

Mechanisms to explain the awarenesses of intuition and spiritual dimensions have been proposed to exist beyond the ordinary spectrum of physical awarenesses, energies or other mechanisms that are acknowledged in conventional science for perceiving the world outside ourselves. Interestingly, there appears to be evidence from quantum physics to support this possibility. Quantum physics acknowledges that interactions between the presence/ awarenesses/ intentions of observers of a quantum physics experiment can produce measurable changes observable in the physical world. If the presence of an observer can alter a quantum physics process, there may well be reason to expect similar effects of an observer upon processes in living beings (Capra, 1975; Radin, 2006).

Much of what we've considered here is about the processes involved in intuitive awarenesses. It's often the case that your motivations for connecting with your intuition are vital generators for awakening these latent collections of recalled information and gnowings. You will connect with these intuitive gnowings and spiritual resources especially when you feel a need to make a difference in the world, to reach beyond what currently exists, in order to birth new awarenesses, ideas and ways forward for greater healing.

Let's expand our examination of these aspects of intuition. There are three main categories of intuition: pattern recognition, parapsychological awarenesses, and spiritual awarenesses.

## 48. Intuition as retrieved memory

*Intuition is always right in at least two important ways;*
*It is always in response to something.*
*it always has your best interest at heart.*

- Gavin de Becker

Our memories are far vaster than we generally believe. Under hypnosis, we can often retrieve incredibly detailed information that is stored outside our conscious awareness.

– A patient presents with depression, gravelly voice, and thick hair. The doctor, who hasn't even thought about a case of hypothyroidism this severe since reading his medical school textbooks many years earlier, recognizes that this is a case of advanced hypothyroidism.

✦ A surgeon asked me (Dan) to see a 23 year-old patient after his appendectomy because he was depressed. His parents reported he had always been something of a loner. As I spoke with him, I felt uncomfortable because his eyes would not meet mine. The diagnosis of mild to moderate Asperger's syndrome came to mind, from having seen children of all ages with such avoidance of another person's looking them in the eyes. Further questioning about his lifelong social behaviors of isolation and awkwardness in communicating with other people confirmed this to be a very likely diagnosis.

I hesitated before sharing this impression, because it suggests an incurable problem, with the person likely to remain in the autistic spectrum and distant from everyone. His parents, however, were extremely grateful because at last they had a possible explanation for their son's issues and could plan to clarify the diagnosis and to help him better. Following a more thorough psychological evaluation, they subsequently reported that my initial impression was correct.

Studies considering the use of clinical intuition in nurses with varying levels of experience confirm intuition can be a valid aid in decision-making. These studies witness that there is a slow but progressively greater development of trust in clinical intuition – according to levels of experience, from nurses who are beginners, through those who are competent, proficient, and expert.[7]

The complexities of modern medical practice place increasing demands upon physicians to continually update their knowledge of ways to diagnose and treat their patients. No single person could possibly keep up with the multitudes of developments in every medical subspecialty. Computers are increasingly being used to sort through the patient's clinical picture –from patients' responses to computer generated questions, laboratory tests, imaging device inputs, and other sophisticated assessment tools, and relying less and less on physician inputs. With continued advances in computer programs, much of the art of medicine may become obsolete. And just a reminder here that I am focused on the body level of wholistic awareness, which is generally the only level that physicians (and the computer programs they develop) will generally consider.

And there is a mirrored shift occurring among physicians who are increasingly relying on data from sophisticated assessment devices more than they are on clinical assessments. There are also strong pressures in large clinical facilities to spend ever less time with patients, with patient visits being limited to just a few minutes. A further incentive in this direction is the decreasing compensation by insurance companies on the one side for physician time spent in discussing the patients' conditions with them, and on the other side, a 'justified' compensation for physician time spent in doing mechanical tasks and physical interventions.

Patients increasingly complain that their doctors don't listen to them, don't give them enough time to explain their concerns, and don't explain the medications they prescribe. And I would have to speculate that there is a corresponding decrease in physicians' development of their personal, clinical pattern recognition.

This fading in reliance on clinicians' personal intuition, as cognitive pattern recognition, is congruent with the prevalent materialist paradigms that guide and inform conventional medical, nursing and psychotherapeutic practice. Intuition, however, can reach far beyond this level of pattern recognition. And in communities of therapists outside of conventional medical practice, intuition is alive and well and flourishing. And the intuition I refer to extends far beyond the limits of pattern recognition.[8]

This level of intuition, pattern recognition, is congruent with the prevalent materialist paradigms that guide and inform conventional medical, nursing and psychotherapeutic practice. Intuition, however, can reach far beyond this level.

## 49. Intuition as psychological pattern recognition

*A person knows the world because they've seen it often before.*
- Agatha Christie

There are people gifted with abilities to recognize patterns in ordinary perceived observations or in written or numerical data that most others would not notice. They can also see possible shifts and improvements in situations, or dangers in proceeding in certain ways, when they consider what can happen if various decisions are made and particular factors are tweaked and changed. These people may gravitate to research in science, to caregiving, detective work with law enforcement agencies, politics, and other such niches where their gifts may bear fruit.

American biologist James Watson and English physicist Francis Crick (Pray, 2008) bring us a much-cited example of scientific discoveries that involve pattern recognition. Watson and Crick started with information that had been gathered and elaborated over more than a century about the components found in genetic materials within the cells of living organisms. They clarified that genetic proteins were linked in double strands with coded sequences, and that the strands were linked in a double helix. Their recognition of this protein pattern gave an enormous boost to the field of modern genetics.**[9]

The pattern recognition of detectives forms the basis for countless books, films and TV shows. Some of the more popular ones include Sherlock Holmes, Hercule Poirot, Nancy Drew, The Hardy Boys, Miss Marple, Inspector Clouseau, among many, many others. These keen observers of facts and of human behaviors put together clues that are present for anyone to see and hear, but that few have the gifts to bring together in order to solve the mysteries behind clever crimes and murders.

Caregivers are also detectives who rely on pattern recognition. People usually come for help, bringing a modest list of clues, including subjective symptoms, physical changes in their bodies, and details of the sequence in which these appeared. It is up to the caregiver to ask the right questions, perform appropriate examinations, and then identify the patterns that enable recommendations for lifestyle changes and administrations of treatments to bring about improvements and cures for that which is ailing and for patterns that are out of alignment.

Clinical pattern recognition may be more subtle. Clinical sensitivity often leads doctors, nurses and other caregivers to recognize when something is going wrong or going well. Postoperative nurses often report a sense of a patient "not being right," though objective signs and symptoms are normal. Often, these sorts of intuitive awarenesses prove correct, and an internal bleed or other serious problem is identified soon after the nurse's intuitive "alarm bells" start to ring. At other times, the nurse will sense that all is well, and similarly, the patient will have an uneventful postoperative course, even following very difficult and arduous procedures (King & Clark 2002).

Pattern recognition appears to a great extent to be an extension of learned knowledge. As healthcare clinicians learn more and become more experienced, they can perceive increasingly subtle patterns of appearance, behaviors, monitored body data (from sophisticated instruments), and laboratory studies, any or all of which can alert them to unusual changes and dangers in their patients.

This is the art and science of any caregiving practice. It is clinical detective work, the gathering of evidence and seeking for the underlying pattern that explains the contributing wholistic dynamics that solve the riddle of what has contributed to or is causing the presenting clinical issues.

Conversely, it is impossible to rule out that some cases of cognitive pattern recognition are not supported or initiated by psychic intuitive awarenesses. We'll consider these below.

> *One night, a policeman saw a man on his hands and knees,*
> *groping around under a street light. He asked what the man was*
> *doing, to which the man replied, "I'm looking for my car key."*
>
> *"Where did you drop it?" he asked. "Over there,"*
> *he replied, pointing down the block.*
>
> *"Then why are you looking over here?"*
>
> *"Because the light is better here," he said.*
>
> — Anonymous

I repeat this well-worn story here to highlight again that people tend to look for answers to their challenges in places where they are more comfortable looking, and conversely, that they avoid looking where they have only dim perceptions, if any, of what might be found. Conventional medicine looks at the physical body to identify problems, where the light is clearer within body-focused paradigms for health and illness and where laboratory diagnostic evidence is easier to see, identify and address.

Wholistic practitioners will help people shine lights into the darker, neglected corners of their body, emotions, mind, relationships and spirit to find deeper answers about what is out of harmony and to explore what can be done to remedy these problems, which then can also contribute to correcting the body's dysfunctions.

I encourage you to explore the patterns and threads of issues in your own life that have shaped you into the person you are. Many of the tools provided in this book can empower you to clarify these patterns through self-healing.

You may also enhance your explorations of the patterns in your life with the facilitation of a trusted family member, friend or caregiver who can help you identify patterns in your life that you could otherwise miss – as we often overlook those issues involving pain or trauma on some level(s) of our wholistic being.

Coming from the other direction, there are also patterns to be discovered and developed to bring more positivity, happiness and harmony into our lives. Here, the advice and support of caregivers can be enormously helpful. They can suggest ways of shifting or remodeling the wholistic structures of our lives in constructive and healing ways that otherwise might take us much longer to discover and implement on our own. And this is not just about their giving us answers to our issues. It is about their guiding us to search where we haven't looked before, or where we were hesitant for whatever reasons to visit, or about suggesting steps we might take for our healing that we might not have considered or would otherwise have been reluctant to take.

NHSPs may be blessed with pattern recognition, as they use their preferred powers of observation of the outer world, along with their logic and reasoning to explore and sort out issues in their lives. These abilities may enable them to be excellent HSPCs.

## 50. Intuition as wholistic bioenergy pattern recognition

*Intuition is seeing with the soul.*
- Dean Koontz

Many of us have abilities to sense the biological energies in and around the body. (More details on this below, including research.) I just point out here that how we perceive these bioenergies is often similar in many ways to how we see something in the outer world through our eyes. Light, reflected from an object, enters out eyes, stimulating nerve cells in the retina at the back of our eyeballs. These cells transmit the perceived light patterns to the visual cortex of our brain, where we interpret their meanings – based on past visual experiences. We learn to interpret what we are seeing through our visual experiences. Similarly, many people need to learn to interpret what the bioenergies that they sense mean – in terms of the wholistic state of the person whose bioenergies they are scanning.

Many people are able to sense bioenergies with their hands held near to or lightly touching another person. The most common sensations are heat and tingling. With practice, some people learn to interpret some or all levels of the wholistic state of the person whose body they are 'reading' through the patterns of sensations in their hands. You can increase the sensitivity and keenness of awareness of hand sensations by practicing sensing these bioenergies through moving your hands around the bodies of people, near the body but not touching them. This also can extend your awareness to include other types of sensations, such as prickliness, stickiness, heaviness, sluggishness or other perceptions. With further practice, we can grow to understand the conditions of health and illnesses in the person we are examining that are associated with these broad ranges of perceptions.

Some people, particularly HSPs, can develop these perceptions and come to learn their meanings to exquisitely fine degrees. Some sensitives are naturally gifted with abilities to perceive and comprehend the meanings of these energetic perceptions without needing the practice doing so. A few, very gifted people see the entire body as a translucent body of energy, and part of their natural gift is that they can identify immediately from what they are seeing when there are disorders in various structures, organs and functions in the body. This is another, even more sensitive level of energetic pattern recognition.

These energetic pattern recognitions can be of enormous help in quickly and deeply identifying and understanding what is going on in the person they are 'reading.'[10]

## 51. Psychic intuition that is well researched

*When you reach the end of what you should know,*
*you will be at the beginning of what you should sense.*
- Kahlil Gibran

It is possible to know information without inputs from our ordinary senses of sight, sound, smell, taste, and touch and the other senses listed in the Section I, discussion of the body. We call these sorts of acquired information *psychic* impressions. They provide another level for intuitive awareness.

Researchers have identified several components of psychic awarenesses.

- Telepathy: The transfer of thoughts, images or commands from one living being to another, without use of sensory cues.
- Clairsentience: Knowledge about an animate or inanimate object, without the use of ordinary sensory cues (sometimes called psychometry in parapsychology and 'vibes' in popular culture). This may appear in the mind of the perceiver as visual imagery (clairvoyance), auditory messages (clairaudience), or other internal sensory awareness, such as taste, smell, or a mirroring of bodily sensations from another person. It is also demonstrated by intuitives who sense the person who had touched or worn a particular item; and to find streams of underground water; among other, similar awarenesses about inanimate materials.
- Precognition: Knowledge of a future event prior to its occurrence.
- Retrocognition: Knowledge of a past event, without reliance on sensory cues or memories of actual experiences. Retrocognition is now well accepted, and has not been studied as a psychic ability since there is always the possibility that a person could have actually perceived but forgotten that they directly sensed the perceptions attributed to psychic impressions.

The above modes of acquiring intuitive knowledge without cues from any of the external senses have been named extrasensory perception (ESP). ESP is distinctly different from cognitive pattern recognition, which is based on facts learned through our ordinary senses and remembered experiences, or on deductions from known facts. Telepathy, clairsentience and precognition are direct awarenesses of information that is not based on ordinary sensory experiences. To illustrate these, let me share a few researched observations.

Surveys of psychic experiences were conducted from the early 1940's on by J. B. Rhine (1964), Louisa Rhine (1967) and other researchers at Duke University in the US, and then around the world. People commonly reported information acquired without ordinary sensory inputs. For example, they had premonitions of dangers before these materialized, particularly when someone else in the family was in danger or far away and in need of help; or were able to project their thoughts and feelings to others.

Spontaneous extrasensory perception (ESP) may occur in people who are not particularly gifted with intuitive awarenesses. It is experienced frequently during dreams, in times of distress, and in response to strong needs of the psychic person. It may also occur spontaneously, for no apparent reason. This does not necessarily mean that no reasons exist, but just that the reasons are not apparent to us.[11]

In another example, J. W. Dunne published a classic series of his precognitive dreams (1973, Orig. 1927). In one of these, he foresaw by several days the eruption of the volcano on the Caribbean island of Martinique in 1902, in which 40,000 people were killed. Clearly this is an event that could impact the collective consciousness of the planet, and would be more 'available' for psychic perception than lesser events. However, Dunne also records many precognitive dreams of no apparent import. In one of his more unusual dreams, he sees himself standing on a bridge, looking at a scene with no memorable features. About 25 years later, he found himself on that very bridge, surveying that particular scene. He could find no special significance in this precognitive experience, which seemed simply to have been a window across time and space. Perhaps Dunne overlooked the obvious, which would be that this dream was motivated by and fulfilled his need to confirm the existence of precognition. There are many such examples in popular literature and on the internet.

People who have well-developed gifts of ESP commonly offer their services as psychics, to shine new light on current situations and providing windows of perceptions into the futures of clients, for a fee.

We have to be cautious here, though, because some have been known to fake having psychic abilities. The more successful fakes are often gifted observers of non-verbal communications, and clever at defrauding people by telling them what they want to hear, or making frightening predictions. These fake psychics listen carefully to verbal clues, displayed on people's faces and in other non-verbal cues. From these they deduce what people are most eager to hear, and may give them false information and false hopes, or may alarm them with fabricated warnings of impending worrisome or dangerous events. They may suggest things that people can do to avert these dangers, and when the dangers don't materialize, the victims of their scams take this to mean that both the predictions and warnings to take action were accurate.

To study intuition scientifically, Joseph B. Rhine, at Duke University in Durham, North Carolina, together with his wife, colleagues and students, ran hundreds of thousands of tests on psychic abilities. Research replications were published from labs in the US, UK, Australia, Germany, France, Japan and other countries around the world. Rhine's basic tool for ESP testing was a deck of 25 Zener cards, with five copies of each of five different symbols in the deck. (See Figure VII-1.)**[12] The deck was thoroughly shuffled, sometimes with a mechanical shuffler, prior to each test of ESP perception.

**Figure VII-1. The cards of the Zener deck**

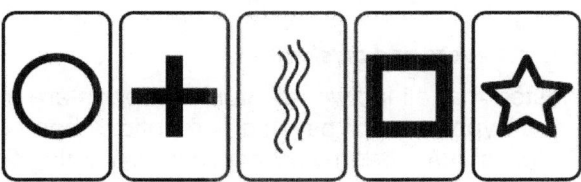

In the telepathy mode of testing, an experimenter looks at one card at a time, while the subject calls out which symbol she intuits is on the card. Cards held by the experimenter are out of the line of sight of the experimental subjects. In this telepathy mode of assessing psychic abilities, the experimenter holds the intent of projecting the image of the card, and the subject holds the intent of reading the mind of the experimenter. When a series of studies following the same protocol is available, we can run a statistical meta-analysis to see how significant the entire series is. A meta-analysis of rigorous research on telepathy demonstrates results that are significant at a level of 10 billion to 1 against these being due to random effects (Radin, 1997).**[13]

In testing the clairvoyant mode of intuitive awareness, the deck is shuffled and the subject psychically 'reads' (intuits) which symbol is on one card at a time, from top to bottom of the deck. After each 'guess' is recorded, the experimenter records the symbol on the card, proceeding in this fashion through the entire deck. Alternatively, after the deck is shuffled, the subject writes down the entire series of 25 guesses prior to the experimenter's turning each card over and recording the order of appearance of each symbol. Two statistical meta-analyses of research on clairsentient abilities are highly significant, the first at a level of 4.8 billion to 1 against these being due to random effects (Bem and Honorton, 1994) and the second at 10 million to 1 (Radin, 1997).**[14]

In the precognitive mode, the subject writes down the entire series of 25 guesses prior to the shuffling of the deck. After it is shuffled, the experimenter records the order of appearance of each symbol in the shuffled deck. A statistical analysis of rigorous research on precognition shows results significant at a level of 10 million billion billion to 1 against these being due to random effects (Honorton & Ferrari, 1989).**[15]

You may ask, why so very many experiments were done on precognition? The probable answer is that this phenomenon, which contradicts our ordinary sense of time in the world, seems so incredible that even parapsychologists were skeptical about it and had to do sufficient research to make it highly, highly, highly unlikely that the results could be due to experimental errors or chance results.

So in studies of each of these intuitive modalities, small but significantly greater than chance numbers of correct guesses were recorded for numerous subjects. When the results of each experimental group was tallied, the deviations from random chance were highly significant. And a few gifted subjects were able to achieve rates of success entirely on their own that were considerably above chance.

Eventually, to save time and energies, experimenters explored presenting series of tests of telepathy and clairsentience to groups of subjects, rather than going through the deck just one person at a time. This proved to be an overall failure, as the average results were not above chance expectations – although some individuals within the groups did achieve significant results. Experimenters were puzzled, but attributed the chance results to distraction or other, unidentified factors related to testing in a group setting.

### *Intuitive perceptions of believers and of 'skeptics'*

'Skeptics' have suggested that all individual intuitive reports are simply coincidences, despite the fact that the hypothesis of psychic perceptions has been put to rigorous, scientific scrutiny. 'Skeptics' have been very active in promoting their agendas of disparaging and denying the existence of ESP. They appear to be well funded, as they are able to mount long-term, ongoing programs of monitoring and editing websites such as Wikipedia. Within just a few hours, the 'skeptics' will eliminate from Wikipedia any reports or even mention of evidence that ESP is extremely well validated in research, as detailed below. (The same happens with entries supporting effectiveness of complementary/ alternative methods).*[16]

And how do such disbelievers deal with the impressive bodies of research confirming the existence of intuitive awarenesses, as well as of psychokinesis and healing? Despite the fact that many of these phenomena are very well researched, most (particularly the spiritual ones), they are still not accepted as real by these disbelievers. A typical reason given for dismissing these researched perceptions is that "They are not published in conventional, scientific, professional journals." This is a nice bit of circular reasoning. They are not published in those journals because those journals won't accept article submissions on intuitive aspects of awareness – because their editors and readers dismiss these as impossible, unscientific, or 'woo-woo thinking.' This is a clear example of neuroplastic blindness.*[17]

> *The non-physical world is nonsense (literally) to five-sensory humans.*
> *It is central to the experience of millions of multi-sensory humans.*
> - Gary Zukav

These so-called 'skeptics' are misrepresenting themselves. The Google definition of a skeptic is "a person inclined to question or doubt all accepted opinions." The self-labeled 'skeptics' of parapsychological phenomena are more than doubters or questioners regarding the existence of intuitive and psychic phenomena. They are rigid disbelievers in phenomena that many people experience, which have been confirmed under rigorous, repeated research protocols (detailed below). I would speculate that these disbelievers are NHSPs, and conversely, that the experiencers of intuitive and subtle energy phenomena are HSPs.**[18] See discussions on neuroplastic atrophy*[19] and cognitive dissonance,*[20] earlier in this book, on why they may be investing so systematically and intensively in disparaging ESP.

A wise parapsychologist, Gertrude Schmeidler, suggested that the random results from group testing should be re-evaluated, assessing separately the results of self-declared believers in ESP and of 'skeptics' – where data were available to identify this factor. When this was done, it was found that the results of the believers were significantly above chance. To everyone's surprise, the results of the 'skeptics' were also significant, but below chance. Taken together in each experiment, the results of the two differing belief groups canceled each other out. Schmeidler dubbed this the 'sheep-goat effect', sheep being the believers and goats the disbelievers. Each group was apparently perceiving and guessing based on psychic awarenesses, but the sheep used their intuition to make correct guesses and the goats apparently used theirs to make incorrect guesses. These results were replicated in parapsychology laboratories around the world. A statistical analysis of rigorous research on sheep – goat effects show results that are significant at a level greater than 1 trillion to 1 against these being due to random effects (Lawrence, 1993).**[21]

I see profound take-home lessons from this research on believers and so-called 'skeptics,' whom I identify as disbelievers. I believe that many such 'skeptics' are probably unable to consciously perceive psychic phenomena for varieties of reasons. What is beyond their bodies is outside their 'selves' and in their lived experience is for them impossible to perceive. Their unconscious minds keep these perceptions outside their conscious awareness. They simply do not see it because their minds reject this information.*[22]

### Intuitive perceptions from a distance

The laboratory research detailed above was done with the test subjects in the presence of the people or objects they were perceiving. People occasionally report that they spontaneously perceive what is happening somewhere in a distant location, when no sensory cues could have provided the reported information, or prior to their occurrence. Louisa Rhine (1967) has an excellent collection of these sorts of reports, including such examples as:

- A woman dreamed of the address where her mother's stolen car had been abandoned by the thieves. She went to that location and found it, 100 miles from where it had been taken (p. 99-100).

- A professional decorator and wallpaper hanger dreamed of a job he was called to do, including the person he was going to meet at the door and the exact location of the room he was being asked to paper. Months later, he found himself in what felt like a familiar location, though he was certain he had never been there before. He explained to the woman at the door that he had dreamed of coming there a while earlier, and asked, "...is this room on the second floor after a right turn beside an umbrella stand?" He was totally weirded out when she confirmed the details, and left without following through on the job. (p. 101-102)

The intuitive connection with families is often a strong one, particularly when one or more of the family members is an HSP.

'Michael' was on a job one day in the early afternoon, tuning a piano for a concert performance that evening. Suddenly he had a vision of his 3 year-old son, 'Nathan,' being at the bottom of a lot of water. Not only was it a visual experience, but Michael also experienced extreme shortness of breath, resembling a panic attack. This was an unusual experience for Michael, who was an HSP but had not had more than an occasional strongly intuitional experience before in his life.

Alarmed, he phoned home, but there was no reply. He recalled that his wife, 'Jane,' had said she'd be going out to visit a friend with Nathan, but did not know which friend it was. He didn't know what to do other than to phone home frequently throughout the afternoon. Finally, around 5:00, Jane picked up the phone.

Michael asked her, with a distinct tone of urgency in his voice, "Jane what happened? What happened to Nathan?"

Jane at first put him off, responding, "What do you mean what happened?"

Michael shared his intuitive perceptions with her, and she then told him that Nathan had been in their friend's pool, playing at the shallow end. He had taken himself, hand over hand along the edge of the pool, till he reached the deep end. His hands slipped off the side of the pool and he found himself at the bottom of the deep waters. He didn't know how to swim. Luckily, there was a 12 year-old boy there who knew how to swim and saw Nathan at the bottom of the pool. He immediately dove in and pulled Nathan to the surface, unharmed.

Everyone was relieved by this near-disaster ending so quickly and well.

Fast forward to 30 years later, when Michael asked Nathan whether he remembered the incident. Nathan acknowledged that he had very clear memories of realizing he didn't know how to swim, and expecting he would die. He didn't know why, but this didn't frighten him at all. At that moment of acceptance, a feeling of calm came over him. Suddenly, he saw a large splash at the surface as the 12 year-old boy swam to the bottom to grab him and pull him to the surface.

✦✦✦ I (Dan) came across an interesting example of group intuitive perception at the Findhorn Foundation in Scotland, where intuition in all its manifestations is an essential aspect of the daily life in their community. The Findhorn Foundation residents wanted an image etched in the glass doors of the large community meeting hall they designed and built. In their usual fashion, they held a group meditation to seek inspiration for this image. An overwhelming majority of the meditators came up with images of flowing water. This made no sense to anyone, as the Community is situated close to the North Sea but the nearest flowing water is about twenty miles away. Repeated meditations continued to produce similar images.

So, despite their inability to make sense of it, they commissioned the etching of a flowing stream of water in these doors. A few months later, a dowser (an intuitive with expertise in locating underground water) visited the Community and casually mentioned that there was an underground stream flowing not far below the surface of the ground, just outside the doors of their hall, and that it could provide water for a reflecting pool that would enhance the beauty of the hall. And his predictions proved true, validating the group intuitive perceptions of flowing water as appropriate for their door design.

Again, 'skeptics' dismiss every and all such intuitive reports as purely coincidental. While this might be the case in some instances, in others (such as those above) it appears highly unlikely that these unusually detailed facts would be reported just by chance, and even more unusual that many of these were perceived ahead of the times of their occurrence or confirmation.

Remote viewing research explores long-distance intuitive perceptions and has confirmed that people can perceive what is happening at a distant location (Jahn & Dunne, 1987). This has been replicated with shielding of the sensitive person who is doing the remote viewing, in order to eliminate the possibility of electromagnetic signals providing the acquired information (Targ & Puthoff, 1974).

In a typical remote viewing protocol, researchers randomly select a remote viewing site from a pool of potential sites that have been identified earlier. One experimenter is given an envelope with directions to the site, which is within an hour's driving radius from the laboratory. The outward-bound experimenter opens the envelope with the directions after leaving the lab, so that he can't give any clues to those remaining in the lab regarding the chosen site. The person being tested in the lab reports to an experimenter in the laboratory what he observes at the distant location. On arrival at that location, the outward-bound experimenter photographs and records whatever he observes. After a series of pairs of remote perceptions and on-site observations have been collected, independent assessors are given all of the pictures plus all of the intuitives' descriptions of the remote sites and are asked to match them. Assessors are blind to the correct matches. Highly significant numbers of successes in matchings were registered by the assessors in many replications of these studies. Meta-analyses demonstrate highly significant results in collections of remote viewing studies.[23]

The most important take-home lesson from these studies and meta analyses is their confirmation that psychic intuition is real and can be helpful in people's lives. While it may not be present or accurate all of the time, it is an inner sense to be listened to when it feels strong or insistent. While we may have difficulties explaining it within the scientific theories and paradigms of today, the evidence strongly supports that these experiences are real and can be extremely helpful. I close this section with the following report from Louisa Rhine (1961):

> ✢ ...a young woman was so upset by a terrifying dream one night that she had to wake her husband and tell him about it. She had dreamed that a large ornamental chandelier which hung over their baby's bed in the next room fell into the crib and crushed the baby to death. In the dream she could see herself and her husband standing amid the wreckage. The clock on the baby's dresser said 4:35. In the distance she could hear the rain on the windowpane and the wind blowing outside.

Her husband ridiculed her and went back to sleep. She was unable to sleep for a long time and finally brought the baby into her bed. She felt foolish when she noticed that the weather was clear and the moon shining brightly on her way back to bed with the baby.

About two hours later, they were wakened by a resounding crash. She jumped up, followed by her husband, and ran to the nursery. There, where the baby would have been lying, was the chandelier in the crib. They looked at each other and then at the clock. It stood at 4:35. Still a little skeptical, they listened to the sound of rain on the windowpane and wind howling outside.

### *Dowsing*

Dowsers are people who can locate water and other materials underground. It appears that dowsers have been doing this for at least 6,000 years, per a cave painting in the Sahara (Fenton, Web ref).

Dowsers use varieties of instruments to augment their awarenesses of the materials or objects that are being sought. All of these devices markedly augment the intuitive awarenesses of the dowser. The dowser focuses on the thought or image of what is being sought.

- The original device is a forked, 'Y' – shaped stick. The dowser holds the two branches of the fork, twisting each branch symmetrically to put tension on it, which bends the base of the 'Y' to point upward. The dowser walks with this stick over the territory that is being explored. When the item is directly underground, the stick will spontaneously twist to point downward.

- Another dowsing tool is a pair of L-shaped rods, with a loose sleeve over the short ends of the 'L,' one of which is held in each of the dowser's hands. The rods are tilted slightly forward and parallel with each other, as the dowser walks over the land that is being explored. When the item is directly underground, the rods will spontaneously twist so that they either converge or diverge.

- Dowsing with the use of a map rather than walking the territory that is being explored directly is another method. The dowser mentally holds the thought of the item being sought and may either move a pen in the air above the map, or a finger on the map, until it feels right to mark the map at a certain point, or may simply hold the thought of the item being sought and wait for inner guidance to direct the pen to a point on the map. Map dowsing can be done at any distance from the target location.

Dowsers often intuitively sense the depth at which the item will be found, or may use their instruments to answer questions about the depth of the item.

– A pendulum may be used with map dowsing or in field dowsing to answer questions about items such as the depth of the item, the amount of water flow available, and so on. The string of the pendulum is held in one hand while the dowser mentally focuses on a question. The direction of the swing of the pendulum indicates 'yes' or 'no' answers to the question. Pendulums may be used in field dowsing, but winds may interfere with its readings.

Pendulums are commonly also used for intuitive medical diagnoses and treatments. Dowsers holds questions in mind and use the pendulum for 'yes' or 'no' answers. I am impressed that the feedback of all forms of dowsing are excellent ways for many people to develop their intuitive gifts, and to enhance their confidence in their intuitive impressions.

Many dowsers also develop their healing gifts. Many healers in various traditions such as Healing Touch use pendulums to connect with intuitive knowledge for assessments and healing.

An additional health benefit identified by dowsers is to avoid areas of geopathic stress – places that negatively influence people who spend time there. People who live in such places may develop illnesses.*[24]

Dowsing research has produced impressive results. The classical use of dowsing is to locate underground streams for wells. Under sponsorship of the German government, physicist Hans-Dieter Betz studied water dowsers in Sri Lanka over a 10-year period. In 691 drillings they achieved a success rate of 96 percent, compared to the 30-50 percent success rates anticipated when drillings in this area are based on geological recommendations. Even more impressive was the fact that the dowsers were able to predict the depth at which water would be found and the amounts of flow, within a 20-30 percent margin of error, prior to drilling.

There have been further studies confirming the effectiveness of dowsing for natural sources of water and other studies that showed no significant results. I have been unable to find a meta-analysis of dowsing studies.

Some municipalities use dowsers to locate gas and electric lines when they've lost the relevant maps. I have spoken with ex-military people who report the US army has used dowsers to locate land mines.**[25]

Dowsers also identify subtle energy lines in the earth, called 'ley lines' or positive earth energy lines, extending for many miles, crisscrossing the planet. It is fascinating that ancient churches and monuments were often built on locations where several of these positive lines meet. Dowsers report that such points of ley line confluences have strongly positive energies.

Dowsers report that there are also earth energy lines and areas on our planet that have negative health effects, which have been called 'geopathic stress.' People who spend any extended length of time in the vicinity of these negative earth energies, are at risk for various illnesses.

Ilse Pope investigated geopathic stress in German and Austrian patients with various disorders:

> "In 1929 a German scientist named Freiherr von Pohl was curious about anecdotal reports connecting ley lines with illness. He convinced Dr. Blumenthal of the Berlin Centre for Cancer Research to review the 54 cancer deaths in Vilsbiburg, a village in Southern Germany with a population of 3,300. This is an unusually high number over the brief period when records were kept of cancer deaths. Freiherr von Pohl drew onto the map of Vilsbiburg all the subterranean water veins which had a strength of above 9 on the Pohl Scale... This scale, which went up to 16, Freiherr von Pohl had worked out over his many years of research into the phenomenon of earth radiation. After three days his plan was compared to the records of the district hospital and it was found... that every single cancer death had occurred exactly above the lines which Freiherr von Pohl had drawn as being above the strength of 9 and therefore cancer producing... When Freiherr von Pohl was called back to Vilsbiburg 18 months later because another ten people had died of cancer, the beds of these ten people again were exactly on the lines he had drawn on the map."

These results were so impressive that they were published in the Journal of the Centre for Cancer Research. While no blinds are mentioned, the last 10 cases occurred in predicted zones.

Ilse Pope mentions Dr. Rambeau, the President of the Chamber of Medicine in Marburg, who used a geoscope, "an instrument used by the Geological Institute to locate geological fault lines." He mapped the geological fault lines in the villages around Marburg. He found that "the beds of all his severely ill patients were above these geological fault lines." He could not locate a house that was not over a geopathic zone in which a person had lived for a long time just prior to the development of cancer, and felt that cases of cancer did not occur on neutral ground. No controls or blinds are mentioned.

In Stettin, Dr. Hager studied the 5,348 cancer deaths that occurred between 1910 and 1931. All were associated with dowsed subterranean water lines. Only 1,575 premises were associated with one cancer death each. All the rest involved multiple deaths. All premises with more than 5 cancer deaths (199 people in 28 houses) were located on crossings of water veins. Five premises were associated with more than l0 cancer deaths each (Pope; von Pohl).

Kaethe Bachler (1989), an Austrian teacher, compiled an excellent review of dowsing. She studied the influence of geopathic lines on children with learning disabilities. She reports that moving the beds or school desks of such children (when these were located over water or Curry crossings)**[26] often resulted in improved school performance. She also found correlations between cancer and such geopathic zones. No controls or blinds are mentioned.

Further research references are available in the endnotes.**[27]

In dowsing, again we have a phenomenon that does not fit within conventional scientific paradigms. The dowsing research has been largely ignored by the medical and scientific communities. And, as always, 'skeptics' in parapsychological phenomena will cite research that has produced no positive results, while generally ignoring the research mentioned here.

Within the wholistic spectrum, there is another possibility to explain some or all of the field dowsing observations. If the planet earth, Gaia, is a living entity, in and of herself, it is possible that dowsers are obtaining some or all of their information from her.

All of the dowsing instruments appear to be moved unconsciously by the dowsers, through subtle muscle control. In essence they are allowing their unconscious mind to guide their muscles in using their dowsing instruments. This appears to be confirmed by the simple test of having dowsers hold their instruments while resting their hands on the edge of a table. No movements of their instruments occur.

So while dowsers point to their dowsing devices as the instruments that detect whatever is being sought, it is the dowsers themselves who are the active instruments, and their devices are more like dials that they themselves activate. This assumption is further supported by the practice of muscle testing, where the intuitive person's body is the instrument for revealing the intuitive perceptions.*[28]

## *Understanding ESP and intuition*

ESP as researchers have defined and studied it may not be the way it actually functions. Intuition, too, functions as a wholistic combination of awarenesses. It is impossible to separate the various ESP modalities from each other.

- An instance of presumed telepathy in card reading experiments actually could be clairsentience, where the intuitive person is 'reading' information from the Zener cards that are in the hands of the person who is testing their psychic abilities, or from the examiner's physical brain (or from their mind – however we define that).
- An instance of presumed telepathy or clairsentience could actually be the results of precognition, in which the intuitive sees the final order of the Zener card series that is written down in the experimenter's records, rather than reading the experimenter's mind or perceiving the cards directly from the cards in the experimenter's hands during the experimental procedure.
- In remote viewing experiments and dowsing, ESP modalities that could be involved may include clairvoyance (for the directions given to the outbound researcher and for the location itself), and precognition (for the impressions recorded by the outbound researcher on arrival at the location). So the intuitive person may perceive what is present at the distant location, may precognitively read the mind of the outgoing experimenter, and/or may precognitively see the results of the report that the outgoing experimenter will bring back to the lab. Clairvoyance and telepathy on the part of the judges could also be postulated.
- Bioenergies may mediate or facilitate many or all aspects of intuition. When people are near each other, this is much more evident, through interactions between people's bioenergy fields.

In short, we are in early stages of clarifying what intuition is and how it works. Isn't it exciting to be exploring our world, on the leading edge of science?!

*WHAT EXAMPLES OF INTUITION HAVE YOU EXPERIENCED?*

*YOU MAY BE SURPRISED IF YOU ASK PEOPLE YOU KNOW TO SHARE INTUITIVE EXPERIENCES THEY OR OTHERS AMONG THEIR FAMILY AND FRIENDS HAVE HAD. I EXPECT YOU WILL FIND QUITE A FEW WHO WILL OFFER INTERESTING REPORTS.*

### HSPs and intuition

HSPs are often highly intuitive, in every sense of this concept, as detailed above. They pick up subtle cues in people's voices, facial expressions, gestures and so on. They sense people's emotions and sometimes pick up their thoughts as well. This provides a radar of that can help HSPs steer their ways through social situations and interactions. It can also provide alerts and warnings of people's negative thoughts and intentions.

In a caring relationship, HSPs will be sensitive to the emotions and attitudes of their partner or spouse, and to those of other members of the family. In trusting relationships this is often a blessing.

While others may think this is a great advantage in navigating through life, HSPs may find it a bit too much of a good thing. Being in groups or crowds may prove distracting, over-stimulating or even overwhelming.

HSP children may be confused by their intuitive awarenesses. These can run the whole gamut of reading people's minds and emotions, seeing into the future, recalling past life memories, communicating with spirits and angels and more. If parents or other family members disparage or dismiss such perceptions, these children may shut them out of their awareness. Their valuable gifts may be cut off forever, or until they grow up and learn they can think and decide for themselves what they want to believe or not.

You can be of enormous help to your intuitive child if you just listen with an open mind and explain that not everyone has these abilities, just like some people can't sing or aren't as strong in lifting things as other people are.

Children may also be confused between seeing something negative happening in the future and thinking they might have caused it to happen, if and when it comes true. Again, you can help them, explaining the differences between sensing a thing happening and making it happen.

You may also find some children worrying about causing bad things to happen because these children have psychokinetic abilities – to move objects through mental intent. There is actually a basis for concern in this regard, because some people, particularly teenage children, have been known to cause objects to move vigorously or even violently around a room when they are upset.**[29] Psychokinesis is discussed next.

## 52. Psychokinesis (PK): Intentionality interacting with matter

*The energy of the mind is the essence of life.*
- Aristotle

Some people find they can move or transform an object through deliberate mental intent, without the use of any physical means or of generally recognized energies. This is popularly called 'mind over matter' and in parapsychology it is labeled 'psychokinesis' (PK). PK has been well studied by parapsychologists, who have confirmed people's abilities – both individually and in groups – to control the roll of dice and the outputs of random number generators.

An additional PK manifestation is in objects moving about, sometimes forcefully or even violently, without apparent intervention or intent of anyone who is present.

Radin and Farari (1991) published a meta-analysis of 59 "studies reported by a total of 52 investigators, involving more than 2 million dice throws contributed by 2,569 subjects" from 1935-1987....**[30] We conclude that this database provides weak cumulative evidence for a genuine relationship between mental intention and the fall of dice."

Gifted people are also able to influence electronic random number generators (RNGs), as well special RNGs in which randomization is controlled by radioactive emissions from substances that ordinarily emit their radiation randomly in any direction, a randomness that is otherwise totally beyond any known influence.

Electronic random number generators have also shown significant deviations from randomness when very large numbers of people are focused intensely on an event. This could be anything, from a global crisis, to a very popular TV event, or a major sports event. This would appear to be a mental influence of a portion of the collective human consciousness.

PK is not just a human ability. Research shows that animals have this ability too. Baby chicks 'imprint' on the first large moving object they encounter after hatching. Normally this is the mother hen. In a research study, chicks were imprinted on a robot, which was programmed through a random number generator to move at random around a small room. Its path was confirmed to be random, covering all sides of the room. The chicks were then put into a small compartment outside one corner of the room, with a glassed-in window facing the room. The robot's path then deviated significantly from its previous random path. Its movements were concentrated closer to the corner of the room where the chicks were located. Chicks who had not been imprinted on the robot did not influence it to deviate from its random path around the entire room (Peoch, 1995).[31]

Another common PK effect is seen in clocks that stop when someone dies.**[32]

## 53. Psychic factors in health and healing

*It is important to use discipline with intuition,*
*and to use intuition with objectivity.*

- Paulo Coelho

Psychic abilities may enable caregivers to perceive information from careseekers' conscious and/or unconscious minds and about the wholistic states of their emotions, relationships and spirit. Likewise, information could be obtained directly from careseekers' bodies, or precognitively from later medical examinations, successful treatments or autopsies.

Many healers and medical intuitives report they deliberately make intuitive assessments in these ways. They may be able to diagnose problems even when they have never had direct contact with the person, from many miles away.[33]

Here is an example of such medical intuition:

✦ 'Betsie,' a 7 month-old baby, had colic and would cry and cry and cry periodically through the night. 'John' and 'Sarah,' her parents, were utterly exhausted from lack of sleep. Their pediatrician referred them to several specialists who were unable to find anything wrong, and reassured the parents that the colic would almost certainly resolve within a few more months.

The parents were desperate to help Betsie stop suffering and to get some decent sleep themselves. They took her to a medical intuitive. When they sat down in the intuitive's office, she admired the baby and asked if she could hold her. As soon as she had Betsie in her arms, she said, "You poor child! You have terrible allergies to cow's milk, don't you?" Identifying the problem through her medical intuition was as simple as that!

And indeed, within two days after the parents switched from cow's milk to a non-dairy formula, the colic stopped. John, a skeptic about medical intuition, thought this might just be a lucky coincidence of the colic coming to an end – as the pediatrician had predicted. Over Sarah's strong objections, he insisted on checking this out by giving Betsie a bottle of milk a week later. When she again cried and cried, Sarah insisted that John had to stay up to care for Betsie that night and the next, since this was his experiment! John learned his lesson and Betsie had no more colic after that.

Two series of intuitive assessments have been published. C. Norman Shealy (1975; 1988) checked the diagnostic impressions of a highly gifted intuitive named Carolyn Myss, reported from a distance, using patients whose diagnoses he knew. He found that she was able to make accurate diagnoses from hundreds of miles away, up to 97 percent of the time, given only the name of the patient. Similarly, Karel Mison (1968) reports from Prague that "biodiagnosticians" were able to achieve between 45 and 85 percent congruence with medical diagnoses.

In another study, by Young and Aung (1997), three psychics reported their impressions of five people with known illnesses. The congruence of intuitive readings with the medical diagnoses was 6-14 % (mean 9 %) and the authors conclude that intuitive assessments are "not to be trusted."

While the research to date has been limited, intuitive assessments appear to be promising clinical approaches for further study.

## *Ethics in intuition*

It is important to consider wholistic spiritual ethical issues as we round out this discussion on intuition. Spontaneous intuitive awarenesses are generally considered to be guided on some level by our higher spiritual selves, our spirit guides, angels or the Infinite Source. It is usually assumed that these are inherently directed by these agencies to be for our own highest good and for the highest good of whoever else is participating in our intuitive awarenesses and communications.

Ethically, our intentionally seeking intuitive awarenesses requires that we set an intention to open to our intuitive connections with others only if and when this is 'for the highest good of all.' When we are seeking to connect with another person, it would be invasive if we sought information via our psychic awarenesses without their permission. This would be like setting up a hidden microphone or camera to spy on them. Most of the gifted and experienced caregivers I know would never use their intuitive abilities without setting this intent prior to connecting with a person when they had not received this person's permission first.

Relevant to HSPs and HSPCs, intuition in all of its manifestations may be very helpful in your relationships. When an HSP is in a caring relationship, his intuitions can serve your mutual highest good. This can be enormously beneficial in matters small and large, such as:

- Drawing your attention to issues, small and large, that need attention, such as feeling the boiler, refrigerator or car might need attention, before any malfunctions are physically evident
- Sensing when it would be good to call someone in your family or circle of friends – to offer support or cheering up
- Identifying issues between you that can benefit from healing, before they fester into sores that are difficult to address and soothe and heal
- Scouting out ways to enhance your mutual enjoyments of each other

## 54. Biological energies (biofields)

*My job is to... correct the "mistakes" in the patient's biofield by means of my own energy...*
- Mietek Wirkus

Many parapsychologists consider healing to be a psychic ability, sometimes calling it 'bio-PK.' In this healing model, intention is the active factor. Most healers consider healing to be a separate and distinct caregiving modality, involving far more than just altering the physical body with PK.**[34]

As mentioned earlier, in addition to using herbal remedies, healing rituals, and healing through intention, many shamans and Western healers report that they see auras of color around people and can palpate these with their hands. They explain that these are biological energy fields (also called Biofields) which are connected with every level of a person – body, emotions, mind, relationships and spirit (Benor, 2008).

Similar reports of healing abilities are found in Western society. Some gifted, natural healers are born with these abilities. Today, many more learn to develop their healing gifts through organizations that offer healing courses and workshops. Some of the more popular organizations include Therapeutic Touch, Healing Touch, Reiki, Qigong and related methods. Some people discover and develop their healing abilities spontaneously, particularly after near death experiences or in times of urgent need. Some conventional caregivers are gifted with intuitive and/or healing abilities, but won't mention them in public because they fear the censure of their licensing boards or the ridicule of their skeptical colleagues.

Many people who are not healers can also perceive biofields around the bodies of people and other living beings (animals and plants). Many sense these fields with their hands, describing heat and cold, smoothness and roughness, tingling, prickliness and other sensations. Far fewer can perceive these visually, as fields of color around living beings, although children under school age often report seeing auras (Peterson, 1987). Some are also gifted with the abilities to use these auras to assess the states of people's bodies, emotions, minds, relationships, and spirit (Brennan, 1988).

Some people who sense auras can also sense the chakras. These are energy fields along the spine that were identified in Eastern writings over the past 5,000 years (Karagulla & Kunz, 1989). The chakras are associated bioenergetically with various body functions. See Table VII – 1.

Some report they also see energy fields around what humans consider to be inanimate objects, such as rocks, earth, water, and air. Some of these more sensitive sensitives also perceive that inanimate objects have consciousness. A rock, a mountain or a river may speak to them. They, in turn, will ask for permission from a locality before entering a new territory. Within wholistic frameworks, it is commonly the spirit or spirits of the locality with whom they communicate.

Conventional medicine, which originated well prior to modern physics, focuses almost exclusively on the physical aspects of living beings and has been slow to absorb that it is also possible to address their bioenergy aspects.

**Table VII–1. The chakras**

| Name | Location of chakra | Level / Endocrine gland / NERVE PLEXUS | Influence on |
|---|---|---|---|
| Crown / Sahasrara | | Apex of skull / Pineal | Higher brain centers, spiritual connection |
| Brow/Third Eye / Ajna | | Brow / Pituitary / DEEP BRAIN CENTERS | Deeper brain centers, eyes, ears, nose, nervous system, visualization |
| Throat / Visuddha | | 3rd cervical / Thyroid / PHARYNGEAL | Voice, breathing, digestive tract, expression, clairsentience |
| Heart / Anahata | | 4th thoracic / Thymus / CARDIAC | Heart, blood, autonomic nervous system, circulation, closeness of relationship |
| Solar Plexus / Manipura | | 8th thoracic / Spleen/pancreas / SOLAR PLEXUS | Stomach, liver, gall bladder, awareness of place in cosmos |
| Sacral / Svadhisthana | | 1st lumbar / Gonads / SPLENC | Reproduction, relating on sexual levels |
| Base/Root / Muladhara | | Base of spine / Adrenals / COCCYGEAL | Spine, kidneys, levels of energy |

In addition to psychic healing, other therapeutic modalities also address aspects of biological energies, including Acupuncture (and its derivatives, such as Shiatsu and Reflexology), Qigong and T'ai Chi.

✦ I've spoken with numbers of doctors who have great gifts of diagnostic intuition. Some of the more sensitive ones are able to diagnose problems instantly. They know whether an abdominal pain is caused by an infection, a blockage, a cancer or some other problem – from perceiving the aura either visually, through touch, or other psychic modes of intuition. Invariably, they have kept these precious gifts completely secret, even from their doctor and nurse colleagues with whom they may have worked closely for many years.

✦ A physician acquaintance of mine in the US reported that she was able to make intuitive diagnoses regularly when lightly touching her patients during a physical exam, and often just by viewing their aura. She found her diagnoses were almost always accurate, and was similarly frustrated that she had to wait for laboratory and scan reports before starting treatments. This could involve unnecessary delays of up to several days. She had never dared mention this to any of her colleagues.

Healing is much more accepted in Great Britain than in many other countries. In the 1970's, a group of healing organizations lobbied the government to be allowed to offer their services in government clinics and hospitals, under the National Health Service (NHS). In one governmental (not medical) decision, 1,500 hospitals were opened to healers, with the provision that the patient could request the healers' services and the local medical unit head nurse and doctor had to approve this. Over the following decades, healers have been active in the NHS, for the most part at the invitation of patients. Many patients reported relief of pains of all sorts, more rapid recuperations from surgery and injuries, decreases in nausea, vomiting and other symptoms.

Gradually, nurses and doctors saw the benefits of healing and some of them would invite healers to help their patients. Some of the nurses developed their own healing gifts. A few doctors started working closely with healers.

Nurses have been great pioneers in integrating healing with conventional care. Largely due to the encouragements and inspiration of Dolores Krieger, RN, PhD and Dora Kunz (a gifted, natural healer), Therapeutic Touch (TT) is being practiced openly by many nurses in hospital and clinic settings. Some of these nurses have also confirmed the efficacy of TT healing with clinical research for their Masters and Doctoral Dissertations, as have nurses practicing Healing Touch. This has not been without challenges, however, from nurses who are unaccepting of the legitimacy or even the possibility of nurse-mediated healing.

✦ A creative solution was devised by 'Terri,' an oncology nurse caught in one such situation. She had had very positive results from her healing on her cancer unit. Patients she treated had less pains from their cancers and less nausea, vomiting, headaches, tiredness and other symptoms from chemotherapy and radiotherapy. They also needed less medications for these symptoms. However, a new supervisor objected to her offering healing and insisted that she stop.

Terri was inspired to impart healing to the chemotherapy bottles, having learned that water is a good vehicle for healing energies. The other nurses noticed that Terri's patients did not complain of nausea, vomiting, headaches or other side effects from their conventional treatments. Her supervisor came to observe how Terri prepared and administered the chemotherapy, but found no fault in her medication management!

✦ 'Joan,' an emergency room nurse, found herself in a similar situation. Subjected to scrutiny and then threatened with sanctions by her supervisor if she did not stop giving healing, she came up with another, similar solution. Joan imparted healing to the dressings she used to bandage people's wounds, again providing relief from pains and facilitating healing for their wounds.**[35]

### *Bioenergy field assessments*

As mentioned above, biofields reflect the conditions of the organism. Healers (and many others) can sense these fields with their hands. Some are gifted with abilities to intuitively identify people's conditions of wholistic health or illness. Others must learn the meanings of the colors of the biofields that they see. Dora Kunz, one of the founders of Therapeutic Touch, was very gifted at seeing auras. She spent several years sitting next to a doctor as they both examined the doctor's patients – each in her own way - in order to learn what the correlations were between the colors and shapes of people's auras and chakras (Karagulla & Kunz, 1989).

YOU MIGHT BE INTERESTED IN EXPLORING YOUR OWN BIOENERGY SENSITIVITIES

- Hold your hands opposite each other, slightly apart. Move them further apart (12-24 inches) and then closer together again, back and forth. What do you sense?

- Close and open your hands rapidly about 20 times, then repeat the process. Do you notice a difference?

- Find someone who will hold a hand up for you to practice with, and move one of your hands near theirs, then apart - as you did with your own hands.

– Repeat this with your other hand. What do you sense?

– Do you notice any other wholistic awarenesses about them?

Most people will sense heat, tingling, very light pressure, or a feeling like holding two magnets near each other when they do these explorations. Some will experience occasional tastes or smells along with the tactile sensations in their hands. I speculate that these unfamiliar bioenergy stimuli to the brain are being deciphered through nervous system pathways that are new to the consciousness of the explorers in these realms. I would guess that the smells and tastes are the brain's ways of bringing these new stimuli into the conscious awareness of the perceiver.

With practice, many can develop increasing sensitivity and increasing awarenesses of the meanings of the various delicate tactile and other sensations. Some can learn to identify a person's condition by the intuitive emotional feelings or intuitive cognitive perceptions they experience while moving their hands through a biofield. For many people, such individualized, personal explorations may be the type of research that impresses them the most.

### Research on biofield assessments

Susan Wright (1988) found highly significant correlations between sensed biofield abnormalities and pains in the neck, upper back, and lower back of 52 people. Her observations could have occurred by chance less than one time in 10,000.**[36]

Gary Schwartz, et al. (1995) report two experiments to establish whether ordinary people who were blindfolded could identify the presence of the hand of an experimenter which was held several inches above one of the experimenters' hands. (Subjects had no claims to any healing abilities.)

In the first experiment, the average of the subjects' guesses were significantly above chance levels.**[37] Subjects' average confidence ratings were also significantly higher for correct guesses than for incorrect ones.**[38] This suggests that they were partially aware of when their guesses were correct. In the second experiment, guesses were 69.8 percent correct, again significantly above chance.**[39] In the combined experiments, results were highly significant.**[40] There were no differences between men and women in percents of successful guessing. Both groups also had higher confidence ratings regarding correct guesses compared to incorrect ones.**[41]

A much-publicized science fair project by a 10 year-old was published in the Journal of the American Medical Association (JAMA), showing no abilities of a series of healers to identify the presence of the hand of the experimenter held near their own hand (Rosa, et al., 1998). This is a very peculiar publication, as the JAMA is a prestigious medical journal for doctors, focusing on formal medical research. It was unheard of for a high school science fair project to be published by a 10 year-old girl in JAMA prior to this one, and no other such article has been published since then. It is also notable that an inadequate literature review is provided in this study, which is another major deviation from the publication standards of this journal.**[42]

I was curious whether different healers visually perceive the bioenergy field by similarly or differently from each other. I set up a pilot experiment in which a panel of eight healers simultaneously observed the same people who had known medical diagnoses (Benor, 1992). The differences between individual readings were far more obvious than the similarities. However, the people being observed validated that seven of the eight intuitive aura readings were accurate. Repeating this pilot study with another four healers who appeared to have more highly developed aura reading abilities produced similar results. I speculate that each of the healers was resonating intuitively with different aspects of the people whose auras they were reading. Further discussion on this a bit later on.

I close this section with a few general observations and speculations. Sensitive people shake their heads when disbelievers question whether what they report about their perceptions of bioenergy fields is true or just a figment of their imagination. In addition to perceiving physical disorders, the sensitives report that these perceptions are enormously helpful in identifying people's emotions. They find it useful to be able to see immediately when people are anxious, angry or sad.

Similarly, interactions between the auras of people who are in close proximity to each other reveal their degrees of psychological closeness to or distance from each other, as well as other information about their relationships. Further aspects of an aura are reported to reveal the person's levels of spiritual development.

After years of exploring these intuitive awarenesses, my take on it is that the biofields of the sensitives interact with the biofields of those they are sensing. The sensitives' consciousness uses their ordinary senses (sight, smell, taste, etc.) to cue them to the presence of the various physical issues, feelings and thoughts that are evident in the biofields of the people they are observing. Sight is the sense that appears most commonly stimulated, but numbers of sensitives have reported that they perceive certain aspects of other people's biofields as smells, tastes or physical sensations in their own bodies.

Completely unrelated to biofields, these sorts of variability in perceptions may occur in people's ordinary senses. Some people are able to perceive colors by touching the surface of an object. Others may see colors stimulated by sounds. These crossed sensory perceptions are called 'synesthesias' (van Campen, et al., Web ref.). Clearly, we have much to clarify yet in these areas of sensory awarenesses.

Some people question the ethics of reading people's bioenergy fields without their permission. Sensitives just shake their heads and say that this is no different from smelling a person's odor. Odors are there for anyone who can sense them, and so is the bioenergy field.

*In summary:*

A variety of theories have been proposed to explain healing. Each of these appears to be a partial explanation. Taken together, they offer the beginnings of several avenues for understanding healing:

- Quantum physics tells us that every physical object can also be addressed as energies. This theory has been well validated and has come to be accepted within the physical sciences. Biological matter can equally well be considered as energy.
- Quantum physics demonstrates that consciousness and intent of the researcher can influence the outcome of processes in the world of physics, and healers say the same about their intents to heal that can alter living matter.
- Parapsychology confirms that conscious intent can influence the physical world (as in the roll of dice and altering outputs of random number generators), so there is no reason this shouldn't be true of living physical bodies as well as of inert physical objects.

- Telepathy may be effective in generating healing through mind-to-mind projections of suggestions for improvements. This would be similar to self-healing that can be generated through verbal and non-verbal suggestions on the part of the caregiver or researcher that activates self-healing on the part of the person receiving any sort of treatment. This is true even when the treatment is an inert substance used as a placebo, where the person receiving treatment is led to expect the treatment to produce beneficial effects.
- Healers say their energy fields interact with the energy fields of healees to bring about healings.
- Healers say their wishes and/or prayers for help from the Infinite Source and/or angels can bring about healings.

Biofields around the body are just one way in which healers connect with their healees. Many healers report they are able to sense the states of health and illness of people from a distance, much in the same way that remote viewing is reported. These reports have numerous clinical case confirmations but only a few research studies have been published on distant clinical assessments so far.*[43]

Coming back to the primary focus of this book, I find that most of those working as psychics and healers are HSPs. Conversely, substantial numbers of HSPs possess some measure of psychic and/or healing abilities. Many of these HSPs have learned to keep their gifts under wraps, because those who do not possess such abilities tend to be skeptical and may be derisive or abusive in dismissing the HSPs because the disbelievers consider them eccentric or crazy.

Psychic abilities are often greatly appreciated by those who possess them. Telepathy and clairsentience may contribute to caregiving relationships – both in the HSP-HSPC relationship and in the relationships of professional caregivers and their careseekers. Caregivers with these abilities, particularly when they are HSPs themselves, can be of extra help to HSPs and their HSPCs.

Healers report that people can use their own biofield to protect themselves against negative energies. There are varieties of ways to do this. The simplest is to make a mental image of your biofield protecting you like the energy fields pictured in Star Trek. I've heard numerous reports from people who say this works for them to prevent feeling the influence of other people's negative thoughts, emotions or intentions. I've also seen numbers of people with various allergies, even with severe multiple allergy syndrome, using this successfully to reduce their sensitivities to whatever they are allergic to.

So here are further tools for reducing HSPs' responsiveness to negativities:
- When you are exposed to other people's negativity, picture your biofield being strengthened to shield you from any negativity that might affect you.
- You may do this similarly if you feel negative energies in various physical locations.
- Taking this a step further, you might offer healing to a place with negative energies, which might be due to earth energies or to residues from human negativity.

## Unusual properties of biological energies

Biological energies may behave in ways that seem unusual from conventional, Western perspectives of the world. While the properties of bioenergy may appear odd within conventional scientific and medical frameworks, they reveal new realms of realities and understandings of our world.

### Biological energies can be imprinted in various materials

Healing energies can be transmitted in water, cotton and other materials. As mentioned above, intravenous medications and cotton wool dressings have been used to convey healing to people and animals. Research also confirms that cotton wool treated by a healer can enhance wound healing in mice (Grad, et al., 1961) and can cure cancers in mice (Bengston, 2017).

An object held, worn or carried by someone for a period of time, or a photograph of a person acquires some of their bioenergies. These bioenergy imprints can be 'read' by clairvoyant people, and can be used for healers to link to the person in order to send them distant healing.**[44]

Living tissues may also contain imprints of and connection with the source of those tissues. There is an amazing report from Claire Sylvia (1997) following her heart transplant. Shortly after waking from her surgery, she started craving beer, which was a completely alien taste for her. Gradually, she became increasingly aware of the deceased previous owner of her transplanted heart. He had been a motorcycle rider with a love of beer. Over time, her awarenesses of his spirit became clearer and clearer, and eventually he guided her to his previous family in his most recent life, where details of her perceptions of his life were verified.

Homeopathic remedies may be effective through bioenergies in those remedies made from living materials (such as plants) that are used to create some of the remedies. In contrast with conventional medications, the greater the dilution of a homeopathic remedy, the greater the potency of the preparation. Remedies are shaken in order to get the therapeutic substance to imprint the solution in which it is prepared. For modern commercial purposes, mechanical vortexing is used rather than hand-held shaking, as in earlier days. While it might appear from a Western scientific standpoint that the process of vortexing can be automated in this way, there are sensitive homeopaths who feel that the attitudes of company personnel who manage the vortexing can make a difference in the qualities of the remedies.

Clinical studies of homeopathic remedies (Boyd, 1946) and laboratory tests[45] have demonstrated that a shaken remedy is effective, whereas an unshaken one is not. Ten seconds of shaking suffices to potentize a solution. Heating potentized solutions to 70-80 degrees Centigrade inactivates them. Another unusual observation is that loss of potency in aging solutions can be reversed by repeated shaking (Jones & Jenkins, 1981). Jacques Benveniste (1998) and other homeopaths suggest that there is a bioenergetic pattern carried by water which brings about the observed healing effects.

Potency can be demonstrated in remedies that are so dilute that they could not contain even a single molecule of the original substance (Davenas et al.; Smith & Boericke, 1968). Studies using nuclear magnetic resonance have also shown alterations in these sorts of very dilute homeopathic solutions (Young, 1975).

Another counter-intuitive observation is that the more dilute the remedy, the more potent are its clinical effects. This is very different from conventional medications, where we are used to seeing greater potency with less dilute medications.

A further strange but repeatedly observed phenomenon is that the efficacy of homeopathic treatments rises and falls repeatedly as the remedies are progressively diluted. That is to say, an effect observed with initial dilutions disappears when greater dilutions are used, then reappears when even greater dilutions are made, etc. This waxing and waning of effectiveness continues in a regular pattern with continued dilutions (Scofield, 1984a; 1984b).

## Bioenergies interact with solar and planetary energy fields

Recent research demonstrates that human heart rhythms are influenced by geomagnetic field fluctuations of the sun and of planet earth (McCraty, et al., 2017). Solar storms, shifts in the solar wind striking the earth, and shifts in the earth's magnetic field are all reflected in heart rate variability of individual people. It is too early as yet to know what, if any, effects these electromagnetic shifts have on consciousness, normal and/or abnormal functions of the human bioenergy field.

## Personal exploration of your own bioenergy sensitivities

Biofield awareness can add to your HSP-HSPC connections, enabling you to sense each others' wholistic states of being (popularly called 'vibes') more clearly. HSPs often do this as a matter of course, even without being conscious of it. Doing it consciously gives you more awareness of each other and also opens up further channels for understanding and helping each other.

You may be able sense the biofield with your hands.

- Hold your hands opposite each other, slightly apart. Move them further apart (12-24 inches) and then closer together again, back and forth. What do you sense? Many people will sense warmth, tingling, a slight 'buzz' feelings, a gentle tug towards the other hand or slight pressure of repulsion – like you can feel with the various poles of a magnet.

- Close and open your hands rapidly about 20 times, then repeat the process. Do you notice a difference? Many people notice an increased intensity of sensations between their hands

- Find someone who will hold a hand up for you to practice with, and move one of your hands near theirs, then apart - as you did with your own hands.

- Repeat this with your other hand. What do you sense? Each person's hand has a subtle different bioenergetic 'signature' of sensations.

- What else, if anything, do you sense?

With practice, many can develop increasing sensitivity and increasing awarenesses of the meanings of the various delicate tactile sensations. For instance, some learn to identify a person's condition on some or all levels of the wholistic spectrum, by the intuitive feelings they experience in moving their hands through a biofield.

With practice and with the development of natural intuitive gifts, people may be able to sense bioenergies solely through holding the intent to be present in a healing manner, without needing to access the biofields manually. This can even be done from great distances, without direct access to another person's biofields.

When we have these abilities, we can also offer bioenergy support to someone we want to help just through the intention to help. Many people do this naturally, without any awareness of the processes that are involved. You may have experienced this by being in the presence of someone who had calm, joyful, exciting or healing vibes.

If you wish to explore this further, I encourage you to read more about it and to seek out training in one of the healing modalities, such as Therapeutic Touch or Healing Touch, which offer courses to learn healing, with ongoing mentoring and supervision. This involves a serious commitment over a period of months. Reiki is an easy way in, requiring only a weekend to pick up the basics, but Reiki has no structure for supervised instruction in more serious applications of healing.**[46]

### Healing powers of objects

As mentioned earlier, physical objects are reported by healers to store healers' healing energies. Cotton wool and water are the most frequently mentioned. In these cases, people intentionally project healing energies into these 'vehicles for healing' and the vehicles are then available for healings of those in need.*[47] In other cases, natural objects and places may inherently possess healing energies that can be accessed by people in need of healings.

#### Crystals

Certain crystals have been found to offer inherent healing benefits for particular problems and/or generally energizing effects. A basis for the healing powers of crystals is suggested by their uses as signal receivers and current rectifiers in crystal radio sets, quartz watches and other devices. It may be that they can serve similar focusing functions for the biological energies that appear to be involved in healing. The natural healing properties of crystals may be enhanced by healers' bioenergies and intentions.

Crystals may be used to make essences, similar to homeopathic remedies and flower essences. Typically, the crystal is left in a bottle of water, for a period of time and the water becomes a vehicle for the healing energies. This suggests a vibrational aspect to their healing powers.

C. Norman Shealy (1992), a neurosurgeon who began investigating complementary therapies for use in pain management, demonstrated highly significant effects of quartz crystals on depression. I know of no other research to confirm the use of crystals for particular problems, though they are used by some healers to augment healing for many ailments.

Here are just a few examples of crystals and their particular benefits.

*Amethyst – Harmonizes relationships*

*Aquamarine – Treats arthritis*

*Black tourmaline – Protects against negativity*

*Fluorite, Black tourmaline – Neutralize irritating energies*

*Opal (gem quality) – Opens and stimulates chakras to higher functions*

Crystals may be used for self-healing. The selection of particular crystals by a healer may be a great help. Crystals may also carry the healing vibrations of self-healing intent, or of a healer who uses them as vehicles for healing intentions and energies.[48]

#### Consciousness appears to interact with matter

As with imprinting of healing properties in cotton and water with deliberate healing intent, there can be healing properties imprinted in matter spontaneously, without relying on deliberate intent of the person preparing the remedies.

Colin Griffiths (1995) discusses the homeopathic remedy that was developed from a piece of stone taken from the Berlin Wall when it was torn down. The wall was built of concrete, incorporating bricks and other debris that had been gathered after the bombings of World War II. The piece of the wall that was used to develop the remedy was brought to Britain by a German woman who gave it to Griffiths as a curiosity, and it lay in a drawer for about a year till he presented it to a homeopath who was psychically sensitive for her intuitive impressions. She instantly felt fear, panic and distress, though she was totally unaware of the source of the little piece of concrete. This encouraged Griffiths to have a homeopathic company prepare a remedy from the stone. When the sensitive woman was given a dose of a 30c dilution of the Berlin wall preparation, she felt that it was so extraordinarily potent that she strongly advised it should be kept separate from other remedies because it might seriously alter them or antidote them.

The Berlin wall had been built in 1961, separating Communist-dominated East Germany from West Berlin, which was a Western enclave buried deep within East Germany. The wall was the product of Communist fears about the infiltration of Western influences, and the source of enormous tensions and conflicts between East and West. Thousands died in attempts to escape to the West, hoping for freedom from East German oppressions and reunification with families which had been torn asunder by the war and its aftermath. With the coming of glasnost (the loosening of state controls in the Soviet Union), the wall was torn down, releasing large floods of people who had been trapped and powerless to oppose the governing authorities.

Griffiths and other homeopaths have found that the remedy prepared from this highly symbolic material is helpful for treating people who are suffering in various ways from oppression, suppression, depression or repression. An example from Griffith follows.

✦A 28-year-old woman had been taking homeopathic remedies for several years to treat depression and a number of other complaints. One day she came to the clinic in deep misery, feeling that nothing was right with her, or had ever been right before, or would ever be right thereafter. She felt deprived in her inner life and her relationships, and in particular she felt short-changed by her parents, who had separated when she was a little girl. She complained of always giving and not receiving in return, of being alienated from her loved ones, and of marking time to no purpose. She had longed for years when she was in East Berlin to be protected from the world, feeling she had never really wished to grow up, and had been pining for the security of her family and the place of her birth, in Berlin.

The woman was given a single dose of Berlin Wall 30c, and after 3 days she reported that she was quite changed.

...She had resolved a number of difficult issues with both her boyfriend and her father and, in the case of the latter, felt that she had established the first proper communication for years. She had also been offered a decent job, after years of doing indifferent work. She felt as though a wall had been broken through that had stood between herself and the rest of the world. She has not needed to come [for further treatment] since.

I think of these as 'metaphoric' remedies, in which the subtle energy vibrations associated with a substance are shaped by the conceptual essence embedded in the material used to create the remedy.

The obvious alternative explanation of suggestion as the causal agent in this case awaits clarification via controlled studies of such metaphoric remedies.

Other intuitives have developed such intuitive, intentional, metaphoric remedies, in the context of homeopathic and flower essence therapies. Madeline Evans (2000) has an excellent book on homeopathy, including essential, esoteric and chakra relevance. Machaelle Small Wright (1988) has these sorts of flower essence remedies.

Homepathic remedies do not stand alone in containing information embedded in physical matter – which can be perceived intuitively by sensitive people. The research on clairvoyance demonstrates similar abilities.*[49]

William Bengston (2007), a gifted natural healer who is also a brilliant researcher, has developed a method for learning healing that involves focusing the mind on a random series of thoughts, after setting the intention to heal. Many people who have no known innate healing abilities, including people who are skeptical about healing, have learned this method and succeeded in curing mice of cancer that is ordinarily incurable. As Bengston notes, this suggests that consciousness is the organizing factor in healings. Bengston concludes (2017), "Healing appears to be fundamentally about 'information' rather than 'energy,' despite the popular use of the latter term."[50]

However, he also reports that mice who have been injected with cancer cells and are in need of healing for their growing tumor will place their bodies next to the left hand of the healers holding their cage. After the mice were cured of their cancers, they no longer positioned themselves next to the left hand of the healers. This suggests that bioenergies may be involved in healing.

My own impression is that psychic healing is a multi-faceted phenomenon that includes components of both bioenergies and of intention. I believe that some healers offer their healing more through bioenergies and others offer healing more through intentions.

### *Healing powers of places*

Most sensitives report that walking in nature feels refreshing, rejuvenating and energetically cleansing. Many healers recommend releasing negative energies from our bodies during healing and directing them deep into the earth for composting and cleansing.

Many sensitives can identify places with positive healing energies, where people can clear their negative energies and conversely, can fortifiy themselves with refreshing, healing energies. Some sensitives also a sense of connection with spirit in places like these. I have come across reports of geographic locations, mountains, boulders, still and flowing waters, particular trees and garden areas, and other aspects of nature where such cleansing vibrations are sensed. Some of these places also appear to support and promote healing.

Many healers suggest that the healing energies of some places in nature may be generated by people who engage in bioenergy or prayer healing in such places. I have heard frequent reports about the healing vibrations that are sensed in healers' treatment rooms, and spiritual or healing vibrations that are sensed in churches and other places of meditation, prayers and healing services.

Shrines have been built at some such locations, and healings have been attributed to visits at various shrines around the world. The most famous and best studied of these is in Lourdes, a little south of Bordeaux in France.[51] So many people have made claims for cures at Lourdes, that the Catholic church created a commission which rigorously reviews these annually. Their medical panel, after detailed investigations, ascertains whether the reported physical changes could have occurred spontaneously or under normal medical care.

The story of Lourdes begins in 1858, when a peasant girl named Bernadette Soubirous was gathering wood by the River Gave, at the base of a cliff known as Massabieille. A vision of the Virgin Mary appeared to her, standing at a split in the rock. Miraculous cures were alleged to have occurred at this spot within a few weeks of the first appearance of the Virgin. This became a healing grotto where millions of people with all varieties of illnesses have come to ask the Virgin for a cure. Thousands bathe daily in the waters of the grotto.

Because a few have experienced miraculously rapid cures of intractable, serious illnesses, much interest has been stirred in religious and medical circles. A local medical board has reviewed cases of cures since 1885, staffed by volunteers and supported by donations from private, nonclerical sources. An independent body, the International Medical Commission (IMC), sits in Paris so they cannot be biased by the emotional atmosphere of Lourdes. There are 25 members of the IMC, all practicing Catholics, 13 from France and the rest from other European countries. Their specialties include surgery, orthopedics, general medicine, psychiatry, and radiology, among others.

If the Commission considers the case inexplicable by ordinary laws of nature, the dossier is submitted to the Archbishop of the diocese of the healed person. He designates a Canonical Commission to review the case afresh. They take separate testimony from the witnesses and express their opinions on whether the case can be considered miraculous by the Church's standards. It is only on the favorable recommendation of the Canonical Commission that the Archbishop may pronounce the cure attributable to the miraculous intervention of the Virgin Mary.

D. J. West (1957), an English physician, critically reviewed 11 such cures that had been declared 'miracles' by the church after extensive medical and ecclesiastical reviews. He presents a thorough analysis of another 11 cases**[52] and a sketchy overview of a further 87. He is clearly a disbeliever in healing miracles.

West points out that in most of his 11 cases there were possible diagnoses which were not seriously entertained by the Board or the Commission (including malingering) and in some cases diagnoses such as tuberculosis were not supported beyond reasonable doubt by the available laboratory data. The declarations of miraculous cures relied heavily on clinical impressions and a variety of testimonies which could conceivably have been erroneous. He concludes:

> Self-evidently impossible cures, involving something like the regeneration of a lost eye or limb, are not in question because they are never claimed. The great majority of the cures concern potentially recoverable conditions and are remarkable only in the speed and manner in which they are said to have taken place. In no case is a sudden structural change confirmed by the objective evidence of X-rays taken just before and just after the event.

In his survey of other cases, West grudgingly notes that there are chronic, infected wounds that had not responded to conventional treatments, and that closed rapidly and completely at Lourdes.

It is still impressive that positive findings remain after the many siftings of the evidence. Although X-ray evidence of instantaneous physical cures is not observed among the Lourdes cases considered in this review, there are witnessed reports from apparently reliable sources testifying to instantaneous total healings of chronic fleshy suppurating wounds. These are impossible to account for in any conventional way. They appear to constitute recoveries from infections of chronic nature, with enormous acceleration of the rate of wound healing. These cures are particularly impressive when they had resisted all conventional treatments.

St. John Dowling reviews another cure which was agreed by the IMC to be medically inexplicable.

✣ Delizia Cirolli was 12 years old in 1976 when she complained of a painful, swollen right knee. She was examined by Professor Millica at the Orthopedic Clinic of the University of Catania in Sicily. X-rays and a biopsy produced the diagnosis of a metastatic neuroblastoma. The family refused the amputation which the surgeon advised. Though they agreed initially to radiotherapy, the family took her home before she had any treatment because she was very unhappy in the hospital. She had another consultation at the University of Turin but again had no treatment. In August 1976 she spent four days at Lourdes with her mother, participating in ceremonies, prayers in the Grotto, and baths in the water. She showed no improvement clinically and X-rays showed advancement of the growth in September. Her condition deteriorated and her mother even started preparations for her funeral. Her neighbors in the village kept up their prayers to Our Lady of Lourdes for a cure and she received Lourdes water to drink regularly from her mother. Just before Christmas she unexpectedly asked to go out and did so without pain. She was unable to go far because of weakness, weighing only 22 Kg (48 lbs.) at that time. Her general condition improved and the swelling in her knee disappeared, though a deformity remained in the knee.[53] She came back to the Medical Bureau at Lourdes yearly from 1977 to 1980. No signs of the typical calcifications of neuroblastoma were found on X-rays of her chest or abdomen.

Though she was cured beyond doubt, the precise diagnosis was debated as to whether it was a metastatic neuroblastoma or a Ewing's tumor. Spontaneous remissions of neuroblastomas occur in rare instances but never after the age of five years, while spontaneous remissions of Ewing's tumors have never been reported. The IMC reviewed the case three times between 1980 and 1982, finally deciding that it was a Ewing's tumor and that its cure was inexplicable. It was not considered relevant that the moment of cure was not at Lourdes. It was left to the church to decide whether this was to be declared miraculous.

Dowling briefly notes how difficult it is for many people to accept that miraculous cures can occur. They tend to doubt the diagnoses of the Medical Board, or to seek other explanations for these unusual improvements in conditions which are normally intractable.

Though opinions vary as to the validity of findings in some cases of Lourdes healings, a core of convincing evidence remains.

Healings of physical illnesses at shrines appear to be rarer occurrences than the media might have us believe. Nevertheless, those which are accepted by the medical and church authorities are among the best documented complete shrine healings available. How similar these are to healings brought about with the direct help of healers remains to be clarified.

The spiritual uplift experienced by pilgrims appears to be much more frequent than cures. This, in fact, is the aspect of healing that many spiritual healers value the most.

While credits for the cures are attributed to the Virgin Mary, it is also possible that the atmosphere of hope and belief in the power of the shrine to facilitate cures might facilitate the healing powers of those people present at the shrine who pray for the cures.

And again, I have known many HSPs who report perceiving calming and healing energies in various places. I would wonder whether those who experience healings at shrines are more likely to be HSPs.

## 55. Psychic healing – as psychic intuition and psychokinesis

> *The imagination of a man can act not only on his own body but even on others and very distant bodies. It can fascinate and modify them; make them ill, or restore them to health.*
> - Avicenna (Persian, 980-1037)

Parapsychologists consider healing to be a psychic ability, combining telepathy, clairsentience and/or psychokinesis. Many healers consider healing to be a separate and distinct, wholistic caregiving modality that involves far more than just altering the physical body. Many of these healers go much further, saying that the origins of our being are not in our body but rather in our spirit, which determines what and how our body should be and how we need to live our lives – in order to learn our spiritual and karmic lessons. Spiritual healing is therefore an alternative name for psychic healing within this perspective.**[54] Unless otherwise specified (as, for example, in wound healing or physical healing), I use 'healing' to refer to psychic healing.

Throughout recorded history, and in every culture around the world today, there are people who are able to offer healing through non-medical methods. These may be called indigenous or shamanic healers. In addition to using herbal remedies and healing rituals, many shamans report that they see the auras of color around people and can sense these with their hands. They explain that these are the body's energy fields, which are connected with every level of a person – body, emotions, mind, relationships (with other people and the world at large), and spirit.

In the modern western world today there are many varieties of healers. Among the more popular are those practicing the following healing methods:

- Therapeutic Touch (TT) and Healing Touch (HT): both of these require class instruction and at least a year's mentorship, and both of which have conducted substantial numbers of research studies, many of them Masters theses and Doctoral dissertations to validate their work. Healing may be given through light touch, with hands held near to but not touching the body, or from a distance. The hands are held where the healer intuits they need to be placed.**[55]

- Reiki, a very popular healing method, is learned in weekend workshops, with an attunement by a Reiki master in which special healing energies are transferred from the Master to the student. Various Japanese symbols are used to convey healing, along with touch and/or distant healing. Specific patterns of hand positions on the body are used. Reiki Masters used to be highly gifted, selected by the originator of the Reiki method and his acknowledged disciples, and given special attunements as induction into their roles as Masters, after long periods of study and practice. Today, a person can become a Master in a long weekend workshop.

- Qigong is a Chinese system of healing and energy medicine, involving breathing, gentle movements, and meditation to purify, enhance, and circulate the life energy called qi (pronounced chi). There are thousands of variations, worldwide, on the theme of qigong (Cohen, 1997).

- Healing in religious settings has been used throughout recorded history. It is most commonly done through prayer and meditation, and may also include the laying-on of hands (Benor, 2006).

– There are indigenous healers in most countries.[56]

Healers report they can send healing through intention, meditation and prayer to people who are located anywhere in the world.

Practitioners of conventional hands-on therapies such as nursing, massage and physiotherapy often report they feel warmth and/or tingling in their hands when working with people. Often, these therapists have struggled with how to let potential clients know they are available for bioenergy interventions, while not weirding out or alienating their nursing and medical colleagues or being brought up before their professional boards for using unconventional and (in the opinions of these conventional practitioners) unconfirmed methods of assessment and treatment.

As the awareness of what is being called 'energy medicine' slowly grows in the Western world, these practitioners are increasingly identifying themselves more openly as bioenergy practitioners or healers.

Intuitive gnowing and the psychic phenomena associated with these sorts of healings, detailed above, have been accepted parts of indigenous cultures around the world, throughout recorded history, and continues to be so today. In indigenous cultures, the shaman (medicine man) is the main healthcare provider. He or she is usually a naturally gifted intuitive and healer, who was apprenticed to an experienced shaman for years before assuming the full role of a shaman. Various shamans often have knowledge and skills in some areas of healing, but not in others. These may include:

– Intuitive diagnosis
  - Information absorbed from the shaman's hands placed on or near the person in need
  - Information obtained through clairsentience, which may be acquired in a waking state, trance, dream, ritual ceremony. Any of these may also include spirit guidance.
– Learned diagnosis and treatments
– Rituals prescribed according to local healing traditions for diagnosis and/or treatments
– Herbal remedies – prescribed according to wisdom acquired from teachers and books, from past experiences, or through intuitive awarenesses (as in walking through the forest and inviting the appropriate plant remedy to call the shaman's attention to itself and to speak to the shaman of ways it can help the person in need
– Intuitive treatments
– Ceremonies for wholistic healing
  - For the individual person in need
  - For the individual and his or her family
  - For the individual and her or his community (demonstrating wholistic awareness of the person as a pixel in the greater picture that is the whole community)

– Divination
- Observing results of ritualized practices, such as casting bones, reading tea leaves, Tarot cards, and other variations on the theme of interpreting patterns in the outer world that reflect the personal worlds of people.
- Interpreting synchronistic occurrences in the lives of people relevant to the required healing and events related to questions being asked.

*YOU CAN EXPLORE DIVINATION YOURSELF*

Hold in your mind a question for which you might ask the help of a shaman, or which you are simply pondering within your own life context. Take any long book you particularly like – that speaks of the breadth and depth of human existence, and crack it open to any page, pointing your finger immediately, without reading the page, to text on one of the two pages in front of you. You may be surprised at the helpfulness of some of the answers you receive.**[57]

### Locus of control in healing

In psychokinesis it is assumed that the person initiating the influence over an inanimate object is causing that object to behave according her wishes. This is commonly the way healing is explained. It is assumed that the healer is manipulating the body, perhaps via the biofield, to bring about the observed physical changes.

Within a wholistic perspective, we may postulate other possibilities as well. The healer might also be influencing the emotions, mind, relationships or spirit of the healee; of the collective of the healee's family; and/or of the entire local community consciousness. When healing occurs at any of these levels, physical changes could then occur as parallel or as secondary effects to shifts in these other levels. In other words, just as a part of an individual's body might draw attention to disharmony in the wholistic life of the individual,*[58] the same might apply at these other levels of participatory existence and experience. Any one individual may take on the spiritual responsibility of drawing attention to disharmonies in the collective consciousness of his family or of her community.

Let's start our considerations of possible further explanations for healing with some observations on the energy aspects of living beings.

### Research on healing

In the past 50 years, scientific research on healers in the Western world has been confirming these reports of successful healing through light touch, with the hands held near the body, as well as by mental intent, and/or prayers. There are many controlled studies of varieties of healers, treating people with diverse problems, compared to control (comparison) groups of people with the same problems who receive other treatments or no treatments. The control group serves as a comparison to measure the benefits of the healing. There are now many studies, published in professional journals, demonstrating statistically significant effects of healing (Benor, 2002; 2008; Jonas and Crawford, 2003; 2006; Council for Healing, Web ref.). There are also many Doctoral dissertations and Masters' theses exploring healing.

Research confirms effects of distant healing, demonstrated in well-designed, well-reported research studies on humans,[59] plants (Solfvin, 1982), cells in laboratory test tubes (Braud, 1989) and cultures (Nash, 1982; 1984), and more.[60] This is impressive confirmation of healers' claims that healing works from a distance.

A meta-analysis of distant healing studies, published in the *Annals of Internal Medicine,* a respected conventional medical journal, assesses the significance of the effects of healing that included prayer, Non-Contact Therapeutic Touch, and other types of distant healing (Astin, et al., 2000). Literature reviews of available databases through 1999 brought to light 100 studies of distant healing. Of the 23 studies that met their inclusion criteria, including 2774 participants, 13 studies (57 percent) demonstrated positive treatment effects, 9 (39 percent) showed no effect, and 1 (4 percent) had a negative effect.

Another two (more rigorous} meta analyses were published in 2015, confirming modestly significant healing effects.**[61] In both series, the authors included only rigorous studies, where alternative explanations other than healing are unlikely to have been the causative agents for the observed effects (Roe, et al., 2015).**[62]

The research supports the use of healing as a therapeutic modality. Healing should, in fact, be a treatment of choice for use as early as possible after a health issue is identified, since healing has no known negative side effects. Healing could also be a useful adjunct in treatments of problems such as pain, for which medications with dangerous side effects are prescribed. Healing could eliminate the need for such medications, or could reduce the required doses of medication.

### Negative effects of healing

People who are new to healing often ask whether there are any negative effects they should look out for. There are no known serious negative physical effects of healing.

Healing is a wholistic modality and may bring about changes on any and every level of one's being. While the end results are positive, some of the effects may be unsettling.

Physical effects, such as major releases of chronic pains and stiffness may occur quite rapidly. Much as they are desirable, these changes may be unsettling because they have not been possible for many months or years.

There is often a general relaxation, which may be experienced as mild weakness. Some people experience tiredness during healing and may even fall asleep. Most people are pleased to have these effects, experiencing them as releases of tensions and anxieties.

Emotional releases may be intense, as healing softens or eliminates blocks to trauma awarenesses that may have been present for a long time. The healing itself often softens the releases, but the healer's rapport, understanding and support also are important factors in how people handle these emotional clearings.

Trauma memories may surface along with the emotional releases. These may be accompanied by feelings that were buried outside of conscious awareness since the time the trauma occurred.

Spiritual awarenesses may be awakened.*[63]

The above releases and changes may bring about shifts in people's relationships, which may be unsettling and may need to be addressed as new issues of their own. People often have unrealistic expectations of complete healing and total clearing of all related issues and residues of whatever problems brought them for healing. Having only partial releases of their issues may be unsettling, disappointing or even frightening. Some changes are so rapid, deep and unsettling that people don't return for further sessions of healing that could have helped them complete their transformations from illness or disability to fuller or complete health. It is here that the healing presence, love, acceptance and psychotherapeutic savvy of the healer may make a big difference in the outcomes of healings.

### *Using bioenergies with negative intentions*

Biological energies and transforming types of intentions may also be used for reasons that are not for the highest good of the healee.

> ✦✦✦ I (Dan) was shocked to see a strong, male healer, who was able to bring about very rapid releases of chronic, disabling problems, use his healing-type intentions to command a woman in his group healing session to kiss him on the lips, even though she had said she would not intentionally do this.

Such deplorable, unethical behaviors are uncommon, in my experience with healers. However, human nature and traumas being what they are, you are wise to seek personal recommendations with healers, just as you would with any other therapist.

Worse yet, I have heard of healers and shamans who have projected negative energies at people with the deliberate intent of hurting or harming them. Clearly, the abilities to manipulate and project healing do not reside only in people who have positive, healing intentions.

And even worse yet, there are groups of people who engage in cult-type rituals in which they invoke negative energies and hurtful intentions. There are even people who gather to worship evil, demonic powers.

### *Explaining healing*

A frequently asked question is, "How can healing work?" Among the many explanations that have been proposed, there are several main candidates that I favor, which I mentioned earlier and summarize here. Each of these is a partial explanation. Taken together, they offer a credible theoretical basis to explain healing. We don't yet know whether healing occurs through varieties of different mechanisms or whether there is a unifying meta-mechanism that we have yet to identify.

- Quantum physics tells us that matter and energy are inter-convertible, as noted earlier. Every physical object can also be addressed as energies. This theory has been well validated and has come to be accepted within the physical sciences. Modern medicine is far behind the times in acknowledging that biological matter (as in people's bodies) can equally well be considered as energy, and that people's problems can be addressed by healers who sense and alter these energies.

- Quantum physics demonstrates that consciousness and intent of the researcher can influence the outcome of processes in the world of physics. There is every reason to expect that consciousness and intent can influence living matter as well.

- Parapsychology demonstrates that consciousness can influence the physical world.

- Healers report their energy fields interact with the energy fields of healees to bring about healings.

- Healers report their personal healing intent can bring about healings.
- Healers report their wishes and/or prayers requesting help from The Infinite Source and/or angelic beings can bring about healings.
- Self-healing can be generated through suggestion on the part of the caregiver or researcher, and through latent self-healing abilities of the person receiving any sort of treatment. This is true even when the treatment is an inert substance used as a placebo, where the person receiving treatment expects the treatment to produce beneficial effects (Benor, 2017).

A hypothesis of disbelievers who question the existence of The Infinite Source, angels and spirits also deserves mention. Some people may feel that taking on the burden of responsibility for bringing about a healing is a heavy one. I have heard the proposition raised that supernatural beings could be nothing more than the unconscious creation of people who would like to pass the heavy burden of responsibility for healings to some inscrutable agent other than themselves. This has also been mentioned by several healers I know, who feel that they can offer more whole-hearted (and therefore more potent) wishes and prayers when they don't feel they, themselves, bear the responsibility for the outcomes.

## 56. Spirits and channeled information

> *Even though our critical arguments may cast doubt on every single case, there is not a single argument that could prove that spirits do not exist.*
> - Carl Jung

This chapter is inspired by my own intuition, which is overriding my left-brain objections that this information fits more comfortably in Section VIII on spiritual awarenesses. My intuition is telling me that readers who are new to this information may be able to absorb it better in this preliminary, left-brain analysis of wholistic healing first, and then also be better able to consider it in a second round of discussions focused on spiritual issues, further on in this book.

Another hypothesis sometimes put forward to explain intuitive awarenesses, inspirations and effects of psychic healing is that these are produced by spirits of people who have passed on from the physical world but remain available to help those of us who are still in the flesh.

In many societies, such abilities to perceive and channel spirit guidance at any level are highly respected and admired. In Western society these are often denigrated, explained away as 'unscientific' and rejected.

> *If you talk to God, you are praying; if God talks to you, you have schizophrenia.*
> - Thomas Szasz

On the other hand, the evidence from intuition research may be taken to suggest that reported communications with spirits of the deceased are not what they appear to be. The memories of those who passed on are still going to be present in the collective consciousness. It could logically be proposed that presumed communications with spirits are unconscious fabrications from collective consciousness memories.

While we cannot rule out this possibility, I find the great specificity of details shared in reports of apparent spirit communications to be so accurate in many details that it seems to me difficult to support this argument. Such minutia seem unlikely to be known or preserved in the unconscious of anyone but the deceased.

I introduce the observations in this chapter at this point because I find that spiritual aspects of our awarenesses are important in wholistic healing.

Many healers report that they are aided by spirits and angels. There are millions of members of spiritualist churches in England and the Americas, where a major portion of the service includes the sharing of messages from spirits to congregation members. These messages often convey information that has strong healing effects on those to whom they are directed.

One of the best known spiritual healers was the late Harry Edwards, who reported clear communications from spirit guides (H. Edwards, 1945; 1953; 1968). Edwards said, "There must be a healer to act as the human instrument or medium for the applied spirit-healing forces. Through him are directed the forces that can transcend and overcome the causes of the illness and restore the physical distortion of harmony. To enable the human instrument to be well used, there must be the willing co-operation of the total organization of the healer: mental, physical, etheric and spirit. Using the human instrument is the spirit-healing Guide or Guides. The two, the healing medium and the healing Guide, become co-operators. The human mind interprets the condition of the patient, and the spirit-healing minds are concerned with the diagnosis and correction of the disharmony" (Edwards 1945).

My own informal surveys demonstrate that there are many gifted people who are able to communicate directly, at will, with spirit healing guides. There are also numerous reports of ordinary people communicating with spirits of their close relatives and friends who are nearing death or who have recently passed on from their physical existence.*[64]

Spirits who appear as the time of people's death comes near, as well as after their passing on, are little acknowledged within conventional medicine and psychology, though they are an extremely common experience during the second stage of grief.*[65] Such communications are usually profoundly moving, emotional and spiritual experiences of the presence of the deceased. Bereavement apparitions, as these are called, usually visit in the first few weeks after the loss, and are more common when the deceased person was psychologically close to the grieving person. This may include seeing and/or hearing the deceased or just sensing they are present.

I was utterly surprised to find a study of bereavement apparitions in the American Journal of Psychiatry, which is absolutely not a New Age publication. This study revealed that two out of three people who had had someone close to them die reported they either saw, heard, or sensed the presence of the departed shortly after their physical death (Vargas, et al., 1989).

The authors of this study, as is typical of most conventional therapists, do not appear to believe in the reality of spirit communications with the living. This is consistent with my own observations over the 45 years that I've been aware of and exploring these reports. The vast majority of conventional medical doctors and psychotherapists completely dismiss any possibility that such reports might be based on real experiences rather than on fantasies and wishful thinking. In my psychiatric training, to their credit, however, the more enlightened among these disbelievers recognized that such reports of bereavement apparitions are not to be taken as signs of psychotic hallucinations. The psychoanalytic interpretation of these experiences, which I was taught 50 years ago, has been that "These are projections of the introjections of the lost object after termination of a close relationship through death." In normal language, this means that psychoanalysts believe people compensate for their feelings of grief and loss through conjuring up vivid, imaginary visions of the deceased. It is also acknowledged that with time, these projections usually resolve 'spontaneously' and there is no need to offer therapy or prescribe medications for these experiences.

My own impression, from having spoken about bereavement apparitions with many people in my private practice, in lectures and workshops, and socially, as well as from extensive reading on this and related subjects, is that the percent of people having such experiences may be even higher than Vargas, et al. reported. Very few of these people I spoke with had volunteered reports of their experiences to anyone, because they feared they were losing their minds – or would be thought by their relatives, friends or conventional physicians and therapists to be seriously deranged and in need of medications or hospitalization.*[66]

## 57. Activating and using our personal intuitive perceptions

> *Ironically, it is when we identify with our spirits rather than our bodies that we are most powerful on the material plane.*
> *Our over-identification with the world does not give us power within the world so much as it diminishes our power here.*
> *It makes us frightened and nervous and full of anxiety.*
>
> - Marianne Williamson

We have seen that many people have intuitive and psychic abilities. Many 'skeptics' have intuitive awarenesses, though these may remain outside their conscious awareness (Lawrence, 1993). So, if you want to develop your abilities, there is a good chance you'll able to do so – even if this has previously not been part of your conscious life experiences.

Your first step in opening to greater conscious connection with your intuitive awarenesses is to set your intentions to do so. You might choose any of these helpful steps as starting points, depending on your individual gifts and personal preferences:

- Ask yourself, "Why am I interested in this now?"
- Having motivations that are for the highest good and healing of yourself and/or of others enhances your chances of opening to spiritual awarenesses.
- It is often helpful to write down your views and considerations on this and other items in this list.
- You may well find further reasons surfacing to your awareness, as you percolate these questions and engage in these explorations.
- Keeping your list on your computer, tablet or mobile phone can enable you to add to your list as new insights arrive, as well as to reorganize your list when you find your understandings about intuition broadening and deepening.
- Read more about whatever areas of intuition speak to you.
- Seek out 'readings' and/or workshops with personally recommended intuitives who can help you.
- Again, I repeat, keeping written records of intuitive information you receive from others or yourself is extremely helpful. Memories alone are often untrustworthy in these explorations of intuition.

Intuition may speak through any of our senses when we get impressions of physical and psychological details of health and illness in ourselves and in others. Some intuitives and healers access intuitive information through the aura - as described above. Others may hear words in their inner dialogue that alert them to explore particular aspects of the assessment; or sometimes the name of a condition may be heard on this inner hotline. Some healers have told me that they recognize certain disorders or diseases by a smell or taste that they perceive when particular issues are present in the people they are assessing. Others have reported they resonate with the problems of healees, sensing pains and other symptoms in their own stomach or other parts of their body that identify for the healers where the problems are present in the healees. These mirrored sensations have been termed telesomatic reactions by Berthold Schwarz (1967).

Intuition may appear as mental imagery. This could be a direct picture that points to the issue, such as seeing a blocked artery to the heart that explains chest pains. It may be a "snapshot" or "film clip" of past trauma that uncovers emotional difficulties, such as sexual abuse that left a woman with severe menstrual pains – relieved when she is helped to release the fear, emotional hurt, shame, anger, other buried feelings and meta-anxieties*67 associated with her traumatic memories.

Sometimes the intuitive impression rises through the unconscious mind much like a dream image, appearing to the conscious mind as a metaphoric explanation for a problem.

> ✦✦✦ My (Dan) first experience of this sort was at a healing workshop, where I was paired for bioenergy sensing exercises with a nurse named 'Sheila.' I got a mental image of someone riding piggy-back on her, whipping her unreasonably to move faster. I had the feeling that she ought to tell this person in no uncertain terms to get off. Hesitantly, I shared this image with her. She burst into tears, saying, "You're absolutely right!"
>
> Perplexed, I asked her to explain. She clarified, "I've been working on this pediatric unit at the hospital for a year. Lately I've felt miserable. I just got a new boss who is younger than me, and because she feels insecure, she's cracking the whip and insisting that I do things her way. She actually doesn't know the routines for many of the special care children we treat, and I've hesitated to assert myself because I don't want to get on her wrong side. But it's not good for the children, and I really do need to tell her to get off my back!"

As with dream analysis, it is best for people to make their own interpretations of the intuitive imagery relating to their issues – even when the imagery and story arise in the mind of the intuitive counselor. When I perceived the image of the person riding piggy-back on Sheila, I could have come up with many interpretations of my own. I would probably never have arrived at the associations she had to this imagery. My imagery, however, was a very helpful stimulus for Sheila – to raise her awareness and to find better ways to deal with issues that were troubling her.

Over the years, I've developed increasing abilities to pick up on people's issues in these ways. I only do this with their permission, always asking that what comes through should be for the highest good of that person and for all. What I perceive is very often helpful, but sometimes may draw a blank.

### *Learning and practicing intuitive awarenesses*

This is an enormously complex subject. I'll offer some basic observations and suggestions, with references for further explorations. Here are some ways to connect with your own intuitions.

Exercises to develop inner awarenesses start with explorations of your own issues. You can access these channels of intuition through any aspect of your being:

- Body responses, as in muscle testing*68
- Visual imagery
  - Look for mental associations and imagery in response to questions you focus on
  - Dreams may offer spontaneous imagery and content, or may answer specific questions are asked before falling asleep, to be answered in your dreams

- Words may come to you mentally when you ask questions
- Pay attention to inner feelings of rightness and wrongness about wishes and intentions you hold
- Practice through interactions with the world at large
  - Offer or seek second person guidance, as with muscle testing, where one person does the muscle testing while the other holds the question in mind
  - Watch for synchronicities
- Ask for personal spiritual guidance, which could come through any of the above.
- Keep notes or a journal on your explorations. This will sharpen your focus, help your memory, and reassure you that you are not engaging in wishful thinking by imagining you thought of something prior to its manifestation in your life.

People often ask, quite rightly, "How can I be sure I'm not just making up what I think are intuitive awarenesses?" The bottom line answer is that we can never be absolutely certain that such occurrences aren't pure coincidences or wishful thinking. However, with practice and experience, we can often build our confidence in a sense of rightness about our intuitive impressions. Muscle testing can also help.

### *Body indicators for intuitive awareness: Muscle testing*

Your body can be enormously helpful in connecting you to your intuitive perceptions. The easiest and most frequently used approaches involve subconscious body movements that connect you with your inner innate and acquired wisdom, intuitions and your personal spiritual awarenesses and guidance. This has been explored for over a hundred years in hypnotic explorations of unconscious awareness, known as the 'ideomotor response.' The hypnotist invites a person to put both hands on their lap or on a table, palms down, and says, "Your right index finger will rise if the answer to my question is a yes, and your left index finger will rise if the answer is a no."

This opens the doors to our unconscious mind to speak through our body, without our conscious, mental guidance directing our body to move. Sources for the responses may include:

- Vast stores of memory in our unconscious mind
- Our intuition
- Interpersonal psychic awarenesses
- Personal Spiritual guidance

Similar muscle testing can be used without the guidance of a hypnotherapist and without being in a hypnotic state. Varieties of muscle movements may be used.

- The most common approach is for a therapist or a friend to press down on your outstretched arm as you focus on a question. Muscle strength indicates a Yes and weakness a No.
- There are many other variations to this approach:
- You lift a weight with your arm extended to the side. This weight should be heavy enough to require distinct effort to raise it. The weight acts similarly

to someone pushing down on your arm. The facilitator supports the weight, then releases the support. Your strong ability to continue holding the weight is a 'Yes' and your arm being pulled downward is a 'No.' (This is also a reassurance to skeptics who might think that a person pressing down on your arm is varying their pressure – rather than your having your muscles stay strong or go weak, in accordance with yes and no responses.)

## *YOU CAN SELF-TEST FOR YOUR OWN YES/NO RESPONSES*

Here are a variety of ways to access your intuition. Your accuracy and confidence will increase the more you explore your intuitive awarenesses. Don't be hard on yourself if you find yourself a slow learner, or if you have only modest intuitive awarenesses. This is like any other aspect of your sensory system. Some people simply have more sensitivity to see or hear or smell or intuit than others.

- Place one hand, palm-down, on a table or on your knee and raise your index finger, while focusing your mind silently on a question. Press down with your other index finger to test for strength in your raised finger. When your raised finger remains strong, this indicates a 'Yes'; and weakness indicates a 'No.'

- Hold out your index and middle finger, spread apart in a 'Y,' and test the strength of these fingers in resisting your other hand, as you press the two fingers towards each other.

- Make a circle by firmly touching the tip of your index finger of one hand to your thumb on the same hand. Hook your opposite thumb through the circle, pressing against the pinching fingers of your first hand until you break the contact between index finger and thumb. Strong resistance to separating your index finger and thumb indicates a 'Yes' and weak resistance a 'No.'**[69]

- Rub the index finger of one hand across the thumbnail of the same hand, in a motion similar to a bow moving across the strings of a violin. Ask yourself, "What does 'Yes' feel like?" and note how your index finger moves and feels. Then ask, "What does 'No' feel like?" and observe how your index finger moves and feels. For many people, 'Yes' feels smooth and 'No' feels rough or sticky. For others, 'Yes' may generate a clockwise movement of your index finger and 'No' a counter-clockwise movement. With practice, this can also indicate a strong or weak 'Yes' or 'No' answer, depending on the intensity of sensations in your fingers.

- Other, individual variations in responsiveness are possible. For instance, standing upright, close your eyes and hold a question in your mind. You set your intent that your body swaying forward indicates a 'Yes' and swaying backward a 'No.'

I find muscle testing to be very helpful. Many other people I know have also reported accurate responses pretty consistently. For other people, muscle testing has been unreliable. I suspect some of the difficulties may reside in beliefs and disbeliefs of the experimenters.

However, research on muscle testing has been greatly disappointing. Most clinical studies have not shown significant successes in obtaining correct responses. A recent lab study (Jensen, 2017) showed significant results, where the questions asked were objectively 'Yes' or 'No' – rather than clinical questions, which could often include answers that were partially 'Yes' or 'No.' This suggests that the previous research, showing no significant benefits of muscle testing, did not focus clearly enough on questions with unequivocally 'Yes' and 'No' answers.

This also suggests that when we are practicing in order to learn muscle testing, we may do a lot better if we use questions that have definitive 'Yes' and 'No' answers. Easy ones to use include:
- The last digit of my office/ mother's/ son's/ etc. phone number is an odd number
- The last digit of [whoever's] address is an even number

*Pendulums offer another form of muscle testing*
- Dangle a pendulum by its string that you hold in one hand, holding your arm out comfortably in front of you. Think of a statement which is true or a question to which you know the answer is 'Yes' and observe the way the pendulum swings. For some, swinging forward and backward is a 'Yes' and swinging left and right is a 'No' (or the reverse). For others, swinging clockwise is a 'Yes' and swinging counter-clockwise is a 'No' (or the reverse).

While many attribute the movements of a pendulum to the instrument itself, the muscle movements of the user of the pendulum are essential to their responsiveness. When the hands of dowsers are rested at the end of a table, the pendulum that dangles from their hand will not move.

*Dowsing rods may be used instead of pendulums*
- These can be pairs of L-shaped rods, where the short arm of the 'L' has a sleeve that allows the rod to swivel back and forth when the sleeves are held in each of your hands and the rod is tilted very slightly downward from the horizontal.

Another variety of dowsing rod is a forked stick, the classical instrument for water dowsing. The stick is shaped like a 'Y,' where each of the two branches of the 'Y' is held in one of the dowser's hands and torsion is applied to force the outward pointing base of the 'Y' to point upward or downward. When walking across an underground water source, the outward pointing branch will flip to point in the opposite direction. There is impressive research confirming the efficacy of dowsing rods in locating good places to dig wells for water, oil and other minerals.*[70]

CAUTIONS: Bioenergetic reversals are possible, in which case your responses in muscle testing (MT) can be reversed. For instance, a 'Yes' may show as a weak arm and 'No' as a strong arm. To check for this, do the MT, saying to yourself, "Yes, Yes, Yes" while testing, and again while testing say "No, No, No." If your MT responses are as expected, you're fine to continue with MT to address your issues. If you are reversed, getting a 'No' response when your muscles move in ways that regularly indicate a 'Yes', give yourself a massage for 15 seconds on your acupressure releasing points (Figure VII2), and then recheck to see that you are no longer reversed. Then continue with your MT for answers to your questions.

**Figure VII-2. Releasing spots/ Tender points**

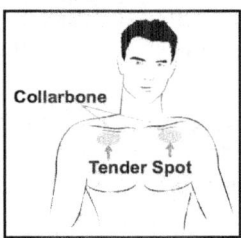

Another way to correct reversals is to alternate tapping for a minute anywhere on the left and right sides of your body, back and forth.

Be aware that there is no intuitive test that is 100% accurate. Just as medical laboratory tests may give false positive or false negative results, so, too, with MT. It is important to share this with students and clients, and always important to remember this for ourselves.

Boosts to reliability may be achieved in several ways.
- Having a trusted friend or therapist do the MT while you hold a question clearly and firmly in your awareness, without stating it out loud
- Having a trusted friend, colleague or therapist ask the questions silently in her mind while you do the MT

When you begin to use MT, it is helpful to explore how it works best for you in as many settings and situations as you can find. Our bodies have innate wisdom that we can access through MT. For example, you might ask these sorts of questions:
- Will this [name the food item] upset my stomach?
- Will my headache clear before this evening so I can go to the party?
- Will this medicine relieve my [specify: backache/ itching/ cramps/ other symptoms or disorders]?
- Will I sleep soundly tonight? (If you're concerned about random waking or nightmares, be sure to include these in your question, not leaving the question vague.)
- Your consciousness includes broad ranges of intuitive awarenesses and you can access these with MT. MT can be used to ask questions about anything and everything in your life, not just about your personal states of being. I recommend being playful in your MT investigations. For instance, you might check out the answers you get from questions like these:
- Will it be quicker getting through this traffic light if I'm in the right lane rather than the left lane?
- Will this avocado be ripe on Saturday, when I need it?
- Will I like eating this new item on the menu?
- Will I enjoy this film?

A few words of caution regarding MT are again in order. MT is far from an exact science, even at its best. Even the most gifted of intuitives are not always accurate in their perceptions and predictions. Even were the results of MT 100 percent accurate, they would still be subject to errors in predicting the future because after an intuitive prediction is made there can be unforeseen, random or purposeful intervening occurrences that alter the courses of events in ways that were unrecognized at the time of the original MT.

Another tricky variable is the wording of the questions we ask, as well as our interpretations of the information we receive. Here are a few common examples of errors in questions posed for MT predictions.

- As a therapist, you ask, "Is this client making a poor choice in deciding to quit his job?" You have not specified what you mean by 'a poor choice.' In the short term, your client may suffer financial challenges following a decision to quit his job, but in the long term he might find a much more satisfying and lucrative job.

- A person has a serious illness and you ask, "Will he die?" The answer you must get in response to this question is 'Yes!' Everyone is going to die. The question you may have intended to ask could have been, "Will he die in less than a month from this serious illness?"

- You're approaching an intersection and ask, "Is it for my highest good to be in the right lane rather than the left lane?" What you probably want to know is "Will I get through this intersection more quickly if I'm in the right lane rather than the left lane?" It might be for your highest good to be in the slower lane for crossing this intersection. Perhaps in that way you will avoid being hit by a car that drives across the intersection at the end of the yellow light, just as you're driving out into the intersection. Another possibility is that by being just that little bit later, you might meet the love of your life or the person who will tell you of a wonderfully profitable investment.

- As a therapist, you ask, "Is it for the highest good for my client to pursue this relationship she is thinking of getting serious about?" The answer you get may be a 'No', but if you immediately share your intuition, you may be doing your client a disservice. By sharing your MT awareness prematurely, you may rob your client of the opportunity to weigh the pros and cons and come to the same decision for herself – thereby developing her skills and confidence in her abilities to cope in life. In effect, you may be infantilizing her. Or it might be for her highest good to enter into this relationship because she has valuable lessons to learn, even though it may have negative aspects to it, So, a second question you might ask through MT could be, "Is it for the highest good for my client to have me share my intuitive awareness with her about this now?"

- And last, but not least, be aware that in many situations the answers to questions may be yes and no at the same time. The English language is misleading in this regard because it only includes the polarities of yes and no in its lexicon. In Russian, da means 'yes' and nyet means 'no.' In Russian slang there is also the word, 'danyet,' which is both yes and no. I suspect that if we examine some of the discrepancies in MT answers, we may find that many of the questions we asked might best be answered most accurately by danyet.

✦✦✦ Despite these cautions, I (Dan) have found MT to be helpful beyond my expectations for many clients and students of TWR/WHEE whom I've trained, as well as for myself. With practice and experience, people are able to achieve subtleties of perception, such as recognizing when an intuitive 'Yes' is a strong affirmative or when it is only a partial, weakly positive response. My personal preference is to do self-muscle testing by rubbing my index finger across my thumbnail, like a violin bow across the violin strings. This provides subtleties, such as where my index finger has slight-to-modest but not totally immobilizing friction when I rub it across my thumbnail, which I take to be a weak 'Yes;' or, conversely, where it has near-complete but not total resistance, which I take to be a partial 'No.'

And I emphasize again that we must remain cautious in using muscle testing. Despite our most diligent practicing with MT, and despite repeated successes, logical questions often remain – keeping us aware and alert to the possibilities of fooling or misleading ourselves through wishful thinking, anxieties about unwanted consequences of our decisions, or errors due to mistakes in asking our questions or in interpreting the MT responses – conscious and unconscious.

> *Our world requires that decisions be sourced and footnoted,*
> *and if we say how we feel, we must also be prepared to elaborate on why we feel that way... We need to respect the fact that it is possible to know without knowing why we know*
> *and accept that - sometimes - we're better off that way.*
> — Malcolm Gladwell

## 58. Integrity: wholistic perspectives

*Integrity without knowledge is weak and useless,
and knowledge without integrity is dangerous and dreadful.*
— Samuel Johnson

I invite you to consider integrity, an important quality often found in generous measures in HSPs and in those that HSPs generally choose to associate with. This is a vitally important, yet often neglected aspect of our lives. It is a somewhat difficult quality to define. Much of this book is about how to come to be more consciously aware of your sense of integrity on every level of your being, so that you can understand it better and include it in every aspect of your life.

Being in integrity is defined as:

1. Firm adherence to a code of especially moral or artistic values: incorruptibility

2. An unimpaired condition: soundness

3. The quality or state of being complete or undivided: completeness
— Merriam Webster's Dictionary

To this I would add:

4. When we honor and respect each wholistic level of our being (body, emotions, mind, relationships with other people and with the environment, and spirit) individually and collectively, we are in a place of personal wholistic unity. We are in a place of wholistic integrity when we adhere to the highest moral, ethical and spiritual standards we perceive and understand for each level, individually and collectively.

Wholistic integrity is guided by principles of adhering to attitudes, actions and relationships that serve the highest good of all. People who are in wholistic integrity frequently have a very deep sense of rightness and wrongness about their states of being in any situation, as well as in their perceptions, feelings, intentions, actions and relationships with other people, the world at large, and spiritual aspects of themselves and others.

Integrity within ourselves may be marked by specific or vaguely perceived and understood feelings, thoughts and intuitive/ spiritual awarenesses which guide us towards our highest good and the highest good of all. These lead us to want to engage more with people and situations that feel right, in ways that feel right, and to avoid others that feel wrong.

Integrity is another awareness that HSPs often possess to heightened degrees in comparison with NHSPs. This awareness of integrity often functions as a protective mechanism for HSPs, alerting them to people and situations in which they feel safe or unsafe.

Awareness of one's personal integrity varies greatly between different people. I've observed in a very general way that those who are more connected with their feelings and intuitions tend to have stronger senses of personal wholistic integrity, while those who relate to the world more through their thinking and outer-world senses tend to be less aware of their degrees of integrity in their personal wholistic spectrum.*[71]

Integrity is an inner compass that points us towards the most healing ways forward in life. Acknowledged good teachers, therapists, business managers and parents (among others) often embody this quality. I share here a few examples from my personal experiences of learning about integrity during my training in medicine and psychiatry.

✦ Maurice Levine was a wonderful Chairman of the Department of Psychiatry in Cincinnati, where I had my first year of residency training. He had a marvelous ability to critique a resident's therapeutic assessments and interventions that were discussed in a psychotherapy supervision seminar. He was able to point out strengths and weaknesses of the clinical summary without ever putting the resident down for errors or commission or omission. Even when we had missed identifying or dealing properly with important issues, Maurice Levine's inputs always came as warm encouragements to delve more deeply into issues we had overlooked, or to intervene in ways we had not yet considered. Maurice Levine was a teacher of great integrity. He always pursued discussions in a manner that was respectful, healing, exploring and explaining what could be improved, while not emphasizing what had been omitted or addressed in less healing ways.

In contrast, many instructors in medical school used their positions to boost their own egos, taking apparent pleasure in putting down the students for not having the correct answers or for other sorts of errors.

The other impressive example of Levine's integrity that stands out in my memory was his sharing about his personal professional reviews. Every ten years he would look back on his professional experiences in the previous decade. "I never fail to surprise myself by seeing how presumptuous I had been on my previous decade review, feeling that at last I really understood what makes people develop their problems and how we can help them to deal with them." This was enormously helpful to me, personally, in appreciating that learning to be a psychotherapist is an ongoing, ever-deepening project for an entire lifetime.

Integrity also rings alarm bells of vague or specific anxieties and varieties of senses of wrongness when we are straying towards being out of integrity, or when we are already there.

✦✦✦ Medical school in the US felt deeply out of integrity to me. At that time in my life I didn't have the clarity of awareness and understanding that I do now, in retrospect, about the specifics of the out of integrity alarm bells I was hearing with my inner HSP sensitivities.

My first disintegrity was within myself. I had let my mother push me to cram four years of undergraduate premedical studies, majoring in psychology, into two and a half years of nose-to-the-grindstone studying. I had had to pack 22 units of courses into each semester, plus very full summer school programs. The purpose of this madness was to save on tuition expenses, plus to see whether I could manage the sort of intensive curriculum I would face in medical school.

After two years in medical school I felt I needed time off – not just from studies but to allow me to explore some of my interests which my mad pace of studies had not permitted previously. I had also just gotten married and needed time to settle into my marriage. I was accepted for a National Institute of Mental Health research fellowship in psychiatry. My wife was seriously worried that I'd never want to return to the grind of medical studies after my year off, after a normal, 9-5 work routine. But I did. And after my year off from intensive studies, I felt a lot more centered, clear and happy with my career choice of psychiatric psychotherapy.

At that time, I didn't conceptualize or sense any of this as a matter of personal integrity, but in retrospect I feel this was an important aspect of what I had been searching for, and was lucky enough to have found.

✦✦✦ A further, much more jarring disintegrity that I experienced was in the dehumanizing medical school and hospital atmospheres.

– First and foremost was the focus on diagnosing and treating bodies rather than people. This was by far the most prevalent attitude among the majority of my instructors.

– A close second was the disempowerment of people, particularly in the hospital environment, where the patient was expected to accept the medical recommendations passively, and preferably without question. As an example, elective surgery was often presented as a treatment of choice, with little discussion of other alternatives, and often with minimal discussion of possible negative outcomes.

I once asked two doctors in obstetrics and gynecology, "What is the primary indication for hysterectomy?" They chuckled, as one of them replied, "Can they afford to pay for it?"

– Nurses, who spend more time with patients than doctors do, often can see when problems are developing following surgery or other treatments, or when there is a downward turn in the course of a patient's illness. Many doctors have difficulties in listening to nurse's observations, viewing nurses as less well trained than themselves and thinking it was therefore not worth listening to them. The better doctors took nurses seriously and immediately responded when they mentioned concerns about people (not 'patients') under their care.

– Medical training was abusive and traumatizing (in the 1960's). Looking back, I see we suffered many aspects of classical brainwashing:

- Students often worked every other night, producing sleep deprivation (a classical technique used in brainwashing)
- Students were often shamed and derided publicly for not knowing answers to instructors' questions
- Students were often afraid to ask questions, because this would reveal their 'ignorance' and open them to being shamed, derided and given lower grades for clinical work
- Women students were often belittled and disrespected
- Many instructors ignored or dismissed any consideration, much less discussion of psychological issues that might be contributing to medical or surgical problems
- I am told that many of these conditions have changed for the better in many medical schools today.

HSPs frequently have a very keen and deep sense of rightness and wrongness about their perceptions and relationships. This begins with sensing specific or vague feelings that lead us to want to engage more with people and situations that feel right, in ways that feel right, and to avoid others that feel wrong. This sort of sensitivity to integrity manifests on each of the wholistic levels of ourselves.

> ✢ 'Lois,' a school counselor, raised a good question in a supervision group at a school where I was consulting. "I can't understand why 'Sonia,' a seventh grader, does well in some of her classes but not in others. It's not a matter of science subjects or social studies or the arts, and not a man or woman teacher difference. There is something about her reaction to various teachers that I can't put my finger on."

> While at that time I was unaware of the HSP trait, I'm pretty sure Sonia was an HSP from the description of her as being a 'delicate flower' who was treasured by some of her teachers but criticized by others for the very same traits.

> We were able to clarify with Lois that those teachers who were finding Sonia a positive student were people with sensitive barometers for emotions, and those having difficulties with her lacked this awareness.

I have seen this sort of issue so many times that it is now one of the first questions I ask in such situations, and not just in schools but also in families, work situations and other groups with ongoing relationships. Whenever I speak with the sensitive people in question, I find them reporting, "I just don't feel right in that classroom." or "I bristle whenever I hear my work manager speaking with me or anyone else." Most often, it's not so much in the 'what' of the interactions, but distinctly in the 'how' of what is going on. And the most common irritating 'how' is that the person in question is not just focusing on the situation that needs addressing, but is being critical, putting people down, or even making them the butt of derision and belittling. In other words, these authority figures are not in integrity. They are taking advantage of their positions of authority to express negativity towards their students or subordinates. And HSPs feel very uncomfortable in this breach of integrity.

> ✢✢ And I clarified with Lois, the school counselor, that Sonia was very sensitive, and 'wise beyond her years.' Lois was able to teach Sonia some self-calming techniques for when she felt distressed, which enabled Sonia to cope much better with her distress in the classes where she felt unsafe with the teachers.

Let's look at how issues of integrity manifest on each level of our being.

**Body** (Wholistic Integrity)

> *Often the hands will solve a mystery*
> *that the intellect has struggled with in vain.*
> - Carl Jung

HSPs need to learn to recognize and attend to their personal needs for being in comfortable sensory surroundings. Initially, as children, or in new surroundings, they may not be clearly aware of the particular stimulations that are irritating, distracting or even overwhelming, and that can make them irritable and frazzled. They may feel uncomfortable with loud noise levels, visual intrusions or distractions, fluorescent bulbs that have a subtle flicker, strong smells, and rough bits of their clothing (such as labels and rough cloth textures), or any other negative perceptions that lead them to feel their bodies are out of integrity.

Sensory overload may be experienced as irritability with overstimulation from noise, too much commotion, or intensity of emotionality that feels somewhere on the spectrum from too intrusive, to annoyingly strong, to insufferably intense, or possibly becoming overwhelming to the point of intolerable distress. HSPs usually withdraw from such situations and learn to avoid them as much as possible.

In situations such as a classroom, workplace, busy streets or public transportation it may be impossible to avoid the over-stimulation or intensities of emotions. HSPs usually withdraw from such situations and learn to avoid them as much as possible. When they are unavoidable, the withdrawal may be inward, into silence and avoidance of interactions with others.

NHSPs may have difficulties understanding and accepting these sensitivities of HSPs. When NHSPs belittle, tease, criticize, pathologize or even bully HSPs for expressing such sensitivities, the HSPs may begin to question whether they are weak, wimpish or in some other ways abnormal. This is where they may lose their integrity, wanting to conform to the expectations of the majority and doing their best to minimize or deny their own sensitivities and accommodate to the expectations of the majority, while ignoring their sense of who they really are and what they need in order to be in integrity.

Our bodies may develop symptoms when we're out of integrity. Common body responses may include various metaphoric hints calling for our awareness of being out of integrity.

- "I can't stomach being in my class (I actually get nauseous) because my teacher can't control the kids and they're completely rowdy and noisy!"
- "I get horrible backaches during some of the meetings we have at my office, because when I speak out in my usual, quiet manner about how to improve the horrible atmosphere, people roll their eyes and dismiss me as a softy or tell me I need to develop callouses on my eyes and ears. There's just one of me and a lot of them, and I don't know how to stand up for what I'm feeling without any support from anyone else."
- "I clench my teeth to the point that I get headaches when my wife and I get into arguments. I've learned to hold off complaining about what's bothering me at those times because I'll only make things worse if I speak out."

Even when HSPs are not criticized, they may find themselves in very stressful situations such as a busy, noisy workplace, bustling streets or public transportation where it's impossible to avoid the over-stimulating sensations. Here, self-calming techniques such as tapping, meditation and various other relaxation and de-stressing methods can be enormously helpful in attending to HSP integrity in dealing with their personal sensory intolerances.*[72]

✦ 'Jessica' was a sensitive psychiatric resident at a clinic where I worked. She came in one morning with the clear appearance of having a migraine – moving slowly, wearing sunglasses indoors, speaking softly, and clenching her jaw with the pain. She had suffered migraines for over six years, with only moderate relief from medications. Using TWR/WHEE, she relieved her current migraine in less than half an hour. She was able thereafter to abort her migraines with tapping as soon as they began.

For reasons that are beyond my understanding, migraines fairly frequently respond with complete and permanent clearing of pains by just addressing the symptoms, without delving into psychological contributors to these headaches – as is often necessary with other sorts of pains. I have to guess that migraines have a strong physical basis for their mechanisms of operation, and that addressing the physical manifestations of the pains in people's nervous systems and muscles clears their pain.

And here we also have to consider biological energies that might be involved in migraines, as well as with other pains and physical, emotional mental, relational and spiritual issues. And then there are the bioenergy and other healing approaches that can be used to address them. These will be discussed briefly under 'spirit', below, and more extensively in Section VII, Subtler sensitivities, biological energy medicine and collective consciousness.

Factors of epigenetics (the mind influencing the expression of an organism's genes) may also contribute to complex wholistic healing processes that have been shown to include our physical genes, our emotions, thoughts and relationships. It is becoming clear that our genes can be affected by our diets, factors related to our geographic locations, our relationships, exercise, sleep patterns and more.[73]

*IN WHAT WAYS DO YOU FIND YOUR BODY CONTRIBUTING TO YOUR SENSE OF INTEGRITY?*

*HOW DOES YOUR BODY ALERT YOU WHEN YOU ARE OUT OF INTEGRITY?*

**Emotions** *(Wholistic Integrity)*

> *We know too much and feel too little. At least, we feel too little of those creative emotions from which a good life springs.*
> - Bertrand Russell

HSPs are often keenly in touch with their feelings and emotions, being much more in integrity than many NHSPs in terms of conscious awareness of these important aspects of our lives. As with physical sensations, however, HSPs may at times be flooded with their feelings, experiencing overwhelm and feeling out of integrity. For instance, boisterous expressions of feelings, including anger may be just part of a day's normal experience for NHSPs, experiences they can shrug off with relative ease. HSPs may find such strong emotions unpleasantly intense or even frightening.

Many NHSPs feel they are in integrity when they are not showing their feelings. A high percent of NHSPs are often unaware that they are even experiencing feelings. So for them, a sense of emotional integrity may be one that is free of experiencing emotions much of the time. Understandably, the emotionality of HSPs can be an irritation or annoyance to them.

HSPs are often repeatedly surprised at NHSPs' responses to the HSPs' expressions of their feelings. HSPs start out in life expecting others to accept their HSP feelings and their sensitivities to others' feelings. HSPs often suffer when NHSPs respond to expressions of feelings with disapproval, dismissal, pathologizing, bullying, rejection or other abuse.*[74]

More subtle, but often equally important, are HSP awarenesses of any holding back on the part of other people from expressing what they are actually feeling. It is quite common for people to put on a pleasant face that covers their discomforts in expressing their own emotions, or minimizing how they resonate with hearing or seeing others expressing their emotions. HSPs often pick up on these shifts away from emotional integrity. HSP children may find these sorts of encounters confusing, particularly in adults, who they assume and are indeed told are role models for children. Discussions and clarifications with an understanding parent or teacher can be enormously valuable to them in such situations.

HSP children will sense the hidden feelings and may be confused by such cover-ups.

– Children's misunderstandings and partial understandings about the worlds of information they are absorbing may be amusing or funny to adults, but often adults will not clarify for children what they are tickled or laughing about. Children may interpret such experiences as rejections of who and how they are as little people.

– It is quite common for people who are grieving to hold back from showing their tears and sadness. Children will often sense the unhappiness of the adults, and again may take this as a personal criticism or rejection. In addition, children may take the lack of NHSP emotionality as an injunction against their expressing their sensitivities and emotions.

– HSP adults may be treated in similar manners by their family, friends and people in their workplace. The HSPs' strong emotional responses to situations that NHSPs would feel are no more than water off a duck's back may be dismissed by the NHSPs as annoying or laughable. The HSPs may feel something is wrong with themselves, rather than that there are just differences in sensitivities at play.

– HSPs who are feeling stressed by the intensity of their emotions often find it extremely helpful to identify and practice stress reduction methods for their sensory and emotional overloads. These help them return to a place of integrity.

My many years of helping people with their personal and interpersonal challenges have shown that despite NHSPs' lack of conscious awareness of their emotions, most of them do experience emotions. And when they do, then even though they are unconscious about their emotions getting stirred, they may be distractible, irritable, easily triggered into frustration or anger, or may have vague feelings of not being their normal selves. With chronic, unconscious emotions percolating beneath the surface of their awareness, their bodies will often 'speak' about their unexpressed feelings.

– Swallowing down their feelings is often associated with stomach aches and can lead to more serious intestinal problems.

– Holding back from hitting someone who angers them may produce pains in their shoulders or back.

– Deep sadness may express itself in chest pains (heartache).**[75]

I've been pleasantly surprised to find that those NHSPs who are open to listening to what their bodies are saying (through various symptoms) about their lives are often able to connect with such meanings behind their symptoms. These are, however, by far the minority of NHSPs. Most NHSPs prefer to get medications to address what they perceive to be purely physical issues.

HSPs, on the other hand, readily connect with what their bodies are wanting them to know. And as soon as they start to listen, the intensity of their symptoms decreases, often quite dramatically.

And here we have questions to ponder about what emotional integrity constitutes for an NHSP. Is it being at peace with burying their feelings and moving on with life, in harmony with their habitual avoidance of emotional awarenesses? Or might this be considered a disharmony or ignoring and avoiding of emotional consciousness? To a great extent, people generally accept that what works in a person's life is ok, as long as they are comfortable with it.

In my experience, even when people are comfortable on conscious levels with ignoring and burying their emotions, their unconscious mind may be objecting to what they are doing. I see strong evidence for this in the persistence of many people's physical symptoms, even to the point of being treated surgically. It is rare for most of these people to consider wholistic approaches. But even when they have joint degenerations and other serious physical conditions, their pains may be markedly decreased if they listen to what their bodies are wanting them to know about their lives; what their bodies are asking them to change in their lives, and to promise their bodies that they will listen to their requests and make the required changes.

Sadly, for the most part, these people remain strongly stuck in their personal place of NHSP integrity in which they deny and avoid feeling their emotions. And in a significant percent of such cases their pains are not relieved with medications or surgery. However, even after they have ignored what their bodies are wanting them to know to such a degree, if they begin to listen to their body, their pains will often decrease.**[76]

*WHAT HELPS YOU FEEL YOU ARE IN OR OUT OF EMOTIONAL INTEGRITY?*

*WHEN YOU'RE OFF-CENTER, WHAT HELPS YOU RECONNECT WITH YOUR EMOTIONAL INTEGRITY?*

### Mind (Wholistic Integrity)

> *Mind has the characteristics of a process more than of a thing;*
> *a becoming, a way of being, more than an entity. Every individual*
> *mind is a process of interaction with whatever it is that exists*
> *apart from ourselves according to its own private history.*
> — Iain McGilchrist

We have enormously complex memories, thoughts and beliefs about ourselves. Our mental sense of integrity is very often firmly locked into conceptual constructs that we've picked up from our family, friends, community, religion, school, general culture, media and other random sources. We hold these as truths and believe them to be self-evident. We generally resist any questions or challenges that might lead us to question or doubt, much less to alter our mental beliefs.

But our cognitive awarenesses of integrity are also intertwined with our wholistic awarenesses of physical, emotional, relational and spiritual aspects of our lives. These add further layers of complexity to our beliefs and thoughts about integrity, which reciprocally influence each of the other wholistic aspects of ourselves.

So we end up with beliefs and thoughts, about which we hold an unconscious, emotional, felt sense of integrity, plus mental beliefs about emotions, with further layers of cognitive senses of integrity, and so on. But in many people, the layers of wholistic awarenesses about our integrity are filtered through their thoughts. And when these other layers contradict their thoughts and beliefs about their integrity, they tend to dismiss them as illogical, unreasonable, invalid, unscientific, nonsensical or senseless. Do you see the circular reasoning here? Our language is very rich in terms for dismissing any part of the wholistic spectrum that is outside the boundaries for what is logical.

The most troublesome part of our mental beliefs as a species is that the majority of humanity are NHSPs. Although they also participate in the rest of the wholistic spectrum of life experiences, much of their awareness of anything outside their thoughts is only partially and dimly perceived by their conscious mind. For them, thoughts are the primary essence of their sense of being.

> *I think, therefore I am.*
> - René Descartes

And people whose primary sense of self comes from what they think about life, the universe and everything[77] hold the opposite views about themselves. They believe (and feel) their thinking ways of addressing the world are logical, reasonable, valid, scientific and sensible.

Some NHSPs are able to acknowledge they have an intuitive sense of integrity. For many of them, their understanding about their intuitive awarenesses is that they recognize whether the pattern of something novel that they encounter fits in with their established cognitive maps of the world.*[78] Others may have a sense of psychic intuition as well.

Some NHSPs have an emotional sense of rightness and wrongness, based on their life experiences and beliefs that they acquired from childhood on. Commonly, they identify these as lessons and rules for living that their parents, other family members, church, school, community and country taught them.

But overall, NHSPs may be at considerable disadvantage in lacking awareness of those parts of the wholistic spectrum outside their thinking consciousness. These are the people who go for medical and surgical treatments of their pains and of many physical problems because that's just what you're supposed to do when something isn't working properly in your body. They have no sense of participating personally in what is happening in their body; no sense that poor diet, lack of exercise, emotional stresses and tensions, tensions in relationships or spiritual issues might be contributing to their physical issues.

When HSPs have similar pains and medical and surgical problems, they are far more often open to listening to what their bodies are wanting them to know about their lives. By listening to their bodies, they are able to reduce and eliminate many of their problems through self-healing.*[79]

Fortunately, some of the new healing methods like TWR1/ WHEE enable us to alter both the emotions themselves and some of our beliefs about the emotions – through addressing the physical symptoms alone. However, in many other cases, unless we also clear the emotional and trauma memories and other issues associated with our physical symptoms, the pain and other symptom relief may be only partial and temporary. But at least this offers some help for those NHSPs who are willing to explore what are to them unreasonable, unlikely, etc. approaches that defy conventional medical and conventional psychological logic, beliefs and practices.

For HSPs and those NHSPs open to using their minds to harmonious collaborations with the rest of their wholistic awarenesses, it is wonderful and fascinating to explore the deeper changes they can make by using these self-help methods.

By focusing your mind on an issue that is painful (on any level of wholistic awareness), alternating tapping on the left and right sides of your body, and then refocusing your awareness on positive feelings and thoughts, you can rapidly reduce and eliminate the pain.

I cannot count the numbers of people I've helped to relieve their chronic pains through self-healing approaches, even when they had suffered their pains for many years. Here are a few examples in which the mind played an important role in facilitating wholistic healing.

- ✦ 'Betty,' a secretary at the clinic where I worked (mentioned above), heard about Jessica's successful relief of her migraines, and asked if I could teach her how to relieve her own migraines, which had been present for three years and were gradually increasing in frequency to about twice a week. Betty didn't have a migraine at the time that she made this request, but I suggested she might learn to use TWR/ WHEE by focusing on her memory of the worst migraine she had ever experienced. She did this, and reported over the next few weeks that her migraines were less frequent and she was able to abort them quickly by tapping when she sensed they were just starting. Within a few weeks, she was free of her migraines.

I would love to see the use of EP for migraines researched properly. My clinical experience has been extremely encouraging. Most of those who have come to me for migraine relief have rapidly and permanently freed themselves of their migraines. In significant numbers of cases they did so without receiving messages from their pains in the same ways that most other pain sufferers do, as in Betty's case. I have no explanation for this.

Far more common are those who find their pains are messengers from their unconscious mind, begging them to connect with issues in their lives that have been festering in their unconscious minds and that are inviting inner housekeeping for wholistic healings, most often related to trauma memories.

- ✦ 'Greta' asked me at a conference where I presented whether I could help her with pain in her cheek that she had suffered for over 40 years. The pain started following a toothache in her late teens, for which she received a dental filling for a cavity in a right upper molar. The dental work itself was extremely painful, as the anesthesia did not work properly. The filling increased her pain, and she had it removed by another dentist, who replaced it with a filling of another material. The pain persisted, and the tooth was eventually extracted. The pain still continued, spreading to a large portion of her cheek.

Varieties of pain medications were prescribed, none of which completely alleviated Greta's pain. After close to 10 years of exploring various medications for her pain, which was diagnosed as neuritis in her facial nerve, the side effects of the pain medications eventually proved to be intolerable. So Greta just learned to live with her pain. It was almost constantly present, interfering with her chewing, speaking and sleeping. The only treatment doctors could suggest was to cut her facial nerve. She refused to do this, as it would have left her with a disfiguring facial paralysis.

With a one-hour lesson in self-healing with WHEE for her pain, Greta was pain free for the first time in over 40 years. A significant part of her relief was related to releasing anger at the first dentist, whom she blamed for starting her on this journey of pain.

A further step in self-healing of painful memories and feelings is to install positive thoughts and emotions to replace those that have been released. TWR/WHEE enables us to do just that. These 'replacement positives' are then strengthened by repeated rounds of tapping and affirmations.

Installing and strengthening positivity is another demonstration of how we can work on every wholistic level of our being. Many people have never experienced this as a deliberate exercise in self-healing. They are often surprised when they build up their positive thoughts and feelings to the maximum of '10' on a scale of '10,' that when they continue to tap to strengthen the positivity, it may increase to '11' or sometimes considerably higher – because they had no sense of how positive they could feel!

*DO YOU SENSE YOUR ARE IN A PLACE OF GREATER INTEGRITY THROUGH EXPLORING YOUR BELIEFS ABOUT INTEGRITY?*

*CAN YOU IDENTIFY ISSUES OR WAYS IN WHICH YOU ARE OUT OF INTEGRITY?*

*WHAT CAN YOU DO TO BUILD AND MAINTAIN YOUR INTEGRITY?*

**Relationships with other people** (Wholistic Integrity)

> *Let there be spaces in your togetherness,*
> *And let the winds of the heavens dance between you.*
> *Love one another, but make not a bond of love;*
> *Let it rather be a moving sea between the shores of your souls.*
> — Kahlil Gibran

Sensitive people feel they are in a place of integrity when they can express their sensitivities and receive respectful acknowledgments and responses to them. They feel out of integrity when they encounter NHSP intolerance of their sensitivities, or bullying that may be anywhere on a spectrum between snide remarks about people being overly emotional, to teasing about blushing or withdrawing into silence when they are treated rudely, to outright, brutal disparagements over HSPs showing feelings or not tolerating rudeness or nastiness. HSPs often report such rejecting relationships with family members, masquerading as encouraging the HSP to "be strong" or to "stop being a baby." With such discouragements, HSPs may come to feel they are actually abnormal. To stay within a place of integrity, HSPs often withdraw and isolate themselves socially. They may be left to their own company, for lack of anyone who accepts them as they are. If they are luckier, they may have the company of just one or of a few, select friends who are also HSPs or who are accepting of their being sensitive. In time, with support of other sensitive people, or just making it as best they can on their own, they often come to live with their sensitivities as an acceptable norm.

Challenging, difficult relationships are not always bad in the long run. Relationships may serve to bring out memories of earlier rejections and trauma residues, and invite people to find the healings that they need in order to resolve these and move forward more positively in their lives.

✦ 'Ernest,' an HSP, and 'Lilly,' an NHSP, came to me for help to deal with the sad death of their 5 year-old poodle, Dina. Dina had been run over three months earlier, when a staple in her leash tore through the old leather strap and she chased a squirrel across the road. She had lingered with severe injuries for close to a week, but then died. While it was no one's fault, this childless couple in their mid-40's were having difficulties overcoming their grief, each in their own way.

Ernest felt depressed, was having difficulties concentrating on his work, and suffered from insomnia. Lilly was irritable and short tempered. She was worrying about Ernest, and very frustrated she couldn't find any ways to help him.

I invited each of them to tell their life story, as I always do. Ernest was the oldest of two children, and he and his sister (two years younger) were doted on by their parents and maternal grandmother. His sister had suffered from leukemia for a year and died at age six. The family was devastated, and after several years of grieving turned all their adoring attentions on Ernest. He grew up lacking for nothing, knowing he could do no wrong in his family's eyes. He did well as an elementary school teacher, enjoying working with grades 1-3. He had been invited several times to consider working towards being a principal, but was never motivated to leave his teaching.

Lilly had grown us as the youngest of three girls in a family stressed by her father's binge drinking and her parents' frequent arguments. Her parents separated when she was twelve. Her father remained in her life only peripherally, with sporadic, irregular contact, though he continued to provide financial support for the family. She, too, had chosen elementary school teaching as her career, which is how she and Ernest had met each other. Though they dearly wanted children of their own, and Lilly had conceived twice, both pregnancies ended in early miscarriages. No specific infertility problems were identified, and they ended up satisfying their parenting urges as teachers and with a series of three dogs.

Their first two dogs had died natural deaths, and their courses of mourning them had not been unusual. They were puzzled and frustrated that Dina's death was hitting both of them so hard.

My speculations were that each of them was experiencing resonations of Dina's death with losses they had experienced earlier in life. Ernest, who had been eight years-old when his sister died, would have been just at the developmental stage where a child comes to understand the finality of death. As we explored his childhood memories, it became clear that his family's intensifying their doting on him had been paradoxically difficult for him, as he felt he was benefitting from his sister's death, and he felt guilty about this. But he never got to discuss any of this with his family, as their way of dealing with their grief was to bury it outside their conscious awareness and move on, focusing their love and caring on him. Ernest was sensitive to his own emotions and readily connected with these memories and feelings. Using EP, he was able to release the residues of his guilt and other aspects of his grief over his sister's death. He then was able to process his grief over Dina's death.

Lilly's stuckness with her grief was related to her distress over Ernest's withdrawal into depression. This had triggered memories of her loss of her father in the divorce. Here, too, EP enabled her to clear the residues of her childhood grief along with the grief over Dina's loss and her feelings of being abandoned by Ernest when he withdrew into his grief over Dina.

The memory residues that Lilly and Ernest carried from their experiences of grief earlier in their lives were like silently festering sores inside each of them. These grief trauma residues were actually challenges, as well, for each of them to identify the troublesome issues from their past that were interfering in their present relationship.**[80] TWR/WHEE enabled them to connect with and then release these feelings and memories. People usually find it helpful to address components of both memories and feelings in order to clear their pains – both current and in their memories.

> *The tools that are necessary to pull the weeds and cultivate the flowers in your garden are emotional awareness, responsible choice, intuition, and trust in the universe. The more you use them, the more you create authentic power. When creating authentic power is your highest priority, you use them continually.*
> — Gary Zukav

And a side note on pets. Pets are members of the family. When they pass on, they are often grieved just as other members of the family would be. Grieving for a pet may be helpful in many ways that go beyond the relationship of the pet's family members with that pet (Lachman, 2006). Having grieved for a pet, people will be more ready to grieve for a person who dies. Likewise, people will be more ready to deal with their own aging, mortality and end of life issues.

## WHAT HINDERS OR CONTRIBUTES TO BUILDING INTEGRITY IN YOUR RELATIONSHIPS?

On broader levels of relationships, when it is to their advantage in important ways, people in a tribe, a clan or society have often asserted their dominance over any other individual, clan, tribe or society weaker than themselves. These are often glaring demonstrations of lacks of wholistic social integrity.

Paradoxically, in many cases we often only become aware of issues of integrity when we sense another person or group of people, organization or government are seriously out of integrity. It is often easier, of course, to sense lapses of integrity in others than in ourselves.

According to the rules of reasoning and logic, the behaviors in question that lack integrity may be in line with principles that are stated and promoted by these individuals or groups of people whom we see as out of integrity. Their behaviors have the appearance of integrity within the limited focus of their conceptualizations and within their spheres of influence. Varieties of examples of the dis-integrity of these attitudes

and behaviors, within broader frames of reference, readily come to mind.
- 'Purifying the German race' applies standards that favor people with characteristics that have no intrinsic superiority outside their self-serving justification for annihilating people who do not have these characteristics. On deeper wholistic levels of consciousness, World War II was predicted by many at the end of World War I, when Germany was shown no mercy and was shamed by the Allies in the Treaty of Versailles. Germany was saddled with huge reparations costs and shamed with a war guilt clause. These terms laid the festering foundation for World War II. And the persecutions and exterminations of Jews, homosexuals, gypsies, the mentally retarded and physically deformed were, in part, displacements of residual griefs and angers from WWI.
- Denigrating women or Black people is a rationalization for denying them civil rights and access to positions of power, not to mention justifying the venting of personal and collective festering hurts and angers after having suffered one's own injustices through various persecutions. Again, we see relationships where some people 'put themselves up' by 'putting others down.'

Such persecutory behaviors provide the perpetrators with a sense of strength, superiority and power over those they designate as 'others.' They also serve as excuses to confiscate the property of 'others' and to take advantage of them in many ways. They often occur in the contexts of long histories of conflicts that have left people with grief, anger and other feelings that fuel the fires of inter-community and inter-racial histories of conflicts. This is ample evidence to suggest these behaviors are serious breaches of integrity.

- Granting vast tax advantages to people who already have vast advantages of accumulated wealth, at the expense of people who are less well off financially, are common abuses of political, economic and social power. They serve to increase the wealth and power of those who measure themselves by these yardsticks. Again, these breaches of integrity are justified with logical arguments, such as suggesting that food, clothing, shelter and healthcare are privileges rather than rights of people under one's jurisdiction.
- Severe breaches in integrity have been demonstrated repeatedly in North American treatment of Indigenous people. Although there are no agreed assessments of the size of the Native American population prior to the formal gathering of census figures in the mid-20$^{th}$ Century, a reasonable estimate is that as many as 10-12 million Native Americans were living north of the Rio Grande River when Columbus arrived in 1492 (Lord, 1997). The population appears to have been decimated by European diseases, against which the local populations had no immunities. In addition, Indigenous people have been repeatedly pushed off their homelands when natural resources of value were discovered. If they did not kill off the Native Americans immediately, they created physical and social conditions on their reservations that have been pretty well guaranteed to continue their decimation in one way or another.

The lack of integrity in relationships between settlers and Native Americans has been most pointedly demonstrated in the very sad history of the Residential Schools of the US and Canada. Both governmental and church residential schools were established, starting in the last quarter of the 19$^{th}$ Century, with the last Canadian residential school closing in 1996. First Nation, Inuit and Métis children were forcibly removed from their homes en masse. The schools were deliberately designed to distance the children from their family and cultural roots. The schools were at such distances from the children's homes that for all intents and purposes, family contact was severed for the duration of the children's time in these schools.

Over more than a century, an estimated 150,000 children were removed from their homes and isolated from their cultures. The Residential Schools severely disrupted Native American culture, and is felt to have been a strong factor in the development of broken families, depression, alcohol and drug abuse, disrespect for women, and more.

Canada officially acknowledged these abuses and officially apologized to its Indigenous population in 2008. The US has yet to do this, although President Obama, in private, signed a Presidential apology resolution in 2010.

Sadly, the Indigenous residential placements of children appear to be continuing in Canada, where more than 150,000 Indigenous children are now in foster care, nation-wide, under local governmental supervision. Most of these are in homes with White parents. In many of these cases the children's placements are due to assessments of inadequate care in their parental homes. To some extent this is credible, as the conditions on reservations can be appallingly stressful – due to lack of governmental supports, pollution of the land and waters from unregulated mining wastes, poor diet, and from cumulative personal and cultural traumas. The province of Alberta is particularly notorious in this regard. "Only nine per cent of Alberta children are aboriginal, yet they account for a staggering 78 per cent of children who have died in foster care since 1999" (Henton, 2014).

The sorts of behaviors listed above are grossly out of integrity when considered in wholistic perspectives that include the needs, views and wishes of the 'others.' These 'others' are those who are not allowed to sit in the boardrooms with those in power; in the seats of government where discriminatory laws are promulgated and enforced; or in the war rooms where campaigns against 'others' are planned, set in motion and executed.

The sorts of questions regarding integrity I raise here often are marked by definitions of right and wrong based on left brain hemisphere considerations of costs and profits. At the same time, they overlook or dismiss right brain hemisphere factors of basic human needs for food, shelter, clothing, safety and healthcare, not to mention dignity and freedom from oppressions.

For many, it is only when they are made aware of extreme examples where integrity is lacking that questions of integrity enter their awareness. The rationales and behaviors of the Nazis, white supremacists, male chauvinists and other such groups are cases in point. Within their groups of adherents and spheres of control, their stated goals are by definition in integrity with their beliefs and aims. However, their behaviors serve the advantage of those who are in power within their spheres of influence, at the expense of others.

From the perspectives of those who are deliberately disadvantaged in many ways, denied their civil rights, attacked, imprisoned and murdered, and kept in varieties of disadvantaged positions, we can pretty clearly say that their persecutors are out of integrity. Stating this more succinctly: Actions that bring advantages to a select group, at the expense of others who are treated unfairly, are out of integrity.

Short of such extreme examples, where the lack of integrity is grossly obvious, there are many instances where questions about integrity may be more difficult to define and delineate within linear, left brain criteria and terminology. We are left with doing our best to decide on matters of integrity through our emotionally and intuitively felt senses of rightness and wrongness.

### Relationships with the environment (Wholistic Integrity)

*The only work that will ultimately bring any good to any of us is the work of contributing to the healing of the world.*
- Marianne Williamson

In countless societies throughout recorded history, people who hold positions of power have felt themselves to be anointed as the beings chosen by the Deity of their culture to administer the resources of the world within their sphere of control. For the most part, humans have been incredibly self-centered, selfish and very short-sighted in relating to the lands in which they dwell. My assessment is that we humans have, for the most part, been sorely out of integrity in this sphere of our wholistic relationships.

This problem is not just a philosophical or theoretical speculation. Humanity, as a whole, actually appears to be working its way towards collective suicide through overpopulating the world, exhausting its resources and polluting the environment, in addition to warming our planet to the point that most life as we know it today is likely to become unsustainable.**[81] All of these behaviors may be dismissed by some people as oversights or ignorance, but this is a weak argument in the world today, when 97% of climatologists agree about the dire need to curtail carbon emissions if we are to avert the irreversible spiral of increasing temperatures on our planet that will bring to extinction the vast majority of life on earth, as we know it today.

*Demanding constant growth on a finite planet is suicidal.*
- David Suzuki

The relationships of many indigenous cultures around the world with the environment has been distinctly different. Their sense of integrity often extends to include obligations to relate in caring and responsible ways to the land, waters, animals, plants, and other aspects of the territories in which they live. There is an acknowledgment that humans are but a small part of the community of all living beings on the planet. We have no rights to assert ownership over other species, nor to assume we deserve greater privileges to resources of land, waters and air than other species do.

For example, in these societies, it is often the custom to ask permission of the spirits of the land, waters and living beings (plants and animals) before entering a new territory. This honors the collective integrity of all that is.

A common Indigenous peoples' invocation at the end of a discussion, group gathering, or prayer, clearly stating this acknowledgment, is to say, "*All my relations.*"**[82]

***Spirit*** *(Wholistic Integrity)*

> *The speech of silence has profound respect for the integrity of meaning as an entity separate from language. In silence, meaning is no longer heard, but felt; and feeling is the best hearing, the best instrument for recording meaning. Meaning is made welcome as it is and treated with respect.*
> — Malidoma Patrice Somé

On the extra-sensitive end of the HSP spectrum are those who can directly read others' physical conditions, emotions, thoughts and relationships – bypassing spoken language and going beyond information obtained through their ordinary senses. These super-aware children and adults often learn very quickly to keep their intuitive impressions to themselves, outside of those few situations and forums where their intuitive gifts are accepted.

✦ Olga Worrall was one of America's most researched, stellar healers in the mid-20th Century. In discussing her struggles to understand integrity, she told the poignant story of listening at age 4 to visitors in her home who were complimenting the family's new brown curtains. She asked her mother, "Why are these people lying about the curtains? They don't like them at all! I thought you said we're not supposed to say things that aren't true!"

Her embarrassed mother told her, in front of these friends, never to say anything impolite like that again. This led Olga to shut down much of her intuitive awarenesses from that point forward, and they were only awakened again years later, when she came to have a clearer understanding of social graces, of NHSPs' discomforts with intuitive awarenesses, and of spiritual and healing integrity.

And on this spectrum are also sensitive children and adults who are precognitive, have reincarnation memories, see spirits, and have gifts of diagnostic and healing abilities. These intuitive/ psychic abilities are parts of the awarenesses and language of the spirit aspects of our wholistic consciousness.*[83]

Further spiritual awarenesses may include communications with the spirits of humans, animals and other spirit beings – some of whom are benign and friendly, and others who may be selfish, manipulative, nasty and malicious. Nature spirits, angels, and the Being of Light/ God/ The Infinite Source are encountered in these realms. They are frequently reported in near death experiences, pre-death experiences, deathbed encounters and during bereavement.*[84]

What we identify as 'spirit' are series of awarenesses that are reported by those who experience them as consisting of dimensions extending beyond physical reality. They seem to be perceived through inner, intuitive awarenesses of the spirit worlds. They may be reported as perceptions of the physical senses, but it is unclear whether they are actually sensed through the eyes, ears, nose, taste buds, touch, or other senses, or whether inner, intuitive/ spiritual perceptions are translated by the mind and/or brain into these more familiar forms of perceptions.

As I mentioned above, I was pleasantly surprised to find a survey of 201 relatives or close friends of people who had experienced the presence of someone close to them, roughly within a two-month period following that person's passing on. This was reported in the American Journal of Psychiatry, which is very conservative when it comes to matters of spirit (Vargas, et al.,1989). Two out of three of the people surveyed, (a surprisingly high percent!) reported that within a few weeks of the death of these people they had either seen the deceased, heard their voice or movements around the house, or intuitively sensed their presence.

These experiences were explained by the authors as a generally unresearched and unreported phenomenon in the literature on grief reactions. It was technically labeled as "preservation of the lost object," where 'object' is a psychiatric term for the internalized image of another person. No mention is made of the possibility that these perceptions might have any validity outside of the wishful thinking and imaginations of those who perceived them.

Another common experience is that there are apparently psychokinetic movements or other changes in objects that accompany these awarenesses. One of the most frequently reported is that a clock or watch stops precisely at the time of the death. This is such a common experience, it has even been immortalized in a popular song.

> *It rang and alarmed in the dead of the night*
> *An alarm that for years had been dumb*
> *And we knew that his spirit was pluming for flight*
> *That his hour for departure had come*
>
> *Still the clock kept the time with a soft and muffled chime*
> *As we silently stood by his side*
> *But it stopped short, never to go again*
> *When the old man died*
>
> *Ninety years without slumbering*
> *His life seconds numbering*
> *It stopped short, never to go again*
> *When the old man died.*\*\*[85]

In general life experience (unrelated to the Vargas, et al. article), many of those who are questioned about bereavement apparitions report them as having the feeling of being the continued, spirit existence of the departed person. This has been my own experience with repeated, casual surveys of acquaintances, holistic conference attendees, and my therapy clients. Another interesting observation I've made is that almost none of the people who responded that they had had such experiences had ever mentioned them to anyone else. This was because they, themselves, feared they might have been having a psychotic perception ('losing their minds'), or that others would suspect that was the case.

The fact that two out of three of these people perceive bereavement apparitions, shortly after someone close to them died, appears to indicate that these are the most common personal experiences of spirit dimensions of reality. I would love to see replications of this research that include separate groups of NHSPs and HSPs, which might shed further light on this phenomenon.

Many NHSPs think awarenesses of spirits are only wishful products of human imagination. They generally explain spirit as an issue of people's beliefs. The truth appears to be that the NHSPs disbelieve the reported experiences of two thirds of all people who grieve over someone close to them who passed from physical existence into spirit dimensions.

Further personal spiritual awarenesses may include communications with spirits of humans (unrelated to bereavement), of animals and other spirit beings – some of whom are benign and friendly, and others who may be selfish, manipulative and nasty. Nature spirits, angels, and the Being of Light/ God/ The Infinite Source are found in these realms. Communications with spirits are frequently reported in near death experiences, pre-death experiences, encounters and during bereavement.*[86]

Integrity in spiritual dimensions of our lives is probably the most difficult of the aspects of the wholistic spectrum to define. From conventional Western perspectives, this is for many people a matter of choice of opinions and beliefs – based on teachings in various religious traditions. Within any of these teachings, being in integrity is based on established beliefs, religious laws and traditional expectations. Adhere to these culturally established ways and you are in a place of integrity within that religious community.

Not sensing these dimensions directly themselves, it is difficult or impossible for most NHSPs to even consider that they may be more than fantasy or wishful thinking – if they are being kind – or dismissing them as delusions and hallucinations if they judge HSPs harshly.

From perspectives of HSPs' with direct spiritual awarenesses, the questions of spiritual integrity become more difficult to define in ways that are universally acceptable. As we sense our ways into personal spiritual awarenesses, different individuals may hold diverse principles and standards to be of greater or lesser relevance and priority.

"Do unto others as you would have them do unto you" is a common starting point. Depending on your values, this could generate acceptance, closeness, warmth, generosity and supportiveness. It could also promote competitiveness in the realms where yardsticks of power and financial success are the measures of personal and collective worth. In the dog eat dog corporate world, when you use your power to enhance your position at the expense of other people, you are simply doing unto others what you expect they will do unto you if they can get away with it.

In offering healing, it is common to ask and pray that The Infinite Source grant us whatever results we are seeing. We may request that these be manifested as requested, or even better than we have conceived, provided these wishes are for the highest good of ourselves, of those whom we are offering to help, and of All That Is. This form of request for wholistic healing acknowledges that as humans, despite our best efforts to be in a place of full, wholistic integrity, our personal vision of the highest good for ourselves and for All may be limited or in some ways flawed or misconceived, due to our incomplete and imperfect perceptions, perspectives and understandings of spirit.

There are serious philosophical questions here. People choose their life experiences in coming into each lifetime. Whether they are or aren't in wholistic integrity is for them to judge within themselves. There may be soul reasons for choosing options that lead to wholistic outcomes with greater suffering for them or for others who suffer as the results of their choices during a given lifetime.

I mention these spiritual awarenesses here briefly, in order to identify the broad range of these awarenesses that can be accessed in wholistic healings. I discuss these in greater detail earlier in this Section.

## *Wholistic, broad-spectrum healings* (*Wholistic integrity*)

When we are ready on multiple levels of our being to let go of old patterns of beingness and to be in a place of broad-spectrum healing, we may be able to experience remarkable recoveries from many types of issues. These transformations are so unusual that it has been hard for people to get their heads around them.

Even researchers in this field have boggled at the inconceivable magnitude of these changes in difficult and incurable problems. For instance, Brendan O'Regan and Caryl Hirshberg (1993) published a collection of 3,000 "spontaneous remissions" they collected from over 800 journals in 20 different languages in the world literature. These included tantalizing medical notes on spontaneous recoveries from cancers, skeletal deformities, hormonal abnormalities, and hundreds of other types of physical issues. However, these published reports never included any in-depth considerations of psychological or spiritual details that might have contributed to the unusual remissions from diseases which, in many cases, were expected to be fatal; and conversely, reports from psychological literature rarely included medical details or documentations of the associated physical problems.

Even the researchers who study these unexplained, dramatic transformations seem to have difficulties acknowledging what they are observing. The very term these researchers use, 'spontaneous remissions,' appears to state that they occurred without cause or explanation. My belief is that such transformations are actually remarkable recoveries that are probably explainable by changes in various wholistic levels of people's beingness, which included their physical bodies.

Let me share just a few of subsequently published remarkable recoveries to give you a sense of some wholistic changes behind such recoveries.

✦ 'Tom,' a 40 year-old married factory worker, was admitted for evaluation of weakness in his right hand and arm that were making it impossible for him to perform at his usual level of competence on the assembly line. Neurological examination was normal, with only a weakness in the muscles of his right hand, arm and shoulder. There was no history of injury, no peripheral nerve or muscle damage, and no spinal or brain lesion could be identified. Psychosomatic consultation revealed that the weakness in this very meek and mild-mannered man had started following an uncharacteristic, major argument with his wife. In short, this was found to be a psychological weakness produced by Tom's unconscious mind to help him control the angry impulses he had been feeling, with a wish to strike his wife. The symptom also served to punish himself for having had this impulse, which his conscious mind deemed to be unacceptable. Brief psychotherapy resolved the symptoms.

✦ Gary Craig (2009), founder of EFT, reports on success in treating Sally, a 51 year-old woman, six years after she had suffered a Traumatic Brain Injury (TBI) in an auto accident. Sally had severe unsteadiness in walking and suffered from inability to tolerate intense or complex stimuli, such as many people talking in a room, or even walking along a carpet with a 'busy' pattern. In a single session of EFT, Sally was cured of her unsteadiness, and in further sessions her sensitivity to complex stimuli was markedly reduced. The EFT treatment was tracked by Donna Bach, ND and Gary Groesbeck, BCIAC with a Mind Mirror III electroencephalograph, which demonstrated interesting changes as Sally's condition improved. Having participated in organizing this report, I (Dan) weigh in with the observations that while it is unclear whether diagnostically it was brain trauma that was reversed or whether it was a post traumatic stress disorder (PTSD) causing these symptoms that was alleviated, the fact is that Sally's condition was dramatically improved.

✦ Patsy Anthony-Green (2009) suffered from Crohn's Disease, which produces inflammation for unknown reasons in the lower end of the small bowel, extending sometimes into the large bowel. Her Crohn's was so severe she had to have the affected portions of her bowels surgically removed. Despite careful adherence to her diet, her intermittent symptoms continued to plague her periodically, and medication side effects made her suffering worse, so she elected to treat herself.

By using EFT, Patsy has been able to halt and then symptomatically clear her Crohn's disease. She found, as with numerous people with this diagnosis, that although there were many anger issues in her life, it was extremely hard for her to identify these, and even harder to express them. In addition, she was able to connect with and clear issues of guilt, fear, loss, betrayal, rejection, death and grief. Part of her journey in searches of good therapists and cures for her issues led her to also connect with awarenesses of spirit survival and spirit communications.

I believe that the dramatic changes seen in remarkable recoveries don't just occur as spontaneous remissions, on their own, for no reason. When we open our awarenesses to issues in the wholistic spectrum, we generally find relevant information. And in fact, on a soul level it may be that our inner, deeper guidance leads us to develop serious symptoms and illnesses in order to open us to spiritual lessons.*[87]

Having said this, let me share another remarkable recovery. This one is for cancer.

✦ In 1957, psychologist Bruno Klopfer (1957) had a patient, Mr. Wright, with an advanced lymphosarcoma. He had cancer masses as large as oranges in his neck, armpits, chest abdomen and groin, and was expected to die from the disease within days. His liver and spleen were hugely enlarged. The lymph duct in his chest was blocked, and two liters of fluid had to be drained daily from his chest. With no further conventional treatments available, he was placed on palliative care by his doctor, Philip West.

Mr. Wright was given an experimental new drug called Krebiozen on a Friday. Over the weekend he regained a lot of his strength and was able to walk around the ward and chat cheerfully with patients and staff. His cancers cleared and he was discharged after ten days.

A few months later, Mr. Wright learned via the news media that new reports made it look unlikely Krebiozen was effective. He immediately went into relapse, returning within a few days almost to the condition just prior to taking Krebiozen.

Dr. Klopfer, who was personally certain Krebiozen is ineffective, nevertheless believed Mr. Wright had had a remarkable recovery due to a placebo response. He therefore told Mr. Wright that the news reports had been based on the fact that earlier supplies of Krebiozen had decomposed during shipment but that new supplies were now available. Mr. Wright was then given shots of water, being told this was from the new batch of Krebiozen. He recovered from his second moribund state even more rapidly than after his initial shot. His tumors melted away, his chest fluid disappeared, he regained his strength, and even returned to piloting his private plane.

Sadly, not long after his second recovery, Mr. Wright read further disparaging reports about the drug being totally ineffective and had another severe relapse. He was admitted to the hospital and died within a few days.

*Placebo reactions are wholistic, broad-spectrum healings*

Placebo reactions are self-healings stimulated by something in the outside world. A sugar pill, water injection or anything else that sets up a belief and expectation that a cure will take place can stimulate people to activate their wholistic self-healing capacities (Benor, 2010a). Even fake surgery was able to stimulate placebo reactions in people who were recommended to have repairs of their knees (Moseley, et al., 2002).

In any group of people with almost any medical issue, the expectation of receiving a cure can strongly stimulate self-healing in about 30% of the group. In the majority of cases this is mainly a decrease in symptoms. But in some cases there are complete cures, when no improvements were expected in the medical, surgical or psychological problems.

For the most part, we have no explanations within conventional science for how these self-healings can happen. Certainly in the case of a terminal stage of cancer, we have no understanding of mechanisms that could explain the disappearance and reappearance of the cancer.

The rapidity of Mr. Wright's two recoveries from advanced cancer suggests to me that an important aspect of such remarkable recoveries may be the activation of patterns of health within the biological energy body, that then guide the physical body to resume its normal structure and functions. Such rapid healings are also seen in some treatments of some bioenergy healers[88], spirit healers[89] and spiritual healers.[90]

My theory is slightly different. I believe these self-healings represent activation of healthy processes on some or all levels of our being. Hypnosis has been known for 150 years to heal underlying psychological causes for physical problems (Rossi, 1986). Energy Psychology is proving similarly effective in relieving physical symptoms and side effects of medications[91], pain;[92] fibromyalgia;[93] phantom limb pain (Leskowitz, 2014), Dyslexia (McCallion, 2012), seizures (Swingle, 200), tinnitus (Pasahow, 2009), Tourette's Syndrome (Chun & Kim, 2008). It is of note that many of these conditions involve the nervous system. I have no suggestion to explain this.

These documented changes that are initiated through hypnosis and by self-tapping on the bioenergy acupuncture meridians confirm that we definitely have considerable self-healing capacities. The alternative possibility of healing by the therapist through bioenergies and/or intent and/or invitation of help from spiritual dimensions remain as other wholistic possibilities.

Most importantly, remarkable recoveries are invitations to spiritual awakenings. They hint, and sometimes shout, that we have far more self-healing potentials and capabilities than Western science generally accepts.

It would be presumptuous to suggest that this mini-encyclopedia of wholistic healing is the be-all and end-all in promoting and implementing remarkable recoveries. It is the author's compilation of what has helped him and his uncounted thousands of clients, students and people who attended his lectures and workshops. Just for inspirations, I'd like to point out a few examples of remarkable recoveries from completely different sources.

✦ Amy Purdy (Web ref.) shares her outstanding recovery from bacterial meningitis that left her without her spleen, kidneys and legs below the knees, the hearing in her left ear, and serious brain damage. Despite these challenges, she has returned to her favorite sport of snowboarding and has won gold medals in competitions. Her self-healing attitude and presence are contagious!**94

✦ Damon Horowitz teaches philosophy through the Prison University Project, bringing college-level classes to inmates of San Quentin State Prison. In this powerful short talk, he reports on a healing of attitude and self-image in an convicted, imprisoned murderer.

✦ Sophie Andrews (Web ref) discusses her personal experiences of being helped by a crisis hotline early in her life, and then going on to found the Silverline phone support service for the elderly. Her Ted talk is well worth listening to – for a sense of how these services can help in crisis and can sometimes be transformative.

WHAT HAS STIRRED YOUR AWARENESS OF INTEGRITY IN YOUR LIFE?

WHAT DO YOU DO TO PROMOTE GREATER INTEGRITY IN YOUR LIFE?**95

*In summary (Wholistic Integrity)*

There are multiple overlaps in the wholistic elements related to integrity. Each wholistic element represents a level of awareness that contributes significantly to the chorus of influences which create and sustain the wholistic entities we are. And each is complemented/ supplemented/ enhanced by the other wholistic elements, just as it supports and enhances them.

Conventional science and medicine are used to considering and addressing each element separately, yet body, emotions, mind, relationships and spirit interact inseparably as a wholistic chorus of awarenesses, energies and intentions. And once we are aware of wholistic healing, the fragmented approaches of conventional science and medicine can be seen to be distinctly out of integrity.

## 59. Collective consciousness of humanity

> *Bread for myself is a material question.*
> *Bread for my neighbor is a spiritual one.*
> - Nikolai Berdyaev

Intuitive awarenesses can extend to include more than one individual. Carl Jung identified this as the 'collective unconscious.' He and many other Jungian therapists after him have noted that there are archetypal images that appear in the unconscious minds of their patients. Patients resonate very deeply with mythic stories that touch on their mental images, dreams, and psychological conflicts. Often, these contribute to resolving their issues.

Probably the most famous example of collective consciousness is a dream Jung encountered in his practice of psycho-analysis, which I repeat here.*[96]

✦ A woman described a golden scarab beetle in one of her dreams. At that moment, Jung heard a tapping on the window. To his enormous surprise, he found this was caused by a scarabaeid beetle, which very closely resembled the one being described by his patient. This synchronicity put an enormous punctuation mark on what Jung had been working very hard to teach this woman. She had been very resistant to considering, much less accepting, that her inner consciousness was interconnected with her lived experiences and with the outer world.

Jung named these sorts of coincidences synchronicities. These are unusual occurrences that are extremely unlikely to happen by chance. Some are so outrageously beyond chance that they appear to be shouting at us to ask what they want to draw our attention to or to tell us.

Here are two examples of synchronicities from over the three decades in which I've known about these intriguing coincidences. The first is from a book and the second, a similar, personal experience:

✦ Dr. Jean Shinoda Bolen (1979) is a psychologist who has studied and written a book on synchronicity. She shares:

"An... initial meeting that had the flavor of synchronicity led to my analysis of an artist who would be particularly significant for me. She had been given my name a few months before and, not knowing anything about me, did not call for an appointment, but carried my name on a slip of paper around with her. Some time later her mother...asked her to be on the lookout for *Psychic Magazine*...

When she was visiting a friend, she spied a copy of *Psychic Magazine* on the coffee table. It was a past issue, worn and nearly a year old. Thumbing through it, curious about her mother's interest, she came across the only article I had written for the magazine in the six years it was published, on psychotherapy and meditation in the treatment of cancer... with my picture and biographical sketch at the end. This unexpected encounter with me in the magazine led her to call the next day, a time when I had an opening. If she had called when she had first gotten my name, I probably would have referred her to someone else, as I had not had time available for a new patient for some time."

Dr. Bolen felt this was a very meaningful coincidence. It suggested to her that special circumstances conspired to arrange for them to work together. This also gave the client a conviction that their work would be important from the start. She relates that she too came to feel that this meeting was of special significance for her own growth.

✦✦✦ I had two clients in my general hospital practice during my residency training who were very similar in their personalities, interests and life styles, and had similar troublesome issues. Both were middle-aged women, single parents, each with a single child under ten years old. Both had previously lived on welfare for years, had started to work in salaried jobs, and both had drinking problems. 'Ann' had been in therapy with me for about six months and was doing extremely well-controlling her drinking, being much more consistent in disciplining her son, and seeing nice changes in his hyperactivity and attitude. 'Bobby' had only been in therapy for two months and seemed to have much less motivation (though no less potential) to make positive changes in her life.

I suggested to Bobby that it might help her to talk with Ann, explaining that Ann had been through similar straits and might have a few ideas which could help. I had checked earlier with Ann and she was agreeable to this. I kept after Bobby for a month but she gave one excuse after another and never followed through on her promises.

Ann came one day for her regular appointment, chuckling about an unusual coincidence. She had been sitting in a hairdresser's chair next to an unfamiliar woman and they started up a conversation. The woman mentioned my name, and you can guess the rest. It was Bobby, and they enjoyed talking with each other, agreeing that they had a lot in common.

Bobby went to the hairdresser fairly frequently, when she could afford it, but Ann did not. Ann had come for a perm prior to her sister's wedding. The chances of this synchronicity happening seem very small.

And indeed, Bobby found a lot of encouragement in befriending Ann, and made much more rapid progress in her therapy thereafter.

I've been interested in synchronicities for many years, and have been bemused at times by the unusual numbers of coinciding points of reference in people's lives that may be noted, as with Bobby and Ann, when they experience synchronicities.

A collective consciousness is supportable if we accept that intuitive psychic abilities reside in each of us. Our individual awarenesses may be linked through our psychic senses to the awareness of every other consciousness in the world. This may explain how intuitive information could be drawn from the collective awarenesses and wisdom of the world – to explain the orchestrations of synchronicities and manifestations (the creation of synchronicities and invitation to the universe to bring into being what we want and need in our lives.*[97] **[98]

*HAVE YOU HAD EXPERIENCES THAT SUGGEST YOU ARE PARTICIPATING IN A COLLECTIVE CONSCIOUSNESS?*

In various parts of Scotland there are enormous groups of starlings that gather together at the end of the day and swarm together in a collective aerial dance that is absolutely amazing and mesmerizing. They illustrate the collective consciousness in action. Millions of these birds collect together in an ever-shifting, magnificent aerial ballet that swirls and shifts across enormous stretches of the skies, with no apparent outward purpose. They just seem to enjoy this unusual, collective ballet of movement, back and forth, round and round in the skies. Regular observers of these 'murmurations' have never seen a collision of one bird with another. See a video of this at the link in the following endnote.**[99] This is a lovely visual image of how I sense the collective consciousness of all of creation interconnecting and acting.

## 60. Family constellations therapy - accessing collective consciousness

*It remains an irrefutable social and individual premise that no culture has ever been able to provide a better shipyard for building storm-proof vessels for the journey of man from the cradle to the grave than the individual nourished in a loving family.*
- Laurens van der Post

Couples' therapy and family therapy can help when there are disharmonies between couples and within families. Patterns of relationships and behaviors between ourselves and others are often influenced by residues of conflicts and trauma residues that shaped and scarred other individuals within our family, with secondary impacts on further members of the family – including ourselves. Family therapy addresses how these issues express themselves in individuals', couples' and families' attitudes, behaviors and interactions.

And, per the discussion in Section V, there is the whole level of the collective consciousness involved in the family constellation group process. To recapitulate: Group participants, each of whom has no knowledge of the families of other group members, volunteer to role play family members of another group member. They are usually able to do this with a very high degree of accuracy, apparently picking up required information from the collective consciousness. Furthermore, the therapeutic interactions of role-players within the group may also lead to healings of the trauma residues from the past and present interpersonal relationships of the actual family members.*[100]

Family constellation therapy extends ordinary family therapy into the collective consciousness of the family, as described earlier.*[101] It demonstrates the existence of a shared consciousness among family members, both within the current generation and connecting with residues of traumas from previous generations. It also demonstrates some of the ways that collective consciousness can function, both in carrying trauma residues and in healing and clearing them.

The collective family awarenesses of traumas may manifest themselves in the lives of individual family members. In many cases, the individuals who are symptomatic did not experience the traumas themselves. But on some level of their consciousness they sense and respond to the trauma residues that were generated by stresses and traumas in other members of the family, often from previous generations.

✦ 'Paul' invited members from a family constellation workshop to represent his family, which included 8 children. The family therapist had the family representatives stand in a line according to the ages of the family members. She then asked each one how they felt. The representatives of the parents and of the first 4 children reported how they felt, but each one also added, "There's someone missing from this family." The representatives of the rest of the parents made no mention of someone missing.

Paul could not at first understand who could be missing, as he had grown up with 7 siblings and each was represented in the constellation group. Suddenly it dawned on him that his mother had mentioned a miscarriage after the fourth child had been born. When a representative for the miscarried baby had volunteered and joined the family constellation group, every family representative who had reported someone was missing no longer felt this was true.

Untimely deaths and other traumas often leave impacts in the collective family consciousness. This workshop demonstration of Paul's family shows how such traumas can be picked up by people who are totally unrelated to the actual family that experienced the trauma, but who connect with them through the collective consciousness.

The essence of family constellation therapy extends the effects of the healing beyond ordinary family therapy,*[102] to include trauma residues from anyone and everyone who experienced the same or similar sorts of traumas, anywhere in the world. Trauma residues from the past or future lives of anyone else in the collective consciousness may also intrude in individual lives in the present. John Payne (2005) also suggests that we can offer healing to the constellation of all participants in our traumas.

Within the wholistic network of relationships, the lessons learned from family constellation therapy suggest that the limits for what we consider to be our relationships may extend far, far beyond conventional understandings of 'family.' Others have suggested that humanity as a whole is a family.**[103]

In a broader wholistic awareness, our consciousness can be perceived to extend to include the environment. That is, we are related to the entire world, with every living and non-living aspect of our world. This means that the current general concept of family is in serious need of expansion!

The same applies to our awarenesses of spirit. And again, we can acknowledge the Native American invocation at the end of many public discussions, "All my relations."

## 61. Manifestation: Activation of our individual and collective consciousness

*What you think is what you get.*
*What you fear is what you will draw to you.*
*What you resist, persists.*
*What you look at disappears - giving you a chance to recreate it*
*all over again, if you wish, or banish it forever from your experience.*
*What you choose, you experience.*
— Neale Donald Walsch (1997)

This chapter suggests that the collective consciousness can be accessed not just for information but also to achieve our needs, wants and wishes in the world we live in.

David Spangler is a spiritual teacher who focused on maximizing the healing potentials in our incarnations. Spangler (1975) observed that it is possible to invite synchronicities to occur. He labeled this application of intuitive abilities 'manifestation.' With practice, it appears possible to get manifestations to occur with increasing frequency and with some degree of reliability.

Here are helpful general recommendations for inviting manifestations into our lives in propitious, helpful, and often surprising manners:

1. Be specific regarding requests. For instance, if you're asking for a new home, you may get better results if you specify its location, size, the number of rooms, and all other features of the house that are important to you.

2. Add some variation of a statement of trust in your higher guidance, allowing that what is granted may be even better than you have wished or asked for.

3. Add that your request should turn out only for your highest good and for the highest good of all.

4. Release your wish to the hands of your higher self, your spirit guides, your angels, and The Infinite Source.

5. Trust that your wishes will be granted. Repeated requests are actually a statement of disbelief or distrust in the power of your initial request. Once you get into that loop of doubts, there is no end to your distrust in the processes of manifestation – which will weaken its effectiveness.

In learning to manifest your needs and desires, you might start with little wishes. It is helpful for development of your spiritual awareness and the growth of trust in your connection with a higher power when you find that the universe responds even to your modest requests. The responses you get may be truly astounding and beyond your expectations and beliefs. It is instructive to convince yourself that these manifestations can be generated by your wishes and needs. To this end, you may find it more convincing if you:

– Record in detail exactly what you are requesting.
– Record the manifestations that come about, reflecting your wishes. It is easy to forget details you have included or excluded in making your wishes, and

most instructive when you compare that which manifests with that which you requested. You may be surprised to see how literal the universe can be in listening to your words.

– Small, even playful requests are allowed! These help us learn to trust in the manifestation process and to gain confidence in our abilities to activated it. For instance, asking for a parking space to be available at your destination is a commonly granted request.

✦✦✦ I've been intrigued with manifestations and have explored them – with increasing successes over four decades.

1. I started out with little requests, such as having a parking spot available at my destinations, particularly in busy shopping areas and in bad weather. Even some of my skeptical family members have come to chuckle over my good luck, and some will tolerate my attributing this to my parking angel.

An important lesson along the way was to be very specific in my requests.

2. I once asked for a spot to be available in front of a busy office building when I was running late. When I arrived, sure enough, there was the available spot, right near the front door... but someone else was pulling into it! Lesson learned: Specify that a spot is being requested for my car at the desired destination! Visualizing my car parked in a spot in the desired location is also helpful.

– Long-term, standing orders for these gifts are also available from whoever or whatever choreographs our synchronicities and manifestations. In other words, multiple manifestations can be included in a single request. You can, so to speak, put all your similar begs in one ask-it.

3. I've shifted to asking for recurrent manifestations, with a long-term, ongoing wish for a parking spot to always be available at my destination. This succeeds most of the time. With needs of special urgency I update and sharpen the focus on my request.

4. When I drive onto limited access highways I've often been nervous because aggressive and inconsiderate drivers sometimes make it difficult to merge onto the highway, especially in big US cities. The access lane is commonly rather short and sharply curved, with limited visibility for the road ahead and the highway behind. I've sometimes had to slow to a stop due to heavy traffic, with other cars behind me starting to accelerate as they round the on-ramp to enter the highway, anticipating they will join a rapidly moving flow of traffic. I've put in a standing request for the road to be clear of cars in my immediate vicinity as I come onto any limited access highway. I've been astounded repeatedly as I merge onto these highways to find them comfortably clear of traffic in my immediate vicinity. In many cases, the highway is very generously clear of traffic, as though putting an exclamation point on the response, to make it clear that my request has been heard and is receiving a full and pointedly helpful response.

– There may be unstated, unidentified circumstances and options surrounding our wishes that can influence them.

When we wish for something, we often focus only on that one item alone. We want the parking spot, the new job, the raise in salary, success with a new relationship we're hoping for or already starting, resolution of conflicts in a current relationship, rapid relief from pain or illness, and so on. Outside our area of focus, perhaps never even within our current consciousness, nor even within our realms of belief of possibility, are all of the countless infinities of possibilities that might unfold if our wish for that one thing would not be granted.

- Those of our wishes for manifestations that are not granted are often as instructive as those that are.

  - By missing getting that parking spot, I might just make it possible to meet someone important, even someone very special in the building, whom I would not have otherwise encountered if I arrived a few minutes earlier. Or I might run into them on my way out of the building or somewhere else, later in the day, because my original wish was not manifested.

  - By not getting the job or success in the relationship I wish for, I might get an even better one, or avoid one that ends up being dissatisfying.

  - By not getting rapid relief from pains or illnesses, I might learn deeply meaningful life lessons that I would otherwise never achieve; or I might offer someone the opportunity to bring more healing into my life and more lessons in offering healing into their life.

  - An excellent illustrations of this aspect of manifestations comes from Bernie Siegel. Bernie is one of my favorite authors and a highly esteemed colleague. Bernie, a surgeon, was making rounds in the hospital when he unexpectedly literally bumped into 'Charlie,' a previous surgical patient of his, in the General Medicine corridor. Charlie was rushing towards the elevator, and in stopping briefly to say hello to Bernie he missed the elevator he had been hurrying to catch. Bernie could clearly see that Charlie was frustrated and upset at not catching his elevator.

Later that day, Bernie again ran into him at the nurse's station. He apologized for having delayed Charlie from catching his elevator, but congratulated him on his good luck in missing it. He explained that the elevator cable had snapped and the elevator car had fallen two stories before the emergency system halted its fall. No one had been seriously injured, but these people were trapped for two hours before the maintenance crew could rescue them. "Realy!?!" said the wide-eyed Charley in amazement. "Well, actually, no." said Bernie. "But it could have been that way."[104]

✦✦✦ Amazingly, just as I was writing Bernie's story into this book, I received an email from Bernie with Happy New Year wishes, notice of his new book, *The Art of Healing,* and the offer of a new article for publication in *The International Journal of Healing and Caring,* of which I am Editor-in-Chief.

In short, our wishes for manifestations can have powerful effects, sometimes extending far beyond our vision and expectations when we make our requests. Our wishes may also influence countless, unknown others as well as those included explicitly in the request for the manifestation. It is therefore prudent and ethical to add to your request something to acknowledge this, such as:

- "I ask that this wish be granted only if it is for my highest good and the highest good of all."
- "I ask that this wish be granted as I stated it or in any ways that it could be better than I anticipated and requested it."

I also accept that there will be times when manifestations are not granted according to my stated wishes. Over the years of making these requests, I've come to see in retrospect that there are situations in which it may be for my highest good and/or for the highest good of all for my wishes to not be granted as I initially envisioned or stated them.

Synchronicities and manifestations may also occur in the collective consciousness of couples, families and groups of like-minded people.

✦✦✦ One of my personal favorite synchronicities occurred after the wedding of my brother, David. He had reserved a hotel room at an undisclosed location for the night after the wedding, as a precaution against any pranks by family or friends, prior to their departure the next day on their honeymoon to Hawaii. On the next day, I was driving in my father-in-law's white, 1958 Chevrolet on a freeway when I glanced over to look at another white, 1958 Chevrolet of exactly the same model in the next lane. I was astonished to see David and Roberta passing us in that car, also borrowed from a relative. We waved and smiled at each other, and have recounted this synchronicity on many occasions since then.

- Share your synchronicity and manifestation experiences with others, and invite them to share theirs with you.
- Read some of the fascinating books written on synchronicities and manifestations.[105]
- As we take them more seriously, increasing numbers and complexities of synchronicities and manifestations will often occur.
- Be aware that unspoken and even unconscious wishes and expectations may activate synchronicities and manifestations. The following is shared by Joel and Michelle Levey (2002):

✦ "Rabbi Zalman Schachter-Shalomi, once helped us to understand the relationship between the active and receptive dynamics of questioning, prayer and intuition. He reminded us that our lives are filled with prayers, albeit mostly unconscious ones. When we are hungry, our prayer for food organizes our attention to look for food markets, restaurants, fruit trees, or other whiffs of dinner on the wind. When we are lonesome, our prayer for companionship organizes our attention to notice people who have partners and those who are potentially available.

Our questions, conscious or unconscious, spoken or unspoken, individual or collective, are prayers, aspirations, and yearnings that infallibly organize our attention and, in the most subtle ways, make us more intuitively receptive to inspiration in whatever forms it may take. As our understanding of this process deepens, we discover that we live in a responsive universe. If you drop a little stone in the pool it sends out and draws back a little wave. If you drop a big stone in the pool, it sends out and draws back a big wave. The moment there is a yearning in our hearts or a question in our minds – consciously or unconsciously – there are echoes of information intuitively available to us. The answer or clues might be revealed in the patterns of a cloud, in a bird's song, or by what a person three seats away is saying. As we learn to listen more deeply, we discover that the answers to our question are always here, though generally speaking our circuits are usually too jammed to hear them (Joel & Michelle Levey, 2002)."

We've seen that individual intuitive/ psychic/ spiritual experiences may be extended into the collective consciousness. I see no reason to believe that the same would not apply for manifestations. And in fact, there is the very common belief among sports fans that wishing and/or praying for the success of a favorite athlete or team can be helpful in promoting their successes. For some, this is perceived to be primarily a psychological boost. It is well known that sports teams tend to perform better on their home turf.

To a certain degree this may have to do with disadvantages to visiting teams in dealing with travel fatigue and disorientation, lack of familiarity with peculiarities of the playing field, plus lack of psychological support on the one side, compared with the opposite experiences of the home team.

But to some degree, I believe that this is also an expression of the collective consciousness that can be much like healing that is sent from a distance. Research (reviewed in the next section) confirms that healing can be effective when it is projected by individuals and groups to people and other living beings who are located at any distance from the healers. These research studies lend support to the belief that manifestations in the physical world (other than healings) may also be brought about through the collective consciousness. So our cheers at the ballpark may be forms of wishes for manifestations.

*IF YOU KEEP A DIARY OF YOUR SYNCHRONICITIES, OR IN ANY OTHER WAYS COMMIT YOUR ENERGIES TO PONDERING AND EXPLORING THESE EXPERIENCES, YOU'LL NOTICE THEM HAPPENING MORE AND MORE. AND YES, YOU'LL WONDER WHETHER IT'S THE NOTICING OR THE HAPPENING THAT IS INCREASING.*

*I HIGHLY RECOMMEND EXPLORING MANIFESTATIONS.*

*IN COMPOSING YOUR REQUESTS:*
  *AIM HIGH*
  *ASK THAT YOU BE GRANTED WHAT YOU ASK – OR EVEN BETTER SPECIFY THAT YOU'RE ASKING ONLY FOR YOUR HIGHEST GOOD AND THE HIGHEST GOOD OF ALL*

It is mainly through exploring and experiencing our personal intuitive awarenesses, and getting feedback from our successes in manifestations, that we broaden, deepen and extend our conscious perceptions beyond the limits of our physical senses. This is how we connect more clearly with our participation in the collective consciousness.

# SECTION VIII. Spiritual Awarenesses

*We are not human beings having a spiritual experience.*
*We are spiritual beings having a human experience.*
- Pierre Teilhard de Chardin

The Spirituality we are addressing here is a personally experienced awareness of transcendent reality.**[1]  Each of us is a part of this reality, just as each drop of water in the seas is a part of the vastness of all of the oceans on our planet. Spirituality informs every aspect of our being, just as every aspect of our being participates in our Spirituality.

Starting in this Section, I capitalize 'Spirit' when I am referring to this transcendent reality, to distinguish it as a special dimension that is distinctly different from our everyday reality.

## 62. Spiritual awarenesses within Western scientific perspectives

*We may be aware of a truth, yet until we have felt its force, it is not ours.*
*To the cognition of the brain must be added the experience of the soul.*
— Arnold Bennett

This is probably the most important section of our consideration of the spectrum of awarenesses and sensitivities of HSPs and HSPCs. I believe we are not physical beings with glimmerings of spiritual fantasies. Nor are we just spectators peering through windows of awarenesses into aspects of the vastness of Spiritual realities, somewhere "out there."

What I share here is not based on religious doctrines, nor on family or cultural beliefs. What I share is derived from all of my personal Spiritual experiences; extensive reading about personal Spiritual experiences of others; research reports; extensive experiences with seekers for inner truths – as a psychotherapist for over 50 years; and with my analyses of all of these through wholistic perspectives.

My distillation of all of the above in explorations of Spirit is that we are Spiritual beings who have come into physical realms to learn about Spirit from earthly perspectives. In the earth dimension, we have only partial awarenesses of the vastness of Spirit.

Most people have only little, if any, conscious perception of Spirit. Some have occasional, spontaneous, very partial personal glimpses of these vast, awesome, inspiring vistas. Some choose to pursue an active development of consciousness of Spirit. These explorations may be through left brain studies of religious teachings and reports of examples of the Spiritual lives of others. Other choose to pursue more experiential, right brain gnowings of Spirit through meditation, deep prayer, sacred dance, communion with nature and other approaches. And some come into gnowing awarenesses through the use of mind-altering drugs. Some are gifted with life-altering openings of windows and doorways into personal Spiritual consciousness. Everyone who has these deeper gnowings acknowledges that they are beyond any possibility of adequate description in words.

From these observations, we can speculate that HSPs may be among some of humanity's more valuable resources for exploring and understanding Spiritual dimensions, as their sensitivities often include broader and deeper awarenesses of Spirit. Similarly, HSPCs may be among our most important interfaces with the portals of awarenesses that HSPs offer us.

Where does Spiritual awareness and personal Spirituality begin or end? Within the wholistic spectrum, the Spiritual is an integral part of who we are, on all levels of our being. It has no beginning or end, and often defies precise definitions in meanings and boundaries that are imposed by limitations of language and written or spoken words. Our understandings of Spirituality are also hampered and limited by personal, cultural and religious beliefs and disbeliefs.*2

Having said that, there are nevertheless some helpful distinctions within the spectrum of our personal experiences of Spiritual dimensions. I use Spirit to designate that part of ourselves which is our connection with Spiritual dimensions. I use 'soul' to designate that part of ourselves which survives from one physical life to the next, which contains memories (usually unconscious) of many of our lifetimes on earth as individual entities. Soul connects with the Spiritual collective consciousness of the universe, and holds purposeful intents to grow and deepen our own wholistic Spiritual awarenesses.

The terms, 'spirit' and ghost are also in common usage to designate the non-physical aspect of people who have reached the end of their physical lives and passed on to dimensions of non-material existence. There are fascinating reports of communications with spirits around the end of people's lives, which we'll consider below.

Many people rely on religious teachings to define and explain what Spirituality is, within their understanding that we can generally know about this but that only in exceptional cases can some few people gnow Spirit directly, as in people who are born as, or transform into, saints or their equivalents.

> ✦ 'Monty,' a gifted intuitive and healer, was quietly bemused one day when we met for a discussion of his healing work. When I observed to him that he seemed preoccupied, he responded, "I'm still deeply moved by having met the person with the purest and most Spiritual energies I've ever connected with."
>
> "Goodness!" I responded, "Tell me more!" I was truly eager to hear about this, as Monty had been around a lot of other healers in his life.
>
> "There's nothing more I can share in words." he responded. "She was a bag lady, sitting on the sidewalk with a tin can for donations. And when I looked into her eyes, I connected with infinity."

While there is much of value in each religion, I am not addressing such teachings here because each religion has its own interpretations of how to connect with and relate to our Spirituality. Some parts of these are based on personal Spiritual awarenesses. But many of these rely on cognitive religious explanations, constructed and refined over many centuries, in many different cultures, by people with Spiritual awarenesses, as well as by followers with less direct Spiritual consciousness, if any. This explains why each religion differs in significant details from the others. Even within single religions, such as Christianity, there are distinct differences between Anglican/ Episcopalian, Assembly of God, Baptist, Catholic, Lutheran, Methodist and Orthodox in beliefs, doctrines, practices, and explanations of Spirit.

Many Eastern religions invite adherents to explore their connections with personal Spiritual awarenesses, through varieties of meditative practices. This brings people into more direct gnowings of Spirit. Eastern meditation masters guide their students to experience directly what Spirit is, rather than instructing them cognitively about Spirit.[3]

Regretably, there also appear to be what I perceive as serious distortions of Spiritual integrity in many religions.*[4] In particular, I note the elevation of men to more privileged, powerful and exalted positions within their families, religions and cultures than are allotted or allowed to women. There are also distortions of Spiritual awareness in the allocation of powers to clergy to mediate between the Spiritual and the secular – thereby distancing people from their own, direct awarenesses and personal connections with Spiritual dimensions.

In contrast with Western religious views on spirituality, there are naturalistic perceptions of Spirituality. It is these I focus on in my discussion in this Section of the book. What I consider here are ways that people connect personally and directly with their experienced Spiritual awarenesses. These Spiritual insights are important parts of our wholistic being. Personal Spiritual awarenesses deserve a separate review and discussion because Spirituality is often overlooked, ignored and neglected in Western society – if not outright disparaged and dismissed.

Personal Spirituality, experienced as inner gnowing, is alive and well and inviting us to reconnect with it. Personal Spiritual awarenesses include a sense of being absolutely real, beyond any question. See, for instance the descriptions of Mellen-Thomas Benedict and of Eben Alexander, a Neurosurgeon, about their near death experiences, for a sense of what this can be.*[5]

Personal Spiritual awarenesses may have liabilities. Our personal experiences are colored by and filtered through our individual perspectives, through perceptual and conceptual filters created by our individual life experiences, family and cultural teachings, beliefs and disbeliefs, our satisfactions and disappointments in life, our joys and sorrows, our epiphanies and our traumas. They are further colored by the linear, logical language we use to describe them. Yet it is possible to sift out the common denominators among Spiritual experiences that are reported by numbers of people, preferably including reports from different cultures, to arrive at core collections of factors that are common denominators among diverse reports on Spirituality.

> *I think the most wonderful things in life are beyond reason,*
> *that is why I think 'why' is often such an irrelevant question,*
> *it is very limited. The real things of life have nothing to do*
> *with 'why.' They are just 'so.' They are just 'thus.' Life is a 'thus'*
> *and until you realize this 'thusness' of life you are stuck.*
> — Laurens van der Post

I am not well versed in comparative religious beliefs, practices or experiences, so I cannot comment on these more than in a general way. But I have lived on three continents and in various parts of the North America. So I feel I've had a broad experience of some of the English-speaking Western world, plus a solid immersion in the Jewish cultural island in the Middle East. I also had a more balanced view of the Middle East than might appear at first sight, as my Jewish father was born and raised in Cairo and worked for most of his life as an administrator in Arab education in British Mandate Palestine and then in Israel. He provided windows of understanding and appreciation of Arab culture and views that markedly broadened my awarenesses about the diverse and conflicting cultural, religious and political views of Arabs and Jews, as well as of overlapping, positive worldviews, life experiences and culturally-colored interpretations of what is important in life.

My most valuable takeaway lessons from my various cultural immersions are that there is no single way of viewing or relating to the world that is THE right or best way for conceptualizing and explaining Spirituality. Considering the differences among diverse cultures and religions in explaining our world, no one on this planet, anywhere or anywhen, can have unbiased views or explanations for what life in the flesh and in Spirit are all about. Our cultural upbringings invariably color how we perceive and explain the world around us.

While this may appear to be a criticism about Spiritual awarenesses, it is in no way intended to question or disparage the diverse personal reports from individual people through the ages about their experiences of gnowing aspects of Spiritual realms. What I want to emphasize is that while there is validity in each report, at the same time there are also cultural and individual biases that invariably color and distort each report, as well.

We also face the unavoidable challenge that each window of perceptions and doorway into experiences of Spiritual dimensions is unique and provides just a tiny number of pixels of perceptions from a canvas that is infinitely vast. In addition, visitors in these realms bring back reports of highly individualized experiences and understandings of these numinous awarenesses. The perceptions, subjective experiences and interpretations of them are usually outside the ordinary experiences of the explorers in these dimensions, and therefore they have no words or concepts that are adequate to describe them. Furthermore, because each report is personal and unique, there will always be questions as to how similar they might be to other explorers' reports. At best, we can collect varieties of reports and look for commonalities amongst them.

What is most commonly reported is a sense of being in a place of unconditionally loving acceptance. Spirits of other beings, often family members and close friends, come to greet and welcome visitors, reassuring them that physical death is not the end of life.

Western scientific research offers methodically developed observations of the physical world. Western science assumes that the mind is the product of the nerves in the brain. However, there has never been anything like clear evidence, nor a consensus on how the brain could produce the entire range of observed mental activities that are reported by people. Despite these limitations of conventional scientific speculations, the majority of scientists continue to believe that eventually the functions of the mind will all be explained by neuroscience.

> *We regard promissory materialism as superstition without a rational foundation. The more we discover about the brain, the more clearly do we distinguish between the brain events and the mental phenomena, and the more wonderful do both the brain events and the mental phenomena become. Promissory materialism is simply a religious belief held by dogmatic materialists... who often confuse their religion with their science.*
> — John C. Eccles

When we apply research methods that work well in the physical world to questions relating to the Spiritual worlds, we are on very shaky ground. There are no objective measures for perceptions of the Spiritual dimensions. There are no objective dimensions of length, weight, depth, or electro-magnetic activity to supplement our personal perceptions in order to make our assessments of Spiritual dimensions more precise.

In research of Spiritual dimensions, we have as our data base only the subjective reports ---of individuals. So the best we can do is to ask educated questions about personal experiences and look for commonalities and/or differences among the various reports.

There are physical effects associated with some psychic/ spiritual experiences that can be measured, such as with psychokinesis and healing. These can validate that people are able to influence the physical world through their intents, without any physical interventions or known, measurable energy influences. But these confirmations of physical effects do not as yet offer us windows into understanding the Spiritual worlds themselves.

Despite these limitations, we will review below many research reports that explore and confirm the observed nature, types and prevalence of these personal Spiritual experiences and their deeply transformative effects – both to arrive at the clearest available descriptions of personal Spirituality and to counter the strong, prevalent Western skepticism and frequent disparagements and dismissals of Spiritual awarenesses.

*WHAT HAVE YOU BEEN TAUGHT TO BELIEVE ABOUT SPIRITUAL EXPERIENCES?*

*HAVE ANY OF YOUR PERSONAL EXPERIENCES GIVEN YOU PAUSE TO WONDER WHETHER THERE MIGHT BE MORE TO YOUR SPIRITUAL AWARENESSES THAN YOU'VE BEEN LED TO EXPECT?*

*HAVE YOU FOUND YOURSELF CONNECTING YOUR PERSONAL SPIRITUAL AWARENESSES THROUGH RELIGIOUS TEACHINGS?*

*WHAT OTHER RELIGIOUS EXPERIENCES HAVE HELPED YOU CONNECT WITH PERSONAL SPIRITUAL AWARENESSES?*

## 63. Spiritual awarenesses – accepting the Spiritual as real

> *All our Power,*
> *All our Magnificence*
> *consists in our reception of the soul's hints.*
> *These become ever clearer and grander*
> *as they are acted upon.*
> - Ralph Waldo Emerson

People commonly think of humans as the pinnacle of evolution on our planet. Those wedded to the religion of Western scientism insist that nothing is real unless it is supported by conventional scientific research, based on replicated measurements, showing consistent results under standardized conditions. Reports of individual, subjective Spiritual experiences are dismissed as wishful thinking, fantasies, delusions, hallucinations or deranged thinking, or products of a damaged brain. This is left brain thinking.

Within this rigid mental set there is a neuroplastic blindness*[6] to and dismissal of reports that push the boundaries of current scientific theories and paradigms. We see these sorts of rejections and dismissals of well-validated evidence, even where the parapsychological explorations of intuitive and Spiritual awarenesses are meticulously well researched and extremely well validated within conventional scientific research paradigms.*[7]

People who trust their individual experiences of the world through their inner senses perceive Spiritual awarenesses as real, valid and deeply meaningful – both personally and collectively. They are able to accept that consciousness extends beyond their immediate physical bodies and includes dimensions of realities that are not measurable within the bounds of current material science, nor contained within the theories or experiments of quantum physics.

> *The difference between Spiritual reality and material reality is*
> *how much of reality are you ready to chew on.*
> - Daniel Benor

Any discussions of Spiritual dimensions are therefore based on reports of the inner experiences of various people, each of whom may describe their perceptions through their personal, familial, cultural, linguistic, religious and other habits of beliefs and understandings. We can, however, distil common denominators among diverse individual reports.

Typically, discussion on these topics start from perspectives derived from our physical perceptions in the physical world. Let's turn this around and consider our world through the perspective that we are Spiritual beings exploring what it's like to have lives in a physical body, in the physical world.

One of the first questions to consider is: Why would anyone wish to leave the wonderful Spiritual dimensions and spend time in a physical existence that is often challenging, difficult, painful, and in many other ways far less pleasant and enjoyable than life in Spiritual realms?

My personal belief is that The Infinite Source realized that light cannot be truly appreciated without the contrast of darkness. So we are living in a relatively dark portion of the universe, with our awareness of the light disconnected to a great degree, in order to provide a contrast that will enhance and deepen the appreciation of living in the light and love of the Infinite Source.

But regardless of reasons and motivations for incarnation, the fact remains that spirits come for sojourns in the flesh and then return to their Spiritual homes.

### *Spirit guides*

People with strongly developed intuitive awarenesses may find guidance from spirits of humans, animals, plants and other parts of nature. This is a very widely accepted and well-developed part of indigenous culture. In many tribes, one of the rites of passage in becoming an adult is to go on a spirit quest, to connect with your guides and to open more into your personal Spiritual awarenesses. The messages received from spirit realms in these rites of passage may guide people for the rest of their lives.

In Western society, intuitives (also called mediums) may develop such awarenesses of spirits. In many cases, the spirits speak to the intuitives, who report the information to the people consulting them. In other cases, the spirits take over the mind and body of the intuitives, and speak directly through the intuitive, using the intuitive's voice. In some cases, the intuitive's voice changes to match the accent and intonation of the deceased spirit. Often, information is conveyed that was of an intimate nature between the deceased and the person seeking the reading, and highly unlikely to be known to anyone but the deceased and the person requesting the reading.

✤ 'Vera' was devastated by the loss of 'Alfred,' her husband, who died of a sudden heart attack at age 59, when she was 51. They had been very happily married for 32 years, raising three lovely children and planning to enjoy visiting with them and their grandchildren in their retirement.

Vera sank into a deep depression that she was unable to overcome, despite many efforts of her family to support and encourage her. She was unable to continue work, and had to take an early retirement three months after Alfred's passing on.

Her younger daughter, 'Molly,' insisted she move in with their family, hoping to cheer her up, as well as to keep an eye on her to be sure she ate and did not follow through on some of her suicidal thoughts, expressed as "I wish I could just be with him again."

Molly mentioned she had heard of a very gifted medium who was able to communicate with spirits. Vera was neither religious not Spiritually inclined, but responded with modest interest, despite considerable skepticism. Vera was quite nervous in going to the session because she worried that nothing was likely to convince her this was real, which would leave her with a great disappointment on top of her bereavement.

'Doris,' the medium, explained that her way of channeling spirits was to invite the spirit of the deceased to speak through her. She recorded her sessions as much for her own interest as to offer her clients a record of the communications, because she had no recall of what transpired when the spirits were speaking through her.

Doris closed her eyes and her head slumped briefly to her chest. When she raised her head, her eyes remained closed but her voice sounded masculine. "Verily, Vera," she intoned, "I'm so pleased to be able to speak to you! I've wanted so much to sit beside you and hold your hand and console you and let you know that I'm more than hunky dory OK!"

Vera broke out in tears as she heard this, and continued to weep openly through most of the session. She was very glad to have the recording, as she hardly remembered anything other than the first few sentences. She later explained that she knew immediately in her heart this was real because Albert had often used the phrase, "Verily, Vera" when speaking with her alone, and they had spent many long, loving hours sitting side by side and holding hands either on the swing on the front porch or on the sofa in front of the TV. "Hunky dory" was also a phrase he commonly used within the family, but not specifically with Vera rather than other family members. Still, this added to Vera's inclination to believe it was a true communication from Albert.

It is very common for such communications to contain 'signature' phrases and details that are very specific to the spirit communicator and the person seeking the connection. Such information is highly unlikely to be known to mediums in their ordinary states of consciousness, so it verifies the authenticity of the channeling.

The fact that Vera was able to converse with Alfred enabled her to move forward in processing her grieving much more gently. It was the process of a less abrupt termination of the relationship, as much as the content of Alfred's reassurances, plus the anticipation of being reunited after passing on herself, that helped Vera work through her grief.

Spirit communications are often great consolations to people who were bereaved by the sudden, unanticipated death of someone close. They are also enormously helpful for unresolved grief and trauma residues of longer durations.

People will also seek out psychics for spirit advice on practical matters, such as whether to make an important investment or purchase. They believe the psychically channeled information is more reliable than advice from living people, because spirits may be able to perceive the outcomes of investments and other information from the future. Here, however, common sense suggests that channeled sources of information may be only as good as the fund of knowledge and innate wisdom of a guide or spirit of a person from earthly existence who is currently residing in spirit dimensions. We would do well to heed the succinct warning from a Native American shaman who was asked why she didn't consult the ancestral spirits. She replied, succinctly, "Dead no make smart."

See much more in later chapters on mind to mind communications among the living*[8] and on Spiritual awarenesses, including research confirming that these are not just beliefs but experiences that can be validated.

## *Awakening and deepening our Spiritual awarenesses*

We may waken to personal Spiritual awarenesses spontaneously, sensing we are part of a greater whole that extends beyond ourselves. We may deepen our connections with many aspects of Spirit. Common invitations and practices for connecting with Spiritual dimensions may include

- Physical activities such as ritual dancing and chanting; total focus in a sports activity ('zoning'); prayer beads, fasting; tai chi, quigong, yoga; tantric practices; participating actively or as an observer in creative arts; other activities performed with focus and intentionality; connecting with the messages your body offers you spontaneously (through symptoms, injuries and illnesses); or seeking connections with your intuition through muscle testing.*9

- Emotional attunement with a friend, with a person in need, with a close partner, a child or other family member
- Being present in each moment with focus and intentionality; meditation; reciting mantras; reading and poetry about inspiring subjects; holding an intention to take every life experience as your participation in the dance of Spirit that is your life, journaling your Spiritual awarenesses and experiences
- Being focused and present in interactions with people; associating and resonating with people who are Spiritually highly developed; group meditation and prayer; Spiritual retreats; acts of service (enhanced with intentionality and loving kindness); asking people who are grieving whether they have had a sense of the presence of the departed;*10 asking people who are approaching death whether they sense angels or spirits of their deceased relatives waiting to welcome them,*11 campaigning for healing our planet
- Being in nature, gardening with intentionality; living simply and in harmony with the environment; being mindful of not polluting or exhausting natural resources, spending time in places that speak to people of Spiritual awareness
- Meditation, prayer, religious practices; looking for synchronicities and manifestations;*12 inviting higher guidance and inspiration into your life

The Spiritual dimensions are all around us and within us. We can open our awarenesses to them and connect with them more deeply through holding a clear and firm intent to do so and through engaging in deliberate practices such as the above.

## *Spiritual emergence and Spiritual emergencies*

Stanislav Grof, MD, and Christina Grof developed this terminology of Spiritual emergence and Spiritual emergencies in the 1980's, to identify challenges we may encounter in the process of opening our awareness to Spiritual dimensions. They created the Spiritual Emergence Network (SEN) to provide support for people who experience serious psychological challenges in opening to Spiritual awarenesses. We may feel such distress as we enter these realms and release our attachments to the familiarity of our physical existence. In instances where the Spiritual awakenings develop rapidly they may be unsettling, particularly if they are stimulated by traumas. We may at times feel uncomfortable, frightened or even overwhelmed. Many have used terminology to describe these Spiritual crises like feeling 'unmoored,' 'untethered,' or 'disconnected from reality.'

These sorts of anxieties and fears are also commonly experienced by people who are entering psychotic states. Since psychotic conditions are far more familiar in Western society than states of Spiritual emergence, many people become frightened by their awakening awarenesses of Spirituality, believing that they are losing their minds. Such fears may become overwhelming. This is not only because Spiritual awakenings are inherently unsettling, but because we're unused to them and fear the unknown.*13

The International Spiritual Emergence Network (ISEN) lists the following typical intense Spiritual emergence experiences:
- Being bombarded with unusual inner experiences and/or information previously unknown
- Having challenges to our old beliefs and ways of being
- Finding it difficult to cope with the demands of everyday life
- Having difficulty distinguishing the transpersonal world from the world of shared reality
- Physical sensations of forceful energies through the body
- Feeling a strong urge to communicate these experiences
- Feeling like you have unusual or paranormal powers and are the only one in the world who knows 'the truth'
- Feeling like you are going to die
- Having telepathic experiences and communication from spirit *14
- These are generally not preludes to or signs of going into a psychotic state. They are signs of letting go of accustomed, left brain ways of thinking, and opening to gnowing the world through intuitive, psychic and Spiritual perceptions.

Conventional therapists, who have very little or no under-standing of Spirit or of Spiritual awakenings, may similarly mistake these for psychoses. It is not uncommon for people in these states to be put on antipsychotic medications or even hospitalized.

In such situations, it's extremely helpful to have the support and help of a knowledgeable friend, Spiritual teacher or therapist who is familiar with experiences of Spiritual emergence. They can provide reassurance that this is not a psychotic breakdown, but rather an opening into transcendent awarenesses. They can offer support and advice in the ways to deal with these profoundly deep awakenings to our Spirit. The ISEN has a website with links and resources for support.*15

As people weather the waves of new feelings and integrate their Spiritual awarenesses, they frequently find themselves coming into inner places of great peace. Their lives are frequently transformed, with new, deep understandings of their roles and missions in life, including expanded wholistic awarenesses inviting involvement in social and environmental activism and healing.

*Bidden or unbidden, God is present.*
- Erasmus

Mirroring the observations of Erasmus, a Dutch, Catholic humanist in the late 15th and early 16th centuries, I would broaden his observation to say that on some level, Spiritual influences (though not always with conscious awareness) are always present. I believe this is the most important aspect of all of our lives.

Some will argue that evil is not Spiritual, but I believe that darkness is an important part of appreciating light, helping us to connect with light in ways we would otherwise not pursue.

*CAN YOU RECALL YOUR FIRST PERSONAL SPIRITUAL AWARENESSES?*

*WHAT PRACTICES HELP YOU OPEN TO SPIRITUAL AWARENESS?*

*WHAT ENVIRONMENTS FACILITATE THESE AWARENESSES?*

*DO YOU HAVE PEOPLE WITH WHOM YOU DISCUSS THESE?*

*ARE THERE PEOPLE WITH WHOM YOU DEFINITELY DON'T DISCUSS THESE?*

*WHAT MORE MIGHT YOU DO TO INCREASE YOUR PERSONAL SPIRITUAL AWARENESSES?*

### Angels

> *...the genus Angelus Occientalis.... Is a general term for a number of species and sub-species to be found in the monotheistic religions of Judaism, Zoroastrianism, Christianity and Islam....These four religions ... believe that the cosmos is divided into Heaven, Earth and Hell and is populated accordingly with angels, humans and demons.*
> — Malcolm Godwin

In the religious traditions of Judaism, Zoroastrianism, Christianity and Islam, God communicates with humans through angels. Traditionally, these are heavenly beings serving God's will as his helpers. Christianity holds Satan to be a fallen angel who is the polar opposite of God. Satan is a being of darkness who seeks to lead humans into dark and sinful ways.

The Old Testament mentions seven archangels but names with clarity only Michael, Gabriel, Raphael and Uriel.**[16] The archangels, particularly Michael, do God's bidding. Michael is often described as a warrior. Gabriel, who sits on the left side of God is sometimes describes with feminine attributes in earlier religious writings. The other archangels are not described in detail in the Old Testament. The New Testament offers more details.

Many people pray to angels for help. Doubters suggest that the only help likely to come from such prayers is the building of hope that something good will materialize in the lives of those praying. Believers have stories to tell about unusual, even miraculous answers to their prayers.

While I know of no formal research on this subject, my own explorations have been fascinating. I detailed these in chapter 61, in my discussion on manifesting what we wish for. Summarizing these briefly, I've found that wishing for parking spaces to be available wherever I go appears to work better when I ask my personal angels for help. Being very specific in my requests increases the likelihood of success.

I know many people who have been helped by angels. Here are a few examples of their experiences.

✦ 'Joanne,' who is a healer and has direct awarenesses of angels, was driving down a narrow road on a hill in a small English town in winter, not aware there was black ice on the road. Her car started to skid just before the bottom of the hill, right where the road made a sharp turn. With stone walls on both sides of the road, she had nowhere to turn, and when she pressed on the brakes, her car started into a skid. She braced herself for the anticipated impact, but was astounded to feel the car turning around the curve in the road, "as though a giant hand was gently but firmly guiding my car safely around that sharp bend in the road." I gave thanks to my guardian angels for their help!

✦ Bernie Siegel, MD, a wonderfully caring doctor, is another great healer who senses the presence of an angel in his life and also in the lives of his patients. He found, however, that in times of dire need he was sometimes forgetting to call upon for angelic help. So he asked if it was ok to give his angel a personalized name so that Bernie would be more likely to call upon him immediately when he was in danger and under stress. His angel agreed. So now his angel is called "Oh, Shit!"

✦✦✦ I have to acknowledge a strong sense of angelic help in bringing me to Canada in 2006, where I met and eventually married a person whom I sense to be a soulmate from several past lives.

I moved away from the US in 2006 for several reasons. First, the US no longer felt a safe place to be. The government's response to 911 left me seriously anxious about the lack of integrity in the Federal government. But even more than that, the increasing concentration of money in the hands of a few, at the expense of the majority of the population, leaving increasing portions of the population with ever-worsening economic and social problems are witnesses to the decline of democracy that cannot end well. In particular, the skyrocketing costs of healthcare, along with the ever-increasing unavailability of medical coverage for these costs for millions of people continues to be a growing concern. Second, I had visited Canada on various occasions and have been impressed with the far greater concern for the general good of all that is a part of Canadian culture. And third, the fact that Canada is further north and global warming is proceeding with little efforts to curb or reverse it made this an attractive option.

I had no conscious awareness at the time when I moved to Canada that I was moving towards anything so deeply positive.

There are many good books reviewing and discussing angelic guidance and protection.*[17] It is worthy of note that in many cases people report being helped during their travels by strangers, often in situations of serious distress and danger. These people appeared exactly when needed, provided the required assistance (such as helping push a car out of a ditch and back onto the road), and then literally disappeared into nowhere when those they had helped looked away for a moment.

Far more important, however, than the physical assistance provided by angels in times of need are the personal transformations in awarenesses brought about by these encounters. We may never be able to fully identify, delineate and describe whatever consciousness guides our personal and collective lives; whatever transcendent consciousness choreographs and shapes the course of history; whatever aspects of ourselves that participate in these deep lessons. But when we open to Spiritual awareness, we are connecting with the Infinite Source that choreographs and guides us through the lessons that are the highest purposes of our lives.

> *The oak sleeps in the acorn. The bird waits in the egg, and in the highest vision of the soul, a waking angel stirs.*
> -Napoleon Hill

HAVE YOU HAD A SENSE OF ANGELIC SUPPORT AT ANY TIMES IN YOUR LIFE?

I ENCOURAGE YOU TO INVITE SUCH SUPPORT. IF YOUR REQUEST ALLOWS FOR MORE THAN ONE OUTCOME, BEST TO BE OPEN TO ANY WAYS IT MIGHT CHOOSE TO MANIFEST, RATHER THAN NARROWING YOUR REQUEST TO A VERY SPECIFIC OUTCOME.

AND ALWAYS ADD AT THE END: THIS REQUEST IS MADE ONLY IF IT IS FOR MY HIGHEST GOOD AND THE HIGHEST GOOD OF ALL.

SOMETIMES THE BEST OUTCOME UNFOLDS FROM A DENIAL OF YOUR REQUEST AS YOU STATED IT.

### *Demons*

God, as described in the Old Testament, included both good and evil in His essence. In the second century BCE, the dark angel who is now called the Devil was identified in Christian texts. Over the centuries, the Devil and his demons were reported to have deliberately led people into minor and major negative behaviors and suffering.

Demons not only influence people to behave in hurtful and destructive ways, but may at times 'possess' people. That is, they may partly or completely take over a person's consciousness and behaviors and do horrible things to others.

Overlapping with demonic possession are instances in which discarnate spirits may do the same. In many cases it is reported that these spirits somehow failed to move through the normal after-death paths of either going into the light or into spirit realms where they undergo various lessons or healings.

There are healers who are able to clear away possessing spirits. They guide them to move on into the Light, thereby relieving the living people of symptoms they had been suffering. Such interventions are definitely not something recommended for anyone without the guidance of an intuitive who is knowledgeable and experienced in doing this sort of spirit psychotherapy. There are also exorcists in the Catholic church who do similar clearings of negative beings who 'possess' (take control over) living human beings.

✦✦✦ Shortly after writing this section of this book, I started to think that there were times when I felt 'not myself.' I was sometimes unusually irritable and short-tempered for no reasons that I could identify, including checking myself to be sure my HSP HuTiST**[18] factors were not lowering my threshold for irritability. The more I observed myself at such times, the more it felt to me that I might be subject to irritations caused by some sort of negative entity or entities.

I contacted a trusted colleague who has considerable expertise and experience in these matters, and with several Skype sessions we cleared a variety of types of entities. I was surprised with how much clearer and more centered I felt, starting right after each session. Muscle testing by the therapist and myself was an essential supplement to these clearings.

Unexpectedly, my voice was much stronger a few days later, though I couldn't know whether this was due to the entity removal or to healing I had received from another healer on the same day as my second entity removal session.

## 64. Reincarnation and past life therapy

> *...The gross material body...is in a very real sense the prison house of the ego-soul, and a central part of human growth is to transcend its limitations...*
> - Daskalos[19]

Many people sense that the spirit of man survives after physical death in an afterlife and returns to live again. These include people in Eastern religions, many in traditional cultures around the world, psychic healers, and growing numbers of people with current-day awakenings of past life memories. Early Christianity included beliefs in reincarnation until it was anathematized by The Council of Constantinople in AD 553.

'Skeptics' in reincarnation dismiss past life memories and past life influences in our lives as being matters of belief but devoid of substance. The disbeliefs of 'skeptics' are strongly contradicted by evidence from research on people reporting past life memories and experiencing transformations in past life therapy.

Several lines of evidence suggest that reincarnation actually occurs. Reincarnation memories arise spontaneously, particularly in children. In a few exceptional instances, there is even recall of fragments of languages from past lives, clearly not learned in the current life, and on rare occasions also including the ability to converse in those languages (Stevenson, 1974a).

A variety of approaches may bring forth memories of previous lifetimes. Explorations with hypnosis and a range of psychotherapies report that immediate symptom relief may be obtained when some patients relive experiences or release residues of emotions from traumas they report they experienced in previous lifetimes.

### *Spontaneous reincarnation memories*

Ian Stevenson (1974b; 1987), a psychiatrist at the University of Virginia, pioneered the exploration of spontaneous reincarnation reports from India, Lebanon, Sri Lanka and other cultures around the world, He meticulously collected first-hand accounts of witnesses corroborating reports of such memories.

Some religions and cultures fully accept reincarnation, such as the Brahmans, Hindus, Jains, Taoists, Vedists and others – particularly in China, India and other far eastern countries.

I spoke with a Druse person when I lived in Israel. The Druse live in northern Syria, Lebanon and Israel. Reincarnation is an integral part of their personal experiences. The Druse report that people often reincarnate within brief periods of time after their physical death, typically within days. They welcome reports of reincarnation memories as links between the family from the previous lifetime and the reincarnated person. If the reincarnated person can clearly describe the previous identity, he or she is welcomed into the folds of their recalled family. In such cases, however, extra precautions are taken (especially by the prominent and well-to-do) to guard against possible fraud by persons who might seek social or monetary advantages in falsely claiming a past life recall in their family.

Successful cases under such circumstances have been found in which multiple witnesses verify the reported events. Particularly impressive are reports of children, in societies where there is little access to media and little mobility. Here is a composite example.

✦ Four year-old 'Ahmed' reported that he was really 'Shari,' and lived in a small town 300 miles from his own village. His persistent and detailed descriptions of persons, places and events, along with altered personality styles in the child when he was talking about his/her previous life, impressed them sufficiently so that appropriate inquiries were made.

Ahmed had never visited the recalled town of his alleged past-life memories, nor had any contact with anyone from there. After his present life family confirmed there was a family in that town with the names Ahmed provided, his family arranged a visit there. Ahmed was taken to the edge of the town. He led witnesses from among his alleged previous family by the most direct route from the edge of town to his recalled former home. Along the way, he pointed out a place where a tree had stood (where no sign of a tree was then evident) and other changes in the houses and surroundings of the home where he claimed he had lived.

On arrival at the home of his previous life, he identified relatives of Shari by name and kinship ties. He disclosed intimate details relating to Shari's family's experiences that no one outside the family could possibly have known. Shari's family verified that Ahmed's statements were almost entirely accurate. An example was a dress that Shari had particularly liked, with odd, brass buttons which Ahmed described in great detail. The dress had been passed on to another family member, who brought out several different dresses for Ahmed to look at. He immediately identified the correct one, which matched his description in every detail.

You might object that Ahmed could have obtained his information from news media or visitors from the town he described. However, his family had no radio (this was before TVs, computers or cellphones were found in his part of the world) and no newspapers were available in his village. Ahmed had never been outside his village, and no one recalled any visitors from outside the village who could have shared with him the minute details he reported.

Stevenson (1974b; 1987) collected large series of such witnessed reports from various countries. He found many cases in which numerous details in reported memories of previous lives were validated by the families of the deceased person. Others have also collected personal reports of past lives.[20]

He also found impressive physical evidence supporting reincarnation. He found people with birthmarks and other physical deformities appearing in the bodies of the current person, corresponding to documented traumas on body parts relevant to experiences recalled from previous lives (Stevenson, 1997). many people who died violent deaths have such birthmarks. For example, a person recalling being killed by an arrow through his chest in a previous life may find a birthmark on her chest in that spot.

In Western society, where reincarnation is not a familiar phenomenon to most people, past life memories are more rarely reported than in societies where it is well accepted. However, it is not uncommon for children in Western countries to report such memories. Children who are 2-6 years old may recall their existence in past lives as well as in spirit dimensions between lives. These may be simple, factual memories, or may include advanced Spiritual awarenesses, sometimes even with a sense of why they chose to incarnate into their current-life family, and their chosen/ agreed/ assigned tasks in this lifetime.[21]

Carol Bowman, in an excellent book on children's past life memories, tells of her son, Chase, who was horribly upset by loud bangs that had any resemblance to gunfire. When he was six, a hypnotherapist simply asked him what his fears were about, and Chase related he had been shot in his wrist during wartime in a previous life. Just sharing his story relieved the eczema he had suffered on that wrist in his current life since infancy. None of the medical treatments he received previously had provided any relief.

Tobin Hart (2003) gives a clear example of a child who would cry in the car from the time he was a baby if the weather was stormy. His mother thought this was just due to thunder or lightning, but when he was nearly two he reported he and his mother had died in a car crash during a storm in his previous life. He was six years old at the time of that fatal accident, and became anxious in his current life as he approached age six (when his mother mentioned these details to Hart). Hart had no further information from the boy's mother to share.

These are the sorts of situations in which TWR/WHEE or other EP methods can be quickly and deeply helpful. Children respond particularly well to such self-healing approaches. One of their major benefits is that once they know how to use them, they are available at any time the children get triggered.

My own, similar, first past life memory is detailed below, under past life therapy.

Not mentioned in the reincarnation literature are child prodigies, who may well be unrecognized reincarnated people demonstrating past life skills.

### Past life therapy

*If you look no further than getting rid of what's wrong, you may never deal with what's brought your life to a standstill. The thing you want to heal from may be the very thing you need to focus on in order to learn.*
  - Marc Ian Barasch

Hypnotic regressions to previous lives have been reported for decades. Connecting with trauma memories from a past life may resolve emotional and relationship issues in one's current life. Typically, people complain of a persistent pain, phobia, anxiety or interpersonal conflict that has not responded to conventional psychotherapy. Hypnotic recall reveals experiences that were lingering in their unconscious mind from previous lifetimes. People will frequently experience intense emotional releases as they recall traumatic past-life experiences, such as the death of a relative or their own deaths. Bringing out the related memories and feelings often frees people from their presenting problems in their current life. This is very similar to trauma residue releases for negative events that people experience in their current lives.

Brian Weiss (1986), a conventional Harvard psychiatrist, was surprised to have one of his patients report past lives during a hypnotherapy session. Though he considered at first this was probably a fantasy, he eventually became convinced that these memories were real. He has since conducted past life therapy sessions with numerous clients, over several decades, with great success in alleviating enormous ranges of emotional and physical problems. He also wrote several interesting and informative books about these people. Here he illustrates how regression relieves a serious symptom.

✦ 'Kathy' had been to see Weiss previously for help with post traumatic stress following a childhood car accident. Sometime later, she came back for help in losing weight, which had resisted all her efforts at dieting. Weiss hypnotized her and suggested that she return to any previous life in which weight issues might be found. She was surprised to find memories of being in a concentration camp, reduced to a skeleton during cold-blooded medical experiments. Her only release in that life came through death. She also remembered being between lives, after experiencing an encounter with a loving, white light. She reported to Weiss:

> ...Kathy floated above her body. And...she found the brilliant light that did not hurt her eyes.
>
> "I never found someone to love in that life," she wistfully observed. Her spirit had starved as had her body.
>
> ... she had died in a state of starvation...
>
> "Is there a connection between these lifetimes and your current weight problem?" I asked...
>
> The answer came quickly and effortlessly. "In this life, I needed the extra weight for protection. I needed to guarantee that I would not starve again." After a pause Kathy added, "But now I no longer need this protection."
>
> Because Kathy had remembered the traumas of starvation, she no longer needed layers of fat to protect her.
>
> Over the next six or eight months, Kathy slowly and steadily lost all of her extra weight. At the time of this writing, she has sustained the loss. Perhaps even more significantly, Kathy has started a wonderful new romantic relationship since losing the weight. Feeling good about herself and liking how she looks definitely played an important part in Kathy's ability to let this new relationship into her life (Weiss, 1994).

It is very commonly reported by past life therapists that when symptoms present in a person's current life corresponding to traumas in past lives are treated with trauma clearing methods, the current life symptoms are relieved.[22] This has been my own experience, both personally and as a therapist. And, getting a little bit ahead of my expansion in this discussion of wholistic Spiritual contributions to healing, I share a further layer of these trauma clearings related to my connecting with the Spirit level of my awareness.

Sometimes we have information available to us but we don't focus our attention on it, and it never enters our awareness. Sometimes, all it takes is opening ourselves to invite this information to come forward and it will surface into our conscious mind.

> ✦✦✦ My own past life memories contributed to my progress in dealing with nighttime urinary frequency. As mentioned earlier, I had suffered several years with a partially paralyzed vocal cord and waking at night to urinate. These improved a lot when I came to a place of deeper forgiveness for my mother for abusing me when I was very young.
>
> Over the previous two decades, I had had occasional past life memories of being a soldier in Greek or Roman times, and brutally abusing women sexually during and/or after several battles. I had done a modest bit of clearing of my horror over

these memories, but in connecting more strongly with memories of having been abused myself by my mother in this lifetime, I revisited these past life memories and did further clearings. This time, my releases were much more intense, and I had further decreases in the frequency of my nighttime urination.

*Research on past life hypnotic regressions*

Research on past life hypnotic regressions produced fascinating results. Helen Wambach gathered two series of past-life memories in several group hypnosis sessions in Southern California. One series had 850 cases; the other had 350. Wambach first sorted the reports by century, and within each century distributed them geographically. In each geographic area, she sifted the cases into their apparent socio-economic groups. These sortings produced percentages of upper, middle and lower classes that closely parallel what is known of population distributions in the respective historical periods. Gender distribution in past lives was split 50 percent male/female in both groups, although the present-life distribution in her first series was 78 percent female. She also studied clothing, food, tools and other items mentioned in past-life recall. There were cases in which verified types of historical items were mentioned that the subjects claimed they had had no conscious knowledge of prior to the hypnotic regressions. There were very few cases of objects misplaced in time.

Wambach's findings suggest in several ways that the reported past life memories were real rather than imagined. If you were a typical Southern California yuppie who came for a past life regression and were producing a narrative (consciously or unconsciously) from your imagination rather than from an actual memory:

— Would you be more likely to see yourself as randomly male or female, or the same gender as your own in your current life?
— Almost everyone I've asked has said they would have a hard time imagining themselves as anything other than their own gender. This strongly contrasts with the 78 percent of the combined groups who were women, yet half of them remembered being a man in their previous life.
— Which social class would you be most likely to choose for your fantasy narrative?
— Most people said they would be middle or upper class citizens in a fantasied past life, again in line with their current life lives. Yet in earlier centuries 80 percent were peasants.
— If you were building an imaginary past life narrative, what is the likelihood you would include clothing and objects that accurately match known styles and technology that were found in the century when you lived that life? And what is the likelihood you wouldn't include items from later or earlier centuries that were out of place in the century you were identifying?

My guess is that most people would have a difficult time creating imaginary settings in which their descriptions accurately matched the items known to have existed in any given single previous century.

These demographic and descriptive findings suggest that the past life memories were likely to have been accurate ones.

## HSP benefits from past life recall and past life therapy

I have found many HSPs with spontaneous memories of past lives. Many more have connected with such memories during the process of exploring current-life traumas. What many discovered was that they had experienced traumas in past lives that were very similar to the ones they had suffered in their current lives. This happens often enough that it suggests a distinct linking of experiences across lives.

This is similar to what we see in repetitions of traumas within the same life of a person. When children were abused, they have a higher likelihood of finding themselves in abusive relationships as adults. One would think that having had an abusive relationship as an adult, the next relationship chosen would be a better one. But often this is not the case. People find themselves in one abusive relationship after another. Several factors appear to contribute to these repetitions of negative choices and behaviors.

- At the time of the abuse and shortly afterwards, people are often in shock. The intense fears, with emotional and physical pains associated with trauma may produce post traumatic stress reactions.*[23]

- People tend to repeat behaviors because these are the patterns of expectations and responses they developed in childhood. Abused women will often return to an abusive relationship even after suffering serious injuries from their partners.

- When trauma memories and feelings are not cleared, they tend to fester inside the trauma survivors. They have fears, phobias, anxieties, depression, temper outbursts, nightmares and more. It appears that some part of a person will invite later life re-creations and repetitions of the trauma situations in an apparent plea for that person to address and clear these lingering memories and feelings from the original trauma. This repetitive pattern appears to be the same, whether the original trauma was in one's current lifetime or in a past life.

- Another common pattern we see is that many people who were abused at any time in their lives tend to become abusive themselves. In part, this is a learned pattern of relating to others. These residues of trauma may linger and fester in a person's unconscious mind for the rest of their lives. And relevant to our focus in this chapter, these residues may linger into future lives as well, unless they are cleared and resolved.

What I suggest about lingering trauma residues from one lifetime into another is not mere speculation. The past life memories that people recall are traumatic experiences more often than not. These appear to follow the same patterns and courses of creating residues of pain, trauma, and so on in future lives, just as the patterns with trauma repeat themselves in a single life. They also can be cleared similarly to the traumas we experience in our current life.

    ✦✦✦ I had my first clear past life memory with the help of 'Billie,' a gifted intuitive. My bike had slipped on wet grass while street biking and I fell on my left thigh. It was a minor fall on soft grass and without a second thought I rode home, a trip of about two miles. The soreness in my thigh seemed at first to be waning, but after two weeks it still ached.

I mentioned this to Billie as a 'by the way' issue when we were discussing other matters. She said she could sense a past life residue related to my continuing ache in my thigh. She held an energetic space for me (over the phone, from about 100 miles away), encouraging me to invite whatever images were attached to this ache to surface.

I saw myself dressed in winter furs, climbing a steep, snowy, mountain pass with a number of other Native Americans. This was a clan I had married into a few years earlier. My wife and baby had both died in childbirth several months ago. I felt that I had little reason to continue with this clan, but did not know where to find my clan of origin. I was limping as we climbed the pass, and with time it became clear that I could not keep up with the others. We had no pack animals and there was no help to be had. We had to climb over the pass to a place where we had stored provisions and where there was a cave for shelter. It was clear that I they could not stay back or go more slowly. This meant that I was not going to survive.

We said our goodbyes, knowing I was doomed to a frozen end to my life. I loosened my furs to shorten my suffering as I ended that life. I held no bitterness towards the clan because these were, of necessity, the ways of our world. An individual would be sacrificed so that the majority could survive. I did, however, feel I had been betrayed by The Infinite Source because of the deaths of my wife and child.

My hip pain diminished modestly, shortly after I started clearing the past life trauma memories from my Native American life using TWR/ WHEE. It was completely gone when I finished this release of traumatic memories and feelings.

Several decades later, I came into a much earlier past life memory. Again, it was a scenario of having moved to a new place, having lost those who moved with me, and feeling alone and betrayed by the Infinite Source. This earlier life trauma probably stimulated the development of the Native American life trauma.

About ten years later, early memories surfaced from my current life, in which I suffered a seriously traumatic early childhood. And here, again I felt I had been betrayed by the Infinite Source. The current life trauma residues have cleared much more slowly than those of my past life traumas. It's pretty clear that in my present life childhood the traumas were many times repeated. The fact that the abuse started in infancy is a further explanation for why the repeated trauma from this life is clearing much more slowly.

Periodically, I connect with additional memories of trauma details from my current life childhood. With time and practice, it is increasingly easy to clear these.

It was helpful to have a few phone sessions with an expert in dealing with early childhood traumas. This gave me more tools and confidence to connect with my inner child. Hypnotherapy has provided further help in uncovering and dealing with aspects of my current life traumas. It has also helped me to do inner child work to re-parent myself.

Most of the past life traumas I've helped people clear were single episodes. These generally clear more quickly and easily than current life traumas. My guess is that the sojourns in between-life realms also offer respite and some measure of healing for the traumas, though obviously not clearing them completely – per the problems apparently created by symptom residues of past life traumas that repeat themselves in the current life.

Numerous explorers in these realms have come to the conclusion that reincarnation appears to be the process of spirits and souls taking the equivalent of elective courses in the material world, with a major in Spiritual development. This has been a repeated observation of people who have had spontaneous past life memories, hypnotic regressions, near death experiences, and researchers who have examined these reports.

There are also reports of between-life memories from periods when people are in spirit world existence (Newton, 2001).

*HAVE YOU FELT UNEXPLAINED AFFINITIES FOR HISTORIC PERIODS OR PLACES THAT MIGHT SUGGEST YOU ARE HAVING VAGUE PAST LIFE MEMORIES?*

*HAVE YOU FELT LIKE YOU'VE BEEN IN A PLACE PREVIOUSLY, WHEN YOU ARE VISITING IT FOR THE FIRST TIME?*

*HAVE YOU FELT YOU'VE KNOWN SOMEONE BEFORE, EVEN THOUGH YOU ARE MEETING THEM FOR THE FIRST TIME?*

*HAVE YOU HAD ANY CLEAR PAST LIFE MEMORIES?*

## 65. Life in Spirit dimensions

> *[I]...define my spiritual journey more as one of listening and tuning to what is than of choosing. The spiritual journey, as I now conceive of it, is a progression from truth to ever-deepening truth...*
> — Ram Dass

While conventional human perspectives suggest that our life on earth is the primary experience of our existence, many people's Spiritual perspectives suggest the reverse is true. This is not a new conceptualization of spirituality. Pierre Teilhard de Chardin was a French philosopher and Jesuit priest who worked as a paleontologist and geologist. In the first half of the 20th century, he taught that we are all participating in the beingness that is God.

The evidence reviewed below suggests our physical life is not our primary, core experience in our total existence. It is only a transitory visit to the physical world. Here we learn lessons contributing to our soul journeys in other dimensions, which we only dimly sense, if at all, from perspective of our physical selves.

Assuming this is true, this places our Spiritual awarenesses as far more important than most people in Western society acknowledge. Let us consider the evidence supporting this view.

### *Bridging between physical and Spirit life*

We've seen reasonable evidence from a variety of anecdotal reports that life after death is not just a wish, a fantasy, or psychotic thinking, or a religious belief. While it is commonly held by many in Western culture that consciousness originates in brain activities and that physical death is the end of consciousness, there are many reports of people declared dead but who came back to life. Their reports of near death experiences (NDEs) are very consistent, even when they come from different personal backgrounds and cultures.

### *The near death experience (NDE)*

> *Death is only what shoves life along its way. It is a doorway to something new. Nothing is annihilated or lost or forgotten. All is carried on to the next place and all experience is shared and remembered. It is a great trick to learn to use this doorway. You must face, confront your death, prepare to die. This changes your place among the webs, gives you courage, shows you how living is a matter of attention.*
> — Kay Cordell Whitaker

Scientists have studied experiences of people who came close to death, or were actually declared dead (on the basis of total lack of responsiveness and sometimes also flat EEGs, EKGs and other vital signs) but later returned to life. Many were cases of cardiac arrest, serious accidents, complications of surgery or other clear causes of death.

In a composite picture of the Near-Death Experience (NDE), people typically feel they are moving out of their bodies in spirit form, passing through a long tunnel towards a bright light at the end. They may hear strange and beautiful music; may meet angels or other spirit beings who welcome them warmly; and may see or in other ways sense the presence of relatives who had passed on earlier.

There is a tremendous sense of well-being and calmness; of knowing and understanding about one's own life and relationships, as well as about the meaning of existence in general. These experiences peak in an encounter with a bright, white light that appears to embody an all-knowing, non-judgmental, all-accepting, all-loving being. Many experience a complete review of all the events in their lifetime, under the guidance of the Being of Light. The review is totally accepting and non-judgmental on the part of this Being, but people may feel regrets and criticisms of themselves over errors or poor choices around things they did or did not do.

Some NDE-ers ask the Being of Light to let them return to physical life to complete unfinished business. Others are led to understand – in words or just by some inner 'knowing' – that a higher authority requires them to return to their physical bodies. Many feel great disappointment upon being told this, as the Spiritual realms feel so good. The next awareness is usually of being back in the body, with only a partial recall for the NDE, which in any case defies adequate description in ordinary language.

In and of itself, the NDE is frequently experienced as a healing. NDE-ers return from death's door with a markedly different, more peaceful and accepting attitude towards themselves and the world around them. Kenneth Ring (1984), a professor of psychology at the University of Connecticut, has studied the NDE extensively. He points out that

"Following their experience, NDE-ers are likely to shift towards a universalistically spiritual orientation. This shift is not found... for... persons who have not had NDEs but who are otherwise comparable...I have found seven essential elements of this coherent world view...

1. A tendency to characterize oneself as spiritual rather than religious...

2. A feeling of being inwardly close to God.

3. A de-emphasis of the formal aspects of religious life and worship.

4. A conviction that there is life after death, regardless of religious... belief.

5. An openness to the doctrine of reincarnation (and a general sympathy... toward Eastern religions).

6. A belief in the essential underlying unity of all religions.

7. A desire for a universal religion embracing all humanity."

Ring emphatically characterizes the profoundly deep transformations the NDE creates in the lives of experiencers of NDEs as the distinguishing hallmark of the NDE. People who return from an NDE no longer fear death and their lives are given completely new meanings by the broader perspectives and deeper understandings they perceive. Other researchers also emphasize transformative effects of the NDE.*[24]

There have been many studies of the NDE. For instance, to clarify how common the NDE is, Pim van Lommel and colleagues (2001) did a 12-year, prospective study of 344 people who had cardiac arrests. They found 18 percent reporting NDEs. This study is of particular interest because subjects were selected for study prior to having their NDE and because it was published in Lancet, a prominent medical journal.

Other studies reveal the NDE is a very common experience in numerous cultures. Another survey reveals that 70% of clergy are told of NDEs by some of their parishioners (Royce, 1985; van Lommel, et al., 2001).

Various conventional theories have been suggested to explain the NDE. One of the most basic ones is that the NDE might simply be a manifestation of death of parts of the brain as perceived by other parts of the brain that are still alive. To clarify whether this is likely, Owens et al. (1990) compared NDE reports of 28 people judged to be medically close to death with NDE reports of 30 people who thought they were close to death but were judged medically to have been in no danger of dying. Significantly more patients who were judged really close to death reported enhanced light perception and enhanced cognitive powers. Other variables did not distinguish between the groups. The experience of enhanced cognitive powers would suggest that the NDE is not a product of a dying brain, since cognitive powers would presumably be declining rather than markedly sharpened if NDE awareness was produced by waning activities of the physical brain.

## Reports from NDEs on a spirit life between physical lives

There have been reports from people returning after NDEs that they met relatives who had died prior to their NDE but whom they had never met or heard of previously. These NDEers were subsequently able to confirm descriptions of the physical appearances, personality characteristics, and/or factual information reported by the deceased. In some cases they had known the deceased prior to their deaths but did not known they were dead.[25]

Further impressive evidence comes from reports of children who had NDEs. Children under the age of eight usually have little understanding of death and are unlikely to have been primed with prior expectations that would lead them to the core experience of the NDE. Yet children report identical experiences to those of adults when they return from their NDEs (Atwater, 1999; Morse with Perry, 1994).

Most remarkable are the NDEs in blind people who were identified by Kenneth Ring and Sharon Cooper (1999). Of the 21 people interviewed, 10 were blind from birth and another 9 were blind from before the age of five years. Fifteen of the 21 subjects (71 percent) reported they were able to see during their NDE. Their vision was typically clear, organized, and immediately comprehensible. In a few cases it was possible to confirm the accuracy of what these blind people reported they had seen during their NDEs. This is very different from blind people whose vision is restored surgically. In such cases it takes a long time for people to make sense of their perceived visual patterns.

The large numbers of consistent NDE reports of continued existence in a spirit world following death suggest this is a real experience. The NDE reports are also consistent with other types of reports about the world of spirits.[26]

Those of us who have not experienced an NDE can still take away many lessons from reports of those who have had NDEs.

- Most importantly, there is the universal NDE awareness that consciousness continues after physical death when people from around the world experience NDEs.
- In after-death consciousness we encounter the consciousness of others who have died and transitioned to spirit existence.

- From the perspectives of spirit consciousness, we and those who were close to us in physical life will often arrive at very different understandings about our physical lives.

    Memories and feelings from disappointments, misfortunes, misbehaviors and traumas from our most recent life will be perceived and understood with more acceptance and forgiveness – of ourselves and of others

    Our relationships in our most recent life will be seen and understood within frameworks of residues from prior past life experiences
- Challenges and traumas in our most recent life will be understood as lessons that our soul either chose of its own volition, or agreed to experience under the tutelage and guidance of our spirit world advisors).

*Pre-death experiences*

Pre-death experiences are reported by people who are close to death. Melvin Morse (1994) collected many stories of psychic and spiritual experiences preceding the time of death by days or weeks. These had very broad overlaps with NDEs in many respects, including:
- Having precognitive awarenesses in dreams and waking visions that their deceased relatives are near or present, extending their love and caring
- Simultaneous perceptions by living relatives and medical staff of the visions that those close to death are perceiving
- Angelic presences that convey helpful information

In addition, people close to the person who was in a pre-death state reported knowing that these relatives or friends were approaching death, even when this was not obvious from any ordinary signs and symptoms.

People may dismiss pre-death experiences as ordinary dreams or coincidences. Because the experiences were new and alien to their cultural norms, they would often question whether they hadn't imagined them out of wishful thinking or fears of death. Many were anxious that they might be losing their minds and would not tell anyone about their experiences. Morse suggests the following reassurances:
- There is no reason to believe you are mentally unbalanced because you have such experiences.
- Most people who have these experiences are mentally healthy.
- People who are losing their minds often have many other experiences of this sort, numerous fears in broad varieties of situations, negative feelings and hallucinations, and loss of control over their emotions and behaviors.

Those reporting pre-death experiences say that these have a feeling of reality that is as valid as any other of their life experiences. They have a quality of reality that is very different from imagined stories or made-up fantasies. Very often:
- They have a Spiritual quality to them.
- They are transformative, producing more positive outlooks and beliefs about life and death.
- They lead to commitments to work for the highest good of all.
- Those who have pre-death experiences are likely to have fewer and less intense anxieties, to feel more positive about the meaning of their life, to have

increased Spiritual awareness, to feel more certain that there is an afterlife, and to live more comfortably with their physical and emotional problems.

The visions and dreams convey information that is coherent, useful, and often relevant to others in addition to the one who is perceiving them. The quality of the process of dying is vastly improved for people nearing the end of their lives, as well as for those family, friends and caregivers who are able to listen to and accept their experiences.

'Skeptics' and those who are not reassured by the above may continue to ask whether these experiences are real, or just wishful thinking. In Morse's experience, criteria which appear to differentiate psychic and Spiritual visions from ordinary dreams and fantasies include two or more of the following:

- Visions and voices are superimposed over ordinary per-ceptions.
- They may appear as solid and sound as real as ordinary perceptions, or may have qualities that immediately distinguish them as visionary – such a mistiness or an awareness of an inner source to the perception rather than it being a physical, outer-world perception.
- The inner experience feels absolutely real, often even more real than everyday experiences.
- Deathbed perceptions that occur in dreams have distinct qualities of uniqueness, clearly distinguishing them from ordinary experiences.
- The experiences often include a unique white light or a Being of Light that is completely loving and accepting of those who perceive it.

Morse presents excellent discussions on the very positive effects of these experiences, with a treasure trove of examples from people he treated and people who shared their NDEs after reading his books. The pre-death experiences often ease the processes of parting between those who are dying and those still alive. They distinctly soften the pains of bereavement.

Most importantly, they open people to spiritual awarenesses. People who are approaching their death, along with those close to them, find peace in the reassurance that physical death is a transition to other dimensions rather than an end to existence. Death of a child or other person who is particularly dear to us may be shifted from being a complete tragedy towards also being a Spiritual awakening.

## Deathbed experiences

*Man's body can be reduced back to the elements of the earth, but the spirit and soul that is of the nature of God is eternal.*
- Alice Steadman

Deathbed experiences, resembling the NDE and pre-death experiences, are often reported by family members, nurses, hospice workers and clergy. Typically, people approaching their death become calm and smile. They may hear celestial, ethereal, 'beautiful music of the spheres.' They may report that they see angels, Christ or relatives who had passed on previously, coming to guide and accompany them on their journey through the process of dying. These spirit beings explain that there is an afterlife and that they need not fear death. The angels they see are not menacing 'angels of death' that are often depicted in various novels and media, but rather luminous, kind, welcoming angels whose presence alone (even without words) is described as soothing and comforting. Often, following these visions, any pains and other distressing symptoms they have will either abate or no longer bother them as much. A Gallup poll survey in 1982 found that 5 percent of dying people were reported to have experienced deathbed visions (Gallup and Proctor). These have been well documented in countries around the world, including the US, UK, Iceland and India (Osis, 1997).

Deathbed experiences from America, England and India are very similar to each other. Some have asked whether deathbed experiences might be produced by processes of brain death or of emotional disturbances. Karlis Osis and Erlunder Haraldsson (1977), both experienced parapsychologists, reviewed the possible alternative explanations for deathbed visions. Their findings point to a distinctness in the deathbed vision from physiological conditions that may produce hallucinations.

In Buddhist traditions, death is a viewed as a crucial state of transition. People prepare for their death over many years, through living their lives unselfishly, with regular prayer and meditation practices. In their experience, at the time of death and in the days immediately following, if the spirit is properly guided and assisted through the prayers of the mourners, it may transition to higher levels of advancement.

✣ 'Harvey' was a 66 year-old businessman who had retired a year and a half earlier after a very successful career in international marketing. His retirement had been marred by the fatal pancreatic cancer which had quickly carried off his wife, 'Ettie,' three years earlier.

He wasn't open to his emotions or to intuitive awarenesses, and was most probably an NHSP. Despite his strong skepticism about spiritual matters, he had tolerated Ettie's interest in healing and her belief in spirits. They had a clear understanding that she was not to mention these interests to any of his business associates, and both were able to live within this agreement. His story was shared by Ettie's sister, 'Kira,' a participant in one of my workshops.

Despite Ettie's experiencing a lot of pain, she had maintained a positive attitude and was at peace with her knowledge that she only had a few months to live following the diagnosis of her cancer, which had already metastasized when it was diagnosed. She was grateful that she could say her goodbyes to their three children and five grandchildren, and to extended family and friends. She told Harvey that she would be waiting for him when his time came to move on, just as her parents and grandparents were waiting to welcome her when she passed on. He patted her hand and told her he was glad she had this belief that made her feel better. She passed on quietly in her sleep a few days later.

Harvey was very disappointed and lonely in his retirement, as he had planned to travel the world with Ettie, exploring places and doing things they had had to put off due to his heavy business obligations. He was probably significantly depressed, though his habits of hiding his feelings kept his family from clearly sensing this. He developed a cough, which he thought was just a lingering bad flu that was going around, but when it persisted beyond four weeks he finally went to a doctor. The chest x-ray showed widely scattered lung masses, suspected to be cancerous, and a biopsy returned the diagnosis of liver cancer.

Harvey decided he would not undergo chemotherapy because there was virtually no hope for a cure, and he preferred to live out his last days without the side effects of chemo. As he became weaker and was bedridden, he experienced dreams that he considered odd. He shared these with Kira, as he knew Ettie had shared her own pre-death 'beliefs' with her.

After a preamble of heavy excuses about wishful thinking and hopeful dreams, he told Kira that Ettie had come to him several times in dreams. She looked younger and very vibrant and happy. She told him not to worry because she and others would be there to welcome him when he made his transition to the spirit world.

What worried him was that he thought he was losing his mind and just creating fantasies to stave off his sadness and disappointments over not getting to enjoy his retirement, and dreaming of Ettie because he missed her so much.

Kira shared that she had been volunteering in a hospice following Ettie's passing, and that what he was experiencing was extremely common. She, herself, had started out skeptical, like him, but after hearing about Ettie's visions, and then hearing similar stories related by numerous other people in hospice over the past year, she had come to feel they were real.

Harvey showed no signs of being moved by these stories that Kira shared. But a few days later, as he was lapsing in and out of his final coma, Kira saw him smiling and saying, "I'm coming, Ettie, I'm coming." On another occasion, one of his children reported he heard him say, "Thank you, Ettie, for sending me your angels to show me the way."

The stories of spirit and angelic encounters of disbelievers and 'skeptics' are often more convincing than those of believers. I encourage you to be supportive in listening to these sorts of stories from people you may visit when they are close to passing on. The spirits, guides and angels are very welcoming, and they (and we) can draw enormous encouragement and hope from their messages.

Even if you don't believe in spirits, God or an afterlife, does it do any harm to just accept that other people believe in all of these? Is there any reason to deny them the hope, solace and healing that these pre-death and deathbed experiences give them?

*IF YOU HAVE THE PRIVILEGE OF BEING PRESENT WHEN SOMEONE IS MAKING THEIR TRANSITION TO SPIRIT EXISTENCE, AND YOU HAVE ANY SENSE THAT THEY ARE EXPERIENCING THE PRESENCE OF SPIRITS, YOU MAY BE ABLE TO REASSURE THEM THEY ARE PROBABLY NOT HALLUCINATING, AND THEY MAY SHARE WITH YOU SOME INSPIRATIONAL VISIONS.*

### *Lessons from NDE's, pre-death and deathbed experiences*

Much of what we can perceive and deduce from NDE research is colored more than a bit by our physical-world understandings of the world we live in, and by religious teachings. Here is an eloquent, first-hand report of profoundly transformative effects of an NDE that suggest deeper ways to understand many aspects of these observations on transitions from physical to spiritual life, within spiritual perspectives.

Mellen-Thomas Benedict is an artist who died of a brain tumor in 1982. He went into the light, and as part of his NDE he asked questions about the universe and the meaning of life. Following his return to life an hour and a half after he was declared dead – with flat EKG and other body function monitors – he went on to study cellular communication and the influences of light upon life, particularly for healing (Bailey & Yates, 1996). He lived until March, 2017.

The content of Benedict's NDE report is remarkable for its scope.[27] He asked the Light to explain the meaning of life. He was led telepathically to perceive that the Higher Selves of all of humanity – of every individual – are joined in a matrix, and that all are connected to the Source.

"[W]e are actually the same being, different aspects of the same being. It was not committed to one particular religion… And I saw this mandala of human souls. It was the most beautiful thing I have ever seen. I just went into it and, it was just overwhelming. It was like all the love you've ever wanted, and it was the kind of love that cures, heals, regenerates…

I was astonished to find that there was no evil in any soul.

I said, "How can this be?"

The answer was that no soul was inherently evil. The terrible things that happened to people might make them do evil things, but their souls were not evil. What all people seek, what sustains them, is love, the light told me. What distorts people is a lack of love."

Benedict's consciousness expanded to encompass all of creation, through all of time. He found it was without beginning or end.

"… I came back with this understanding that God is not there. God is here…" (Benedict, Web ref).

Similar reports have been shared by others. While details of individual experiences differ in many minor respects, the broader picture of unconditional acceptance and love, communications that are felt to be absolutely true beyond any doubt or question, life reviews and decisions to stay or return to physical life, all remain similar across these reports.

Here are a few further observations, from the NDE shared by Eben Alexander, a neurosurgeon, who was in a coma and close to death, due to a severe infection of the meninges (lining) of his brain. He was greeted in his NDE by a beautiful female guide.

… She looked at me with a look that, if you saw it for a few moments, would make your whole life up to that point worth living… It was not a romantic look… not a look of friendship. It was a look that was somehow beyond all these… beyond all the different types of love we have down here on earth. It was something higher, holding all those other kinds of love within itself while at the same time being more genuine and pure than all of them.

Without any words, she spoke to me… and I instantly understood that it was true. I knew so in the same way that I knew that the world around us was real – was not some fantasy, passing and unsubstantial.

The message had three parts, and if I had to translate them into earthly language, I'd say they ran something like this:

"You are loved and cherished, dearly, forever."

"You have nothing to fear."

"There is nothing you can do wrong."

The message flooded me with a vast and crazy sensation of relief. It was like being handed the rules to a game I'd been playing all my life without ever fully understanding it. (Alexander, 2012, p. 40-41)

Conversations that Alexander had with this being and others were not in sequential words, as in ordinary human language. Information arrived in waves of understanding that transcended earthly language. He comprehended immediately whatever was being conveyed, even when the ideas were so complex that they would have required extensive explanations and even serious study to absorb these if they had been spoken in ordinary human language.**[28]

In left hemisphere terminology, we might say that thoughts conveyed within the spirit realms (as during NDEs) carry with them a sense of being true and real beyond any question. The same applies to emotions experienced in these dimensions. Alexander's experiences of emotions were very different in the NDE realms from what he felt during life on earth. He experienced them more deeply, with a total immersion in whatever he was feeling, along with very strong resonations of emotions from his surroundings. This led him to feel that "inside" and "outside" were not separate.

### *Life after physical death, between physical lives, and before birth*

People have reported memories from their existences in spirit dimensions, following their previous lives on earth.

- Most commonly described are the post-death reviews of their lives, immediately after physical death, in the presence of The Being of Light. These reviews are with total acceptance and no criticisms from the Being of Light.

- Between-life communications are telepathic, whether with spirits of other people, with angels or the Being of Light. There is a very warm, loving, accepting atmosphere in the existence between lives.

- There are loving reconnections with relatives, friends and other significant people and pets from our most recent physical life.

- There are also reconnections with other people from previous lives, and the recognition in many cases that you have spent numbers of other lives together, in addition to your most recent one. In most cases, these relationships were different in each lifetime. You might have been the child of the other person in your most recent life, but were their parent in a previous one, and their spouse, little brother or sister in yet another.

- Classrooms are attended, with teachers from advanced realms of existence providing orientation and education in spiritual advance-ment.

- Lessons may focus on experiences from previous lives, particularly on how relationships with other people evolved and how you behaved towards them and responded to their behaviors towards you.

- Subjects are explored in these Spiritual classes that are beyond descriptions, explanations or comprehension within our earthly under-standings of existence.

- Support and healing are provided by spirit guides, angels and other beings of light.

- People who died traumatic deaths, or while still suffering residues of serious traumas earlier in any of their physical lives, may be taken to a spirit-world equivalent of a hospital, a place of total peace, love, safety and healing, for recuperation, rehabilitation and illumination.

- During parts of our sojourn in Spirit dimensions, there are careful considerations and discussions about choices for our next life outside the Spirit dimensions.*[29]

- One's own soul, a part of ourselves that is more deeply conscious, wise and spiritually connected to higher awarenesses and understandings, participates in these growth-promoting studies, healings and life choices. At times, there is a certain amount of firm persuasion involved in these deliberations.

✦ 'Millie,' a wise healer, reported a memory of "sitting with my guardian angel on the edge of time, contemplating my next incarnation." She was distressed to see some of the challenges that awaited her, and complained, "But I didn't agree to that!!" Her last memory of this conversation was that she received a very firm push back into physical existence, with her angel's words echoing in her mind, "Oh, yes, you did!"

Overall, these dimensions of existence are described as places of love, light and healing.

It is unclear why very few people have any recall of their between-lives experiences. My speculation is that the lessons we undergo in earthly existence are much more strong and impacting when we have no recollections whatsoever of our between-physical-lives existence. Were we to remember with any clarity, after being born, what the Spirit world is like, the impacts of our challenging experiences in the physical world would probably be considerably weakened.

There is also the incredibly positive experience of constant, gnowing communications while in spirit worlds. Feelings and thoughts are shared from heart center to heart center. Many have described these messages as coming through a language of love. There is no need to speculate or guess whether the being transmitting the communication is being honest or sincere. What is shared is relayed with complete openness and without hidden personal agendas.

There are also spirit places of darkness and negativity, where people who are strongly attached to negativity congregate and have mutually depressing, frightening experiences of deceptions, violence, anger and despair. These are not places of punishment for failures to adhere to religious beliefs and practices, but rather places for lessons in experiencing evil and extreme negativity that may be reflections of their behaviors towards others when they were in the physical world. I have not pursued explorations about these realms of darkness, but have spoken with people who report memories of having experienced unpleasant sojourns in these realms.

Some also recall past lives on planets orbiting suns in distant galaxies and nebulae. They report existences that would rival the best of science fiction stories.**[30] Some lives were in humanoid forms, but others were as energy beings that defy accurate descriptions in human language and concepts. And on the positive worlds, collective consciousness is the rule rather than the exception.

Some recall lives on negative worlds, where they perpetrated and experienced nastiness and evils of all sorts. On worlds that are primarily negative, it is reported that the love and caring they sense from positive beings and positive worlds are perceived as being alien and uncomfortable.

### Relationships of spirits with people who are physically alive

Many spirits who contact the living are the surviving entities of deceased people. The most commonly reported communications are from deceased relatives to family members who are still living. There are also spirits who choose not to incarnate but nevertheless are involved with living people.

The motivations for spirit communications often falls into one or several of the following categories.
- To express the ongoing love and concern of the deceased for the living
- To explain that physical death is just a transition to another, continuing state of consciousness
- To reassure that the experience of transition from life to death is a release and relief from suffering, rather than frightening, painful or traumatic
- To provide helpful factual information, such as "The key to the safety vault is hidden in the bottom of the sugar bowl, which you never allow to get empty."
- To provide psychological support, such as "You're feeling totally devastated because I'm no longer there, but just be patient because in three weeks you'll start to come to a place of acceptance and healing."
- To offer warnings, such as "Bob is going to come around to console you, and you're going to feel attracted to him, but be really cautious before you make any commitments to a serious relationship. You'll find he's not the person you think he is."
- To offer general advice and guidance, which for the most part is not consciously perceived by the living

There are also spirit guides who provide advice, intuitive guidance and protection. For most people, this occurs on a totally unconscious basis. For sensitive people there may be direct awareness and communication with spirits and guides.

People who have traumatic deaths may end up stuck in spirit form but unable to move on into the light. Some may be perceived by the living as ghosts who are attached to particular locations. These ghosts may communicate with people living in distant locations and times, in ways that are perturbing or even malevolent. Many of the more gifted intuitives are able to communicate with them and help them connect with their angels or the Being of Light and move on into the higher Spiritual dimensions.

There are also psychologically and spiritually disturbed as well as malevolent spirits, and apparently non-human entities as well, that can pester or persecute living people on Earth and may cause them to behave in very unusual ways, such as becoming uncharacteristically angry, anxious or even psyhotic, or to suffer various physical disturbances. As mentioned earlier, sensitives and healers are often able to deal with such ghosts and malevolent spirits.*[31]

### *Gaia, our planet*
There are sensitives who perceive a distinct consciousness associated with planet Earth, often referred to as Gaia. Humans are actually just a small part of a collective consciousness that includes Gaia and all conscious beings who dwell on her. Sensitives report that each species of animals, plants, bacteria, algae, viruses and other life forms on our planet has their own, species-specific collective consciousness.

It appears from these reports that Gaia promotes and supports life on this planet, which is situated at just the right distance from the sun to create temperatures and other conditions here that are conducive to life as we know it.

Other parts of our planet that are not generally considered by Western culture to be alive are acknowledged by Indigenous peoples and some Eastern cultures to be alive and deeply sentient. The rocks and mountains, streams and rivers, the air and its winds and weather are all also conscious sub-units of Gaia. People who resonate with these awarenesses often communicate not only with the animals, trees and other plants, but with particular rocks, mountains and waterways as well.

Dora van Gelder (1978) describes angels who choreograph aspects of weather on earth. She reported that these manipulations of the weather are intended to rebalance various atmospheric and planet energies.

And again I note that some of the more sensitive human intuitives add that Gaia is a traumatized being. She has suffered the repeated traumas of five major extinctions of the majority of living species on Earth over the 4.5 billion years of her life. Gaia has also been stressed by the current human challenges that threaten to produce another major extinction (Benor, 2014).

There are reports, as well, that each of the planets in our solar system has its own, distinct consciousness and personality, as does our sun. Similarly, there are reports that other stars and their planets are conscious sub-units of our galaxy.

It is reported that within our galaxy there are areas of suns and solar systems that are primarily places of darkness and negativity, and other areas that are all or mostly places of light and positivity. So, too, with galaxies and nebulae around our universe.

Is this all myth and speculation? I would say that it is not. Reports of these perceptions are frequent enough in literature by and about intuitives that they are difficult to ignore. These reports are also pretty much consistent, coming from many parts of the world, over many decades. Furthermore, to me and to other sensitives whom I respect, these reports carry a sense of gnowings that feel real.

### *The Infinite Source / All that Is / God*
Every known culture has its beliefs, mythologies and religions to explain how the world was created. Most identify a Creator and/or various gods who brought this world into existence, along with all its living beings.

To recap, as relevant to our discussion on Spirituality, the NHSP majority usually view and explore the subject of divinity either as theoretical, philosophical considerations or as beliefs based on religious teachings and traditions. Psychologically, it is often suggested that these beliefs are largely fantasies humans have created in order to lessen their fears of dying. Or it is dismissed as a pre-scientific or non-scientific, mythic explanation for what are natural processes of planetary formation and biological evolution. In contrast, many HSPs experience direct awarenesses of spiritual dimensions, including in some cases personal perceptions of the Divine as a loving, healing presence.

Again, as with HSP and NHSP differences over emotions, and with disbelievers' dismissal of reports of intuitive, psychic and Spiritual awarenesses, the chasms dividing the sides are often unbridgeable. To explain this situation from the perspective of those who experience the Divine as tangibly real, an analogy has been proposed: We all live in the equivalent of a tall building, with each floor representing one of a progressively refined levels of intuitive awarenesses as one goes up in the building. The floor of each level in the building is a one-way mirror allowing residents of that level to see down through their floor and the floors below it to lower levels but not allowing them to see through the mirrored ceiling of their own level to higher levels. Through personal Spiritual development we advance from one floor of the building to the next, higher one above where we currently life.

> *We are all sparks of the Divine flame,*
> *seeking our ways back home to the Source.*
> - Jewish mystical tradition

The Creator is often identified as masculine. Many theories have been proposed to explain why this should be. I am not well versed in theology, so I cannot speak with any authority about the historic and cultural roots and developments of these beliefs. However, I offer some personal and professional views and observations.

What speaks to me most strongly is the theory that men suffer from lack of a deep, significant purpose in life in comparison with women. A girl knows from her observations of her mother and of other women, starting in her earliest years, that she has the important responsibility of bringing life into the world and of nurturing and raising her children till they leave home. This gives a deep meaning and purpose to her life. While a man participates in the creation of life, after the procreative act his contributions are not absolutely essential. In most societies, his contribution in terms of the efforts and responsibilities in child care and child rearing are very limited, compared to the responsibilities the woman carries.

In societies where life is lived close to the land, a man has the responsibilities of hunting, fishing and/or farming, for providing adequate shelter, and in standing guard to assure the safety of his family, clan and community from animal predators and human marauders. These tasks provide some measures of existential satisfactions. But compared to women, men remain less important to the continuity of life and the transmitters of the legacy of family wisdom and traditions that are passed on from one generation to the next. Men have had to create reasons and invent explanations to boost their self-image in order to feel they have an important, significant purpose in life. And for the most part, all of these gender role contributions to men's existential satisfaction are not within their conscious awarenesses.

An outcome of these differences is that men have more time available to sit around and think about issues and challenges in their lives, and to come up with ideas and theories to explain the world. Their inborn tendencies to left brain hemisphere dominance endows them with greater inclinations to create stories, collect oral and written records, and build themselves community roles to boost their egos and self-images. Their responsibilities for protecting their families and communities are strong motivators to be physically strong and aggressive, and their mentality of measuring their value by their strength compete for leadership roles in their communities.

With men's inclinations to be left-brain hemisphere dominant. Their focus in life pursuits is far more often on the external world than on their internal worlds. Competition in sports, other feats of strength, combat and in moving up their social and career ladders provides them with a measure of satisfaction and sense of purpose and achievement in life. A further factor is that many men, particularly in the technologically developed world, tend to be dominating in their relationships with their spouses and families, which is also carried over into their roles and behaviors within their modern workplaces and communities.

Similarly, men have also dominated in serving as leaders in their religious communities. Having men in charge allows them to tweak, if not color some (if not many) of the teachings of the founders of their religions to their masculine and personal views and preferences, to serve to their advantages. They come from a place of left brain interpretations of spiritual teachings, which self-empowers them – as religious leaders – to be the interpreters and enforcers of their communities' religious doctrines. Were women to be in charge, they would most likely turn more often, in at least some measure, to the gnowings of direct Spiritual awarenesses for guidance. This would likely include contradictions of male-friendly interpretations of the doctrines, and disempowerments of masculine leadership. Is it any wonder that men in many cultures have resisted including women in their societies' leadership hierarchies? This has been true in Judeo-Christian and Muslim societies for many centuries.

For example, in Jewish tradition, up to the 4th Century women participated in the Torah readings on the Sabbath. There was even discussion about whether women could do all the Sabbath Torah readings. At some time later they were completely prohibited from reading the Torah on the Sabbath.

To a modest degree there is now a shift in some religious groups towards greater inclusion and empowerment of women within the clergy. This may shift religious views towards greater reliance on Spiritual gnowings and to more direct communications with the Infinite Source.

In strong contrast to people in modern society, there are indigenous communities with traditions of consulting the wise mothers and grandmothers for advice on important decisions – in preference to responding to competitive, testosterone-driven advice of the men. Women are often the leaders in their communities.

In further contrast, many of the indigenous societies base their connections with the world on their wholistic relationships with themselves, their families, the environment and Spirit. Rupert Ross (2003), a retired Crown Attorney in Ontario, Canada, has a magnificent book detailing the totally different attitudes of Native**[32] people who were raised in the traditional hunter-gatherer societies of North America. In their early years, their children are only told what to do or not do when they are facing a life-threatening danger. Otherwise, they are very strictly left to learn from their experiences of making wise and unwise choices. They are also encouraged to connect with their intuitive awarenesses to help with their decision making.

Misbehaviors and acts of poor judgment represent a lack of full and proper focus on the issues at hand. Problems that arise are not seen as willful errors or misdeeds, but as neglecting to maintain one's connection with all aspects of creation, particularly the guidance of spirit. Therefore, it is a return to the full flow of consciousness that determines the path to follow that is best for all. The spirit world is the ultimate guide for all that happens and is experienced. It is the challenge of all people to discern the most healing path that is promoted by the spiritual world.

Basic Native ethics include:

1. Non-interference in any other individual's personal path of learning (a deeply ingrained attitude that is absolutely adhered to, even under great stress and duress)

2. Anger must not be shown

3. Praise and gratitude are respected

4. Carefully considering all aspects of action before responding to challenges

5. Choosing the right time to speak and act

Similarly, Rupert Ross observes, it is virtually unheard of for one Native person to tell another what to do or to criticize what they have done. This applies even to situations of violence and abuse between people. Even in discussing the most negative behaviors, their focus is on very gently suggesting how a person can do better even after grossly antisocial behaviors, such as getting drunk, beating up or even raping, injuring or killing another person.

Ross cogently argues that the attitudes evolving from these Native ways have profoundly deep effects on shaping the lives of their people. First and foremost, people are left to rely largely on their feelings and intuitive senses of rightness and wrongness in any and all situations – and particularly in new and unknown circumstances. As hunter gatherers, foraging in in new territories and in ever-changing environments, having their wholistic awarenesses keenly tuned from their lifetimes of always having to rely on themselves to decide what to do was a tremendous advantage.

At even more basic levels, the guiding principles of Native society "…include respect for the natural sphere, an emphasis upon careful and sensitive consensus-building, a focus upon a rehabilitative and preventative response to social turmoil and an insistence upon family and community responsibility for the mental, emotional, spiritual and physical health of each member." This is in stark contrast to white man's rules which emphasize punitive punishments for misbehaviors, which are seen as sinful. Perhaps as important as the above are the Native social rules and teachings that place very high values and priorities on honoring one's personal, intimate interconnections with environment and Spirit. When each of us, individually and collectively, is an integral part of the world, it is our responsibility to be the best little pixel we can be on the big screen.

The above attitudes and rules are in stark contrast to white man's rules. The white man emphasizes parental responsibility and control over his children, under rigid commandments that are to be obeyed throughout life without question. In adulthood, punitive punishments are set in place for serious misbehaviors, which are seen as sinful – both during life and in the hereafter. The white man sees himself as his brother's keeper and feels responsible for recommending better actions and correcting transgressions against social rules. Misbehaviors deserve punishment, and the courts are set up to determine whether lack of adherence to the rules of society merit the meting out of civil or criminal sanctions or punishments.

### Theodicy: The study of good and evil

The question of continued belief in Divine goodness in view of the existence of evil and the suffering experienced in our world has a whole branch of its own in the philosophy of religions. The focus of these studies are questions about how a God who is infinitely good could allow evil to exist. These questions are asked particularly regarding the Holocaust and countless other human experiences of mass murders and genocides, but clearly, they touch anyone who has experienced serious disappointments, mistreatments and traumas.

> *Would we still have heroes if we had no villains?*
> - Anonymous

Within our own lives, any one of us may be challenged when we are targets of the malevolent behaviors of others. It is all the worse when these injuries are parts of the perpetrators' self-seeking behaviors. This is particularly evident today, as there are increases in the accumulations of wealth in the hands of a few, at the callous expense

of the general population (McQuaig & Brooks, 2010). Have you suffered or known of others who experienced:
- Disappointments or serious financial strains or disasters when insurance companies delay or deny payments for medical problems or major property damages?
- Serious side effects of medications, where the drug companies' liabilities are limited by laws they have promoted through their influences on politicians and governments?
- Poor healthcare, despite the high costs of medical treatments?
- Loss of employment, without compensation, due to automation of jobs you used to do?
- Loss of employment, without compensation, after complaining about sexual harassment?
- Deterioration of your children's school systems due to insufficient funds, due to taxation that allows the rich to pay little or no taxes relative to their profits and incomes?

Ironically, the rich will die as well as the poor from the results of climate change and/or other evils generated by humans. They may have the means to stave off their deaths a bit longer than those with less resources, but they, too, will die in the end from the horrors they are perpetrating on this world.

Within some religious traditions there are those who hold religious beliefs that the faithful members of their tradition will ascend to heaven when the world is either all good or all evil. Wanting to ascend to heaven, but being doubtful the world will ever reach a point of being all good, numbers of these people are said to be working towards making the world all evil.

Some mystic traditions state that our planet is just one, typical world, in a universe full of both light and darkness. But gifted intuitives and some who have had near death and other spiritual experiences report that:
- Our universe has a stronger measure of darkness than many others.
- Our planet has a stronger mixture of light and darkness than many others.
- Those souls who choose to come to this planet agree to do so because this offers opportunities to learn more intense lessons and to better understand the differences and relationships between light and darkness, good and evil, forgetting unconditional love and remembering/ knowing unconditional love.

Without darkness, one wouldn't know the light as light. Gifted intuitives report that in most other universes, and in many places in our own universe, there may be just a whiff of darkness that suffices for this contrast; and there are also places where darkness or light strongly prevail, without the contrast. We have been either very brave or very foolhardy to choose to incarnate on this planet![33]

✦✦✦ My personal sense of Spiritual awareness is that we are all parts of the Infinite Source, gathering our experiences on this planet to bring back with us when we return from our journeys into denser realms of experience, where we distance our consciousness from the Infinite Source.

I sometimes speculate whether the Infinite Source itself might have gotten bored with knowing everything about everything. Could it be that All That Is therefore created beings who periodically forgot their connection to their own higher selves and to the Infinite Source, and worked their ways back into remembering their connection to Spirit? We would not know light as light in the same ways that we do when we contrast it with darkness that we have personally experienced. And the same applies to our connections with Spiritual light and with our experiences of traumas and darkness.

## WHAT IS YOUR SENSE OF YOUR CONNECTION WITH THE INFINITE SOURCE?

*Psychology disappears in the language of sheer facts and personality dynamics and structures. It also disappears in a reaction against the interior life as it chases into the world as a psychology of things. The secret of being psychological is to leave this Newtonian world altogether and speak from a place of intense sensation, impression, and reverie.*
- Thomas Moore

## 66. Spirit inspires every aspect of our existence

> *God is the mind that imagines physical reality.*
> *We are each like a cell in that mind.*
> - Peter Shepherd

We've considered our connections with Spirit within ourselves in various sections of this book, and in chapter 24 we lightly reviewed some of the possible meanings of life. Let's reconsider these issues again, in the light of having reviewed many more aspects of Spiritual awarenesses.

While every facet of our being is interlinked and intertwined with every other facet, Spirit is the most broad and deep of these. The modern Western world has largely overlooked, ignored and dismissed our personal Spiritual awarenesses, as well as the experienced participations of Spirit in our lives. Most of us have been raised in cultures where matters of Spirit have been fragmented into various religious perspectives and are segregated into activities within religious frameworks. From the prevailing, predominantly left hemisphere perspective of our world, spirituality is a matter of beliefs rather than a living reality.

Opening to personal Spiritual awarenesses requires that we connect our consciousness with Spiritual dimensions. We participate in these, whether we are conscious of them or not. Ignoring and forgetting our Spiritual awarenesses is a participation in the darkness that makes it possible, by contrast, to appreciate and understand the light. So, in actuality, those who live lives in darkness are also contributing to appreciations of the light.

Living in darkness and negativity leaves residues of negativity in our soul at the end of our physical lives. In Eastern traditions, this is called 'bad karma." Bad karma incurs a cosmic debt, which we can work off in future lives by suffering negativity ourselves, so that we understand the pain we have caused others. We can neutralize our bad karma by living positive lives, in which we offer love and caring to others and do not incur further negative karmic debts.

HSPs, by virtue of their greater sensitivities, often connect more readily to conscious Spiritual perceptions and participations in enhancing our connections and re-connections with the light. If you are an NHSP in a relationship with an HSP, you have the potential to connect with the Spiritual dimensions more clearly and strongly – either through vicarious appreciations of your HSP's Spiritual awarenesses or through opening to developing your own.

Here, too, as in other aspects of our being, our Spirituality is expressed in every wholistic level of our being.

- Treating your body with respect is an important foundation in your wholistic integrity. Many of us take our bodies for granted, assuming they will serve us adequately, regardless of how we treat them.

  - Eating food that has been grown in ways that are considerate to the plants and animals and to our local and planetary ecosystems that provide us with nourishment aligns our intentions and our Spiritual selves with the highest good for all.

  - Avoiding toxic chemicals contributes similarly to our respect for our bodies.

- Giving thanks for the levels of physical health that we enjoy will heighten our Spiritual awareness of our participation in the physical world. If we treat our own bodies with respect, we are more likely to be considerate of the physical health of other people and of all other life on our planet.
- Our emotions can heighten our Spiritual awareness.
  - When we feel happy, we can give thanks to The Infinite Source for our good fortunes and for the people and circumstances that help us feel good.
  - When we are unhappy, we can ask for Spiritual support to deal with whatever is weighing upon us and leading us to feel frustrated, angry or sad.
  - One of the most central experiences of Spirit is love. While amorous love is generally high on the list of HSP-HSPC relationships, spiritual love can be waaay stronger, deeper and more profoundly satisfying and healing in our lives.
- Our thoughts can connect us with Spirit.
  - Regular spiritual practices such as meditation and prayers enhance our participation in Spirit.
  - When we walk our daily paths, conscious of our Spiritual connections, with each of us being a ray of light from the Infinite Source, then each experience and each act strengthens our connections with Spirit.
  - Challenging and negative experiences can be addressed as invitations to bring more light into the world.
- Interactions with other people are invitations to share and enhance our Spiritual consciousness
  - Group celebrations can multiply our joyous connections with the wonderment of being alive.
  - Reaching out to others who are in need is not only a blessing to them but also an opportunity for ourselves to invite the presence and support of Spirit in our lives.*[34]
- Interactions with the environment are invitations to expand our Spiritual horizons.
  - Offering our support to environmental initiatives, both personal and financial, brings healing to all
  - Sending our healing wishes and energies to endangered individuals, species and to our entire planet is a blessings for all.

*WHAT SPIRITUAL AWARENESSES AND EXPERIENCES HAVE YOU HAD?*

*WHAT ARE ACTIONS, PRACTICES AND INITIATIVES YOU CAN PROMOTE TO BRING MORE SPIRITUAL CONNECTIONS AND AWARENESSES INTO YOUR LIFE?*

*WHAT ARE YOU DOING IN YOUR LIFE TO PARTICIPATE IN THE LIGHT RATHER THAN THE DARKNESS?*

## 67. Grief and trauma in the collective consciousness of humanity

*So many parts of ourselves we have pushed away come up in grief.
That is why grief has this enormity of potential for healing.*
- Stephen Levine

I believe that unresolved personal grief and trauma reactions of uncounted numbers of individuals on our planet have been accumulating over thousands of years, carried over from one life to another. These trauma residues may be expressed through the collective consciousness. Each individual contributes to the collective consciousness of humanity in diverse ways. Very directly, we share our thoughts and feelings with each other through our daily physical interactions, including individual conversations and other levels of verbal communications. We share our experiences and views with many others through social media, airwaves and cable media, news media and books.

There is also a collective consciousness that transcends physical communications through our sensory organs. We reviewed rigorous research confirming the existence of extrasensory perceptions, including telepathy, clairsentience, precognition and retrocognition, in Section VII. These individual intuitive awarenesses provide much broader and deeper avenues for participating in the collective consciousness of humanity.

The research and anecdotal evidence reviewed in this book provides a basis to suggest that just as each individual collects memories of similar experiences as categories of information in her or his memory, the same occurs in the collective consciousness of humanity. Countless people suffer active grief and trauma, and contribute their feelings of hurt, anger, guilt, and more to the collective consciousness. It appears likely that such unresolved feelings accumulate over time. As with individuals who have unresolved trauma and grief memories, the collective consciousness might respond with depression, anger, and with suicidal thoughts and behaviors.

There appears to be very suggestive evidence that humanity as a whole is suffering from a collective PTSD. Many of the problematic behaviors exhibited by humanity as a whole resemble those of individual people with unresolved grief and trauma reactions. Angers, violence and suicidal behaviors in particular are recurring issues we often see and hear about – reported very generously in the media. There are grossly unbalanced numbers of reports of violence (contrasted with reports of positive experiences) that are broadcasted and published in many of these media outlets.**[35]

Another confirmation of the presence of unresolved grief and trauma residues is evident in humanity's morbid interest in media reports of violent accidents, crimes, murders, wars and other mayhem. Until recently, I had not found a satisfying explanation for the morbid preferences of most people for items of violence and death in the media. I now believe this gruesome behavior may represent individual and collective ways of lessening some of the tensions and feelings from accumulated personal grief and trauma memories and feelings in many people's individual lives and in the collective consciousness as a whole. Sadly, however, our focus on violence and trauma in the media does not help us to clear our own trauma residues.

And our collective angers from our own traumas and grief reactions are expressed in discriminatory and persecutory behaviors towards vilified individuals and minorities, as well as in wars and genocides. Here again, I propose that people may be venting on 'others' many aspects of their individual and collective grief reactions and trauma residues that have been buried outside their conscious awareness.

> *Grief is the garden in which anger and hate and violence can grow.*
> - Michael Pritchard

When we avoid strong, buried feelings, they tend to fester and get triggered by other life circumstances, as we saw in the individual examples above. These responses are just as likely to manifest in the collective consciousness as they do in single participants/contributors to the burdens of feelings that are buried in the collective consciousness.

Behaviors common to individuals which suggest grief reactions that are exhibited by humanity as a collective include: many people feeling drained of energies, apathetic, too weak to deal with these serious demands and challenges, and avoidance of facing and dealing with underlying thoughts and feelings about humanity's many flirtations with extinction.**[36]

In cases of grief caused by major natural disasters, outbreaks of illnesses and wars, it is often the case that the best thing survivors can do at the time of the original traumas is to bury their feelings and move on. This gives them their best chance for survival, as they are then not burdened or incapacitated by their conscious awarenesses of grief. We can be certain that numerous experiences of losses with unresolved grief have occurred over the many thousands of years of human life on this planet. We can be equally certain that understandings and resources to deal with these feelings were unknown and/or unavailable in the past.

Grief that is unexpressed and never cleared to the point of resolution is often triggered in individual people later on in their lives. Unresolved grief appears likely to be contributing to the current day drift of humanity towards self-destruction and collective suicide. Aspects of accumulated individual grief that may be expressed through the collective consciousness may explain the numerous self-created and self-perpetuating challenges that threaten the survival of humanity and of most other living beings on our planet. These challenges include:

– Global climate change

- Overpopulation
- Major pollutions of our air, land and waters
- Increasing ocean acidity and de-oxygenation – contributing to extinctions of fish, whales and other ocean life
- Numerous other extinctions, including vitally important species ETC
- Depletion of numerous resources essential for life, as in erosion and loss of irreplaceable topsoil
- World hunger and starvation
- Increasing local, national, international and global social dysfunctions
- Social and religious conflicts, ongoing wars and impending conflicts over limited resources
- Major investments in wars at the expense of education, healthcare and social services
- Nuclear disasters – civilian and military

– The reluctance of the majority of people to consider that most or all of humanity could be dead within 100-200 years, or perhaps even sooner

Precipitating events of a PTSD may involve the death of someone close; witnessing someone being injured or killed in an accident or act of war; or experiencing secondary trauma through hearing the reports of severe traumas of other people (as in psychotherapists, first responders, emergency room personnel, and court stenographers). We may also mourn the loss of some aspect of our own body functions or health.

The behaviors seen in PTSD and grief reactions have broad overlaps.
- Cognitive and emotional intrusions ('flashbacks' to images and feelings of the trauma or grief)
- Avoidance of situations that trigger memories of the trauma or grief
- Negative alterations in cognitions and mood (anxieties, depression and suicidal thinking and suicidal behaviors)
- Alterations in arousal and reactivity (anger, temper outbursts, insomnia, nightmares)
- Everyday functioning is impaired

These are reactions described and exhibited by many people when they discuss their thoughts and feelings about their countries and their nations' relationships with other countries. The same applies for people of just about every ethnic group, relative to other ethnic groups they particularly disparage. There is hardly a nation or ethnic group I know of that does not do this.

And politicians capitalize on this, stirring traditional prejudices and hatreds, rooted in traumas, to justify going to war, and this conveniently distracts people from political ineptitudes in dealing with economic and social issues at home.

This brings to mind an apocryphal quote:

> *Beware the leader who bangs the drums of war in order to whip the citizenry into a patriotic fervor, for patriotism is indeed a double-edged sword. It both emboldens the blood, just as it narrows the mind...*
>
> *And when the drums of war have reached a fever pitch and the blood boils with hate and the mind has closed, the leader will have no need in seizing the rights of the citizenry. Rather, the citizenry, infused with fear and blinded with patriotism, will offer up all of their rights unto the leader, and gladly so.*
>
> *How do I know?*
>
> *For this is what I have done.*
> *And I am Caesar.*
> - Source unknown

### Grief and trauma in the collective consciousness of our planet

I hope we've reached a point in these discussions where I can stretch your belief systems and challenge your disbeliefs a bit further. This is vitally important to understanding the state of the world and our places in it today.

The rate of extinctions on our planet has been escalating dramatically over the past century. In the previous 500 years, the number of extinctions were about 5 species in a year. Today, it is estimated that species are disappearing somewhere between 1,000 and 10,000 faster than that. At this rate, between a third and half the species living today could be gone in another 30 years.

There were five previous mass extinctions, due to shifts in climate from volcanoes, asteroids hitting the planet and other natural causes. Our current mass extinction is being caused by human pollution, over-fishing, destroying natural habitats, and worst of all, by global warming. This process is very likely to gain momentum because when one species goes extinct, others will follow because of the interlinking of ecosystems that make one species depend on others for their survival.

And again, contrary to conventional human disbeliefs, members of other species are conscious beings. This includes animals, plants, insects, bacteria, yeasts, algae and all other living organisms. And each member of each species participates in the collective consciousness of that species. And each species is collectively aware of other species and participates in a planetary, interspecies collective consciousness.

And they are dealing with the traumas of disruptions of their habitats, and grieving the losses of members of their species, as well as the losses of other species with whom they interacted over many thousands of years. They are also suffering anticipatory grief over their own extinctions.

Gaia, herself, has grieved the decline of life that she supported into existence and nurtured for many hundreds of thousands of years. Gaia and the other planets in our solar system, and our sun as well, have residues of trauma from the fragmenting of the planet that used to live between Mars and Jupiter, which left the asteroid belt we know today.

You are probably asking, and rightly so, "How can anyone make such far-reaching claims regarding individual and collective consciousness of other living beings?" "And of planets and suns???" And you can probably guess that my answer is that these are the observations and reports of numbers of highly intuitive people who are able to connect with other species and intelligent beings through their gnowing awarenesses. And they are validating each others' impressions that I summarized above.

But not all is doom and gloom. There is a growing acceptance that the major extinction we are experiencing has some positive aspects to it. The ecosystem we have on Gaia today is one that guarantees interspecies conflicts and repeated traumas. The fact that so many species have to kill and eat other species guarantees continual repetitions of traumas. This is not a necessary fact of life. It is reported that there are many worlds in this universe where food and energies for life are acquired as most plants do it, without having to kill other organisms for their nourishment. It is predicted that the mass extinction underway is going to be a very thorough one. It will eliminate all but a few species who can survive in a sulfurous atmosphere. And new forms of life will eventually evolve and flourish in that atmosphere. They and Gaia will have learned well the lessons of our current ecosystem, so they can avoid ongoing traumas in the collective consciousness from the devouring of one species by another.

And the spirits of the many beings who are dying in this mass extinction will transition to Spirit lives, where they can recover from individual and collective traumas. Alternatively, they may carry their traumas with them into their lives on other planets throughout the universe. There, they will have further opportunities to learn and grow wiser, individually and collectively.

*In summary:*
People around the world are behaving in ways that suggest they are suffering from a chronic, long-standing collective PTSD. I have found no other theory to explain why humanity is being so very creative, in so many ways, in threatening the continuation of all life on our planet as we know it today.

## 68. Offering healing for the collective trauma and suicidality of humanity

> *Modern civilization can survive only if it educates the heart, which is the source of wisdom, for modern man is now far too clever to survive without wisdom.*
> - E. F. Schumacher

Just as we can send healing to a single individual, it is possible to send healing to the entire human race. There is every reason to believe we can reduce the intensity of the collective human trauma that has accumulated over countless generations.

Ordinarily, healing is sent to an individual in need of help for issues of physical and/or psychological health. Healing is also sent for people's relationships with their partner, spouse, or another family member, as well as for an entire family. Healing may also be sent to groups of people who are in danger, as in passengers on an endangered boat, a community threatened by fire or other natural disaster, or a group of people threatened by war. As reported in the healing therapy and prayer traditions, there appear to be no limits to the power of prayer to help any numbers of people. Therefore, there would seem to be no reason that intentional healing or prayers would not be effective when sent to the entire human population of our planet.

There also appear to be no limits to the distances over which intentional, psychic influences can be projected. Research confirms that healing from a distance, also called 'absent healing,' can be effective in addressing individual and group problems of people and other living beings who are many miles away. As we saw in chapters 54 and 55, research confirms effects of distant healing and of intents for other effects in the physical world, demonstrated in well-designed research studies.

Proxy healing (also called surrogate healing) is a variant of distant healing that is commonly used in Energy Psychology and in other healing methods, such as Kinesiology and Healing Touch. When a person in need is not present in the therapist's office, a proxy person may be used as a focus for projecting the healing. The intent during this healing process is held for healing of the absent person who is in need of the healing.

Numerous anecdotal reports attest to successful results with proxy healing. The only systematic review of proxy healings I've found describes a collected series of 100 reports of individual proxy healings. David Feinstein (2013), found that proxy healing was successful in every reported case. While I would speculate that this unusually high rate of positive results involves selective reporting of successful cases,**[37] the fact remains that this is a substantial series of documented successes with proxy healing.

We must be cautious, however, in offering distant healing or proxy healings when they have not been requested by the intended recipients. Many people who are new to healing through conscious projection of healing intents are eager to promote more healing in the world in ways they believe could be helpful. They think that sending the intent that others should "Be more loving" or "Be more caring" or "Be more considerate and generous to others" will promote improvements in the world. Many believe that healing comes from a higher power and wish to share with others what feels healing to themselves in these ways, such as "May Christ's love be accepted by all" or "May the devil be driven out of those who behave in evil ways." Further along on the spectrum of such beliefs are those who send out prayers for the rapid progress to Armageddon and the end of the world, so that they and other 'True Believers' will ascend to heaven. Countless other variations on these approaches are promoted by various religious and healing groups.

*Do not change your beliefs because you want other people to change theirs. Change your beliefs because your new beliefs announce more accurately who you are.*

*Yet even as you change, do not be surprised if other people change, and if the world around you changes. For the change in you will act as a catalyst in producing change in others.*
- Neale Donald Walsch (1997)

From perspectives of those who might benefit from healing, there may be reasons behind the illness, pains, angers, and negative behaviors. It is quite common for people to find that their illnesses bring them deep lessons – which are a different form of healing. Therefore, it's possible that healers who are sending healing, however well-meaning, could be interfering with or even blocking these important life lessons.

A way to send healing that is in greater integrity is to hold an intent that is respectful of the independence of the healee to choose whether to accept the healing or not. One offers healing with the intent that it should be "for the highest good of the healee and for the highest good of all." This is an acknowledgement that neither the healer/ therapist nor the healee/client may know what is ultimately for the best of the client in the long run.

In offering healing for the collective consciousness, we may simply invoke an intent, such as the following one, after completion of a healing for oneself. Similarly, this could be done when a therapist is providing healing to an individual – in which case either or both participants in this healing could recite the following invocation, silently or out loud:

If it is for my highest good and the highest good of all

I / We invite anyone and everyone

Anywhere and everywhere

Anywhen and everywhen

Who is ready to [accept this healing/ clear their pain and trauma issue(s)/ etc.] with [me/ us] to do so.**[38]

And I / We invite you to pay this forward when you offer healings to others

In this way we open doorways of healing for others to resonate with – as and when they are ready to do so. And we are not pushing our views or healing wishes upon anyone. We are just inviting them to participate in the healing wishes/ intentions/ energies/ Spiritual healing spaces that we are generating.

Research confirms that In addition to helping individuals, distant healing has been effective in influencing groups of cells and organisms (Braud 1989; Nash 1982; 1984). This supports the likelihood of benefits of proxy healing for problems in the collective unconscious.

A decrease in the intensity of the collective trauma and grief memories could decrease the intensity of collective residual hurts, angers, depression and suicidality that have accumulated over uncounted generations, during the entire existence of the human species and of other living beings.

*Everyone has something they can do. Whatever means you
have to make the world a better place, you need to do it.
Even if we won't see the fruits of this in our lifetime, start now.*
- Daniel Goleman

Proxy healing through inviting the enhancement of positive feelings and thoughts in the collective consciousness may also alleviate some of the selfish human behaviors that are contributing to the brutal, negative behaviors of humans – which are, in turn, creating further grief in many beings on this planet.

> *There is an important link between deep change at the personal level and deep change at the organizational level. To make deep, personal change is to develop a new paradigm, a new self, one that is more effectively aligned with today's realities. This can occur only if we are willing to journey into unknown territory and confront the wicked problems we encounter. This journey does not follow the assumptions of rational planning. The objective may not be clear and the path is not paved with familiar procedures. This tortuous journey requires that we leave our comfort zone and step outside our normal roles. In doing so, we learn the paradoxical lesson that we can change the world only by changing ourselves. This is not just a cute abstraction; it is an elusive key to effective performance in all aspects of life.*
> - Robert Quinn

### Suggestions for offering healing for the collective planetary consciousness

In addition to offering proxy healing to the human collective consciousness, we can also extend our proxy healing to those of other species whom we are genociding. The bees, the polar bears, and fish in the seas whose entire populations are being fished out of existence; the trees in the forests and other plants that are being cleared for wood and to open up land for more human homes, or for grazing animals to supply hamburgers for fast food chains; all these living beings and countless others, too, suffer individual and collective traumas that cry out for releasing and healing.

Proxy healing for humans, animals and plants that are dying in distress could alleviate some of the collective grief that continues to accumulate in the collective consciousness of all living beings. This could help them have a more peaceful and healing transition out of this life.

Increasing numbers of people are sensing we may be too late to avert the human mass extinction that appears already to be well on its way on our planet. Interestingly, Helen Wambach (1978), who explored past life memories in group hypnotic regressions,*[39] also explored future life memories (Snow, 1993). She found considerable similarities and overlaps among the future life reports of her subjects. While these are interesting, they are obviously difficult to assess when predictions are made for the distant future. Most troubling in Wambach's series, however, is that only about five percent of her hypnotic subjects were able to identify lives in the years 2100-2200, suggesting the possibility of a catastrophic decrease in the planetary human population.

Even if it should be true that we are facing a drastic decrease in population in the coming century, we may yet be helpful to many souls through clearing their individual and collective PTSDs before they leave their current lives for unknown futures. We may likewise be able to send our healing to those who have transitioned into spirit lives, carrying trauma with them from the multiple disasters humanity has been and continues to be generating.

And if we are indeed too late to save most or even all of the life on our planet as we know it today, we may console ourselves in some measure by recalling that Gaia has survived five earlier major extinctions. She can survive this one, too. And perhaps our proxy healings will help her and those creatures that evolve next, hopefully to live their lives in more healing ways in the spaces we vacate. And hopefully, as well, these will survive with healing lessons learned through the collective consciousness of all life on our planet, including Gaia herself.

And again we must keep in mind that members of other species are conscious beings. This includes animals, plants, insects, bacteria, yeasts, algae and all other living organisms. And each member of each species participates in the collective consciousness of that species. And each species is collectively aware of other species and participates in a planetary collective consciousness. And other species reincarnate just as humans do. Only they remember doing so, and therefore also hold awarenesses of having further chances to live satisfying lives in the future, although their current lives may be fraught and traumatic. They are also suffering anticipatory grief over possible deaths and extinctions of individuals and of whole species.

Gaia, herself, has grieved the decline of life that she supported into existence and nurtured for many hundreds of thousands of years. Gaia and the other planets in our solar system, and our sun as well, also have trauma residues from the fragmenting of the planet that used to live between Mars and Jupiter, which left our asteroid belt.

You are probably rightly asking, "How can anyone make such claims regarding individual and collective consciousness of other living beings? And of planets and suns???" And you can probably guess that my answer is that these are observations of highly intuitive people who can connect with other species and intelligent beings throughout the universe through their growing awarenesses. And they are validating each others' impressions, although their individual reports contain only partial truths because they are common in diverse intuitive impressions.

## WHAT WARNINGS AND LESSONS WOULD YOU PROPOSE TO INCLUDE IN OUR COLLECTIVE LEGACY?

> *...Here in birth the preamble of life on earth there is the immutable provision that creation is not a program in conformity but rather is committed to diversity and to an increase through diversity of new and more and more options and revelations of areas of creation to swell the great flow of becoming to which the stars, the nebulae and the foam and spray of the Milky Way bear witness and quicken the sense of unclaimed realities beyond.*
> — Sir Laurens van der Post

You might be asking what these last few chapters have to do with HSPs. Due to their greater emotional and intuitive sensitivities, HSPS are more often aware of the impending planetary disasters than NHSPs. Many HSPs feel the distresses, pains and grief of those humans and other species who are leaving this planet, due to human depredations on this planet. At the same time, HSPCs who are NHSPs are also more likely to become aware, through their relationships with their HSPs, of these perils and impending disasters of our times.

## SECTION IX. Summary

*Be the change you want to see in the world.*
*Nobody else can do it for you.*
*We are now recruiting.*
*Perhaps you will join us,*
*Or already have.*
*All are welcome!*
*The door is open ...*
*        - Brian Piergrossi*

Being an HSP can be a blessing. Having greater sensitivities in one's body awarenesses (including both inner- and outer-world senses), emotions, relationships, intuitions and Spiritual awarenesses opens many doorways to experiencing life more deeply and fully.

Being an HSP can also be a challenge and a burden. You may feel stressed by overloads in any of your areas of sensitivity.

Relationships, in particular, can often bring out the best and the worst of these sensitivities, for both participants in the relationships.

Being an HSPC can feel like a privilege and a blessing, opening you to new ways of perceiving, experiencing and interacting with your outer and inner worlds. Similarly, you may find this relationship enormously challenging – both in getting along with your HSP and in developing more sensitivities yourself.

### *So, again, what's it all about?*

*I INVITE YOU TO CONSIDER YOUR OWN ANSWERS TO THIS QUESTION*

*A GOOD WAY TO APPROACH THIS MIGHT BE TO TAKE A VISUAL STROLL THROUGH THE TABLE OF CONTENTS OF THIS BOOK.*

*CONSIDER HOW THE VIEWS AND APPROACHES DETAILED IN EACH SECTION MIGHT CONTRIBUTE TO YOUR PERCEPTIONS, OPINIONS AND UNDERSTANDINGS ABOUT:*

*WHO YOU ARE*

*HOW YOU RELATE TO AND THROUGH YOUR BODY, EMOTIONS, MIND, RELATIONSHIPS AND SPIRIT*

*WHY YOU'RE HERE, IN THIS TROUBLED, CHALLENGING WORLD NOW*

*WHAT IS THIS WORLD ALL ABOUT, FROM YOUR PERSPECTIVE?*

My understanding of life, the universe and everything is that each of us is on this earth for personal, wholistic Spiritual lessons, as well as for interpersonal and collective consciousness lessons. Some of these lessons are pleasant, while others are not. Whichever we are experiencing are grist for our Spiritual mill. We learn at least as much from our negative experiences and errors as we learn from our positive experiences and successes.

Often, we learn more from the negative ones, because they can resonate with similar experiences earlier in this life or in past lives, inviting us to clear the similar trauma residues. In many cases, it appears that the earlier traumas in our current and past lives may actually have predisposed us to experience similar ones in our current life, or even to create them.

A frequent question I'm asked is, "Do our life lessons ever end?" The best answer I've found is from Richard Bach.

*Here is a test to find whether your mission on earth is finished:*
*If you're alive, it isn't.*

And from what people have reported from near death experiences, deathbed, Spirit and other Spiritual communications, we can anticipate even deeper lessons to continue after physical death.

Should we indeed end up participating in another extinction on our planet, in the long term our experiences will be enormously helpful lessons, not only to ourselves, but to others throughout our universe. And this extinction will be a deep lesson to ourselves and to others in some of the ways we might choose not to behave selfishly and destructively - towards ourselves and others.

## Looking and moving forward, re HSP issues

No one knows for certain about whether we are past the point of no return on our way to extinction. We hope and offer our energies towards avoiding this. What we do know is that we are living with various life challenges, on every level of our being.

If you are seeking help to deal with HSP or HSPC issues, I encourage you, dear reader, to trust that you will find the healings you want and need through the methods described in this book and/or in other resources referenced in the endnotes. Should you feel the need for counselling or therapy, seek out teachers and caregivers who are recommended by people you trust.

I welcome your sharings about your HSP and HSPC experiences, and feedback on your experiences with these recommended approaches that have helped countless people in my several decades of practice – myself included.

And I wish you good wholistic healings.

# SECTION X. My Journey in Writing this Book

*To travel is to take a journey into yourself.*
*- Danny Kaye*

My journey of writing this book has taken two years. They have been eventful years that included clearing masses of trauma memories and feelings from the earliest years of my life – with the strong motivation of healing my partially paralyzed vocal cord.

This has indeed been a journey into myself in numerous ways. I've used my own methods, detailed in this book, with the additional help of numbers of healers and complementary/alternative therapists.

As I wrote explanations for each aspect of the approaches I've reviewed, I considered how each was relevant to my journey. This thoroughly validated my convictions that it is difficult to begin to understand who I am and how I got to be where I am when I'm analyzing any specific part my journey – in isolation from my whole being.

This is far more complex than is conceptualized or taught in most Western healthcare programs. And the neuroplastic blindnesses of most conventional teachers, courses and training programs in which I've participated, and in the countless books I've read, are so completely entrenched that I hesitate to hope this book will be read by many people outside the HSP and complementary/ alternative therapies communities.

Despite these challenges, I believe that there are enough open-minded people who will find enormous benefits from exploring the self-help and therapist-guided approaches so that this book will find a home on the shelves of many happy explorers in the wholistic realms of healing.

### *Appreciations*

My journey through life has been marked by times when I felt challenged in various ways and sought the help of many varieties of caregivers in the community of conventional and complementary alternative therapies. Most recently, many of my issues have been in relation to awakening and adjusting to being an HSP.

There were numerous times when I had different types of psychotherapy at various ages and stages of my life, from my teen years to the present. These helped me achieve personal insights, as well as to understand much more deeply how psychotherapy can be helpful. I resonated particularly with Transactional Analysis, Gestalt Therapy (two-chair work). Muscle Testing and several types of Energy Psychology.

I give special thanks to the following people in the healing community who have personally helped me enormously on my wholistic healing journey in recent years:

**Judith Landau, MD**, helped me through marital, family constellation, and intuitive insights and therapies.

> Judith Landau, MD, DPM, LMFT, CFLE, CIP, CAI, CRS, President and CEO of Linking Human Systems, LLC, and ARISE® Network, and President of LINC Foundation, Inc., is a child, family and community neuropsychiatrist. She has specialized in mental health, trauma, addiction and co-occurring disorders for 40+ years, facilitating resilience and healing for individuals, families and communities through collaborative care. She developed the Evidence-Based, Best Practice Transitional Family Therapy (TFT); the first integrative family systems model; Invitational Intervention® ARISE® Comprehensive Care; LINC Community Resilience; and LIFE (LINK Individual Empowerment), all based on TFT. She is a Senior Fulbright Fellow and an Isangoma or traditional African healer and a member of 4 Winds Indigenous Healers, committed to bridging traditional wisdom and western science.

**Wendy Hurwitz, MD** has been of tremendous support in my wholistic healing journey, with uniquely insightful and wonderfully helpful energetic assessments over the phone.

A graduate of Yale School of Medicine, Dr. Hurwitz is a nationally recognized expert on stress. A former medical researcher for ABC News, Dr. Hurwitz is an expert in two fields: Mind/Body Medicine and Energy Medicine. She has used energetic assessments for over two decades in her own work with clients. Based in New York City, Dr. Hurwitz offers consultations in person and by phone.

Dr. Hurwitz helps organizations and individuals achieve peak performance by enhancing vitality and welness. She provides individual energetic assessments, personal consultation, training, lectures, seminars, and workshops. Dr. Hurwitz has provided training for AT&T, Unilever, Lowe Worldwide, the FDNY, and has been an invited guest speaker at the United Nations.

**Andrea Rose**, provided intuitive awareness concerning my health and relationships.

Through higher sense perception of sight, felling, hearing, smelling, tasting, and knowing; I am aware of the human energy field (aura) which contains the thoughts, feelings, emotions and experiences of others, and the universal energy field (life energy) which is intelligence at the heart of creation surrounding and penetrating everything. Being able to subtly perceive in such a ways helps me to develop compassion, understand- ing and a greater connection with others and the sacredness of life. In order to remain balanced with the different frequencies found through artificial energy (electromagnetic radiation) and natural human energetic residue (mental, emotional, and physical, and relational; I use various methods such as meditation, yoga, biodynamic craniosa- cral therapy, flower essences, sound healing and forms of energy therapy for myself as well as for others. This allows me to perceive, resonate and regulate my energy in order to utilize it for self healing and to support others in their own inner healing creat- ing greater health, growth and change.

**Michael Dragoman, DC**, helped with spinal manipulations and laser therapy for my vocal cord and voice issues.

Celebrating 25 years of chiropractic practice and over 15 years of acupuncture experience. Winner of two research awards for outstanding contributions to the field of chiropractic from the Canadian Memorial Chiropractic College in 1987 and 1988, and recognition from the RAND Corporation for his research contributions in 1995. Graduate 2013 of the course in Biological Medicine taught by the renowned Dr. Thomas Rau, founder of the ParaCelsus Clinic in Switzerland. Biological Medicine aims to restore health and well-being using principles of natural healing.

**Harry Kalajian,** an intuitive healer, for insights and bioenergy therapy for my voice and lungs. Harry writes:

I work with my inner guidance that points out the areas that need to be healed. Finding energy that is stuck in the body causing pain and replacing it with a Loving and freeing energy using touch and sound.

***Jim Mc Aninch*** and ***Tom Greenhalgh,*** work with First Responders and other caregivers who have suffered serious psychological traumas, helping with evidence-based Thought Field Therapy (TFT) and healing. Jim and Tom helped me address the partial paralysis of my vocal cord. I immediately experienced the sensations of a strong healing, with modest physical heaviness and tiredness that lasted several days. Over the following several weeks, for the first time in my life, my memories opened to specific experiences in the years of abuse I had experienced during my early childhood. Although not within their conscious intention in offering their healing, this was of enormous help to me in clearing my trauma, using Energy Psychology methods, on deeper levels than I had achieved over several previous years. Here is how they explain their approaches:

> We have developed an assessment and treatment method known as FAST-AIDE®. This method combines a variety of energy modalities and concepts with both human and digital assessment methods to provide psychological and often physical relief from emotional life events.
>
> FAST-AIDE® has been used primarily with Public Safety Personnel, Military Veterans, those challenged by Addictions, and in the world of Crisis Intervention. A key component is the removal of the need to talk about the challenge the client faces, a major component of many traditional treatment methods. The option to talk about their challenges is still available to clients if they would like to do so. This model has recently been used and tested in a residential Drug and Alcohol Treatment Center with hundreds of clients using the model and reporting significant and lasting results after only a single session.

***Barbara Stone, PhD, LISW***, for help in clearing negative energies and entities. Barbara writes:

> Many HSPs may sense and be influenced by energies, some of which are not helpful, from realms beyond our ordinary senses. They may be affected by the presence of earthbound spirits that have not yet crossed into the Light and by various other detrimental energetic interference patterns from other dimensions. Barbara Stone's Soul Detective protocols identify the multiple origins of these problems and treat each contributing factor with a win-win solution for transforming the invasive energy as well as healing the client so the results will last.

***LeRoy Malouf*** has taught me to let go of residues of negative experiences and of attachments to outcomes of positive and negative expectations and anxieties.

> The Energetic Well Being Process (EWBP©) was created by LeRoy Malouf to unearth and remove energetic root causes of acute and chronic symptoms and issues that interfere with day-to-day life, such as back pain, headaches, digestive issues, allergies, depression, stress, relationship difficulties, work-related challenges and ADHD, just to name a few problems we help people to clear.
>
> LeRoy assists you in becoming the best version of yourself to create and support a meaningful life, filled with joy, balance and Energetic Well Being.

Through higher sense perception of sight, felling, hearing, smelling, tasting, and knowing; I am aware of the human energy field (aura) which contains the thoughts, feelings, emotions and experiences of others, and the universal energy field (life energy) which is intelligence at the heart of creation surrounding and penetrating everything. Being able to subtly perceive in such a ways helps me to develop compassion, understanding and a greater connection with others and the sacredness of life. In order to remain balanced with the different frequencies found through artificial energy (electromagnetic radiation) and natural human energetic residue (mental, emotional, physical, and relational) I use various methods such as meditation, yoga, flower essences, sound healing and forms of energy therapy for myself as well as for others. This allows me to perceive, resonate and regulate my energy in order to utilize it for self healing and to support others in their own inner healing creating greater health, growth and change.

*And if it is for my highest good and the highest good of all,*

*I / We invite anyone and everyone*

*Anywhere and everywhere*

*Anywhen and everywhen*

*Who is ready to accept this healing with me to do so.*

*And I / We invite you to pay this forward when you offer healings to others*

# ENDNOTES

## Abbreviations and notations
1. See details for developing your PPSH in ch 2.

## Introduction
1. Indeed, this was not a good thing happening! It was the start of the Yom Kippur War, with Israel responding to attacks from Egypt in the Sinai and from Syria in the Golan Heights.
2. Benor, 2009; 2002; 2004; 2005; 2006.
3. More on TWR/WHEE in ch. 29.

   a. Healing Research: ETC. Volume 1, (Popular Edition), Spiritual Healing: Scientific Validation of a Healing Revolution, Bellmawr, NJ: Wholistic Healing Publications, 2nd Edition (2009). The Popular Edition eBook discusses what spiritual healers say they do and how they believe it works, with a thorough but light review of the research literature. The Professional Supplement provides a much more detailed annotated bibliography of the research, including statistical analyses. https://danielbenor.com/product/ebook-healing-research-vol-i-pop-ed-spiritual-healing/

   b. Healing Research: ETC. Volume 1, (Professional Supplement), Spiritual Heal-ing: Scientific Validation of a Healing Revolution, Orig. Southfield, MI, 2001, Vision Publications. Now owned by Wholistic Healing Publications, Bellmawr, NJ. The Professional Supplement eBook provides a much more detailed annotated bibliography of the research, including statistical analyses. https://danielbenor.com/product/ebook-healing-research-vol-i-professional-supplement-to-Chapters-4-5/

   c. Benor, Daniel J. Healing Research, Volume 2: (Professional edition) Consciousness, Bioenergy and Healing Bellmawr, NJ, 2004, Wholistic Healing Publications. This eBook discusses complementary/ alternative medicine from a wholistic perspective, addressing body, emotions, mind, relationships and spirit. It considers ways in which problems develop in each of these areas and diverse approaches for dealing with them. 1500+ references https://danielbenor.com/product/ebook-healing-research-vol-ii-pop-ed-how-can-i-heal-what-hurts/

   d. Benor, Daniel J. Healing Research, Volume 2: (Popular edition), How Can I Heal What Hurts? Wholistic Healing and Bioenergies, Bellmawr, NJ, 2005, Wholistic Healing Publications This eBook is a lighter version of the Professional Edition, written for a lay audience, with fewer references but with 100 pp. discussing methods for self-healing. https://danielbenor.com/product/ebook-healing-research-vol-ii-pop-ed-how-can-i-heal-what-hurts/

   e. Benor, Daniel J. Healing Research, V. 3, Personal Spirituality: Science, Spirit and the Eternal Soul, Bellmawr, NJ, 2006, Wholistic Healing Publications. This eBook reviews research suggesting there is reason to believe in survival of a spirit after physical death. https://danielbenor.com/product/ebook-healing-research-vol-iii-personal-spirituality/

## SECTION I. Foundational introduction
1. Benor, 2001; 2002; 2004; 2005; 2006; 2009
2. Healing in this use of the word is discussed in, ch. 54.
3. You will find detailed discussions of spiritual awarenesses in Sections VII and VIII
4. Energy Psychology (EP) is a family of approaches involving tapping on the body while focusing your mind on your problems in various ways. Details in ch. 29.
5. See fuller discussion of wholistic healing http://www.ijhc.org/variations-on-the-theme-of-healing/
6. See ch. 29 for more on TWR/WHEE.
7. For Energy Psychology (EP) methods see The Association for Comprehensive Energy Psychology (ACEP) http://www.energypsych.org/ and brief summaries in ch. 15.
8. More on meta-anxieties in ch. 6.
9. Other authors have been helpful in expanding on HSP awarenesses, and in contributing to making HSPs feel more comfortable, functional and safe in a world they often find unsettling

and challenging:
- Elaine Aron, PhD, (1996; 2000; 2006; 2010) has been the leading light in identifying, observing, researching and helping HSPs. Her pioneering books cover very broad aspects of HSP awarenesses and ways of dealing with HSP issues in ourselves and in our relationships.
- Ted Zeff, PhD (2004; 2007; 2010; 2013; 2015) has written an outstanding series of books on ways to survive and thrive in a world that often sees the HSP as different but doesn't recognize that 'different' isn't something bad or a sign of weakness, emotional instability or mental derangement. In each of his books, he presents an excellent, broad spectrum of practical suggestions for dealing with HSP stresses and challenges.
- Jamie Williamson (2014) sensitively details what HSP children are like, with some suggestions for helping them.
- Barrie Jaeger (2004) explores varieties of ways that HSPs can adapt in the workplace.
10. See details of building your PPSH in ch. 28.
11. See details for creating an internal, personal place of peace and safety and healing (PPSH) in ch. 28.
12. Lazarou, Pomeranz & Corey, 1998; Starfield, 2000; Thomas, Cohen, et al., 2007
13. The true figures on medical causes of death may be considerably higher than is commonly appreciated. Gotzsche (2013) observes that death certificates assign an International Classification of Disease (ICD) code for the cause of death. Causes of death not assigned an ICD code, including many medically caused problems like human and medical system errors, are not identified.

## SECTION II. Understanding the HSP and HSPC: explanatory frameworks

1. Aron, 1996; 2000; 2006; 2010.
2. Zeff, 2004; 2007; 2010; 2013; 2015
3. Benor, 2001; 2002; 2006
4. Intuitive and spiritual awarenesses are discussed in greater detail in Sections VII and VIII.
5. More on this below, under Spirit
6. See more on Energy Medicine in ch. 53-55.
7. More on TWR/WHEE in ch. 29 and in Benor, 2009.
8. More on this in ch. 25, Emotions, overwhelm.
9. See Alexander (2012) and Benedict (Web ref.) for wonderful descriptions of the richness of communications during near death experiences.
10. There are numbers of medical doctors who brilliantly address the human aspects of their professions. Among my favorites are Bernie Siegel, Allan Hamilton, and Samuel Shem.
11. More on intuition earlier in this section in the discussion on emotional/ energetic resonations; below on the Spirit aspect of wholistic healing; and in Section VII on Understanding intuitive perceptions.
12. Detailed in Section IV.
13. More details on de-stressing in ch. 23, HSPs, their HSPCs and other family members, and Section V. Supports for the HSP and HSPC: resources and therapies.
14. The most common psychological emergency is for suicidal thoughts and feelings.
15. Goldstein, et al., 2012; HeadCase, web ref.
16. Much more on how we form our beliefs and change them – or not – in later Chapters of this Section.
17. More on maintaining and changing our beliefs in ch. 10 on neuroplasticity.
18. For more on bullying see ch. 15.
19. More on our relationships with the environment in this Chapter, below.
20. More on personal Spiritual awareness/ Gnowing in ch. 53-55.
21. Coping with traumas is more fully discussed in ch 15.
22. See more on disbelievers in aspects of this book's contents in Section VII. Chapter 51. Psychic intuition that is well researched.
23. See especially the reports from near death experiences of Mellen-Thomas Benedict (Web ref) and Eben Alexander (2012), discussed in ch. 62.
24. See Section VII.
25. More on centeredness in Ch. 13. Observing ego

26. In further discussions from this point on, I will identify the so-called skeptics as 'skeptics.'
27. Lazarou J, et al., 1998; Brennan, 1991; Moore,TJ. et al., 2007; US Food and Drug Administration; Law, web ref.; UK statistics on medical deaths compared with battlefield deaths in Iraq and Afghanistan.
28. For those who find it helpful to examine research explorations of these Jungian polarities, as related to HSPs, Elaine Aron (2010) is most helpful.
29. Elaine Aron (2010) adds many helpful observations on Jungian typologies relevant to HSPs.
30. More on the HSP and Jungian perspectives in Aron, 2006.
31. More on synchronicities in Section VII, as collective consciousness. See also Bolen, 2005; Castleman, 2004; Mansfield, 1995; Peat, 1987; Vaughan, 1979.
32. More on spiritual awarenesses, including synchronicities, in Sections VII. and VIII, and esp. in ch. 59 on collective consciousness.
33. It might appear at first glance that Paula Underwood Spencer got her ears mixed up, but she didn't. The left ear connects to the right brain and the right ear to the left brain.
34. Tables 1-3 are taken from Benor, 2004; 2005.
35. See more in Sections IV and V on how awareness of these brain hemisphere differences can be helpful in relationships of HSPs and their significant others.
36. More on NHSP-HSP relationships in ch. 25.
37. Chinese medicine has been practiced for thousands of years and offers much wisdom and healing. The concepts of yin and yang are worthy of brief mention here, in parallel with Western concepts of masculine and feminine, as well as with right brain and left brain aspects of our awarenesses. Yin and yang are polar opposites that must be balanced in order for life to proceed in harmony. See an excellent discussion on this in Kaptchuk, 1984.
38. There are also diurnal shifts of activities in the body, occurring roughly in 24 hour cycles. These may involve the central nervous system (brain), peripheral nervous system (nerves and nerve plexuses in the body, hormones, temperature control, and more.
39. Ernest Rossi and Brian Lippincott review ultradian rhythms, as related to mind-body communications (Web ref.).

    "In a wide-ranging series of studies Werntz et al (1982a; b) found that subjects could voluntary shift their nasal dominance by forced uni-nostril breathing through the closed nostril. Further, this shift in nasal dominance was associated with an accompanying shift in cerebral dominance to the contralateral hemisphere and autonomic nervous system balance throughout the body (Klein, R. et al. 1986). The ultradian nasal cycle is not only a marker for cerebral hemispheric activity, but it also could be used to voluntarily change the loci of activity in the highest centers of the brain and autonomic system that are involved in cybernetic loops of communication with most organ systems, tissues and cells of the body. Some of these investigators hypothesize that this nasal-brain-mind link may be the essential path by which the ancient practice of breath regulation in yoga led to the voluntary control of many autonomic nervous system functions for which the Eastern adepts are noted (P. Brown, 1991; Rossi, 1991).

    These relationships inspired a recent Ph.D dissertation by Darlene Osowiec (1991) who assessed hypothesized associations between the nasal ultradian rhythm, anxiety, symptoms of stress and the personality process of self-actualization. She found that: "(1) there is a significant positive correlation between self-actualizing individuals having low trait anxiety and stress related symptoms and a regular nasal cycle... and (2) non-self-actualizing individuals with high levels of trait anxiety and stress-related symptoms exhibit significantly greater irregularity in the nasal cycle..." These results are reminiscent of the ancient texts that emphasize that an irregular nasal cycle, particularly one in which the person remains dominant in one nostril or the other for an excessively long period of time are associated with illness and mental disorder (Rama, et al, 1976)."
40. See more on Oliver Sacks' experience at https://www.lrb.co.uk/v04/n11/oliver-sacks/the-leg
41. Hippocrates noted that if a person's leg was immobilized for 50 days, he might lose his ability to use it, despite the fact that nothing seemed wrong with it any more.
42. See ch. 41 on the five love languages.
43. More on our personal intuitive and spiritual awarenesses in Sections VII and VIII.
44. More on bullying in ch.15 on dealing with trauma.
45. See details for developing your PPSH in ch 2.

46. See more on the PPSH in ch. 28.
47. The Subjective Units of Distress Scale (SUDS) ranges from 0 – 10.
48. More on life lessons in Section VIII.
49. More on meta-awarenesses in ch. 42.
50. Berne, 1996; Stewart & Joines, 1991
51. More on the PPSH in ch. 28. See details of this and other therapeutic methods in Sections V and VI.
52. More on inner child work in Ch. 12.
53. More on trauma later in this Section, ch. 15. See two-chair work in ch. 31. See TWR/WHEE in ch. 29.
54. Protecting yourself with a bioenergy shield is describe in ch. 55.
55. De-stressing with TWR/WHEE is explained in Chapter 29.
56. See sections IV, V and VI for a spectrum of ways to understand yourself and your relationships, to clear stresses, as well as to clear anxieties, traumas, and other issues that leave you more vulnerable to getting triggered and make it harder to stay centered.
57. Zukav, 2010, has excellent discussions on clearing issues that push us off center.
58. The PPSH process for HSPs and HSPCs is described in ch. 28.
59. See Sections IV, V and VI for varieties of approaches that can help you stay centered.
60. On bioenergies and other psychic perceptions see Section VII.
61. For your interest, you might want to see the extremes to which people may go in rigid thinking. Strawson (2018) reviews and discusses a book in which consciousness itself is denied.
62. For a clear example of prejudice against women when they first joined the police force in Sweden, see Krlen 1997. This is also a fascinating story of the reincarnated Anne Frank.
63. Past life traumas are also a factor here, discussed in ch. 64.
64. You may want to skip this report, or to be prepared to use self-treatment, de-stressing methods such as the PPSH explained in, ch. 28 or tapping methods of Energy Psychology (EP) in ch. 29.
65. There is an even more severe level of trauma discussed below, called a complex PTSD, in which people are so severely hurt, repeatedly, over long periods of time, often in one generation after another, that they become shadows of human beings (Herman, 1992). Also graphically described in Ross, 2014.
66. You may want to skip this report, or to be prepared to use self-treatment, de-stressing methods such as the PPSH explained in, ch. 28 or tapping methods of Energy Psychology (EP) in ch. 29.
67. For more on EMDR see http://www.emdria.site-ym.com/.
68. For more on helping with suicidal thoughts and feelings see the discussion later in this Chapter. On cognitive dissonance see Section II, ch 14 and on neuroplastic blindness ch. 10.
69. See Ted Zeff (2010) for counteracting this common, anti-HSP social pressure by encouraging sensitivities in boys.
70. You may want to skip this report, or to be prepared to use self-treatment, de-stressing methods such as the PPSH explained in ch. 28 or tapping methods of Energy Psychology (EP) in ch. 29.
71. See details of the PPSH in ch. 28.
72. See two-chair work in ch. 31.
73. See TWR/WHEE in ch. 29.
74. See meta-anxieties in ch. 42; ch. 29, TWR/WHEE.
75. See Brooks Gibbs video at https://www.youtube.com/watch?v=7oKjW1Oljuw.
76. See TWR/WHEE in ch. 29, NLP in ch. 32, P.E.T. in ch. 25, relaxation in ch. 40 and meditation in ch. 42.
77. See discussion on grief in ch. 16, the next one in this Section.
78. You may want to skip this report, or to be prepared to use self-treatment, de-stressing methods such as the PPSH explained in Section V, ch. 28 or tapping methods of Energy Psychology (EP) in ch. 29.
79. Neurolinguistic Programming (NLP), discussed in ch. 32.
80. Neglected common job personnel who also experience indirect PTSD include Emergency Medical Services personnel, including drivers; 9-1-1 phone operators; court stenographers; and air traffic control personnel.
81. "People with childhood histories of trauma, abuse and neglect make up almost the entire criminal justice population in the US…. Seventy-five percent of perpetrators of child sexual abuse report to have themselves been sexually abused during childhood. People with childhood histories of

trauma, abuse and neglect make up almost the entire criminal justice population in the US.... Seventy-five percent of perpetrators of child sexual abuse report to have themselves been sexually abused during childhood" (van der Kolk, 2005).

82. For anyone working on traumas originating in childhood, van der Kolk (2005) is very strongly recommended.
83. See Right and Left Brain functions in ch. 8.
84. More on trauma in the collective consciousness in Chapters 59, 60, 67.
85. Herman, writing 25 years ago, is a strong advocate 'flooding' therapy, in which trauma victims were led to revisit their trauma memories again and again and again until the memories lost their intensity. This has been found to actually intensify their traumas in many cases.
86. Grief and mourning are detailed in the following Chapter of this Section.
87. See meta-anxieties in ch. 6. and ch. 42, which also addresses installing meta-positives. In this case, people who released their trauma responses will have also released meta-anxieties about not letting go of their trauma anxieties – which their unconscious mind saw as helping to protect them against getting into situations where they might again be traumatized.
88. More on this in ch. 35.
89. For more on EMDR see http://www.emdria.org/
90. More on EP at http://www.energypsych.org/
91. See more on TWR/WHEE methods in in Section I. Introduction; ch. 29; Benor, 2009
92. Helpful lists of suicide alert signs are detailed by WebMD http://www.webmd.com/depression/guide/depression-recognizing-signs-of-suicide#1 and Suicide.org http://www.suicide.org/suicide-warning-signs.html
93. See ch. 37, active listening
94. See more on proxy healing in ch. 67, on Sending healing for the collective planetary consciousness.
95. On inner child work see ch. 12.
96. On family constellation therapy see ch. 36
97. On past life therapy see ch. 64.
98. More on 12-step programs in Ch. 35
99. Narcotics Anonymous is one of a spectrum of '12-step programs' for group support in dealing with addictions. More on this in Ch. 35
100. See ch. 33 on homeopathy.
101. See ch. 34 on flower essences.
102. See more on emotional pains which express themselves through one's body in ch. 29, TWR2/WHEE: Listening to body messages and TWR2/WHEE: Deeper Clearings, and in-depth discussion in Benor, 2005; 2005.
103. More on observing ego in ch. 13.
104. More on marital and family therapy in ch. 30 and on family constellation therapy in ch. 36.
105. More on past life issues in ch. 64.
106. Post Traumatic Stress Disorders are discussed in ch. 15.
107. More on trauma in the previous Chapter.
108. More on spirits and spiritual awarenesses in Sections VII and VIII and in Benor, 2006.
109. More on spirits and spiritual awarenesses in Sections VII and VIII and in Benor, 2006.
110. You may want to skip this report, or to be prepared to use self-treatment, de-stressing methods such as the PPSH explained in, ch. 28 or tapping methods of Energy Psychology (EP) in ch. 29.
111. See Winch, Guy. How to fix a broken heart, Ted Talk.
112. More on pre-death and deathbed spirit encounters in Benor, 2006; R. Smith, 1998; Wills-Brandon, 2000.
113. See ch. 67. Grief and trauma in the collective consciousness of humanity
114. See excellent discussion on this by Knox (Ted Talk).

### SECTION III. Understanding the hsp: alternative or additional diagnoses

1. For a list of ADHD symptoms see Centre for ADHD Awareness, Canada
2. For a touching video about what it feels like to have serious ADHD see Bokstavsbarn, Web ref.
3. See ch. 17.

4. See 'ADHD' in References for various ADHD resources.
5. For specific criteria for a diagnosis of ODD see American Psychiatric Association's Diagnostic and Statistical Manual of Mental Disorders (DSM-5)
6. International OCD Foundation2. https://iocdf.org/about-ocd/treatment/meds/
7. On your PPSH see ch. 28.
8. International OCD Foundation2. https://iocdf.org/about-ocd/treatment/meds/
9. See meta-anxieties in ch. 42; ch. 29, TWR/WHEE
10. For specific criteria for a diagnosis of Narcissistic Personality Disorder see The American Psychiatric Association (2013).
11. See discussion on observing ego in ch. 13.
12. See also HSPC First Aid and Stress Management methods for your HSP who is triggered into distress by their trauma in ch. 27 – 39.

## SECTION IV. HSPs, their HSPCs and other family members

1. Zukav, 2010 has excellent discussions on how the evolution and processing of our close relationships can help us come into deeper awarenesses of ourselves.
2. More on being part of a larger wholeness in Sections VII and VIII, and Benor, 2015.
3. Bellaium Glutamate (E 625), Natrium Glutamate, Yeast Extract, Anything "hydrolyzed" or "hydrolyzed protein", Calcium Caseinate, Sodium Caseinate, Yeast Food, Yeast Nutrient, Autolyzed Yeast, Textured Protein, Soy Protein, Soy Protein Concentrate, Soy Protein Isolate, Whey Protein, Whey Protein Concentrate, Whey Protein Isolate, Vetsin, or Ajinomoto. And there are other pseudonyms as well.
4. For options in complementary/ alternative methods of treatments which have almost no known serious side effects, see Section V,; Benor, 2004; 2005.
5. Aron (2000) has an excellent discussion on HSP sexual relationships
6. See ch. 41, The Five Love Languages
7. Listening is in fact one of the best ways to help. See Andrews, Web ref.
8. Body memories are discussed in Section II, Chapter 15 on Trauma
9. See details of the PPSH in ch. 28.
10. See "I-messages" in Parent Effectiveness Training (P.E.T.), later in this Chapter.
11. See many more suggestions for helpful approaches in dealing with HSP issues in the Sections VI and VII.
12. More on helpful mental approaches in your relationships in Section VI, General wholistic approaches to facilitate health and healing; Benor, 2017b.
13. See ch. 41 for the Five Love Languages
14. See Jungian perspectives on thinking and feelings, as well as discussions on left and right hemisphere preferences in ch. 7.
15. See the Five Love Languages in ch. 41.
16. On meta-issues see ch. 6, and ch. 42.
17. See de-stressing methods in Sections V and VI. The SUDS and SUSS scales are, respectively, ratings from 1 (not at all) – 10 (the strongest it could be), explained in ch. 1.
18. On building positivity see ch. 42.
19. Although the book title suggests P.E.T. is just for parents and children, these approaches are incredibly helpful in any discussion, particularly when the issues under consideration are sensitive and emotions are running high.
20. See also 'conjugations' in Section IV, general wholistic considerations of relationships.
21. A medium is someone who can communicate with spirits of people after their physical death. More on mediums in ch. 65.
22. Spiritual awarenesses and experiences are considered in detail in Sections VII and VIII.
23. For more precise assessment of children's HSP qualities see http://hsperson.com/test/highly-sensitive-child-test/
24. For Observing Ego see ch. 13.
25. See ch. 29 for more on TWR/WHEE.
26. See the five love languages in ch. 11
27. More on mistaken diagnoses in HSPs in Section III.
28. To explain the HSP see Aron, 1996; 2010; Rosenshein, 2013; Zeff, 2004; 2010; 2013.

29. For more on using TWR/WHEE with children see ch. 29; Benor, 2009.
30. More on bullying in ch. 15.
31. Varieties of de-stressing and self-healing approaches are detailed in Sections IV – VI.
32. See ch. 28, Your PPSH
33. Aron, 1996; 2010; Benor, 2018; Rosenshein, 2013; Zeff, 2004; 2010; 2013.
34. More on bioenergies in ch. 54.
35. More on healing in ch. 55.
36. Moe on past lives in ch. 64 and 65.
37. Much more on spiritual awarenesses in Sections VII and VIII.
38. More on spiritual issues of HSPs in Sections VII and VIII.

## *SECTION V. Supports for the HSP and HSPC*

1. See two-chair work in ch 31.
2. See TWR/WHEE for tapping away stress and distress in ch. 28.
3. See the five love languages of (Chapman, 2007) in ch 41.
4. See TWR1/WHEE in ch. 29.
5. See muscle testing ins ch. 57.
6. See ch. 29 on sore spot massage.
7. For two-chair work see ch. 31.
8. See ch. 29 on TWR/WHEE.
9. See TWR/WHEE in the next chapter of this Section.
10. Mechanisms explaining how TWR/WHEE works are explained in Benor, 2013.
11. See 28 in this Section.
12. For two-chair work see ch. 31.
13. Moore, et al., 2007.
14. See ch 16 on grief and bereavement.
15. See the severe case of 'Ken' under meta-anxieties, ch 6, Mind, where the child had to be dragged from the car by his parents and held by the vice principal so he wouldn't run back to the car.
16. Much more on metaphoric roots of pains in Benor, 2004; 2005.
17. See Ch. 31 on two-chair work for clarifying messages from your body.
18. See Ch. 31 on two-chair work for clarifying messages from your pains.
19. More on meta-anxieties in ch. 42.
20. See ch. 13 on observing ego.
21. On neuroplasticity see Ch. 10.
22. Todd's story begins in Ch. 7.
23. Goldenberg, 2016; Minuchin, 1974; Minuchin & Fishman, 1981; Nichols, 012.
24. Non HSP Companion
25. See also Family Constellation Therapy for transpersonal expansions of family therapy in ch. 36.
26. See Ch. 31 on two-chair work for clarifying inner messages.
27. See ch 16 on grief and bereavement.
28. See Figure VII-2 for the releasing spots/ tender points
29. The term, vibrational medicine, is sometimes used more broadly, to include what I call bioenergy healing (discussed in ch. 54 and 55.
30. See ch. 51-53 on intuition.
31. More on homeopathic remedies as biological energy medicine in ch. 54.
32. Davenas et al.; Resch & Guttman
33. Davenas et al., 1988; Smith & Boericke, 1968
34. Gebhardt, 1929; Humphreys, 1849.
35. Case description courtesy of J. Steele.
36. Case related to me by a UK homeopath.
37. Intuitive awarenesses are discussed in ch. 46-51.
38. Kaminski & Katz, 1994; M. Wright, 1988.
39. Flower Essence Society, Web ref; Gurudas, 1989; Harvey & Cochrane, 1989; Howard, 1994; Johnson, 1996; Kaminsky & Katz, 1994; Pettit, 1996; White, 1994.
40. Alternative English spellings: Ki or Chi.

41. Sanskrit dates back 3,000 years in India, which shows that acupuncturists have been aware of the chakra energy centers for a very long time.
42. More on chakras, including a diagram, in ch. 54 on biological energies (biofields).
43. New scientific methods have also been developed to demonstrate the existence of the meridians. Jean-Claude Darras, a physician and president of the World Union of Acupuncture and P. de Vernejoul, a physician who heads the Department of Biophysics of Neckar Hospital in Paris, injected radioactive chemicals at acupuncture points and followed the course of distribution of these materials with a Geiger counter at the body surface. They demonstrated that connections exist between acupuncture points, along lines identical with the meridians described by acupuncturists. Similar research completed decades earlier had been rejected due to difficulties in verifying the findings.
44. These research challenges mirror similar problems in applying western research methods to other wholistic therapies, such as homeopathy and flower essences.
45. Other studies report benefits in treatment of asthma, chronic obstructive pulmonary disease (COPD), ear, nose and throat (ENT) problems, allergic rhinitis, sinusitis (especially in children), Menière's disease (middle ear problems) in younger people, trigeminal neuralgia, facial paralysis, and susceptibility to recurrent infections. Benefits were noted in reduction of pain, less need for medications, and more rapid recovery. Other applications of acupuncture showing significant effects include: facilitating labor and delivery; relief of menopausal symptoms; treatment of depression; enhancement of physical performance; treatment of enuresis, and of frequent, urgent and painful urination; nocturia; tinnitus; weight reduction; and chronically dry mouth.

    Acupuncture is also finding modest successes in a wide range of treatments of addictions, including long-term (average 20 years) alcoholics, cocaine addicts (average use 13 years), smokers, enhancing drug detoxification from nicotine, heroin and alcohol.

    See many references for research of the above problems in Benor, 2004, p. 188ff.
46. See ch. 29 for more details on energy psychology.
47. Marich, 2012, discusses how 12-step programs can help people with trauma.
48. On Family Therapy see Goldenberg, Stanton & Goldenberg, 2016; Minuchin, 1974; Nichols, 2012.
49. On Family Constellation Therapy see Mason Boring, 2013; Reddy, 2012.
50. On anchoring emotions see NLP in ch. 32.
51. On bundling see ch. 30.
52. Here is one Eliza link you can visit: http://manifestation.com/neurotoys/eliza.php3/
53. On love languages see ch. 41
54. On Jungian typologies see ch. 7.
55. On HSS see Ch. 9.

## SECTION VI. General wholistic approaches

1. This is my adaptation of a similar healing intent that is taught in the tradition of Hawaiian Ho'oponopono, in which the invocation is:
    I love you
    I'm sorry
    Please forgive me
    Thank you.
2. For more on healing the collective consciousness of humanity and or our planet see ch. 59 – 61; ch. 67, 68.
3. See P.E.T in ch. 25.
4. More on a healthy diet in ch. 40.
5. More on toxic foods at:http://civileats.com/2010/11/16/after-super-size-me-in-conversation-with-morgan-spurlock/

    Fast food app. The Super Size Me app gives you the fastest and most convenient access to full nutrition facts for all major chain restaurants in the US and Canada, helping you decide what you want - and what you don't want - to eat. Now all the details you need to be an informed consumer are right at your fingertips, constantly updated, and optimized for fast use as a mobile app.

6. De-stressing with TWR/WHEE is explained in ch. 29.
7. See much more on biological energy fields and energies in ch. 55.
8. More on sensing fields in ch. 55.
9. More on acupuncture in Birch, 1996; Kaptchuk, 1984. Other derivatives of acupuncture include shiatsu; reflexology; diagnoses of tongue, ear and iris.
10. Walther, 1981; Weil, Web ref.
11. For Energy Psychology see Association for Comprehensive Energy Psychology (ACEP), web ref.
12. See more in Section VII, ch. 54; Figure VII-1; and Bruyere, 1989; Judith, 1987; Karagulla & Kunz, 1989; Motoyama, 1981.
13. Benor, 2001; 2002; Brennan, 1988; 1993.
14. See long-term effects of trauma in ch. 15; ACE study
15. A few more details on diet in ch 25. Body.
16. See other cases involving obesity in ch 15 on Trauma, and ch 38 on Past Life Therapy
17. On meta-anxieties see ch. 10 on neuroplasticity; This was, in fact, a complex post traumatic stress reaction, with repeated traumas over 3-4 years. See discussion of complex PTSD in ch. 15, under severe and long-term residues. On meta-anxieties see ch. 10 on neuroplasticity; ch. 42. More on my lessons from my voice issues below.
18. See Gibbs, et al., 2002 for a more recent review of wart treatment by suggestion.
19. See discussions of neuroplasticity in ch. 10; and cognitive dissonance in ch. 14.
20. We all know Jim Carrey for his comedy, but he is now spreading joy This voiceover was taken from Jim's speech at MUM Graduation in 2014. Full talk can be seen here https://www.youtube.com/watch?v=cCDAiFrWNP0
21. Zukav (2010) has excellent descriptions and explanations of how couples can overcome negativity and build positivity in their relationships by addressing issues that come up between them.
22. More on bringing ever-increasing positivity into your life in ch. 61 on manifestation.
23. More on anchoring with NLP in ch. 32.
24. More on bullying in ch. 15.
25. Kabat-Zinn (2013) is my favorite book on mindfulness meditation.
26. AMRA, web ref; Flaxman & Flook, web ref; Goyal, Singh & Sibinga, 2014
27. Meditation research: Chalmers, Web ref; NIH Meditation research, Web ref; TM.org, Web ref; UCLA Semel Institute, Web ref; WebMD Web ref;
28. Much more on clearing trauma in in Section II
29. More on spiritual awarenesses in ch. 62-66.
30. See also various ways to say things to each other in respectful ways under Parent Effectiveness Training later in this chapter.
31. See Forgiveness website; The Youtube of Elva and Stranger has an outstanding example of interpersonal forgiveness of trauma.
32. More on reincarnation and current life issues related to past life experiences in ch. 64.
33. More on my hoarseness odyssey in ch. 64. Reincarnation, and past life therapy
34. See Forgiveness website; The Youtube of Elva and Stranger has an outstanding example of interpersonal forgiveness of trauma.
35. For more on global challenges see ch. 66-68.
36. For more on dealing with global challenges see ch. 66-68.
37. Equivalent to a district attorney in the US.
38. More on intuitive and spiritual awarenesses in Sections VII and VIII.
39. For more on dealing with global challenges see ch. 66-68.

## SECTION VII. Subtler sensitivities, biological energy medicine and collective consciousness

1. More on spiritual experiences in Section VII.
2. See listing of the PA on the AAAS site https://www.aaas.org/aaas-affiliates#p and website of the PA at http://www.parapsych.org/.
3. I use the 'Infinite Source' as a hopefully more generic and neutral term for what is commonly referred to God, the Lord, the Creator, Allah, and other names that have been used in various religious contexts. Some people in religions groups have come to assume exclusive relationships

between themselves and the infinite source, to the exclusion of people of other faiths and religions. Please feel free to substitute whatever name suits you if you feel the Infinite Source does not speak to you.
4. Gladwell, 2005: Inglis & West, 1989; Jovanovic, 1995; Karagulla, 1957;
5. For detailed intuition research with highly significant research see ch. 51.
6. Feynman, Richard. (1997).
7. King and Clark 2002; Offredy 1998; Polge 1995.
8. Dreyfus and Dreyfus (1986) discuss pattern recognition as a factor in intuitive awareness.
9. It is of note that two other scientists, Maurice Wilkins and Rosalind Franklin, also made significant contributions to this discovery (Science History Institute).
10. Brennan, 1988; 1933; Karagulla, 1967; Karagulla & Kunz, 1989
11. For spontaneous psychic experiences see L. Rhine, 1961; 1964.
12. Zener is sometimes spelled as Zehner.
13. Meta-analysis of studies of telepathy (Radin, 1997) demonstrate significant mind-to-mind communications ($p < 10 \times 10^{-8}$).
14. Meta-analysis of studies of clairsentience demonstrate significant awareness of the inanimate world around us (Bem & Honorton, 1994) - ($p < 4.76 \times 10^{-8}$ and (Radin, 1997) - ($p < 10 \times 10^{-5}$).
15. Meta-analysis of studies of precognition (Honorton & Ferrari, 1989) demonstrate significant abilities to connect with awarenesses across time ($p < 10 \times 10^{-24}$).
16. See Wikipedia's biases against complementary/ alternative medicine in ch. 6.
17. More on neuroplasticity and neuroplastic blindness in ch. 10.
18. Gary Zukav (2010) has an excellent discussion on 5-sensory people compared to multisensory people.
19. Section II, ch. 10 on neuroplasticity.
20. Section II, ch. 14 on cognitive dissonance.
21. Meta-analysis (Lawrence, 1993). of studies of the sheep/goat effect of $p<10 \times 10^{-8}$.
22. See discussions on neuroplasticity in ch. 10;
23. Jahn and Dunne, 1987; Targ and Puthoff, 1974.
24. More on geopathic stress below.
25. For those interested in dowsing research, further observations are summarized in Benor, 2004; and in details of dowsing in Bird, 1979..
26. In Germany and Austria a regular grid of energy lines running 3 to 4 meters apart has been identified. This is called the Curry net.
27. O. Bergsmann, a Viennese consultant in medicine, explored the effects of geopathic stress on 24 laboratory parameters. These included electrodermal response; heart rate; systolic blood pressure; orthostatic changes in blood pressure (changes when people rise from recumbent positions); time required to warm fin- gertips that were cooled in a standard manner; tendon reflex time; muscle electrical potentials; blood sedimentation rate; circulating immunoglobulins; and levels of calcium, potassium, zinc, serotonin, tyrosine, and tryptophan in the blood. Three dowsers identified areas of geopathic stress and neutral areas in eight hospital rooms around Austria. The stress areas involved crossings of water lines or crossings of water and earth energy lines. Bergmann studied the 24 pa- rameters in 985 people. Each subject was given the battery of tests three times: after sitting for 15 minutes in a neutral area, after 15 minutes in a stress area, and after another 15 minutes in a neutral area. Subjects did not know which were the stress areas.

Results showed significant changes in 12 parameters. The serotonin level is the only test identified specifically by the reviewer of this German report (Schneck). Serotonin levels change with mood and sleep, and changes in this vari- able may be related to sleep disturbances and depressions reported by people suffering from geopathic stress.

Herbert Douglas (1974) investigated 34 cases of arthritis. he dowsed under- ground veins of water that crossed precisely under the affected part of each arthritic's body. In 18 out of the 34 cases he was able to convince the patients to move their beds. In each case there was partial or complete improvement within one day to three months following the relocation. No controls or blinds were instituted in this study, so effects of suggestion cannot be ruled out.

Vlastimil Zert of Czechoslovakia reports that tree tumors are also found more frequently over geopathic zones, and other studies have shown various further anomalies occurring over geopathic zones.

In one very interesting summary of dowsing research, Herbert L. König et al. mention that infrared radiation from human bodies is altered when they stand above geopathic zones.

Petschke (1953a; b) performed extensive experiments on laboratory blood test results in relation to geopathic zones. In 62 series he observed differences in re- sults when tests were run over a neutral zone, in a dowsing zone, and at a crossing of dowsing zones – all carried out in the same area, only a few meters apart. He found that the blood sedimentation rates were either accelerated or retarded over dowsing zones and over crossings, relative to the rates over neutral zones.

E. Hartmann (1967; 1976) repeated these tests in the homes of people who had died of cancer. He had several sedimentation tubes that were placed 6 cm apart in a rack, with some of the tubes over the point in the bed where the cancerous organ would have been positioned and others outside of this zone. The sedimentation rates in the tubes over the geopathic zones deviated markedly from those that were not over these zones. Germination of seeds of vegetable such as cucumbers and corn was suppressed over these zones. No blinds or controls are mentioned.

Changes in the weather were also noted to alter the sedimentation rates in the above-mentioned studies.

28. More on muscle testing in ch. 57.
29. This is called the 'poltergeist' effect, and may also include fires starting spontaneously in unusual places (Manning, 1974; Goss, 1979).
30. "The estimated effect size for the full database lies more than 19 standard deviations from chance while the effect size for the subset of ball anced, homogeneous studies lies 2.6 standard deviations from chance."
31. You can find more detailed summaries and discussions of psychokinesis and of other parapsychology research in excellent books by Dean Radin (1997; 2006).
32. See more on clocks stopping when someone dies in Section VII, Integrity, wholistic aspects of spirit.
33. Orloff 1996; Schultz 1998; Shealy 1975; 1988
34. PK = psychokinesis; 'mind over matter'
35. The effectiveness of cotton wool to convey healing has been confirmed by Bernard Grad in formal research, detailed near the end of this chapter.
36. $p < .0008-.0000l$.
37. 58.5 %,: $p < .02$
38. $p < .004$
39. $p < .00001$
40. $p < .00005$
41. $p < .007$
42. For a more formal discussion of the flaws in this article see Cox, 2004. For an annotated bibliography of healing research available at the time of publication of the Rosa, et al. article see Benor, 2002.
43. See details above, in this section.
44. 'Reading' the energies of an object is called 'psychometry' in parapsychology.
45. Davenas et al., 1988; Resch & Guttman, 1987
46. See Healing Touch: Healing Touch International/ Healing Beyond Borders; Therapeutic Touch: Therapeutic Touch International Association. For Reiki I recommend you search for local personal recommendations.
47. More on imprinting healing energies in physical objects earlier in this chapter.
48. See much more on healing properties of crystals in Holbeche, 2016; Sibley, 2016.
49. See more on information and meaning the is perceived in matter in this section, ch. 51
50. Bengston, 2007, 2012, 2017; Bengston & Krinsley, 2000.
51. Dowling, 1984; Myers & Myers, 1894; West, 1957.

52. Of West's cases, 9 were from years prior to the founding of the IMC.
53. Medically called genu valgum.
54. Spiritual healing has been a very popular name for healing in the UK. There are numerous healing organizations there. They joined in a Confederation in the 1970's, lobbying the British government for permission for healers to visit patients in hospitals at the patient's request, with the approval of the attending physician and the nurse in charge of the ward. With one governmental decision, about 1500 hospitals were opened to healers on this basis. Healing has gained acceptance among the public and among doctors, as evidence for healing has become evident on a case by case basis.
55. See Healing Touch: Healing Touch International/ Healing Beyond Borders; Therapeutic Touch: Therapeutic Touch International Association. For Reiki I recommend you search for local personal recommendations.
56. See for example Canadian Indigenous healers described in Ross, 2014.
57. Another variation of this form of divination is possible if you have access to a collection of books on shelves. Hold a question in your mind for which you are seeking clarity. Pick one number each for A. The particular bookshelf; B: the shelf within the bookshelf; C. The number of the book as you count the books from the left side of the shelf; 4. The page number within your selected book. Read that page and see what the universe might want you to know in answer to your question.
58. See more on parts of the body 'speaking' for the whole person under Section II, ch. 6 on wholistic healing; and ch. 31 on two-chair explorations of symptoms.
59. Braud & Schlitz, 1983; Byrd, 1988; Goodrich, 1974; W. Green, 1993; O'Laoire,1997; Radin, 1995), animals (Snel & Hol, 1983)
60. See annotated bibliographies to 2000 in Benor, 2001; 2002; and healing references, with abstracts where available, to 2014 at http://www.councilforhealing.org/researchonhealing/
61. The first meta-analysis focused on results of healing intent on biological systems, excluding studies on humans, which could be subject to placebo effects. This included "…49 non-whole human studies from 34 papers." A second meta- analysis focused on "57 whole human studies across 56 papers."
62. "The combined weighted effect size for non- whole human studies yielded a highly significant r of .258, but outcomes were heterogeneous and correlated with blind ratings of study quality; 22 studies that met minimum quality thresholds gave a reduced but still significant weighted r of .115. Whole human studies yielded a small but significant effect size of r = .203. Outcomes were again heterogeneous, and correlated with methodological quality ratings; 27 studies that met threshold quality levels gave an increased r = .224.

    … Results suggest that subjects in the active condition exhibit a significant improvement in wellbeing relative to control subjects under circumstances that do not seem to be susceptible to placebo and expectancy effects. Findings with the whole human database suggests that the effect is not dependent upon the previous inclusion of suspect studies and is robust enough to accommodate some high profile failures to replicate. Both databases show problems with heterogeneity and with study quality and recommendations are made for necessary standards for future replication attempts."

    Google definition of 'r': The main result of a correlation is called the correlation coefficient (or "**r**"). It ranges from -1.0 to +1.0. The closer **r** is to +1 or -1, the more closely the two variables are related. If **r** is close to 0, it means there is no relationship between the variables.
63. Discussed in Section VIII.
64. Discussed in ch. 65.
65. On grief see ch 16.
66. More on this in Section VIII.
67. On meta-anxieties see ch. 6.
68. On muscle testing see the next topic in this section.
69. This has been called the "Bi-Digital O-Ring Test" or BDORT.
70. See dowsing research details in ch. 51.
71. See detailed discussions on thinking vs. feeling and intuition vs. outer world focus in ch. 7; and on Left vs. Right Brain preferences in ch. 8.
72. More on self-calming methods in Sections V and VI.

73. On epigenetics see Francis, 2012: Gerald & Gerald, 2015.
74. More on HSP traumas in ch. 15.
75. Much more on what I call 'metaphoric symptoms' in Benor, 2004; 2005.
76. More on listening to your body and dealing with physical symptoms in ch. 29, 31 and 32.
77. The phrase, "life, the universe and everything" has made its way into common language from the science fiction series of books by Douglas Adams, Hitchhiker's Guide to the Galaxy.
78. More on intuition in ch. 45-51.
79. See TWR/WHEE and other Energy Psychology approaches that are particularly helpful for these sorts of problems in ch. 29.
80. Zukav, 2010 has excellent discussions and suggestions for individuals and couples working on developing and maintaining 'authentic power," which I see as being very close to wholistic integrity.
81. See more on Healing the Collective PTSD of Humanity in Benor, 2014; 2015.
82. For a wonderful, in-depth discussion on the interrelationships of all of Creation see Ross, 2014.
83. More on intuitive awarenesses, including research, in ch. 45-51.
84. More on awarenesses of spirits, angels, and the Infinite Source in ch. 56.
85. For a classic rendition of this song by Johnny Cash see Doll & Work.
86. See Pre-death experiences and Deathbed experiences in ch. 65.
87. More on inner guidance and spiritual awarenesses in Sections VII and VIII.
88. Benor, 2002a; 2008.
89. Edwards, 1945; 1953; 1968.
90. Casdorph, 1976; Kuhlman, 1969.
91. Church & Palmer-Hoffman, 2014; Bakker & Hoffman, 2015
92. Benor, et al., 2014; Church, 2014; Church & Brooks, 2010; Ortner, et al., 2014; Stapleton, et al., 2016.
93. Benor, et al., 2014; Brattberg, 2008.
94. Interestingly, Eben Alexander, a neurosurgeon, had a remarkable recovery from bacterial meningitis too, which included a wonderful near death experience (NDE), detailed in ch. 65.
95. Zukav, 2010 has excellent discussions for individuals and couples working on developing and maintaining 'authentic power," which I see as being very close to wholistic integrity.
96. This is described as well under synchronicities, ch. 7.
97. See ch. 61.
98. For research confirming individual intuitive and psychic abilities see ch. 45-53.
99. The collective consciousness of starlings is wonderfully demonstrated in a Ted Talk by Don Tapscott, an analyst of innovation and the impacts of technology. He illustrates his talk with stunning images of murmurations, starting at 14 min. 15 sec. in his talk at
https://www.ted.com/talks/don_tapscott_four_principles_for_the_open_world_1/details
100. See more on marital/ couple and family therapy in ch. 30.
101. Details of family constellation therapy in ch. 36.
102. More on conventional family therapy in ch. 36.
103. Edward Steichen put together a 'Family of Man' collection of wonderful photographs in the New York Museum of Modern Art in 1955 that beautifully illustrates the commonalities connecting people all over our world.

## SECTION VIII. Subtler sensitivities, biological energy medicine and collective consciousness

1. It is unclear whether there is a single Spiritual reality or multiple such realities, or whether this question makes any sense within the Spiritual dimension (or dimensions).
2. More on this in ch. 8, The mind and the brain.
3. On deep effects of meditation see Goleman, 1977; Ray, 2008.
4. See ch. 58 for more on integrity.
5. See more on NDEs in ch. 65.
6. See ch. 10 on neuroplasticity.
7. See research in ch. 51-55.
8. See ch. 51-57.
9. See muscle testing in ch. 57.
10. See bereavement apparitions in ch. 65.

11. More on pre-death and deathbed experiences in ch. 65.
12. See details of manifestations in ch. 61.
13. Gersten, 1997 has a good discussion on enlightenment vs. psychosis.
14. http://www.spiritualemergencenetwork.org/what-is-spiritual-emergency/
15. http://www.spiritualemergencenetwork.org/resources/ and http://spiritualemergence.info/
16. Other angels mentioned by name include Metatron, Remiel, Sariel, Anael, Raguel and Raziel.
17. For more on angels see Godwin, 1993; Inglis & West, 1989; Jovanovic, 1995. See also: Benor, 2006; Giovetti, 1993; Moolenburgh, 1992; Price, 1994; Steiger, 1995; Virtue, 1999.
18. Hunger, tiredness, stress and trauma.
19. Daskalos is a very gifted healer described in Markides,1965.
20. Gershom, 1996; Kelsey & Grant, 1967; Morse with Perry, 1994
21. Bowman, 1997; Hart, 2003; Morse with Perry, 1994; Stevenson, 1987
22. Dethlefsen, 1977; Kelsey & Grant, 1967; Netherton & Shiffrin 1978
23. See ch. 15 on Trauma.
24. See the detailed report of Mellen-Thomas Benedict later in this Section.
25. Alexander, 2010; Moody, 1975. Ring, 1980; 1984; Ring & Cooper, 1999; Taylor, 2009
26. More on these experiences later in this chapter.
27. Benedict, Web ref.
28. Interestingly, another remarkable recovery from bacterial meningitis was reported by Amy Purdy, who lost her spleen, kidneys and both of her legs below the knees, detailed in ch. 58, on wholistic, broad-spectrum healings.
29. For pre-birth memories see McCarty, 2012.
30. The Cantina scene from Star Wars offers a very modest suggestion of what some of these beings might be like, though I rather doubt that they would be meeting in a barrrom. https://www.youtube.com/watch?v=g6PDcBhODqo
31. Angels and demons are discussed in Ch. 63.
32. Ross uses 'Native' for the currently favored term, 'Indigenous,' to identify the pre-European, northern people of Canada.
33. Cannon, 2001; 2007; 2008; 2012; 2015
34. More on sharing positivity with others in ch. 25, 26, and 42.
35. See Benor, 2015 on Healing the collective PTSD of humanity.
36. See Benor, 2014, on Human addictions and our march to collective suicide
37. This is also called 'the file drawer effect' – of selectively leaving reports of unsuccessful cases locked away, unreported, in a file drawer.
38. This is my adaptation of a similar healing intent that is taught in the tradition of Hawaiian Ho'oponopono, in which the invocation is:

    I love you

    I'm sorry

    Please forgive me

    Thank you.
39. More on Wambach's research in ch. 64.

# REFERENCES

'12-steps': *Proactive 12 Steps* http://proactive12steps.com/list.htm. Printable copy of the 12 steps, with suggested and standard wording, plus observations and suggestions for each step, see: http://proactive12steps.com/list.htm

12-step sponsorships Q & A: chrome-extension://oemmndcbldboiebfnladdacbdfmadadm/http://www.aa.org/assets/en_US/p-15_Q&AonSpon.pdf

ACE study: See Stevens

ADHD': MY ADHD http://www.myadhd.com/index.php?page=Assessment_Tools

ADHD & You http://www.adhdandyou.com/hcp/children-adhd-screening.aspx

ADHD Adult Self-Report Scale (ASRS-v1.1) Symptom Checklist Instructions https://add.org/wp-content/uploads/2015/03/adhd-questionnaire-ASRS111.pdf

Adverse Childhood Experiences (ACE) Study: See Stevens

Alexander, Eben (2012). *Proof of Heaven: A Neurosurgeon's Journey into the Afterlife.* New York: Simon & Schuster.

American Psychiatric Association (2013). Personality disorders. In *Diagnostic and Statistical Manual of Mental Disorders* (Fifth Edition ed.). Washington, DC: American Psychiatric Publishing Inc

AMRA (American Mindfulness Research Association) https://goamra.org/.

Anderson, J., Lu, D-F. Strybol, N., Hess, S., & Mangione, L. (2015). *Healing Touch Research Brief.* Lakewood, CO: Healing Beyond Borders.

Arama. http://www.jewish-wisdom.com/index.php?submit=author&a=Arama

Aron, Elaine N. (1996). *The Highly Sensitive Person – How to Thrive When the World Overwhelms You.* New York, NY: Broadway Books.

Aron, Elaine. (2000). *The Highly Sensitive Person in Love.* NY: Broadway Books.

Aron, Elaine N. (2006). The clinical implications of Jung's concept of sensitiveness. *J. Jungian Theory And Practice.* 8(2), 11-43.

Aron, Elaine. (2010). *Psychotherapy and the Highly Sensitive Person: Improving Outcomes for that Minority of People who are the Majority of Clients.* New York: Routledge/Taylor & Francis Group, p. vi

Aron, A. Ketay, S. Hedden, T. Aron, E. Markus, H. R. Gabrieli, J. D. E. (2010). Temperament trait of sensory processing sensitivity moderates cultural differences in neural response, Special Issue on Cultural Neuroscience. *Social Cognitive and Affective Neuroscience* 5: 219–226. doi:10.1093/scan/nsq028.

Association for Comprehensive Energy Psychology (ACEP) http://www.energypsych.org/

Astin, John A. Harkness, Elaine Ernst, Edzard, (2000). *The efficacy of distant healing: a systematic review of randomized trials, Annals of Internal Medicine,* 132, 903-910.

Atwater, P.M.H. (1999). *Children of the New Millennium: Children's Near-Death Experiences and the Evolution of Humankind.* New York: Three Rivers Press.

Bach remedies http://www.bachcentre.com/centre/shop/books_eu.php

Bach, Richard. *Illusions: The Adventures of a Reluctant Messiah Delacorte.* Press/ Eoleanor Friede 1977.

Bachler, Kathe (1989). *Earth Radiation.* Manchester, England: Wordmasters 1989.

Bailey, Lee Worth & Yates, Jenny (1996). *The Near-Death Experience: A Reader.* New York: Routledge .

Bandler, Richard & Grinder, John (1982). *ReFraming: Neuro-Linguistic Programming and the Transformation of Meaning.* Moab, UT: Real People Press.

Barry, Lynda (2008). *What It Is.* Drawn and Quarterly.

Batiste, Marie & Henderson, James Sa'kej Youngblood (2008). *Naturalizing Indigenous Knowledge in Education: A Synthesis Paper.* (Unpublished manuscript). Quoted in Ross, 2014.

Bell, Christopher (2015). *Ted Talk: Bring on the female superheroes!* https://www.ted.com/talks/christopher_bell_bring_on_the_female_superheroes?language=en

Belsky, Jay; Pluess, Michael (2009). Beyond Diathesis Stress: Differential Susceptibility to Environmental Influences (PDF). *Psychological Bulletin* 135(6): 885–908. doi:10.1037/a0017376

Bem, DJ. and Honorton, C. (1994). Does psi exist? Replicable evidence for an anomalous process of information transfer. *Psychological Bulletin.* 115, 4-18

Benedict, Mellen-Thomas. *Near-Death Experience* http://www.near-death.com/reincarnation/experiences/mellen-thomas-benedict.html

Benor, Daniel J. Council for Healing, a non-profit organization that promotes awareness of a broad spectrum of healing http://councilforhealing.org

Benor, Daniel J. Discussion of wholistic healing http://www.ijhc.org/variations-on-the-theme-of-healing/

Benor, Daniel (1992). Intuitive diagnosis. *Subtle Energies,* 3(2), 41-64.]

Benor DJ (2000). Distant healing. *Subtle Energies and Energy Medicine.* 11(3), 249–264.

Benor, Daniel J. *The International Journal of Healing and Caring*, an open access, peer reviewed publication since 2001 (http://ijhc.org)

Benor, Daniel J. (2008). *Healing Research, V. 1 - Scientific Validation of a Healing Revolution.* Popular Edition, Bellmawr, NJ: Wholistic Healing Publications, 2nd Edition. https://danielbenor.com/product/ebook-healing-research-vol-i-pop-ed-spiritual-healing/ *[The Popular Edition discusses what spiritual healers say they do and how they believe it works, with a thorough but light review of the research literature.]*

Benor, Daniel J. (2002a). *Healing Research, V. 1 Professional Supplement.* Orig. Southfield, MI, Vision Publications, Now owned by Wholistic Healing Publications, Bellmawr, NJ. https://danielbenor.com/product/ebook-healing-research-vol-i-professional-supplement-to-chapters-4-5/ *[The Professional Supplement provides a much more detailed annotated bibliography of the research, including statistical analyses but does not include the sections on individual healers or discussions on what healers say they do and how they do it, and anecdotal reports and assessments of healers' work.]*

Benor, Daniel J. (2002b). *Intuition (Editorial).* International J Healing and Caring, 2(2), 1-17 http://ijhc.org/2016/03/intuition-daniel-benor/.

Benor, Daniel J. (2004). *Healing Research, V. 2 - Professional edition, Consciousness, Bioenergy and Healing.* Bellmawr, NJ: Wholistic Healing Publications. *[This book discusses 1500+ references on complementary/ alternative medicine from a wholistic perspective, addressing body, emotions, mind, relationships and spirit. It considers ways in which problems develop in each of these areas and diverse approaches for dealing with them.]* https://danielbenor.com/product/ebook-healing-research-vol-ii-consciousness-bioenergy-and-healing-pro-ed/

Benor, Daniel J. (2005). *Healing Research, V. 2 – Popular edition, How Can I Heal What Hurts?* Bellmawr, NJ: Wholistic Healing Publications, 2nd Edition. *[This book is a lighter version of the Professional Edition, written for a lay audience, with fewer references but with 100 pp. discussing methods for self-healing.]* https://danielbenor.com/product/ebook-healing-research-vol-ii-pop-ed-how-can-i-heal-what-hurts/

Benor, Daniel J. (2006). *Healing Research, V. 3. Personal Spirituality: Science, Spirit and the Eternal Soul.* Bellmawr, NJ: Wholistic Healing Publications. *[This book reviews research suggesting there is reason to believe in survival of a spirit after physical death.]* https://danielbenor.com/product/ebook-healing-research-vol-iii-personal-spirituality/

Benor, Daniel J. (2007). *Reaching Higher and Deeper – Workbook for Healing Research, Volume 3: Personal Spirituality.* Bellmawr, NJ: Wholistic Healing Publications https://danielbenor.com/product/ebook-healing-research-vol-iii-personal-spirituality/

Benor, Daniel J. (2009). *Seven Minutes to Natural Pain Release: Pain is a Choice and Suffering is Optional - WHEE for Tapping Your Pain Away.* Bellmawr, NJ: Wholistic Healing Publications (2nd Ed.)

Benor, Daniel J. (2010). *WHEE for Grief and Bereavement* ebook https://danielbenor.com/wp-content/uploads/2015/03/WHEE-BOOK-GRIEF-BEREAVEMENT100914.pdf
http://www.danielbenor.com/product/ebook-whee-for-pain-2/

Benor, Daniel J. (2010a). *'Placebo' Is the Medical Term For Self-Healing.* International J Healing and Caring, 2, 1-15.

Benor, Daniel J. (2013). *Energy psychology – a discussion of practices and explanatory theories.* International J. Healing & Caring, 13(2), 1-23.

Benor, Daniel J. (2014). *The Sixth Mass Extinction and The Monkey Grasping Trap: Human addictions and our march to collective suicide.* International J Healing & Caring, 14(1), 1-10.

Benor, Daniel J. (2015). *Healing the Collective PTSD of Humanity.* International J Healing & Caring, 15(2), 1-21. http://ijhc.org/2015/11/healing-the-collective-ptsd-of-humanity-daniel-benor/

Benor, Daniel. Rossiter-Thornton, John. and Toussaint, Loren (2016). *A Randomized, Controlled Trial of Wholistic Hybrid Derived from Eye Movement Desensitization and Reprocessing and Emotional Freedom Technique (WHEE) for Self-Treatment of Pain, Depression, and Anxiety in Chronic Pain Patients.* J Evidence-Based Complementary & Alternative Medicine. DOI: 10.1177/2156587216659400 (Demonstrating benefits for pain, depression and anxiety) http://journals.sagepub.com/doi/full/10.1177/2156587216659400

Benor, Daniel J. (2017a). *Caregiver factors contributing to healing.* International J Healing and Caring, 1, 1-16.

Benor, Daniel J. (2017b). *Renovating the Boxes We Build and Live In.* International J Healing and Caring, 1, 1-16.

Benveniste, Jacques (1998). *Understanding digital biology* http://www.digibio.com/cgi-bin/node.pl?nd=n3. (accessed 5/3/03).

Berne, Eric (1996). *Games People Play.* New York: Random House (reprint of much earlier original). Details of games and related materials http://www.ericberne.com/games-people-play/

Betz, Hans-Dieter. *Unconventional water detection: field test of the dowsing technique in dry zones, part 1.* J of Scientific Exploration 1995, 9(1), 1-43. (Also as: 2nd ed. GTZ Deutsche Gesellschaft fur Technische Zusammenarbeit 1993).

Birch, Stephen & Hammerschlag, Richard, (1996). *Acupuncture Efficacy: A Compendium of Controlled Clinical Studies.* Tarrytown, NY: National Academy of Acupuncture and Oriental Medicine, Inc..

Bird, Christopher (1979). *The Divining Hand: The Five Hundred Year Old Mystery of Dowsing.* New York: EP Dutton.

Bolen, Jean Shinoda (2005). *The Tau of Psychology: Synchronicity and the Self.* New York: Harper & Row. Bolen, Jean Shinoda. *The Tao of Psychology: Synchronicity and the Self.* HarperSanFrancisco.

Boyd, WE (1946). An investigation regarding the action on diastase of microdoses of mercuric chloride when prepared with and without mechanical shock. *British Homeopathic J,* 36, 214-223.

Braud, William G (1989). *Distant mental influence of rate of hemolysis of human red blood cells.* In: Henkel, Linda A./ Berger, Rich E (eds); *Research in Parapsychology 1988.* Metuchen, NJ/ London: Scarecrow 1989, 1-6.

Braud, William & Schlitz, Marilyn (1983). Psychokinetic influence on electrodermal activity. *J. of Parapsychology,* 47(2), 95-119.

Brennan, Barbara A. (1988). *Hands of Light: A Guide to Healing Through the Human Energy Field.* NY: Bantam.

Brennan, Barbara A. (1993). *Light Emerging.* NY: Bantam.

Brennan, TA. Leape, LL. Laird, NM. et al. (1991). Incidence of adverse events and negligence in hospitalized patients: Results of the Harvard Medical Practice Study I, *New England J.Medicine,* 324:370-376.

Bruyere, Rosalyn L & Farrens, Jeanne (1989). *Wheels of Light: A Study of the Chakras.* Sierra Madre, CA: Don.

Briggs Myers test http://www.truity.com/test/type-finder-research-edition

Byrd, Randolph C. (1988). *Positive therapeutic effects of intercessory prayer in a coronary care population.* Southern Medical J. 81(7), 826-829

Campbell, Joseph (1978). *The Masks of God.* New York: Penguin.

Campbell, Joseph (1989). *This Business of the Gods.* Caledon, East, Ontario, Canada: Windrose Films.

Canadian Resource Centre for Victims of Crime. *Restorative Justice in Canada: what victims should know.* 2011. https://www.crcvc.ca/docs/restjust.pdf

Cannon, Dolores (2012). *The Convoluted Universe, Book 1.* (10th ed) Ozark Mountain: Huntsville, AR.

Capra, Fritjof (1975). *The Tao of Physics.* Boulder, CO: Shambala.

Castleman, Tess (2004). *Threads, Knots, Tapestries: How a Tribal Connection is Revealed through Dreams and Synchronicities.* St Paul, MN: Daimon Verla.

Caulfield, Timothy (2015). *Is Gwyneth Paltrow Wrong About Everything?: When Celebrity Culture and Science Clash.* Viking.

Center for Biological Diversity. *The Extinction Crisis.* http://www.biologicaldiversity.org/programs/biodiversity/elements_of_biodiversity/extinction_crisis/

Chapman, Gary (2007). *The Heart of the Five Love Languages.* Chicago, IL: Northfield.

Chess, Stella/ Thomas, Alexander. *Temperament in Clinical Practice.* Guilford Press 1968.

Murray, Christopher J.L. & Frenk, Julio (2010). Ranking 37th — Measuring the Performance of the U.S. Health Care System. *New England J Medicine.* 362:98-99 January 14, 2010 DOI: 10.1056/NEJMp0910064 http://www.nejm.org/doi/full/10.1056/NEJMp0910064

Church D, Stern S, Boath E, Stewart A, Feinstein D, Clond M. (2017). Emotional Freedom Techniques to Treat Posttraumatic Stress Disorder in Veterans: Review of the Evidence, Survey of Practitioners, and Proposed Clinical Guidelines. *Permanente J.* 21. doi: 10.7812/TPP/16-100.

Cohen, Kenneth S. (1997). *The Way of Qigong: The Art and Science of Chinese Energy Healing.* New York: Ballantine.

Cohen, Kenneth (2003). *Honoring the Medicine: The Essential Guide to Native American Healing.* New York: One World/ Ballantine

Council for Healing http://councilforhealing.org

Cox, Thomas (2004). Transgressing the boundaries of science: Glazer, scepticism, and Emily's experiment. *Nursing Philosophy.* 5, 75–78

Dabney, M. Ewin & Bruce N. Elmer (2006). *Ideomotor Signals for Rapid Hypnoanalysis: A How-to-manual.* Springfield, IL: Charles C. Thomas.

Dalebout, Katie (2016). *Let It Out: A Journey Through Journaling.* Hay House.

Davenas, E et al. (1988). Human basophil degranulation triggered by very dilute antiserum against IgE, *Nature,*333, 816-818.

Davis, Laura. *Allies in Healing.* NY: HarperPerennial 1991.

Davis, Laura F & Bass, Ellen (1992). *The Courage to Heal: A Guide For Women Survivors of Child Sexual Abuse.* New York: HarperCollins.

Diehl, Manfred; Elnick, Alexandra B.; Bourbeau, Linda S.; Labouvie-Vief, (1998). Gisela Adult attachment styles: Their relations to family context and personality. *J Personality and Social Psychology,* 74(6), Jun, 1656-1669. http://dx.doi.org/10.1037/0022-3514.74.6.1656

Doll, Erich & Work, Henry Clay. *My Grandfather's Clock.* See lyrics and hear them sung by Johnny Cash http://www.metrolyrics.com/my-grandfathers-clock-lyrics-johnny-cash.html.

Dossey, Larry (1993). *Healing Words: New York.* Harper San Francisco 1993.

Douglas, Herbert (1974). *A further look at dowsing and arthritis.* American Dowser (February), 14(1), 37-40 (continued in: American Dowser 1974, 14(2).

Douillard, John. http://lifespa.com/sneaky-names-for-msg-check-your-labels/#.

Dowling, St. John (1984). Lourdes cures and their medical assessment. *J of the Royal Society of Medicine,* 77, 634-638.

Dreyfus, H. & Dreyfus, S. (1986). *Mind over machine: The power of human intuition and expertise in the era of the computer.* Oxford: Basil Blackwell.

Dunne, J. W. (1973). *An Experiment with Time.* London: Faber and Faber (Orig. 1927).

Edwards, Harry (1945 ). *The Science Of Spirit Healing.* London: Rider (estimated date).

Edwards, Harry (1953). *The Evidence for Spirit Healing.* London: Spiritualist Press.

Edwards, Harry. *Thirty Years a Spiritual Healer.* London: Herbert Jenkins 1968.

Edwards, Jenny (2016). *Healing in Rwanda: The Words of the Therapists.* International J. Healing and Caring, 1, 1-16.

Elva, Thordis and Stranger, Tom, *South of Forgiveness.* https://www.ted.com/talks/thordis_elva_tom_stranger_our_story_of_rape_and_reconciliation

Evans, Madeline (2000). *Meditative Provings.* Holgate, UK: Rose Press.]

Feinstein, David. Energy psychology treatments over a distance: The curious phenomenon of "surrogate tapping". *Energy Psychology* 2013, 5(1), 1-12.

Fenton, Bruce (2015). Dowsing Research. *Scientific & Medical Network.* MARCH 26.https://explore.scimednet.org/index.php/2015/03/26/dowsing-a-review/

Feynman, Richard (1997). *Surely you're joking, Mr. Feynman!* W. W. Norton.

Flaxman, Greg and Flook, Lisa. *Brief Summary of Mindfulness Research* http://marc.ucla.edu/workfiles/pdfs/marc-mindfulness-research-summary.pdf

Flower Essence Society http://www.fesflowers.com/

Forgiveness http://www.forgivenessweb.com/

Francis, Richard C. (2012). *Epigenetics: How Environment Shapes Our Genes.* Norton.

Gallup, George Jr. with Proctor, William (1982). *Adventures in Immortality: A Look Beyond the Threshold of Death.* New York: McGraw-Hill.

Gersten Dennis (1997). *Are You Getting Enlightened or Losing Your Mind? A Spiritual Program for Mental Fitness,* New York: Random House.

Gerstenberg, F. X. R (2012). Sensory-processing sensitivity predicts performance on a visual search task followed by an increase in perceived stress. *Personality and Individual Differences* 53: 496–500.doi:10.1016/j.paid.2012.04.019.

Gerald, Michael C. & Gerald, Gloria E. (2015). *The Biology Book: From the Origin of Life to Epigenetics, 250 Milestones in the History of Biology.* New York: Sterling

Gersten, David (2004). Recovering the Soul. International *J Healing and Caring.* 4(3), 1-5.

Gibbs, Brooks https://www.youtube.com/watch?v=7oKjW1Oljuw

Gibbs, S., et al. (2002). Local treatments for cutaneous warts: systematic review. *British Medical J.* Aug 31; 325(7362): 461. https://www.ncbi.nlm.nih.gov/pmc/articles/PMC119440/

Gladwell, Malcolm (2005). *Blink: The power of thinking without thinking.* New York, NY: Little, Brown and Company.

Godwin, Malcolm. *Angels: An Endangered Species.* New York: Simon & Schuster 1990/ London: Boxtree 1993.

Goldenberg, Irene; Stanton, Mark. & Goldenberg, Herbert (2016). *Family Therapy: An Overview* (SAB 230 Family Therapy) 9th Edition. Independence, KY: Cenberg.

Goleman, Dan (1977). *The Varieties of Meditative Experience,* New York: Dutton.

Goodrich, Joyce (1974). *Psychic Healing – A Pilot Study* (dissertation) Graduate School, Yellow Springs, Ohio.

Gordon, Thomas (1975). *P.E.T. – Parent Effectiveness Training,* NY: Penguin.

Goss, Michael. *Poltergeists: An Annotated Bibliography of Works in English, circa 1880-1975.* Metaden, NJ/London: Scarecrow 1979.

Goyal, Madhav; Singh, Sonal; Sibinga, Erica M.S. (2014). Meditation Programs for Psychological Stress and Well-being. *JAMA Internal Medicine.* doi:10.1001/jamainternmed.2013.

Grad, B., et al, (1961). The Influence of an Unorthodox, Method of Treatment on Wound Healing in Mice. *International J. of Parapsyhology,* 3, 5-24.

Grad, B., et al, *The Influence of an Unorthodox, Method of Treatment on Wound Healing in TOM* Graves, Tom (1976). Dowsing Techniques and Applications. Turnstone Books. Mice, *International J. of Parapsychology* 1961, 3,

5-24.

Green, William Michael (1993). *The Therapeutic Effects of Distant Intercessory Prayer and Patients' Enhanced Positive Expectations on Recovery Rates and Anxiety Levels of Hospitalized Neurosurgical Pituitary Patients: A Double Blind Study (dissertation)*. San Francisco: California Institute of Integral Studies.

Griffiths, Colin. *The Berlin Wall, a remedy proved by group meditation*. Promethius Unbound 1995, Spring, 25-30.]

Grof, Stanislav/ Grof, Christina. *Spiritual Emergency: When Personal Transformation Becomes a Crisis*. New York: Putnam/ England: Thorsons 1995.

Gurudas, (1986). *Gem Elixirs and Vibrational Healing, Vols. I, II*. Channelled by Kevin Ryerson, Boulder, CO: Cassandra.

Gurudas, (1989). *Flower Essences and Vibrational Healing*, San Rafael, CA: Cassandra.

Hamilton, Allan J. (2008). *The Scalpel and the Soul: Encounters with Surgery, the Supernatural, and the Healing Power of Hope*. Penguin/Tarcher.

Hamne, Gunilla & Sandström, Ulf (2017). Shift a nervous system – and you shift the world! *International J. Healing & Caring* 17(3), 1-12.

Hart, Tobin (2003). *The Sectret Spiritual World of Children*. Makawao, Maui, Hawaii: Inner Ocean.

Hartmann, E. (1967). *Krankheit als Standortproblem*, Heidelberg: Haug Verlag.

Hartmann, E. (1976). *Krankheit als Standortproblem*. 3rd ed, Heidelberg: Haug Verlag.

Hartung, John G. & Galvin, Michael D. (2003). *Energy Psychology and EMDR: Combining Forces to Optimize Treatment*. New York: Norton.

Harvey, Clare & Cochrane, Amanda. *Encyclopaedia of Flower Remedies*. London: Thorsens 1995.

Herman, Judith (1992). Trauma and Recovery: The Aftermath of Violence – from Domestic Abuse to Political Violence. NY: Basic Books.

Hawken, Paul (2007). *Blessed Unrest: How the Largest Movement in the World Came into Being and Why No One Saw It Coming*. New York, NY: Viking Penguin.

HeadCase http://www.headcasecompany.com/concussion_info/stats_on_concussions_sports

Healing Touch: Healing Touch International/ Healing Beyond Borders http://HealingBeyondBorders.org. Educating and Certifying the Healing Touch®.

Hellinger. Bert (2001). *Supporting Love – How Love Works in Couples Relationships*. Phoenix, AZ: Zieg, Tucker & Theisen, Inc.

Hemi-Synch research https://hemi-sync.com/learn/research-papers/

Henton, Darcy (2014). *Deaths of Alberta aboriginal children in care no 'fluke of statistics.'* Calgary Herald 01.08. http://www.edmontonjournal.com/life/eaths+Alberta+aboriginal+children+care+fluke+statistics/9212384/story.html

Holbeche, Soozi (2016). *The Power of Gems and Crystals*. London: Piatkus

Honorton, C. & Ferrari, DC. (1989). Future telling: A meta-analysis of forced-choice precognition experiments, 1935-1987, *Journal of Parapsychology*. 53, 281-308.

Howard, Judy (1994). *Growing Up with Bach Flower Remedies: A guide to the use of the remedies during childhood and adolescence*. Saffron Walden, UK: CW Daniel.

Inglis, Bian & West, Ruth (1989). *The Unknown Guest: The Mystery of Intuition*. London: Coronet.

*Integrative Practice, Principles and Research*. Haren, The Netherlands: Homeolinks Publishers 2010

International OCD Foundation. https://iocdf.org/about-ocd/treatment/erp/

International Spiritual Emergence Network http://www.spiritualemergencenetwork.org/resources/

Jaeger, Barrie (2004). *Making Work Work for the Highly Sensitive Person: Learning to Bend, Not Break, When Work Overwhelms You*. New York: McGraw-Hill.

Jahn, Robert G. & Dunne, Brenda J. (1987). *The Margins of Reality*. San Diego, CA and London: Harcourt, Brace Jovanovich.

Jahnke, Roger (2002). *The Healing Promise of Qi: Creating Extraordinary Wellness Through Qigong and Tai Chi*. New York: Contemporary/McGraw-Hill.

Jeffrey, Francis. *Working in Isolation*. In: Wolman. Benjamin B. & Ulman, Montague (Eds) (1986). Handbook of States of Consciousness. Van Nostrand Reinhold.

Jensen, Anne M. (2017). *Assessing the validity of muscle response testing (MRT): A series of diagnostic test accuracy studies, Advances in Energy Psychology: Proceedings of the 7th Annual Research Symposium, Association for Comprehensive Energy Psychology*. San Antonio, TX.

Johannes, Christopher K. & van der Zee, Harry E. (Editors). *Homeopathy and Mental Health Care*

Johnson, Steve (1996). *The Essence of Healing: A Guide to the Alaskan Flower, Gem, and Environmental Essences*, Homer, AK: Alaskan Flower Essence Project.

Jonas W. & Crawford C. (2003). Science and spiritual healing: a critical review of spiritual healing, "energy"

medicine, and intentionality, *Alternative Therapies Supplement: Definitions and Standards in Healing Research*, 9(2), A56-71.
Jonas W. & Crawford C. (2006). *Healing, Intention and Energy Medicine: Science, Research Methods and Clinical Implications*. Churchill Livingstone, 2006.
Jones, RL. & Jenkins, MD (1981). *Plant responses to homeopathic remedies*, British Homeopathic J, 70, 120-128.
Jovanovic, Pierre. *An Inquiry into the Existence of Guardian Angels: A Journalist's Investigative Report.* New York: M. Evans 1995.
Judith, Anodea (1987). *Wheels of Life: A User's Guide to the Chakra System.* St. Paul, MN: Llewellyn.
Jung, Carl, (1955). *Synchronicity: An Acausal Connecting Principle.* Princeton: Princeton University Press.
Kabat-Zinn, Jon (2013). *Full Catastrophe Living (Revised Edition): Using the Wisdom of Your Body and Mind to Face Stress, Pain, and Illness.* Bantam.
Kaminsky, Patricia & Katz, Richard (1994). *Flower Essence Repertory.* Flower Essence Society.
Kanigel, Robert (1991). *The Man Who Knew Infinity.* Washington Square Press.
Kaptchuk, Ted J. (1984). *The Web That Has No Weaver.* New York: Congdon and Weed.
Karagulla, Shafika (1967). *Breakthrough to Creativity: Your Higher Self Perception.* Santa Monica: DeVorss.
Karagulla, Shafika & Kunz, Dora van Glelder (1989). *The Chakras and the Human Energy Fields.* Wheaton, IL: Quest/Theosophical.
Kindlon, D. & Thompson, M. (1999). *Raising Cain.* New York, NY.
King, Lindy & Clark, Jill Macleod (2002). Intuition and the development of expertise in surgical ward and intensive care nurses, *Journal of Advanced Nursing*. 37(4), 322-329.
Kiszkowski, P & Szydlowski, H. (1981). *The low frequency electromagnetic field as a signal carrier in dowsing.* Psychoenergetic Systems, 4 189-197.
Klein, Gary A. (2002). *Intuition at Work anthology.* New York: Doubleday Business.
König, Herbert L. (1968). *Der BIO-Resonator als Höchstfrequenzresonanzpule.* Wetter Boden Mensch
König, HL et al. (1981). *The divining rod phenomenon.* Chapter 10 in Biological Effects of Electromagnetism, New York: Springer 194-217.
Krieger, D. (1979). *The Therapeutic Touch.* Englewood Cliffs, NJ: Prentice-Hall.
Krieger, D. (1987). *Living the Therapeutic Touch.* New York: Dodd Mead.
Krieger, D. (1993). *Accepting Your Power to Heal: The Personal Practice of Therapeutic Touch.* Santa Fe, NM: Bear & Co.
Kubler-Ross, Elisabeth (1975). *Death: the Final Stage of Growth.* New Jersey: Prentice-Hall.
Kwong, Evelyn (2017). https://www.thestar.com/news/gta/2017/04/14/toronto-womans-viral-tweet-sets-off-cat-in-the-square-craze.html.
Lachman, Larry (2006). The Disparaged Grief: Pet loss and 20 years of 'fighting the good fight'. *International J Healing and Caring.* 6(3), 1-6.
LaGrand, Louis E. (1997). *After-death Communication: Final Farewells*, St. Paul, MN: Llewellyn.
Law, Ron former executive director of the New Zealand National Nutritional Foods Association and member of a New Zealand government working group advising on strategies for reducing medical errors. http://laleva.cc/petizione/english/ronlaw_eng.html
Lawrence, Tony. *Bringing home the sheep: a meta-analysis of sheep/goat experiments.* Proceedings of 36th Annual Parapsychology Convention 1993, Fairhaven, MA: Parapsychological Association.
Lazarou J, Pomeranz BH, Corey PN. (1998). Incidence of adverse drug reactions in hospitalized patients: a meta-analysis of prospective studies. *JAMA* . Apr 15;279(15):1200-5.
LeShan, Lawrence (1974). *How to Meditate*, New York: Bantam.
Leskowitz, Eric (2001). Medical intuition, In: Shannon, Scott (ed). *Handbook of Complementary and Alternative Therapies in Mental Health.* San Diego, CA: Academic/Harcourt, 269-286.
Leskowitz, Eric (2017). The zone: a measurable (and contagious exemplar of mind-body integration. *J. Alternative and Complementary Medicine.* 23(5), 1-2.
Levey, Joel & Levey, Michelle, in Klein, Gary A. (2002). *Intuition at Work Anthology.* New York: Doubleday Business.
Levine, Stephen (1984). *Meetings at the Edge: Dialogues with the Grieving and the Dying, the Healing and the Healed*, London & New York: Anchor/Doubleday.
Licht, C., Mortensen, E. L., & Knudsen, G. M. (2011). Association between sensory processing sensitivity and the serotonin transporter polymorphism 5-HTTLPR short/short genotype. *Biological Psychiatry, 69,* supplement for Society of Biological Psychiatry Convention and Annual Meeting, abstract 510.
Linde, K, et al. (1997). Are the clinical effects of homoeopathy placebo effects? A meta-analysis of placebo-controlled trials, *Lancet*. 350: 834-84 www.ncbi.nlm.nih.gov:80/ entrez/ query.fcgi?cmd=Retrieve&db=PubMed&list_uids=9310601&dopt=Abstract

Lipton, Bruce H. (2005). *The Biology of Belief: Unleashing the Power of Consciousness, Matter and Miracles.* Santa Rosa, CA: Mountain of Love/ Elite Books.

Lord, Lewis (1997). How Many People Were Here Before Columbus? One of the few certainties: The Indian populations of North and South America suffered a catastrophic collapse after 1492 *U.S. News & World Report*, August, 68-70. http://www.bxscience.edu/ourpages/auto/2009/4/5/34767803/Pre-Columbian%20population.pdf

Maby, Joseph Cecil & Franklin, Thomas Bedford (1939). *The Physics of the Divining Rod. Being an account of an experimental investigation of water and mineral divining.* London: Bell & Sons.

MacEnulty, John. Email blog. 8/29/2003.

Manning, Matthew. *The Link.* New York: Holt, Rinehart and Winston 1974.

Mansfield, V. (1995). *Synchronicity, Science, and Soul-Making: Understanding Jungian Synchronicity through Physics, Buddhism, and Philosophy.* Open Court. Chicago.

Markides, K. (1985). *The Magus of Strovolos: The Extraordinary World of a Spiritual Healer.* London/ Boston: Arkana.

Markova, Dawna (1991). *The Art of the Possible: A Coimpassionate Approach to Understanding the Way People Think, Learn & Communicate.* Conari, p.26.

March, Jenny. *Cassell's Dictionary of Classical Mythology.* Copyright 1998 by Cassell and Co. Entry on Gaia. http://www.greekmedicine.net/mythology/mythology.html, March, p. 324. See also discussions on Gaia at Gaia theory http://www.gaiatheory.org/overview/

Marich, Jamie (2012). *Trauma and the Twelve Steps: A Complete Guide For Enhancing Recovery.* Warren, OH: Cornersberg.

Mason Boring, Francesca, (2013). *Feather Medicine, Walking in Shoshone Dreamtime: A Family System Constellation.* Llumina Press.

Mayo Clinic. http://www.mayoclinic.org/diseases-conditions/borderline-personality-disorder/basics/treatment/con-20023204.

McCarty, Wendy Anne (2012). *Welcoming Consciousness: Supporting Babies' Wholeness From the Beginning of Life - An Integrated Model of Early Development.* Santa Barbara, CA: Wondrous Beginnings Publishing (Orig. 2004).

McGilchrist, Iain (2009). *The Master and his Emissary: The Divided Brain and the Making of the Western World.* London, England: Yale University Press.

Mcquaig, Linda & Brooks, Neil (2011). *The Trouble with Billionaires: Why Too Much Money At The Top Is Bad For Everyone.* Penguin.

Mercola, Joseph. http://mercola.com.

Milan School, paradoxical intervention approaches https://postmoderntherapies.wikispaces.com/Milan+Family+Therapy.

Minuchin, Salvador (1974). *Families and Family Therapy*, London: Tavistock.

Minuchin, Salvador & Fishman, Charles (1981). *Family Therapy Techniques.* Boston: Harvard University.

Mison, Karel (1986). Statistical processing of diagnostics done by subject and by physician, *Proceedings of the 6th International Conference on Psychotronic Research*, 137-138.

Moody, Raymond A. (1975). *Life After Life*, New York: Bantam.

Moore, Michael (2015). *Where to Invade Next?* (Film).

Moore, TJ. Cohen, MR. et al. (2007). Serious adverse drug events reported to the food and drug administration, 1998-2005, *Archives of Internal Medicine, 167*:1752-1759.

Morse, Melvin with Perry, Paul (1994). *Parting Visions: An Exploration of Pre-Death Psychic and Spiritual Experiences.* New York: Villard/ Random House.

Motoyama, Hiroshi (1981). *Theories of the Chakras: Bridge to Higher Consciousness.* Wheaton, IL: Theosophical.

Myers, AT/ Myers, FWH. (1894). Mind-cure, faith-cure and the miracles of Lourdes, *Proceedings of the Society Psychical Research*, 9, 160- 209.

Myss, Caroline (1996). *Anatomy of the Spirit: The Seven Stages of Power and Healing.* New York: Harmony.

Newton, John (2001). *Journey of Souls: Case Studies of Life Between Lives.* St. Paul, MN: Llewellyn (orig. 1994).

Nash, Carroll B. (1982). Psychokinetic control of bacterial growth, *J. of the Society for Psychical Research*, 51, 217-221.

Nash, Carroll B. (1984). Test of psychokinetic control of bacterial mutation, *J. of the American Society for Psychical Research*, 78(2), 145-152.

Nelson, Bradley (2007). *The Emotion Code.* Wellness Unmasked Publishing.

Newton, Michael & Duff, Michael (2000). *Destiny of Souls: New Case Studies of Life Between Lives*, St Paul, MN: Llewellyn.

NHS Choices: Your health, your choices. http://www.nhs.uk/Livewell/fitness/Pages/Whybeactive.aspx

Nichols, Michael P. (2012), *Family Therapy: Concepts and Methods* (10th Ed). Pearson.

'OCD' International OCD Foundation, https://iocdf.org/about-ocd/treatment/erp/

Offredy, M. (1998). The application of decision-making concepts by nurse practitioners in general practice. *Journal of Advanced Nursing.* 28, 988-1000

O'Laoire, Seán, (1997). An experimental study of the effects of distant, intercessory prayer on self-esteem, anxiety, and depression, *Alternative Therapies*, 3(6), 38-53.

Oldham, John M. (2015). *Personality Disorders and DSM-5.* American College of Psychiatrists Annual Meeting, Tucson, AZ – February 19. https://www.acpsych.org/content/documents/oldham.pdf

Omalu BI, DeKosky ST, Minster RL, et al. (2005). Chronic traumatic encephalopathy in a National Football League player. Neurosurgery. Jul;57(1):128-34; discussion 128-34.

Orloff, Judith, *Second Sight: The Personal Story of a Psychiatrist Clairvoyant.* New York: Warner 1996.

Osis, Karlis/ Haraldsson, Erlendur (1977). *At the Hour of Death.* New York: Discus/ Avon.

Owens, JE. Cook, EW. Stevenson, I. (1990). Features of "near-death experience" in relation to whether or not patients were near death, *Lancet, 336*, 1175-1177.

Page, Christine (2004). *Beyond the Obvious; Bringing Intuition into our Awakening Consciousness.* London: C.W. Daniel Company, Ltd.

Patel, Meera Lee (2015). *Start Where You Are: A Journal for Self-Exploration.* Tarcher/Penguin.

Payne, John L. (2005). *The Healing of Individuals, Families & Nations: Transgenerational Healing & Family Constellations.* Forres, Scotland: Findhorn. See book review with quotes that more fully express my summaries of Payne's observations and suggestions: http://ijhc.org/2016/01/ijhc-book-reviews-september-2010/

Peat, F. David (1987). *Synchronicity: The Bridge Between Matter and Mind.* New York and London: Bantam.

Peoch, R. (1995), [Mentions research on chicks imprinted on a robot programmed by a random number generator] Network *(Journal of Scientific and Medical Network, UK)*, vol. 62. Discussed in http://paranormal.se/psi/pk/djur.html.

Perls, Fritz (1992). *Gestalt Therapy Verbatim.* Gestalt Journal Press.

Petschke, H. (1953a) *Uber Beziehung zwischen der Blutkorperchensenkungsreaktion radioiisthetischen Befunden und meteorologischen Vorgiingen.* Medizinische 39: 1263

Petschke, H. (1953b) *Uber Beziehung zwischen der Blutkorperchensenkungsreaktion radioiisthetischen Befunden und meteo* List of References 315 *rologischen Vorgiingen.* Medizinische 52: 1759-1761

Pettit, Sabina (1996). *Energy Medicine: Pacific Flower and Sea Essences*, Victoria, BC Canada: Pacific Essences (Box 8317, V8W 3R9).

Polge, J. (1995). *Critical thinking: the use of intuition in making clinical nursing judgements.* Journal of the New York State Nurses Association. 26, 4-9

Pope, Ilse (1987). A view of earth energies from Continental Europe, *J of the British Society of Dowsers,*32, 130-139.

Pray, L. (2008). *Discovery of DNA structure and function: Watson and Crick.* Nature Education 1(1):100. https://www.nature.com/scitable/topicpage/discovery-of-dna-structure-and-function-watson-397

Radin, D., et al, (1995). Remote mental influence of human electrodermal activity, *European J. Parapsychology*, 11, 19-34.

Radin, Dean (1997). *The Conscious Universe.* New York: HarperCollins.

Radin, Dean (2006). *Entangled Minds: Extrasensory Experiences in a Quantum Reality*, New York: Paraview Pocket Books/ Simon & Schuster.

Radin DI and Ferrari DC. (1991). Effects of consciousness on the fall of dice: A meta-analysis, *Journal of Scientific Exploration*, 5, 61-84.

*Ramanujan, The Man Who Knew Infinity*, Starring Dev Patel, 2015, based on this book.

New Zealand. Relative risks of hospital care, pharmaceutical drugs, traffic accidents, foods and dietary supplements. http://laleva.cc/petizione/ronlaw/relative_risks_bubbles3.pdf

Rando, Therese A. (1991). *How to Go On Living When Someone You Love Dies.* New York: Bantam Books.

Ray, Reginald A. (2008). *Touching Enlightenment – Finding Realization in the Body.* Boulder, CO: Sounds True Inc. .

Reddy, Michael (2012). *Health, Happiness, & Family Constellations: How Ancestors, Family Systems, and Hidden Loyalties Shape Your Life.* ReddyWorks Press.

Reiki. http://reiki-light.co.uk/a-brief-history-of-reiki/

Resch, G. & Gutmann, V. (1987). *Scientific Foundations of Homeopathy.* Berlin: Barthel & Barthel.

Rhine, J. B, (1964). *Extrasensory Perception.* Boston: Branden.

Rhine, Louisa E, (1961). *Hidden Channels of the Mind.* New York: William Morrow.

Rhine, Louisa E, (1967). *ESP in Life and Lab: Tracing Hidden Channels.* New York: MacMillan.

Ring, Kenneth. *Life at Death: Scientific Investigation of the Near-Death Experience.* New York: Coward, McCann & Geoghegan 1980.

Ring, Kenneth. *Heading Towards Omega*, New York: Morrow 1984.

Ring, Kenneth & Cooper, Sharon (1999). *Mindsight.* William James Centre for Consciousness Studies, UK.

Rocard, Yves (1964). *Le Signal du Sourcien Paris: Dunod.* (French, cited in Hansen 1982)

Roe, Chris. Sonnex, Charmaine. Roxburgh, Elizabeth C. (2015). Two meta-analyses of noncontact healing studies *Explore*; 11, 11-23.

Ronningstam, E., & Weinberg, I. (2013). Narcissistic Personality Disorder: Progress in Recognition and Treatment. *J of Lifelong Learning in Psychiatry*, Spring XI(2), 167-177. http://focus.psychiatryonline.org/data/Journals/FOCUS/926935/167.pdf

Rosa, Linda et al, (1998). A close look at Therapeutic Touch, *J. American Medical Association*, 279(13), 1005-1010.

Rosenshein, Julie B. (2013). *Parenting the Highly Sensitive Child: A guide for parents & caregivers of ADHD, Indigo and Highly Sensitive Children.* Bloomington, IN: Balboa/ Hay House.

Ross, Rupert (2006). *Dancing with a Ghost: Exploring Aboriginal Reality.* Penguin Canada.

Ross, Rupert (2014). *Indigenous Healing: Exploring Traditional Paths.* Penguin Canada.

Royce, D. The near death experience, a survey of clergy attitudes and knowledge, *J Pastoral Care* 1985, 39, 31-42.

Sacks, Oliver (1998). *A Leg to Stand On.* Touchstone Reprint.

Schneck, G. (1993). Book review of Bergsmann, O. *Risk Factor Place, Dowsing Zone and |Man: Scientific Study Investigating Place-Related Influences on Man*, University Publishing House Facultas 1990, reviewed in: J of the British Society of Dowsers, 239, 236-238.

Schulz, Mona Lisa (1998). *Awakening Intuition: Using Your Mind-Body Network for Insight and Healing.* New York: Harmony.

Schulz, Mona Lisa (2005). *The New Feminine Brain – How Women Can Develop Their Inner Strengths, Genius, and Intuition.* New York. Free Press.

Schwartz, Gary E. Russek, Linda G. Beltran, Justin (1995). Interpersonal hand-energy registration: evidence for implicit performance and perception, *Subtle Energies*, 6(3), 183-200.

Schwarz, Berthold E. (1967). Possible telesomatic reactions, *J Medical Society of New Jersey*, 64, 600-603.

Scofield, AM. (1984). Experimental research in homeopathy: A critical review, *British Homeopathic J* Part I –73(3), 160-180; Part II – 1984b, 73(4), 211-226.]

Shapiro, Francine (1995). *Eye Movement Desensitization and Reprocessing.* New York: Guildford.

Shealy, Norman (1975). The role of psychics in medical diagnosis, In: Carlson, Rick (ed), *Frontiers of Science and Medicine*, Chicago, IL: Contemporary.

Shealy, Norman (1988). *Clairvoyant diagnosis, In: Srinivasan, T. M, Energy Medicine Around the World.* Phoenix, AZ: Gabriel, 291-303.

Shealy, C.N. (1979). Effects of transcranial neurostimulation upon mood and serotonin production: a preliminary report. *Il dolore,* Vol. 1, No. 1, 13-16.

Shealy, C.N., Cady, R.K., Wilkie, R.G., et al. (1989a). Depression: a diagnostic neurochemical profile & therapy with cranial electrical stimulation (CES). *The Journal of Neurological & Orthopaedic Medicine & Surgery*, Vol. 10, Issue 4, (December). pp. 319-321.

Shealy, C.N., Cady, R.K., Wilkie, R.G., et al. (1989b). *Depression: a diagnostic neurochemical profile and therapy with cranial electrical stimulation (CES).* Energy Fields in Medicine, the John E. Fetzer Foundation, Kalamazoo, MI, pp. 446-457.

Shealy, C.N., Cady, R.K., Veehoff, D., et al. (1992). (The neurochemistry of depression. *American Journal of Pain Management*, Vol. 2, No. 1, January pp. 13-16

Shealy, C.N., Cady, R.K., Veehoff, D.C., et al. (1993). Non-pharmaceutical treatment of depression using a multi-modal approach. *Subtle Energies*, Vol. 4, No. 2, pp. 125-134]

Shem, Samuel (2012). *The House of God.* Reissue edition, Berkley

Siegel, Bernie. Approximate quote from my memory, verified with Bernie.

Siegel, Bernie (2013). *The Art Of Healing.* New World Library.

Silbey, Uma (2016). *The Ultimate Guide to Crystals & Stones: A Practical Path to Personal Power, Self-Development, and Healing.* Skyhorse.

Smith, Rodney (1998). *Lessons from the Dying.* Boston: Wisdom.

Smith, Rudolph & Boericke, Garth W. (1968). Changes caused by succession on NMR patterns and bioassay of bradykinin triacetate (BKTA) succussions and dilutions, *J of the American Institute of Homeopathy*, 61, 197-2 12.

Snel, Frans & Hol, P. R. (1983). Psychokinesis experiments in casein induced amyloidosis of the hamster, *European J. of Parapsychology*, 5(1), 51-76.

Snow, Chet (1993). *Mass Dreams of the Future: Do we face an apocalypse or a global spiritual awakening? The choice is ours, Featuring hypnotic future-life progressions by Helen* Wambach, Crest Park, CA: Deep Forest.

Solfvin, Gerald F. (1982). sorins Psi expectancy effects in psychic healing studies with malarial mice, *European J. of Parapsychology*, 4(2), 160-197.

Sorin, Sergey. http://samvitwellness.org/bio-field-viewing
Spangler, David (1975). *The Laws of Manifestation*. Forres, Moray, Scotland: Findhorn Foundation.
Spiritual Emergence Network http://spiritualemergence.info/
Staggs, Sara. Symptoms & Diagnosis of PTSD. http://psychcentral.com/lib/symptoms-and-diagnosis-of-ptsd/
Steichen, Edward (2016). *Family of Man: 60th Anniversary Edition*. New York: Museum of Modern Art.
Stevens, Jane Ellen. *The Adverse Childhood Experiences Study — the Largest Public Health Study You Never Heard Of, Part Two*. http://www.huffingtonpost.com/jane-ellen-stevens/the-adverse-childhood-exp_4_b_1943772.html (More on the ACE study at: Jane Stevens blog: Aces too High https://acestoohigh.com/author/jestevens/; The Adverse Childhood Experiences study: a springboard to hope http://acestudy.org/index.html; Adverse Childhood Experiences (ACEs) https://www.cdc.gov/violenceprevention/acestudy/; For more detailed, formal testing see the ACE quiz on line. http://www.npr.org/sections/health-shots/2015/03/02/387007941/take-the-ace-quiz-and-learn-what-it-does-and-doesnt-mean)
Stevenson, Ian (1974a). *Xenoglossy: A Review and Report of a Case*, Charlottesville, VA: University of Virginia.
Stevenson, Ian (1974b). *20 Cases Suggestive of Reincarnation*. Charlottesville, VA: University of Virginia.
Stevenson, Ian (1987). *Children Who Remember Previous Lives: A Question of Reincarnation*. Charlottesville, VA: University of Virginia.
Stevenson, Ian, (1997). *Where Reincarnation and Biology Intersect*. Westport, CT: Praeger.
Stewart, Ian & Joines, Vann (1991). *TA Today*. Chapel Hill, NC: Lifespace. Bokstavsbarn, https://www.youtube.com/watch?v=EQ71vgRzCA4
Suicide Alerts: WebMD http://www.webmd.com/depression/guide/depression-recognizing-signs-of-suicide#1
Suicide.org http://www.suicide.org/suicide-warning-signs.html
Surowiecki, James (2005). *The Wisdom of Crowds*. New York: Anchor/Random House.
Sylvia, Claire & Novak, W. A (1997). *Change of Heart*. Boston: Little, Brown..
Tamblyn, R. Eguale, T. Huang, A. et al. (2014). The incidence and determinants of primary nonadherence with prescribed medication in primary care: a cohort study. *Annals of Internal Medicine*. 160(7):441-450. DOI: 10.7326/M13-1705.
Targ, R. & Puthoff, H. (1974). Information transmission under conditions of sensory shielding, *Nature*, 252, 602-607.
Tavris, Carol & Aronson, Elliott (2007). *Mistakes Were Made (but not by me)*. Orlando, Harvest/Harcourt.
Taylor, Jill Bolte (2009). *My stroke of insight*. Penguin; also Web reference: http://www.ted.com/talks/jill_bolte_taylor_s_powerful_stroke_of_insight#t-14408
Taylor-Reilly, David, et al. (1986 ). Is homeopathy a placebo response: Controlled trial of homeopathic potency, with pollen in hayfever as model, *Lancet*. (October), 881-886. 65-74.
Thackara, W.T.S. http://www.theosophy-nw.org/theosnw/world/med/me-wtst2.htm
Therapeutic Touch: Therapeutic Touch International Association (TTIA) http://therapeutictouch.org/.
Thomas, JM; Cohen, MR, et al. (2007). Serious adverse drug events reported to the food and drug administration, 1998-2005, *Archives of Internal Medicine*. 167:1752-1759.
Tiller, William A. (1997). *Science and Human Transformation: Subtle Energies, Intentionality and Consciousness*.
Tiller, William A. Dibble, Walter E. & Kohane, Michael J. (2001). *Conscious Acts of Creation: The emergence of a New Physics*, Walnut Creek, CA: Pavior
Today I Found Out http://www.todayifoundout.com/index.php/2010/07/humans-have-a-lot-more-than-five-senses/
Tromp, Sol W. (1949). *Psychical Physics: A Scientific Analysis of Dowsing, Radiesthesia and Kindred Divining Phenomena*, New York: Elsevier 1949.
Twelve-steps programs: *see 12-Steps*
US Food and Drug Administration acknowledgment of Medicine as the 4th leading cause of death. www.fda.gov/Drugs/DevelopmentApprovalProcess/DevelopmentResources/DrugInteractionsLabeling/ucm114848.htm (Accessed 29 March 2014) The third leading cause of death after cancer and heart disease is not stated here. Recently, deaths from Alzheimer's Disease have brought them into third place on this list.
van Campen, Crétien (Editor), Berman, Greta & Galeyev, Bulat. Bibliography: *Synesthesia in Art and Science*. https://www.leonardo.info/isast/spec.projects/synesthesiabib.html
van der Kolk, Bessel A. (2005). Developmental Trauma Disorder. Psychiatric Annals; May; 35(5); *Psychology Module* 401-408. http://www.wjcia.org/conpast/2008/trauma/trauma.pdf
van Gelder, Dora (Kunz) (1978). *The Real World of Fairies*, Wheaton, IL: Quest/ Theosophical.
van Lommel, Pim, et al. (2001). *Near-death experience in survivors of cardiac arrest: a prospective study in the Netherlands*, Lancet, 358, 2039-2045.
Vargas, Luis A, et al. (1989). Exploring the multidimensional aspects of grief reactions, *American J Psychiatry*,

146(11), 1484-9.
Vaughan, Alan (1974). Investigation of Silva Mind Control claims, in: *Research in Parapsychology* 1973, Metuchen, NJ: Scarecrow.
Vaughan, Alan (1979). *Incredible Coincidence: The Baffling World of Synchronicity.* Scranton, PA: Harper and Row.
von Pohl, Gustav Freiherr (1987). *Earth Currents: Causative Factor of Cancer and Other Diseases*, Diessen nr Munich: Jos C. Hubers Verlag 1932; Frech-Verlag GmbH (English, ISBN 3-7724-9402-1).
Walsh, Froma & McGoldrick, Monica (Eds) (1995). *Living Beyond Loss: Death in the family.* New York: W. W. Norton.
Walsch, Neale Donald (1997). *Conversations With God: An Uncommon Dialogue.* Charlottesville, VA: Hampton Roads Publishing Company, Inc.,.
Walsch, Neale Donald (2004-2006). *The Little Soul and the Sun, Adapted from Conversations With God, Books 1 and 3.* New Spirituality Network, a service of Humanity's Team
Walther, S. (1981). *Applied Kinesiology, Vol. I. Basic Procedure and Muscle Testing.* Pueblo, CO: Systems DC.
Wambach, Helen (1978). *Reliving Past Lives: The Evidence Under Hypnosis.* New York: Harper and Row.
Wardell, D. Kagel, S. Anselme, L. (2014). *Healing Touch: Enhancing life through energy therapy.* Bloomington, IN: iUniverse.
White, Ian. (1994). *Australian Bush Flower Essences.* Forres, Moray, Scotland: Findhorn Foundation.
Weiss, Brian (1988). *Many Lives, Many Masters.* New York: Simon & Schuster 1994.
Weiss, Brian (1996). *Only Love is Real, New York.* Warner/ London: Piatkus.
Weizenbaum, Joseph. http://www.manifestation.com/neurotoys/eliza.php3
West, DJ. (1957). *Eleven Lourdes Miracles.* London: Helix.
Whitmont, Edward C. (1980). *Psyche and Substance: Essays on Homeopathy in the Light of Jungian Psychology.* Berkeley, CA: Homeopathic Education Services and North Atlantic Books.
Whitmont, Edward C. (1993). *The Alchemy of Healing: Psyche and Soma.* Berkeley, CA: Homeopathic Education Services and North Atlantic Books.
Wilber, Ken (1981). *No Boundary: Eastern and Western Approaches to Personal Growth.* Boulder, CO: Shambala.
Wilber, Ken (2000). *Integral Psychology: Consciousness, Spirit, Psychology, Therapy.* Boston: Shambhala Publications.
Williamson, Jamie (2014). *Understanding the Highly Sensitive Child: Seeing an Overwhelming World through Their Eyes.* http://Ebookbydesign.com.
Wills-Brandon, Carla (2000). *One Last Hug Before I Go: The Mystery and Meaning of Deathbed Visions.* Deerfield Beach, FL: Health Communications, Inc..
Wilson, Lori (2005). *De-mystifying - Medical Intuition.* Toronto, Ontario, Canada: Lori Wilson Educational Corporation.
Wright, Machaelle Small (1988). *Flower Essences: Reordering Our Understanding and Approach to Illness and Health.* Jeffersonton, VA: Perelandra.
Wright, Susan Marie (1988). *Development and Construct Validity of the Energy Field Assessment Form* (dissertation) Rush University College of Nursing.
Young, D. & Aung, S. (1997). An experimental test of psychic diagnosis of disease, *Journal of Alternative and Complementary Medicine,* 3(1), 39-53.
Young, TM. (1975). Nuclear magnetic resonance studies of succussed solutions, *J of the American Institute of Homeopathy*,68, 8-16.
Zeff, Ted (2004). *The Highly Sensitive Person's Survival Guide: Essential Skills for Living Well in an Overstimulating World.* Oakland, CA: New Harbinger.
Zeff, Ted (2007). *The Highly Sensitive Person's Companion: Daily Exercises for Calming Your Senses in an Overstimulating World.* Oakland, CA: New Harbinger.
Zeff, Ted (2010). *The Strong Sensitive Boy: Help Your Son Become a Happy, Confident Man.* San Ramon, CA: Prana.
Zeff, Ted (2013). *Raise an Emotionally Healthy Boy: Save Your Son From the Violent Boy Culture.* Prana.
Zeff, Ted (2015). *The Power of Sensitivity: Success Stories of Highly Sensitive People Thriving in a Non-sensitive World.* Prana.
Zert, Vlastimil (1979). Psychotronic research as an active assistance in modern bioengineering, *Proceedings of 4th International Conference on Psychotronic Research.* Seo Paulo, 123-130.
Zukav, Gary (2011). *Spiritual Partnership: The Journey to Authentic Power.* HarperOne.
Zukerman, Marvin (1994). *Behavioral Expressions and Biosocial Bases of Sensation Seeking.* NY: Cambridge University Press.

# INDEX

## Author Names

### A
*Adelaja, Sunday... 282*
*Alcorn, Robert... 40*
*Alexander, Eben... 460, 487, 517, 528*
*Ampère, Andrè... 371*
*Anda, Robert... 152*
*Anonymous... 60, 67, 165, 166, 217, 242, 304, 378, 494, 520*
*Arama... 68*
*Aristotle... 391*
*Aron, Elaine... 12, 13, 23, 30, 33, 46, 47, 73, 89, 96, 184, 226, 314, 517, 518*
*Astin, John... 411*
*Atwater, PMH... 482*
*Avicenna... 408*

### B
*Bach, Edward... 299*
*Bachelard, Gaston... 108*
*Bachler, Kaethe... 388*
*Bailey & Yates... 486*
*Bakker (Tammy Faye) & Hoffman... 528*
*Bandler, Richard... 292*
*Barasch, Marc Ian... 474*
*Barry, Lynda... 114, 240*
*Battiste & Henderson... 363*
*Bell, Christopher... 87*
*Bem and Honorton... 382*
*Benedict, Mellen-Thomas... 460, 486, 487, 517, 529*
*Bengston, William... 400, 404*
*Bennett, Arnold... 458*
*Benor, Daniel J.... 5, 97, 263, 368, 463*
*Benveniste... 400*
*Berdyaev, Nikolai... 447*
*Berne, Eric... 101, 519*
*Betz, Hans-Dieter... 387*
*Birch... 524*
*Blake, William... 299*
*Boese, Paul... 358*
*Bolen, Jean Shinoda... 447, 518*
*Bowman, Carol... 474, 529*
*Boyd, WE... 294, 400*
*Braud, William G... 411, 504, 527*
*Brennan, Barbara... 354*
*Brilliant, Ashleigh... 365*
*Burgess, Frank Gillette... 292*
*Burnett, Carol... 101*
*Burton, L. A.... 316*
*Bush, Marabai... 272*
*Byrd, Randolph... 527*

### C
*Cannon, Dolores... 529*
*Capra, Fritjof... 374*
*Carmichael, Amy... 206*
*Carrey, Jim... 344*
*Castleman, Tess... 518*
*Caulfield, Timothy... 62*

*Chapman, Gary... 334, 522*
*Chess, Stella... 211*
*Christie, Agatha... 377*
*Chun & Kim... 445*
*Church, Dawson... 138, 528*
*Cochrane, Archie MD... 127*
*Coelho, Paulo... 392*
*Cohen, Kenneth S... 408, 517*
*Cox, Thomas... 526*
*Craig, Gary... 12, 332*
*Crick, Francis... 377*

### D
*Dabney, M... 94*
*Dalebout, Katie... 353*
*Daskalos... 472, 529*
*Dass, Ram... 120, 272, 480*
*Davenas, E... 400, 522, 526*
*de Becker, Gavin... 375*
*de Chardin, Pierre Teilhard... 209, 457, 480*
*Descartes, René... 432*
*Dickens, Charles... 197*
*Diehl, Manfred... 190*
*Doll, Erich... 528*
*Dossey, Larry MD... 5*
*Douglas, Hebert... 525*
*Douillard, John... 203*
*Dowling, St. John... 406, 526*
*Dragoman, Poole Heather... 12*
*Dunne, JW... 381, 385, 525*

### E
*Eccles, John C.... 461*
*Edison, Thomas... 371*
*Edwards, Harry... 414, 415, 528*
*Edwards, J... 161*
*Einstein, Albert... 74, 329, 369, 371*
*Eliza... 318, 523*
*Elva, Thordis... 524*
*Emerson, Ralph Waldo... 254, 463*
*Erasmus... 467*
*Evans, Madeline... 404*

### F
*Faraday, Michael... 371*
*Feinstein, David... 503*
*Felitti, Vincent... 152*
*Fenton, Bruce... 386*
*Feynman, Richard... 371, 525*
*Flaxman, Greg... 524*
*Francis, Richard C... 528*
*Frost, Robert... 247*

### G
*Gallup, George Jr... 485*
*Gauss, Karl... 371*
*Gerald, Michael C... 528*
*Gersten, David... 158, 529*
*Gibran, Khalil... 203, 237, 324, 380, 434*
*Gladwell, Malcolm... 423, 525*
*Godwin, Malcolm... 468, 529*
*Goethe, Johann Wolfgang von... 219*
*Goldenberg, Irene... 522, 523, 533, 541*
*Goleman, Daniel... 203, 505, 528*
*Goodrich, Joyce... 527*

*Gordon, Thomas... 110, 232, 233*
*Goss, Michael... 526*
*Goyal, Madhav... 524*
*Grad, Bernard... 400, 526*
*Green, William Michael... 527*
*Griffiths, Colin... 403, 541*
*Grof, Stanislav... 466*
*Guiley, Rosemary Ellen... 326*
*Guillemets, Terri... 224*
*Gurudas... 522*

**H**
*Hamne, Gunilla... 161*
*Haraldsson, Erlendur... 485*
*Hartmann, E... 526*
*Hart, Tobin... 474, 529*
*Harvey, Clare... 522*
*Hawken, Paul... 359, 362, 363*
*Hellinger, Bert... 97, 307*
*Henton, Darcy... 438*
*Herman, Judith... 156, 158, 159, 519*
*Hill, Napoleon... 470*
*Hippocrates... 33, 92, 518*
*Hockney, David... 89*
*Honorton, C... 382, 525*
*Honorton & Ferrari... 382, 525*
*Howard, Judy... 522*
*Hubbard, Elbert... 304*
*Hurwitz, Wendy MD... 513*
*Hustvedt, Siri... 183*

**J**
*Jaeger, Barrie... 84, 517*
*Jahn, Robert G... 385, 525*
*Jami, Criss... 75*
*Janov, Arthur... 340*
*Jeffrey, Francis... 77*
*Jensen, Anne M... 419*
*Johnson, Samuel... 424*
*Johnson, Steve... 300*
*Jonas, W... 410*
*Jones & Jenkins... 294, 400*
*Jones, RL... 294, 400*
*Josephson, Brian... 293*
*Jovanovic, Pierre... 525, 529*
*Judith, Anodea... 524*
*Jung, Carl... 34, 73, 75, 76, 79, 84, 113, 414, 427, 447*

**K**
*Kaptchuk, Ted... 518, 524*
*Karagulla & Kunz... 394, 396, 524, 525*
*Karagulla, Shafika... 394, 396, 524, 525*
*Kaye, Danny... 511*
*Keller, Helen... 95, 204*
*Kelvin, Lord... 371*
*Kennedy, John F.... 74*
*King, Lindy... 377, 525*
*Klein, Naomi... 360, 361, 362*
*Klein, R... 518*
*Klopfer, Bruno... 444*
*König, Hebert... 526*
*Koontz, Dean... 379*
*Krieger, D... 396*
*Kubler-Ross, Elisabeth... 171, 178*

*Kunz, Dora... 394, 396, 524, 525*
*Kwong, Evelyn... 131*

**L**
*Lachman, Larry... 436*
*Landau, Judith MD... 512*
*Lawrence, DH... 50, 383, 416, 525*
*Lawrence, Jerome... 65*
*Law, Ron... 518*
*Lazarou, J... 517, 518*
*LeShan, Lawrence... 350*
*Leskowitz, Eric... 6, 351, 445*
*Levey, Joel... 455, 456*
*Levine, Stephen... 425, 499*
*Linde, K... 297*
*Lord, Lewis... 371, 437, 524*
*Louv, Richard... 250*

**M**
*MacEnulty, John... 364*
*Manning, Matthew... 526*
*Mansfield, V... 518*
*March, Jenny... 486*
*Markides, K... 529*
*Mason Boring, Francesca... 523*
*McCallion... 445*
*McCarty, Wendy Anne... 178, 529*
*McCraty, et al.... 401*
*McGilchrist, Iain... 66, 431*
*Michael Nichols... 536, 542*
*Minuchin, Salvador... 522, 523*
*Mison, Karel... 392*
*Moody, Raymond A... 529*
*Moore, Michael... 522*
*Moore, Thomas... 496, 518*
*Moore, TJ... 144*
*Morrison, Van... 76*
*Motoyama, Hiroshi... 524*
*Mridha, Debasish... 91*
*Myss, Caroline... 392*

**N**
*Nash, Carroll B... 411, 504*
*Newman, Catherine... 201*
*Newton, Michael... 479*
*Nichols, Michael... 522, 523, 542*
*Nouwen, Henri... 225*

**O**
*Offredy, M... 525*
*O'Laoire, Sean... 527*
*Oldham, John M... 192*
*Omalu, Bl... 62*
*Orloff, Judith... 526*
*Osis, Karli... 485*
*Osler, Sir William... 49*

**P**
*Pasahow... 445*
*Pascal, Blaise... 74, 198*
*Pasternak, Boris... 45*
*Patanjali... 371*
*Patel, Meera Lee... 353*
*Payne, John L... 309, 310, 311, 451*
*Peat, F. David... 518*
*Peoch, R... 391*

Perls, Fritz... 282
Petschke, H... 526
Pettit, Sabrina... 522
Piergrossi, Brian... 507
Planck, Max... 130
Plato... 321, 367
Poincaré, Henri... 371
Polge, J... 525
Pope, Ilse... 388
Pray, L... 377
Pritchard, Michael... 500

**Q**
Quinn, Robert... 505

**R**
Radin, Dean... 374, 382, 391, 525, 526, 527
Ramanujan, Srinivasa... 126, 127
Rambeau... 388
Ray, Reginald A... 528
Reddy, Michael... 308, 523
Reeve, Paul... 12
Resch, G... 522, 526
Rhine, J.B.... 380, 381, 525
Rhine, Louisa... 384, 386
Ring... 481, 482, 527, 529
Robbins, Tom... 111
Rodgers and Hammerstein... 124
Roe, Chris... 411
Romanyshyn, Robert... 181
Rosa, Linda... 397, 526
Rose, Andrea... 513
Rosenshein, Julie... 241, 521, 522
Ross, Rupert... 156, 159, 178, 363, 493, 494, 519, 527, 528, 529
Royce, D... 482
Ruiz, Don Miguel... 218
Russell, Bertrand... 429

**S**
Sacks, Oliver... 92, 518
Schachter-Shalomi, Zalman... 455
Schlitz, Marilyn... 527
Schmeidler, Gertrude... 383
Schneck, G... 525
Schumacher, E. F.... 503
Schwartz, Gary... 397
Schwarz, Berthold... 416
Scofield, AM... 401
Semmelweis, Ignaz... 127, 128
Shakespeare, William... 43, 171
Shapiro, Francine... 12
Shealy, C. Norman... 6, 392, 402, 526
Shepherd, Peter... 497
Siegel, Bernie... 5, 454, 469, 517
Smith, Rodney... 520, 522
Smith, Rudolph... 520, 522
Snow, Chet... 505
Solfvin, Gerald... 410
Somé, Malidoma Patrice... 440
Sontag, Susan... 353
Spangler, David... 452
Sparks, Nicholas... 331
Spencer, Paula Underwood... 81, 518

Staggs, Sara... 155
Steadman, Alice... 484
Stedman, ML... 359
Steichen, Edward... 528
Stevens, Jane Ellen... 152
Stevenson, Ian... 472, 473, 529
Stewart, Ian... 519
Suzuki, David... 439
Sylvia, Claire... 400
Szasz, Thomas... 414

**T**
Tagore, Rabindranath... 336
Tapscott, Don... 528
Targ, R... 385, 525
Taylor, Jill Bolte... 86, 297, 529
Taylor-Reilly... 297
Teilhard de Chardin, Pierre... 209
Tertullian... 260
Tesla, Nikola... 371
Thackara, WTS... 367
Thomas, JM... 211
Thornton, L Thd, RN, MSN, AHN-BC... 6
Tzu, Lao... 350

**U**
Upledger, John E.... 253

**V**
van Campen, Cretien... 398
van der Kolk, Bessel A... 156, 520
van der Kolk, Bessel A.... 133
van der Post, Laurens... 275, 450, 460, 506
van der Zee... 294
van Lommel, Pim... 481, 482
Vargas, Luis... 415, 441
Vaughan, Alan... 79, 518
von Pohl, Gustav Freiherr... 388

**W**
Walsch, Neale Donald... 201, 244, 452, 504
Walther, S... 524
Wambach, Helen... 476, 505, 529
Ward, Artemus... 129
Waterman, Robert D... 55
Weiss, Brian... 474, 475
Weizenbaum, Joseph... 318
West, D.J.... 405
Wheatley, Margaret... 322
White, Ian... 438, 522
Whitmont, Edward C... 296, 297
Williamson, Jaime... 517
Williamson, Marianne... 416, 439
Wills-Brandon, Carla... 520
Wirkus, Mietek... 394
Wolfgang von Goethe, Johann... 219
Worrall, Olga... 440
Wright, Machaelle Small... 404, 444, 445, 522
Wright, Susan Marie... 397, 444, 445, 522

**Y**
Young, D... 294, 392, 400
Young, TM... 294, 355, 392, 400

**Z**
Zeff, Ted... 3, 5, 12, 30, 47, 130, 220, 517, 519, 521, 522
Zert, Vlastimil... 525

*Zukav, Gary*... 383, 436, 519, 521, 524, 525, 528
*Zukerman, Marvin*... 89

**Topics**

**A**
*Abuse. See Bullying*
    *emotional abuse*... 155
    *physical abuse*... 169, 355
    *sexual abuse*... 111, 134, 156, 214, 332, 358, 417, 519
*Acupuncture*... 330, 523
    *acupuncture points*... 301, 330, 395, 523
    *chakras*... 18, 301, 394, 402, 523
    *meridians*... 301, 302, 330, 445, 523
    *points*... 264, 270, 289, 295, 301, 303
*Addiction*... 304
    *Al-Anon*... 306
*Adverse Childhood Experiences (ACE)*... 152
*Alcohol and Substances*... 164, 304
    *abuse*... 164
    *addiction*... 304
    *Alcoholics Anonymous (AA)*... 304
    *treatment*... 304, 306
*Allergies*... 51, 67, 109, 250, 269, 392, 399
*American Psychiatric Association*... 155, 192, 521
*Anchoring*... 292, 523, 524
*Angels*... 374, 468, 529
*Anger*... 63, 172, 213, 217, 229
*Anxieties*... 34, 60, 62, 133, 268
    *meta-anxieties*... 31, 59, 139, 141, 177, 188, 193, 209, 254, 265, 269, 271, 339, 357, 417, 516, 519, 520, 521, 522, 524, 527
    *meta-positives*... 62, 158, 212, 344, 520
*Arama*... 68
*Aristotle*... 391
*Association for Comprehensive Energy Psychology (ACEP)*... 12, 516, 524
*Attachment styles*... 35, 190
*Attention Deficit Hyperactivity Disorder (ADHD)*... 34, 184
*Avicenna*... 408

**B**
*Bach remedies*
    *eating healthy, regularly*... 326
    *exercise*... 203, 327
    *food*
        *comfort eating*... 331
        *cravings*... 331
        *obesity*... 110, 152, 153, 203, 269, 307, 326, 331, 333, 524
        *overeating*... 332
        *supplements*... 326, 327
    *HSPs and their HSPCs*... 235, 236
    *relaxations*... 328
        *muscle relaxation*... 328
    *rescue remedy*... 299
    *systematic desensitization*... 329
    *Transactional Analysis (TA)*... 101
*Bias*
    *confirmation bias*... 120
*Biological energy (bioenergy)*
    *assessments*... 152, 396, 397
    *fields*... 26, 41, 51, 294, 330, 389, 394, 396, 398, 401, 524
    *interacting with matter*... 391
    *medicine*... 379, 394
    *research*... 396
    *sense*... 329, 397
    *unusual properties*... 399
*Body*... 26, 50, 62, 121, 203, 237, 285, 325, 326, 427, 521, 524
*Borderline Personality Disorder*... 192
*Brain*... 34, 520, 527
    *emotional intelligence (EQ)*... 85
    *left and right hemisphere preferences*... 521
    *left brain*... 463
    *neuroplasticity*... 91, 93, 100, 517, 522, 524, 525, 528
    *right brain*... 458
*Bullying*... 64, 138, 139, 144, 148

**C**
*Chakra*... 18, 301, 394, 395, 396, 402, 404, 523
*Chinese cosmology*... 301, 302, 351, 408, 518
*Closeness*... 40, 190, 192, 198, 200, 204, 226, 311, 318, 319, 398, 442
*Cognative Behavior Therapy (CBT)*... 13, 60, 188, 272, 328
*Cognitive dissonance*... 125, 130
*Collective consciousness*... 410. *See also Consciousness*
*Companion*... 136
*Confirmation bias*... 120
*Conjugations*... 354
*Consciousness*... 121, 364, 372, 402, 447, 516
    *cognitive dissonance*... 125, 130
    *collective family constellation*... 40, 308, 451, 520, 528
    *conscious intuition*... 198, 224, 300, 369, 371, 389, 517
    *healing for humanity*... 322, 503, 520
    *interacting with matter*... 391
    *intuition*... 28, 50, 69, 73
    *of humanity*... 15, 25, 40, 70, 86, 157, 179, 202, 235, 307, 309, 311, 323, 350, 359, 362, 364, 365, 368, 372, 381, 391, 414, 424, 429, 439, 442, 447, 450, 452, 455, 459, 469, 489, 494, 499, 501, 502, 503, 505, 520, 523, 528, 529
    *planetary collective consciousness*... 401, 502, 505, 520
*Council for Healing*... 24, 410
*Cravings*... 89, 103, 160, 165, 263, 270, 296, 306, 331, 332, 333
*Creativity*... 81, 219, 371

**D**
*Death*... 6, 39, 41, 42, 50, 56, 66, 68, 72, 73, 88, 96, 127, 152, 155, 168, 171, 172, 173, 175, 176, 177, 178, 179, 180, 203, 268, 286, 308, 327, 364, 370, 386, 388, 394, 415, 435, 440, 441, 444, 460, 461, 465, 466, 470, 472, 474, 475, 479, 480, 481, 482, 483, 484, 485, 487, 488, 490, 495, 499, 501, 516, 517, 520, 521, 528, 529
*Deathbed experiences of spirits*... 179, 440, 484, 509, 520

*Lessons from NDE's, pre-death and deathbed experiences*... 486
Depression... 37, 40, 53, 77, 95, 96, 103, 110, 134, 136, 151, 152, 162, 163, 164, 166, 167, 171, 172, 179, 192, 194, 263, 276, 295, 298, 304, 306, 307, 309, 327, 331, 351, 356, 375, 402, 403, 436, 438, 439, 464, 477, 499, 501, 504, 514, 520
Diagnoses (Alternative or Additional)
    Attachment styles... 190
    Attention Deficit Hyperactivity Disorder (ADHD)... 184
    Borderline Personality Disorder... 192
    Narcissistic Personality Disorder (NPD)... 194
    Obsessive Compulsive Disorder (OCD)... 188
    Oppositional Defiant Disorder (ODD)... 186
        oppositional children... 186
    Post Traumatic Stress Disorder (PTSD)... 34, 93, 134, 137, 156, 161, 444, 477, 519, 524
Dowsing... 386
    (diseases from) geopathic stress... 387, 525

## E

Ego, observing... 113, 114, 115, 116, 117, 118, 119, 169, 176, 189, 194, 238, 272, 345, 472, 517, 520, 521, 522
Emotional Freedom Techniques (EFT)... 12, 13, 18, 160
Emotions... 49, 53, 121, 204, 206, 238, 307, 331, 350, 429, 517
    emotional intelligence (EQ)... 85
    HSPs and their HSPCs emotions... 36, 235, 372
Energy Medicine... 330, 365, 445, 516, 519, 520, 524, 528
    biological energy... 26, 40, 51, 236, 251, 293, 296, 301, 318, 379, 394, 400, 402, 429, 445, 522
    body energy... 516, 518
    psychology... 111, 129, 143, 160, 165
Energy Psychology (EP)... 12, 13, 28, 39, 111, 129, 143, 160, 165, 188, 263, 277, 303, 306, 330, 445, 503, 512, 516, 519, 520, 524, 528
Environment
    dowsing for geopathic stress... 387
    human disregard for... 64
    relationships with the environment... 49, 64, 67, 123
    wholistic aspect... 67
Evil. See Theodicy
Extrasensory perception (ESP)... 367, 380, 381, 382, 383, 389
Eye Movement Desensitization and Reprocessing (EMDR)... 12, 160, 165

## F

Family
    constellation therapy... 307, 310, 372, 450, 520, 522, 523, 528
    family relationships... 307
    family therapy... 275, 281, 450, 523
Findhorn Foundation... 385
First aid for HSP distress, anxieties and triggered states... 254
Five love languages... 208, 226, 334, 518, 521, 522
Flower Essence Society... 522
Food
    comfort eating... 51, 270, 326, 331, 332, 333
    cravings... 103, 160, 165, 263, 270, 296, 306, 331, 332, 333
    overeating... 111, 134, 331, 332, 333
Forgiveness... 355, 358, 524
Freud... 101
    Eric Berne (TA)... 101

## G

Gaia (planet earth)... 68, 362, 368, 389, 490, 502, 506
Geopathic stress... 387, 388, 525
Gestalt Therapy... 282
Gnowing... 366, 517
God (The Infinite Source; All That Is)... 26, 42, 50, 65, 127, 128, 136, 172, 178, 244, 264, 274, 290, 350, 414, 440, 442, 459, 467, 468, 470, 480, 481, 484, 486, 487, 491, 494, 497, 524. See also All That Is; Infinite Source
Grief... 147, 171, 179, 499, 501, 520
    Collective consciousness of grief and trauma... 465, 499
    initial stages of grief... 172, 175
    middle stages of grief... 172, 175
    resolution stage of grief... 177
    unresolved grief... 39, 149, 156, 175, 178, 179, 215, 223, 229, 258, 259, 307, 308, 309, 310, 465, 499
Group therapy... 129, 159, 289

## H

Healing... 26, 40, 321, 350, 395, 408, 503, 526
    collective consciousness grief and trauma... 307, 499
    Healing the collective consciousness... 323
    intuitive healing... 74
    proxy healing... 164, 272, 503, 504, 505, 520
    psychic healing... 373, 408
    Qigong... 373, 394, 395, 408
    Reiki... 19, 26, 129, 373, 394, 402, 408, 526, 527
    Therapeutic Touch (TT)... 396, 408
Healing touch... 12, 18, 154, 251, 329, 330
Highly sensitive person (HSP)
    challenges of the HSP-HSPC... 220
    children. See HSP children
    companion (HSPC)... 136, 184, 187, 194, 198, 203, 204, 207, 210, 215, 220, 225, 229, 230, 235
    explanatory frameworks... 37, 91, 135, 161, 237, 241, 245, 247, 249, 251, 274, 276, 281, 307, 390, 430, 473, 474, 482
    family of HSPs... 135, 161
    first aid for anxieties, distress, triggered states... 59, 91, 254
    places of peace, safety and healing (PPSH)... 37, 40, 91
    Relationships with other people... 354
    resources and therapies for HSPs... 37, 91, 135, 161, 237, 241, 245, 247, 249, 251, 273, 274, 276, 281, 307, 390, 430, 473, 474, 482
    sensitivity of HSP... 37, 91, 135, 161, 237, 241, 245, 247, 249, 251, 273, 274, 276, 281, 307, 390, 430, 473, 474, 482
    supports for the HSP... 37, 91, 135, 161, 237, 241, 245, 247, 249, 251, 273, 274, 276, 281, 307, 390, 430, 473, 474, 482

*understanding the HSP...* 37, 91, 135, 161, 237, 241, 245, 247, 249, 251, 273, 274, 276, 281, 307, 390, 430, 473, 474, 482
High sensation seeker (HSS)... 89
Homeopathy... 293, 294, 296
    Homeopathic research... 297
    Self-help with homeopathy... 298
HSP children
    Body... 237
    Emotions... 238
    in school... 249
    in separation and divorce... 247
    intuition... 390
    Mind... 239
    Relationships with the environment... 250
    Relations with extended family... 246
    relations with other people... 241
    Spirit... 250
HSP companion (HSPC)... 30, 522
    challenges... 46, 58, 164
    family... 198, 458
    first aid... 254, 260
    giving each other some space... 47
    relationships... 198, 458
    relationships in extended family... 198
    relationships in general with other people... 458
    relationships in general with others... 198
    relationships in school... 458
    relationships in separation and divorce... 458
    relationships in the environment... 260, 458
    sensitivities... 254, 260
    support... 165
    therapies... 148
    understanding the HSP... 32, 33, 75
HSPs and their HSPCs... 36, 275, 322
    Relationships with the environment... 235
    Spirit... 236
Hunger, tiredness, stress, trauma (HuTiST)... 59, 63, 187, 204, 207, 215, 218, 221, 223, 225, 254, 257, 261, 352, 470

**I**
*Infinite Source (God; All That Is)...* 12, 26, 42, 70, 123, 172, 173, 261, 264, 350, 364, 368, 373, 374, 393, 399, 413, 440, 442, 452, 463, 464, 470, 478, 491, 493, 495, 498, 524, 528
Inner child... 34, 108, 111
Inspiration... 371
Integrity... 424, 425, 427, 429, 431, 434, 439, 442, 446, 526
International Spiritual Emergence Network... 467
Intimacy
    How close is close enough?... 106
    Levels of intimacy... 106
Intuition... 73, 364, 369, 371, 375, 376, 377, 379, 416. See Healing
    brief overview... 369
    clairsentience... 367, 380, 382, 389, 399, 408, 409, 499, 525
    creativity with intuition... 499, 525
    ethics... 393
    inspiration... 499, 525
    manifestation... 56, 80, 391, 418, 452, 453, 454, 455, 482, 523, 524
    muscle testing... 466, 471, 525
    pattern recognition... 371, 374, 376, 377, 379
        psychological pattern recognition... 377
        wholistic bioenergy... 379
    precognition... 367, 380, 381, 382, 389, 499, 525
    psychic... 6, 41, 56, 309, 378, 380, 381, 382, 383, 386, 389, 393, 394, 395, 399, 404, 408, 409, 414, 416, 418, 432, 440, 448, 456, 461, 467, 472, 483, 484, 491, 503, 519, 525, 528
    retrieved memory... 375
    telepathy... 50, 367, 381, 382, 389, 408, 499, 525

**J**
Jung
    Carl Jung... 73
    Jungian Perspectives... 73, 228
    synchronicities... 79, 447
    typologies... 30, 518, 523

**L**
*Life, what is it all about?...* 43, 201, 460, 508
Love... 63, 208, 209, 324, 434, 521

**M**
*Manifestation...* 452
Marital/ couples therapy... 18, 117, 166, 224, 226, 231, 233, 259, 275, 281, 307, 357, 359, 520, 528
Medication... 18, 40, 70, 138, 164, 185, 203, 266, 288, 294, 297, 396, 411, 444
    medication side effects... 40, 203, 444
Meditation... 466, 524
Mental judo... 186
Meridians. *See* Acupuncture
Meta-issues
    anxieties... 59, 209
        meta-meta-anxieties... 60
    confidence... 209
    expectations... 209
    positive thoughts and felings... 209
    thoughts and feelings... 55, 77, 92, 99, 100, 113, 117, 141, 142, 151, 154, 160, 161, 163, 202, 211, 227, 262, 263, 265, 266, 282, 292, 316, 332, 340, 343, 344, 345, 348, 353, 364, 380, 434, 499, 500, 501, 517, 519
Mind... 49, 55, 62, 121, 218, 239, 336, 431, 522
    Preventive installing of positivity and meta-positivity... 338
Morning sickness (pregnancy)... 269, 303
Motion sickness... 269
Muscle testing... 258, 298, 389, 417, 418, 419, 423, 466, 471, 522, 526, 527, 528

**N**
*Narcissistic Personality Disorder (NPD)...* 35
Near Death Experiences (NDE)... 366, 394
Neurolinguistic Programming (NLP)... 40, 154, 292, 519
Neuroplasticity... 91, 92, 93, 94, 95, 97, 98, 100, 130, 138, 272, 383, 463, 512, 519, 525
    body... 92
    feelings... 93
    meta-awarenesses... 98
    thoughts... 91

## O

*Obesity (overweight)...* 152, 269, 332
*Observing Ego...* 113, 272, 517, 521
   developing... 118
   full awareness... 115
   partial awareness... 114
*Obsessive Compulsive Disorder (OCD)...* 35, 188
*Oppositional behaviors...* 144, 187
*Oppositional Defiant Disorder (ODD)...* 35, 186
   mental judo... 186, 187
   oppositional children... 186
*Overeating...* 111, 134, 331, 332, 333
*Overwhelm...* 209

## P

*Parapsychology...* 398, 412
   dowsing... 386
   precognition... 367, 372, 380, 499, 525
   psychokinesis (PK)... 391, 526
   reports... 463, 482, 491
   research... 412, 526
      clairsentience... 367, 380, 382, 389, 399, 408, 409, 499, 525
      dowsing... 386, 387, 420
      precognition... 367, 389
      Psychokinesis... 13, 372, 390, 391
*Parent Effectiveness Training (P.E.T.)...* 230, 232, 521
*Past life memories...* 373, 474, 519
   children... 41, 42, 251
   HSP benefits... 390, 472, 476
   hypnotic... 93, 339, 418, 476, 479, 505
   reincarnation... 41, 366, 440, 472, 473, 474, 479, 481, 524
   research... 474, 476
   spontaneous... 479
   therapy... 477
*Pattern recognition...* 55, 56, 371, 374, 376, 377, 378, 379, 380, 525
   psychological pattern... 377
   wholistic bioenergy patterns... 379
*Personality...* 35, 192, 521
   shadow aspects of personalty... 76
*Placebo...* 445
*Place of Peace and Safety and Healing (PPSH)...* 189, 215, 242, 258, 260, 266, 274, 292, 313
*Planet Earth (Gaia)...* 68, 490
*Positivity*
   meta-positivity... 338
   preventive installing... 338
*Post traumatic stress disorder (PTSD)...* 156. *See also Trauma*
   complex PTSD... 519, 524
   post traumatic growth... 159
*Precognition...* 372, 380
*Pre-death experiences...* 483
*Pre-death spirit awareness...* 179, 484, 486
*Pregnancy...* 296
   morning sickness... 269, 303
*Psychic*
   awareness... 382, 399, 408
   disbelievers... 366, 413, 419
   distant awareness... 392, 399, 408

   factors in health and healing... 392, 399, 408
   healing. *See Healing*
   intuition... 372, 380, 393, 408, 517. *See Intuition*
   manifestation... 56, 80, 372, 380, 391, 408, 418, 452
   pattern recognition... 55, 56, 371, 374, 376, 377, 378, 379, 380
   research
      telepathy... 372, 390, 391
   skeptics... 381, 382
   spirits... 41, 50, 70, 414, 415, 459, 464, 465, 479, 488, 489, 502
   telepathy
      ... 13, 372, 390, 391
*Psychokinesis...* 13, 372, 390, 391
   research... 391, 408
*Psychology...* 17, 24, 81, 124, 154, 165
   Conventional Psychology... 124
   Indigenous Psychology... 70, 156, 159
   Modern Psychology... 51, 72, 86, 91
   Western Psychology... 26, 72, 83, 88, 392, 399
*Psychotherapy*
   family... 22, 28, 38
   family constellation... 40, 307
   group... 372
   individual... 77, 78

## Q

*Qigong...* 373, 394, 395, 408

## R

*Reiki...* 19, 26, 129, 373, 394, 402, 408, 527
*Reincarnation...* 472, 524
   past life therapy... 129, 373, 472, 474, 477, 520, 524
   spontaneous memories... 477
*Relationships with other people...* 64, 65, 122, 219, 354, 434
   active listening... 40, 316, 318, 520
   collective... 447
   communicating... 41, 53, 81, 144, 204, 251, 279, 334, 354, 375, 390, 415
   conjugations... 354, 521
   deepening sensitivity... 34, 416
   focusing on positives... 322
   HSPC - HSP... 22, 34, 37
   HSP – HSPC... 203
   Parent Effectiveness Training (P.E.T.)... 230, 232, 521
   reparenting... 287
   touching base with each other... 322
*Relationships with the environment...* 49, 67, 123, 235, 250, 362, 439
   animals... 16, 42, 46, 67, 123, 251, 268, 269, 297, 362, 363, 391, 394, 400, 439, 440, 442, 464, 478, 490, 491, 497, 502, 505, 527
   planetary... 401, 491, 497, 502, 505, 520
   plants... 67, 123, 235, 251, 298, 362, 363, 394, 400, 410, 439, 464, 490, 491, 497, 502, 505
   reparenting... 287
*Research*
   healing research... 18, 19, 24, 41, 42, 69, 88, 152, 186, 302, 327, 352, 360, 366, 367, 372, 381, 388,

391, 397, 400, 410, 456, 476, 503, 504, 516
intuition... 69, 73, 367
parapsychology... 380, 383, 391, 526
Resentments... 144, 145

**S**
Self-help. *See* Meditation, TWR/WHEE, Energy Psychology
Spirit
deathbed experiences... 179, 440, 484, 485, 486, 529
inspires our exisitence... 497, 529
lessons from Spirit awareness... 342, 343, 354, 480
life between physical lives... 485, 529
near death experiences (NDE)... 42, 366, 394, 440, 442, 460, 479, 480, 517
past life therapy... 472
personal spiritual awareness... 458, 497
planetary... 491, 497, 505
pre-death experiences... 485, 486, 529
research... 458
transitioning from physical to Spirit life... 485, 486, 529
Spirit guides... 464
Spirit life
Western scientific research... 461
Spirits
ghosts... 42, 283, 364, 490
relating to live people... 368, 413, 414, 415
Spiritual Emergence Network... 466
Stress... 27, 29, 42, 51, 59, 70, 76, 90, 93, 98, 108, 112, 117, 133, 134, 161, 171
anxieties... 31, 34, 51, 59, 62, 133, 135
de-stress... 40, 117, 133, 149, 161, 167, 180, 199, 209, 215, 221, 242
geopathic... 388, 525
stress hormones... 133, 154, 255
Subjective Units of Distress Scale (SUSS)... 13, 228, 261, 265, 266, 521
Suicide... 138, 153, 161, 162, 163, 164, 172, 439, 500, 520, 529
Synchronicities... 79, 80, 176, 418, 447, 448, 452, 453, 455, 466, 518, 528

**T**
Theodicy... 494
Therapeutic Touch... 19, 26, 129, 373, 394, 396, 402, 408, 411, 527
Therapy
Cognitive Behavioral Therapy (CBT)... 60, 188, 328
Energy Psychology (EP). *See above*
Family Constellation Therapy... 307, 310, 311, 372, 450, 522, 523
Gestalt Therapy... 282
Marital/ couples therapy... 244, 275, 277
Neurolinguistic Programming (NLP)... 40, 154, 292, 519
Polarity Therapy... 373
Primal Therapy... 340
Transactional Analysis (TA)... 34, 101, 102, 129

Two-chair explorations and clearing... 282
Thought Field Therapy (TFT)... 161, 291, 303, 334
Trauma... 29, 146, 154, 156, 157, 194, 352, 411, 451, 521, 524, 529
dealing with trauma... 138, 158, 159, 161, 518
dissociation... 156
family trauma... 311
long-term physical effects of... 411
meditation... 350, 351
mild trauma... 146
moderate... 29, 146
psychological... 30, 133, 138, 146, 154, 164
severe... 149, 156, 159, 161, 172
Twelve-step programs... 304
Two-chair explorations and clearing... 40, 111, 129, 141, 167, 255, 258, 270, 282, 283, 284, 285, 286, 287, 290, 291, 334, 344, 347, 348, 356, 357, 358, 519, 522, 527
body symptoms... 267, 285
reparenting ourselves... 287
TWR/WHEE... 12, 40, 50, 52, 58, 61, 111, 136, 141, 161, 165, 167, 169, 170, 174, 178, 187, 188, 189, 211, 233, 239, 241, 246, 247, 260, 263, 265, 268, 269, 272, 273, 274, 279, 281, 282, 286, 287, 290, 291, 306, 313, 314, 321, 326, 344, 347, 349, 358, 423, 428, 434, 436, 474, 516, 519, 520, 521, 524, 528
bundling issues... 272
children... 273
Energy Psychology (EP)... 28, 39, 111, 160, 165, 188, 306, 330, 516, 519, 520
methods... 263
preventive installing of positivity and meta-positivity... 338
TWR1/WHEE: Symptoms and positive resources... 114, 258, 263, 266, 267, 268, 270, 432, 522
TWR2/WHEE: body messages... 263
TWR2/WHEE: deeper clearings... 270
Typologies... 518, 523

**U**
Ultradian brain rhythms... 87, 518
US Food and Drug Administration... 518

**V**
Vengefulness... 144, 146
Vibrational medicine... 293
Void (following trauma release)... 158
Vomiting (pregnancy)... 269, 303, 395, 396

**W**
What is life all about?... 201, 508
WHEE. *See* TWR/WHEE
Wholistic
HSPC – HSP wholistic issues... 199
wholistic approaches to facilitate health and healing... 40
wholistic awarenesses... 19, 42, 53, 202, 343, 397, 431, 433, 467, 494
wholistic beingness... 106, 208
wholistic considerations of HSP children... 237
wholistic dysfunctions... 202
wholistic EP... 165, 205, 209, 241, 346

*wholistic healing. See* Wholistic healing
*wholistic healing framework... 23*
*wholistic perspectives... 27, 201, 424, 438, 458*
*wholistic psychotherapist... 18*
*wholistic relationship... 209*
*wholistic sensitivities... 228, 231*
*wholistic spectrum... 26, 50, 63, 70, 71, 114, 131, 132, 154, 237, 272, 298, 300, 352, 389, 401, 424, 432, 442, 443, 444, 458*
*wholistic spectrum of our beingness... 26*
Wholistic healing... 26, 49, 50
   *bioenergy... 26, 49, 50*
   *body... 26, 41*
   *building positive physical relationships... 242*
   *emotions... 204, 219, 238*
   *engaging in wholistic healing... 69*
   *environment... 424, 439*
   *HSPs and their HSPCs... 203, 204, 219*
   *individual issues... 70*
   *mainstream attitudes... 71*
   *psychic... 373*
   *spirit... 424, 440*
   *wholistic healing therapies... 24*
*wholistic perspectives... 27, 201, 424, 438, 458*

# Z
*Zener cards... 381, 389*

## ABOUT THE AUTHOR

**Daniel J. Benor, MD, ABIHM,** has been searching over four decades for ever more ways to peel the onion of life's resistances, to reach the gnowing that we are all cells in the body of the Infinite Source.

His principal work is through wholistic healing – addressing spirit, relationships, mind, emotions, and body. He teaches TWR/ WHEE, a potent self-healing method, for adults and children who are dealing with psychological and physical pain, stress, trauma, cravings, and other issues.

Dr. Benor founded The Doctor-Healer Networks in England and in North America. He authored *Healing Research, Vol. 1–3* and many articles on wholistic healing. He is the Editor-in-Chief of the International Journal of Healing and Caring.

Dr. Benor appears internationally on radio and TV. He is a Founding Diplomate of the American Board of Integrative Holistic Medicine; Founder and Past Coordinator for the Council for Healing (http:// councilforhealing.org); and has served for many years on the advisory boards of the journals *Alternative Therapies, Subtle Energies, Explore;* the Advisory Council of the Association for Comprehensive Energy Psychotherapy (ACEP), Canadian Association for Integrative Energy Therapies (CAIET), Emotional Freedom Techniques (EFT), and the Advisory Board of the Research Council for Complementary Medicine (UK). Dr. Benor teaches TWR/ WHEE in lectures, workshops and teleseminars.

See  http://danielbenor.com    http://twrapp.com    http://ijhc.org

www.ingramcontent.com/pod-product-compliance
Lightning Source LLC
Chambersburg PA
CBHW060307240426
43661CB00059B/2683